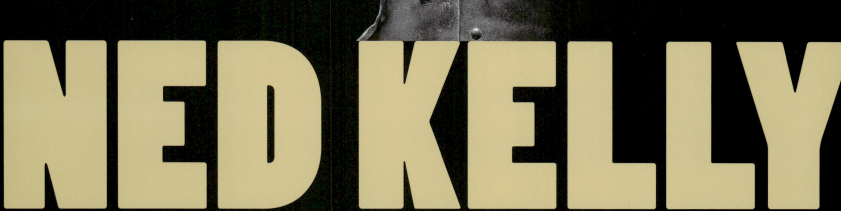

NED KELLY

KEITH McMENOMY   THE AUTHENTIC ILLUSTRATED HISTORY

Hardie Grant Books

The original source material contains references to the imperial system of measurements and currency. For clarity, the metric equivalent has been included for distance and area where possible. Currency remains in the original imperial values.

LENGTH AND AREA

1 inch = 25.4 mm
1 foot = 30.5 cm
1 yard = 0.914 m
1 mile = 1.61 km
1 acre = 0.405 ha
1 square mile = 2.59 square km

WEIGHT

1 pound = 454 g
1 stone = 6.36 kg
1 hundredweight = 50.85 kg
1 ton = 1.02 tonnes

CURRENCY

When decimal currency was introduced in 1966, two Australian dollars equalled £1. This, however, bears no resemblance to the exchange values of the eighteenth century. In some cases, inflation and depreciation of currency since the 1870s has been in the order of one hundredfold.

To approximately compare value, consider that a good stock saddle cost £8 in 1870. In 2001, a good stock saddle would cost around $800. Farm labouring wages varied seasonally but in 1875 Joseph Evans (William Evans, *Diary of a Welsh Swagman* 1977) earned 17s 6d for a six-day working week with food and lodging. He paid 6d for a newspaper, the same for a hotel meal, 1s for a bed and 6d for a glass of beer. In 1870 Mrs Kelly charged 1s for a glass of brandy. In his Jerilderie letter, Ned boasted that after leaving prison in 1874 he never worked for less than £2 10s as a sawmill overseer. Miners at this time received £4 2s for one ounce of gold.

♣

Published in 2001
by Hardie Grant Publishing
12 Claremont Street
South Yarra Victoria 3141, Australia
www.hardiegrant.com.au

All rights reserved. No part of this publication may be reproduced, stored in a retrieval system or transmitted in any form by any means, electronic, mechanical, photocopying, recording or otherwise, without the prior written permission of the publishers and copyright holders.

First published by Currey O'Neil Ross Pty Ltd in 1984
Copyright © Keith McMenomy 2001

National Library of Australia Cataloguing-in-Publication Data:

McMenomy, Keith.
    Ned Kelly: the authentic illustrated history

    Bibliography.
    Includes index.
    ISBN 1 74064 020 9.

    1. Kelly, Ned, 1855–1880. 2. Bushrangers – Australia – Victoria – Biography. 3. Victoria – History. I. Title.
364.1550924

Edited by Dale Campisi
Designed and typeset by Phil Campbell
Printed and bound in Singapore by Tien Wah Press.

Every effort has been made to locate copyright material used in this book. The publishers would like to hear about any omissions or errors.

CONTENTS

	PREAMBLE: Two Sides to One Story	vi
	ACKNOWLEDGEMENTS	xi
1	**FORMATIVE YEARS:** Beveridge, 1850–64	1
2	**LUCK OF THE IRISH:** Avenel, 1864–67	12
3	**RETURN TO THE CLAN:** Greta, 1867–70	24
4	**A SECONDARY EDUCATION FOR THE KELLY CHILDREN,** 1870–74	41
5	**THE COMING OF AGE,** 1874–78	52
6	**AN ILL-FATED VISIT TO THE KELLY HUT:** The Fitzpatrick Incident, 15 April 1878	68
7	**FROM HORSE-STEALING TO HOMICIDE:** Stringybark Creek, 28 October 1878	82
8	**FROM OBSCURITY TO OUTLAWRY:** October–December 1878	98
9	**THE EUROA HOLD-UP:** 9 December 1878	108
10	**EVADING THE POLICE FORCE:** December 1878–February 1879	118
11	**THE JERILDERIE HOLD-UP,** 8 February 1879	134
12	**THE GREAT DISAPPEARANCE, PART ONE:** February–June 1879	144
13	**THE GREAT DISAPPEARANCE, PART TWO:** June 1879–June 1880	158
14	**DEVIL'S ELBOW:** The Death of Aaron Sherritt, 26 June 1880	173
15	**THE LAST STAND:** Glenrowan, 26 June 1880	182
16	**AFTERMATH OF A TRAGEDY,** June-July 1880	218
17	**THE PRELIMINARY HEARING:** Beechworth, 6 August 1880	232
18	**THE TRIAL, MELBOURNE:** 18 October 1880	244
19	**TO A HIGHER COURT:** Two Weeks to 11 November 1880	256
	ABBREVIATIONS	274
	NOTES	274
	PICTURE SOURCES	284
	BIBLIOGRAPHY	287
	INDEX	290

PREAMBLE
TWO SIDES TO ONE STORY

The pictorial or visual side of the Kelly story has never been adequately presented, and that is where this work differs from others on the subject. The early camera was not free from manipulation. Moreover, photographs are human constructs – context and presentation can influence the interpretation of the subject. Studio portraits attempt to flatter, while mug shots tend to brutalise the subject. Nevertheless, the images can provide a powerful insight into the people and places as they appeared, fixed at a particular time, or viewed in sequence to reveal change over a lifetime. With a subject that is continually discussed with prejudice and agenda, photographs obviously have significant historical value. Drawings and paintings provide information, sometimes as much about the artist as the subject – scenes and sitters can be treated impartially, romanticised or caricatured, but they still provide valuable insight. The documents, letters, maps and artefacts also help fill gaps in our knowledge and help transport us back to very different times.

This book began with my discovery as a student that pictorial material existed but had never been fully assembled. Since then, with four decades of on and off research, with luck and the help of friends, archivists, librarians and descendants of the Kelly family, a concise collection has materialised.

I found that many people were suspicious or treasured their photographs, so the only way to gain copies was to take a camera with me around the vast amount of land significant to the Kelly story. I have photographed in cells, museums, in kitchens, on verandas, in office corridors and on the roof of police stations. One marvellous old man even had a photograph under the battered seat of his truck; it was his most valued keepsake. Some pictures turned out to be bogus and I also made mistakes, but I was often rewarded. I have climbed all over 'Kelly Country', time and again, to get the right locations and the right light.

That this collection exists at all is due in large part to the efforts of early photographers who made a living recording the events and 'likenesses' of participants. Those we know of, Arthur Burman and John Lindt of Melbourne, lugged their cumbersome wet-plate equipment into the wild backblocks to record some of the events. James Bray of Beechworth recorded the images of so many who figured in the Kelly story and arrived at Glenrowan in time to record the siege. Oswald Madeley, from Benalla, was equipped with new dry plates, allowing much faster exposures, so he braved the gunfire at Glenrowan to get the first pictorial news-scoop of a national tragedy. W. E. Barnes of Wangaratta was another significant contributor. Charles Nettleton, who held the contract for prison portraits in Melbourne for over 25 years, took many of the prison identification photographs shown here. He usually worked outdoors, near a cell set up as a darkroom. At Pentridge, he photographed Harry Power and at the old Melbourne Gaol, he took the two remarkable plates of Ned Kelly the day before he was hanged.

To complement the photographs and other illustrations, I have made use of many first-hand narratives left by the people who were there. These accounts have survived in personal memoirs, statements to the press, depositions and official reports. I have also included some conflicting statements for comparison and balance. I have attempted to show – as far as is possible – those involved as they were, and let them describe the events as *they* saw them happen.

Over the years, a vast amount of material (books, films, plays, poems, songs and magazine articles) has appeared with amazing regularity – *Outlaws of the Wombat Ranges* even appeared during the Kellys' career in 1878. Songs and poems also flourished from about the same time; some were even composed by the outlaws. More books have been published about the Kellys than any other subject in Australian history. So much has been written that it might even be said that the story suffers from over-exposure. As a journalist once quipped, 'Ned Kelly rides again, and again, again and again'.

To some academics and historians, Kelly has become something of a wild colonial bore – his life history sifted and re-sifted by an unending line of writers – many of them with only one eye on accuracy and neither on impartiality. Yet the subject remains one of the most moving and intriguing chapters in Australian history.

This will not be the last word on Ned Kelly; many questions still remain unanswered. Who was present at the Fitzpatrick incident? Was Ned Kelly married, as he claimed at Jerilderie? Did he intend to declare a republic in the north-eastern district of Victoria?

On a wet winter's day in 1911, two men in a jinker picked their way along a drowned track leading out of Glenrowan – a small nondescript bush town in the north-eastern backblocks of Victoria. One was journalist B.W. Cookson; the other was an unnamed photographer. The Sydney *Sun* had assigned Cookson to interview survivors of the Kelly ou break – an event that had occurred over 30 years before. The Kelly gang, a group of four bush criminals including two Kelly brothers, had been the most prominent outlaws in the whole country. They had shot dead three policemen, outwitted the Victorian police force and terrorised Victoria and New South Wales for two years. They had held up whole towns, robbed banks of over £4,000, and murdered a police spy. Finally, they had been surrounded in a bush shanty at Glenrowan – only a few kilometres across the ranges from their mother's hut. Three of the outlaws died in the fight that followed. Their leader, Edward 'Ned' Kelly, was captured, tried and hanged in Melbourne Gaol. Ever since, the gang's career has been the subject of a great deal of discussion.

Whether the outlaws, and more particularly their leader, were colonial Robin Hoods or just ingenious thugs has become an evergreen debate. For his assignment, Cookson went to the gang's old stamping ground to throw more light on the story. He interviewed police who had chased the gang and sympathisers who were closely connected to the outlaws. Most importantly, he spoke with Ned's mother and brother – who lived alone in poverty and privation in their hut near Greta. Accompanied by a few grandchildren, Mrs Kelly, elderly and feeble, gave her version of the Kelly outbreak – that so-called romantic drama which Australians so often enjoy hearing. Here are some extracts from the interview interspersed with Cookson's own quaint observations:

It were impossible to regard with any but feelings of the liveliest interest the mother of those desperate men, the fame of whose exploits has rung throughout the world, and whose names will be remembered in Australia long after recollection of much better men has passed. This shrivelled face, with its petrified aspect of grim despair, had been proudly pressed, in the fresh bloom of youthful motherhood, against the baby faces of men who had since out-

Ellen Kelly/King and granddaughters Lilian, left, and Alice Knight, 1911.

raged almost all the laws of the community, and who had long ago perished miserably, like wild beasts, in expiation of their crimes. They are dead. But she who brought them into the world and who for long dreadful years, suffered and wept for them and their grave misdeeds, she has been spared – spared to a life that is but a living death, bowed down in agonising memories, and quite devoid of hope.

She has much to tell – much more than there is space for the telling. And her hearers encourage her as they find occasion or opportunity. Naturally, for she was very old, the story of her life, as she tells it, is fragmentary and incomplete. There is such a very great deal that she could not remember.

Going back to the early history of the family, Mrs Kelly said that her husband, John Kelly, made some money on the goldfields, and bought a farming property at Beveridge.

In 1865 he got into trouble, and died not long afterwards.

There were seven children, [Anne, Edward, Margaret, James, Daniel, Catherine and Grace]. With these children Mrs Kelly took up the land at [west] Greta, on which the old Kelly homestead still stands. Here she and her children lived, happily enough, if roughly, till the visit of Constable Fitzpatrick. 'People blame my boys for all that has happened. They should blame the police. They were at the bottom of it all . . . I remember it all as if it were yesterday . . . Before that black day when Fitzpatrick came we were all living so happily at the old homestead – that's about a mile and half from here, on the other side of the road. We were not getting too rich, but were doing all right. It was a lonely life, but we were all together, and we all loved each other so dearly. Dear little Kate! I can see her now, bustling about the place, keeping things tidy, helping outside whenever she got the chance; always bright and cheerful, just like a sunbeam about the house.'

'The trouble began over a young Constable named Fitzpatrick. That was in April 1878. He came over to our place over there and said he was going to arrest Dan. He started the trouble. He had no business there at all, they tell me, no warrant or anything. If he had he should have done his business and gone. He tried to kiss my daughter Kate. She was a fine, good looking girl, Kate; and the boys tried to stop him. He was a fool. They were only trying to protect their sister. He was drunk and they were sober. But his story was believed. If he'd been badly hurt he would have richly deserved it. But I never hurt him – before God I didn't. They swore I hit him with a shovel. It was untrue. Why did he want to interfere with my girl? He stayed there to make trouble; and there was trouble. That was the end of the happiness for us. After that, nothing but misery. And it has been nothing but misery ever since.

At the memory of her forcible severance from her family the old woman broke down and wept bitterly. On recovering somewhat she proceeded, slowly: 'Oh, you can't imagine what I suffered. You can't understand what it means to us poor people in the bush, to be taken away from all that we have – our children. But they took me away, and I had to stay in prison for years. And for nothing – nothing at all. Because I never touched that Constable at all. I had no part in his being hurt. That was all his own fault. I declare this to you now, declare it before the God I shall soon see, and by my hope of salvation after a life of dreadful trouble, that I did nothing to Fitzpatrick.'

The old woman had many tales of what she called the persecution by the police to tell. Her daughters had been, she said, subjected to continued and studied indignities. Police would come at all hours of the night to search the house; and they would pull the girls out of bed and turn their beds upside down in the most rough and brutal fashion. 'The girls could have told you more about these things than I can', she said wearily. 'They had to suffer. And it was the conduct of the police all through – the brutal ill-usage that we had from them – that made all the trouble. But I don't know much of what happened after Fitzpatrick came that day. But the things that the girls have told me the police used to do were simply brutal and without excuse at all. If they had been trying to provoke the boys to break the law and retaliate they could not have done more than they did.'

That was Mrs Kelly's version, but there was another conflicting interpretation and one that had gained as much support as that of the Kelly survivors. Thirty years before Cookson took down the old woman's story in her lonely little hut, a carriage passed along the track outside carrying a group of gentlemen from Melbourne – that was in 1881, only months after Ned Kelly's execution. These men were conducting a royal commission into 'the circumstances preceding and attending the Kelly outbreak' and the state of the Victorian police force and its administration. Implicit in this term 'outbreak' was the official, bourgeois view that the episode was an example of social disease which had broken out among the poor or 'criminal class'. The seven commissioners held 66 meetings and visited the northeastern district and principal towns associated with the gang's exploits. They examined as many as 66 witnesses, among them police of all ranks, local squatters, members of parliament, civilians who had survived the tragedies, and police spies. Significantly, only one of those interviewed was in any way a sympathiser of the gang.

The royal commission recommended a thorough overhaul of the police force: a number of senior officers were retired or demoted and many police from all ranks were sacked. The royal commission also outlined the circumstances that it found to have caused the Kelly outbreak. Here is a small excerpt from that report, representing officialdom's version of the Kelly saga.

Amongst the many predisposing causes which operated to bring about the Kelly outbreak must be included the unchecked aggregation of a large class of criminals in the North-Eastern district of Victoria, all of whom, either by ties of consanguinity or sympathy, were identified with the outlaws . . . Mrs Kelly, upon the death of her husband, settled at the Eleven-mile creek, near Greta, where, with the younger portion of her family, she at present resides. Her place was regarded for years as the resort of lawless and desperate characters, including Power, who is said to have given Ned Kelly his first lesson in bushranging. Edward Kelly, the leader of the outlaws, was born in 1854, at Wallan Wallan [sic], and from an early age was regarded by the police as an incorrigible thief. In company with Power the bushranger he, on the 16th of March 1870, robbed Mr

McBean; and on the 25th of April stuck up Mr John Murray, of Lauriston. Kelly was arrested for the latter offence on the 4th of May following but escaped conviction owing to want of identification. He was implicated in several outrages; and at Beechworth, in 1871, he received a sentence of three years for receiving a stolen horse. He led a wild and reckless life, and was always associated with the dangerous characters who infested the neighbourhood of Greta until the shooting of Constable Fitzpatrick, on the 15th April 1878, when he took to the bush. Daniel Kelly was born in 1861, and from the age of 16 years was, with his elder brother Ned, a noted criminal. Joseph Byrne, the third outlaw, was born in 1857, and lived with his parents, who were of Irish extraction and respectable antecedents, at the Woolshed, about seven miles from Beechworth. When 16 years of age he was in trouble, and from the first appears to have developed vicious and cruel propensities . . . he was also believed to have been connected with numerous cases of horsestealing in the North-Eastern district, which ultimately led to his joining the Kelly gang. Steve Hart, the fourth member of the gang was born in 1860, and was the second son of Richard Hart, of Three-mile creek, near Wangaratta. Stephen, at an early age, became associated with disreputable persons, and carried on a system of stealing horses and planting them until such time as rewards were offered by the owners for their recovery. He received a sentence of imprisonment in July 1877, and subsequently was sent to gaol for ten months for horsestealing.

The incident, however, which seems to have immediately precipitated the outbreak was the attempt of Constable Fitzpatrick to arrest Dan Kelly, at his mother's hut, on the 15th of April 1878. This constable appears to have borne a very indifferent character in the force, from which he was ultimately discharged. The arrest was attempted to be made in consequence of a Gazette notice to the effect that a warrant had been issued at Chiltern against Dan Kelly and Jack Lloyd, on a charge of suspected cattle [sic] stealing. Fitzpatrick's efforts to fulfil what he may have considered his duty proved disastrous. He was entrapped by accepting the invitation to accompany Dan Kelly into the hut, where he was attacked by several members of the family, and shot in the wrist by Ned Kelly. Warrants were in due course issued against Fitzpatrick's assailants; and those arrested, including Mrs Kelly and a relative [sic] named Williamson, were sentenced to long terms of imprisonment for the offence of assault with intent to kill. The alleged severity of the punishment inflicted upon the mother of the outlaws has been the subject of comment in the course of the inquiry, and Captain Standish considers that it formed one of the many causes which assisted to bring about the Kelly outrages.

It may also be mentioned that the charge of persecution of the Kelly family by the members of the police force has been frequently urged in extenuation of the crimes of the outlaws; but, after careful examination, your Com-

missioners have arrived at the conclusion that the police, in their dealings with the Kellys and their relations, were simply desirous of discharging their duty conscientiously; and that no evidence has been adduced to support the allegation that either the outlaws or their friends were subjected to persecution or unnecessary annoyance at the hands of the police.

The question of whose Kelly story is closer to the truth, as much as the undisputed details, has helped fuel the controversy since the Kellys were outlawed in 1878.

If this book is to be dedicated to anyone it is not just to the Kellys, but to everyone who was involved in the tragic saga. They all still deserve a fair hearing.

ACKNOWLEDGEMENTS

I have met some remarkable people and gained much assistance while assembling this project. No one has offered more support over a longer period than Ian Jones. We have been sharing discoveries since the early 1960s – exchanges that always seem to be in my favour. Without the unfailing inspiration, encouragement and assistance from him and so many others, this collection could not have been so comprehensive.

Phillip Adams encouraged me in the early stages. Sue Galley motivated me to do a marketing proposal and negotiate its initial sale. John Ross, bless his soul, recognised the book's potential. The editor of the first edition, Helen Duffy, worked tirelessly for me while I was at the other end of the globe. More recently, commissioning editor Tracy O'Shaughnessy revived interest in this amended, bigger and better compilation. Dale Campisi applied his eagle eye and patiently untangled tortured prose. Foong Ling Kong helped nurse the project to completion, while Phil Campbell achieved the graphic design equivalent of re-inventing the wheel.

Many hours were spent in the wonderful old reading room of the State Library of Victoria and the catacombs of the government archives. Dianne Reilly and Mary Lewis at the State Library of Victoria were very helpful and supportive as were staff at the National Library in Canberra and the State Library of New South Wales. Baiba Berzins and Patricia Jackson at the Mitchell Library in Sydney helped me uncover invaluable material.

A list of specific acknowledgments appears with endnotes but I cannot give due credit to all those supportive people in other government departments. The former Museum of Applied Sciences in Melbourne, Victorian Government Lands Department (Lands Victoria), Tony Morabito, Titles Office, Government Statist Office and the Victorian Railway Archives (VicRail). Government archivist Harry Nunn, and all those at the Public Records Office of Victoria, provided valuable material. Various managers of the Victorian Police Historical Unit – Peter Wilson, Peter Free and Martin Powell – have given unreserved assistance.

I am equally grateful to the following institutions and local historians for their assistance and permission to reproduce items from their collections over the past 40 years. Lansdowne Press, the Council of Adult Education, Harold Baigent, Art Gallery of New South Wales, Alice Livingstone, Geelong Regional Gallery, Veronica Filmer, Melbourne Diocesan Historical Commission, Catholic Archdiocese of Melbourne, Rachel and Phillip Naughton. The Royal Historical Society of Victoria, the North-Eastern Historical Society, Brenda Leitch, Joan Wood, Joan Canny. The Benalla Historical Society, Norma Grubb, the Burke Museum in Beechworth, Wangaratta City Council, Rod Shaw, the Jerilderie Shire and the Euroa Camera Club.

I have been shown genuine kindness and trust by many Kelly–Quinn descendants, including the Cleves, Lloyds and Griffiths, Elsie Pettifer and Leigh Olver, John Spencer and Marie Donnelly. Thanks also to Mr B. Hiscock, Bridget Griffiths and Colin Boyd of Benalla; Patience Stewart, John Payne and Matt Quinlan, formerly of Beveridge; William Gould of Wangaratta; Mr D. Stribling and Mrs Lomer of Euroa; Ethel Middleton, Pat Kelly and Mr C. Lefoe, formerly of Avenel; the Tobin and Johnson families of Kilmore; Bernie Laffan and Steve Brown of Wallan. Lionel McKenzie, Mr J. T. Parkinson, Mr E. W. Swan. Liz Archer, Dagmar Balcarek, Annette Hall, Graham Moore, Mr J. Murphy, Kevin Passey, Garry Dean, Edgar Penzig, Peter Smith and Mrs Proute Webb.

1 FORMATIVE YEARS
BEVERIDGE, 1850–64

Edward 'Ned' Kelly most likely 'first drew breath', as he put it, under a bark roof on Big Hill at Beveridge, Victoria. At that time, Beveridge was a small, scruffy coach-stop 38 kilometres (24 miles) north of Melbourne on a track being constructed as the Sydney road. In hindsight, the event was significant, but was not formally registered. Estimates of Ned's birth vary between mid 1854 to mid 1855. Ned was most likely born in November or December 1854. A neighbouring squatter's wife, Mrs David Gorman, acted as the midwife and Father O'Hea, visiting Catholic priest from St Pauls, Coburg, was said to have baptised the boy.

Ned was the first son and third child of poor Irish immigrants, Ellen (nee Quinn) and John 'Red' Kelly. In 1854, Ellen was 22 years old. She arrived in Victoria as a child with her parents and siblings as free settlers from Northern Ireland. John was then 34 and had reached Port Phillip via Van Diemen's Land (Tasmania) five years earlier. John, however, did not arrive free; he had been imprisoned for seven years for theft.

The Kellys' first daughter, Mary Jane, was born at Wallan East three months after their marriage in November 1850, but died during infancy. A second girl, Annie, was also born at Wallan East in 1853. Like many early settlers' wives, Ellen was regularly pregnant for more than two decades.

If Ned was born in December 1854 it confirms family legend that he was born at the time of the Eureka Stockade. The 1850s were a period of great change and turmoil in Australia. The new colony of

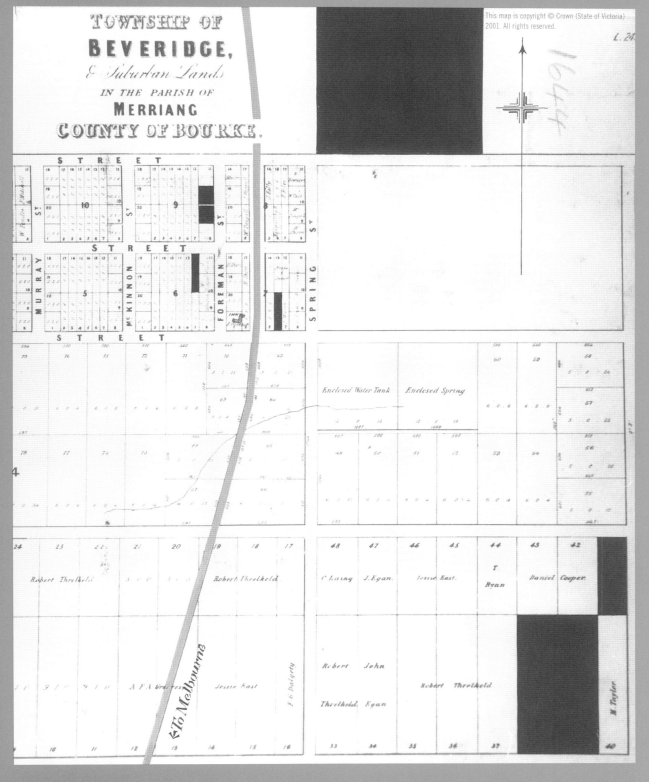

Top: Township of Beveridge plan, original 1852 survey. Records show Ned's father made considerable investment in land between 1854–64. The eastern portion of the town is shown. The grey strip indicates the Sydney road at the time and the black areas indicate properties owned by John 'Red' Kelly. The largest (top) was their first farm of 41 acres. The two smaller allotments in the town proper were owned between 1855 and 1859; the two fronting Foreman Street came with the transaction for their second farm. This was the area (bottom right) of 21 acres in the south-eastern corner of the township reserve.

Bottom: John Kelly's signature was shakily recorded on all but one of his Beveridge land dealings. This one was on the 1859 purchase transaction with Charles McDougall for the last property he ever owned. The line above it refers to an earlier proclamation date.

Overleaf: The Quinn homestead at Merri Creek, Wallan, as it survived a century later. The building, spacious for the period, contains six rooms all lined with hand-split and stained palings identical to John Kelly's home. The area under the main roof is divided into three large rooms with three bedrooms formed under a skillion along the rear wall. Outside, gnarled trees and ancient shrubs, known as 'Kelly's garden', still struggle for life.

Above: Interior of the Quinn kitchen. In the 1850s, the Quinns (and Kellys) would have prepared meals and relaxed around the open hearth. One journalist said of the home, 'it is evident, even today, that the Quinns were comparitively well-to-do. Whereas most settlers' homes of the period were bark and [slab], the Quinn home was externally clad in sawn boards . . . a good deal of the interior was similarly lined and the frame timbers had been roughly squared, no doubt by hand-operated adze. Everything spells comfort as it was known in those days . . . the kitchen [had] a huge open fireplace complete with elaborately made and still functional spit crane capable of handling the roasting of a whole sheep. Nearby is a built-in bread oven'.

Top: Quinn forge door. A variety of brands burnt deep into the old timber record initials on the Wallan East property. On the outside, almost obliterated by a century of weather, three initials of 'EK' and 'K' survive in and around the lower brand, presumably carved by young Edward in the 1860s.

Victoria experienced phenomenal social and economic development, even though conditions were still largely primitive. In July 1851 Port Phillip was administratively separated from New South Wales and gold discoveries triggered a population boom in both colonies. Farmers, tradesmen, merchants and publicans benefited as much as the thousands of diggers who tramped past within sight of the Kelly property.

John Kelly also shared in that prosperity. Ellen recalled he 'made some money on the gold fields', which helped them gain independence. He also worked as a stockman, no doubt with his in-laws, who 'shortly after breaking out of the diggings, in consequence of the increased value of stock . . . were dealing in and breeding horses and cattle'. At Beveridge land sales in February 1854 'Red' Kelly was one of the first to purchase a town allotment as well as a 41-acre block 'including buildings etc.' on the subdivision's northern edge. At the time, there was already a scattering of buildings and a hotel offering them the prospect of selling dairy foods.

During the next few years, Kelly speculated on small land purchases in the township while running dairy cows and undertaking building and carpentry work. Yet despite entrepreneurial efforts and 'hard work' he evidently did not prosper. Nor did the township; Beveridge gained churches, a school and a blacksmith along with inns and a scattering of rough timber huts and houses but never developed according to expectations. Land and commodity prices were temporarily inflated in the early 1850s because of the gold rushes. Kelly paid dearly for his 41 acres and over-extended himself, suffering later as values plunged.

There was little to romanticise in the Kelly family's precarious and extremely harsh living situation. This was no novelty to many Irish settlers, whose former living conditions were among the worst in western Europe. Many first-generation settlers such as the Kellys had considerable difficulty in the first few decades if they did not modify agricultural and grazing practices to the fragile (if rough) terrain and unreliable weather. Frequent droughts could extend over several seasons, native pastures were eaten out, and water supply was always critical. The small acreage Europeans were accustomed to was impractical here. Weather ruled and ruined the lives of those without expertise and capital resources to improve pastures or conserve fodder. Child mortality increased each summer as water supplies diminished. Many could manage only a fragile subsistence on the edge of starvation and were eventually forced off their holdings. Interestingly, the Quinns prospered in the same

QUINN CLAN 1880

Mary Anne McGlusky b.1809
married **James Quinn** b.1803 in 1824

Patrick Quinn 1825-1850	John 'Jack' Quinn b. 1830	Mary Anne Quinn b.1831 m.1857 to Robert Miller	Ellen Quinn b.1832 m.1850 to John Kelly (1820–1866) re-m.1874 to George King	Catherine Quinn b.1837 m. John Lloyd 1852	Jane Quinn b.1840 m. Thomas Lloyd 1857	James Quinn b.1840	William Quinn b.1843 m. Mary Comerford	Margaret Quinn b. 1845 m. Patrick Quinn 1866	Grace Quinn b. 1847 m. Patrick O'Farrell 1875
		Mary Miller Alexander Miler Jane Miller Margaret Miller Catherine Miller Christine Miller Grace Miller Elizabeth Miller	Mary Jane Kelly b. 1851, d. 1850s. Anne Kelly 1853–1872 m. Alex Gunn 1869 Edward 'Ned' Kelly b.1854, d. 1880 Margaret Kelly b.1857, m. William Skillion 1873 James Kelly b. 1859 Daniel Kelly b. 1851 d. 1880 Catherine Kelly b 1863 Grace Kelly b. 1855 Ellen Kelly b. 1870 d. 1872 Ellen King b. 1873 John King b.1875 Alice King b. 1873	Thomas Peter Lloyd b. 1857 Charles Lloyd John Lloyd Silas Lloyd Mary Lloyd Dorothy lloyd Esther Lloyd Bridget Lloyd b.1855 m. Isaiah Wright 1874	Mary Lloyd b. 1858 m. John McElroy John Lloyd b. 1859 d. 1879 Winifred Lloyd b. 1860 m. J. McGaffin Catherine Lloyd b. 1863 m. William J. Cleave Bridget Lloyd b. app.1864 m. J. Jones Margaret Lloyd b. app.1876 Jane Lloyd b. app.1878 Thomas Lloyd b. app.1879 Ellen Lloyd b.1880			Daisy Quinn b. 1878 Francis Quinn b. 1880	James Quinn b. 1869 m. Sarah McCarthy Patrick Leopold Quinn b.1871 Mary Quinn b. 1873 Myles Quinn b. 1875 Elizabeth Quinn b. 1879	Stewart O'Farrell William O'Farrell Martin John O'Farrell

JOHN 'RED' KELLY'S BROTHERS AND SISTERS WHO EMIGRATED IN 1857

Edmond Kelly b. 1820	Thomas Kelly b. app. 1825	Mary Kelly b.1828	Anne Kelly b. 1833 m. John Ryan 1857	James Kelly b. 1835	Daniel Kelly b.app. 1839
Family unkn.	Ditto.	Ditto.	Thomas Ryan b. 1857 Joseph Ryan b. 1859 John Ryan b. 1860 Mary Anne Ryan Ellen Ryan Julia Ryan Sarah Ryan b. 1867 James John Ryan b. 1869 Johannah Ryan b. 1872 Elizabeth Ryan		Family unkn.

Farmhouse of a dairyman and his family in 1859. Kelly parents and up to seven children ate and slept in the one large room. Most of the north end was occupied by the open fireplace. A line of pegs in auger holes hanged their few belongings and clothing along the south wall. Subsequent purchaser Stewart's wife recalled that she wept on the first night they moved in because the house was in such a poor state. The mud floor and open drain remained. A broken window pane had a tin plate nailed in the opening – small things that mattered. The photograph, taken 100 years later, shows it from the rear and east side; the only external changes were an iron roof and veranda.

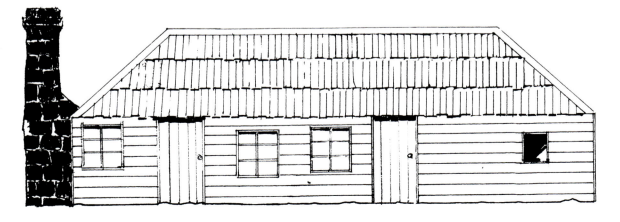

Elevation of original house, west side. Author's reconstruction of the original form. The structure was typical of bush huts with split weatherboards, shingle roof, low walls with doors dropping from the eaves.

FORMATIVE YEARS

Above: St Francis's Church Melbourne, where the young Irish couple were married on 18 November 1850 in a simple ceremony by Father Gerald Ward; so started one of the most dramatic and pathetic tragedies in Australian history.

Right: Reverend Father Charles O'Hea was appointed to the mission of St Paul at what was later Coburg. It was no easy charge including the post of Pentridge Stockade and the vast parish. The likeable, robust character, 'his genial face alive with humour', won the affection of a scattered flock, the Kellys among them. Oral tradition has it that he baptised young Edward and was the family's counsellor. His good influence on young Ned was renewed years later at Pentridge and finally at the Melbourne Gaol.

district, so the Kelly problems possibly had other contributing causes.

In 1854, John borrowed money to purchase more land, but was forced to mortgage the larger acreage. In 1856 he helped the Quinns build a large and comfortable timber homestead on newly acquired land on the north-east side of Herne's swamp. This purchase totalled 700 acres freehold and adjoined the rented land at Wallan East — evidence of the Quinns' relative wealth and ability to manage local conditions. By contrast, in May 1857, Ned's father sold the 41 acres and half his town allotment to pay debts, netting only about half the original price.

Nevertheless, John 'Red' Kelly had been confident enough with local prospects in the mid-1850s to encourage his three brothers, two sisters and a husband to emigrate from Ireland. They arrived in July 1857 when Victoria's economic conditions were in temporary decline. Yet even this must have represented considerable improvement on Tipperary, devastated by the potato blight, famine-fever and typhus, which claimed about one third of the total Irish population in previous years. These Kelly uncles and aunts formed families of their own. Red's brothers, James and Edward, and sister Anne (married to John Ryan) initially settled nearby. Ellen's sisters all married too, in contrast to three of her Quinn brothers. All of these unions eventually expanded into a vast and important network of filial support — scattered initially between Beveridge and Kilmore, and later throughout north-east Victoria and the Riverina in New South Wales.

By 1856, John and Ellen Kelly had four children, including Ned's baby sister Margaret, born at Beveridge. They presumably lived on the quarter-acre town allotment until purchasing another half-acre in 1858 fronting Arrowsmith Street. Red may have built on these lots or provided accommodation for relatives, possibly renting grazing land to complement dairying with carpentry work. In February 1859 Red bought two more town allotments in Beveridge, and three larger lots on the southern edge of the town amounting to 22 acres. The larger lots were relatively flat with stony rises, contained some lightwood and box timber, and were within a few hundred metres of the settlement's natural spring and water reserve.

In the north-east corner of Lot 41 he built a two-roomed, split-weatherboard, shingle-roofed cottage with a large bluestone chimney. It was rudimentary in comparison with the Quinn home, but typical of most bush dwellings. It was without refinements such as verandahs, wall-linings, ceilings or timber floors. The main room, 8.8 by 3.9 metres (29 by 13 feet), partitioned with calico or hessian, accommodated their growing family. An earth drain between the two doors in the main room divided the living from the sleeping quarters. A small dairy or coolroom, 2.4 by 3.9 metres (8 by 13 feet), occupied the south end, and outside they dug a deep stone-lined well to provide a permanent water supply. The family settled here in time for the birth of their second son, James.

In 1861 a Catholic chapel school opened, bringing better prospects and opportunities for the Kelly children. It closed several times in the first two years, but by 1863 Thomas and Sarah Wall had an average of 36 pupils of mixed denominations. No early academic records survive but between 1861 and the 1863, Anne, Edward and Margaret Kelly, along with their cousins the Ryans, were among the children attending. Ned was remembered by a schoolmate, Frederick Hopkins, as 'a tall and active youngster who excelled all other boys at school games'. Another identified him as 'just an ordinary young fellow; there were wilder boys around'. At home, more siblings arrived to crowd the hearth and ash corner (where family socialised and visitors bedded down). Daniel, 'Dan', was born in 1861 and Catherine, 'Kate', in 1863.

John and Ellen Kelly's reputation at Wallan and Beveridge survived in contradictory versions. One property owner at nearby Kalkallo described them as 'rough characters' and suggested that 'Red was responsible for the level of stock theft at the time'. Thirty years later the royal commissioners claimed that while at Beveridge, Red 'became notorious as an expert cattle stealer, and his house was known as the rendezvous of thieves and suspected persons'. But there was no evidence to support these accusations. Several reputable biographers have since pointed out that nothing at all connected Red with unlawful activities at that time. By contrast, he was consistently recalled by Beveridge residents as a quiet, inoffensive and retiring individual.

Ned's father's reticence was not surprising. He was an ex-convict, transported for stealing two pigs in Tipperary, not for shooting at a landlord as wrongly claimed by the royal commissioners. Recent research in Ireland indicates that he may also have informed on accomplices, one of whom was shot dead trying to escape. Red was given seven years' imprisonment, customary for an agrarian first offence, but had to serve them at the other end of the globe with little or no prospect of ever seeing his homeland again. He spent six of these in Van Diemen's Land without serious misdemeanours, but in misery according to his children.

This background was not so unusual for the time. Large numbers of freed transportees crossed to the mainland for better opportunities and to escape the stigma of their past. Surprisingly, for a colony of supposedly 'free settlers', almost one third of the adult male rural population in Victoria at this time were ex-convicts. Even so, Red Kelly would have been acutely aware that knowledge of his background could invite surveillance, if not harassment. To his credit he drew no official attention for seventeen years after arriving at Port Phillip.

According to a Wallan settler who knew the Quinns and Kellys, 'they were just an ordinary family, not well off, hard-working like most . . . Kelly was a quiet man who kept to himself a lot . . . Mrs Kelly wore the pants'. Complementing (or compensating) for her partner, Ellen was indeed assertive when required, independent and sometimes hot-tempered, yet remembered affectionately, too, as a local midwife. Alcohol abuse likely contributed to family hardship. It was endemic in country towns during that period and particularly so at Beveridge in the 1850s and 1860s. An unsubstantiated legend held that Red kept a poteen still and imbibed his product freely, and Ellen acknowledged her husband had a particular affection for brandy. Yet significantly, John and Ellen had no problems with the law at Beveridge.

Some of their relatives were not so fortunate. Ned's grandfather James Quinn had an unblemished record and was able to discipline his sons until their

Above: Beveridge Catholic School, exterior.

Overleaf: Beveridge Catholic School, interior. The school was designed in 1857 and opened periodically from 1861 to serve as both school and church. It faced west in Spring Street, halfway up the slope from the natural spring and within sight of the Kelly hut. The impressive Gothic style would have contrasted sharply with the surrounding primitive township. The Kelly children, living in an earth-floored bush hut, must have been impressed attending school and worshipping in such an elegant interior with plastered walls, stained-glass windows, milled timber floors and the lofty beamed ceiling.

late teenage years, but their interest in livestock and brawling brought occasional trouble. A critical turning point came in 1856 when Ned's 16-year-old uncle James 'Jimmy' Quinn was first accused of stock theft from the Tallarook Run; a charge that was dismissed. Four years later at Kilmore, Jimmy served six weeks in prison for violent assault and faced another, although unsuccessful, charge for horse-stealing. In 1861, he got four months for illegally using a horse. Earning the epithet 'Mad Jim', he was intermittently wanted for violent assault or stock theft over the next three decades and this was to have an indelible influence on his nephews. Uncle John 'Jack' Quinn was cleared of accusations in 1860–61. In the next five years, nineteen charges were listed against some clan members for drunken brawls or alleged stock offences. Significantly, twelve of these failed. As John McQuilton (1979:71) pointed out, the failed charges indicated either incredible incompetence by the police involved or, as oral tradition claimed, over-zealous attention directed to the wrong suspects. Eventually, however, Ned's uncles James Quinn, Thomas and John Lloyd, and James Kelly were all gaoled.

It is important to acknowledge that most of Ned's relatives were not habitual endemic criminals or thugs. More accurately, they were archetypal 'wild colonials'. They reacted against the oppression experienced by European-born, particularly (but not only) Irish Catholic parents. This first generation of white settlers – skilled and adept at bush life – were more independent and confident in comparison to their elders. The younger males in the Quinn, Lloyd and Kelly clans were aggressively egalitarian, and passionately loyal to their own working class – even if occasionally argumentative. As Patrick O'Farrell (1987:136) generalised, they were 'pugnacious, colourful, and vigorously Irish'.

Top: Kilmore, as it was in the early 1860s. The town was the marketplace and centre of a predominantly Irish district stretching south, taking in Wallan and Beveridge, as far down as Donnybrook. The Kellys and Quinns sold their livestock here and bought hardware at stores like Fitzgerald's (right). They drank at impressive hotels like the 'Red Lion' or small shanties in the back streets. Occasionally they ended up before magistrates in the courthouse on the hill behind the dray.

Bottom: Kilmore courthouse, where eight-year-old Ned Kelly was taken by his mother to testify on behalf of uncle James Kelly in 1863. It was the boy's first unhappy introduction to the law.

This often irritated respectable officials, police and authoritarians determined to maintain class distinctions. Although there were significant exceptions, the Protestant majority in the Australian colonies assumed social superiority over Irish Catholics, considering many to be uneducated and wild primitives. The extended family, including the older generation, generally despised the notion of social superiority while worshipping equal rights. Referring to such widespread colonial sentiment, one immigrant observed: 'in this country everybody

FORMATIVE YEARS 9

Settlers travelling up-country by dray. This contemporary engraving gives some idea of the adventure involved. Relocating was a taxing exercise. Livestock went with family and furniture; note the ducks peering out from the load. Children too had to pitch in to drive the cattle along unfenced and often still timbered tracks.

addresses one another by the name of "mate" – a very equalising expression', but another complained: 'we found the company of our Irish partners rather difficult to take. Drinking, swearing and fist-fights amongst them, to be forgotten in a few minutes, were surprising and inexplicable to us.' Excitement and drama compensated for the monotony of bush life and frequently it was drinking sprees at local shanties or arguments at bush races that got out of hand and caused trouble for the clan. Such behaviour was also an indelible formative influence for the younger generation, including Ned.

The Quinn, Lloyd and Kelly menfolk worshipped horses. This was not surprising as they were the ultimate social equaliser and status signifier as well as means to mobility and freedom. Riding hacks were beyond the means of many citizens, their value representing more than a year's wages, not including saddle and bridle. Most of the rural population in this period relied on 'Shank's pony', walking distances which now seem extraordinary. Ten to 20 kilometres (six to twelve miles) was not unusual for adults or children to walk to reach a township or school. Others 'hitched' a ride on a dray or wagon, or for longer journeys bought a seat on the mail coaches. Several generations of Quinn, Lloyd and Kelly males, on the other hand, were reluctant to walk anywhere, and would only run for sport, money or freedom. The show-offs among them favoured partly broken or semi-wild mounts, to the alarm of pedestrians. Other aspects of Ned's relatives' stock-management practices caused difficulties. There is no surviving evidence that the clan became 'notorious as local cattle stealers', as claimed by the royal commissioners – only two uncles were convicted of stock theft up until the early 1860s – but there is little doubt that some of them were involved in borderline practices. They were said to occasionally muster unbranded 'scrubbers or cleanskins' that strayed in the unfenced, timbered ranges to the east and north of Wallan and further afield.

They also occasionally made use of straying or unbranded horses. 'Borrowing' a horse was not necessarily illegal at the time, depending on consent of the owner or duration of use. Generally, borrowing was tolerated if the animal was not mistreated and returned within a few days. It was also hard to police, as fencing was minimal – if it even existed – on many properties so horses strayed and borrowers could not always be identified. Rewards also tended to encourage desperadoes to exploit the opportunity for fraud, planting stock and later claiming the bounty.

Otherwise, occasional anti-social behaviour attracted police attention, which in turn produced fierce resentment from the Quinn clan, who viewed it as harassment. Uncle James carried a particularly bitter attitude towards some of those he called the 'traps'. Yet it is inaccurate to attribute this resentment simply to criminality, sectarian prejudice, or a simple feud between wild colonials and the police. The clan's problems and alleged offences were invariably either agrarian – disputes over livestock – or breaches of the peace. As to racial and religious bigotry, this was a powerful and insidious dividing influence at the time, but the Quinn clan had English, Scottish, German and Protestant friends as well as enemies. Adding to complications, allegiances within the clan shifted. There were feuds and occasional litigation occurred between clan families and even individual family members.

It was significant that in the wider community, Irish immigrants formed most of the unskilled and poorest labouring social group; partly an effect of former cultural deprivation under British rule. Fierce resentment accumulated through centuries of ill-treatment and exploitation was passed on to successive generations 'as mother's milk' to nourish nationalist spirit. One effect of this was the widespread antagonism felt towards Irish-born police who then made up most of the rank and file in the Victorian force. Almost half of these were ex-members of the hated Irish Constabulary. Catholic and Protestant Irishmen numerically dominated the police force, the legal and judicial institutions, as well as the prison population in Victoria until the 1870s. The difficult and essential job of policing invited enmity from countrymen who considered it social treachery, so native-born Australians shunned enlistment during this period.

These social dynamics were of critical importance to the Kelly–Quinn experience. The system of law enforcement was less than adequate after the chaos of the gold rushes. Favouring the chances of nefarious bushmen, there were few police in country districts in the 1850–60s and these were generally overworked with non-policing duties. On the other hand, they were poorly paid by local standards and relied on convictions for official merit and promotion. Added to this was a reward system offered by livestock owners that tended to corrupt some citizens as well as police. Both unscrupulous civilians and police sometimes planted livestock to claim rewards. This was a tempting means to augment income and a troublesome practice. Opportunistic police could be over-zealous in laying charges, civilians could also use police and country courts to lay unfounded complaints to settle scores. Adding to already difficult relations, pastoralists and squatters acted as magistrates, sometimes manipulating the police force and court system to protect their interests. Irish–Australian policemen, understandably, did not appreciate contempt from the community. Any display of pride and defiance – the egalitarian spirit cherished by bushmen generally and larrikins in particular – was considered 'flashness' by police, sometimes resulting in brutal treatment. Relations between a complex network of competitive and opposing elements of the population were therefore volatile.

Despite community antagonisms, only a very small percentage of Ned's relatives were ever convicted, but the few disreputable ones affected everyone. The next generation of children was drawn into the occasional traumatic conflicts, chases, arrests and trials, growing up to view the police generally as their natural enemies and henchmen for the wealthy – colonial officials, bankers, squatters and merchants. As one instance, a mere eight-year-old Ned was taken to the Kilmore Court in April 1863 as a witness for his uncle James Kelly. James was charged with stealing cattle from a Beveridge blacksmith – his third charge for stock offences in twelve months, the previous two being dismissed. The young boy confirmed his mother's testimony that uncle Jim was at their hut at the time the animals were taken. But the word of the complainant's wife was accepted over theirs and James received three years' imprisonment. The Kellys were not believed, so were either wronged or had lied. Either way, the little boy's first recorded contact with the law was not a positive one.

The family's Beveridge experience might not have been unhappy overall but it was definitely a financial slide. After James's conviction Ellen and John Kelly were concerned enough with prospects to sell out and leave the district later that year. The Quinns made the same decision and advertised for a buyer between 1860 and 1864. Encroaching development persuaded them to look for quieter pastures further away from Melbourne.

Grandfather James illustrated his dissatisfaction in the only confrontation with local authorities and the Roads Board in 1860. Against his wishes, the extension of the Merriang Road was surveyed through his farm on the east of Herne's swamp, only three kilometres north-east of the Kelly hut. So, when the contractor and his party arrived at Quinn's boundary, he bailed them up with a shotgun and ordered them off. The case was referred to the attorney general. Eventually Quinn's rights were upheld and he was compensated, but the road went through. To make matters worse, the north-eastern railway was surveyed across his western paddocks in 1863–64, dividing his land even further. This encroachment was too much and the Quinns decided to leave before the line was completed. It has been misconstrued that the family retreated solely because of rigorous police attention, but the transport extensions seem to be the main contributing factor.

Meanwhile, in January 1864, the Kelly property at Beveridge sold to a local farmer and carpenter, James Stewart, for £80, a deal that did not even realise John Kelly's improvements. A proportion of this sum, their only remaining asset, evidently went to repay debts. Stewart's wife recalled being reduced to tears because the Kelly cottage was 'in such a poor state' by the time they arrived. Despite ten years of work at Beveridge, unsuccessful investments and perhaps alcoholism thwarted the family's efforts.

The Kellys loaded their dray, farewelled their friends and family and headed away up the old Sydney road. Travelling past Kilmore, commercial centre of the Irish community, then eighteen kilometres (eleven miles) beyond Seymour and the Goulburn River, they rattled down a long winding grade with their belongings piled high and their hopes with them, to the township of Avenel on Hughes Creek.

2 LUCK OF THE IRISH
AVENEL, 1864–67

The Kellys' new home at Avenel, north of the Great Dividing Range, was a stark contrast to the windswept plains of the Merri Creek catchment. It was a larger settlement, but one still in its rough infancy. Situated near a natural watercourse, on a flat plain surrounded by hills, it took its name from nearby Avenel Run. In 1864 the township comprised two hotels, a general store and post office, blacksmith, tollhouse, school, police station and a courthouse. In the clearings between the tall timber, there was a scattering of buildings, gardens, orchards and vineyards. The remaining members of the local aboriginal tribe camped on the outskirts of the new settlement.

The Kellys did not purchase property in this new location. They rented a house near Campion's store before moving to an unfenced 40-acre block that they leased from the widow Mutton. This was about 1.6 kilometres (one mile) north-west of the Sydney road on the edge of the settlement. They occupied a slab and bark hut and lived in similar hardship to that experienced at Beveridge. The decision to rent land possibly indicates that Red's health was beginning to deteriorate.

The *Duffy Selection Act of 1862* prompted many of the Kellys' relatives to move even further north – beyond the Kellys at Avenel. For the same financial outlay, the Kelly family could have selected a viable acreage further on, with the prospect of eventually owning it. Although, this would have been more isolated and required clearing and improvement.

If Ned's father was broken in spirit and body, as some have claimed, there was still plenty of energy

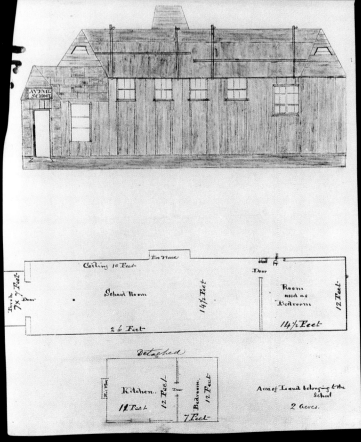

Top: Avenel bridge and toll-gate on Hughes Creek: the township as the Kelly family saw it. The camera has captured the rough nature of the place and quiet plodding pace there in the 1860s. Smoke obscures a group of heavy covered wagons and their teams near the large tree beyond the bridge. The line of white telegraph posts leads from the photographer who was on the east side of the crossing, up past the tollhouse to Esau Shelton's Royal Mail Hotel. In 1864, Avenel had around 30 buildings; most of the town allotments were unfenced, apart from the gardens and orchards of the more prosperous residents. As Eliza Mutton recalled, interest always centred on passing traffic. The arrival of the police coach was of great interest, 'especially to the children, who could see the prisoners staring out from the iron bars of the coaches, or being transferred in fetters to the lockup for an overnight stop'.

Left: Avenel common school, 17 September 1874. The building had high slab walls, a large bark roof, chimney, and a small shingled porch facing onto the street. The main structure was twelve metres long (40 feet) and the classroom was eight by 4.3 metres wide (26 by 14 feet). An average of 45 pupils divided into four classes that shared the space. The floor was wooden and walls canvas-lined, with minimal lighting and ventilation. The room was fitted with wall-desks on two sides, two twelve-foot desks, 68 feet of forms to sit on, two small blackboards and a set of maps.

Overleaf: Hughes Creek, where Shelton's rescue took place.

Far left: Schoolmaster James J. Irving was a stern disciplinarian who occasionally 'boxed' pupils' ears and used a leather strap on those who did not perform well. According to the visiting inspector, he was not particularly well organised, but was nevertheless a qualified and experienced teacher. Ned did well under his stern eye and Irving, when asked later, confirmed that 'all the Kellys behaved well at school'.

Top left and middle: Elizabeth and Esau Shelton, Richard Shelton's parents, gratefully presented Ned with a green silk sash with heavy bullion and gold-plated metallic fringe. The colour was emblematic of Irish heritage. Sashes were worn around the waist and popular since the gold rush to identify national groups. By contrast, English immigrants favoured red.

Below: Richard Shelton. The undated portrait was taken about the time of his rescue. He was between six and seven years old when Ned – about four years older – pulled him to the creek bank and back to life.

Facing page: Avenel township and surrounds. Portion of an early map shows the Sydney road cutting across two channels of Hughes Creek in the bottom right corner. Apart from the railway, which came later, the area is shown as the Kellys knew it, with the land rented by them shown in black.

in his growing family. The older children, Annie, Ned and Maggie, commenced school in the slab and bark-roofed school run by James and Henrietta Irving. James was a strict but capable and experienced teacher, conducting four grades in the same large room. While 56 pupils were enrolled, nearly a third of these were regularly absent. This may have been for a variety of reasons. Children were regularly required to work at home and sometimes, the weekly four-pence cost to attend the school was simply too much. Irving was also known to deliver stern punishments to students who did not perform well. As L.J. Blake (1980:8) pointed out, you could generally tell which children were poor: the most roughly clad ones came from the huts of bush workers, itinerant teamsters and impoverished farmers who eked out a small subsistence. Those better presented were the offspring of innkeepers, tradesmen or storekeepers. Lack of shoes often distinguished the two groups.

The meticulous diary entries of Schools Inspector Brown preserved some details of Ned's school performance. On 30 March 1864 he tested 39 Avenel students who were over the age of seven – young Edward and Margaret Kelly among them. Both passed reading and writing. Ned passed his third-grade spelling but failed arithmetic, grammar and geography – but so did the rest of his classmates, so it may have been due to poor teaching or difficult questions. Eventually, Brown passed 25 of the 36 Avenel children.

The following year, Ned entered fourth grade but his sister Maggie, having failed arithmetic, stayed in second grade. On 30 March 1865 Schools Inspector Brown repeated the tests. This time Ned passed arithmetic as well as reading and writing.

Around September 1864, when a severe drought was beginning to take hold across most of the country, the Kelly children were treated to some additional excitement. The Quinns, with their fully laden wagons and livestock, passed through Avenel on their way north to take up a pastoral run at Glenmore in the King River valley district.

The Quinns' decision to move north was a considerable one, and eventually most of the filial network followed in their wake. The two married

LUCK OF THE IRISH

CAPTURE AND DEATH OF MORGAN, THE BUSHRANGER—[DRAWN BY N. CHEVALIER, ESQ.]—See Page 10.

A matter of example; the death of Morgan, from a contemporary drawing by Chevalier. While the Kellys attended school at Avenel, they were also absorbing other formative influences. 1865 was a peak period for bushranging and its violent consequences. On 9 April 1865 at Peechelba station in north-eastern Victoria, bushranger Daniel Morgan was shot in the back. Few had sympathy for Morgan, who was considered to be a pathological murderer, but enduring public affection remained for Ben Hall and John Gilbert, shot dead soon after in New South Wales. In the same colony fourteen years later, the Kellys rode through Jerilderie at the peak of their career shouting 'Hoorah for the good old times of Morgan and Ben Hall!'

Lloyd aunts and their families eventually settled at Greta, and the Millers would later select Nillahcootie near Mansfield. The remote cattle station Ned's grandparents and remaining unmarried aunts and uncles took up included 10,125 hectares (25,000 acres) with a carrying capacity of only 400 head – indicating how untamed the land was.

The £2,000 investment to purchase the lease was a very considerable amount for the time – evidence of the Quinns' accumulated wealth – but it was also a risky venture. The new homestead was as far away from development and social distractions as one could find. But the isolation offered them freedom and land – a marvellous and wild expanse of 63 square kilometres (39 square miles) of mountainous country and river valley – a lofty monarchy where only they ruled.

The motivations of the Quinns, Kellys and Lloyds energised young Ned. Land, space, freedom – to work, play, love and compete – formed the essence of family aspirations and action. They were not primarily motivated by desire for wealth or the easier prospects of a coming civilisation. For them, social position rested on respect in the working-class bush community – from prowess in bush skills, excelling at physical activities and strong family ties. For many Irish–Australians, 'land was life itself' – the key to self-realisation and wellbeing. Conservatives in the community would criticise them for being a 'wild lot' but the Quinns and the Kellys viewed this as living life to the full – a positive quality to be passed on to their children. This ethos was as influential to young Ned as his formal education with Father O'Hea at Mass, and at school with James Irving's wall-charts and British world-view.

Ned may have worshipped his mother and grandmother, but his role models were a battling father, tough grandfather and uncles whose standing rested on how they fared in the struggle to survive. The reality of bush life was seldom romantic; rural work at the time was hard, dreary and unrelenting. In the face of floods, droughts, bushfires and child mortality, it was often heartbreaking. Avaricious banking practices and over-zealous policing did not

Top: The Avenel lock-up, where Ned's father was gaoled on several occasions. In photographer Thomas Washbourne's plate, a trooper obligingly poses at the door with a customer who shows reluctance to enter the solid, but dark and draughty place.

Above: Campion's store. William Campion and unnamed bystanders pose outside Avenel's busiest establishment in the 1860s. As well as being storekeeper, post-master and correspondent for the local school, Campion was also registrar for births and deaths.

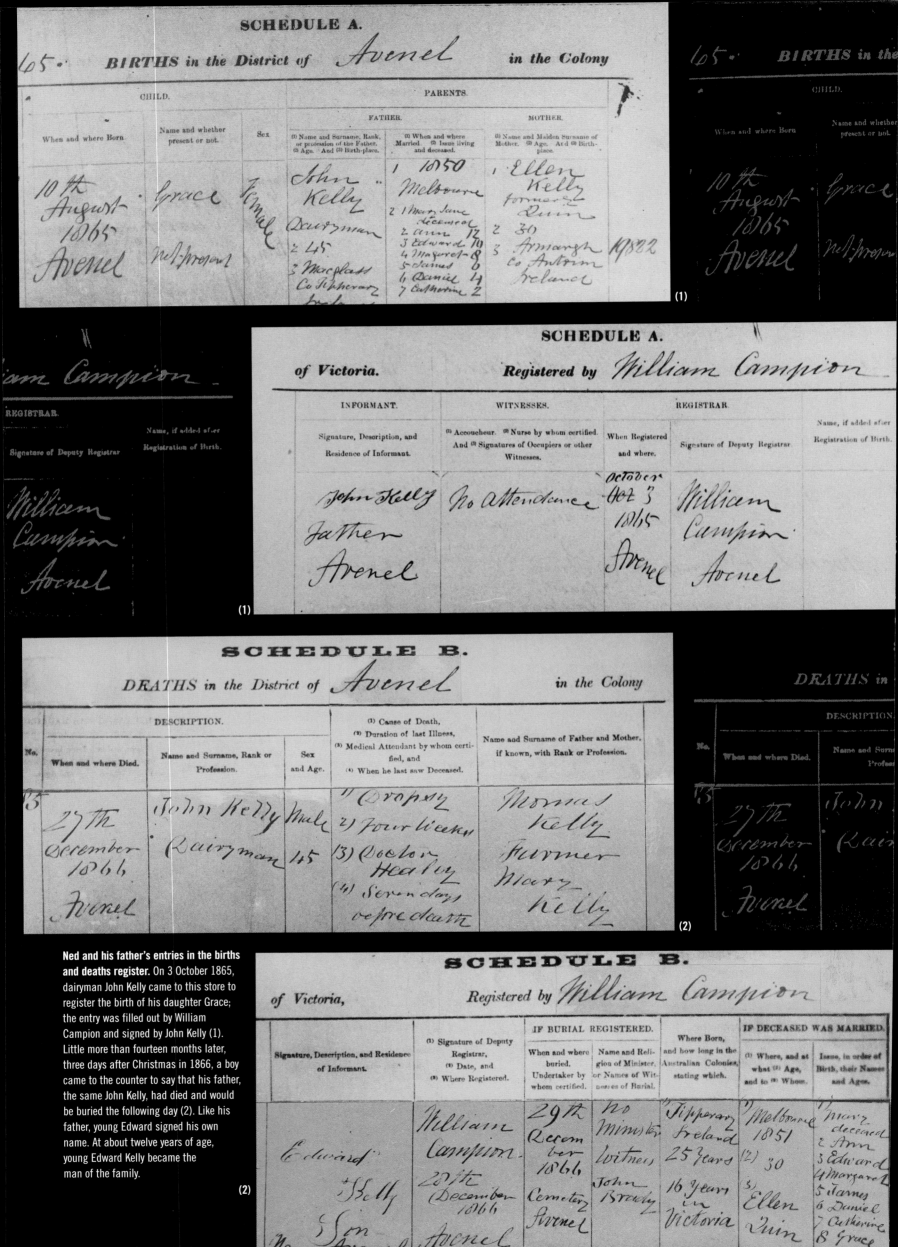

Ned and his father's entries in the births and deaths register. On 3 October 1865, dairyman John Kelly came to this store to register the birth of his daughter Grace; the entry was filled out by William Campion and signed by John Kelly (1). Little more than fourteen months later, three days after Christmas in 1866, a boy came to the counter to say that his father, the same John Kelly, had died and would be buried the following day (2). Like his father, young Edward signed his own name. At about twelve years of age, young Edward Kelly became the man of the family.

help matters either. In contrast to more peaceful citizens, games for these Irish–Australians males were sometimes as rough as their work. Pastimes of 'furious riding', drinking and brawling compensated for the loneliness. Several generations of Quinns and Kellys were also remembered as fine sportsmen: some as foot-runners but most often as equestrians.

Around this time in the mid-1860s, when Ned was eleven years old, he heroically saved the life of a young classmate. Each day on their way to school, Richard and Sarah Shelton took a shortcut across Hughes Creek from their home at the Royal Mail Hotel. On one occasion, Richard, six or seven years old, slipped into a deep waterhole. He was on the point of drowning when Ned dived in and, 'at the risk of his own life', rescued the little boy from a watery grave. Young Ned became a local hero, earning considerable esteem. Richard's parents were so grateful that his father, publican Esau Shelton, presented Ned with an impressive green silk sash with a heavy bullion fringe. A lifetime later, this small reward was still among Ned Kelly's most valued possessions. The public recognition and appreciation must have been pivotal in his early experience – a rare exception to family setbacks and humiliations.

The year 1865 was also significant beyond the Kelly family. In January, the British Government announced it would cease convict transportation to Australia – the system that had banished (or liberated) his father to the other side of the globe. On 9 April, newspapers reported the end of the American Civil War – followed less than a week later by the brutal assassination of their president, Abraham Lincoln.

Much has been made of the influences of an ex-convict father and lawless uncles on the Kelly children. But the influence too often ignored was the nineteenth-century trend of hero-worshipping bushrangers. During the convict period, local bush robbers, dubbed 'bushrangers', sometimes became heroes – and not only to the poor. In a country without war – and therefore without legitimate opportunity for gallantry and violence, the exploits of some law-breakers were covertly viewed as admirable. Although there were exceptions, bushrangers cultivated the English highwaymen stereotype, avoided bloodshed except towards police, and were considerate to women and children. They usually robbed the prosperous, because it was more profitable, and subsidised supporters among the poor, on whom they relied for shelter and hiding. With a show of gallantry, real or feigned, they built up an aura of romantic glamour around what was usually a desperate and miserable life. Their example provided excitement in the difficult lives of bush people and urban dwellers alike. Some policemen – those who abused their powers or were seen to represent harsh authority – were just as often considered to be the villains.

'On the Tallarook Ranges', from Cassell's picturesque *Australasia*.

Bushranging first became prevalent during the gold rushes, but between 1861 and 1865 it reached a climax when Frank Gardiner, Ben Hall and John Gilbert inspired so many others. With characteristic humbug, newspapers filled their columns with extensive reports of disgraceful but daring exploits. One desperado of the period – an exception to the highwaymen stereotype – was Daniel Morgan, a pathetic and cruel murderer who terrorised southern New South Wales for nearly two years. Morgan came close to, if he was not part of, the Quinn family history. In the first week of April 1865, he returned to Victoria – visiting stations and former employers on the upper King River. On 6 April, Morgan arrived at Whitfield station, on the Quinns' northern and river boundary, intending to shoot the owner, Evans, who had fired buckshot into Morgan's back in a previous skirmish. Evans was away so Morgan burnt the haystacks and granary and left saying he would call at Degamero station, opposite the Quinn homestead. That lucky owner was also absent. The manager there claimed that the Quinns 'harboured the bushranger'. Years later the belief was still popular, although never proven. Morgan was ambushed three days later on 9 April at Peechelba station, north-west of Wangaratta, shot in the back without opportunity of surrender.

Within a month, Ben Hall and John Gilbert were killed under similar circumstances. Police in Victoria and New South Wales adopted the unofficial practice of not allowing surrender when cornering bushrangers, even when the culprits were greatly outnumbered. As Ian Jones (1995:23) observed, this practice tended to diminish any moral lesson and embittered impressionable bush youths. In December that year, in the Kelly's own neighbourhood, a small-time bushranger calling himself 'Lowry' was also arrested after a series of hold-ups on the Sydney road and sentenced to four years for shooting with intent and horse-stealing. It was suggested he knew the Kellys, and years later the association was renewed.

During winter and spring of 1865, physical factors such as the worsening drought impacted directly on the Kellys at Avenel. At this time, they occupied a bark-roofed hut some distance from the south-eastern corner of their property. This dwelling was apparently more primitive than their Beveridge home – probably because it was on rented land. The owner's daughter and Ned's fellow pupil, Eliza Mutton, remembered: 'the family had a hard struggle to make ends meet . . . and knew what it was to go hungry'. At this stage, the Kellys gained most of their income by selling milk and butter to Campion's store, the hotels and local householders. But by May 1865, the paddocks were still dry without the autumn rain, forcing Red to kill off stock in order to minimise loss. Unable to support his wife and six children by dairying, he also sold beef in and around Avenel. This aroused the suspicion of some unsympathetic neighbours.

The Morgans, more substantial landowners, were based about 2.5 kilometres (1.5 miles) downstream from the Kellys, but possibly rented land adjoining them. If relations between the struggling Irish-Catholic Kellys and the Methodist Morgans were not good in early 1865, as oral tradition maintains, they got worse that May when Philip Morgan lost a heifer calf. When he went looking for it along the creek, he passed by the Kellys hut and noticed hind-quarters hanging on a hook. He returned later with Constable Doxey and a search warrant. Everything was there but the complete hide (including brand), which the law required him to keep. Ned's father was arrested and appeared in the local courthouse on charges of cattle-stealing and unlawful possession of a hide. The first charge was dismissed but the latter was upheld. The family maintained it was a 'trumped-up charge', and to their dismay Red was fined £25 or given the alternative of six months' imprisonment with hard labour. Kelly's worst fears were realised. Instead of alleviating the family's desperate predicament, he added to it. The family had no savings and it appears Kelly served out the time with some remission, either at the Avenel cells or Kilmore Gaol.

On his return on 3 October 1865, Red registered the birth of another daughter, Grace, at Campion's store – almost two months after she was born. By this time, the Kelly children no longer attended school, probably due to financial difficulties. On 12 December 1865, Red was arrested again for being drunk and disorderly. He lost five shillings surety a week later when he did not turn up to court, but this settled the case.

The following year signalled even more unhappy developments. The children did not return to the Avenel school in 1866. They were required to help at home or the family was too proud to ask for exemption from fees. Little was recorded of the family at this time, although the wife of one unsympathetic neighbour claimed 'they were light-fingered people who had a tendency to pick up things that were not nailed down'. Most of 1866 passed with uneventful struggle and mounting desperation. By August it was noted that Red had fenced in five acres of their leased land. By this time, eleven-year-old Ned had most likely committed his first offence. In the October issue of the *Police Gazette*, a traveller's chestnut mare was reported missing at Hughes Creek. The *Gazette* noted that it was 'supposed taken to Quinn's Station, King River . . . by Daniel Kelly'. Ned used his brother's name as an alias and this referred to an overland trip to visit his grandparents. Although nothing came of the incident, this was the first official reference to his alleged delinquent ventures.

Meanwhile Ned's father was in more serious trouble – but not with the authorities. When he returned from gaol he was a sick man, dogged by anxiety for his wife and seven children, and broken-hearted at the collapse of all his hopes for them. His health collapsed in the spring of 1866 when he

Early postcard: 'A Family Hut' by L. H. Davey.

'Bush burial, F. McCubbin 1890, collection Geelong Gallery, purchased by public subscription 1900.'

developed dropsy, and by December he was bed-ridden. Doctor Heeley was called out from Seymour late in the month, but by this stage Red was beyond treatment. Two days after a sad Christmas, 46-year-old John 'Red' Kelly died at their hut. The following day, twelve-year-old Ned registered his father's death at Campion's store and became the man of the family. On 29 December Red Kelly was given a pioneer's burial in the corner of the cemetery opposite the courthouse.

Without Red, the family was destitute. At 39, Ellen was left alone with seven children to support, in an age without social welfare. Within a few months, she took out her bitterness and frustration on relatives and neighbours alike. Her sister-in-law, Anne Ryan (nee Kelly), settled temporarily in Avenel, possibly to lend help, but she and Ellen got into a fight which ended in court six weeks after Red's funeral. They charged each other with assault. Ellen was found guilty, ordered to pay 40 shillings damages, five shillings costs or spend seven days in the lock-up. By 28 May, the feisty women were back in court – but this time united against Anne's landlord. Thomas Ford claimed Ellen had damaged his property and charged her with abusive and threatening language. Ellen counter-claimed, with Anne as her witness, that he had assaulted her. However, both Ellen and Ford were found guilty! Ellen was fined another 40 shillings or seven days' detention. Both were bound to keep the peace for six months on a £50 bond – a considerable sum at the time. Ellen's fine was generously paid by friends and she was allowed to go home to her bewildered children.

These various dramas with the law, compounded by the death of her husband and their desperate circumstances, prompted the family's next move. Ellen and the children packed their animals and belongings and headed off again, even further away from civilisation.

It was around this time that Michael 'Black' Kelly (no relation) accused Ned of interfering with livestock after one of his mares disappeared. Black Kelly reported his suspicion – after the Kellys had departed – that twelve-year-old Edward Kelly had taken the animal to Violet Town, their assumed destination. Ned was listed in the *Police Gazette* as 'charged with Horse Stealing' and rated a description in the June edition. The horse may have re-appeared as no warrant was issued and nothing came of this mention in the wanted list.

Ned, his mother and siblings, possibly accompanied by one of the Quinn uncles, travelled 100 kilometres (about 63 miles) north-east in their dray along the rutted Sydney road. It would have taken several days at a pace of only six kilometres per hour and at night, the family camped under their vehicle. They passed through Euroa, Violet Town and Benalla on the Broken River, then finally branched off due east at a coach-stop called Winton. The Kellys stopped just beyond Futter's Range at the small settlement of Greta, situated on Fifteen Mile Creek at the edge of the rich Oxley plains. Here, 209 kilometres (over 130 miles) inland from Melbourne, against the spectacular backdrop of the Victorian Alps, Ellen's sisters, Catherine and Jane Lloyd, were also struggling to survive with large families of young children. But in Greta, John and James Quinn had moved in with their sisters to help support their large families.

John Kelly was given the same sort of funeral that artist Frederick McCubbin observed so poignantly in 'bush burial'. One kilometre along the track from their hut on Hughes Creek, a grave was sunk in the uncleared, unfenced south-west corner of the Avenel cemetery reserve. With only the company of a friend, John Brady, the family said their last farewells, and like thousands of others in his time, John was left without even a stone to mark his existence.

3 RETURN TO THE CLAN
GRETA, 1867–70

The Kelly family's move north from Avenel was a major turning point in their lives. It distanced them from their many sad memories and bad luck. In Greta, Ellen and her family joined her sisters, Catherine and Jane Lloyd, where they would be closer to the Quinn parents at Glenmore station.

However, the move was not solely motivated by a wish to be closer to family. Under the *Land Selection Acts*, the government was progressively releasing farm blocks from the edges of vast pastoral leases and making them available to 'selectors' with little capital. Ellen and others in her clan recognised the opportunity to improve their lot.

Ned's family took up residence in Greta township, in a big old rambling timber house that had previously been a hotel. They lived with Catherine and Jane Lloyd and their children, and also John and James Quinn. With fourteen rooms under the main roof, it was one of the largest local buildings – and necessary as the combined household totalled 22 at the dinner table!

At this time the aunts were supporting themselves by farming while both Lloyd husbands were in prison. The Quinn uncles lived with them at intervals to handle the heavier work and to buy and sell stock for them. The women grazed a herd of cattle on leased land in and near the township. They fattened pigs for sale, kept fowls and milked cows, and were growing and harvesting wheat during Ellen's stay. It is likely that the Kellys brought their own livestock with them, but Catherine Lloyd said that 'Mrs Kelly lived with us but had no [financial] interest in the place'.

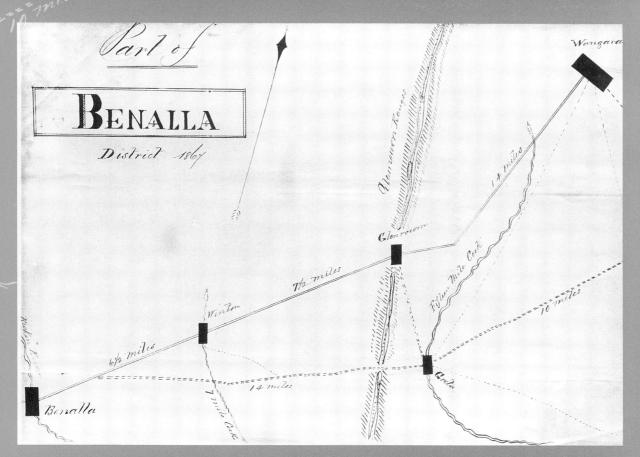

Greta and district. While the Kellys made their way north along the Sydney road, a settler on the Oxley plains was drawing, with painstaking effort, this plan of the locality they chose for a new life. What is shown as the Glenrowan Range was described on official maps as 'Futter's Range'. Adding to confusion, north of Glenrowan was locally referred to as the 'Warby Range'.

Proeschel's 1860s 'Desk and Traveller's Map' of the north-eastern Murray District of Victoria. The heavier dotted line indicates the telegraph. Greta was on the old route to Beechworth but also to the country south along the King River to Glenmore station, located just below the 'Y' of Murray. The Kellys and Lloyds were within 48 kilometres of their parents.

The settlement of Greta was situated on the Fifteen Mile Creek (out from Benalla) at a bridge and coach-stop. At Greta, the road, or track as it was then, branched in three directions – left towards Wangaratta, ahead on the old route to the Beechworth diggings, and right to the south-east through Moyhu, the upper King River and eventually Glenmore station.

The township consisted of a small collection of rough buildings scattered around the bridge and crossroads and was the central village for the five vast pastoral leases that surrounded it. It was often described as picturesque because of the park-like setting among tall, ancient red gums. The people in the area were small farmers, owners of a few cattle, carriers on the roads, and were generally in poor circumstances. The township had a school, hotel, store, blacksmith and even a shoemaker. At the time it did not have a church, police camp, or apparently, a post office.

At the rear of their house the Lloyds owned a detached brick building near a piggery and large stockyard. They allowed an elderly schoolmaster, John Lyons, to lease and renovate this building as the first local common school. The younger Kelly children most likely attended along with their cousins but no records survive. Schools Inspector Brown included Greta in his north-eastern circuit in 1867 and was told by the Lloyd children that their fathers, Tom and Jack, were both 'away from home at Pentridge'. They had been arrested at their Greta stockyards in 1865 with cattle belonging to a neighbour and were sentenced at Beechworth to five years' imprisonment. The Quinn brothers were allegedly implicated in the same trouble but were not charged, so they moved in to help their sisters manage.

The Kellys' stay turned out to be a brief one. Ellen and the children had just settled in before another tragedy befell the already disadvantaged families. Early one morning in January 1868 the Kellys and Lloyds narrowly escaped being incinerated when their home was deliberately burnt to the ground. Adding to their misery, the arsonist was Ned's uncle, James Kelly.

After release from prison and the death of his brother John 'Red' Kelly in 1866, James had kept in touch with the family. Ellen recalled 'he sometimes stopped for a few days and had shown me acts of kindness'. Like Ned's father, James had an affection for alcohol, which also got him into trouble. A week before the fire, he turned up drunk and mischievous and the women sent him away. He returned on 27 January to make peace with them but was drunk again, made an offensive remark to Kate Lloyd and a fierce brawl resulted. One sister broke a gin bottle over his head and Ellen chased him through nearby O'Brien's Hotel with a stick. Later that night, Kate Lloyd was woken to see the outside wall on fire and James Kelly illuminated by the flames. The building burned quickly as it was tinder dry from the drought that had gripped the area. The sisters only had time to wake the children and escape.

Uncle James Kelly was found hiding in the Greta shoemaker's shop, arrested, then tried at Beechworth the following April. To the probable horror even of the homeless Kellys and Lloyds – Ellen and Ned were almost certainly in court – he was sentenced to death for a vicious, drunken prank. This was handed down by judge (later Sir) Redmond Barry, whose presence on the Victorian Judicial Bench was one of the most unfortunate coincidences in the experience of the whole Kelly family. The sentence was later reviewed and mitigated by the Executive Council to fifteen years hard labour and James went back to prison for the rest of his useful life. The severity of the judgment was intended to demonstrate brute official force and had been handed down by an expert.

So the Kelly family's lives were redirected once again. According to Joseph Ashmead, neighbours at Greta took up a collection for the families left with little more than the clothes they were wearing. Ellen was able to rent a cottage in Wangaratta and took in washing and dressmaking for a time while Ned may have stayed with Quinn and Lloyd relatives at Greta.

Judge Redmond Barry was the Kellys' social antithesis and nemesis rolled into one. He was a great cultural benefactor but not known for compassion as a judge. Instead, he was 'intoxicated with the awful power of his position', and known as 'the hanging judge'. A pillar of the Protestant ascendancy and Victorian colonial society, Barry was born of the landed Anglo–Irish establishment. But the Fenians drove his relatives from their country house (and his childhood home) and torched it. Consequently, he was not warmly disposed to democratic principles or to the landless Irish. He believed the 'lower orders' should be taxed and kept down, 'placed little faith in reformation and rehabilitation, and his sentencing ... was designed to keep those who had fallen foul of the law out of society for as long as possible'. He applied this formula with extra rigour towards ex-felons who he viewed as 'a hateful threat'. His prejudices had clear and dire consequence for the Kellys.

'H.L. Houten, Bush farm, Victoria, 1876, oil on canvas, 41.2 x 61cm. Art Gallery of New South Wales, photo: Jenni Carter for AGNSW'

'A Bush Farm in Victoria, 1876'. H.L. Houten admirably conveys the positive aspects of life in remote districts for settlers like the Kellys. No photograph has surfaced of the original Kelly hut, but from descriptions this painting captures the scale and character well; even if the immediate locality is less hilly. The small building stood on the south side of the track where it intersects the Eleven Mile Creek. The interior was divided into five compartments with blankets and calico partitions. It most likely had a detached kitchen and smokehouse. A visitor recalled that the hut was 'about twelve feet across, and is built of slabs, with a bark roof. There are not many trees immediately about the place but the timber is heavy beyond a brush fence.' The hut accommodated a constant flow of visitors and extended family. Their recollections of weekend dances, card-games and sporting competitions are in stark contrast to the 'squalid grog-shanty' image promoted by police.

In mid-1868, the chance came to take over a land selection. Possibly helped and encouraged by her brothers, Ellen moved to the outlying Greta district to take up an 88-acre (35 hectares) block on the Winton track. The selection was five kilometres (three miles) west of Greta on the Eleven Mile Creek in the Lurg parish.

This would have been a daunting task for the widow and mother of seven. She was required to develop and cultivate an uncleared and unfenced portion of bush eighteen kilometres (eleven miles) from the nearest large town, but the land offered them a preferable existence and independence. It provided the children with a focus for their energy and the opportunity to develop rural skills. While isolated, there was an availability of water, although the creek sometimes dried up in summer. There was already a large slab hut with a bark roof, located on the south side of the road where the creek met the regularly trafficked route to Wangaratta, Beechworth and up-country.

The Kellys' selection, 57A, was in a line of 88-acre blocks along the south side of the track. They were the smallest in the district and cut from the north-west boundary of Robert McBean's Kilfeera station only two years earlier. The sub-divisions were much to the displeasure of McBean, who had tried to purchase them back several times. The surrounding country was as wild as it was remote. It was only 'fair' agricultural ground, elevating slightly to the south and situated in a wide basin between two low arms of Futter's Range.

While some Kelly biographers have romanticised their situation, and others have emphasised the wretchedness, their new home was not unusual or shameful for bush settlers. Their hut was crude and uncomfortable by urban middle-class standards, but the place was still popular with a steady stream of visitors and lodgers. The difficulty was not only in living conditions hard to imagine today, but in what was expected of them as selectors.

The *Land Selection Acts* were both a blessing and a bind. They were based on the commendable democratic ideal of unlocking vast tracts of pastoral leases to a population of small agriculturists. They were nevertheless framed in such a way that some degree of failure was inevitable. Within the rules of the system, settlers had to clear and cultivate the land and were not allowed to take outside work. These provisions were an attempt to ensure the quick cultivation of the land, but they were difficult to meet when droughts were frequent and the land was only fair quality.

The system favoured those with expertise, those first into an area and those with capital. Settlers like Ellen Kelly with little or no financial backing could rent the land for £11 per annum and, providing conditions were met, they would own their block within eight years.

Selectors like the Kellys often had to break the rules of the *Land Selection Acts* in order to survive and raise the rental money. It was common for selectors' daughters to take outside work and for sons to take seasonal work such as shearing, fencing, clearing or stock-work on stations. Even if the rules could be 'got around', frequent droughts reduced or wiped

Unidentified selector at Lurg. The Kellys provided much-needed social contact for lonely bush workers like this neighbour. His hut was smaller than that of the Kellys, but typical of most accommodation. Each year it was necessary to undertake clearing or initially ring-barking as shown here, boundary fencing, pasture improvement and cultivation. Selectors had to occupy their blocks and were not allowed to work outside. If these conditions were not met or rents maintained, forfeiture could follow. Experienced farmers who selected ample fertile ground in higher rainfall zones or near permanent water and markets could manage and even prosper within these constraints. But battlers like this fellow and the Kellys faced difficult odds. Hardship arose from geographic, climatic and economic limitations.

out productivity. Only those in high-rainfall areas could set aside fodder for these regular setbacks.

Adding to the difficult nature of selection, pastoralists who lost acreage to selectors applied their considerable power and capital to undermine attempted land reform. Under the *Land Selection Acts*, individuals could purchase only one block per year. Pastoralists got around this by using family members and employees to buy on their behalf. With their prior knowledge of the land's capabilities, they 'peacocked' the best portions, particularly water frontages, rendering alienated land near useless for farming.

While the *Land Selection Acts* were manipulated by pastoralists and selectors alike, it was pastoralists who took the most advantage. Station owners sat on local councils, roads boards, stock protection society boards, parliament, and acted as magistrates. While there were philanthropic exceptions, many primarily served the interests of their propertied class, manipulating legislation, handing out fines and disadvantaging selectors – applying law and order – but adding to poverty and social unrest. As selections were abandoned or forfeited for non-compliance, they were picked-off by wealthier entrepreneurs (sometimes neighbours).

As Ann Galbally (1995:184) has noted, men such as the Kellys' neighbour, squatter and magistrate Robert McBean, were able to disseminate their version of the rural situation to friends and fellow members of the Melbourne Club, those who held ultimate power – the judges and police chiefs. The Quinns were social exceptions in this situation. While pastoralists, they were not well-educated, gentry or power-brokers and were in fact despised by some of their well-connected neighbours.

So it was within these socio-economic and geographic circumstances that Ellen and her children took on their selection at the Eleven Mile Creek. But if the task was difficult, Ellen was far from naïve after decades of experience on small land-holdings. She knew she could not rely solely on agricultural returns. While she was aware that it was outside the law, Ellen planned to support the family and subsidise the necessary land improvements by opening her hut as a shanty – an unofficial 'sly grog-shop'. If the place was not ideal for agricultural purposes, it was for a wayside stop offering accommodation, meals and refreshments to carriers, travellers and neighbouring selectors. The eldest girls would assist with housekeeping and gardening, while the boys would help with clearing, fencing and stock work.

The Kellys' first months at Lurg passed uneventfully, but not so for uncle James Quinn. He

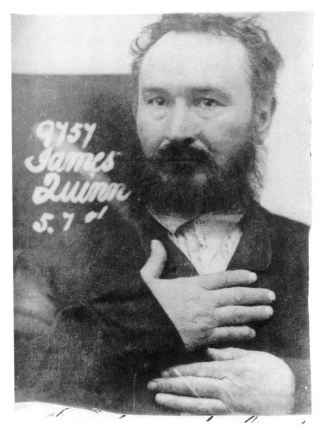

helped Ellen settle at the Eleven Mile Creek and was probably living with them and the Lloyd aunts, while actually a fugitive.

Both James and John Quinn used the Kelly and Lloyd stockyards for cutting and branding cattle and to break horses. During this time, James was wanted for assault and grievous bodily harm at Greta and had successfully evaded arrest for two years. When he heard that the complainant had sailed for England, James gave himself up and was remanded at Benalla in September 1868. From this time Ned had to abandon any further schooling and within a year his younger brother James began working for local hawkers (travelling merchants). According to one local, the younger children were 'growing up wild for want of schooling' after their move to the Eleven Mile Creek.

1869 was another tough year for the Kellys. It brought more drought and social problems. By this stage, fifteen-year-old Ned was helping boarders to clear trees, split timber for fencing, and cultivate the land. Among the less agriculturally minded visitors to their home that year was a fugitive directed there by the Lloyd uncles. Irishman Henry Johnstone would trade on the roads as 'Harry Power' – one of

James 'Jimmy' Quinn was probably one of the worst influences on the Kelly children as a result of his most redeeming feature – affection for his sisters. James was the wildest of a wild family and was gaoled regularly for nearly two decades. Nearly all of his convictions resulted from violent assault; even nephew Ned had to run for his life in August 1870. Quinn was six feet tall and solidly built. One eye was turned, his face was scarred and his left hand 'deformed from a gunshot wound'.

Overleaf: Colony of Victoria in the 1870s.

RETURN TO THE CLAN 29

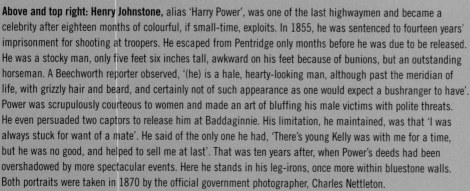

Above and top right: Henry Johnstone, alias 'Harry Power', was one of the last highwaymen and became a celebrity after eighteen months of colourful, if small-time, exploits. In 1855, he was sentenced to fourteen years' imprisonment for shooting at troopers. He escaped from Pentridge only months before he was due to be released. He was a stocky man, only five feet six inches tall, awkward on his feet because of bunions, but an outstanding horseman. A Beechworth reporter observed, '(he) is a hale, hearty-looking man, although past the meridian of life, with grizzly hair and beard, and certainly not of such appearance as one would expect a bushranger to have'. Power was scrupulously courteous to women and made an art of bluffing his male victims with polite threats. He even persuaded two captors to release him at Baddaginnie. His limitation, he maintained, was that 'I was always stuck for want of a mate'. He said of the only one he had, 'There's young Kelly was with me for a time, but he was no good, and helped to sell me at last'. That was ten years after, when Power's deeds had been overshadowed by more spectacular events. Here he stands in his leg-irons, once more within bluestone walls. Both portraits were taken in 1870 by the official government photographer, Charles Nettleton.

Above: Robert McBean contributed more than anyone to the capture of Power. He was an astute manager and exerted considerable influence in the Benalla district. He was also on friendly terms with Jack Lloyd and employed Jack's son, Tom Lloyd, on Kilfeera station while the father acted as his 'insider' with the clan. After persuading Jack to betray the bushranger, and after getting back the gold watch he is shown wearing, McBean secretly paid Lloyd instalments of the £500 he was promised through his brother-in-law, James Quinn.

the last of the highwaymen. He had escaped from garbage disposal duty outside Pentridge Gaol in February and headed north-east for shelter among friends. Police speculated that he would find help with Kelly relatives at Beveridge, the Lloyds at Greta, or with Ellen Kelly at Lurg, among others. They were correct; he called on the Lloyd aunts at the Fifteen Mile Creek in March or April – around the same time that their husbands were released from prison. Thereafter, he stayed with the Kellys.

Ellen was not overwhelmed by Harry Power, recalling him as 'a brown-paper bushranger who could not make tucker either for himself or his friends'. But to Ned, he was a celebrity and a potential mentor.

In April 1869, the family had a festive expedition to St Patrick's Church in Wangaratta for Anne Kelly's wedding to a young selector, Alex Gunn. They both lived at the already crowded Kelly hut and Annie continued working for her mother as housekeeper.

At this time too there was romance in Ellen's life. Ellen possibly met William Frost while in Wangaratta as he was a boundary rider at nearby Laceby. He became a regular visitor at the Kelly hut on weekends that year and after Ellen became pregnant in June 1869, Frost said he would marry her.

1869 also brought more close shaves with the law. In May, Robert McBean reported that sheep had been stolen from his Kilfeera run. In their investigations, police found mutton at the huts of Kelly neighbours, selectors Gunn (possibly a relation of Alex) and Stewart at Lurg.

At that time, Kilfeera extended up to the southern boundary of the Kelly selection on the Greta road. On the northern side of the road was Springs station and less than a kilometre west was Emu station. Five kilometres east was the Myrrhee run. Stock from all these big properties (including unmarked and unbranded animals) occasionally strayed along the road.

At the court hearing in June 1869 at Benalla, fourteen-year-old Ned, who gave his occupation as a splitter, testified that he had a small flock of unbranded sheep that he kept on the Myrrhee station. The boy swore he sold Gunn two sheep on the day the meat was discovered. The judge was not convinced and Gunn and Stewart were fined. A few weeks earlier, uncle Tom Lloyd also made local news after a drunken brawl at Greta where a trooper had to fire his revolver over the brawlers' heads to subdue them. He was fortunate only to be fined.

Then in August 1869 Ellen's 66-year-old father and Ned's grandfather James Quinn died from dysentery at Glenmore station. His body was brought down to Moyhu cemetery, east of Greta near the King River, where he was given a pioneer's burial. With James Quinn senior gone, the extended family lost their strongest moderating influence. His sons Jack, Jimmy and William (eldest brother Patrick had drowned in the Murray in 1850) took over the property for their mother. This involved legal transfer and brought the family under police scrutiny once again. Discussing the death of Quinn senior, one detective wrote unflatteringly:

the deceased is the father of James and John Quinn at present residing on Glenmore station, the former of which is at present committed for trial for assault with attempt to rob. John is one of the most reputed cattle stealers in the district. Their brother-in-laws Thomas and John Lloyd are only discharged from Pentridge some short time and are at present residing in the locality of Greta where the Quinns often resort . . . The Quinns and Lloyds are suspected of harbouring Power the bushranger since his appearance in the district.

The detective was right about Power and Jimmy Quinn but there was no firm evidence for the accusation against John (or 'Jack', as he was

John 'Jack' Quinn was a great rider and stockman but neighbouring pastoralists had nothing positive to say about him. One wrote 'the young Quinns [as distinct from James senior] are continually in the habit of "duffing" whatever stock they can lay their hands on'; another claimed 'they are known horse and cattle stealers and suspected harbourers of bushrangers'. Jack was under surveillance for over two decades, charged several times, but never convicted of an offence. After the family sold the Glenmore lease to a neighbour, Lewis, in 1875, Jack led a rather nomadic existence living 'amongst a few of his friends in turn' while becoming a successful horse-breeder. Police attempted to prosecute him under the *Vagrancy Act* until it was shown that he ran over 300 horses and cattle on land leased from stations near Hedi and Moyhu. This portrait was taken when John was 40 years old. His crooked nose was broken in a fight and his cheek bears a scar.

known) for he was never convicted of an offence. Neighbours opposed transfer of the lease to the sons, and one feared retaliation if this became known. But as John McQuilton pointed out (1979:72), only one neighbour reported stock stolen between 1864 and 1869 and the stock was recovered by the owner. The Quinns were highly unpopular for mustering 'clean-skin' strays, but seldom mentioned is that the Quinns also reported stock stolen during this period. Nor did they have any luck prosecuting those who killed their livestock. However, with the death of James Quinn senior, the clan began to live up to police expectations.

Power was provided with shelter at Glenmore and by May 1869, it was noticed that 'the old fox' occasionally had a young assistant who stayed at a distance during hold-ups. At that time Dr Rowe, of Mount Battery station near Mansfield, observed two suspicious characters sunning themselves on the hill overlooking his horse paddock. Stalking within range, he fired at them with a long-distance rifle, spraying gravel in their faces. Both jumped on their horses and fled. Power later admitted that it was him and 'young Kelly'.

This period saw increasing trouble and growing notoriety for the family. Their home had become an unofficial public house. The children were without the steadying influence of a father and were exposed to the examples of their wild uncles and the rough company that lodged at their hut. While these lodgers provided the family's income, they attracted even closer attention from police. In turn, this generated increased resentment of authority and more reckless behaviour ensued.

In September 1869, another incident drew police to the Kelly hut. One afternoon, as Anne sat sewing in the front doorway of the hut, a Chinese pig and fowl dealer came along the track and asked for a drink. She gave him creek-water – obviously not what he expected – and he flew into a rage. Ned heard the shouting from the paddock nearby where he was splitting and grubbing trees with a boarder, William Skillion and his mother's employee, William Grey. Ned went to see what the problem was and got into an argument with the traveller, whose English was very poor. Ned chased him down the track, and may have even beaten him with a stick.

Two weeks later, the *Benalla Ensign* devoted two columns to the boy's first appearance before a court as an accused, charged with assault and robbery. He had spent his first week and a half in the Benalla cells. With the help of an interpreter, Ah Fook alleged that he had been robbed as well as beaten. He had no witnesses and Anne Kelly, William Skillion and William Grey contradicted his story. The arresting sergeant Whelan testified that ferocious dogs had been set loose on him at the hut while Kelly 'ran into the bush at full speed', which he interpreted as evidence of the boy's guilt. Without enough evidence, the case was dismissed. According to the local reporter, 'the young lad left the dock inwardly rejoicing'.

Ned's association with Harry Power lasted until 1870; all the while he was tutored in a new way of life. He travelled with Power as far west as Kyneton and east across the Great Dividing Range into Gippsland near Bairnsdale. It was dangerous for a fourteen-year-old, but the travel offered escape from the drudgery at home, a chance to acquire more money than he could earn labouring, and achieve some social status. As Patrick O'Farrell (1987:140) put it, bushranging was light work offering high returns, adventure and the prospect of fame. It is apparent that from an early age, Kelly was determined to rise above anonymity and sought a 'larger than life' reputation. His involvement with Power was one step towards emulating and out-distancing his wild uncles.

An understanding of Kelly's complex and sometimes contradictory personality rests partly on consideration of these early developments, the cultural baggage, influences and prejudices that comprised the backdrop to his delinquent development. His early experiences did not necessarily justify his or his family's actions – but they help illuminate his motivations. It must be remembered that many poor bush settlers, equally hard-pressed, survived without drifting outside the law.

With 'Old Harry', as the clan called him, Ned worked from bases in the Greta district and upper King River. Power was generally careful not to commit robberies too close to his hideouts. He vigilantly chose to rob an assortment of travellers, carriers and coaches at strategic points between towns. He even disarmed an unfortunate constable. He avoided roads – sometimes covering distances of up to 100 kilometres a day to keep ahead of pursuers. Coach passengers, pastoralists and merchants were prime targets, while the poorest settlers were generally left in peace. Local sympathisers (who sheltered Power and provided him with information) were generously rewarded.

Credited with an ungovernable temper, Power usually acted coolly and affably towards his victims, cultivating the 'gentleman highwayman' image, but with a shotgun and two pistols levelled. On one occasion, he paused melodramatically to pray that a victim would co-operate. For all of Power's victims, the sight of his weapons and a mixture of courtesy, bluff and bluster ensured that he never had to shoot

---

Facing page: Power's Lookout. Two bushmen perch on the spot where thirty years before, in the early months of 1870, a bushranger and a boy watched out across the summer haze for the sign of approaching police. The view looks south-east and the floor of the King River valley can be seen in the distance. The valley is still timbered down to a few paddocks along the river as it was in the time of the Quinns, whose Glenmore homestead was directly below. Power vividly remembered the view from his spectacular bivouac. In gaol he asked a visitor if he had ever seen the ranges: 'It's there ye'll see the finest sights in the world. Ay! It's grand to be on the ranges, and to breathe the beautiful pure air, and to see Mount Feathertop far above ye, and, down below, for miles and miles, the beautiful country. There's water all the year round, and it's always cool and pleasant. That's the place for a man to live.'

Wangaratta police barracks and courthouse, as the Kellys knew it. Ellen appeared here in May 1870 when she escaped being prosecuted for selling illegal spirits. In April 1871 Ned, Alex Gunn and Wild Wright were held here on remand before transfer to Beechworth. Ellen's two youngest boys were hauled before this bench too in September 1871; again the charge was dismissed because of their age and intimacy with the owner, Jim's employer, Mark Krafft. The view looks north along Murphy Street, on a wet winter's day in 1866, showing the police station, with cells at rear and courthouse beyond.

anyone. Kelly, as the impressionable apprentice, was tutored in such showmanship.

Ned also learned to modify his language in the company of others. Nineteenth-century bush workers favoured foul language while in their own company (part legacy of convict background). Bullock drivers were most obvious in this way as they urged on their teams. Conversation was embroidered with profanities, oaths and curses while semantics were obscured with slang. The Quinn clan were no exception to this habit but as Ned acknowledged later, generally modified their language in the company of women.

Along with elocution lessons, Kelly learned the survival skills necessary for a fugitive existence. Power introduced Kelly to places where provisions could be obtained without betrayal and remote hideouts where stolen horses could be rested. He also showed him obscure tracks between settled river valley systems, and paths across the superb Victorian Alps.

By its sheer isolation Glenmore station provided one ideal retreat. Located on the King River flats, the Quinn homestead was between a bend in the river and lagoons near the western edge of the range. Their stockyards blocked access to a bridge and a wide, steep gully behind. Halfway up this gully, the Quinns cut toe-holes and drilled spy-holes inside a tall hollow tree that Power could use as a 'watch-box' or lookout. Further up the gully, about 1.6 kilometres (a mile) from the house, Power built a mia-mia for his camp. On a magnificent rocky outcrop overlooking the camp and the homestead below, he could get a commanding view as far as visibility would allow along the valley in both directions.

Power eventually made serious tactical errors. In March 1870 he stole a horse from a squatter neighbour of the Quinns on the King River and a few days later bailed up the influential pastoralist, Robert McBean. McBean's combined leases, Fern Hills and Kilfeera stations, comprised 68,000 acres or 106 square miles (27,540 hectares). This huge tract of country adjoined the Quinn's western boundary in the south and extended 105 kilometres (65 miles) north-west to the back boundary of Mrs Kelly's 'pocket-handkerchief sized block'. McBean was checking fences three kilometres from Kilfeera homestead and about eight kilometres south-east of the Kelly selection when he sighted two horsemen. He caught up with them and the stocky figure turned out to be Power. He initially thought his companion, the 'youth who remained in the background', was Ned Kelly. Power took the magistrate's valuable horse, saddle and bridle, but more importantly, an heirloom pocket-watch. This incident made McBean a powerful enemy for Power. He foolishly said he had been on the lookout for McBean to settle with him 'for having impounded some cattle belonging to Mrs Lloyd' – ignoring the fact that Mrs McBean had intervened to redeem the same animals. His slip implicated the Lloyds and later he offered to return the watch through them for £15, so providing an irresistible opportunity to the owner.

In April, Power and his boy were robbing travellers near Seymour. By the beginning of May they were 187 kilometres (116 miles) south-west of Kyneton holding up a number of people near Lauriston. One victim, detained for hours, described the assistant as 'twenty years [a considerable overestimation], five feet nine or ten inches tall, light build, sallow complexion, smooth face, surly, with the appearance of a half-caste'. Interestingly, a supposed double of Power, also with a young companion, was alleged to be conducting hold-ups in the north-east at this time. In April a warrant was issued and Kelly's uncle Jack Lloyd was arrested.

Robert McBean also approached his friend, Chief Commissioner of Police Charles Standish, at the Melbourne Club and urged him to increase the bounty for Power's capture. The squatter was sure that a sufficient reward would induce Lloyd to lead them to Power on the pretext of retrieving the watch. So a reward of £500 was gazetted in late April 1870 – then the equivalent of four to five years' labouring wages. Senior police applied pressure on Lloyd to lead them to Power, offering him freedom and money – to be paid secretly in instalments to avoid suspicion of his co-operation.

By this time, Ned had ceased to enjoy Power's company. Frank Hare (1892:93) wrote that Kelly left Power because he 'had such an ungovernable temper that he thought Power would shoot him. He told me that when they were riding in the mountains, Power swore at him to such an extent, without him giving any provocation, that he put spurs to his horse and galloped away home'. Kelly rode nearly 200 kilometres in three days and arrived emaciated and exhausted.

By this time, Ellen Kelly had just given birth to a daughter, also named Ellen, fathered by William Frost. Ned barely had time to settle in when four police burst into the hut at dawn on 6 May to arrest him. A contingent of mounted troopers, including an Inspector Nicolas, escorted the exhausted and starved 'cub' down the track to the Benalla police station where he was charged with two counts of highway robbery and locked in the cells.

Coincidently, his mother was also waiting to appear in court at Wangaratta. Not long before the birth of her youngest child in March, another traveller had stopped to ask for a drink. Ellen served him a glass of brandy and he 'treated the lady to a

Capture of Power, the bushranger. His hideout was on the side of a crescent-shaped range behind the Quinn homestead. The family had a small army of fierce dogs and a pet peacock said to be the best alarm, which perched on the roof at night. But early on Saturday morning, 5 June 1870, driving rain kept all silent as the police crept past. At first light black tracker Donald pointed out a blue wisp of smoke above the trees high up the mountain. 'The small fire and a few cooking utensils around it came into view,' superintendent Nicolson wrote, 'throwing myself into the gunyah upon the prostrate body of the occupant, I seized and held him securely by the wrists . . . superintendent [Hare] and sergeant [Montfort] appeared almost immediately and catching the man by his legs . . . with one simultaneous heave we swung our prisoner outside, and then the Sergeant quietly handcuffed him'. As they climbed down the mountain to the Quinn stockyards the alarm went off with all strength. 'When near the house I observed three men standing near the porch, and another known as "Red George" outside . . . for an instant a large bush intercepted our view, but when we cleared it . . . the men had disappeared and in their places stood three rather tall women in black, who silently stared at us . . . We passed without exchanging a word. Poor Power gave his friends an inquiring wistful look, to which came no answer'.

Kelly's note to Babington reveals his anguish on returning to the Eleven Mile Creek; again he used his young brother's name as a rather thin alias. It reads: 'I write these lines hoping to find you and Mistr Nickilson in good health as I am myself at present. I have arrived safe and I would like you would see what you and Mstr. Nickelson could do for me I have done all circomstances would alow me which you now [know] try what you con do answer letter as soon as posabel direct your letter to Daniel Kelly greta post office that is my name at presa[nt] Edward Kelly. Every one looks on me like a black snake send me an answer as soon as posable.'

glass of brandy also', paid her two shillings and went on his way. The following month she was among a number of people in the district summonsed for 'selling liquor without a license'. Mrs Kelly appeared at the Wangaratta courthouse on 9 May 1870, while her son was still in the cells at Benalla. Fortunately for Ellen, the detective could not positively identify her, so the case was dismissed.

Ellen was less fortunate with her baby. Frost had reneged on the promise of marriage and in early February 1870, at the upper King River, was shot in an attempt on his life (although there was no apparent connection between the events). The following year, Ellen had to sue him for maintenance, succeeding only months before baby Ellen died.

A few days after Ellen's court appearance, Ned gained more celebrity status and notoriety at the Benalla court. In the lead-up to his case, local newspapers confidently described him as 'the bushranger Kelly, the juvenile Highwayman, and companion of the notorious Power'. He even rated brief mention in metropolitan Melbourne newspapers. At his first remand, one reporter noted:

The court was crowded with spectators, who appeared anxious to ascertain the result of the charge. Kelly seemed quite indifferent to the danger of his position. While casting eyes among the crowd, he smiled complacently and assumed a jaunty air. Previous to his appearance in the Benalla Court, and while confined in the lockup, he 'sang like a bird', and appeared proud of his position . . . the misguided youth evidently considers himself a character to be admired.

He was remanded several times, tried on two counts and acquitted, as Robert McBean declined to swear Kelly was Power's accomplice. Ned was then remanded to appear at Kyneton in connection with the Lauriston hold-ups. The long case was engineered by police with the co-operation of McBean to delay verdict and allow further interrogation of Ned for information on Power. Instead of being transferred directly to Kyneton, he was transported to Melbourne and interviewed at Richmond depot by the three most senior officers of the police force.

The chief commissioner, captain Frederick Charles Standish, with superintendents Charles Hope Nicolson and Francis Augustus Hare were officers, gentlemen and members of the Melbourne elite. They would have offered an interesting contrast to the scrawny, ill-educated bush youth they interrogated in the cells. Their impressions revealed as much about themselves as their captive. The aristocratic Standish was offended by Kelly's lack of

Wild Pat Quinn, the Dubliner, shown here in his best cord breeches and starched collar. Wild Pat married Ellen Kelly's sister, Margaret, at Mansfield in 1866 and settled with her family at Glenmore. Dubbed 'Wild Pat' by an already wild Quinn family, he was staying at Mrs Kelly's hut with James Quinn in August 1870 when the memorable difference occurred between the two uncles and young Ned. This cost him three years of freedom. The plate is taken from an undated tintype.

personal hygiene and Hare was offended by his foul language, recalling him as 'a flash, ill-looking young blackguard'. Nicolson was equally imperious but also recognised more exceptional qualities in the boy. In exchange for information, Kelly was offered a share in the reward and guarantee (to avert suspicion) that he would be kept detained until after Power's capture. In the hope of reforming him, Nicolson also offered to find him a position on a pastoral station well away from his home surroundings. Kelly declined the reward but gave details about the bushranger's movements and the Glenmore hideout.

Young Kelly was transferred to Kyneton and by 29 May was still being held there on remand. This was extended so he would not be implicated in the capture or take warning to Power. Meanwhile, the police superintendents redirected their attention to Jack Lloyd. Through McBean, the 'Pentridge bird' agreed to act as intermediary and betray his old friend. Exchange of the pocket-watch would be the means of Power's entrapment. Lloyd was discharged from custody and on a rainy winter's day in June made his way through the ranges east of Benalla with McBean's £15. He was accompanied by Nicolson, Hare, sergeant Montfort and black tracker Donald. Due to bad weather and rough terrain, it took them two days to reach Glenmore homestead. Lloyd visited his Quinn relations and made the exchange with Power, who had been staying at the house during the day and sleeping in his mia-mia at night. Mrs Quinn senior tried to warn Power of impending danger, but her son Jimmy was also involved in the treachery. Under cover of driving rain, the police crept past the homestead to the bushranger's hideout and surprised him at dawn on Sunday 5 June, taking him back to Beechworth.

The Lauriston charges were dismissed after witnesses could not positively identify Kelly. He was released on Friday 3 June and a sympathetic sergeant Babington paid for his board at a local hotel until brother-in-law Alex Gunn rode down to collect him a week later. At Beechworth, Henry Johnstone, alias Harry Power, was sentenced the following October to fifteen years' imprisonment, leaving Ned Kelly's life as abruptly as he had entered.

The drawn out exercise was a significant lesson for the apprentice bushranger. It demonstrated how the law could be manipulated – on this occasion to his advantage. He also experienced the exhilaration of being a celebrity, if a notorious one. His court appearances drew crowds, local and city newspapers reported his case, and the most senior police officers in the colony had interviewed him. Indicating that the authorities expected to hear more of the bushranger's apprentice, Kyneton police were instructed to forward seventeen portraits of the boy to headquarters in Melbourne.

Rumours circulated that Kelly was the betrayer, a view promoted by Power, even though Ned had been in Kyneton until a week after the capture, spending seven weeks in custody. When Ned returned home he was despised 'like a black snake'. His short, sad note to sergeant Babington in July 1870, the only surviving example of Kelly's handwriting apart from his signatures, indicates the boy's disillusionment and alludes to unkept promises made by Nicolson. It should have been apparent from Kelly's continuing poverty that he did not gain from the association with Power or his capture. Interestingly, only days after the note was posted, Ned got into a brawl with some family members.

Uncle James and his brother-in-law 'Wild Pat Quinn, the Dubliner', got into a disagreement with young Ned in August 1870. Wild Pat was staying at the Kelly hut, along with James Quinn, when the argument occurred. The brawl was possibly over Power's betrayal, as Ned and James Quinn were both partly involved. The *Benalla Ensign* reported 'young Kelly was being pursued by James Quinn when he made for Greta police station, shouting out for help. Senior constable Hall came to Kelly's rescue and told him to go into the station yard where he would be safe'. This followed after Hall had urged Kelly on to entrap the Quinns. James, annoyed at losing Kelly, began abusing Hall. Hall ordered him into the yard, but Quinn refused and a struggle ensued. In the midst of the fighting Wild Pat rode up, took off his stirrup iron, and inflicted a dreadful wound on the back of Hall's head, rendering him insensible. Hearing the noise, constable Archdeacon came out and tried to arrest the Quinns but was also beaten by Wild Pat. When Hall came to shortly after, he again tried to tackle the assailants but was laid prostrate once more by Pat's stirrup iron. The two ruffians then got away. Pat was captured at gunpoint two days later at the Eleven Mile Creek and James Quinn surrendered shortly after. Both went to prison: James got three months and Patrick was given three years for what had been his first offence. Young Kelly, for the time being, escaped their wrath.

Editorials appeared in Melbourne and north-eastern newspapers demanding prosecution of the whole clan for harbouring Harry Power. Power incriminated all of them, saying, 'first and last they had heaps of money from me, for I paid the whole family [Quinns, Kellys and Lloyds] well', but still no charges were laid. Instead, as a preventive measure, a police station was built on the flats within half a kilometre of the Quinns' house at Glenmore run. While the station may have been effective in checking on the Quinns' activities, there was nothing else to occupy the troopers – there was hardly another home within sixteen kilometres. The hostile Quinns went on about their work and one trooper went insane because of the isolation.

4 A SECONDARY EDUCATION
FOR THE KELLY CHILDREN, 1870–74

Like their relatives, the Kelly family escaped conviction for their association with Harry Power. But rather than being wiser for it, Mrs Kelly's delinquent son was in more trouble by October the same year. At Wangaratta, on 19 November 1870, he was found guilty of assault and indecent behaviour in Greta township.

During winter and spring the north-eastern district experienced record floods. The Broken River washed away the Benalla bridge, cut communication with the northern section of the town and all the country beyond. All the flat land from Winton across to Greta and the Oxley plains was a chain of lakes.

During the 1870 floods, Ned's brother James was working for a hawker, Ben Gould, who got bogged on the road near the Eleven Mile Creek. Gould stayed with the Kellys at their hut, waiting for drier weather. A rival hawker of Gould's, Jerimiah McCormick, was also stranded with his wife and wagon further along the road in Greta. Early one morning, one of the McCormicks' horses strayed along the road outside the Kelly selection. Gould sent James to take the horse back to them, but instead of thanking the eleven-year-old, they abused him, drove out to the Kelly hut and accused Gould and the Kellys of working their horse. Ned later recalled that he was astounded to hear the McCormicks accuse Gould and his brother of working their horse when they had been so kind as to return it. Ned and James Kelly always maintained that they did not use the horse, but the version handed down by Ben Gould years later suggests that they did.

41

Top: Murphy Street, Wangaratta 1866, looking south-east. It was here that Ned unknowingly paraded the Mansfield postmaster's chestnut mare. The Star Hotel, where he celebrated freedom for a few days and dazzled the publican's daughters, was on the corner of Warby Street, background left. The Kelly family were familiar with all the major centres in the area, regularly travelling to Wangaratta to buy supplies, attend church, cattle sales and to defend themselves or prosecute others.

Above: Benjamin Gould, the hawker, regularly stayed at the Kelly hut on his way to and from the country beyond Greta. He became a close friend of the family during their first years in the district and probably employed eleven-year-old James Kelly as a favour to the struggling widow. Gould was originally from Nottingham, England, and an ex-convict in Van Diemen's Land (Tasmania). As a 'grossly violent' prisoner, he received extra punishment at Port Arthur and Norfolk Island. Upon release in 1853, he immediately crossed Bass Strait to join the gold rush. He led an exciting life, including one clash with bushrangers, before settling in the north-eastern district at Euroa. He was described affectionately as a small squirt of a man, a born trader who could sell anything. He had flags and anchors tattooed on his arms, carried a small whisky flask in his pocket and was remembered for his honest and colourful personality. Gould believed that rival hawker Jeremiah McCormick was encroaching on his territory. This strengthened the belief that Ned Kelly, whether innocently or through his own devilment, got involved in what was simply a professional feud. The significance of the incident revolved around the question of whether or not Ned Kelly did use McCormick's horse to pull Gould's wagon out of the bog. Ned and James Kelly always maintained that he did not, but a later version from Gould suggests that he did. This portrait was taken in 1879 when Ben was 43.

That same afternoon, Kelly, Gould and Jack Lloyd were branding and cutting calves in Greta when they decided on a joke to repay McCormick's ingratitude. McCormick's wife was without children, so Gould wrapped some calf's testicles and attached a note of instructions. It was given to Lloyd's young son, thirteen-year-old Tom, who gave it to Mr McCormick, saying, 'Ned Kelly gave me this parcel for Mrs McCormack' [sic].

When Ned rode past their camp that evening on his way home, the irate hawker was blocking the track. Sure enough, the pair got into a fight when McCormick called Ned a liar and said he would welt him. Kelly claimed that he accepted the challenge and was about to dismount when 'Mrs McCormack struck my horse in the flank with a bullocks shin-bone, it jumped forward and my fist came in collision with McCormack's nose and caused him to lose his equilibrium' [sic]. Ned wanted to finish the fight, but McCormick got up and ran to the police camp. Ned received his first sentence of three months hard labour for assault, a further three months for the obscene parcel and was bound to keep the peace for twelve months. So fifteen-year-old Edward Kelly joined his uncle, Wild Pat Quinn, in Beechworth Gaol – who was breaking stones for trying to thrash Ned two months earlier. Superintendent Nicholas, who was in charge of the whole police district, commented in November that 'Young Kelly was a terror to the locality, and persons were afraid to prosecute him'. He also speculated that Kelly would have joined Lowry, a bushranger operating at that time.

Young Kelly was nearly sixteen when he was released on 29 March 1871. Almost immediately, he was headlong into more strife. He went home for a few days, and then to Wangaratta to celebrate a short freedom. At his mother's place he had met a stranger called Wild Wright, a friend of his brother-in-law Alex Gunn. Wright had lost a chestnut mare during his stay at Mrs Kelly's and had to borrow one of Ned's horses to get home to Mansfield. He asked Kelly to keep his horse if it was found and they

Top: Police barracks, Greta. Some less than reputable officers were posted at Greta. The police station was established in 1870, initially in this brick building on the north side of Curlewis Street, with a portable timber lock-up outside. This was the site of fierce brawls and uncomfortable accommodation for a number of the clan and 'Greta mob', as local larrikins dubbed themselves. Senior constable Hall and constable Archdeacon were beaten up by the Quinns where these gentlemen are posing. Eight months later, on the same spot, constable Hall had another violent experience trying to arrest the boy he had earlier protected. Ned recalled, 'when Wild Wright and my mother came they could trace us across the street by the blood in the dust and which spoiled the lustre of the paint on the gate-post of the barracks'.

Above: The township of Greta. In 1867 the township was having a brief revival as centre of an area just opened for selection. This engraving was made in 1880. The view looks down Curlewis Street, which twisted past stumps and tall trees near Lawrence O'Brien's Hotel. The hotel was under construction in April 1871 when Hall tried to shoot Ned. The single-storey building beside it was either their original premises or Murdoch's Greta store. In 1867–68, the Lloyds and Kellys lived on the block next to O'Briens Hotel. Opposite is the police station.

Right: Curlewis Street Greta, 1880–81. This view shows various buildings opposite the hotel, and to the left of previous scene, including out-buildings and stables of the police camp.

A SECONDARY EDUCATION

Inset: Senior constable Edward Hall was considered particularly suitable to run the new police station at Greta. The Irish-Protestant weighed more than 102 kilograms (over sixteen stone) and was as heavy on government horses as he was on larrikins. He was no ornament to the police, however, having previously been charged with assault and perjury at Eldorado, forced out and transferred to Broadford only to leave there in similar disgrace for vindictive and violent behaviour. As Professor John Moloney put it (1980:54,63), Hall was a mischievous perjurer as well as a uniformed thug. The chestnut mare had not been advertised as missing when he confronted Kelly on the Greta bridge. Records confirm that Ned was still in Beechworth Gaol when Wright took the animal. This technicality was overcome when Kelly's charge was amended. It embittered Kelly that he received three years for 'receiving' when the actual culprit, Wright, was sentenced to only eighteen months. The fact that Hall pistol-whipped and tried to shoot an unarmed youth was noted but, instead of censure, he was rewarded. Afterwards, Hall feared revenge from Kelly's friends, refused lone mounted-patrol duty and put on too much weight. He was dismounted and transferred out of the district in 1871.

Facing page: Ned Kelly's record sheet. On the day of his entry to Beechworth gaol, the particulars of prisoner Edward Kelly were recorded. Ned's head-scars resulted from the pistol-whipping from senior constable Hall. The identification photographs show how young he was, though not as young as the (incorrect) year of birth entered. Kelly may have signed his name at the top of the sheet, entered his place of birth, incorrect date of birth, and religion. The other details were entered by an official.

would exchange later. On the way to Wangaratta, Ned found the horse and took it with him. He later wrote that it was a remarkable 'chestnut mare, white face, docked tail . . . branded (M) as plains as the hands of a town hall clock'. For the few days he stayed in Wangaratta, he even allowed the daughters of the publican, Peter Martin, to ride the horse. But on his way home the proud horseman was stopped on the Greta bridge by senior constable Hall. He asked him to come to the police camp and sign some papers. He went, but refused to dismount and go inside the barracks. Hall tried to drag him from his horse, saying he was under arrest, and Kelly resisted violently.

During the furious brawl, Hall admitted bludgeoning the boy with a revolver four or five times, and also snapping his revolver two or three times, but it misfired. Ned 'rooted both spurs into his thighs, and he roared like a big calf attacked by dogs'. Hall called for assistance from men looking on – Cohen, Barnett, Lewis, Thompson and Jewitt. Finally, the six men got Ned tied up and dragged him, covered in blood, to the small lock-up beside the police station. There he was told that his horse was gazetted as stolen.

Even after all this, the excitement was not over. Senior constable Hall could not stop Kelly's bleeding skull. He sent an urgent despatch to Wangaratta for a doctor and two troopers. By this time, Kelly's friends had heard through a bush telegraph that he had been arrested. Just on dark, a group including the Quinns rode into Greta and surrounded the police camp shouting and threatening to rescue the prisoner. Hall got the help of a blacksmith, armed him, lit a large fire outside the lock-up, and loaded every gun in the station. But by the time Doctor Hester and two police arrived things had quietened down. Kelly was treated and taken to Wangaratta early the next morning.

This time 'Edward Kelly, known as young Kelly', as the papers now familiarly called him, was kept in custody under remand for three months before trial. At several of his appearances during this period, the justices jotted in the margin of the court records that they were most unwilling to bail the prisoner. Police Superintendent Barkly mentioned in reporting the arrest to headquarters that . . . it was the accomplishment of a timely and much needed check on young Kelly's career. On 2 August 1871, Kelly, his brother-in-law Alex Gunn and Wild Isaiah Wright were brought to trial at Beechworth. Kelly was the first brought forward, and was defended by a Mr Brown.

The Mansfield postmaster appeared and testified that the horse tethered outside the courthouse was his, and that it was stolen on 19 March. An ex-convict, James Murdoch, was produced for the Crown and swore that Kelly told him he got the same horse 'on the cheap . . . from the Plenty Ranges'. Evidence was also given of the arrest, the fight, and Kelly's possession of the horse when arrested. For the defence, Mr Brown first proved that Ned Kelly was in Beechworth Gaol until 29 March and therefore could not have stolen the horse. A stockman testified that Wright had taken the mare from Mansfield. William Williamson, a lodger at Mrs Kelly's, swore that Wright brought the mare to the Eleven Mile Creek, mislaid it, and asked Kelly to keep it if anyone found the animal. However, it could not be denied that Kelly was in possession, and it was not proven that he was unaware it was stolen. So the jury found him guilty of receiving.

Ned's brother-in-law, Alexander Gunn, was arraigned on the same day for stealing another horse from a Mansfield schoolmaster. It disappeared the same day as the postmaster's chestnut mare, and also from the same vicinity. It emerged from lengthy evidence that Gunn had followed Wright's example and may have taken the animal at Wright's suggestion. The jury found Gunn guilty of horse stealing. Isaiah Wright was then tried for the theft of the same horse as Kelly and in contrast was treated with curious leniency. After conclusive evidence was brought against him, he was only found guilty of illegally using the horse. The only explanation for the leniency of the verdict was a local petition of Wright's good character and the fact that he had not actually sold the animal. The sentences passed on the three appeared just as inappropriate. Wright was given eighteen months and Alex Gunn was given three years' hard labour. Kelly was also given three years' hard labour, twice the term received by the culprit who was proven to have stolen the mare.

On the day of his conviction, an embittered

No. 10926 193 Name, Edward Kelly 74/1648 [No. 64 P.]

Native Place, Victoria
Year of Birth, 1856
Arrived in Colony { Ship, — Year, — Bond or free, — }
From where, —
Religion, R. Catholic

	On Conviction.	On Discharge.
Education—Read or write	Both	Both
Height	5.10	
Weight	11.4	
Build	Med	
Complexion	Sallow	
Color of Hair	D. brown	
Color of Eyes	Hazel	
Trade or Calling	Laborer	

No. 466 Date, 20/6/43
No. 925 Date, 24/1/44

No description

Particular Marks,
Scar top of head, 2 scars crown of do., scar front of head, eyebrows meeting, 2 natural marks between shoulder blades, 2 freckles lower left arm, scar ball of left thumb, scar back of right hand, 3 scar left thumb

When and where convicted,
2nd August 1871
Genl. Sessions Beechworth

Offence,
Receiving a stolen horse

Sentence,
3 Years H.L.

Remarks,
Freedom by remission
February 2nd 1874

Criminal History and Remarks—
3 mos. for assault
3 mos. for obscene language
12 mos. for assault in default of bail (bail found) — These convictions on same date at Wangaratta Police Ct.

To be returned to Detective Office Melbourne

J. H. Gardiner
Superintendent
14.3.43

N.B.—Margin not to be written on.

ENTRANCE TO THE PRISON.

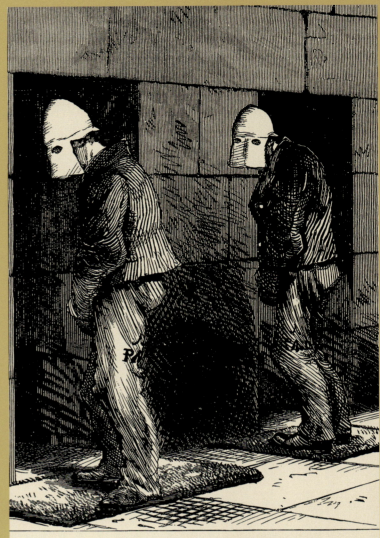

WAITING FOR EXAMINAITON.

SOLITARY CONFINEMENT.

THE EXERCISE YARD.

Facing page clockwise from top left: Prison life as experienced at Pentridge gaol. Entrance to the prison; waiting for examination; solitary confinement; exercise yard; (this page) prisoner's school. These sketches were made at the time Ned Kelly was an inmate in 1873. Biographers have generally given little attention to the effects of wasted years and a brutalising process that entrenched anti-social habits. One symptom of the degradation surfaced in distinctive habits of speech. Foul vocabulary embellished and punctuated the speech of ex-convicts and larrikins like the Quinns and Kellys. The commonplace euphemism of 'bugger' for offensive males was adopted from convict language. Uncle Tom Lloyd described Pentridge as 'hell'; both he and Ned swore they would never go back. This grim establishment originally covered 64 hectares (160 acres) and was located eleven kilometres (seven miles) north of Melbourne.

Prisoners bathed, scrubbed, were shaved and given a close haircut; a process repeated weekly. Their dark grey uniform was branded and numbered. 'They wear the white cap', a visitor noted, 'coming low down over the face and with two holes for the eyes, which prevents them from seeing each other's faces. New arrivals went to A division, spending a month there for each year sentenced. It is not better than solitary confinement. Each (un-heated) cell is furnished with a folding bedstead, bedding without a mattress, a small table, a stool, a patent water-closet, a pair of slippers, a slate and a few books . . . [However] here the culprit spends twenty three hours of the day.' Conditions in B and C divisions were less severe with allocation to outdoor work-gangs. Nine hours labour, six days a week, Sundays for worship and tuition.

In the prison schoolroom, Kelly would have sighted his former employer, Power. In the winter of 1873, Ned was transferred to the prison hulk *Sacramento*.

Left: One of the prison hulks moored off Point Gelibrand. The converted hulks were anchored well beyond swimming distance from the shore. They were painted yellow and the area where they were moored was marked as prohibited. The prison hulks were essentially floating dungeons and were among the most inhumane punishments during the 1850s and 1860s when Harry Power spent time in one. By 1873, when Ned Kelly served part of his gaol term on the *Sacramento*, conditions were improved but nonetheless harsh. The *Sacramento* was the last prison hulk to survive, kept for special purposes until as late as 1878.

A SECONDARY EDUCATION 47

The many false faces of Ned Kelly. It is a surprising anomaly that there are more pseudo-portraits of young Ned Kelly than of any other single figure in Australian history – surprising because of the number of genuine portraits in existence. The fraud started as early as 1878 when police only had access to the two prison photographs taken in 1873 and 1874. The dates may have been wrongly attributed as he looks older with close-cropped hair.

Artists and illustrators of the day added beards to earlier portraits to bring his appearance up to date. Nearly all of these early frauds were engravings (above). One of the best photographic forgeries (opposite, top left) was copyrighted in 1880 by William J. Burman. He billed it as 'Ned Kelly's portrait, the latest as yet photographed' on leaving Pentridge. Only close examination of the original reveals that it was the 1873 portrait with new shoulders pasted on and additional hair and beard carefully painted over. When portraits could be reproduced in books, more forgeries of the 1873 original appeared (opposite, bottom right). At least four faked Kelly faces have appeared over the years, with those shown being the most successful efforts. Writers and journalists, out of ignorance or lack of concern for accuracy, have kept them appearing. Perhaps as a reaction to this, Jack Cato (1955:33) in his *Story of the Camera in Australia* refers to the last gaol portrait taken of Kelly (see page 263) as the only real photograph of him ever taken – a remarkable inaccuracy in itself.

Edward Kelly entered Beechworth Gaol for three more years of bad influence. For the next eighteen months he lived in the heart of Beechworth, but in another world. He worked in the chain gangs employed daily on the May Day Hills, straddling the north and south sides of the town. In February 1873 he was transferred with a few fellow convicts to Pentridge Gaol where his former employer, Harry Power, was spending the rest of his life.

While at Pentridge, Ned met another old family friend. Father Charles O'Hea was still at St Paul's Mission and still visiting Catholic chaplain at Pentridge – nine years after he had farewelled the Kelly family from Beveridge. The men resumed a friendship remembered long after. Father O'Hea has even been credited with providing, during this prison term, the most powerful single influence for good in Kelly's life. But if that was true, he had very little time. Kelly was only in Pentridge for a few months before he was moved, in mid-winter, to the *Sacramento* – the last of the prison hulks moored in Hobson's Bay off Point Gelibrand.

Prison hulks were used in Melbourne until 1878 when the *Sacramento* was finally taken out of service. On the recommendation of a royal commission into penal discipline in 1870, gangs of selected convicts confined in prison hulks and on temporary shore establishments were put to labour on public works – among these the bluestone embankments along the Yarra River and the Williamstown defences. They were paid a small wage for their labour, payable only on release. From late winter until early summer 1873, Ned Kelly worked in the quarries and on the battlements and sea walls. Each night, with the gangs making up these work parties, he was rowed back to the dreadful yellow-painted hull that served as their sleeping quarters. When Ned served his time on the *Sacramento* it housed relatively privileged convicts; fifteen years earlier the same hulk had been one of the most inhumane floating dungeons for society's worst offenders. Despite the better treatment of 1873, however, the short stay would have been an unforgettable experience. Still, only one mark was recorded against his behaviour – six days were added to his sentence for handing tobacco to a fellow prisoner. In spring, Kelly was transferred to the Battery, presumably the temporary quarters on the Williamstown gun emplacements. Then, on 2 February 1874 he gained two-thirds of maximum remission of his sentence for good behaviour and was released.

Back in the north-eastern district at Greta, life at the Kelly household did not improve during Ned's absence. After four years on the Eleven Mile Creek, degenerated circumstances were taking their toll. Their 'fair' agricultural land was found to be not so fair. A constable Flood who arrived at Greta in 1871 remembered they 'seemed to have a very miserable way of living'. Mrs Kelly later said the 'land was very poor, and wouldn't grow anything scarcely'. The Kellys were not known to have grown crops or

James Kelly. In April 1873, at the Beechworth Assizes, Justice Williams sentenced fourteen-year-old James Kelly to five years imprisonment for his first offence of helping Tom Williams, an employee of his mother, to sell stolen cattle around Greta. This would have given Ned even more reason to resent the law.

cultivated more than a small acreage near the hut during this period. Mrs Kelly maintained that the land was only suited to grazing her small herd of cows and certainly not for successful dairying. The Kellys depended on the income made by providing accommodation. Despite their poverty, Ellen persisted year after year in clearing and fencing whenever she could get help or afford labour. The hardship of the life, in a locality far from social comfort, education or religious influence, has never been clearly conveyed; nor have the effects it produced.

The Kellys' reputation continued to plummet as the family got into more trouble with the law. In 1871, Ned's brothers, Jim and Dan Kelly, got into their first scrape with local authority. Jim had left his job with Ben Gould to work for another hawker and carrier, Mark Krafft, but returned home after his eldest brother's third arrest in April. Krafft camped at the Kelly hut on Eleven Mile Creek in September and rested his horses in Mrs Kelly's horse paddock. Early the next morning Jim, then twelve years old, and ten-year-old Dan Kelly sneaked them for a ride. Krafft did not appreciate the joke and called constable Flood from Greta to have the young boys arrested. They were taken to Wangaratta, locked in the cells, and brought before the court two days later. In desperation, Mrs Kelly attended and stood up to cross-examine the hawker on her sons' behalf. The case was dismissed 'on account of their youth and their intimacy with the owner of the horses – one of the brothers being a [former] servant of the person'.

A series of court appearances recorded the regular dramas in Kelly family life at the time. In September and October Ellen successfully sued William Frost at Benalla court for support of their child. To celebrate that success, Anne, William Skillion and Ellen stayed in town with their friends, Anne and James Murdoch. As a result, after three days of carousing, all were arrested and charged with 'furious riding' about the town streets. They were let off on a technicality. The following month Ellen employed a servant, Tom Williams, who lived with the family for nearly two years. She had only just gained his help when she lost part of her income. Permanent boarder and labourer, William 'Bricky' Williamson, got into another one of Jimmy Quinn's violent shenanigans, which ended in imprisonment.

In January 1872 Jimmy Quinn went to Black Springs near Greta to help his sister Margaret with harvesting while husband Pat was still 'inside'. But he spoilt the friendly gesture by assaulting his sister for interfering with amorous advances towards another visitor from the Kelly hut, Jane Graham. The same weekend he savagely bludgeoned an elderly splitter living nearby, suspected of informing others about Quinn's behaviour. Margaret went over to plead with him to stop and 'Bricky' Williamson, who was with Quinn, also tried to call him off. Judge Barry later sentenced Williamson to eighteen months for his involvement. 'Mad' Jimmy got four and a half years for both assaults and in a case pending from 1865 (another serious assault) he had two more years added, relieving the community of his bad temper for a considerable period. While brother James was causing havoc at Margaret Quinn's, Ellen was fully occupied with her sick baby who contracted diarrhoea in early 1872. By the time a doctor arrived from Benalla she could not be saved and died on 28 January. Frost had supported his child for only three months.

It was a dramatic and sad period at Greta. At this time, Anne, Ellen's eldest daughter, was also getting into strife. She had an unfortunate and unhappy marriage, even by Kelly standards. They had no home or land of their own – husband Alex had to forfeit his selection – and their first child died in March 1871. Soon after, Alex borrowed a horse and went to prison along with Wild Wright and Ned.

A Victorian selector's homestead.

In January 1872, Anne was escorted to Benalla by a new constable at Greta, Ernest Flood, to give evidence against three men accused of stealing horses from the Kelly selection. Flood, married and a father, took more than a professional interest in young Annie. She bore his child in November 1872 but died two days later from convulsions. The unfortunate nineteen-year-old girl was buried in the garden beside the Kelly hut by Ned's uncle William Quinn, who was living with them at the time. Understandably, Flood was not on good terms with the family, but to add malice to injury, he brought an unsuccessful charge of theft against Ellen and employee Jane Graham, on the very day of Annie's death. Annie's daughter and namesake survived for little more than a year and died from diphtheria. Flood, on the other hand, was admonished for his adultery but not disciplined.

Flood continued the police policy of harassing the family while stationed at Greta. Superintendent Nicolson would later direct that police officers should endeavour, 'without oppressing the people, or worrying them in any way . . . whenever they [Kellys, Quinns, Lloyds] commit any paltry crime, to bring them to justice, and send them to Pentridge even on a paltry sentence, the object being to take their prestige away from them . . . flashness helped to keep them together and it is a very good way to take the flashness out of them'. This supported the clan's belief that they were being persecuted, and as Ian Jones (1995:80) pointed out, Nicolson's order was in direct contradiction of Police regulation 183 which prohibited 'a harassing and vexatious course of conduct towards . . . those who are desirous of earning an honest living'.

By March the following year, young James Kelly was into more trouble with another of the Kelly household. He and his mother's employee, Tom Williams, were arrested after selling a number of stolen cattle between Greta and Wangaratta. Tom was the ringleader and acted as salesman, while his fourteen-year-old accomplice acted as driver. Williams signed receipts for the sales in the name of Jim's cousin, Tom Lloyd, and told their customers he needed the money to get his father out of trouble. They even sold one heifer to Mrs Kelly, possibly why the boys were undefended at Wangaratta in April. Both were found guilty on two counts of cattle-stealing. Williams bravely stood up in court to say he had led Kelly into it and the jury asked that their youth be taken into consideration. It was not; Tom Williams, at seventeen, was given five years' imprisonment. James Kelly, only fourteen, was given the same. It was never established who had actually stolen the animals.

So the family's bad reputation and their bitterness against the law steadily grew. By 1873 five of Mrs Kelly's household – Ned Kelly, Jim Kelly, Alex Gunn, boarder William Williamson and employee Tom Williams – were all in prison. At the same time, three of their relations – Pat Quinn, Jack Lloyd and Jimmy Quinn – were also behind stone walls. Three of the eight were serving sentences for assault, and the rest for offences to do with livestock.

5 THE COMING OF AGE
1874–78

Young Ned Kelly was the first convicted criminal from Mrs Kelly's household to make his way home from prison in February 1874. By that time, there were already distinct changes occurring in the north-eastern district. A new age had reached Victoria; the railway followed the old Sydney road north for nearly 300 kilometres (over 180 miles) to Wodonga on the Murray River, and the age of true isolation was drawing to a close. New settlers coming into the area were sounding the death knell for the squatting era. Towns lying in the path of the railway – like Benalla, Glenrowan and Wangaratta – saw prosperity; others, such as Greta, began their decline. At the Eleven Mile Creek, Ned would have found even more changes.

During young Ned's absence, his sister Anne had died, his brother Jim was gaoled, and he had gained a new brother-in-law. In September 1873 his sister Margaret married one of the lodgers at the Kelly hut, William Skillion. Together, they settled on the third selection west of the Kellys, along the track towards Winton.

Apparently, Mrs Kelly had been waiting for Ned's homecoming before she too started a second marriage. On 19 February 1874, only a week or so after Ned arrived home, she was quietly married to George King. Both the mother and daughter's ceremonies took place at the parsonage of the Reverend Gould in Barkly Street, Benalla. This was a Methodist church – evidence of a drift away from their Catholic faith.

Only the immediate family attended Ellen's second marriage. The marriage certificate records the

Facing page: Ned Kelly's prison portrait.

Beechworth Gaol
Pentridge.

287

No. 10926 Name Kelly, Edward

Height	5ft 10	Sentence	Three Years H.L.	Death		
Weight	11st 4					
Complexion	Sallow	Serve				
Hair	Dk Brown	Two & a half years				
Eyes	Hazel	Date of Conviction	2.8.71	29 October 1880		
Nose	Medium					
Mouth	Medium					
Chin	Medium					
Eyebrows	Dk Brown	Offence	Receiving a Stolen horse	Murder		
Visage	Broad					
Forehead	Low					
Date of Birth	1856	Where and before whom tried	Beechworth Gaol Sess J. Hackett Esq.	Melbourne Central Crim. Court Sir Redmond Barry		
Native place	Victoria					
Trade	Labourer					
Religion	R. Catholic					
Read or Write	Both					

Scar top of head, Two scars crown of do, Scar front of head, eyebrows meeting, two natural marks between shoulder blades, Two freckles lower left arm, scar ball of left thumb, Scar back of right hand, Three scars left thumb.

Single, Mother Ellen Kelly living at Greta, or Devil's river, Uncle James Kelly a farmer at Wintridge & another James Quinn now at Beechworth awaiting trial and John Lloyd an uncle a prisr at Pentridge 3 Con to same day at Wangaratta pol. Ct. Vz 3 Mo. 3 Mo. & 12 Mo. in default of bail — Bail found.

When received	Offences, Sentences, &c.		Extensions by—				
			Visiting Justice		Superintendent		
			M.	D.	M.	D.	
	Brothers James No 10861 Daniel No 9491						
Beechworth Gaol	21.8.73 Handing to fellow pris. two patches of tobacco Sus. dp 7 days	5			7		Beech
Pentridge 19.2.73							
Sacraments 25.6.73	Jan wants dis 2 prox						
Battery 25.9.73	2. 2.74 Freedom by remission P. earned 2.10.11						
Melbourne Gaol 27.10.80	11 November 1880. Executed at 10 am						

Half-yearly Report				
Date	Superintendent's	Favorable	Unfavorable	Days absent, &c.	Attendance at School as Monitor

scrawled crosses of the bride, bridegroom and witness William Skillion. The fourth witness to the union, Edward Kelly, signed his full name in a clear hand. His mother recorded her age as 36 (when she was actually 42) and George King gave his age as 25 and his birthplace as California. The event went unnoticed outside the family, even by a number within the clan, and Ellen King, as she became legally, would continue to be known and described as 'Mrs Kelly'.

Edward Kelly is said to have told friends after release in 1874 that he would rather face the gallows than go to gaol again. His immediate effort may have been toward reform. Soon after his mother's second marriage, he left home and was without conviction for three years.

The rest of the family also settled down at that time, receiving hardly any police attention. When William Williamson returned to the Eleven Mile Creek from his prison sentence, he took up the selection between the Kellys and Skillions and resumed boarding at the Kelly hut. At last, the clan was living peacefully.

Ned took up work as a tree feller at J. Saunders and R. Rule's sawmills, then for Heach and Dockendorf. He later wrote, 'I never worked for less than two pound ten a week since I left Pentridge'. This was a considerable wage at the time. Skilled farm ploughmen earned five shillings for a fifteen-hour day, or £1 10s for a six-day week.

One of the mills that employed Kelly was said to have been on Red Camp station, near the Quinns' former Glenmore run, north of Mansfield. If this was correct, it was probably while there that he caught up with Wild Isaiah Wright. Either to settle the score for his three-year sentence, or simply as a sporting challenge, Ned fought Wright in a bare-knuckled boxing match in August 1874. The only record of the event is preserved in the photograph taken to commemorate Ned's victory. It has been suggested that the fight took place at Beechworth, organised by Edward Rogers of the Imperial Hotel.

Ned continued to work in sawmills until 1875. Intermittently, he tried other ventures, such as building. A stone house at Chesneyvale, near Winton, was recorded as one 'built by the Kelly brothers ... in 1875'. His three years' experience in the gaol quarries and public works at Point Gelibrand would have taught Kelly the skills of a stonemason. He was probably helped by his younger brother Dan, then fourteen years old, and possibly by their stepfather George King. The house was built of pink granite quarried in the Warby Ranges, 25 kilometres away. The construction alone was a major feat: some of the blocks measured three feet square and six feet long, and the whole building sat

Left: James Kelly, prison portrait.

Facing page: Another of Ned Kelly's record sheets.

on a made-up bank overlooking Lake Winton. In a stone on the rear wall, they carved the inscription '1875' before leaving the completed homestead. Oral history indicates that in the following year or two Ned, Dan and George also built the new timber house for Ellen at the Eleven Mile creek.

These buildings were erected between other ventures. Ned was in the timber business between 1875–76 as 'overseer for Saunders and Rule Bourkes water-holes sawmills'. The mill was on Burke's Hole farm, near Greta, and probably supplied the sawn lumber for the Kelly house. Until 1875, the property and mill was owned by a Wangaratta butcher and councillor. When he was declared bankrupt, the property went to a company, John Saunders and Rule of Greta, and they employed Ned Kelly as the foreman to run the mill. The plant included a two-storey building, thirteen-horsepower steam engine and travelling rack benches. Most importantly, it was probably the most responsible, honest position Kelly ever held.

During his time at the Saunders and Rule mill, he seems to have had only one skirmish with the law. In January 1876 a warrant was issued at Oxley for Ned Kelly on a charge of horse-stealing. The animals in question, a chestnut mare and foal, belonged to none other than his uncle, John Quinn of Glenmore station. It is not known if Kelly was arrested, but some months later a young boy named Michael Woodyard, living at the Kelly hut and

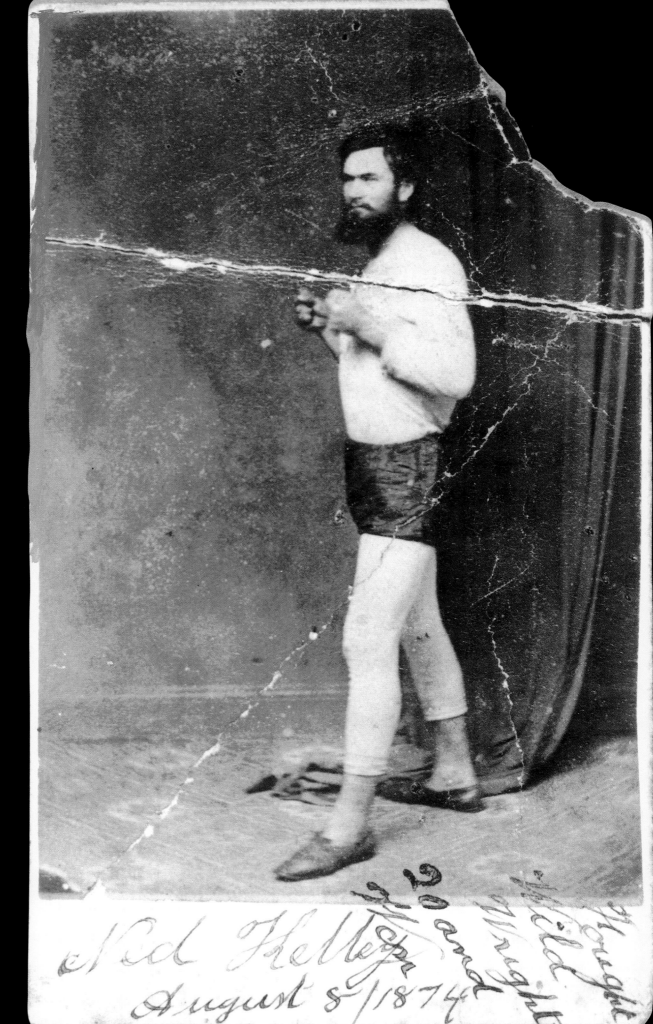

Possibly the most characteristic photograph ever taken of Edward Kelly. The photographer, John Chidley, later settled in Melbourne but the match almost certainly took place at Beechworth. Ian Jones (1995:77) writes that it was organised by publican and entrepreneur Edward Rogers, held at the sports-ground behind his Imperial Hotel and on the banks of Spring Creek. The occasion was evidently an important and seriously conducted one. Kelly wore silk trunks over his long underwear and special boxing-pumps. They fought bare-knuckled and Kelly showed confidence in his boxing ability. He once boasted that 'while I had a pair of arms and bunch of fives at the end of them they never failed to peg out anything they came in contact with'. In 1879, when world heavyweight champion Jem Mace visited Melbourne, Kelly publicly challenged him to a match, but it did not eventuate.

employed by Ned's mother as farm help, was arrested and sentenced to three years' imprisonment for the same theft. Woodyard later said he had been 'dragged into the trouble by the Kellys and Quinns'.

By the age of 21, Ned Kelly was becoming widely known in the north-eastern district. To the local police he was still a dangerous and hardened young criminal and the leading spirit among a close-knit and hostile clan of law breakers. It was during this period that police superintendent Hare claimed 'Ned Kelly had grown into a man and had become so hardened to crime as to be perfectly reckless'. More sympathetic historians have since pointed to this period, apparently free from police convictions, as the one time in his life when he seriously attempted to lead an honest existence. To some of the local population in the north-east, Kelly was definitely gaining, and seemed to encourage, a reputation for leading a 'wild and reckless life'.

Top left: In 1874, Wild Isaiah Wright must have been an unsettling opponent for twenty-year-old Ned. A police bulletin described Wright as a native of Northern Ireland, about 28 years of age, medium build, about five feet eleven, with fair hair, beard and moustache. Another remembered him as 'a young man, six feet one inch in height and weighing thirteen and a half stone without any spare flesh . . . [who] possessed a thorough knowledge of the noble art'. He was also mentioned as having a flowing beard and a loud, though musical voice.

Bottom left: John McMonigle. The 25-year-old Irishman worked under foreman Edward Kelly at Bourke's Sawmill near Greta during 1875–76 and became one of his closest friends.

Above: Edward Kelly at Bray's studio, Beechworth, not dated but 1874–75. This very rare image provides another contrast to the prison mug shots, showing Ned in his best tweeds, trying to lead an honest life as a sawmiller. From 1874 he wore the long beard and favoured a waist sash, another old-fashioned habit. A Mrs Woods later asked Kelly at the Milawa Hotel why such a strapping young man should be horse-stealing and he replied, jokingly, 'Madam, what is a man's lot, can not be blotted out'. Before his last trial he remarked candidly, 'I do not pretend to have led a blameless life or that one fault justified another'. By twenty-one he had no difficulty posing as a respectable stockman. William Elliot wrote that he was 'a well-made athletic young man . . . with rather a pleasing countenance'.

Overleaf: Westerly view from the Bald Hill, or 'Kelly's lookout' at Lurg.

THE COMING OF AGE

Right: James Whitty, Moyhu squatter. Whitty's 46 square kilometre holdings (eighteen square miles) on the Boggy Creek and King River was a prime target for the Kelly horse-stealing raids. Whitty 'leased 11,000 or 12,000 acres of Bank lands' at Moyhu from 1877, including Myrrhee station, and was one of the largest individual land holders on the lower King River. Pastoralists like Whitty and the Byrne brothers came in for vehement criticism in Ned's letters for alienating selectors and unfairly impounding poor people's stock while more than seven unfenced roads cut through their territory. Interestingly, Whitty and his partners, John and Andrew Byrne, were staunch Roman Catholics and Irish patriots, like the elder generation of Kellys and Quinns.

Above right: Aaron Sherritt, a member of the Kelly horse-stealing gang, was a more avid follower of the Greta mob's flash dress. He displays the style that almost amounted to their uniform. The high 'larrikin heel' boots, tight strapped trousers, sash around the waist and chin strap worn under the nose, were all their distinctive characteristics of clothing. Sherritt was remembered as 'being flash as lucifer … [like] an advance agent for a circus'. Another said, 'his parents, sisters and brothers were respectable and well conducted people, his father having been in the police force in the old country. He was a strapping, tall, well made young fellow … but gave himself up entirely to a disreputable life.'

Young Ned Kelly was seldom shy in voicing his opinions at local gatherings and public meetings. On one occasion, he was forcibly ejected from a church in Wangaratta. Like his Quinn uncles, he made a habit of riding unbroken horses into the towns to the alarm of pedestrians. He was told by a policeman on at least one occasion that 'he had better find another place to show off his horsemanship', after careering about the main street on a bucking animal. The same trooper also admitted that Kelly was a 'grand rider'.

At local sports meetings, young Ned was also remembered for his physical prowess and what must have been a mixture of vanity and love of showmanship. The only entertainments in what was still a scattered community were sports meetings, occasional race meetings, the annual ploughing matches, picnics and church dances. These functions were well attended and, in the Kelly locality, were held at Moyhu, Oxley, Greta, Glenrowan and Winton. The Kelly and Quinn clan also held impromptu matches at their various homes. John and James Quinn, Ned's wild uncles, had been recorded winning prize whips and bridles in Greta as early as 1865 and he inherited their love of action. The picnic sports at Glenrowan, held in a paddock near Harvey's orchard, were probably the most popular local event in the 1870s and attracted people from as far as Benalla and Wangaratta. Joseph Ashmead, son of a Winton farmer, recalled how Ned Kelly amused and impressed onlookers at these functions. He would ride at full gallop, bend from the saddle to snatch a handkerchief from the ground, show the same precision standing or lying in the saddle at break-neck speed, and would hurdle fences while kneeling on his horse's back.

Back at work, Kelly held his position as mill foreman until around September 1876. John McMonigle, working at the mill under Kelly then, said that their income virtually ceased when the Beechworth branch-line was completed in September 1876.

Saunders and Rule were also contracted to supply the Gippsland railway, still under construction, and arranged to transfer their whole plant overland. According to McMonigle, he and some of the men were sent with half the equipment and Ned Kelly was to follow with the rest, but the plant arrived in Gippsland without its foreman. The reason Kelly left a lucrative and responsible position remains one of the biggest mysteries of his career. After nearly three years of apparently honest work Ned Kelly returned to the life that had led him to gaol six years earlier.

Top left and above: James Kelly returned home from prison in 1877. He was eighteen at the time and was released early for good behaviour. Jim probably felt like a stranger at the Kelly hut. Mug-shots show that he was a boy when he went to prison four years earlier, and returned a man. This possibly motivated him to leave for New South Wales soon after. While in prison, he learned the shoemaking trade and was qualified upon release. James worked for a time as a shoemaker in Hay, but by June 1877 was following his brother's example. He was arrested, tried and sentenced to three more years for horse-stealing at Wagga Wagga. Once again he was photographed and off to 'college', as he called it, this time at Berrima and Darlinghurst Gaol in Sydney.

Left: Stephen Hart, along with John O'Brien, were two more members of the Greta mob convicted in 1877. In late July, both were arrested for horse-stealing and went to Beechworth Gaol. Later in the year, they were joined by more of the group: Dan Kelly, John and Tom Lloyd. Hart lived with his parents on a 230-acre selection near the Three Mile Creek and Wangaratta racecourse. He was short and lightly built but had great skill in horsemanship. A local resident recalled: 'Steve Hart used to wear a bright sash, and [hurdle] the railway gates in Wangaratta on the way to and from the Three Mile'. Hart is pictured in his Sunday best and spurs. The photograph was taken by James Bray at Beechworth.

Facing page inset: Joseph Byrne, Aaron Sherritt's lifelong friend, was an unlikely recruit of the Kelly horse-thieves. Byrne was the eldest son of 'a respectable woman who had a well-conducted and clean dairy farm' in the Woolshed Valley; his brothers and sisters were decent citizens. Joe was quiet, supposedly educated, handsome, and appears to have been gifted, yet he took to delinquency and crime for no apparent reason. A schoolmaster described him as 'a person who would rather follow than take the initiative . . . who seemed of a nervous, retiring disposition . . . such as is commonly seen in the countrified Australian youth who has spent the greater part of his life on the back-blocks'.

THE COMING OF AGE 61

Bird's-eye-view of Benalla, as the Kellys knew it. The town was divided in two by the Broken River. Bridge Street, with most of Benalla's business houses, is shown in the foreground right. In September 1877 Tom Lloyd and Ned Kelly got William Cain, a Benalla publican, to endorse cheques, among them one from a man named Baumgarten made out to the name of Thompson. The cheques turned out to be in payment for stolen horses and Thompson was Ned Kelly's alias. A barman at one of Benalla's seventeen hotels remembered that 'Ned Kelly was of a cordial disposition, but Dan Kelly was inclined to be sullen or morose . . . At times, under the influence of drink, they would gallop up and down the streets shouting and singing, for which they were fined several times'.

Early in 1877, Kelly left home again – this time possibly after a season of shearing. He headed to the upper King River where his uncles John and William Quinn were making a successful business running in wild and unbranded horses. According to police and local squatters, this business was not considered respectable and the Quinns were suspected of yarding most of the stock off neighbouring stations. Not long after joining them, their nephew came under the same suspicion. Kelly himself described what followed:

During my stay there I ran in a wild bull which I gave to Lydicher, a farmer, he sold him to Carr, a publican and butcher who killed him for beef, sometime afterwards I was blamed for stealing this bull from James Whitty of Boggy creek. I asked Whitty at Oxley racecourse why he blamed me for stealing his bull. He said he had found his bull and never blamed me but his son-in-law Farrell told him he heard I sold the bull to Carr. Not long afterwards I heard again I was blamed for stealing a mob of calves from Whitty and Farrell which I knew nothing about. I began to think they wanted me to give them something to talk about.

James Whitty was one of the largest land holders on the King River near Moyhu. The man described as his son-in-law was constable Farrell.

While Kelly was trying to quash these accusations, police visited his mother's home in April 1877 and made inquiries after him. In a letter to a friend shortly after, Ned complained that he was not being allowed to live in peace. His friend maintained: 'he told me distinctly that he was being persecuted by the police . . . he could not do as he liked; anything that occurred, he was put down for it'. One of the policemen who visited the Kelly hut had been district superintendent Nicholson, the same one from seven years earlier. The observations Nicholson made in writing, and the orders he issued after his inspections, have often been quoted as evidence to confirm Kelly's claim that police were out to get him and his family.

Superintendent Nicholson also gave a graphic description of the first Kelly hut:

I visited the notorious Mrs Kelly's on the road from Greta to Benalla. She lived on a piece of cleared and partly cultivated land on the road-side, in an old wooden hut, with a large bark roof. The dwelling was divided into five compartments by partitions of blanketing, rags and etc., There were no men in the house, only children and two girls of about fourteen years of age, said to be her daughters. They all appeared to be existing in poverty and squalor. She said her sons were out at work, but did not indicate where, and that

their relatives seldom came near them. However, their communications with each other are known to the police. Until the gang is rooted out of this neighbourhood one of the most experienced and successful mounted-constables in the district will be required in charge at Greta.

Nicholson's observations of the Kelly home were revealing but evidently prejudiced. Marilyn Lake (1985:92) has pointed to the discrepancy between Nicholson's description and Ned's image of 'rural abundance' in his letters. When police searched the Kelly home, they upset milk dishes, broke tins of eggs, emptied bags of flour and meat from casks, destroying all their provisions. As Lake pointed out, neighbours clearly found the home more prepossessing than Nicholson did. Police acknowledged it was a social heart of the selector community. Visitors such as William Williamson, Michael Woodyard, Bill Skillion, William Grey and Jack Daniels became employees and long-term boarders. Jane Graham worked as housekeeper; Ann Murdoch, wife of the Greta storekeeper, cooked meals there. Mrs Kelly's brothers and sisters were frequent guests.

Ned Kelly always maintained that police persecution and the unjust accusations of squatters against the family decided his course after leaving the sawmill. He tried to hold up the same reason as justification for starting 'wholesale and retail horse and cattle dealing' – with other people's livestock. It was also the reason he gave for gathering others into the illegal venture and so – though he never admitted it – formed the first Kelly gang in late 1876 or early 1877. Leaving his uncles at the King River, Ned Kelly was joined by his youngest brother Dan and stepfather George King and devised what was to be their full-time occupation.

There were even hints that they had plans beyond mere horse and cattle-stealing. A boy who worked for Mrs Kelly said 'they were then under arms'. William Williamson, their friend and neighbour, said that William Skillion went to Melbourne in 1877 and bought 'ammunition . . . four revolvers and one rifle'. Williamson also later said that Ned Kelly had 'it in mind for a long time to hold up the Seymour Bank'. But for the meantime, the Kellys concentrated on livestock.

Kelly's reasons for returning to crime seemed thin enough, but worse when it was discovered that many animals stolen by them were not taken from wealthy squatters. Locals testified that 'more horses were stolen from Greta than any other part; large mobs, sometimes fourteen or fifteen plough horses [were taken] from farmers . . . in one night'. It is impossible to find out how large the Kelly stock-thieving business was because no complete official statistics were kept, including recovery rates. Station owners and the police commissioner of the time 'deposed to the almost incredible extent to which, for many years, cattle stealing was carried on with impunity'. A constable Fitzpatrick – not a reliable source – mentioned that 'James Whitty's Moyhu station alone lost £500 worth of horseflesh on one year [1877]'. Ned Kelly claimed to have stolen 280 head of horses. Nevertheless, it appears that the police exaggerated the problem to justify their actions and Kelly, too, was probably boasting.

John McQuilton's research (1979:57–9, 1988) separated cattle from horse losses in the period and related these to the rest of the colony. General livestock losses reported in the north-east were, at times, up to 50 per cent of the Victorian total but tended to correspond with droughts when stock strayed in search of water. These peaked in 1869 (185 cattle reported), 1874 (121 reported) and 1876 (146 reported). The figures for horse losses are also indicative; in 1863 (116 horses reported stolen), 1871 (109 reported) and 1877 (122 reported). These totals did not include recovery rates. This was particularly significant in regard to horses – where borrowing was tolerated – and up to 80 per cent of the lost stock was recovered by the owners themselves. Reported losses of both cattle and horses indicate peaks but no proportionate increase. McQuilton linked stock theft in the region to selection failure – conflict resulting from the poverty of selectors in contrast to the wealth of neighbouring pastoralists. It was undoubtedly a major contributing cause in the Kelly case.

The system used by the Kellys in their 'horse and cattle dealing' was very similar to one used by a gang of Omeo horse-stealers years earlier, and supposedly used by the Quinn uncles on the King River. They stole stock in Victoria and then smuggled them across the border into New South Wales where they could be sold with minimal chance of being identified. On the return trip, stock from New South Wales was smuggled back into Victoria and sold in the same way. The Kellys recruited friends to carry out their raids and to help in the long drives to distant markets. Eye-witnesses later showed that at least six or seven men made up the gang, and on each trip a number were changed to avoid recognition. It later emerged that Dan Kelly's friends (and cousins), Tom and John Lloyd, were mixed up in the affair. Others were attracted from outside Greta. Two of these were Aaron Sherritt and Joseph Byrne, who lived on the Woolshed diggings near Beechworth. Three years later Sherritt described their partnership with the Kellys at length. He repeated Ned's claim that they 'used to steal horses wholesale [and] made raids from about Wagga to Albury, took them by a back-track to Melbourne, and on their return would pick up a number of horses in Victoria and take them over to Wagga or Albury for sale'.

For their long droving trips, the gang picked out little-known tracks through the ranges and unpopulated bush country. Their droving area stretched from the Riverina right down to the settled districts near Melbourne – a distance of more than 320 kilometres (200 miles). In the north-east, they established holding paddocks separate from their families' properties so as not to implicate them. Their most secluded block was in the wild and unmapped Wombat Ranges, 22 kilometres (fourteen miles) north of Mansfield and west of the upper reaches of the King River. On a partly worked-out alluvial goldfield, within the rim of a lofty mountain basin, they found an abandoned log house, repaired it, and cleared 28 hectares (70 acres) surrounding it for their use. At Sebastopol, within the Woolshed diggings near Beechworth, Aaron Sherritt took up 42 hectares (106 acres) as a selection. Not long after, the Kellys and Joseph Byrne were known to help clear and fence it. They also used a paddock kept by Byrne at Barnawartha, eight kilometres (five miles) south of the Murray opposite one of their crossing-places near Howlong. A Beechworth detective noted, 'they had ample paddock space [and] indeed, all their arrangements were as perfect as in any properly conducted business'.

When the Kelly gang reached these properties with stolen livestock, they went to great lengths to alter and manufacture brands. They did this by 'blotching', 'over-branding' and 'faking' – techniques that were considered quite modern. If a horse was branded H on the near shoulder, they would turn it

Inset: Constable Lonigan was one trooper very unpopular with Kelly after a brawl at Benalla in September 1877. Kelly is said to have told him during the fight, 'if I ever shoot a man Lonigan, you will be the first'.

Ned Kelly and Joseph Byrne were described as 'good-looking, well-dressed men' who had no trouble passing as well-to-do young squatters. One of the party used to act as master, and the others as servants; the master always going ahead to make arrangements where the horses were to be paddocked for the night. They would make for some squatter's station where they were unknown, ask permission to put their horses into his stockyard, on the pretence that they had met a stranger who wanted to purchase a mob of horses; the stranger being one of their own party . . . At last they would agree to a price, and would then ask the squatter to allow them to go into his office to draw up a receipt. After this the squatter would be asked to witness it. The supposed buyer would start off towards Melbourne, and the sellers appear to return to New South Wales. If, by chance, the horses were claimed by their owners, the receipt would be produced and they would then avoid arrest. Not everything went smoothly; copycats tried similar exploits, but were generally unsuccessful.

Jim Kelly came home from prison in August 1876, released early for good behaviour, but soon left for New South Wales. It is not known if he was involved in Ned's business circle but by June 1877 he was caught at Kiandra and violently resisted arrest. Under the alias of 'Wilson', Jim and an associate, Tom Manly, were charged over stealing horses at Wagga and each given four years hard labour. Then in July 1877 one of the Greta mob, the publican's son, John O'Brien, and two friends, Stephen and Richard Hart of Wangaratta, were arrested for 'illegally using and stealing horses'. It is not certain whether they too were in the Kelly horse-stealing gang at that time. John O'Brien was given eight months and Steve Hart was given twelve months hard labour. Two months later the Kellys and Lloyds were in trouble too, although not for cattle-stealing.

In September 1877, Ned was known as the leader of the Kelly gang and hero of the Greta mob. On a visit to Benalla he was arrested one evening by a supposed friend, constable Alexander Fitzpatrick, for 'being drunk and for having ridden his horse across a footpath' and spent the night in the cells. Next morning, Ned was escorted from the station to the courthouse by no fewer than four troopers. Among them was sergeant Whelan, who had arrested him as a boy for the alleged assault on Ah Fook and again in 1870 for highway robbery with Harry Power. Also in the escort was trooper Fitzpatrick. While the four policemen and their hung-over prisoner crossed to the corner opposite the courthouse, Fitzpatrick tried to handcuff Kelly. The gesture may only have been a flurry of efficiency, but it was not appreciated.

into HB conjoined by getting a pair of tweezers, pulling up the hairs into a B, then by pricking the skin with a needle dipped in iodine. This burns up the skin, and for about a month afterwards it looks like an old brand; new brands were also put on in this fashion, and they could never be detected. With the brands altered, the gang avoided the Murray River bridges by swimming their mobs across using 'forcing yards'; small high-railed stockyards usually erected on a steep bank, upstream and opposite a sandbank where the animals could land safely. The mobs were then divided into smaller groups, driven to saleyards and sold openly, let loose near a town to be impounded and bought cheaply on receipt, or were simply sold off to settlers and stations along the way.

Like his brothers, Dan Kelly left home at an early age. In 1875–76, he went shearing in the Riverina and Monaro High Plains beyond Kiandra. At the end of the season, he returned to his mother's selection and began knocking about with a group of young locals called the 'Greta mob'. They were seen together on hotel verandas, at dances and at local sports and race meetings. By 1876 the Greta mob were known in Beechworth, Benalla and Wangaratta. 'Dan Kelly looked quite a youth beside his brother . . . His countenance was sallow, and devoid of the colour of health one would expect to see in a young fellow used to outdoor life and exercise . . . he looked of a quiet, morose temperament, and one who would rather shun an act of violence than commit one'. Dan Kelly made no effort to hide his bush background, nor here to imitate the 'flash dress' style of the Greta mob. He wears a coat several sizes too large, possibly inherited from elder brothers, and his trousers are held up with rope. This and the matching portrait were printed by Burman's Melbourne studios, but evidently copied from originals taken in the north-east.

William Baumgarten and his brother Gustav were among the first of a long line of bystanders to suffer by the misguided deeds of the Kellys. German settlers at Barnawatha, the two brothers were married, prosperous and respected, with little reason to buy stolen stock. Sergeant Steele of Wangaratta arrested them in October 1877 with several of James Whitty's horses, which they proved they had bought from Ned Kelly under his alias, 'Thompson'. There is every reason to believe Kelly's statement that 'they paid full value for the horses and could not have known they were stolen'. There is also indication that they served as scapegoats because of police failure to apprehend the Kellys. At the second trial the following year Gustav was acquitted, but nearly twelve months later – despite character references by leading Beechworth citizens and distinct lack of evidence – William Baumgarten was sentenced to four years' imprisonment for receiving stolen horses.

Kelly knocked Fitzpatrick unconscious on the spot, and bolted across the main street into King's boot-maker shop. The three troopers and a revived Fitzpatrick tackled him in the store, and even King himself dived into the affray while a crowd gathered outside to watch. Despite outnumbering him, they could not get the handcuffs on. Kelly almost had his trousers torn off and uniforms were shredded in the struggle. Finally, constable Lonigan caught Kelly by his genitals and Fitzpatrick grabbed him by the throat. The fight was only halted when an elderly J. P., William McInnes, came into the shop, rebuked the police, and told Kelly to go quietly. Kelly, satisfied he had come out of it well, held out his hands and invited the J. P. to put the manacles on him. McInnes accompanied all of them into court to see that the incident was reported accurately. Sergeant Whelan requested that Kelly be sent for trial as he had 'assaulted the police' but it was rejected. Ned was treated quite leniently, probably on the recommendation of McInnes. He was fined a total of £3 1s for resisting arrest, costs, and damage to uniforms.

Less than a week later, more of the gang were in trouble. Dan Kelly, John and Thomas Lloyd pulled a prank at Winton one evening that resulted in charges being laid against them. Warrants were issued for their arrest, and the three of them went into hiding at the Kelly farm in the Wombat Ranges. Police search parties combed the Greta district for nearly three weeks. Inspector Brooke Smith of Wangaratta even appealed to Ned Kelly to give the boys up, but he refused. Later, Ned met constable Fitzpatrick on the road into Benalla, their friendship apparently having survived because Fitzpatrick didn't charge him for knocking him unconscious. Fitzpatrick advised him to make them [Dan Kelly, John and Tom Lloyd] give themselves up:

I told him I did not think there was anything serious against them, so accordingly the following morning he brought them into Benalla, came galloping up to the police station and told me he wanted me, so I went down the street with him. He said the four of them had ridden in that morning from wherever they had been hiding . . . So I arrested the three of them, read the charges to them, and brought them to the lockup.

No one would have been more shocked than Ned Kelly at the result of their trial on 19 October 1877. Dan Kelly and both Lloyds were found guilty of 'wilfully damaging property belonging to David Goodman', a hawker who owned a shop in Winton. Each was sentenced to three months' imprisonment at Beechworth Gaol and ordered to pay £2 10s damages. Tom Lloyd was later given an extra three months for 'common assault' on Mrs Goodman. The incident occurred after Dan Kelly arranged to deliver some meat to Mrs Goodman and to pick up some groceries – an exchange that the Kellys frequently undertook to get supplies. Dan arrived at the shop after closing time and the Goodmans refused to open up. Dan and the Lloyds broke the door in and got their rations.

Beyond that, the details are unreliable. The main witness, Goodman, was later sentenced to four years' imprisonment for the evidence he gave in this same case. So Dan Kelly and the Lloyds – not even suspected of the horse-stealing they were guilty of – served sentences on perjured evidence. The remaining members of the Kelly gang at the time (Ned Kelly, Joseph Byrne, George King, Aaron Sherritt and Allen Lowry, alias William Cooke) resumed business with increased vigour. In October 1877 a number of horses were found at Wodonga that had earlier disappeared from James Whitty's pastures. Another stolen horse was found in Byrne's paddock at Barnawatha, but he was not arrested. The police, however, did arrest two wealthy German migrants for claiming the horses at Wodonga. The Baumgartens were arrested along with Studders, Kennedy and Cooke for being implicated in the wholesale trading of stolen stock. The police had been patiently waiting to discover a key to the whole scheme.

William Cooke (or Lowry) was charged at Beechworth for stealing the horses from Whitty and others near Greta. The Baumgartens, Kennedy and Studders were charged with knowingly receiving stolen horses. Cooke was loyal to Ned Kelly and the other four men had almost certainly not known the horses were stolen, so the Kellys were not immediately implicated. The subsequent trials attracted much publicity throughout the district, and no one would have followed the proceedings with more interest than the Greta police.

The police had little trouble convicting William Cooke, who was sentenced to eight years' imprisonment. But it was difficult to convict those charged with buying the stolen livestock as the evidence was threadbare. Subsequent juries could not agree, and the trials dragged on for nearly ten months, through into 1878. As the cases progressed, more was learned of the real culprits. It slowly emerged that a man named Thompson had been the horse-dealer in charge and had traded all the stolen animals. The description, in every case, tallied with Edward Kelly.

Ned admitted later that:

> when the horses were found on the Murray river, I wrote to Mr Swanhill of Lake Rowan to acquaint the auctioneer and to advertise my horses for sale. I brought some of them to that place but did not sell. I sold some of them in Benalla, Melbourne and other places, and left the colony and became a rambling gambler. Soon after I left there was a warrant for me and the police searched the place [Eleven Mile Creek] and watched night and day for two or three weeks.

It was the end of full-time horse-stealing for Ned Kelly and company. When he disappeared, the rest of the troupe dispersed. Whether Kelly went shearing in New South Wales, or into hiding at their farm in the Wombat Ranges, is not known. It does appear that he still had a number of horses unsold when he took off. He instructed Joseph Byrne and the recently released Dan Kelly and John Lloyd to dispose of them. On 15 March 1878, at least a month after he had disappeared, a warrant was issued for Ned Kelly on charges of horse-stealing.

Dan Kelly, the Lloyd cousins and Byrne may have been the only ones of the original band left by that time. Ned vanished; Aaron Sherritt returned to work his selection at the Woolshed Valley; and George King vanished completely.

By 1878, Mrs Kelly was carrying her third child with George King, but she never saw him again. Joseph Byrne and Dan Kelly stayed at the Kelly hut, and the Lloyds lived at home in February and March without any attempt at concealment. By this stage, more information had emerged from the Baumgarten trials still in progress at Beechworth. Two men had been seen driving stolen horses through Chiltern and their descriptions matched Dan Kelly and John Lloyd. By April the police thought they had enough to support charges and on 5 April, a warrant was issued for their arrest. Notice of the warrants was published in the *Police Gazette* within a week of issue and soon came to the attention of the Benalla police.

By coincidence, superintendent Nicholson was inspecting the Benalla district – just twelve months after his report on the Kellys – when the warrants were brought to the attention of sergeant Whelan at the Benalla police station. On 15 April, sergeant Whelan despatched none other than constable Alexander Fitzpatrick to take charge of Greta police station while its officer-in-charge, senior constable Strahan, was supposedly visiting a Riverina shearing shed where Ned Kelly had been reported working. Fitzpatrick was made aware of the warrants before he left, and Whelan told him he could call in and arrest Dan Kelly on his way. The constable left after lunch on 15 April and on the way stopped at 'Lindsay's', an unlicensed shanty at Winton, for a few drinks. About an hour before dusk, he took the track to Mrs Kelly's new hut to see if Dan Kelly was at home.

6 AN ILL-FATED VISIT TO THE KELLY HUT

THE FITZPATRICK INCIDENT, 15 APRIL 1878

Constable Fitzpatrick did not arrest Dan Kelly or reach Greta police station that April evening. At 2 a.m. on 16 April, Lindsay, the shanty-keeper and owner of the Winton store, took Fitzpatrick back to Benalla. Fitzpatrick had a slight flesh wound on the wrist and smelled of brandy. He told a remarkable story of the night's events.

I was proceeding to Greta on duty, having been instructed to relieve Senior Constable Strahan at that place. I had to pass the residence of Mrs Kelly, and called there; it was between 4 and 5 o'clock. Mrs Kelly and the children were in the house. I stayed there about an hour or more, and hearing a man chopping up the hill I went to him to see if he had a license; it was [William] Williamson chopping he said he had a license and I left him. Seeing two horsemen ride towards the Kellys' house I followed them. When I got there [William] Skillion was leading the horses away, and I asked him who had been riding; I said, 'this is Dan Kelly's mare, where is he?' He replied 'up at the house I suppose'. I saw Dan Kelly come out of a hut and after speaking to him about some stray horses I told him I would have to arrest him under a warrant out against him for horse-stealing. He said, 'very well, but let me have something to eat first, as I have been out riding all day'. I consented to this and went after him into the house; it was then getting dusk.

Mrs Kelly was in the room and while Dan was getting his supper, she said to me, 'you won't take Dan out of this tonight'. Dan replied, 'shut up mother, it's all right'. Just afterwards Ned Kelly came in the door, and without a word fired at me with a revolver. I was about a yard and a half inside, rather behind the door with my back towards it; Mrs Kelly was standing with her back to the fire. The first shot did not strike me and he immediately fired again, the bullet lodging in my left arm, immediately above the wrist. Mrs Kelly at the same time rushed at me with a shovel striking a heavy blow on my head, and making a large dent in the helmet I wore. I had raised my arm to guard from the shovel when he fired the second shot. I knocked the shovel down with my right hand, and then turned to draw my revolver, but it had been taken out of my belt; Dan Kelly had it in his hand. I then seized the revolver held in Ned's hand, saying, 'you cowardly wretch, do you want to murder me?' We struggled for the pistol. The pistols were all aimed at me. When I said 'do you want to kill me?' Ned Kelly called out, 'that will do boys'. He turned to Skillion and said, 'you bastard, why didn't you tell me who was here?' and then turning to me said, 'if I had known it was you Fitzpatrick, I would not have fired, but none of the other buggers would have left here alive'. The wound in my arm was bleeding all the time, and I fainted. When coming round again, I heard the men talking. Ned Kelly told Williamson that Bill [meaning Skillion] would have given that bugger a pill the other day if he had not prevented him and Skillion said he had a pill in for Sergeant Steele one of these days. Williamson and Skillion soon after left, and I got up from the floor, when Ned said he was sorry it had happened as it was me; that he should get into trouble over it. I saw my revolver on the table; it was taken asunder with the charges drawn. I took it up, and Ned Kelly took it from my hand; he also took all my ammunition, and asked had I more. I examined my wrist; it was swollen and the bullet was seen under the skin. He said he must have it out of that, and took a rusty razor to cut it out. I told him I wished to go home and get a medical man to remove it, but he refused. I then said I would operate myself and taking a sharp pen-knife I cut it out; and it was a small ball. Kelly's sister was present. Ned Kelly took the bullet, and my arm was bandaged by Mrs Kelly. It was then that I went outside, Ned Kelly followed me. He said, 'now look here, I spared you and you must spare me. How will you manage to say you were shot?' I replied I would not mention it. He then said, 'you had better say this, that you went to arrest Dan, who was in company with Williamson; that you had your revolver out, and in putting the handcuffs on, it went off and shot you; and that Dan took the ammunition.' He also compelled me to make an entry in my notebook. I wanted to get away then but Ned would not return my revolver. He said, 'if you go home and say I shot you, you'll get no credit for it. Government won't reward you; I'll give you five hundred after Baumgarten's case is over.' Mrs Kelly told Ned to say that if I told of it, I'd not be alive long; they had plenty of friends about. I went and got a horse from behind the house, where Dan had tied him, not to be seen. My hand was very painful. Dan brought my revolver and handcuffs and I went away.

Constable Alexander Fitzpatrick, Beechworth 1878. His account of the affray at the Kelly home might have been accepted without question if his reputation and subsequent behaviour had not revealed his lack of integrity. Fitzpatrick's career in the Victorian police force was brief and uncommendable. He joined at the age of 21 in April 1877 and his first posting was to Benalla in August 1877. Within a month of his arrival, he had made disreputable acquaintances, developed a drinking habit, and was unpopular with his superiors. Fitzpatrick almost certainly capitalised on his friendship with Edward Kelly. In September, he arrested him for being drunk, which led to a fierce brawl. Three weeks later he persuaded Kelly to surrender his brother and cousins from hiding. This led to their sentences at Beechworth. In both instances, Fitzpatrick used his supposed friendship to achieve the arrests. He rescued his reputation by them – albeit at the expense of the Kellys. There is strong indication that he tried the same approach at the Kelly hut in April 1878, but by this stage, the Kellys had realised his technique.

Above: Selections on the Greta road; first survey 1866. The land subdivisions are misleading; even by 1878 many of them had not been released for selection and remained in the three pastoral leases contained in the area. The selections held by Mrs Kelly (block 57A), William Williamson (block 57), and her son-in-law William Skillion (block 56) were located on the Greta–Winton road, shown centre. The landmark known as 'Bald Hill' or 'Kelly's Lookout' is located on block 50, between the Kelly and Lloyd selections (blocks 31 and 32).

Right: Constable Fitzpatrick in later life. After the trial of Mrs Kelly and the two selectors, Fitzpatrick's story was questioned and he was dishonourably discharged in April 1880. During his three years as a policeman, he pleaded guilty to a number of charges. He admitted that he was not fit to be in the Police force, as 'I had associated with the lowest persons in Lancefield, and could not be trusted out of sight, and never did my duty'. He also commented that 'there are many constables in the force who have done more serious things than I did, and have remained in the force and got promotion'. In 1881 it was reported that Mr Fosbery, Inspector General of Police N.S. Wales, and Captain Standish, express in strong terms their adverse opinions of Fitzpatrick, while the present acting Commissioner of Police, Mr Chomley, describes him as a liar and a larrikin.

Previous pages: Ruins of the Kelly homestead.

Ned showed me out of the panel, and I started off for Benalla . . . spurred on until coming to Winton to Lindsay's. When I dismounted I could not stand, and the two Lindsays helped me in and gave me brandy. Mr Lindsay bound up my wrist.

Ned claimed that he was not at the house on the day of the incident or anywhere near Greta in April 1878. But his mother implied (and Tom Lloyd openly admitted) that he was present. This was further substantiated by evidence given by Ryan and Harty in October at the trial. Ned also claimed that Fitzpatrick gashed his wrist on the door lock and gave convincing reasons in later letters that he would not have fired three shots into a room crowded with his family. Although this too has been contradicted. After the trial, William Williamson said that the constable had been shot. Either way, the police were soon after the Kellys.

Later that morning after the constable's return, warrants were issued at Benalla for the arrest of the Kelly brothers, their mother and the two farmers. Police from Wangaratta arrived at Greta the following afternoon. The party included a sergeant Steele, detective Brown and senior constable Strahan, whose absence had been the reason for Fitzpatrick's assignment. Steele said,

we watched Mrs Kelly's place for some considerable time from the hill opposite the house. At nine o'clock in the evening we arrested William Williamson. I went to Skillion's place but could not find him then, so we took Williamson to Greta and returned again at about one o'clock in the morning and arrested Skillion. We also arrested Mrs Kelly. She had not been in her bed at all during the night; I was there on three occasions and she had not been to bed. James Quinn was in the house. We took Williamson, Skillion and Mrs Kelly to Greta, and then brought them on to Benalla in a dray.

The following day, Dan Kelly's cousin, John Lloyd, was also arrested on the charge that Dan had resisted. He was taken to Benalla and remanded in court with his aunt and the two other men, but there was no sign of the Kelly brothers.

After the first remand at Benalla on 18 April, the events, as alleged Fitzpatrick, were telegraphed to papers all over the district as an alarming outrage. The

Dan Kelly never made public his version of what occurred with Fitzpatrick. From the conflicting accounts it seems most likely that he or his brother heaved the constable through the back door where he gashed his wrist on the protruding latch. It seems totally implausible that shots were fired in a small room crowded with the Kelly family. The photograph was distributed by Burman's Melbourne studio, but was probably taken at Beechworth. The engraving taken from the photograph was published in 1878 in the *Illustrated Sydney News*.

Kate Kelly. According to the family, the argument with Fitzpatrick started after he made advances toward fifteen-year-old Kate Kelly. Mrs Kelly claimed that he pulled Kate onto his knee and 'tried to kiss her, and the boys tried to stop him. He was drunk and they were sober, but his story was believed.' Ned corroborated this version in a later speech but forbid their solicitors, Zinke and Bowman, permission to call Kate or Grace Kelly as witnesses at the trial. Neither of the girls – who witnessed the entire event – ever gave details.

newspapers accepted Fitzpatrick's allegations, which appeared unchallenged as a substantiated account – which it was not. A Beechworth paper exaggerated: 'on Monday evening last the town of Benalla was thrown into excitement by a report that a constable had been shot by the notorious Kelly'.

The condition and nature of his wound were similarly embellished: 'The poor fellow arrived at the camp here about 9 o'clock in a very weak state, and medical assistance was at once procured for his wound, the bullet having passed through the wrist.'

He had in fact arrived five hours later when the whole town was asleep. The doctor who examined his arm could only cautiously testify that one wound 'might have been caused by a bullet' and that they 'were merely skin wounds'. Shortly after the first local reports, stories appeared in Melbourne and national journals. The Kelly family had gained their first headlines in the distant capital of the colony.

Williamson, Skillion and Mrs Kelly (with her newborn child Alice) were remanded in custody for four weeks before they appeared again in the Benalla court. The case was not heard by the regular judiciary, but three honorary justices. In January 1878, Premier Berry had sacked over two hundred public servants, including police magistrates and judges, on what became known as 'Black Wednesday'. This move caused disruption and delay and every level of the judicial system.

All three accused pleaded not guilty. At the suggestion of their Beechworth counsellor, My Zinke, they reserved their defence. The Crown case was presented and sworn evidence was given before all three prisoners were 'committed for trial at the Beechworth assize court on 9 October 1878'. This meant another wait in custody of nearly five months because of the Berry Government measures.

It was reported that Mr Zinke asked that Mrs Kelly might be allowed bail, as she had a young baby at nurse, and the Beechworth Gaol was a most unfit place for her confinement. Mr Chomley said he would make no objection, and bail was fixed at two sureties of £50 each, and herself in a like amount.

The large amount could not be raised, so Mrs Kelly and baby Alice went to gaol in Beechworth. Almost a month later, this small item appeared in a column of the *Ovens and Murray Advertiser*.

MRS KELLY. A day or two since, Mr W. H. Foster attended at the Beechworth Gaol and admitted to bail this woman, who had been committed to trial for aiding and abetting an attempt to murder constable Fitzpatrick, at Greta. It was an act of charity, as the poor woman, though not the most reputable of characters, had a babe in her arms, and in the cold gaol without a fire, it is a wonder the poor little child lived so long during this bitter wintry weather.

In reality it was not an act of charity; she was only released after the required bail had been produced.

The trial was held in October – six months after their arrest. By that time, neither Daniel nor Edward Kelly had been apprehended. They had been sighted watching their mother's hut from Bald Hill in July but disappeared before police could reach them.

The cases were heard at an unfortunate time for the accused. The Baumgarten horse-stealing cases were still being heard in that October session – ten

Above: The new Kelly homestead featured glazed windows, lace curtains and timber partitioned rooms — vast improvements on their old slab hut. The replacement was built between April 1877 and 1878 on a rise several hundred metres from the road and across the creek from the old hut. Despite devotion to their mother, the three Kelly brothers were away from home too often to put much into developing the land, but this building venture was an effort to make their mother's last pregnancy more comfortable. Mrs Kelly looked fondly upon this period. 'Before that day when Fitzpatrick came we were so happy. We were not getting too rich, but we were doing all right. It was a lonely life, but we were all together, and we all loved each other so dearly.' The small boy on the veranda is either Ned Kelly's youngest step-brother, John King, or one of the Skillion children; another child surveys the photographer from the right. The path in the foreground led to the old hut, which by 1878 was used as the men's quarters. The track to the right led to a large stockyard. The plate was taken between 1878 and 1880.

Left: Kelly house, from the south; a sketch based on later photographs. The new Kelly home was walled with slabs laid horizontally and let into grooved posts, the gable ends were split-paling, and the chimney was timber, lined with clay or sheet-iron. The roof and ceilings were made from sheets of flattened stringybark, held down with jockey rails. A passage ran from front to back door. Two main rooms occupied the front off each side; a living room and kitchen on the right (east side) and bedroom on the left (west). Two more bedrooms were under the skillion roof. The row with Fitzpatrick took place in the room on the right with the tall window.

Ellen Kelly was illiterate, only 1.675 metres (5 feet 5 inches) tall and of thin build, but she was an extraordinary, spirited identity. Described as 'of that class known as bush-women, hardened by a rough and almost savage life [she was, nevertheless] agreeable in her way'. Marilyn Lake (1985:93) noted that Ellen belonged to a rural subculture whose ethos and practices were antagonistic to a then strict ruling middle-class. This allowed such women a wide range of physical expression and Ellen railed against the genteel role model of feminine gentility. Like other Kelly/Quinn women, she would not be intimidated, and could be abusive and assaulted enemies. She and her daughters were sexually active and entered defacto relationships. Ellen loved horse-riding but rode 'furiously' and 'astride' like a man. She was willing to defend herself while socialising in restaurants or hotels when fights broke out; scars on her forehead and cheek bore witness. In 1878 she was 46 and had borne twelve children that are known. Three – Mary Jane, Anne and Ellen (Frost) – had died. She had three children by George King: Ellen (1873), John (1875) and Alice (1878), born only two days before the Fitzpatrick incident. Ned Kelly remarked, 'My mother has seen better days; she struggled up with a large family, and I feel . . . more keenly than I can express the unjust treatment meted out to [her], arrested with a baby at her breast and convicted of a crime of which she was innocent'. Here Ellen is shown with granddaughters Lilian, left, and Alice Knight at Lurg in 1911.

months after the first trials. Ned Kelly had been clearly established as the ringleader behind the robberies and that his young brother was implicated. This undoubtedly influenced the trial of their mother and neighbours. One Beechworth paper commented, 'the calendar is the heaviest for years, and the cases are of a very grave nature', which may have prompted unusually stern measures. Another influencing factor was the judge, Redmond Barry. He was not known for his leniency at the best of times and, as a result of 'Black Wednesday', was probably more overworked than at any other point in his career.

All three were arraigned together in the Beechworth court, charged with 'aiding and abetting a murder' and pleaded not guilty. It was noted that Williamson 'exercised his right to challenge five times', before a jury of twelve could be assembled. A Mr Bowman now appeared for the prisoners and Mr Chomley again appeared for the Crown. The Crown case remained as it had at the Benalla hearing. Constable Fitzpatrick was first called to repeat his sworn statement, which he did with elaboration on earlier readings. He admitted not having the required warrant at the time of his visit and that he had been drinking at Lindsay's in Winton both before and after the affray, but he still expected people to believe his story. He denied being drunk; punching the dent in his helmet to make it appear that Mrs Kelly had struck him; and concocting the entries in his notebook. He did confess, however, that he made his notes some days after the event.

The next witness was a Dr Nicholson of Benalla, who gave guarded testimony about the nature of Fitzpatrick's wound. He stated that he found two wounds, 'one a jagged one and the other a clean incision'. He added that 'they might have been produced by a bullet, that is the outside wound'. Chomley showed two bullets to the doctor that were claimed to be cast from a bullet mould found in the Kelly hut four weeks after the arrests. The doctor said either bullet might have caused either of the wounds. He then qualified his remark by saying, 'there could not have been much loss of blood'. Mr Bowman completely overlooked the opportunity to expand on the doctor's testimony, and in answer to only three questions the doctor replied: 'I did not probe the wound so I do not know if the two wounds were connected. There was a smell of brandy on him. A constable present said Fitzpatrick had some brandy at Lindsay's. It was merely a skin wound.' In answer to the prosecutor he concluded 'he was certainly not drunk'.

Two more witnesses were called for the Crown. David Lindsay described himself as a farmer and

Top left: Ned's brother-in-law William Skillion (or Skilling) was not pardoned, but should have been. Police correspondence to chief commissioner Standish in 1880 revealed that information had been received by them that 'Joseph Byrne was present at the Eleven Mile creek affray' and, as Williamson and Kelly said, had been wrongly identified by Fitzpatrick as Skillion. His association with the Kellys ended sadly: he lost his freedom, his selection and his wife. Maggie and her cousin Tom Lloyd visited him at Pentridge in October 1880, probably to tell him that they were in a defacto relationship and wanted to raise a family.

Top right: William 'Bricky' Williamson boarded with the Kelly family during the 1870s, eventually taking up the selection on their west boundary. He was first drawn into trouble by Ned's uncle James, and received eighteen months hard labour for trying to break up a fight. Just as innocently he was caught up in the Fitzpatrick incident for being a spectator. After the 1881 royal commission into the Kelly outbreak, he said, 'I was granted a pardon for a thing I did not do ... that was worse than the sentences'. The portrait comes from his prison record sheet.

Left middle: Superintendent C. H. Nicolson, who issued orders that 'police were never to go near the [Kellyl house alone', was sitting in the Wangaratta police station discussing the Kelly brothers when sergeant Steele received news of the 'murderous attack'. According to Steele, Nicolson gave no instructions, orders or even advice. It was nine o'clock the following evening when they arrested Williamson at Greta — more than 24 hours after the so-called outrage. It has been suggested that the delays were deliberate, perhaps encouraged by Nicolson or other officers to allow the Kelly brothers to escape, thereby drawing out the political value of the pursuit ('Black Wednesday' occurred only four months earlier). [Premier] Berry made no secret of his view that the Police service could be carried on altogether without officers. Ned Kelly observed that 'Berry would have sacked a great many of them [policemen] only I came to their aid and kept them in their billets and good employment.'

Above: Sergeant James Whelan, Benalla. There are many theories about possible motives behind Fitzpatrick's trip to the Kelly hut against orders — and the obvious leisure taken by him and the other police after the alleged incident. The constable took three hours returning from Winton to Benalla — a journey that could have been made in an hour. When Fitzpatrick finally reached there, sergeant James Whelan was summoned from his bed, but took no action. This delay was never explained. Word of the incident was not even sent to Wangaratta until the next day.

Left: Sergeant Steele and his party arrested Mrs Kelly at one o'clock on a cold and frosty night. Williamson and Skillion had been declared armed and desperate, yet Williamson was at the hut on his selection and Skillion was woken in bed at his home. Neither had gone into hiding and no firearms were found in their homes — circumstances their own counsel overlooked at the trial. Williamson was given a full pardon and released in 1881 — indication of his innocence and the constable's perjury.

storekeeper and gave evidence that Fitzpatrick had come back to his store between ten and eleven o'clock. He was wounded and faint and said that Ned Kelly had shot him and that the two accused were there. Lindsay gave Fitzpatrick some brandy and water, but denied he was drunk. Sergeant Steele then gave evidence of the arrests.

On Thursday 11 October, Mr Bowman urged that no credence could be placed on Fitzpatrick's uncorroborated story, which was exceedingly improbable. He said he would produce two witnesses to prove that Skillion was not present at all; and if one part of the evidence for the Crown was proved false the jury could not believe the rest. He argued that the constable knew nothing of the matter because he was drunk. Francis Harty was then brought forward and swore that Skillion had arrived at his Winton property at five o'clock on the Monday concerned with another man he did not know. Skillion had four horses on grass in his paddock. He had tea with Harty, paid him for the care of the animals and left at 7.30 p.m.

Questioned by Mr Chomley, Harty admitted buying a mare from Ned Kelly on 15 April and said he offered to provide bail for Mrs Kelly. He also stated that Skillion was Mrs Kelly's son-in-law. Joseph Ryan, a young Lake Rowan farmer, then entered the witness box. He swore he had been with Skillion that afternoon and supported Harty's evidence. He said he and Skillion had gone over to Kelly's later that evening but 'the row was all over'. Under cross-examination, he said he also bought a horse from Ned Kelly that day and produced the receipt drawn up by them. He also had to acknowledge that his mother was a sister of Mrs Kelly.

Amazingly, that concluded Mr Bowman's case. Mrs Kelly and Williamson remained virtually undefended beyond the attempt to discredit Fitzpatrick's charges. Bowman did not produce either of the two younger Kelly daughters who had witnessed the whole affair; nor did he produce Margaret Skillion to support the evidence regarding her husband. The Crown prosecutor was left to summarise. He said the facts of the case were proved, the alibi set up by Ryan and Harty was useless, and that they had committed perjury. The jury retired for two hours and returned late in the afternoon with the verdict: all three were found guilty. Five days later, at the conclusion of the trial, they stood before Sir Redmond Barry again to receive his judgment.

In the cells beside the court that day, pastoralist William Baumgarten and farmer Samuel Kennedy had finally been convicted of 'receiving' the horses stolen by Ned Kelly. Judge Barry made an example of the two men who had survived ten months of uncertain juries. Baumgarten was sentenced to four years and Kennedy to six. He made no secret that Williamson, Skillion and Mrs Kelly were to serve a similar purpose. Barry said he 'hoped this would lead to the disbanding of the gang of lawless persons who have for years banded themselves together in the neighbourhood of Greta against the police'. He then sentenced Mrs Kelly to three years' imprisonment and Williamson and Skillion to six years' hard labour. A Beechworth editor wrote in comment of the trial, 'the only pity is that Ned Kelly, one of the most notorious young desperadoes ever known in these parts, has managed to escape detection'.

Facing page, clockwise from top: The gaol and courthouse, Ford Street Beechworth in the 1870s. According to constable Fitzpatrick, it was known that Ned Kelly was a very few miles out of Beechworth when his mother and Williamson and Skillion were being tried. He was reported seen in the Woolshed Valley, mounted and armed. A few days after the trial, Fitzpatrick was transferred to Melbourne for his own safety. After we were sentenced, Williamson wrote, 'Fitzpatrick was escorting us to the gaol. He had a handkerchief to his eyes, and said, "Well Billy, I never thought you would get anything like that". In the Gaol yard Mrs Kelly said to me, "Now they will play up [meaning her sons] . . . there will be murder now"'. It is on record that Kelly made several attempts at peaceful settlement.

After the trial, John Quinn and Isaiah Wright propositioned Benalla magistrate, Alfred Wyatt. They promised that if Ellen Kelly was liberated, an arrangement would be made by which the Kellys (Ned and Dan, against whom there were warrants) would give themselves up. The words were, I think, 'They shall be brought in if the old woman is let out'. Wyatt told them he was unable to make proposals on behalf of the government but would convey their offer. He passed it on to the police, but nothing happened. Afterwards, Williamson added, 'Ned sent word to us to hang something out of the window of the cells we were in, and he would come and stick up the Gaol and rescue us. But I did not like the idea of it, and persuaded Skillion not to have anything to do with it.' Shortly after, Mrs Kelly was transferred to Melbourne Gaol, and Skillion and Williamson went to Pentridge.

The two-storey Beechworth courthouse.

Interior of the Beechworth court, showing the witness box and dock. The clan was attacked again after the Fitzpatrick incident. One article read, 'Mrs Kelly is a notoriously bad woman'. The Benalla *Ensign* proclaimed the Kelly family are notorious in this district and their names are as familiar as household words. The father, a man of ill-repute died some years ago . . . the house of the family has been the rendezvous of thieves and criminals for years past and indeed has been the centre of a system of crime that almost surpasses belief.' William Williamson rejoined, 'the Judge never read the evidence; he got it all out of the papers before the trial. The papers already had us convicted. When he was summing up to the Jury, he said, "Well gentlemen, you all know what this man Kelly is"."

The warrant is a duplicate of the one Fitzpatrick should have been carrying at the Kelly homestead. Ironically, the Kellys need not have resisted it. The same one was issued for Dan's cousin, John Lloyd, who was arrested and arraigned at Beechworth three weeks later. His accusers could not produce anything against him and he was released; as Dan Kelly likely would have been.

at me — no word spoken until shot
was fired — had hair in it — it
was not the edge of the Shovel struck me
I know Mrs Skillion did not see her
I got home about 2 in the morning
I did not call & ask Mrs Skillion if
her husband was at home — have been
in the force about 12 months — I lost my
revolver after 2 shots had been fired
I had seen the bullet mark in the back
before. I went back to look — found 2 Slabs
of bark removed — Williamson muttered
something which I did not hear. Skillion
did not say anything — Don't know
of any pistols were found at the hut — Saw
a revolver there before — The Shovel was
like a Contractors Shovel worn down
had no instructions to arrest Kelly —
was going to relieve Sergt Strachan
Miss Kelly was in the house while the
firing was going on She sat down &
cried

Taken & Read over this 19th day
of October 1878 at Benalla before me

Sergt Whelan had informed me there
was a warrant out for Dan Kelly

Alexander Fitzpatrick
a Const 2867

Top left: Francis Harty was one of only two witnesses called for the defence. His testimony was discredited because of his known friendship with the Kellys. Harty remarked in Fitzpatrick's hearing that 'Ned Kelly is the best bloody man that has ever been in Benalla. I would fight up to my knees in blood for him — I have known him for years. I would take his word sooner than another man's oath.' Sergeant Whelan at Benalla reported, 'I have also been informed that Harty, who lives at the Bald Hill near Winton, has been endeavouring to sell cattle for the Kelly family since the shooting affair and that he has had the use of cows to milk from Mrs Kelly since.' Another dossier revealed that Ned Kelly used to keep horses in Harty's paddocks so that the police would not see too many grazing at the Eleven Mile.

Above: One of the strongest indictments against Sir Redmond Barry and his lack of impartiality towards the Kellys was a remark he was said to have made when sentencing Mrs Kelly: 'if your son Ned were here I would make an example of him for the whole of Australia — I would give him fifteen years'. The statement is said to have decided Ned Kelly on the course he took, but appears to have no substantiation beyond family legend. There was a general feeling that the sentences were particularly harsh. A Benalla magistrate later volunteered that he 'thought that sentence upon the old woman, Mrs Kelly, a very severe one'. Another notable citizen in Beechworth stated that 'if policy had been used or consideration for the mother shown two or three months would have been ample'. Even the then chief commissioner of police conceded two years later: 'I believe the outrages would never have occurred if it had not been . . . for the anger and indignation of the Kellys at their mother having received that severe sentence'.

Left: The record of the Quinns, Kellys and Lloyds most likely influenced the trial. The list, compiled from police and penal records and published in an 1881 royal commission report, is amended to show the clan's record until the October 1878 trial.

Facing page: The cause of an outbreak. The last page of Fitzpatrick's statement about the affray at the Eleven Mile Creek.

AN ILL-FATED VISIT TO THE KELLY HUT 81

7 FROM HORSE-STEALING TO HOMICIDE
STRINGYBARK CREEK, 28 OCTOBER 1878

While Mrs Kelly waited six months for her trial, Ned and Dan retreated into the Wombat Ranges, nearly 50 kilometres away. During winter and spring in 1878 they lived on Daniel Kelly's secluded farm in the dense bush. It was the same farm they had established as stock thieves and the same spot where Dan and John and Thomas Lloyd hid from police in September 1877. The farm was only a few miles west of the remote hideouts Harry Power had shown Ned Kelly eight years earlier.

The brothers were not alone in the wilderness that year. Joseph Byrne, a partner in their horse-stealing and a close friend of Ned's, also joined them. Byrne had intermittently lived with the Kellys at Greta since 1877 and had witnessed the Fitzpatrick incident. He, too, had reason to avoid the police.

They had no trouble getting rations; Byrne was not known in the south at Mansfield, where he was said to have made frequent visits. Friends also brought supplies from Greta up the Fifteen Mile Creek and Ryan's Creek. In June, the company swelled. Their cousin, Tom Lloyd, and a young Stephen Hart were both released from prison and soon joined the Kellys. Hart was an early acquaintance of the Greta mob, and one with whom Dan Kelly had renewed friendship in Beechworth Gaol. Both Hart and Lloyd were attracted by the new business the enterprising Kelly brothers had started during their forced seclusion.

In watersheds to a number of creeks in the area, there were small alluvial gold deposits partly worked out and abandoned years earlier. The Kellys went over these spots and found 'payable quantities' of

Above: The dark and steep Wombat Ranges rise like a wall in front of Mount Battery (right). They stretch ten miles north towards Tatong and Greta and east and west to Barjarg and the King River. A Mansfield editor of the time wrote that the ranges were of an: 'almost unimaginably impracticable nature, save to the few who have been accustomed to cross its gloomy recesses since boyhood. The hills are steep, woods pathless and gullies deep, dark and winding. Vast gorges, bounded by almost perpendicular ranges, monotonous in outline and of endless extent, form a labyrinth territory from which the most experienced bushman might well despair of extricating himself.'

Left: The Kelly farm. The map is a detail from an 1884 survey, by which time the farm had been deserted for six years.

A visitor wrote of their hideout: 'Situated on a small rise in the midst of a basin, bounded on the east by Ryan's creek on the west by a very high and steep mountain, forming part of the Wombat Range, on the north by a small creek flowing down from between the hills, and on the south by a medium sized ridge, which, however, is high enough to effectually conceal the hut from view in that direction. Reining in my horse on the crest of this ridge, and taking a glance at the scene which lay before me, I could not but be struck with wonderment that such a perfect settlement should have existed so long within half a dozen miles of selections without its existence being discovered. A farmer named Jebb lives within four, and another named Harrison within six miles of it, and yet neither — at least so they assert — were even aware that the Kellys were in the locality, although the latter must have lived on this spot for many months, or they could have never got matters into such an improved state. The plateau contains altogether, I should say, about seventy acres, and this is fenced in on three sides (north, south and east) by a sapling dogleg and brush fence, the west side requiring no fencing owing to the steepness of the hill which constitutes its boundary.'

FROM HORSE-STEALING TO HOMICIDE

Dan Kelly's house on Bullock Creek. 'I came back with the full intention of working a still to make whisky as it was the quickest means to obtain money to procure a new trial for my mother . . . We had a house, two miles of fencing twenty acres of ground cleared for the purpose of growing mangel wurzels and barley for the purpose of distilling whisky. We had a place erected close to the house for the purpose of erecting a small distill, so if anyone informed on us, they would not get the most valuable or main distill that was further down the creek with the sugar and other requisitions. We were also digging for gold. We had tools and sluice bores and everything requisite for the work . . . and we were making good wages as the creek is very rich . . . The police were not satisfied with frightening my sisters . . . lagging my mother and infant, and those innocent men, but should follow me and my brother into the wilds where we had been quietly digging neither molesting or interfering with anyone.' Yet there is little doubt that the Kellys had already decided on the course they intended taking. Much later, Ned himself admitted: 'our horses were poor and our firearms were bad, and we wanted to make a rise'.

gold. They sank shafts and set up elaborate sluices in the creek – gaining enough to put towards legal costs for the three awaiting trial. According to Ned Kelly, they also erected two whisky stills and sowed a 20-acre crop near the house to produce the ingredients. A floating population of close friends came and went as they pleased. These friends sold the gold for them and brought back supplies such as newspapers, tools and equipment. Evidence of their industry, and indication of their more serious pastimes, was gained two years later. A Melbourne journalist found their valley with the help of a local bushman and came back with a fascinating story of what he had seen.

Immediately surrounding the hut some twenty acres have been cleared, the trees ringed, and the timber – principally swamp gum and peppermint – placed in heaps ready for burning. The ground had even been raked, so as to give the grass every chance to grow, and the aspect of the whole place denotes that the Kellys had lived in this secluded retreat many a long day before the Wombat murders took place; and as a proof that someone knew of their existence I may mention that on a peppermint tree within a short distance from the hut the name of 'J. Martain' has been carved in the sapwood of the tree after the sheet of bark had been taken off to put on the roof of the hut. In the creek flowing to the north of the hut a considerable amount of gold-digging has been done, sluicing being the principal means employed, and from appearances gold has been got in payable quantities, and the workings are of such an extent that it would be utterly impossible for any four men to carry them on under a period of several months.

Perhaps, however, the most startling sight of all is the appearance of the hut and its immediate surroundings. Imagine a house erected of bullet-proof logs, fully two feet in diameter, one on top of the other, crossed at the ends after the fashion of a chock and log fence, and with a door six feet high by two feet six inches wide, made of stiff slabs, and plated with iron nearly a quarter of an inch in thickness which was loop-holed to fire through. The door is on the north side, opposite the gold-workings in the creek, and a well-built log chimney occupies the greater part of the west end of the hut. Such was the home of the Kelly Gang for some months before the police murders. Its interior was fitted up just as substantially as its exterior, and in a manner calculated to withstand a long siege, there having been every provision made for the storage of flour, beef, tea, sugar, and other necessaries of life and to show that in fresh meat, at least, they were not wanting, we discovered portions of several carcasses, together with seven or eight heads of cattle, with bullet holes in the centre of the forehead, lying outside the hut, which may have belonged either to 'scrubbers' out of the ranges, or the fat bullock of some not far distant squatter or farmer, but most probably the latter. Empty jam and sardine tins, old powder flasks, cap boxes, broken shovels, old billy cans, glass bottles, door hinges, and a great variety of other articles were to be seen all round the hut.

But the crowning wonder of all was the evident pains taken by the Kellys to improve themselves as marksmen. In every direction – taking the hut as a standing-point – we saw trees which were marked with bullets, from five to fifty having been fired into each, at ranges varying from twenty to four hundred yards. The bullets, being afterwards chopped out, were melted down and converted again into their former state. On one small tree a circle of charcoal six inches in diameter had been traced, and into this two or three revolver bullets had been fired, one striking the black dot meant to represent the bullseye in the centre, and the other two being close to it. Some of the bullets had gone to a depth of four inches into the trees and consequently a great deal of chopping had to be done to get them out; and there was abundant

Stephen Hart was one of the men who panned for gold and practised his marksmanship with the Kellys. Nineteen-year-old Hart came to the farm after his twelve-month sentence at Beechworth Gaol. Hart had an unspectacular history, no serious police record, and no evident qualities apart from horsemanship when he joined the Kellys. He left school at an early age to help on the family selection and later worked as a 'butcher boy' with a Mr Gardiner of Oxley Plains. It was there that he met his Greta mates. By 1877, the association had earned him his first prison sentence. He was released in June 1878 and returned to his father's property near Wangaratta before joining the fugitives. One person said later that he was slightly built and looked wiry, about five feet seven in height. He had a round face, dark hair and complexion, grey eyes with black eyebrows almost meeting. He looked of a hasty and sullen temper, easily ruffled, and his face at times wore a vindictive cruel expression. He was quick and active in his movements but spoke very slowly, and appeared to be completely under the domination of his leader [Ned Kelly]. Other unkind bulletins noted a 'slightly hooked nose' and 'sinister expression'. The portrait is by Wangaratta photographer, W. E. Barnes.

Overleaf: Police graves in Mansfield cemetery.

Above left: Joseph Byrne taught the fugitives their mining techniques. In 1878, Byrne was 21 years old and had lived all his life at Sebastopol on the Woolshed diggings near Beechworth. Like Ned Kelly, he was the eldest son of a widow and had two brothers and four sisters. After leaving school Byrne became a close friend of Aaron Sherritt – probably the single, strongest bad influence in his early life. As a young man he was described as a 'nice fellow and well behaved'. Beechworth bookseller and J. P., James Ingram, said 'there was never anything in his deportment anyone could take exception to'. In contrast to Sherritt, Byrne was 'quietly spoken' and 'not flash'. After several minor misdemeanours, including a fine for illegally using a neighbour's horse, Byrne received his first gaol term in 1876. Along with Sherritt, he was sentenced to six months at Beechworth Gaol for 'illegal possession of meat'. In January 1877, the pair got another six months for 'assaulting a Chinaman' who tried to stop them swimming in his Woolshed dam. Shortly after, they met the Kellys and began horse-stealing. By 1878 Byrne was reported engaged to Aaron Sherritt's eldest sister, but must have been rarely home to see her – at 21 he had become a full-time criminal. Curiously, Byrne had a conservative, refined side to his character. He was well read and had more than amateur literary ability. He also had other unlikely qualities: influenced by the Chinese population on the Woolshed, he could be understood in Mandarin, knew many Chinese customs and was addicted to opium – prompting the occasional description of him as a 'half Chinaman'.

But Joseph was evidently not timid; police were warned in October 1878: 'There is a man named Billy King – but that is not his proper name – about twenty five years, five feet ten inches high, stout build, thin features and fair whiskers, small very fair moustache, blue eyes, small hands, thick legs, who is now a mate of the Kellys, and has been stopping at Kelly's since last year; he was in Kelly's house when constable Fitzpatrick was fired at; he wanted the Kellys not to let Fitzpatrick get away alive . . . he is a man that would fire on anyone that would attempt to arrest him; he is a dangerous man.' Billy King was later identified as Joseph Byrne.

Above right: Tom Lloyd junior. Included in a police file of October 1878 were the descriptions of two Kelly cousins – both Lloyds – 'thought to be with the Kellys at the Wombat'. Thomas and John Lloyd were not brothers, but their fathers were, and named their eldest sons after each other. Tom Lloyd junior, shown here as he looked in 1879, was 22 years old, 'well made in proportion to his height' with 'fair features', supposedly bearing a close resemblance to James Kelly. Tom admitted being at Dan's farm on the Saturday night, but arrived after the incident was all over. Tom remained one of the Kellys' closest friends – one of the few who held their complete trust. He was involved in many of their exploits, acting as a scout and spy, but upon Ned Kelly's insistence, he always kept out of sight during public appearances. In 1879, Lloyd was reported as the 'unidentified fifth member' of the Kelly gang.

evidence, too, to prove that the more practice the outlaws had, the more they improved in the use of revolver and rifle, the shooting at some marks on the trees being very wide, and on others remarkably straight and dead into the bullseye.

The Kellys felt a need to practise their marksmanship. In April 1878 a £100 reward was offered for each of the brothers. Police parties searched Greta and the surrounding country in regular patrols. Others raided the Kelly home on a number of occasions, only to find the daughters and young children being cared for by their elder sister Margaret Skillion. In October, Ned Kelly left the ranges and went into hiding near Beechworth to follow the progress of his mother's trial.

In a letter to a member of parliament, Kelly clearly expressed the effect that the verdict had on him.

I heard how the police used to be blowing that they would shoot me first and then cry surrender . . . coupled with the conviction of my mother and those innocent men [it] certainly made my blood boil and I don't think there is any man born could have the patience to suffer what I did.

But Kelly did not suffer it. He returned to his brother and mates and a week later they were warned of two police parties approaching them from both Mansfield and Greta.

I was not there long and on the 25th of October I came on the tracks of police horses between Table Top [mountain] and the Bogs. I crossed them and went to Emu Swamp and returning home I came on more Police tracks making for our camp. I told my mates and . . . we came to the conclusion our doom was sealed unless we could take their firearms, as we had nothing but a gun and a rifle . . . We approached the spring as close as we could get to the camp. The intervening space being clear we saw two men at the logs they got up and one took a double barrel fowling piece and one drove the horses down and hobbled them against the tent, and we thought there was more men in the tent those being on sentry. We could have shot those two men without speaking but not wishing to take life we waited.

One of the two disguised police in the clearing, kneeling at the fire with only a fork in his hand, was Thomas McIntyre. He gave this account:

On the morning of the 25th day of October sergeant Kennedy and constable Michael Scanlon, Thomas Lonigan and myself went in search of the Kelly brothers, charged with attempting to murder constable Fitzpatrick, we camped at Stringybark creek at about twenty miles from Mansfield. On the following morning at about 6 o'clock sergeant

Top: Thomas Lonigan could identify the Kellys by sight and so was included in the search party. 'Both constables Scanlon and Lonigan were said to have misgivings when ordered to join the pursuit of the Kelly brothers . . . it is a remarkable fact that, when leaving Violet Town, Lonigan returned twice a considerable distance to bid his family farewell; and moreover, declared that he knew he would not return alive from the expedition. Scanlon too, appeared to have gloomy forebodings, though a brave and fearless man, for he called out to the wardsman of the [Mooroopna] hospital. "I may never come back, and, if so, you can take my dogs", an animal upon which he set great value.' Lonigan migrated from Sligo in 1867 and joined the Victorian police force in 1874. In 1878 he was 37; the eldest of his four children was only ten years old and his family were left in desperate circumstances after his death.

Middle: Thomas Newman McIntyre said his brush with the Kelly gang 'created a cloud which cast a shadow over my life'. Understandably, he was not impressed with them: 'Ned Kelly and the two strangers were cool, and held their weapons steadily. Dan Kelly was nervously excited and laughing with a short laugh, almost hysterical . . . I may state here that the words "fellow" and "man" did not seem to be in their vocabulary. I use [these] for the word [bugger] which they made use of throughout their conversation.' Dan Kelly and Hart, he said, 'were two bush larrikins, having all the vices of that species, and not being possessed of the steadying influence of mature years, they were two exceedingly dangerous men. Byrne was a nervous man, thoroughly under the control of Ned Kelly.'

Bottom: A sketch, thought to have been made by McIntyre, showing how the Kellys first appeared when they called 'bail up!' from the speargrass. Compare the position of the logs with the following photographs of the camp.

FROM HORSE-STEALING TO HOMICIDE

The clearing on Stringybark Creek 1878. Ned Kelly laid great emphasis on the fact that the police were heavily armed and went to unusual trouble to disguise their identity. He claimed that this indicated their intention to ambush and shoot him without choice of surrender. New South Wales police had done the same to the bushranger 'Midnight' only a few weeks before; an incident that strongly influenced Kelly's actions that afternoon. The papers reported that 'all the constables wore plain clothes, in fact, they were disguised as diggers out on a prospecting tour'. An artist who accompanied the photographer described the spot where the constables camped: 'The two troopers stood at the fire made at the burnt end of the log shown in the middle, and Lonigan fell a few yards away from the fire. The two dark posts in the centre are the remains of a burnt digger's hut. When Scanlon and Kennedy were heard approaching Kelly knelt behind the butt of the fallen tree near the stump on the left hand, and set McIntyre on his right. One of the others concealed himself in the tent, and two made for the speargrass. Scanlon was shot near the tree in the background, between the stump and the fallen tree.'

The clothes the Kellys wore were also of particular interest to the artist: 'From Trooper McIntyre I get the following descriptions of the dress of the Kellys . . . Edward Kelly wore what is known as a Sydney soft-crown hat with a black velvet band, dark, very short coat, vest and trousers, and a bright red sash. A string from the hat under the nose was indulged in by all four bushrangers, and the hat was worn tipped well over the eyes — a style peculiar to all the 'Greta Mob', as the Quinns, Kellys and etc. are nicknamed. Edward Kelly stands six feet, and his moustache is cut square across the mouth. Daniel Kelly had no whiskers and no beard, and wore a light stylish suit of clothes, with Billy Cock hat. The first unknown man was very fair, thin whiskers and etc; and had not the villainous

expression of the others. The second unknown man had a few straggling hairs on his face, wore light clothes and a flat hat; and had a cruel expression of countenance.'

Photographer Arthur Burman, or one of his operators, visited Stringybark soon after the tragedy. The police reconstructed the incident with McIntyre's help, and he may even be one of the men shown. The plate is taken from where the police pitched their tent next to a ruined shingle hut (only the burnt posts remain). The man on the right is supposed to represent Kennedy's position when the firing started, but he was actually some distance further away. The men at the log represent an armed Kelly and constable McIntyre.

Kennedy and constable Scanlon departed upon mounted patrol down the creek, the sergeant ordering me to remain at camp and do some cooking. About five o'clock in the afternoon, I was making some tea, I was unarmed, my revolver being at the tent, constable Lonigan was standing beside me at the fire. I heard someone singing out 'Bail up, hold your hands up!' I turned round and saw four men with guns pointed at us, two of them identified as Edward and Daniel Kelly, from their descriptions. I immediately held my hands up without moving. Constable Lonigan endeavoured to get behind a tree, three or four yards off; before he could do so he was shot. The four men then came rushing towards me and I heard constable Lonigan say 'Oh Christ I'm shot'. They then ordered me to hold my arms up and demanded to know if I had any firearms. I replied I had not. They asked me where my revolver was. I said it was in my tent. Edward Kelly then came to see if I had any and searched me. At this time, I was fifteen paces from the tent.

When he found I had no firearms, he told me to hold my hands down. They then searched Lonigan, taking his revolver from him, searched the tent and took the firearms and ammunition. Edward Kelly, looking towards where constable Lonigan was, said, 'Dear, dear, what a pity it is that man tried to get away'. He said this regretfully. Addressing me, he said, 'You're all right'. One of the other men, whom I can identify, asked me to have some tea, and asked me for some tobacco. I gave them some and had a smoke myself. Daniel Kelly suggested that I should be handcuffed, producing a pair of our own. Edward Kelly said 'Mmm, there's something better than handcuffs here', tapping his gun, which he had reloaded. He said to me, 'Don't attempt to go away. If you do I shall track you to Mansfield and shoot you at the Police station.' He asked me when I expected my two mates to return. I told him I did not know and thought they had been bushed . . . as I expected them long ago.

He asked me several other questions about horses, asked me who had the rifle with him; I told him the party on patrol had it with them. He asked me who they were. I told him sergeant Kennedy and constable Scanlon. He said Kennedy he had never heard about but Scanlon was a flash bugger. I asked him what he intended to do with the men. I said 'Surely you don't intend to shoot them down in cold blood, because I would rather be shot a thousand times myself than give any information about them, the one being father of a large family'. Kelly said, 'No, I don't shoot any man that holds his hands up. If he surrenders I won't shoot him.' I then asked him what he intended to do with me, 'Do you intend to shoot me?' He said, 'No, what would I want to shoot you for? I could have shot you half an hour ago if I liked.' He said at first he thought I was constable Flood, 'And if you had been I would have roasted you at the fire!' They then concealed themselves, expecting the other constables would return.

Kelly hid himself by the fire and told me to stand close to him, and said 'That bloody Fitzpatrick has been the cause

Top: Mounted constable Michael Scanlon was stationed at Mansfield and was a close friend of Kennedy. Thirty-six years old and single, he had worked through the country north of Mansfield before joining the police force. He came from Lake View, Killarney, in 1863. All four of the police search party were Irish immigrants — chasing four Australian-born Irish sons.

Bottom: Sergeant Michael Kennedy left a wife and five children in Mansfield to pursue the Kellys. It was generally believed that Kennedy had been given information of the Kellys' whereabouts and that he did not camp on Stringybark Creek by accident. McIntyre later said that he wondered why they were in that locality and not on their intended route. It has been suggested that Kennedy told Scanlon of the Kellys' whereabouts and they set out to secure the Kellys and the £200 reward on their own. McIntyre and Lonigan certainly had no idea they were near the Kellys as they casually shot at parrots on the Saturday afternoon — noise heard clearly by the Kellys.

A traveller riding through Strathbogie on the Sunday reported 'two or three people shot in the country' — before McIntyre reached Mansfield, proving that another person witnessed the shootings.

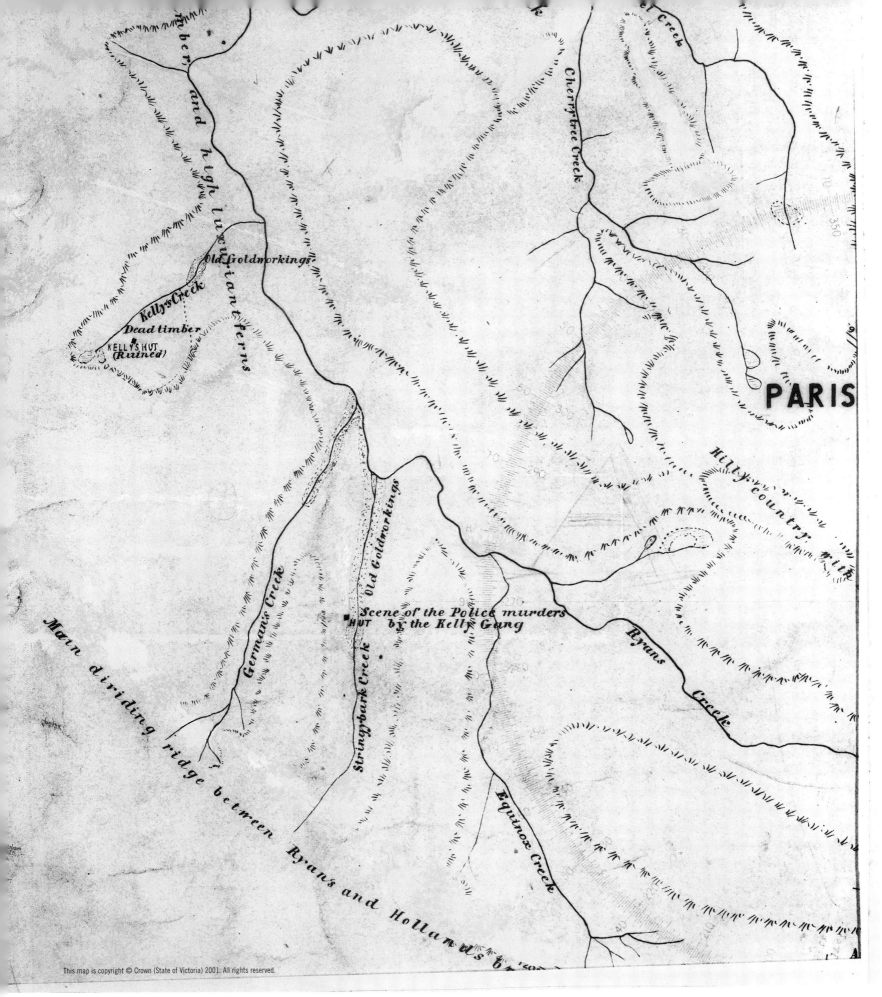

The first map surveyed in the area, 1884. The police camp was only two kilometres south-east of Dan Kelly's farm. The timber and undergrowth in the area was extremely heavy, reducing visibility to a few metres. This explains why Kennedy and Scanlon, when riding down Ryan's Creek and within a few hundred metres of the Kellys' boundary fence, did not discover them. When McIntyre escaped, he rode north-west toward the Kelly hut before veering around over Holland's Creek. When Kennedy retreated, firing as he ran from tree to tree, he followed McIntyre's path, possibly hoping to catch up with him.

of all this. Those people lagged at Beechworth were lagged innocently, they had no more revolvers in their hands that night than you have, and that's the cause of me and my two brothers turning out'. He asked me what became of the Sydney man, referring to the murderer of sergeant Wallings. I told him he was shot by the police. He said, 'Yes! And I suppose you buggers came out here to shoot me!' I said 'No, we came out here to apprehend you'. He said, 'What brings you out here at all? Isn't it a shame to see such fine strapping big fellows in a lazy loafing billet like the Police force.' I told him we were ordered to come out. 'Well', he said, 'If I let you go you will have to leave the police!' I told him I would. I then asked him if I could get the other two men to surrender, what would he do with us. He said 'The best thing for you to do will be to get them to surrender. If they escape I will shoot you; if you let them know in any way that we are here, you will be shot at once. If you get them to surrender I will allow you to go in the morning. But you'll have to go on foot as we want your horses. We'll handcuff you up all night as we are going to sleep here ourselves.'

I asked him if he would promise me faithfully to allow us to depart. He said he would. I said, 'You won't allow any of the other men to shoot us'. He said they could please themselves, that he would not shoot us. During this time none of the other men were in hearing, there was one in the tent and the other two were in the scrub waiting the arrival of sergeant Kennedy and constable Scanlon. Before Kelly's mates could be informed of our agreement about the promise, sergeant Kennedy and constable Scanlon came in sight. Kelly said, 'Hush lads, here they come!' and said to me 'You sit down on that log or I'll put a hole through you!' I said 'Oh Kelly, for God's sake don't shoot the men and I will get them to surrender'. Kelly made no reply. Kennedy then came slightly in advance of Scanlon and I went towards sergeant Kennedy and got within a yard of him, when Edward Kelly and the others cried out, 'Bail up! Throw up your hands!' sergeant Kennedy grasped the case of his revolver and immediately some shots were fired. I said, 'Oh sergeant! You had better dismount and surrender'.

Constable Scanlon threw himself off his horse and endeavoured to get behind a tree and at the same time trying to get a Spencer repeating rifle, which he carried, off his

Above: The 'old gun used by the gang' was a sawn-off muzzle-loading 1850s English Enfield .577 calibre rifle carried by Ned Kelly at Stringybark Creek. The barrel was originally tied on with waxed string. Ned Kelly described it as 'a bloody old crooked musket, in which, if you held it up to your shoulder, you could see the curves', useful for 'shooting round a corner'. Dan Kelly also carried a rifle, but it is unknown whether Byrne and Hart were also armed. Of the police arms Kelly wrote: 'I asked McIntyre why they carried Spencer rifles, breech-loading fowling pieces and so much ammunition, for whereas the police were only supposed to carry one revolver and six cartridges in the revolver they had eighteen rounds of revolver cartridges each, three dozen for the fowling piece, and twenty one Spencer rifle cartridges, and God knows how many they had away with the rifle. This looked as though they not only meant to shoot me but to riddle me . . . I said I did not blame them for doing their duty but I could not suffer them blowing-me to pieces in my own native land.'
F. A. Hare wrote: 'Aaron Sherritt told me it was quite by accident that Joe Byrne and Steve Hart happened to be with the Kellys when they attacked the police. They were always great friends and companions . . . but they had no idea of shooting the police the afternoon they started to attack the police camp. Their chief aim was to secure some good firearms and horses, and they were under the impression that all they would have to do was to cover them with their rifles and the police would surrender. Instead of this they had to shoot the police to save their own lives. McIntyre stated that Byrne and Hart were "dreadfully cut up at the turn things had taken" and mentioned Kelly threatening to shoot Byrne if he did not obey orders.'

Top: Mansfield from the Longwood road. Shops closed and business came to a standstill for more than a week when McIntyre told of Ned Kelly's promise to shoot him at the police station.

shoulder. Before he could do so I saw him fall and the blood spurt out from the right side as he fell. At this time there was a great number of shots being fired by Kelly's party and none by the police, as they had no time to do so. Sergeant Kennedy at my suggestion, surrendered, after endeavouring to draw his revolver from the case. As the firing continued I thought that Edward Kelly did not intend to keep his word and spare our lives. I therefore seized sergeant Kennedy's horse, which was nearest me, and mounting it, I rode off, and whilst doing so I heard Daniel Kelly, one of the bushrangers, cry out 'Shoot that bugger! Shoot that bugger!' After this remark a great number of shots were fired but none of them hit me. Kennedy was quite close to me when

Discovering sergeant Kennedy's body. It took five days and four successive search parties before Michael Kennedy's body was found in the timber just north of German's Creek. The shire president, who helped with the search, said: 'a young man, Sparrow, sang out "here is something, here it is!" Thus we found poor sergeant Kennedy. He was lying some six feet from a tree that had been grazed by a bullet, and there was a jagged hole right through his chest. I had supplied myself with two new cornsacks, and one I put over his head and the other over his feet, and lashed them with saddle-straps.'

On the previous Tuesday, an inquest found Lonigan and Scanlon had been 'wilfully murdered during the execution of their duty by the Kelly brothers and two men whose names were not known'. Scanlon and Lonigan were buried the same afternoon in the Mansfield cemetery. On Friday 1 November, some 200 people gathered for the last rites of Kennedy as he was buried near the graves of his men. Bishop Moorhouse said in his sermon the following Sunday, 'we should pity the poor wretches who have caused us to mourn over the recent disasters'.

While dramatic, Burman's photographs are a subtle fraud. The body lies in the same position as Kennedy did and the men must have been in the party who found him, but it is a reconstruction. In the second, more widely published frame, a bullet-hole has been added for effect.

I rode away and made no remark on my leaving. I rode a short distance north and turned west, the scrub was very thick and I got a buster off my horse, falling, I remounted and rode a little distance further. I was then, I think, about two miles from the camp. Finding then that my horse was giving up, I thought it had been wounded, and so dismounted and let the horse go. I ran a short distance and concealed myself in a Wombat hole and then made a short memoranda in my book of what occurred. (Entry: Ned Kelly, Dan, and two others stuck us up while we were unarmed. Lonigan and Scanlon are shot. I am hiding in a Wombat hole until dark. The Lord have mercy on me. Scanlon tried to get his gun out.) I remained concealed in it until dark and then left my hiding place. Taking off my boots so as not to make any noise, I walked for about an hour and rested myself, then put my boots on and started. By the aid of a small compass and a lighted match I took an observation and went towards the telegraph line on the road to Mansfield. I travelled on foot all night until about 3 o'clock the following afternoon, when I reached Mansfield.

Only the Kellys, Byrne and Hart knew what happened after McIntyre's lucky escape. Ned Kelly was the only one who gave details — and his version noticeably sheltered the others from blame.

While I was talking to McIntyre they appeared in the open. I had just time to fall, the fire very nearly burning my knees. McIntyre then walked up to Kennedy and spoke to him. Kennedy smiled. I then called out, 'You wretches! Throw up your hands!' Scanlon swung his rifle round and fired at me, I then fired at Scanlon and he fell forward, I still kept him covered, thinking he was shamming. When the horse moved he rolled off. During this time Kennedy had dismounted on the offside of his horse and laid the revolver over the horse's rump. He fired at Dan Kelly as he came running up, grazing him on the top of the shoulder. McIntyre then jumped on Kennedy's horse and rode away. Kennedy made for a tree, still firing. Kennedy and I were firing at each other, he retreated from tree to tree. One of his shots went through my whiskers, and the other through the sleeve of my coat. Kennedy was a very good shot; the reason he got so far is that I took up Scanlon's rifle, but had to throw it away again as I could not understand how to use it. I then followed Kennedy up. When he slipped from behind a tree I thought I was then done for, as he fired and the ball grazed my ribs.

He then ran, and I immediately fired and hit him on the shoulder as he was getting back behind a tree. He ran again and I followed, when he wheeled round and raised his hands I fired, and shot him through the chest. When I hit him on the shoulder he must have dropped his revolver, and the blood running down his arm formed into a clot, which I took for his revolver. Knowing he had one shot left when he wheeled around, I thought he was going to fire; but I knew afterwards he was throwing up his hands. I was sorry I shot Kennedy, and would not have done so if I thought he was going to surrender. I had a long conversation with him when he was lying wounded. We wanted to leave the ground, but I did not like to leave him in a dying state; so I shot him. I respected Kennedy . . . he could not live or I would have let him go . . . Had they been my own brothers I could not help shooting them, or else lie down and let them shoot me, which they would have done had their bullets been directed as they intended them . . . I put his cloak over him and left him as honourable as I could and if they were my own brothers, I could not be more sorry for them; with the exception of Lonigan.

Sub-inspector Pewtress, officer-in-charge at Mansfield, had been sent to the district to recuperate from illness. He had no knowledge of the bush, but after questioning McIntyre, immediately organised a search party. With two constables, an exhausted McIntyre, the local doctor and five other volunteers, they made off for the mountains and what must have been the most terrifying night of their lives.

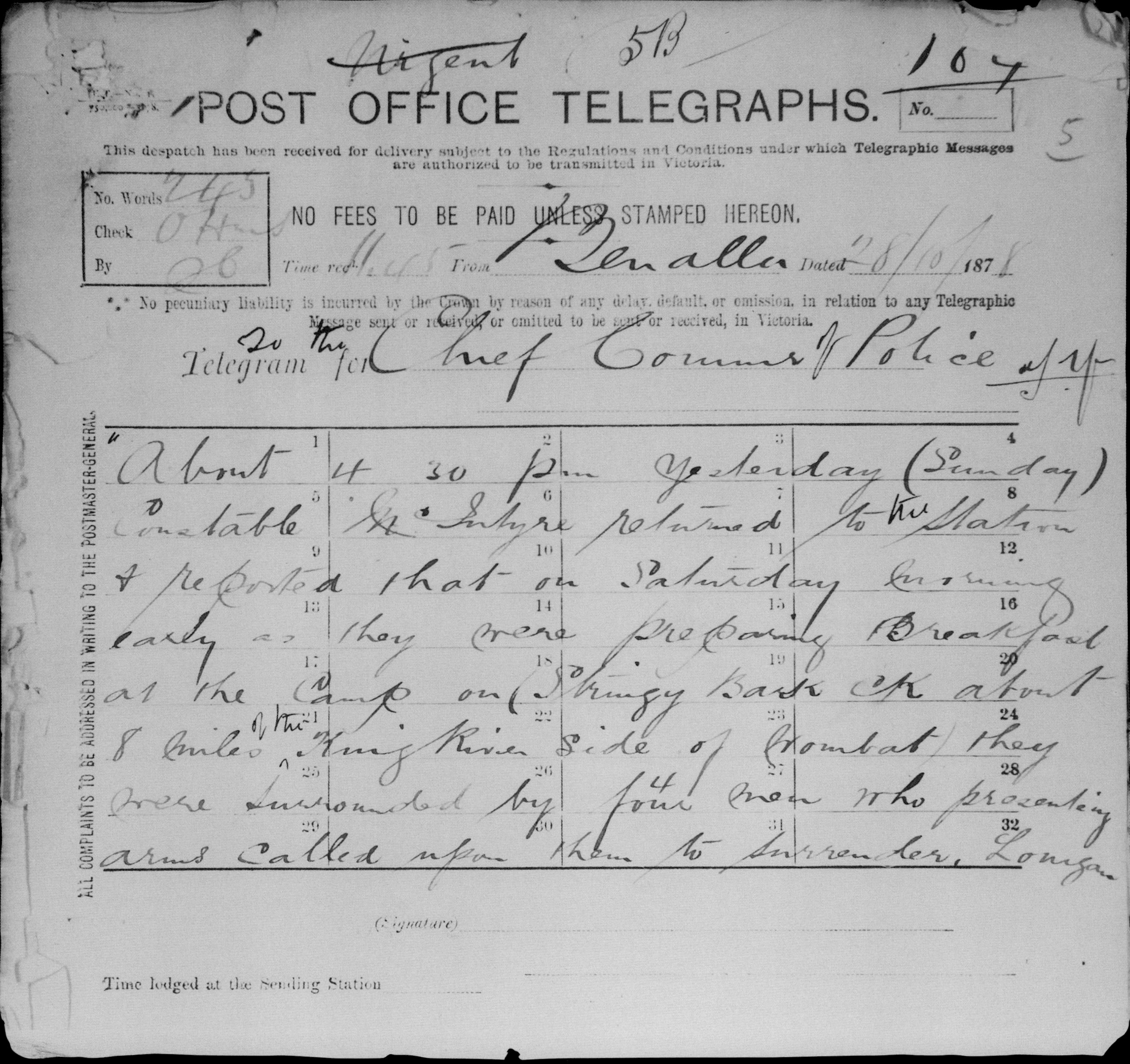

POST OFFICE TELEGRAPHS

No. Words 245
Check 0 Hrs
By 26
Time recd 11.15
From Benalla
Dated 28/10/1878

Telegram to the Chief Commr of Police &c

"About 4.30 pm Yesterday (Sunday) Constable McIntyre returned to the Station & reported that on Saturday morning early as they were preparing Breakfast at the Camp on Stringy Bark Ck about 8 miles on the King River side of Wombat they were Surrounded by four men who presenting arms Called upon them to Surrender, Lonigan

---

MURDER OF TWO CONSTABLES.
MANSFIELD, 27th October.

News has just reached Mansfield that Constables Lanigan and Scanlan have been shot dead by four bushrangers, at Stringy Bark Creek, about twenty miles from here. Constable M'Intyre escaped, and has just arrived with the intelligence. His horse, however, was shot down from under him. Sergeant Kennedy is also missing. Sub-inspector Pewtress, Dr. Reynolds, Mr. Collopy and others left just now on horseback to scour the country in search of the murderers, and to bring home the dead bodies. The bushrangers are supposed to be the notorious Kelly's party, for whom the constables were in search.

Above: The first news to reach Melbourne of the Stringybark tragedy was this 245-word dispatch sent on Monday morning to captain Standish, chief commissioner of police.

Left: The brief details of the murder of two constables were last-minute inserts into Melbourne newspapers such as the *Age*. A constable Meehan, despatched from Mansfield on the Sunday afternoon, did not reach Benalla until two hours after news of the ambush had been telegraphed the following day. It was believed that he too was missing, feared captured by the Kellys. The unfortunate constable — thinking he was being followed — left the road, abandoned his horse and even took off his boots to make less noise, travelling nearly all the way in his socks. The second police group, who entered the Wombat Ranges from Greta on the same day as Kennedy, were scheduled to meet the first group at the head of the King River. They waited there without seeing anyone until the following Tuesday, when news of the ambush reached them.

Above: The Mansfield police station. A slight diversion occurred as the first search party was about to leave Mansfield on the Sunday night. A number of people, gathered at the police station and on their way to church, watched as Wild Isaiah Wright and his brother rode past. Probably stimulated by the audience, Isaiah shouted 'Dogs! Curs! Cowards! Follow me if you want to catch the Kellys, I'm going to join the gang! Come out a little way and I'll shoot the lot of you!' With the police in pursuit, Wright yelled: 'all the police in Mansfield can't catch me!' The pair were later caught and charged with using threatening language. Tom Wright, a deaf mute, was later released. The picture was taken some time before the shootings; sub-inspector Pewtress is believed to be standing, with sword, in the centre.

Left: Doctor Samuel Reynolds accompanied the first search party in heavy rain and pitch darkness to find the bodies of Lonigan and Scanlon. Riding single file in melancholy silence through dense timber, the searchers could hear nothing but rain pattering on leaves, the occasional mournful cry of a mopoke or crashing of a wallaby through the undergrowth. The party waited with the horses about 300 metres from the site while the inspector, constables and doctor went to discover the bodies where they had fallen. They identified them by striking matches under shelter of their coats. After some time, Kennedy's body could not be found and fear of an ambush grew. The doctor examined Scanlon and Lonigan, who were lying on their backs with every pocket turned inside out. He bound the heads with bandages and the men tied the corpses on either side of a packhorse 'which seemed to have some instinctive horror of travelling with its load'. Back in Mansfield, Reynolds' post-mortems substantiated Kelly's later claim that they were not riddled with bullets after death.

8 FROM OBSCURITY TO OUTLAWRY
OCTOBER–DECEMBER 1878

After news of the shootings was telegraphed to Melbourne and the neighbouring colonies, the tragedy became one of national alarm. The crime, unparalleled in the colony at the time, had a profound effect on public imagination.

The undermanned north-eastern police district, with only 79 men including officers in September 1878, was suddenly flooded with reinforcements. By December, 100 mounted police were engaged in the Kelly pursuit. The Kelly brothers had graduated from horse-stealing and assault to homicide – which could only lead to one fate. The Berry Government reversed its former policy and spared no expense in apprehending the offenders.

On Wednesday 30 October, two days before sergeant Kennedy's funeral, parliament rushed a bill through all stages in a single day. The result was the Felons Apprehension Act 1878, which effectively outlawed the Kellys. Six days later, proclamations were published calling for the gang's surrender at Mansfield by 12 November.

As news of the shootings spread through the north-eastern district, fear spread with it. A police superintendent testified that:

at the time we could get little or no assistance from the inhabitants. The people all through the country were in such a state of terror. Civility was shown to us in every town but no information given. The people seemed to be more afraid of the gang than confident in the police.

McIntyre's version of the ambush was the only one available, and newspapers soon coloured his report

V. R.

£1,000 REWARD!!!

FOR THE KELLY GANG.

GO AND SEE
THE GREAT PICTURE
OF THE
NOTORIOUS BUSHRANGERS,
Painted by Fry from a photograph taken on the ground where the Murder of Sergeant Kennedy was committed.

Every Visitor will be presented with a photograph of the Notorious Ned Kelly.

Now on View opposite Theatre Royal.

GOVERNMENT ADVERTISEMENTS.

TO DANIEL KELLY, of Greta, in the colony of Victoria.

Whereas, on the fourth day of November, one thousand eight hundred and seventy-eight, a Bench Warrant was issued in pursuance of the "Felons Apprehension Act 1878," under my hand and seal in order to your answering and taking your trial for that on the twenty-sixth day of October, one thousand eight hundred and seventy-eight, at Stringy Bark Creek, near Mansfield, in the Northern Bailiwick of the said colony, you did, in company with one Edward Kelly and two other men whose names are unknown, feloniously and of malice aforethought kill and murder one Michael Scanlan.

And whereas, in pursuance of the "Felons Apprehension Act, 1878," I did on the fourth day of November, one thousand eight hundred and seventy-eight, order a summons to be inserted in the Government *Gazette*, requiring you, the said Daniel Kelly, to surrender yourself on or before the twelfth day of November, one thousand eight hundred and seventy-eight, at Mansfield, in the said colony of Victoria, to abide your trial for the beforementioned crime of which you the said Daniel Kelly stand accused.

These are therefore to will and require you the said Daniel Kelly to surrender yourself on or before the twelfth day of November, one thousand eight hundred and seventy-eight, at Mansfield, in the said colony of Victoria, to abide your trial for the beforementioned crime of which you so stand accused, and hereof you are not to fail at your peril.

Given under my hand and seal at Melbourne, this fourth day of November, in the year of Our Lord one thousand eight hundred and seventy-eight.

WILLIAM F. STAWELL, Chief Justice of the Supreme Court of the Colony of Victoria.

TO EDWARD KELLY, of Greta, in the colony of Victoria.

Whereas on the fourth day of November, one thousand eight hundred and seventy-eight, a bench warrant was issued in pursuance of the "Felons Apprehension Act 1878," under my hand and seal, in order to your answering and taking your trial for that on the twenty-sixth day of October, one thousand eight hundred and seventy-eight, at Stringy Bark Creek, near Mansfield, in the Northern Bailiwick of the said colony, you did, in company with one Daniel Kelly and two other men whose names are unknown, feloniously and of malice aforethought kill and murder one Michael Scanlan.

And whereas, in pursuance of the "Felons Apprehension Act 1878," I did on the fourth day of November, one thousand eight hundred and seventy-eight, order a summons to be inserted in the Government *Gazette*, requiring you, the said Edward Kelly, to surrender yourself on or before the twelfth day of November, one thousand eight hundred and seventy-eight, at Mansfield, in the said colony of Victoria, to abide your trial for the beforementioned crime of which you, the said Edward Kelly, stand accused.

These are therefore to will and require you, the said Edward Kelly, to surrender yourself on or before the twelfth day of November, one thousand eight hundred and seventy-eight, at Mansfield, in the said colony of Victoria, to abide your trial for the beforementioned crime of which you so stand accused, and hereof you are not to fail at your peril.

Given under my hand and seal, at Melbourne, this fourth day of November, in the year of Our Lord one thousand eight hundred and seventy-eight.

WILLIAM F. STAWELL, Chief Justice of the Supreme Court of the Colony of Victoria.

TO A MAN whose name is unknown, but whose person is described as follows:—

Nineteen or twenty years of age, five feet eight inches high, rather stout, complexion somewhat fair, no beard or whiskers, a few straggling hairs over face, rather hooked nose, sinister expression, supposed to be identical with William King, of Greta, in the said colony.

Whereas on the fourth day of November, one thousand eight hundred and seventy-eight, a bench warrant was issued, in pursuance of the "Felons Apprehension Act, 1878," under my hand and seal, in order to your answering and taking your trial for that on the twenty-sixth day of October, one thousand eight hundred and seventy-eight, at Stringy Bark Creek, near Mansfield, in the Northern Bailiwick of the said colony, you did, in company with one Edward Kelly and one Daniel Kelly and another man whose name is unknown, feloniously and of malice aforethought kill and murder one Michael Scanlan.

And whereas, in pursuance of the "Felons Apprehension Act, 1878," I did, on the fourth day of November, one thousand eight hundred and seventy-eight, order a summons to be inserted in the Government *Gazette*, requiring you, the said man whose name is unknown, but whose person is described as aforesaid, to surrender yourself on or before the twelfth day of November, one thousand eight hundred and seventy-eight, at Mansfield, in the said colony of Victoria, to abide your trial for the beforementioned crime of which you, the said man whose name is unknown, but whose person is described, as aforesaid, stand accused.

These are therefore to will and require you, the said man whose name is unknown, but whose person is described as aforesaid, to surrender yourself on or before the twelfth day of November, one thousand eight hundred and seventy-eight, at Mansfield, in the said colony of Victoria, to abide your trial for the beforementioned crime of which you so stand accused, and hereof you are not to fail at your peril.

Given under my hand and seal, at Melbourne, this fourth day of November, in the year of our Lord, one thousand eight hundred and seventy-eight.

WILLIAM F. STAWELL, Chief Justice of the Supreme Court of the Colony of Victoria.

TO A MAN whose name is unknown, but whose person is described as follows:—

Twenty-one years of age, five feet nine inches high, very fair beard long on chin, fair complexion, hair and moustache; supposed to be identical with Charles Brown, of King River, in the said colony.

Whereas on the fourth day of November, one thousand eight hundred and seventy-eight, a bench warrant was issued in the pursuance of the "Felons Apprehension Act, 1878," under my hand and seal, in order to your answering and taking your trial for that on the twenty-sixth day of October, one thousand eight hundred and seventy-eight, at Stringy Bark Creek, near Mansfield, in the Northern Bailiwick of the said colony, you did, in company with one Edward Kelly and one Daniel Kelly, and another man whose name is unknown, feloniously and of malice aforethought kill and murder one Michael Scanlan.

And whereas in pursuance of the "Felons Apprehension Act, 1878," I did, on the fourth day of November, one thousand eight hundred and seventy-eight, order a summons to be inserted in the Government *Gazette*, requiring you, the said man, whose name is unknown, but whose person is described as aforesaid, to surrender yourself on or before the twelfth day of November, one thousand eight hundred and seventy-eight, at Mansfield, in the said colony of Victoria, to abide your trial for the beforementioned crime of which you, the said man, whose name is unknown, but whose person is described as aforesaid, stand accused.

These are, therefore, to will and require you, the said man, whose name is unknown, but whose person is described as aforesaid, to surrender yourself on or before the twelfth day of November, one thousand eight hundred and seventy-eight, at Mansfield, in the said colony of Victoria, to abide your trial for the beforementioned crime of which you so stand accused, and hereof you are not to fail at your peril.

Given under my hand and seal, at Melbourne, this fourth day of November, in the year of our Lord, one thousand eight hundred and seventy-eight.

WILLIAM F. STAWELL, Chief Justice of the Supreme Court of the Colony of Victoria.

8-12-15

Top left: The notorious bushrangers. The Stringybark Creek tragedy started what was to be the longest sustained newspaper scoop in the colony's history. Editors and photographers were not the only ones to profit by it. Melbourne's Princess Theatre staged a highly sensational drama 'Fleeced, or Vultures of the Wombat Ranges' – a performance that enjoyed far bigger audiences than it deserved. The advertisement shown, from Adelaide's *Frearson's Weekly*, probably prompted similar enthusiasm.

Above: The Supreme Court proclamations appeared in the *Government Gazette* and country papers. Hart and Byrne were not recognised at Stringybark Creek and not positively identified until 9 December, so all mention until then was of 'two others' or 'two supposed to be identical with William King and Charles Brown', but the police had little doubt who they were. On the Sunday after the shootings, Steve Hart was thought to be among the gang at Greta and on 3 November, he was suggested as the person who led the Kellys under the One Mile Creek bridge. On 7 November, police told Mrs Byrne that her son had his 'head in a halter' and she 'could save him if she liked'. The indignant widow replied 'he has made his bed, let him lie on it'.

Left: 1873 identification plate of Edward Kelly, apparently distributed to police after October 1878. The beard and rakish moustache have been crudely drawn on with pen and Indian ink – an attempt to bring his appearance up to date.

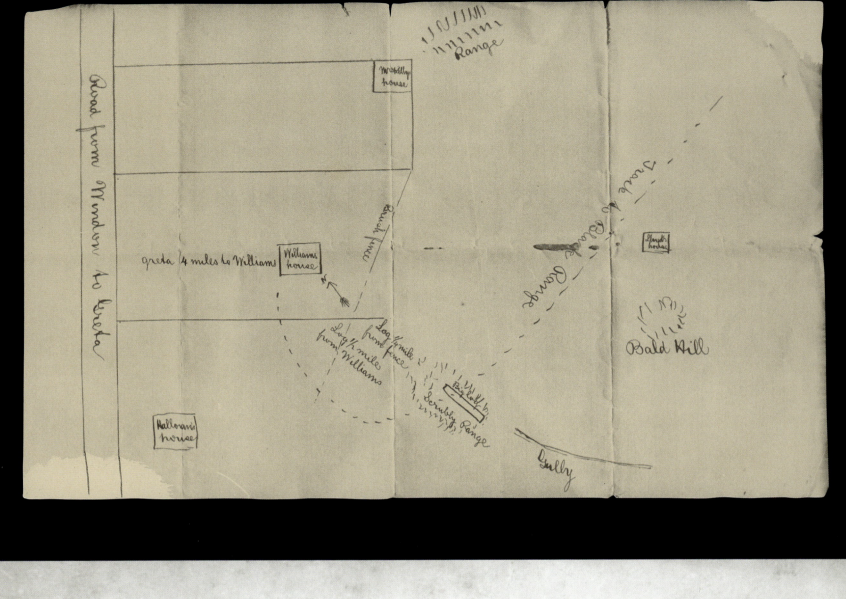

THE KELLY GANG—From an original Photograph.
Steve Hart. Dan Kelly. Ned. Kelly.

Above: Portrait of the Kellys. The only surviving copy of an undocumented postcard distributed in the 1890s. The photograph, taken during their career when more than 100 police troopers could not get within sight of them, was thought to be a forgery but is possibly a genuine article. The composition and poor quality of the picture would have been corrected by a forger. Judging from their characteristics, the men can be identified with some confidence. The man on the grey horse in the centre could be Ned Kelly and the man on the right might be Steve Hart.

Facing page, top: This sketch of the Kelly selection is part of the information that William 'Bricky' Williamson gave to police. 'The Kellys are certain to get supplied with rations from Mrs Skillion, which she would plant for them. Mick Henny 40 years, 5 feet 7 inches grey hair and Mrs Kelly's other daughter [Kate] sixteen or seventeen years, are stopping there and are acquainted with a large log where they plant food for the Kellys to take away; the log, marked an the attached sketch, is about a quarter of a mile from the south angle of my fence, is in a scrubby range, it is the only log about the place and lying north and south. It has a hollow large enough to hold two or three people in. If the log was found to contain food, it would be well to watch it, as the offenders would come in the night and take it away.' If Williamson's statement is true, the log must have been avoided in case of such a betrayal. It was found empty and showed no sign of use.

Facing page, bottom: Typical Kelly country. 'This area constitutes a large and diversified extent of territory, about 1,600 square miles. It is in parts well suited to agricultural purposes, and settlement of late years there has been rapid and permanent; but in the main, especially to the north east it consists of mountain ranges with innumerable spurs forming deep ravines and slopes so heavily timbered, covered with scrub, and encumbered with huge boulders that, for the greater part it is inaccessible.'

Above: The Kellys wrapped their firearms in a coat or blanket and held them in front of the pommel of their saddles. In the photograph, all three men hold such bundles. In this enlargement of the man on the right, two barrels appear to be sticking out from under his hand. The photograph was not given any publicity, and from the identifications on the card, the photographer certainly did not know his subjects. The sharp detail of the horses indicates a dry-plate exposure — so the image must have been taken late in the gang's career.

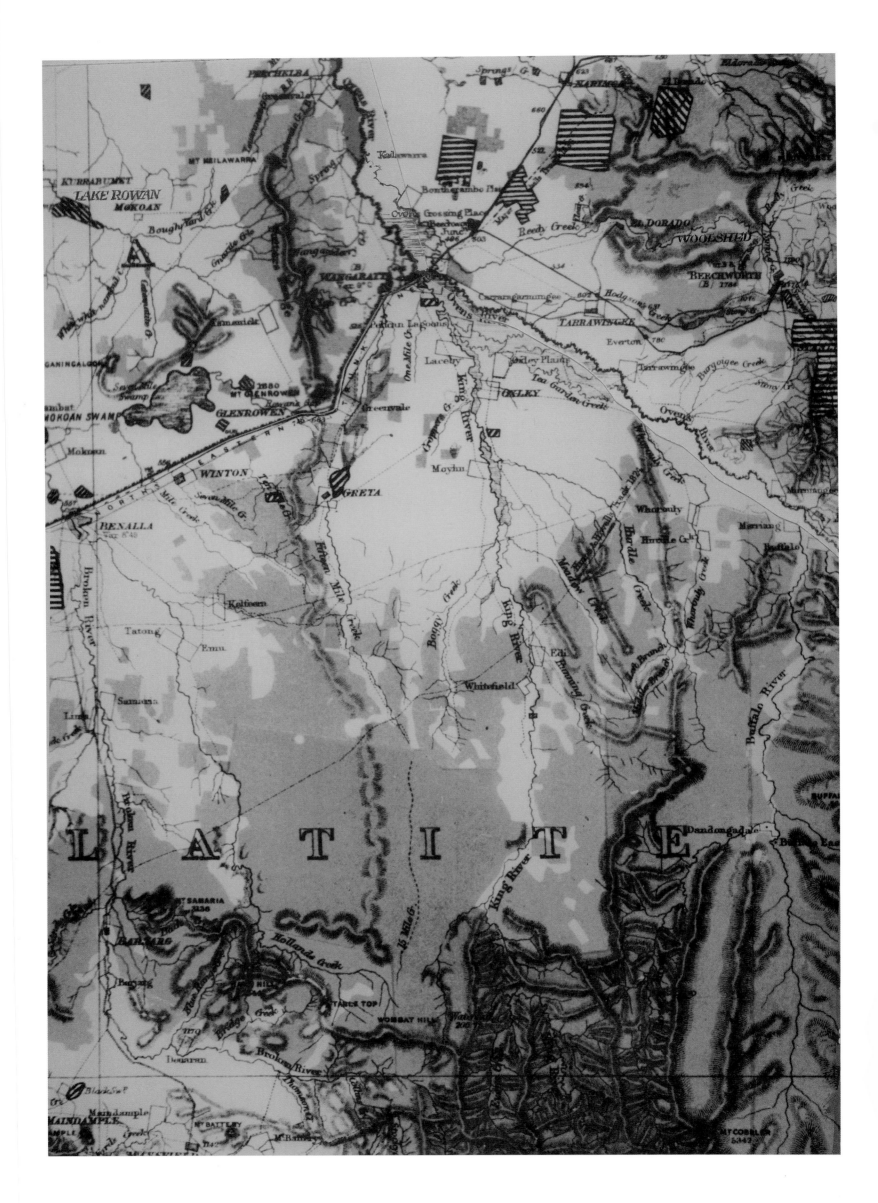

Above and left: Victorian police engaged in the Kelly pursuit always wore plain clothes while on patrol – an attempted disguise that backfired. From the beginning, contradictory reports came from all parts describing armed horsemen thought to be the Kellys, but who were actually policemen. The Kellys always concealed their guns, but the police did not. The embarrassing climax came in December 1878 when a party of troopers from New South Wales opened fire on a Victorian search party. The Kellys used the confusion to their advantage and often posed as police – 'with the assistance of the handcuffs and revolvers they got at the Wombat but their youth and looks ought to be against them'. Nevertheless, it has been suggested that these troopers in disguise, photographed by Barnes at Wangaratta, were in fact William Strickland (left) and his brother Richard (right) – both Kelly sympathisers (see also pages 130–31). The mounted trooper wears regulation uniform with the 1878 British-style helmet.

Facing page: A field of operations. In 1881, a royal commission identified 'Kelly country' as: 'the triangular tract lying between the points formed by the townships of Mansfield, Benalla and Beechworth, together with the country lying to the west of the railway . . . including the vicinity of Lake Rowan, the Warby Ranges and the neighbourhood of the Woolshed. Another person pointed out: The Kellys had not one, but three vast ranges of wild and trackless hills in which to hide, and in each of the three they had a small colony of sympathising kinfolk and "bush telegraphs". Greta was the centre of the Kelly clan and below their home stretched a hundred miles of ranges. Steve Hart's people lived near Wangaratta, with the Warby Ranges behind them. Byrne's family resided at the Woolshed, at the back of which ran a hundred square miles of unpopulated hills. If the police were searching the Greta country, the outlaws withdrew to the Warby Ranges amongst Harts friends; if these were being explored, they . . . found allies amongst Byrne's acquaintances . . . They had three separate tracts of almost inaccessible country, each of them rich in supplies and helpers.'

The map shows the area as it was in 1884. The named rectangles were pastoral stations home paddocks; the striped rectangles were reserves. The Warby Range is noted by its official name 'Futter's Range'.

FROM OBSCURITY TO OUTLAWRY 103

Top: Search party on the Kelly track. The royal commission reported that 'the action of the police immediately after the Wombat murders showed the utter unpreparedness of the authorities'. To their embarrassment, it was to be the pattern for the next two years. The Kellys were seen and reported at Greta, Oxley, the Murray flats, Sebastopol and Wangaratta, but the troopers were always too late to get within sight of their prey. On Monday 4 November the gang's tracks were shown to sergeant Steele, who took no action. Inspector Brooke Smith from Wangaratta was given the same information, later said to be the best opportunity ever given for their capture. His official censure read: 'Two days were allowed to elapse before starting in pursuit . . . then, when the unmistakable tracks of the outlaws were discovered and Kennedy's horse found, this officer deliberately disobeyed orders by returning to quarters with his party. The following day, from sheer laziness, he kept his men waiting three hours, the next day they had to start without him . . . he rode slowly, loitered in the rear and altogether conducted the affair . . . so that his party should not overtake the outlaws.' Other police parties followed tracks at Lake Rowan and Glenrowan with more enthusiasm, but the same result.

Bottom: Attempted surprise. One of the most publicised blunders made by police included its most senior officers. The Kellys had been seen at Aaron Sherritt's parents home at Sebastopol on 2 November, but the sighting was not reported for three days. Before daybreak on 7 November – five days after they were seen – a party comprised of chief commissioner Standish, superintendents Nicolson and Sadleir, three newsmen and nearly 50 police, galloped out of Beechworth toward Sebastopol. As the cavalcade moved across the granite May Day Hills, they made a lot of noise – 'like thunder, and the people heard us a mile off'. They raided both Aaron Sherritt's and his parents' home, but found them empty. They also searched Mrs Byrne's hut in the Woolshed, but again found nothing. The men dispersed at Mrs Byrne's hut, refreshments were brought from a nearby house and the small army dissolved into an impromptu picnic. In Melbourne the following day, long articles ridiculed the police over an episode that was laughingly known as the 'Charge of Sebastopol' and 'The Rat's Castle Fiasco'.

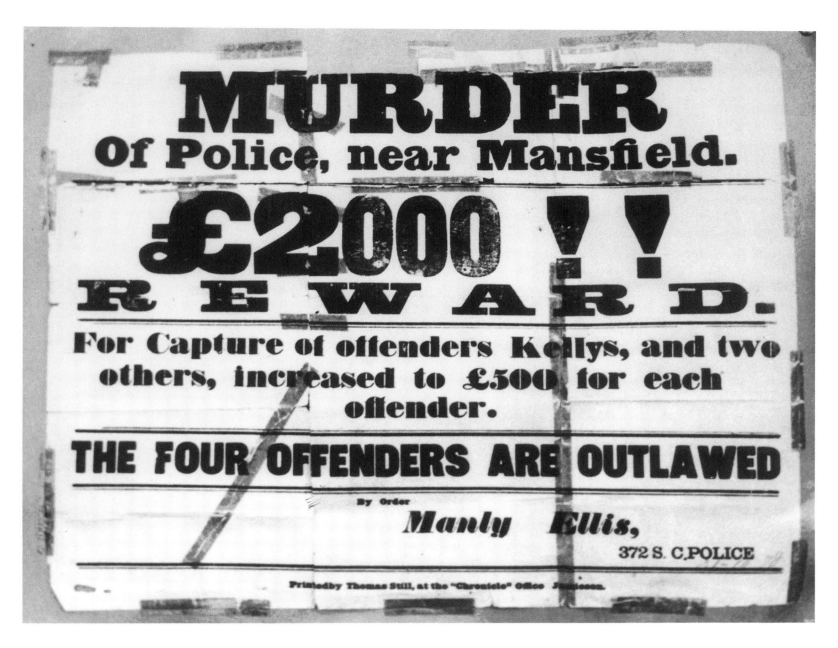

with wild suppositions. There was little sympathy for the Kellys in the weeks following the national head-lines. Even in their own home district, help must have been limited to close friends and relatives. At Glenrowan, Ned Kelly's saw-milling friend, Jack McMonigle, sent word to Mrs Skillion that 'he did not hold with murder' and wanted nothing to do with her brothers. From Pentridge Gaol four days after the shootings, 'Bricky' Williamson, a member of their family circle since 1871, agreed to tell the police all he knew of the Kellys: their plans, habits, hiding places and anything of use in their capture.

Williamson told inspector Green that:

they have a tent 8 x 20 feet, and a fly, which they take with them, together with about a month's rations . . . They are likely to be camped at the head of one of the creeks, and as far back as they can keep; probably the Rose river, Hurdle creek, which is very scrubby, or the Cut-a-way creek, from which places they could see the police coming. This is a most dangerous place, as the offenders could roll down big stones on anyone following them. They would plant their horses on the Rose river about seven miles above Conolly's station; the horses might be hobbled, but being quiet, they are more likely to be without them . . . They will not come from the ranges except when the way is clear, as Mrs Skillion can signal to them when the police are about by hanging a white sheet on a line fastened from the end of the house to a sapling, which can be seen at a great distance . . . the Kellys are likely to get food from their own place [Eleven Mile Creek], but they are more likely to get it at Skillions . . . they would probably get rations at Mick Millar's, near the Buckland . . . they will not be about Buffalo or Morse's creek. They will keep clear of any place where diggers are working. They have some store where Gold is purchased, which Power tried, but missed the gold which was secured on a horse outside, and which Power neglected to examine . . . If pushed they would take food

The cost of living rose toward record heights for the Kellys. After Stringybark the £200 reward was raised to £1000.
After their failure to surrender, and more fruitless attempts at capture, the enticement reached a staggering £2000. This poster was produced by Thomas Still at the *Chronicle*, Jamieson.

Thomas Lloyd was one of many approached for information about the Kellys. Police thought Tom would be a good prospect, but in fact he was a close sympathiser. Superintendent Sadleir revealed that 'proposals were made to old Tom Lloyd, but he also declined . . . and added that the Kellys would trust no one who had been through Pentridge. We suggested that as he, Lloyd, was sure to find his way into Pentridge again, it would be well for him to have some friends in court. His only answer was, "Pentridge is hell, and no one will ever find me there again".'

from any of the farmer's houses about. There is a store at Merrijig, on the Devil's [Delatite] river, where they would likely get food; it is kept by a relative of the Lloyds, on the wife's side. Jack Quinn [on the Black Range Creek] would allow them to come to his house and take rations . . . The Kellys will keep to the ranges, as Ned Kelly told me often that it would be no good for him to try and get away as everybody knew him well, and also that he would be suspicious of persons putting him away. If they do leave the ranges they are certain to stick up and make a haul. They would likely try the Seymour Bank, as Ned Kelly had it in view for a long time to stick it up. They would keep to the bush until they got to Seymour, and return the same way. Mrs Skillion would probably get the haul.

The Kellys did get help among their friends and Williamson's information did not lead to their capture. Tom Lloyd, returning with supplies on the Saturday evening, said he met the Kellys on the Wombat Ranges after the shootings and was told the grim news. He said they all discussed their future over an evening meal of police rations. The four others decided to make for New South Wales to hold up the bank at Howlong – rendering Williamson's prophecy wildly inaccurate. The Kellys threw their mining tools down a shaft, covered them with clay and abandoned the farm. Tom Lloyd said he went with them to Greta before returning home. On the Sunday when McIntyre was struggling through the bush to Mansfield, the Kellys visited another cousin near Greta, William Tanner, who 'gave them a meal and change of clothing'. On the Sunday night, four men with two pack horses were seen riding through Oxley.

Further east at the Ovens River, a man called at the Pioneer Bridge Hotel and 'purchased a bottle of brandy. The other men stood with their horses at the bridge'. At Everton, the same four bought 'several boxes of sardines and some horse feed' then rode off in the direction of Sebastopol and the Woolshed. By the following Wednesday morning, they were camping on the Murray flats a few miles west of Wodonga. Here, they encountered a labourer and asked him for bread. He obliged, and during their brief conversation one of the men told him he was 'Kelly the bushranger' and that 'he intended calling on a man named Whitty of Moyhu about a case of horsestealing'.

The same day, the Kellys moved further west along the Murray River and tried to find a spot to cross. It was flooded to its highest level in years – making it difficult to cross and they nearly drowned trying to swim back from an island. Even a punt they hoped to use at Bungawunnah was sunk at its moorings. They called at the homestead of William Baumgarten (who was in prison for receiving horses stolen from James Whitty) and spoke to his wife. Mrs Baumgarten later told the police they had 'come out from the lagoons, off the island right under her house, camped there till sunset, and then disappeared'.

The Kellys were nearly captured that night. Police had spoken to the labourer who had met the gang earlier that day. From the information they obtained from him, they decided to try the Baumgarten farmhouse.

The woman of the house blamed Ned Kelly for getting her husband into trouble, told her story to the police, and pointed out where the Kellys had forded one of the branches of the Murray. Harkin's party started in pursuit but found the crossing no longer fordable and headed for another crossing . . . Standing up to their necks in water were the four bushrangers, concealed by the reeds, not many yards from where the police turned away. Their weapons under water and they themselves benumbed with cold, the gang could have offered no resistance had it been the fortune of the police to see them; but they did not.

Three days later, the Kellys were reported at the home of the Sherritt family at Sebastopol, evidently while Byrne visited his fiancée – Aaron Sherritt's sister. At dawn the next day, Sunday 3 November, a woman living on the outskirts of Wangaratta was woken by the sound of horses passing under the One Mile Creek bridge near her house. She said she 'saw four young men riding four horses. Two horses with packs were in front, and four others were running ahead bareback.' They were headed for the Wombat Ranges. The gang abandoned sergeant Kennedy's pack horse at the foot of the mountains before making a camp on top of the range. They were later tracked 20 miles north-west to their uncle's farm near Lake Rowan. There they visited another cousin, Joe Ryan, who had given evidence at their mother's trial. On 11 November they were seen riding south toward Greta. Then they disappeared from sight.

On 12 November, the Mansfield community quietly waited for the Kellys to surrender their lives as demanded eight days earlier. The courthouse was kept open all day – but the Kellys were not forthcoming. On 15 November, the Victorian governor, Sir George Ferguson Bowen, outlawed the two Kellys and their unknown comrades. Despite the complicated legal jargon, its meaning was quite clear. It allowed anyone to shoot them dead on sight – with or without warning. Acting police commissioner Chomley directed that [the Kellys]:

if found at large armed or there being reasonable ground to believe that he is armed it shall be lawful for any of Her Majesty's subjects whether a Constable or not and without being accountable for the using of any deadly weapon in aid of such apprehension whether its use be preceded by a demand of surrender or not to apprehend or take such outlaw alive or dead.

The edict also held that anyone who helped the outlaws or withheld information would be subject to prosecution. The Act even gave the police power to raid any house – without a written warrant. In essence, the authorities had declared war on the four men – excluding them from any right or consideration and, by force, recruited the support of the whole community in achieving their destruction. By not surrendering, the Kellys had revoked their citizenship.

Long afterwards, it was disclosed that the gang spent the rest of their first month of outlawry in and near Futter's Range. They camped on Emu station, south of their mother's empty hut on the Eleven Mile Creek and right under the eyes of the watching police. They were supplied with food by their sister, Margaret Skillion, then living on her hus-

'**A Bush Home**' by L. H. Davey.

band's selection with the other Kelly daughters and King children. The outlaws also got shelter and help from their uncle, Tom Lloyd senior, at his farm on the south of Bald Hill. In late November, Francis Harty sheltered the Kellys on his farm near Winton. The gang were rumoured to have hidden in the crops of another selector even closer to Benalla and watched the train loads of police running up and down the line in search of them.

In the first week of December, the Kellys were again reported a few miles out of Violet Town on the north-eastern line – some 25 kilometres (sixteen miles) south-west of Benalla. While camped near Violet Town, Ben Gould, their old family friend, provided the gang with food. Gould was then living in Euroa – the scene of more Kelly exploits on Monday, 9 December 1878.

9 THE EUROA HOLD-UP
9 DECEMBER 1878

On Wednesday 11 December 1878 a short message was tapped along the wires with news of another Kelly exploit. The following day, Melbourne newspapers devoted nearly a third of their editorial space to the details; the *Argus* published more than 10,000 words. The following is an extract.

**RE-APPEARANCE
OF THE BUSHRANGERS**

THE OUTRAGE AT EUROA

The telegram which we published yesterday with regard to the re-appearance of the Kelly Gang of outlaws at Euroa has been fully confirmed. The particulars to hand show not only that the offenders have performed a daring exploit, but also that they feel themselves masters of the situation. That they have outwitted the police is obvious, and until some explanation is given, the public cannot fail to hold the opinion that an outrage has been perpetrated which ought to have been prevented. It was stated in the press more than once that the gang would in all probability stick up and rob some bank, and thus good warning was given to the authorities, yet here we have the township of Euroa, situated in the bushranging district and possessing a branch of the National Bank, left without protection, with the exception of a solitary policeman. There are about 100 members of the police force exclusively engaged in hunting the gang but notwithstanding the number in the field, the outlaws seem to have had little difficulty in evading them, and whilst the bulk of them were sent into the ranges and away towards the Murray, the outlaws coolly disported themselves at Euroa, and insulted the whole country – through the utter contempt they displayed for the law.

Seven Creeks Hotel and store, Euroa. Besides 'Bricky' Williamson's warning from Pentridge, Pat Quinn also informed police that his nephews intended robbing a bank at Bright, Seymour, Avenel or Euroa. The raid was one of their most daring exploits; the detail of planning put into it was equalled only by the coincidences that helped it. The gang knew everything about the bank: its business hours, occupants and their habits. They knew the door was left ajar for the stationmaster to deposit his cash after the 3.30 p.m. goods train had passed through. By arriving after closing time, they could stay inside without raising suspicion. Obvious flukes added to their spectacular success: just two hours prior to the raid, magistrate Wyatt told police in Benalla that he was sure the Kellys were near Euroa, but he was ignored. The chance presence of James Gloster gave them foolproof cover – his wagon and new clothes misled everyone they met in the town. This view of Euroa dates from 1883 and shows the Sydney road – one kilometre from the railway and the bank. The Kellys rode past the hotel and store shown and across the white-painted bridge on the far right.

THE STICKING UP OF FAITHFULL CREEK STATION

(BY ELECTRIC TELEGRAPH)

(FROM OUR SPECIAL REPORTER)
EUROA Wednesday, 11 p.m.

Euroa is a small township on the North Eastern line, nearly 100 miles from Melbourne. It has a population of some 350 inhabitants but a considerable amount of business is, however, done in the place, as it is the outlet for a large Agricultural district reaching down the valley of the Goulburn River. At the back of it, and but a short distance away, are the Strathbogie Ranges. These are a continuation of the Glenmore Ranges, and the same country continues right up to Mansfield, and still further to the North East and South East. The ranges are lofty and thickly timbered, giving excellent cover for any persons trying to escape from justice.

About three miles further along the line is the Faithfull's Creek station, the homestead of which is only about a stone's throw from the railway line. From what can be learned it appears that shortly after noon on Monday one of the employees on the station named Fitzgerald was just sitting down to dinner in his hut, when a bushman quietly sauntered up to the door, and taking his pipe out of his mouth, inquired if Mr McCaulay, the overseer, was about. Fitzgerald replied, 'No, he will be back towards evening. Is it anything particular? Perhaps I will do as well.' The bushman said, 'No, never mind; it is of no consequence', and then walked away from the hut door. Fitzgerald continued to eat his dinner without taking any notice of the man, but happened to glance after him. A minute or two subsequently he saw him beckoning to some person in the distance. About five minutes later two more rough-looking characters joined the bushman. They were leading four very fine horses, in splendid condition. There were three bays and a grey. The bushman then proceeded to the house, and walking in, met Mrs Fitzgerald, the wife of the employee mentioned, who was engaged in some household duties. The old dame, considerably surprised at the

THE EUROA HOLD-UP 109

stranger walking in without an invitation, asked him who he was and what he wanted. He said, 'I am Ned Kelly, but do not be afraid, we shall do you no harm, but you will have to give us some refreshments, and also food for our horses. That's all we want.' She was naturally surprised, and at once called out for her husband. Fitzgerald left his dinner in the hut, and walked over to the house where his spouse introduced him to the stranger, saying 'There's Mr Kelly; he wants some refreshment and food for his horse'. By this time Kelly had drawn his revolver, evidently to show them that there was no joking on his part, and Fitzgerald, no doubt thinking discretion the better part of valour, accepted the inevitable, and resignedly said, 'Well, of course, if the gentlemen want any refreshment they must have it'. Ned Kelly then entered into conversation with the people, making several inquiries about the station and the number of men employed on it. To all his questions satisfactory answers were given. While this was going on the other two men – one of whom was Dan Kelly – found out the horse-feed, and were busily engaged feeding the horses, while it was noticed by Fitzgerald and his wife that a fourth man was standing at the gate, evidently keeping watch.

After getting all the information he could out of Fitzgerald, Kelly made the man go into a building used as a store and fastened the door on him, leaving the woman at liberty, and at the same time repeating the assurance that no harm was intended to anybody. As the station hands came up to the huts to get their dinner they were very quietly ordered to bail up, and were unresistingly marched into the storehouse and locked up with Fitzgerald, no violence being offered them, as they went quietly. Later in the afternoon Mr McCaulay, who had been to one of the out-stations, came quietly homewards, and when crossing the bridge over the creek, which led up to the station, he

Top: Benjamin Gould passed his knowledge of the town on to the Kellys. Gould boarded at Garrett's store right up until the day of their visit and did not take caution to hide his sympathies. Mr Scott, the Euroa bank manager, wrote three days after the robbery: 'I am still more of the opinion that the man Ben Gould is a confederate, he has been hanging around here a great deal of late, gets by train German sausage and Corned beef but does not appear to sell any . . . He told me 10 days ago that the Kellys were as well fed as I was, only they could not get vegetables.' Several days after the robbery, police arrested Gould for 'giving aid to the Kellys in robbing the Euroa Bank'. The charge was modified several times while he was remanded in Beechworth Gaol with other alleged sympathisers. Finally the attorney general refused to proceed with the case and Gould was released, but not until he had spent months awaiting trial. Police intelligence later identified James Gloster and his assistant, Beecroft, as other 'insiders', possibly recruited by Gould. The portrait was taken around 1903 by Howship of Benalla.

Bottom: Aiding the outlaws. This letter, confiscated by police, was said to show he was buying far more meat than he was selling to his customers; but again nothing could be proved. Gould later admitted to having assisted the outlaws for nearly two years.

noticed with some surprise the quietness that reigned about the place, and the absence of the station hands about the huts. However he did not give it a second thought, and proceeded on his way until nearing the storehouse, when he suddenly reined up. This was in consequence of Fitzgerald calling out from the building, 'the Kellys are here, you will have to bail up'. He could not believe this at first, but almost immediately Ned Kelly came out of the house, and covering him with his revolver, ordered him to bail up. McCaulay, without dismounting said 'What is the good of your sticking up the station? We have got no better horse than those you have.' Ned Kelly replied, 'We are not going to take anything. We only want some food and rest for our horses and sleep for ourselves.' McCaulay, seeing it was no good to offer any resistance, at once dismounted and surrendered, but they did not treat him the same as the others, allowing him to remain at liberty, but at the same time keeping a watchful eye upon him. Even then McCaulay did not believe it was the Kelly gang but when Dan Kelly came out of the house he recognised, he said, 'his ugly face' at once from the portraits he had seen of him. He said to them, 'Well, as we are to remain here, we may as well make ourselves as comfortable as possible, and have our tea.' The Kellys were, however, too cautious, and would not all sit down at once. Two of them had their meals, while the other two kept watch until they were relieved. They also took great care that some of the prisoners should taste the food first, being apparently afraid of poison being administered to them. About this time a hawker named Gloster, who has a shop at Seymour, but is in the habit of

Top: Faithfull's Creek run, otherwise known as Younghusband's station, was owned by Younghusband and Lyle, and managed by McCaulay. The station comprised 11,000 acres and stocked 5,000 sheep. The building that the gang held up was not the main homestead, but the manager's – 140 metres east of the railway. Five hundred metres further east was the Sydney road and the Strathbogie Ranges. The manager's homestead was faced-brick with a slate roof, situated about five metres from the creek. According to one captive, the Kellys had little fear of capture: 'Ned Kelly said "I have seen the police often, and have heard them often", he did not seem a bit afraid, but, on the contrary, laughed at them and their efforts to capture he and his mates. The other ruffians seemed to have as little dread for their pursuers. I asked Hart which way he was going when he left the station and Kelly answered carelessly, "Oh, the country belongs to us. We can go anywhere we like". He said, however, that he was getting sick of bushranging life.'

Bottom: Demanding refreshments. Ned Kelly gave Mrs Fitzgerald and a number of other station employees some small change from the proceeds of the robbery – which not everyone returned. Dan Kelly gave Gloster's assistant £2 and constable Lonigan's watch and asked him to hand them to the police in Euroa to be forwarded to his widow. Before leaving, Ned Kelly also went to the storeroom and asked for Mr McDougall's watch. He handed it to him, saying it was a keepsake from his dead mother. Kelly shivered and whispered 'no, we'll never take that from you'. The engraving shows the interior of the kitchen, with the outlaw demanding refreshments from Fitzgerald and his wife.

YOUNGHUSBAND'S STATION.

DEMANDING REFRESHMENTS

The new rig-outs 'valued at £14'. Ned Kelly was described as: '27 years, about six feet high, built in proportion. Dark brown hair, dark brown whiskers, and a beard and moustache worn long. He took a blue sac coat, brown tweed trousers and vest, elastic side boots, brown felt hat, grey striped crimean shirt and a lavender tie. Dan Kelly was recorded as 18 years, five feet six inches, dark brown hair, blue eyes, sallow complexion, scar on left cheek. Wore black paget coat, dark grey tweed trousers and vest, Rob Roy shirt and a black tie, elastic side boots, a light felt hat . . . worn under the nose.' After discarding their old clothes, the outlaws burnt them. In the ashes, portions of a woman's hat were found — supposed to have been in one of the outlaws' swags. The hat supports the theory that Hart, who was young and light, carried feminine disguise and sometimes wore it travelling. Rumours had also circulated that a woman, supposed to be Kate Kelly, was riding with the outlaws through the bush. The photograph shows Gloster's wagon tethered in Railway Street Euroa, several years after the Kellys took it to the Euroa National Bank. Gloster was never charged over his alleged involvement.

travelling about the country with a general assortment of clothing and fancy goods, drove his wagon up to the entrance of the station.

According to his usual custom, Gloster unharnessed his horses, and made preparations for camping out for the night. Having made all in readiness, he walked up to the station to get some water to make his tea with. When he reached the men's hut he was told the Kellys were here, and that he would have to bail up. McCaulay, knowing this man Gloster to be a plucky fellow, was afraid that he might draw his revolver, and that there would be bloodshed. However Gloster got his water from the kitchen, and was going back to his cart, when Ned Kelly called out to him to stop. He turned around and looked at the man, but supposing it was only a lark, he went on his way. Daniel Kelly immediately raised his gun, and was about to fire, when Ned Kelly prevented him from doing so, and at the same time McCaulay called out to him to 'bail up' in order to prevent bloodshed. Gloster, who appears to have been a pretty obstinate fellow, took no notice of the threats of the Kellys or the entreaties of McCaulay, and steadily continued on his way, and got up into his cart. Ned Kelly appeared to be losing his temper, and went down to the cart followed by his brother Dan. Ned then put his revolver to Gloster's cheek, and ordered him to come out of the cart, or he would blow his brains out. Several angry words passed between them, and it was only by the endeavours of McCaulay that Kelly was prevented from shooting Gloster. Ned Kelly at last said he would let him off this time, and at the same time praised his own moderation by saying that not one man in a hundred would have dealt so leniently with him after the manner in which he behaved. Dan Kelly was eager for blood, as he expressed a strong wish 'to put a bullet through the wretch'. Gloster was at last marched up to the storeroom, and locked up with the other prisoners. The four ruffians then proceeded to thoroughly ransack the hawker's cart, and provided themselves with a new fitout. They made regular bush dandies of themselves, and helped themselves pretty freely to the contents of the scent-bottles which they found among his stock. They also took what firearms he had.

Before going to bed for the night, the Kellys opened the door of the storeroom, and let the party out for a little while to get some fresh air, but at the same time keeping their revolvers in their hands and watching their prisoners very closely. While they were all smoking their pipes together, a friendly conversation took place between the gang and their prisoners.

FURTHER STATION INCIDENTS

Early next morning they were all up, and breakfast having been partaken of, one of the gang was sent by their leader, Ned Kelly, to render the telegraph wires unfit for use. There are wires on both sides of the line. On the west side there is a single line belonging to the railway department, while on the opposite side are four lines used for the general business of the colony. These are sustained on light iron poles. In order to destroy the railway telegraph line the earthenware insulators were broken and the line fell to the ground. A great more damage was, however, done to the other lines, as the ruffians took some stout limbs and smashed seven or eight of the cast-iron poles, and then twisted the wires into an inextricable maze. The Kellys appeared to be very uneasy when the trains passed up and down the line, as the homestead is close to the line. The passengers were plainly seen from the homestead looking at the broken telegraph wires.

During the morning four platelayers passed the spot, and they were at once bailed up and marched into the storeroom along with the other prisoners. About one o'clock in the afternoon on Tuesday four men, Messrs. Casement, Dudley, Tennant, and McDougall, passed the homestead in a spring-cart, and went to a level crossing and gate on the railway line near the creek. Mr Casement owned property on the opposite side of the station and line, and the four men were returning from a kangarooing expedition in the Strathbogies, inside the cart they had a rifle and a gun. Tennant was on horseback and the other two were riding with Casement. As they neared the gate two men approached them, one on horseback and one on foot. Both of them held up handcuffs in their left hands and carried guns in their right, and called, 'Bail up! Surrender or you'll be shot.' Dudley, who was driving answered, 'What right have you to arrest us?' thinking they were troopers, and he kept going. The mounted man rode up to the cart and presented his revolver at Dudley's head, shouted, 'I'll shoot you dead on the spot if you give me any cheek'. He accused the men of stealing the vehicle, and leaving his companion guarding them, went over to Tennant who had reached the gate, and took hold of his horse's bridle. Tennant called out to him to let go, to which the stranger replied by ordering him to dismount, at the same time tightening his grip on the bridle and saying 'Bail up! I am Ned Kelly.' Tennant said, 'Mind what you are about or it will be the worse for you', to

Railway Street, Euroa, in the 1870s. The National Bank is on the left and De Boos' North Eastern Hotel in the centre. J. H. Graves testified that: 'Byrne was in the town of Euroa for days before the bank robbery with Gould the hawker. Mr De Boos recognised Byrne as having been in his hotel two days before the robbery'. Steve Hart also enjoyed his anonymity. He had lunch at the same hotel on the day of the hold-up and later met the town's only constable outside. Hart walked out towards him, grinned and said 'good day' as the trooper went past. On his way back to Faithfull's Creek, Hart even met and spoke briefly to Alfred Wyatt, the local magistrate.

'The prison' and 'cutting the telegraph wire' at Faithfull's Creek. In total, there were 22 men locked in the station's storeroom. The fact that they did not overpower Byrne was questioned afterwards, but answered with good reasons. He had two guns 'and his belt stuck full of revolvers'. The building was made of heavy slabs, and the only doors and windows were on the front where Byrne was watching. It has been suggested that some of the prisoners were planted by the gang to warn of resistance. Upon returning from Euroa, the outlaws passed signals to Byrne, which were returned – evidently pre-arranged to show that everything was all right. Mr Scott, the bank manager, said that none of the women [captives at the station]: 'were molested as far as I learnt; in any way, or even locked up . . . though from some remarks dropped by Dan Kelly – who appeared the greatest ruffian of the lot and a thorough type of the larrikin – he did not desire to leave them untroubled. Mr McDougall recalled that although domineering in giving their orders, no attempt at violence or roughness was made on any of us. Ned Kelly conversed freely asking questions as to the movements of the police, and the '"kickup" which the gang had created among the [police] force'. On the Tuesday night, the outlaws put on a trick-riding performance for their captive audience. 'Before leaving they amused themselves by giving exhibitions of horsemanship, of which they were very proud, allowing the men to stand outside the lockup under guard to witness these feats. Ned Kelly in particular distinguished himself as a horseman, galloping about, lying or sitting upon his saddle in all kinds of apparently impossible positions.'

which Kelly replied, 'Good God! Will you get down. I am Ned Kelly, and if you won't I will blow your brains out.' Tennant thereupon dismounted, and saying 'Oh, if that's the case, let's load our guns', at the same time making for the cart into which he jumped with the evident intention of doing as he said.

Kelly was evidently losing his temper, and again said, 'Good God, won't you come out of the cart?' Some more angry words passed between them, and at last Kelly, in a paroxysm of passion, threw his rifle on the ground, and, clenching his fists, said, 'Come and have it out with me fairly. That is the fist of Ned Kelly, and it will not be long before you feel the weight of it.' Tennant, however, declined to accept the challenge, but deemed it advisable to get out of the cart before there was any more trouble. Kelly then ordered them to open the gate leading up to the station; but again Tennant refused. Kelly then put his revolver between Tennant's teeth, and swore that if he did not at once open the gate he would blow his brains out. To prevent such an occurrence Tennant did as he was ordered, and he and his companions were sent to join the others in captivity.

Soon after this the afternoon train stopped and a man got out, who proved to be a line repairer, sent down from Benalla to see what was wrong with the telegraph line. As soon as the train passed out of sight the man was made prisoner, and also locked up in the store. When this was done, Ned Kelly went to Mr McCaulay and asked him to write a cheque for him on the National Bank at Euroa. This McCaulay refused to do, but in searching the desk Kelly found a cheque for £4 and some odd shillings. He said that would answer his purpose as he only wanted it to gain entry into the bank. McCaulay said that of course he could not prevent him from taking it, but he would not sign any cheques. The gang now prepared to make a start, Kelly saying they were going into the township, and that all the crowd would have to remain locked up until they came back, and then, for the first time, he made McCaulay go into the store and be locked up. He decided to leave one of the gang named Byrne as sentry over them, and in order to secure their quietness while he was away one of the prisoners was taken out and kept covered with Byrne's rifle, with the intimation that if he or any of the party attempted to escape he would be shot. This preliminary business having been satisfactorily settled, three of the ruffians left the station, Ned Kelly driving Casement's spring-cart, Dan Kelly driving the Hawker's cart, and the third man accompanying them on horseback, the party proceeding direct to Euroa.

STICKING UP THE BANK

Top: Sticking up the bank. Manager Scott wrote: 'He then forced his way into my room and I saw it was Ned Kelly. Taking his stand near the end of the table at which I was sitting, he presented his revolver at my head and called upon me to bail up. He was followed by another man called 'Steve' or Stephen Hart, who had a revolver in each hand. I did not bail up at first, and they called again upon me to do so. I had a revolver but it was lying in the drawer on the opposite side of the table from me . . . On their again ordering me to throw up my arms I said 'It is all right' and raised them . . . Hart then kept guard over me while Ned Kelly ransacked the bank.' After all the money was collected (£2,060 in total, which represented a fortnight's profit for the National Bank in Australasia), Scott offered his guests a drink, supposedly playing for time, but probably for his nerves. The outlaws refused whisky so Mrs Scott filled a jug from the water bag on the back veranda. Scott was made to taste it before they drank to the health of all present. F. A. Hare wrote of Mrs Scott's bewilderment at Ned Kelly [she could hardly believe he was]: 'the person he represented himself to be; he was a tall, handsome man, well-dressed with the hawker's clothes on, and spoke so kindly to her'.

Right: Euroa National Bank is situated in the busiest part of the town, 50 yards from the railway station and 20 from C. L. De Boos' Hotel. The manager's residence was at the rear of the building, reached by a passage running through the centre of the bank from the front door. The smaller buildings at the back were servants' quarters.

THE BANK.

THE EUROA HOLD-UP 115

Euroa Railway Station 1879.

The bank was in full view of the Euroa railway station. Workmen were putting finishing touches to it on 10 December and watched the Kellys come and go. One of the men working on the new railway building observed: 'Mr Scott walk slowly to his trap, looking round on either side . . . another person behind him [gave] him a push forward but [he] thought it was a friend acting in a jocular manner.'

THE BANK ROBBERY

The next appearance they made was at the National Bank at Euroa, where in a most impudent manner in broad daylight they cleared out the money in the bank, and made prisoners of the 12 persons living there, without any person in the township being a bit the wiser. The bank was closed at the usual business hour, 3 o'clock, and at a quarter to 4 o'clock the two clerks, Messrs. Booth and Bradley, were engaged in balancing their books, while Mr Scott, the manager, was in his room close by. A knock was heard at the door, and Mr Booth asked Mr Bradley, who was nearest the door, to open it, and see who it was. On the door being opened a bushman presented a cheque of Mr McCaulay's for £4, saying he wanted it cashed. He was told he was too late, and he then asked to see Mr Scott, the manager. Mr Bradley said it was too late for that day, as all the cash was locked up. Up to this time the door had only been partially opened, but the man then pushed his way in, saying 'I am Ned Kelly'. He was immediately followed by another of the gang and both drew their revolvers and forced the clerks to go into the manager's room, which was just behind the banking chamber. As soon as they got in Ned Kelly ordered Mr Scott to go and tell the females in the house what visitors they had. It should here be said that in addition to Mr Scott and the two clerks, there were also in the house Mrs Scott, her family of five children, Mrs Scott's mother, and two female servants. Mr Scott, in going to inform the women of what had taken place, had to cross the main passage which runs through the house, and he then saw a third man, who proved to be Dan Kelly, keeping watch at the back door, he having also brought in the two servants from the out-buildings. As soon as they were all assembled in the passage, Ned Kelly demanded the money in the bank. As Mr Scott kept one key to the strong room, and Mr Bradley the other, Mr Scott replied that it was not altogether in his charge. Kelly at once turned to Mr Bradley, and putting his revolver to his head, said he would hold him responsible for the money, and he had better get it at once. After some little delay and hesitation, Mr Bradley handed him over the keys, and Kelly then proceeded to search the strong chest. He took all the money and notes out of it, and placed it on the counter, there was about £1,900 in notes and nearly £300 in gold. Ned Kelly went outside, and brought in a small gunnybag, into which he stuffed the notes and gold. Turning to Mr Scott, he said, 'I see you have a buggy in the yard. You had better put the horse in, as I will have to take the whole of you a little way into the bush, and it will be more comfortable for the women than the carts we have. Mr Scott said his groom was away, and Kelly thereupon went outside and harnessed the horse and buggy himself, having previously told the females to get themselves and the children ready for a journey. Before leaving the place, however, he put the bank books back in the strong-room, and locked the place up, and also fastened the side door. The whole party then went into the backyard, where the hawker's wagon was standing. Mr Bradley, Mr Booth and three of the children were then placed in the wagon, and Dan Kelly took the charge of them. Mrs Scott and her mother, with the other two children and one of the women servants, were placed in Mr Scott's trap, which Mrs Scott was ordered to drive. The other cart, which was that taken from Casement, was driven by Ned Kelly, and in it were placed Mr Scott and one of the servants. The third man of the gang rode on horseback, and was recognised by one of the servants as a man named Stephen Hart, whom she had seen in Wangaratta. This is the man whose name was mentioned in the outlawry proclamation as a man supposed to be King. After proceeding some distance on the road, Dan Kelly lost sight of Ned, who had been bringing up the rear, and he then arranged that Hart should ride back and see what had become of him. Dan then took his seat at the back of the wagon, in order to see that Mrs Scott closely followed him in the trap, and they then drove rapidly to the Faithfull Creek station.

The women were allowed to go on to the house, and Byrne, who had been keeping sentry over the prisoners, opened the door and allowed the captives to come out. Ned Kelly arrived directly afterwards, and took the money out of his cart, and securely strapped it on the front of his saddle. About a quarter to 9 the ruffians prepared for a start, but before doing so Ned Kelly locked all the captives up with the exception of McCaulay. Kelly directed McCaulay to keep the rest of the prisoners for three hours longer, and at the same time impressing upon him the fact that the gang would be in the vicinity, and if he let any of the prisoners go before the hour fixed he would be held responsible for it. Kelly and his mates then rode off in the direction of Violet Town.

THE PRISON

10 EVADING THE POLICE FORCE
DECEMBER 1878–FEBRUARY 1879

On the night of Tuesday 10 December police superintendents Nicolson and Sadleir were at Albury when news of the Euroa incident reached them. They were following information found in a confiscated letter saying that the gang were planning to cross the Murray River – evidently a well-prepared diversion. Nicolson reached Euroa on Wednesday morning. 'At daybreak they attempted to pick up the tracks of the outlaws. There were footprints of horses leading in every direction. The sympathisers who had been confined with the other prisoners at Faithfull's Creek . . . had mounted their horses, and kept riding around the station in every direction.' Two days of searching failed to produce any results. Superintendent Nicolson was recalled to Melbourne and chief commissioner Standish and superintendent Hare took over the Kelly hunt on 13 December.

The Euroa robbery saw the start of a swing in public opinion. While condemning the impertinence of the Kellys, newspapers made no secret of their success and the utter defeat of the authorities, which did as much for the Kellys' cause as their financial prosperity. People began to feel sympathy for the outlaws who, despite having nothing to lose and no reason to respect their captives, avoided violence and were courteous and well behaved. They even explained their actions to their captives – contradicting their former image as violent ruffians. While Ned Kelly was a criminal, and not well educated, he possessed an outstanding sense of politics and knew the strong propaganda value of his tactics.

Facing page: The December *Australasian Sketcher* did not get on-the-spot drawings at Euroa, so they featured this fearsome full-page cover to hide their shortcomings. The men appear to be dividing money, but are actually shown playing cards. The editor explained, 'Our artist has given an imaginary view of a camp of the gang of outlaws whom the police are now searching for in the ranges around the King river. The sketch tells its own tale, one of watchfulness and strained attention, listening for the sights or noises to indicate the approach of the avengers of blood and agents of justice.'

Superintendent Hare said of the Kelly pursuit: 'there were peculiar difficulties connected with this undertaking... Firstly these men were natives of the district... they knew every inch of the ground, bushes and mountains; they had hiding places and retreats known to few, if any, but themselves... Secondly, these men might disappear into the bush, and with their knowledge of the locality, ride hundreds of miles without coming near a dwelling-house, or meeting a human... lastly – what aided them more than anything else – they commanded an enormous amount of sympathy among the lower orders. It was a well-known fact that they had friends and adherents, either open or semi-veiled, all over the colony. The families of the Kellys, Harts and Byrnes were large ones... The Kelly family are the most prolific I have ever met in my life. There was no part of the colony from which we did not receive reports of them; in every part the Kellys had a cousin, an aunt, or something... And outside their family the sympathy they obtained was almost as great, though it was more of a meretricious order... [sympathisers were] always talking in their favour and picking up the news... The gang was lavish with its money. They subsidised largely, instituted a body of spies known as 'Bush telegraphs' who kept them fully informed and aided them on every possible occasion to avoid capture... the gang never behaved badly to a woman, but always treated them with consideration and respect. In like manner they seldom, if ever, made a victim of a poor man. And thus weaved a certain halo of romance and rough chivalry around themselves.'

Hare's estimation of their connections was not exaggerated. A north-eastern magistrate claimed to have counted 77 direct relatives in an area between Mansfield and southern New South Wales, and Kyneton and Tallangatta.

On 13 December, the Victorian Government lifted the gang's reward to £2,500; two days later 50 non-commissioned officers and men of the garrison artillery were withdrawn from the forts guarding Port Phillip and sent to reinforce the police. In parties of seven, the troops were billeted in Seymour, Avenel, Euroa, Violet Town, Wangaratta, Chiltern and Wodonga. More were despatched later to Shepparton and Beechworth. The troops guarded the banks to allow more police to join the hunt. By this stage, there were nearly 200 policemen on call and the cost of the pursuit went up as the numbers increased. In addition, all police engaged in the chase were on an extra 5 shillings per day – almost double their regular pay.

The police followed what they called a 'direct pursuit method' – literally chasing the outlaws. They sent patrols all over the country with or without reported appearances. The idea was to flush out the fugitives, keep them on the move and break their spirits. But after four weeks, the strategy had only exhausted police and publicised their failure. Friends and supporters of the Kellys informed them about approaching police, so the gang could avoid them accordingly. In contrast to their pursuers, they were at home in the bush and, as Ned Kelly himself later explained, 'as long as police strange to the districts... were going amongst them... they could laugh at their efforts'.

During this period, Kelly had enough leisure time to come up with another unexpected move. Buried in a Euroa news report was this mention: 'Kelly also stated that they had written a long letter to the Legislative Assembly, giving the whole circumstances that had led them into their present career. Mrs Fitzgerald was induced to obtain the postage stamps to enable them to forward this precious document, of which more will probably be heard.' The letter was most likely posted from Glenrowan on 14 December and reached its recipient, Donald Cameron MLA, three days later. Cameron handed the document to Premier Berry who heavily censored the document (eliminating all charges against the police) before passing it on to a very disappointed press. The original went to the Crown Law Department and the following is quoted from the only surviving copy.

Dear Sir,
Take no offence if I take the opportunity of writing a few lines to you wherein I wish to state a few remarks concerning the case of Trooper Fitzpatrick against Mrs Kelly W. Skillion and W. Williamson and to state the facts of the case to you. It seems impossible for me to get any justice without I make a statement to some one that will take notice of it as it is no use in me complaining about anything that the Police may choose to say or swear against me and the public in their ignorance and blindness will undoubtedly back them up to their utmost. No doubt I am now placed in very peculiar circumstances and you might blame me for it but if you knew how I have been wronged and persecuted you would say I cannot be blamed. In April last an information was (which must have come under your notice) sworn against me for shooting trooper Fitzpatrick which was false and my mother with an infant baby and Brother-in-law and another neighbour was taken for aiding and abetting and attempting to

murder him a charge of [which] they are as purely innocent as the child unborn. During my stay on the King River I run in a wild bull which I gave to Lydicher who afterwards sold him to Carr and he killed him for beef. Sometime afterwards I was told I was blamed for stealing this bull from Whitty I asked Whitty on Moyhu racecourse why he blamed me for stealing his bull he said he had found his bull and he never blamed me for stealing him. He said it was Farrell who told him that I stole the bull. Sometime afterwards I heard again I was blamed for stealing a mob of calves from Whitty and Farrell which I never had anything to do with and along with this and other talk I began to think they wanted something to talk about. Whitty and Burns not being satisfied with all the picked land on King River and Boggy Creek and the run of their stock on the certificate ground free and no one interfering with them. Paid heavy rent for all the open ground so as a poor man could not keep any stock and impounded every beast they could catch even off Government roads if a poor man happened to leave his horse or bit of a poddy calf outside his paddock it would be impounded. I have known over 60 head of horses to be in one day impounded by Whitty and Burns all belonging to poor men of the district they would have to leave their harvest or ploughing and go to Oxley and then perhaps not have money enough to release them and have to give a bill of sale or borrow the money which is no easy matter and along with all this sort of work Farrell the Policeman stole a horse from George King and had him in Whitty and Jeffrey's paddocks until he left the force and this was the cause of me and my stepfather George King stealing Whitty's horses and selling them to Baumgarten and those other men the pick of them was sold

Chief commissioner captain Frederick Charles Standish did more to impede the Kelly pursuit than anyone involved. He became an indifferent officer and uninspiring leader. After fleeing gambling debts in England and failing as a gold-digger, he gained his commissions through well-connected friends in Melbourne. His greatest problem was constant boredom. Standish rewarded subordinates who shared his love of pleasure and 'dismissed from consideration officers of a more serious disposition'. In this way he played his favourite superintendent, Frank Hare, off against fellow officers Charles Nicolson and John Sadleir, so hampering operations.

The Kelly hunters. Superintendent Hare, fourth from right, is pictured with a group of constables who pursued the Kellys. At Hare's feet is Moses, a Victorian Aboriginal tracker. Although captioned 'in the Kelly country', the photograph was taken in the Benalla police paddock. The men posed against artificially arranged foliage to hide the post-and-rail fence in the background. The troopers with Hare were recruited from his own Bourke district. He wrote, 'I had a splendid lot of fellows in my party. There was not a weak spot in any of them. No work was too much for them, day or night and I never heard a grumble. Several were equal to any bush-riders in the world.' The recruits, however, had no knowledge of the district or the people they were after. Hare later admitted, 'Ned Kelly knew all our camps in the Warby ranges . . . He told of all our movements, and described the men.'

Standish in camp. Even more trouble was taken with this contrived 'Kelly country' setting, intended to look like the police headquarters in the ranges, which never existed. The incorrectly rigged tent, foliage, campfire, and even a dog were all props provided by the enthusiastic photographer.

at Howlong and the rest was sold to Baumgarten who was a perfect stranger to me and I believe an honest man. No man had anything to do with the horses but me and George King William Cooke who was convicted for Whitty's horses had nothing to do with them nor was he ever in my company at Peterson the German's at Howlong. The brands was altered by me and George King and the horses were sold as straight. Any man requiring horses would have bought them the same as those men and would have been potted the same and I consider Whitty ought to do something towards the release of those innocent men otherwise there will be a collision between me and him as I can to his satisfaction prove I took J. Welshe's black mare and the rest of the horses which I will prove to him in next issue and after those horses had been found and the row being over them I wrote a letter to Mr Swannell of Lake Rowan to advertise my horses for sale as I was intend to sell out. I sold them afterwards at Benalla and the rest in New South Wales and left Victoria as I wished to see certain parts of the country and very shortly afterward there was a warrant for me and as I since hear the Police Sergeant Steel, Straughen [sic] and Fitzpatrick and others searched the Eleven Mile and every other place in the district for me and a man named Newman who had escaped from the Wangaratta Police for months before the 15th of April. Therefore it was impossible for me to be in Victoria as every schoolboy knows me and on the 15th April Fitzpatrick came to the Eleven Mile and had some conversation with Williamson who was splitting on the hill seeing my brother and another man he rode down and had some conversation with this man whom he swore was William Skillion this man was not called in Beechworth as he could have proved Fitzpatrick's falsehood as Skillion and another man was away after horses at this time which can be proved by eight or nine witnesses the man who the trooper swore was Skillion can prove Williamson's innocence besides other important evidence which can be brought on the prisoners behalf. The trooper, after speaking to the man, rode to the house and Dan came out he asked Dan to go to Greta with him. Dan asked him what for and he said he had a warrant for him for stealing Whitty's horses. They both went inside Dan was having something to eat The trooper was impatient and Mrs Kelly asked him what he wanted Dan for and he said he had a warrant for him. Dan said produce your warrant and he said he had none it was only a telegram from Chiltern. Mrs Kelly said he need not go unless he liked without a warrant. She told the trooper he had no business on her premises without some authority besides his own word. He pulled out his revolver and said he would blow her brains out if she interfered in the arrest Mrs Kelly said if Ned was here he would ram the revolver down his throat. To frighten the trooper Dan said Ned is coming now, the trooper looked around to see if it was true Dan dropped the knife and fork which showed he had no murderous intention clapped Heenan's hug on him took his revolver and threw him and part of the door outside and kept him there until Skillion and Ryan came with horses which Dan sold that night the trooper left and invented some scheme to say he got shot which any man can see it is impossible for him to have been shot. He told Dan to clear out that Sergeant Steel or Detective Brown would be there before morning as Straughen [sic] was over the Murray trying to get up a case against Dan and the Lloyds as the Germans over the Murray would swear to any one, and they will lag you guilty or not. Next day Skillion, Williamson and Mrs Kelly with an infant were taken and thrown into prison and were six months awaiting trial and no bail allowed and was convicted on the evidence of the meanest man that ever the sun shone on I have been told by Police that he is hardly ever sober also between him and his father they sold his sister to a Chinaman but he seems a strapping and rather genteel looking young man and more fit to be a starcher to a laundry than a trooper, but to a keen observer he has the wrong appearance to have anything like a clear conscience or a manly heart the deceit is too plain to be seen in the white cabbage-hearted looking face. I heard nothing of this transaction until very close on the trial I being then over 400 miles from Greta. I heard I was outlawed and £100 pound reward for me in Victoria and also hundreds of charges of horse stealing was against me besides shooting a trooper. I came into Victoria and enquired after my brother and found him working with another man on Bullock Creek. Heard how the Police used to be blowing that they would shoot me first and then cry surrender. How they used to come to the house when there was no one there but women and Superintendent Smith used to say see all the men I have out to day I will have as many more tomorrow and blow him into pieces as small as paper that is in our guns and they used to repeatedly rush into the house revolver in hand upset milk dishes empty the flour out on the ground break tins of eggs and even throw the meat out of the cask on to the floor and dirty and destroy all the provisions which can be proved and shove the girls in front of them into the rooms like dogs and abuse and insult them. Detective Ward and Constable Hayes took out their revolvers and threatened to shoot the girls and children whilst Mrs Skillion was absent – the oldest being with her. The greatest murderers and ruffians would not be guilty of such an action. This sort of cruelty and disgraceful conduct to my brothers and sisters who had no protection coupled with the conviction of my mother and those innocent men certainly made my blood boil as I don't think there is a man born could have the patience to suffer what I did. They were not satisfied with frightening and insulting my sisters night and day and destroying their provisions and lagging my mother with an infant baby and those innocent men but should follow me and my brother who was innocent of having anything to do with any stolen horses into the wild where he had been quietly digging and doing well neither molesting or interfering with anyone. And I was not there long and on the 25th of October I came on the tracks of Police horses, between tabletop and the bogs I crossed them and went to Emu Swamp and returning home I came on more Police tracks making for our camp. I told my mates and me and my brother went out next morning and found Police camped at the Shingle hut with long firearms and we came to the conclusion our doom was sealed unless we could take their firearms, as we had nothing but a gun and a rifle, if they came on us at our work or camp we had no chance only to die like dogs as we thought the country was woven with Police and we might have a chance of fighting them if we had firearms as it generally takes 40 to one. We approached the spring as close as we could get to the camp. The intervening space being clear we saw two men at

Moses, Hare's favourite tracker, was employed in the first three months of the pursuit. Unlike Standish, Hare had a realistic respect for the abilities of Australian Aborigines. Hare described in great detail, and with typical European conceit, the 'wonderful powers these blacks have in following tracks' – a respect also shared by the Kellys.

the logs they got up and one took a double barrel fowling piece and one drove the horses down and hobbled them against the tent and we thought there was more men in the tent those being on sentry. We could have shot those two men without speaking but not wishing to take life we waited. McIntyre laid the gun against the stump and Lonigan sat on the log I advanced my brother Dan Keeping McIntyre covered I called on them to throw up their hands McIntyre obeyed and never attempted to reach for his gun or revolver. Lonigan ran to a battery of logs and put his head up to take aim at me when I shot him or he would have shot me as I knew well I asked who was in the tent McIntyre replied no one. I approached the camp and took possession of their revolvers and fowling pieces which I loaded with bullets instead of shot I told McIntyre I did not want to shoot him or any man that would surrender. I explained Fitzpatrick's falsehood which no policeman can be ignorant of. He said he knew Fitzpatrick had wronged us but he could not help it. He said he intended to leave the force on account of his bad health his life was insured the other two men who had no firearms came up when they heard the shot fired, and went back to our camp for fear the Police might call there in our absence and surprise us on our arrival. My brother went back to the spring and I stopped at the logs with McIntyre, Kennedy and Scanlan [sic] came up, McIntyre said he

Mr Donald Cameron MLA was very nearly the victim of his own politics on 13 November 1878. Cameron had asked Premier Berry whether he would cause a searching inquiry to be made into the origin of the Kelly outbreak, and the action of the authorities in taking the preliminary steps for the arrest of the criminals. He added that statements made in the Benalla district pointed to the conduct of certain members of the police force as having led up to the Mansfield Murders and maintained that police efforts since had been 'scandalous'. Berry answered Cameron by openly promising that 'if reliable information were to reach him that difficulties were interposed, by want of proper organisation among the police or any other circumstance . . . he would, of course, institute an inquiry.' The Kellys mistook these remarks as a genuine opportunity to state their case. Cameron recognised it would be political suicide if he was identified as spokesman for the outlaws. To avoid this, he handed the Kellys' 22-page document on to Mr Berry. The premier either realised the potential discredit to his government if the alleged corruption was proved, or completely disbelieved it as he too did absolutely nothing. This chance at negotiation could have saved the colony £100,000, but the opportunity was missed.

would get them to surrender if I spared their lives as well as his, I said I did not know either him Scanlan or Kennedy and had nothing against them and would not shoot any of them if they gave up their firearms and promise to leave the force as it was the meanest billet in the world they are worse than cold blooded murderers or hangmen. He said he was sure they would never follow me any more. I gave him my word that I would give them a chance. McIntyre went up to Kennedy Scanlan being behind with a rifle and revolver – I called on them to throw up their hands. Scanlan slewed his horse around to gallop away but turned again, and as quick as thought fired at me with the rifle and was in the act of firing again when I shot him. Kennedy alighted on the offside of his horse and got behind a tree and opened hot fire McIntyre got on Kennedy's horse and galloped away. I could have shot him if I choose as he was right against me but rather than break my word I let him go. My brother advanced from the spring Kennedy fired at him and ran as he found neither of us was dead. I followed him he got behind another tree and fired at me again. I shot him in the arm-pit as he was behind the tree he dropped his revolver and ran again and slewed round and I fired with the gun again and shot him through the right chest as I did not know he had dropped his revolver, and was turning to surrender, he could not live or I would have let him go. Had they been my own brothers I could not help shooting them, or else lie down and let them shoot me which they would have done had their bullets been directed as they intended them. But as for handcuffing Kennedy to a tree or cutting his ear off or brutally treating any of them, is a cruel falsehood. If Kennedy's ear was cut off it has been done since. I put his cloak over him and left him as honourable as I could and if they were my own brothers I could not be more sorry for them with the exception of Lonigan I did not begrudge him what bit of lead he got as he was the flashest and meanest man that I had any account against for him Fitzpatrick Sergeant Whelan Constable O'Day and King the bootmaker once tried to handcuff me at Benalla and when they could not Fitzpatrick tried to choke me. Lonigan caught me by the privates and would have killed me but was not able Mr McInnis came up and I allowed him to put the handcuffs on when the Police were bested. This cannot be called wilful murder for I was compelled to shoot them in my own defence or lie down like a cur and die. Certainly their wives and children are to be pitied but those men came into the bush with the intention of shooting me down like a dog and yet they know and acknowledge I have been wronged. And is my mother and her infant baby and my poor little brothers and sisters not to be pitied more so who has got no alternative only to put up with the brutal and unmanly conduct of the Police who have never had any relation or a mother or must have forgot them. I was never convicted of horsestealing I was once arrested by Constable Hall and 14 more men in Greta and there was a subscription raised for Hall by persons who had too much money about Greta in honour of Hall arresting Wild Wright and Gunn. Wright and Gunn were potted and Hall could not pot me for horsestealing but with the subscription money he gave £20 to James Murdock [sic] who has recently been hung in Wagga Wagga and on Murdock's evidence I was found guilty of receiving knowing to be stolen which L. Wright W. Ambrose I. Ambrose and W. Hatcher and W. Williamson and others can prove I was innocent of knowing the mare to be stolen and I was once accused of taking a hawker of the name of McCormacks horse to pull another hawker named Ben Gould out of a bog. Mr Gould got up in the morning to feed his horses, seen McCormack's horse and knew he had strayed sent his man in with him about two miles to where McCormack was camped in Greta. Mr and Mrs McCormack came out and seen the waggons bogged and accused him of using the horse. I told Gould that was for his good nature Mrs McCormack turned on me and accused me for catching the horse for Gould as Gould knew he was wicked and could not catch him himself Me and my uncle was cutting and branding calves and Ben Gould wrapped up a pair of testicles wrote a note and gave it to me to give to Mrs McCormack. McCormack said he would fight me I was then 14 years of age, I was getting off my horse and Mrs McCormack hit the horse he jumped forwards and my fist came in collision with McCormack's nose who swore he was standing 10 yards away from another man and the one hit knocked the two men down, however ridiculous the evidence may seem I received 3 months or £10 fine for hitting him and 3 months for delivering the parcel and bound to the peace for 12 months. At the time I was taken by Hall and his 14 assistants, therefore I dare not strike any of them – as Hall was a great cur, and as for Dan he never was tried for assaulting a woman. Mr Butler P.M. sentenced him to 3 months without the option of a fine and one month or two pounds fine for wilfully destroying property a sentence which there is no law to uphold and yet they had to do their sentence and their prosecutor Mr D. Goodman since got 4 years for perjury concerning the same property. The Minister of Justice should enquire into this respecting their sentence and will find a wrong jurisdiction given by Butler P.M. on the 19th of October 1877 at Benalla, and these are the only charges was ever proved against either of us therefore we are falsely represented. The report of bullets having been fired into the bodies of the troopers after their death is false and the coroner should be consulted. I have no intention of asking mercy for myself of any mortal man, or apologising, but I wish to give timely warning that if my people do not get justice and those innocents released from prison and the Police wear their uniforms I shall be forced to seek revenge of everything of the human race for the future. I will not take innocent life if justice is given but as it is the Police are afraid or ashamed to wear their uniform therefore every mans life is in danger as I was outlawed without any cause and cannot be no worse and have but once to die and if the Public do not see justice done I will seek revenge for the name and character which has been given to me and my relations while God gives me strength to pull a trigger. The witnesses which can prove Fitzpatrick's falsehood can be found by advertising and if this is not done immediately horrible disasters shall

The Cameron letter contained Kelly's confession to the Stringybark Creek shootings and was held by the Crown Law Department. The original seems to have disappeared, and only one hand-written copy survives. It was said to have been written in red ink on 22 pages of foolscap and, according to the pencilled note on the Crown Law copy, was posted at Glenrowan. The letter was written like a speech, strongly rhetorical and in parts over-stated, yet it remains Kelly's most persuasive statement. Initially, it was ridiculed, misquoted and then completely ignored. The embarrassment of the politicians at receiving it was equalled only by captain Standish's alarm, shown by his urgent telegram on 18 December. All Kelly's letters have been the subject of much study and debate in more recent years and have been criticised as convincingly as they have been praised. Nonetheless, many of Kelly's accusations are confirmed from other sources.

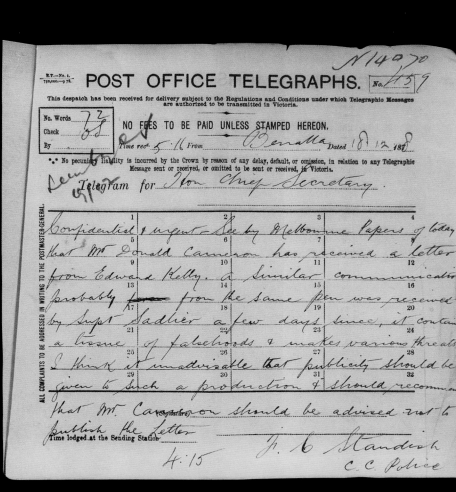

follow. Fitzpatrick shall be the cause of greater slaughter to the rising generation than St Patrick was to the snakes and frogs in Ireland. For had I robbed, plundered, ravished and murdered everything I met my character could not be painted blacker than it is at present but thank God my conscience is as clear as the snow in Peru and I hear a picked jury amongst which was a discharged Sergeant of Police was empanelled on the trial and David Lindsay who gave evidence for the Crown is a shanty-Keeper having no license is liable to a heavy fine and keeps a book of information for the Police and his character needs no comment for he is capable of rendering Fitzpatrick any assistance he required for a conviction as he could be broke any time Fitzpatrick chose to inform on him. I am really astonished to see members of Legislative Assembly led astray by such articles as the Police for while an outlaw reigns their pocket swells Tis double pay and country girls. By concluding as I have no more paper unless I rob for it if I get justice I will cry a go. For I need no lead or powder to revenge my cause, and if words be louder I will oppose your laws. With no offence (remember your railroads) and a sweet good bye from Edward Kelly a forced outlaw.

When the Kelly letter reached Melbourne, parliament was in recess and not due to re-open for another seven months — they had missed their opportunity. In addition, Premier Berry left the colony a few days after he saw their letter, showing the outlaws their effort had been largely wasted. The government was in no mood for negotiation and on 4 January 1879, a drastic police move was sanctioned. On the following Saturday, 20 men were arrested under the provisions of the *Felons Apprehension Act 1878* as Kelly sympathisers. An *Argus* correspondent wrote:

both here and at Benalla the excitement was very great, and a crowd of persons assembled to get a glimpse of the prisoners. The names of the five arrested at Benalla were John McElroy, Thomas Lloyd senior, James Quinn, John McMonigal and Francis Harty. These men were all of the labouring class, but were described as farmers and selectors. The charge against them was brought . . . for having given information to an outlaw and his accomplices, contrary to the fifth section of the Outlawry Act . . . The names of those arrested at Mansfield were Isaiah Wright, who is well known about the district as Wild Wright, John Hart, Robert Millar [sic], John Lloyd, Daniel Delaney and William Perkins.

The other nine men who arrived under guard at Beechworth Gaol were Jack Quinn, Richard Strickland, William Strickland, Joseph Ryan, James and Daniel Clancey and Walter and John Stewart. Benjamin Gould joined them under the recently altered charge of 'withholding information relative to the Kelly gang'. Initially there was mixed reaction to the arrests. There was little objection to the arrest of men known to be the gang's closest supporters. The Lloyds and Wrights had openly watched police movements in Benalla since the first week after Stringybark Creek. On the day of the arrests, old Tom Lloyd sent a telegram home with a cryptic instruction to let the four bulls out of the paddock. Francis Harty and James Quinn were arrested on the Kelly selection, which they were looking after for Mrs Kelly while she was in gaol. Two days after the arrest of Harty and Quinn, the Kellys were seen at Greta asking about the arrest and threatening the police. Superintendent Hare wrote, 'It was found these sympathisers were annoying the police in every possible way, watching every move we made. For example, the gang left Euroa on three bay horses and a grey. For months after we got reports from every side of the district of three men riding bay horses and one on a grey. The sympathisers and lads in the country did it on purpose. One or two men were watching the police at all times; a man named Isaiah Wright was one.'

From the beginning, objection was raised about the method used to arrest sympathisers — many of the men had no connection with the outlaws. Police were encouraged to exaggerate the importance of their suspects, resulting in nearly half of them being wrongly implicated. In the following week, public opinion — if newspapers are an indication — took a decided stand. A Mansfield telegram ran: 'There is a

The Melbourne *Punch*, like most press, were as unkind to the unsuccessful police in 1879 as history has been to them since. When this cartoon appeared on 16 January 1879, it was typical of editorial criticism of the time.

POPULAR IDEA RESPECTING KELLY CATCHING.
Whipper (who has never been beyond Keilor Plains).—I SAY, AIN'T IT SHAMEFUL THEY DON'T CATCH THE KELLYS? WHY DON'T THE POLICE JUMP ON THEIR HORSES AND RIDE 'EM DOWN?"
Snapper (who has been as far as Dandenong).—" NO SIR, YOU'RE WRONG—QUITE WRONG—STRATEGY, SIR—STRATEGY'S THE THING—WAIT FOR 'EM BEHIND A TREE!!"

Bank in the bushranging district. The Kelly robbery caught the banking companies as much by surprise as the police, and caused a major internal stir throughout the colony. Gold and coin reserves were reduced and restricted in country offices and some small branches were closed. The *Hamilton Spectator* observed: 'One effect of the Kelly scare is that by Thursday's train three bank managers, one of whom was from Portland and two from Hamilton, left for Melbourne in charge of treasure belonging to their respective banks. The managers took with them about £25,000. It is not so much from fear of the Kelly Gang that the banks are organising an escort system of their own, but rather from an apprehension that in the present lawless state of the colony the immunity enjoyed by the Mansfield Gang will cause a bad example to be imitated by others.'

Overleaf: Left, Police caves on the Woolshed. Right, Wild Isaiah Wright's prison record.

sort of reaction set in here, as some persons think that the police have gone too far in their arrests'. A Melbourne paper worried aloud that 'a very unhealthy sympathy with the outlaws prevails throughout the district'. A Beechworth editor ran a leading article headed 'A dark prospect' outlining the spreading sympathy and its possible influences.

The growing storm did have some effect. On 18 January, the 21 arrested sympathisers were remanded for a third time at Beechworth – still without any evidence produced against them. Six of them (Miller, the Stewarts, Perkins, William Strickland and Delaney) were released that day, apparently because of public pressure. The police applied for a further remand of the others, claiming their witnesses were engaged in the bush pursuing the outlaws or were too frightened to testify. A Melbourne solicitor representing the remaining men said, 'The whole affair was making a laughing stock of Justice. Were the case heard in Melbourne, five words would set the men free, as there was absolutely nothing proved against the accused.' But because none of them could afford an appeal to the Supreme Court, their remands dragged on.

There was never any doubt that the arrests were necessary to prevent the supply of food and shelter to the outlaws. The police action had the support of the magistrates – and would have had the general community's – but it backfired for two reasons. First, there was no conclusive evidence to back up the charges. Secondly, none of the female sympathisers was arrested. The Kelly women continued the work, which completely cancelled out the effect the arrests might have had on the outlaws. That no evidence was produced of the arrested men's guilt overshadowed the fact that among them were some of the gang's most active sympathisers. It made their confinement illegal, a tactical blunder on the part of the police. It alienated the population from the authorities, gave the Kellys further incentive, and the public a reason to side with them. On 25 January, the remaining fourteen were remanded again. Around the same time, Ned Kelly is said to have posted a second note to the Berry Government – this time to the acting chief secretary, Bryan O'Loghlen.

Sir,
I take the liberty of addressing you with respect to the matter of myself, my brother and my two friends, Hart and Byrne. I take this opportunity to declare most positively that we did not kill the policemen in cold blood, as has been stated by that rascal McIntyre. We only fired on them to save ourselves, and we are not the cold-blooded murderers which people presume us to be. Circumstances have forced us to become what we are – outcasts and outlaws, and, bad as we are, we are not as bad as we are supposed to be.

But my chief reason for writing this is to tell you that you are committing a manifest injustice in imprisoning so many innocent people just because they are supposed to be friendly to us. There is not the least foundation for the charge of aiding and abetting us against any of them, and you may know this is correct, or we would not be obtaining our food as usual since they have been arrested.

Your policemen are cowards – every one of them. I have been with one party two hours while riding in the ranges, and they did not know me. I will show you that we are determined men, and I warn you that within a week we will leave your colony, but we will not leave it until we have made the country ring with the name Kelly and taken terrible revenge for the injustice and oppression we have been subjected to. Beware, for we are now desperate men.
Edward Kelly

No. 12313 **Name** Wright Isaiah

Height	5ft 11in
Weight	134.2lb
Complexion	Fresh
Hair	Brown
Eyes	Hazel
Nose	Short
Mouth	Medium
Chin	Medium
Eyebrows	Lt Brown
Visage	Square
Forehead	Medium
Date of Birth	1849
Native place	Ireland
Trade	Labourer
Religion	Ch of Engd
Read & Write	R & W

Sentence	Three Years HL	Six Years HL
Date of Conviction	13.10.74	16.2.83
Offence	Receiving a horse knowing it to be stolen	Horse Stealing
Where and before whom tried	Beechworth Cir Court Fri Jus Fellows	Beechworth Genl Ses M Cha Skinner

Scar inside corner left eyebrow, large scar right cheek, pimple right cheekbone, scar left side of nose & throat, scar back of head, 4th & little left fingers contracted, upper joint right forefinger injured, scar right thumb.

2.8.71 18 mos HL. Per the "Carlton" from Liverpool to Geelong in 1858. Married wife maiden name Bridget Lloyd in Mansfield proper name. 25.2.97 Cruelty to a horse 20/= 3 days impt. Obs Lang 20/= 3 days impt Euroa PS (Arrested 18/1/1900)

	When received	Offences, Sentences, &c.		Extensions by— Visiting Justice		Superintendent	
				M.	D.	M.	D.
to Pentridge	13.10.74 26.1.75 1st Class 19.7.75 2nd Class 22.8.76 4th Class 23.10.76 5th Class 11.5.77 6th Class						
	27.10.74	2.6.75 Quarrelling	7 days HL		4.		1.
Hulk Sacramento	21.1.76	26.7.75 Talking	Indef 10y.				7.
		9.8.75 Having worsted	" 7 days				5.2.
Pentridge	31.3.76	20.9.75 Playing on the 19th inst	" 5 "				2.
		24.9.75 Quarrelling	" 2 "				2.1.
Hulk	1.11.76	5.11.75 Talking at dinner	" 1 "				2.
		12.1.76 Away from labor	" 2 "				7.
Sandridge	11.1.77	28.3.76 Improper language	" 7 "				
		4.3.76 Assaulting a prisoner	14 days HL		14.		
		14.3.76 Having prohibited articles	1 Month HL	1.			7.
Beechworth Gaol to Pentridge	16.2.83 1.3.83	28.4.76 Insolence	Indefd 7 days				4.2.
		12.4.76 Carelessness at work	" 4 "				2.
		28.6.76 Having a black eye	" 2 "				1.
		27.10.76 Annoying prisoner	" 1 "				
		25.2.76 Misconduct	10 days HL		10.		

May 1877 wants Dis 19 inst
10.5.77 Freedom by promission Pay of £3.2.8
19.4.86 Disorderly at Divine Service 2d Cls 3 days G 3.
14.5.86 Having knife concealed 3 days G 3.
27.6.87 Tobacco Dis Prob 3 days G 3.

Sept 1887 wants Dis 26 Prox,
26/10/87 To freedom

James Quinn

Robert Miller

Henry Perkins

Walter Stewart

Daniel Clancey

James Clancey

John Stewart

Among the 21 men held in Beechworth Gaol for being Kelly sympathisers, eight were relatives of the outlaws, possibly twelve were active sympathisers, and seven had some criminal record. Fourteen of them were of Irish descent, three were Scottish and the rest English. The arrest of **Robert Miller** caused the greatest outcry. A Melbourne newspaper claimed to have made inquiries and found that 'this man is a hard-working respectable farmer who is as ignorant of the Kellys' movements as the police themselves . . . the police suspected him because his daughter [openly admires her cousins] and is a grand horsewoman.' Another agreed: 'He is said to be a quiet, harmless old man. He was taken from his harvest work just as he was getting in his small crop. On his journey to Benalla in the conveyance, when asked to take a cup of tea, he burst into tears, and said he wanted nothing while in handcuffs. Miller was married to a sister of Mrs Kelly, but his wife is dead.' After two weeks, and a local petition, he was released.

Henry Perkins was released on 18 January, but without the same sympathy. He and his son were the only selectors on the Wombat Range earlier in 1878 and lived not far from Stringybark Creek. Sergeant Kennedy interviewed them before the shootings and newspapers did not hide the belief that Perkins had betrayed him to the Kellys.

Walter Stewart, of Rutherglen, admitted to having 'served sentences with Dan Kelly, the Lloyds and Steve Hart'. Two revolvers and several guns were found in his home – the only apparent reason he and his brother John Stewart were arrested. The Stewarts were also let out on 18 January.

Daniel and James Clancey, of south Wangaratta, were friends and neighbours of the Hart family and suspected 'bush telegraphs' for the gang. A newspaper mentioned that 'one of the Clanceys was known to be always on the lookout for information . . . seen hovering about the railway stations whenever troopers were passing to and fro . . . and sneaking away on a fleet horse with the news.'

Richard and William Strickland were described in detective reports as close friends of the Quinns and Kellys. Of the other three men shown, Michael Haney was a farmer on the Ralmattum Range (five kilometres from Euroa) and suspected of harbouring the outlaws before their raid. Daniel Delaney, from Greta, was another old friend. John Hart, apparently no relation to Steve, was a horse-breaker and close friend of the Quinns, and supposed to have been a partner of the Kellys during their horse-stealing days.

Wild Isaiah Wright, seen here without a beard, was the most colourful of the sympathisers and the biggest troublemaker in and out of prison. He was married to Ned's cousin Bridget Lloyd, and held a selection near Mansfield for some years. Wright rivalled James Quinn junior for the number of times spent in gaol – both spent much of their younger adult lives behind bars.

Richard Strickland

William Strickland

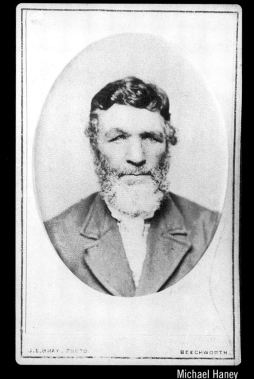
Michael Haney

Daniel Delaney

John Hart

'Wild' Isaiah Wright

It was never explained why the sympathisers at the Woolshed were not arrested, but there were two possible reasons. Overtures were made to Joe Byrne, offering him a free pardon if he betrayed the others. The police were also trying to recruit his friend, Aaron Sherritt, as an informer. If that was the reason, it paid off. During the first week in January 1879, Sherritt walked into the Benalla police station. He met with superintendent Hare and told him Dan Kelly and Byrne had visited his selection at two o'clock the previous afternoon. Hare recorded their first interview:

he [Joe Byrne] had always been his most intimate acquaintance; and sat down beside him; he had been his schoolfellow and with him in crime nearly all their lives. He said Dan Kelly was very suspicious, and would not get off his horse, and did not get near him. He said they sat talking for a long time, and then asked him to join them, as they were going to cross the Murray, and intended going to Goulburn where the Kellys had a cousin in New South Wales. He said they urged him for a long time to go as a scout. He . . . refused to go with them, and, after some pressing Joe Byrne said, 'Well, Aaron you are perfectly right; why should you get yourself into this trouble and mix yourself up with us?' He said they . . . kept looking around and watching every move that was made. He gave me the brands of the horses they were riding – Byrne was on a magnificent grey horse, and the other a bay.

Sherritt was given £2 for the information.

The following day, Victorian and New South Wales police were dispatched to watch the Murray River upstream from Albury. On 8 January, when nearly all the police not watching bridges were concentrated on both sides of the river near Albury, the Kelly gang were crossing it at Burramine, nearly 100 kilometres downstream.

Overleaf: Scene near the Buffalo Mountains.

11 THE JERILDERIE HOLD-UP
8 FEBRUARY 1879

According to Tom Lloyd – who claimed to have acted as a scout – the Kellys borrowed a boat from a publican named Burke and crossed the border at Burramine. They did it 'in two trips and swam their horses behind them, refreshing them after a long ride'. From there, they headed northwest into the Riverina district of New South Wales, out into the seemingly limitless red dust plain. The country was unwrinkled and broken only by occasional stunted timber and scrub for almost 75 kilometres to the Billabong Creek.

The Kellys reached Billabong Creek – three kilometres from Jerilderie – at 'about tea time' on Saturday 8 February 1879. They were not recognised at the Woolpack Inn that night, but a week later Samuel Gill's *Jerilderie Gazette* reported on what had been the most memorable few days in the town's history.

THE KELLYS AT JERILDERIE
KELLY AT DAVIDSON'S

It appeared that Ned and Dan Kelly called on Saturday night at Mrs Davidson's Woolpack Inn, where they had a great many drinks. Ned Kelly entered into conversation very freely with the barmaid, informing her that they had come from the back-blocks of the Lachlan. They asked a number of questions of the barmaid respecting Jerilderie. Ultimately the conversation turned on the Kellys, when they asked what did the people in Jerilderie say about the Kellys? They were informed that the Jerilderie people thought they were brave. The barmaid sang, by way of amusement, 'The Kellys have made another escape'. After several more drinks the Kellys engaged two beds, and said they would

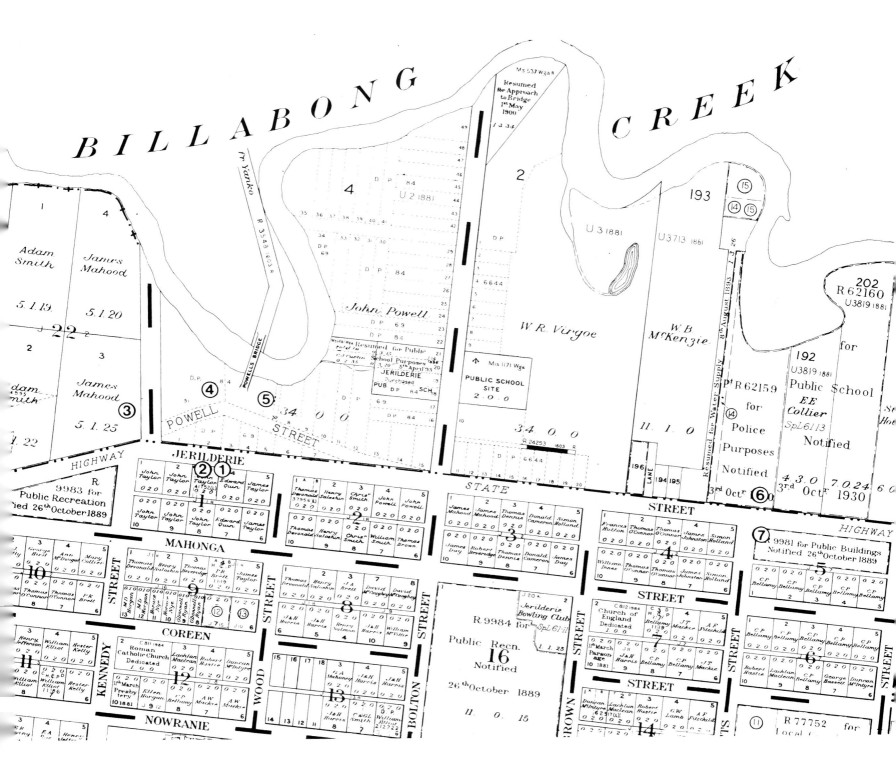

take a ride into Jerilderie and return again. They then mounted their horses and rode away, joining Hart and Byrne, who were only a short distance from the Hotel.

THE ATTACK

About midnight on Saturday the police barracks were surrounded by Ned Kelly, Dan Kelly, Hart and Byrne. Hart was placed at the west end of the barracks, Ned Kelly in front, Dan Kelly and Byrne at the rear of the premises. One of the gang shouted out – 'Police. Police! Get up, there is a great row at Davidson's Hotel.' Constable Richards, who was sleeping in a room at the rear, replied, got up, and went in the direction of the sound. In the meantime Devine had got on his trousers, opened the front door, and asked what was the matter. Constable Richards had, by this time, got round to the front door close to Devine, when Kelly, presenting two revolvers, saying, 'Hands up, I'm Kelly', and in an instant the other men came up with their revolvers, at the same time telling the police if they moved they would be shot. The idea Ned Kelly had in placing his men in different positions was this – when Devine opened the door and stepped onto the verandah he was covered by a man from behind, who could have shot him if he offered any resistance, or even if he had been armed. After securing the two policemen they were guarded by two of the gang, while the other two compelled Mrs Devine to go with them (in her night-dress) and show them where the arms and etc were kept. They kept strict watch till morning, when they locked the police in the lockup, and kept sentry over the premises on Sunday and Sunday night. On Sunday morning mass was celebrated in the Courthouse, distant 100 yards from the barracks, and as it is usual on these occasions for Mrs Devine to get the Courthouse ready for the service, about 10 a.m. she did so, but was accompanied by Dan Kelly, who escorted her to

Jerilderie, New South Wales. According to an 1879 handbook, 'settlers around Jerilderie are reputed to be the most wealthy and enterprising in the Riverina district'. It listed five hotels in the town, a courthouse, school, police barracks and lock-up, a bank, five stores, a population of 550 but not one church. The town's main commercial area was centred around Powell Street and Jerilderie Street – leaving the police station (6) and courthouse (7) particularly isolated. Other locations of interest were the bank (1), Cox's Royal Mail Hotel (2), the Gill's *Jerilderie Gazette* office (3), McDougall's Albion Hotel (4) and the telegraph office (5).

THE JERILDERIE HOLD-UP 135

Bailing up the police. The Melbourne artist who produced this picture took a very rough guess at details. The police station was actually built of slab with a front veranda. The lock-up resembled a small log cabin and was located a few yards to the right of the barracks. Only Ned Kelly was mounted – the other three did not appear until he had bailed up the two policemen.

Police recorded the Kelly visit with professional restraint: 'Week ending 15th of February 1879. 12pm. 8inst. While Senior Constable Devine and Constable Richards in bed, man called any police at home. On going to end of verandah was covered by man who said move and I'll shoot you I'm Kelly put up your hands. Three others of the Kelly Gang rushed from behind and surrounded both Constables – got Senior Constable's wife to show where arms were. Confined both Constables and Mrs Devine and family together with prisoner at barracks from 12pm.8inst. to 7pm. 10inst. Gang robbed bank Monday. Returned to barracks 4pm took two government horses, saddles, bridles, two cross belts, revolvers and other articles belonging to kits.'

and from the Courthouse, where he closely watched everything that was done by Mrs Devine. During Sunday the blinds of the barracks were all down. The two Kellys dressed out in police uniform, and during the day frequently walked from the barracks to the stable. On Sunday night Mrs Gill sent her two little children up to Mrs Devine's intending to go up shortly after, but the children returned saying Mrs Devine was not at home. Mrs Gill then took a walk in the direction of the barracks, and seeing a light there went up close to the door, when the light was put out. Mrs Gill then turned and went home, thinking that Mrs Devine might be going to bed, and took no further notice of the occurrence. During the time the police were locked up the Kellys conversed freely with Devine about the shooting of the three Constables, and stated that Kennedy fought to the last, but he denied having cut off his ear. Ned Kelly asked Devine if there was a printer in the town; that he wanted to see him very particularly, as he wanted him to print hand-bills and the history of his life. Kelly also read to Mrs Devine several pages of what he wanted printed, but Mrs Devine could not remember anything about it on Tuesday. Kelly also told Devine that he intended shooting him and Richards, but Mrs Devine begged them off, Ned Kelly said that if Devine did not leave the force in a month he would shoot him. On Sunday night Edward Kelly again rode up to Davidson's Hotel where he had a great many drinks, and entered freely into conversation with the barmaid and the two Miss Davidsons, who had not the remotest idea that he was the notorious Kelly. It is reported that Ned Kelly got so tight he had to be assisted into the saddle by the barmaid. He stopped at the Hotel until midnight, when he returned to the barracks. During Sunday night two of the gang would sleep while the other two kept watch, and so on until morning. On Sunday the revolvers were cleaned, every bullet being extracted, and the weapons carefully re-loaded for the dangerous work of the next day, which, we are glad to say, terminated without the loss of life. Early on Monday morning Byrne brought two horses to be shod, and Hart bought some meat in the butcher's shop. A little later Byrne went into one of the shops and bought a number of articles.

THE SURPRISE

No one in the town had the slightest idea that the Kellys were in Jerilderie. Several persons saw Ned and Dan Kelly, dressed in police uniform, in company with Constable Richards, coming down the town about 11 am on Monday, but had not the slightest idea they were the Kellys. They were taken for fresh police, and certainly from their outward appearance they looked to all intents and purposes like Constables, more especially when they were seen with Constable Richards. The townspeople could not realise the idea that the Kellys were here until they saw the Telegraph poles being cut down, and Ned Kelly walking in front of the Telegraph Office, revolver in hand. Shortly after 11 am Ned

Top: The Jerilderie courthouse was directly opposite the police station. 'The 9th happened to be visiting Sunday for Father Kiely to say mass, as usual, in the Courthouse. Mrs Devine was accustomed to prepare the altar for the service, and so on this occasion did so, but Dan Kelly accompanied her to see that she left no communication for the priest.'

Middle: Jerilderie Street, just before the Kellys raided the town in 1879. The view looks south-west from Wood Street. James Rankin, storekeeper Harkin, and the newspaper editor Samuel Gill, all fled the bank and were chased by Ned Kelly. The bank is located between Harkin's store and the Royal Mail Hotel. Gill got away and hid in the creek before escaping to an outlying station. He later stated, 'the three of us walked into the bank, there was no one in, but the way papers were strewn about showed something was wrong. Rankin knocked . . . a voice from the ante-room answered, "There in a moment" and in jumped Ned Kelly, calling "Stand". My companions made a rush for the door and I ducked down behind the counter then bounded in front of Harkin. Unfortunately, Rankin fell in the doorway, and I had to jump over him. In the meantime, Kelly jumped over the counter, caught Rankin, and overtook Harkin three or four yards up the verandah; but he could not catch sight of me, and I made good my escape.'

Bottom: The Royal Mail Hotel, some years later. This detail shows just how close the hotel was to Tarleton's safe. The window on the extreme left obscured by the tree was the bank's west window. The townspeople were held in the bar and parlour behind the man on the left. Most of them believed the gang had friends in the hotel and around the town during their stay — scouts who came over the border before them and returned afterwards. Schoolmaster Elliott wrote, 'there is no doubt that the outlaws had spies on the alert all day . . . it was significant that the two bankers had not left the town ten minutes when Ned Kelly came down.'

Bank of New South Wales. From left: clerk J. Mackie, Edwin Living and manager John Tarleton. The veranda of the Royal Mail (extreme right) was extended east along the rest of the block by 1879. The bank had barred windows but, like its occupants, provided no security against a hold-up. The branch was part of the hotel building and was previously used as an assembly hall. 'When it was rented by the bank in 1875, it was partitioned off into compartments . . . the Bank in 1875 constructed a porch inside the front entrance with a door leading into the room on the east [right] side where banking transactions were carried on. Right across this room to the south was the counter. Behind the counter were the teller's and junior's desks and the safe . . . at the end of the centre passage a back door opened onto the rear verandah of the Hotel. It was often mistaken by strangers – both sober and drunk – for part of the hotel.'

Aaron Sherritt said later, 'when the Kellys contemplated a robbery such as sticking up a bank, Byrne wrote down the plan, and then the party decided what part each of them was to take in the affair. Of the Jerilderie raid, Ned Kelly said he thought they made a mess of it.' Living remembered: 'while walking with Ned Kelly he said to me, "I have made a great blunder over this affair. I should not be surprised if we were caught this time" from other remarks I am of the opinion that he had originally intended sticking up the bank on Sunday.'

Ned Kelly and Steve Hart were not strangers to Jerilderie; Kelly 'was known to several when passing through in previous years' – a fact he confirmed during the raid. He was also supposed to have stayed, on one occasion in 1875, 'for a week at the Royal Mail Hotel'. In 1878, Steve Hart had made several trips to the town selling horses – probably for the Kellys while they were hiding in the Wombat Ranges. On his last trip he had argued with J. M. Curtin and was reported looking for him during the hold-up.

and Dan Kelly, with Constable Richards, entered the Royal Mail Hotel. Poor Richards was compelled to introduce the Kellys to Cox, the landlord of the Hotel, and Ned Kelly explained that he wanted the Bar Parlour for a few hours, as he was going to rob the bank, and, intended to fill the room with any townspeople who happened along. The astonished Mr Cox himself was the first prisoner placed in the room, and for the next hour everybody who came to the Hotel was marched into the same room till it was crowded. Then Byrne was despatched to the bank to fetch over the staff of that institution.

BANK TELLER LYVING'S [sic] NARRATIVE

About 10 minutes past twelve on Monday morning I was sitting at my desk in the bank when I heard footsteps approaching me from the direction of the back door. I at first took no notice, thinking it was the manager, Mr Tarleton. The footsteps continued approaching, when I turned round on the office stool and noticed a man. I immediately accosted the fellow, who looked rather stupid, as if he had been drinking. On asking him who he was and what right he had to enter the bank by the back way, he levelled a revolver at me, answered that he was Kelly, and ordered me to bail up. The fellow, who afterwards turned out to be Byrne, ordered me to deliver up what firearms I had. I replied that I had none. Young Mackie, who was standing in front of the bank, then came in, when Byrne told him to jump over the counter, which he did. He then told us to come with him to Cox's Hotel, and remarked that they had all the police stuck up. We went into the Hotel where we met Ned Kelly, who asked for Mr Tarleton, and was told he was in his room. We went back to the bank, but could not find the manager in his room. Ned Kelly said to me, 'You had better go and find him', I then searched, and found the manager in his bath. I was at first a little alarmed at not finding the manager in his room, and at first thought he had got some clue that the bushrangers were in the place, and cleared out. On finding the manager in his bath I said to him, 'We are stuck up; the Kellys are here, and the police are also stuck up'. Byrne then got Hart, and left him in charge of the manager, who was subsequently taken over to the room where all the others were kept prisoners. Ned Kelly took me into the bank and asked me what money we had in it. I replied that there was between £600 and £700, when Kelly said, 'You must have £10,000 in the bank here'. I then handed him the teller's cash, amounting to about £691. Mr Elliott, the schoolmaster, then came into the bank, and as soon as Kelly saw him he ordered him to jump over the counter, Mr Elliott replied that he could not, but Kelly made him, and they then tried to put the money in a bag, but not having one sufficiently large, Ned Kelly went and brought another, and we put the money into it. Kelly asked if we had more money, and was answered 'No'. Kelly then obtained the teller's revolver, and again requested more money. He then went to the treasury drawer, and requested to know what was in it, and was told by me that it contained nothing of any value. Kelly insisted on it being opened, and one of the keys was given to him, but he could not open it, owing to the manager having the second key, which was required to open it. Byrne then wanted to break it open with a sledge hammer, but Kelly brought the manager from the Royal Hotel and demanded the key, which was given to him, and the drawer was opened, when the sum of £1450 was taken out by Kelly and placed in a bag, Kelly then took down a large deed box, and asked what it contained, and was told that it contained a few documents which were of no use. He replied that he would burn the contents, but Mr Tarleton argued with him, and Kelly took one document and put it in the bag, and then expressed his intention of burning all the books in the office. He, however, left the rest of the papers, and said he would come back and see if there were any deeds to town allotments. The whole party then went into the Royal Hotel. Daniel Kelly was in the hotel, and Ned Kelly took two of the prisoners out to the back of the hotel, where they made a fire and burnt three or four of the bank books. In the meantime Mr Rankin and Mr Gill, seeing the bank door open, went in, and were immediately met by Kelly, who ordered them to bail up. Both gentlemen at once made off, Mr Rankin running into the hotel, and Mr Gill in some other direction. Ned Kelly ran after Rankin and caught him in the hotel. Kelly caught him by his collar, and asked him why he ran away, at the same time telling him to go into the passage, and that he intended to shoot him. Several persons called out to Kelly not to fire, and he did not.

He then called Hart by the name of 'Revenge' and told him to shoot the first man that attempted any resistance, and told Rankin if he attempted anything he would be the first person shot. Kelly then asked for Gill, and took Richards and me with him to look for Gill. The policeman had his revolver with him, but Kelly had previously withdrawn the cartridges. We went up to Mrs Gill's house and saw Mrs Gill. Kelly said to her, 'I have a statement here which contains a little act of my life, and I want it published by Mr Gill; will you take it?' She refused to do so. I then took the paper, and promised to have it published. The party then went to McDougall's hotel, where Ned Kelly took a blood mare out of the stable, and remarked that he would take the animal, but would return it in three weeks. The party then went to the Telegraph Office where we met Byrne, who had cut the wires. Ned Kelly then broke the insulators at the office with his revolver, said he would have the poles cut down, and after this he took the postmaster and his assistant to the Royal Hotel and left the party there. Kelly then returned to the bank and obtained my saddle and a pair of riding

Schoolteacher William Elliott was captured in the bank after dismissing his children for lunch: 'when told that his latest capture was the schoolmaster, Kelly ordered him to write out a notice giving the children a holiday and he (Kelly) would sign it, in honour of his visit to their town.' Elliott kept a diary and compiled a detailed account of the Kelly raid. While he was impressed with Ned Kelly, he had no sympathy for the outlaws and urged that 'only his example kept the four desperadoes together'. Elliott also took notes of Kelly's speech in the Royal Mail Hotel: 'He said that he and his family had been persecuted and harassed almost continually by the Victorian police . . . ever since he was a lad of fourteen . . . the outlaw spoke of the time Fitzpatrick came to arrest his brother Dan for horse stealing . . . added that the Constable was a confounded liar . . . said these lies got his mother into trouble and drove him and his brother away from their home; even then they were hunted for like wild beasts. He said, had the police surrendered no harm would have come to them . . . "Had the police shot us", the outlaw said, "they would have been praised by the people and the papers for their courage, but as it turned out they were shot; we were denounced as murderers and blood-thirsty ruffians. And yet, where is the difference? We all had to risk our lives in the encounter."'

trousers belonging to Mr Tarleton, and also a gold chain and gold watch. The saddle was then put on McDougall's mare, and Dan Kelly mounting rode away, but returned in five minutes. Dan Kelly and Hart then both kept guard at the hotel, and Ned Kelly informed the postmaster that if he attempted to mend the wires before next day, or offered any resistance, he would be shot. He also told Mr Jefferson that he intended to take him a few miles into the bush and then liberate him. He informed those present that he intended sticking up the Urana Coach that night, and would shoot anyone who attempted to give warning . . . the gang then rode in the direction of the police camp.

Kelly was bitterly disappointed that he was not able to get his **'Jerilderie Letter'** published. This account expanded on the Cameron letter and was a revealing 8,300-word document: part autobiography, part self-defence. Kelly finished the previous account with 'I need no lead or powder to avenge my cause, if words be louder' – and this was his second attempt. Dictated mostly to Joe Byrne and possibly other helpers, it embellished the same themes and arguments: inequities and miscarriages of justice, persecution and deceit of local police towards his family and the unjust imprisonment of his mother, two neighbours and alleged sympathisers. Again, he claimed the shooting of the policemen was self-defence. The written argument is emotionally charged but most of it stands up to scrutiny in essential detail. The prose rambles but is full of literary allusions and puns – highlighting how Kelly saw his cause as social rebellion. The writing contradicts the idea that the gang were simple, illiterate thugs.

BANK MANAGER TARLETON'S NARRATIVE

Mr Tarleton stated: 'I had returned from a long ride of about forty miles, and after looking over the letters I went to have a bath, the day being a very hot one. I was just about to turn the tap of the shower when the teller burst open the door, and in an excited manner said, 'We are stuck up at last, the Kellys are here now'. I said, 'Oh rubbish', and thought it was only a joke, but when I saw the two men following him, both having a revolver in each hand, I realised the position fully. Mr Lyving said, 'It is no use resisting; the police are locked up, and they have got about twenty people bailed up in the Royal'. I replied, 'Oh well, all right; as soon as I have done my bath I will come in'. Hart was left in charge of me while I finished my bath. Whenever I approached him he levelled two revolvers at me. He searched my clothes for firearms, but they contained none. I began to question him about the past movements and future intentions of the gang, but, after answering one or two unimportant questions, he apparently got tired, saying, 'Come, no more of these questions. I will not have any more.' I replied that it was quite immaterial to me whether he answered them or not. When I was habited in a silk coat, a pair of trousers, and a smoking cap, he ordered me to come out, and took me with him into the Royal Hotel. As we passed in I saw Byrne hit the Chinese cook of the hotel a tremendous blow under the ear because the celestial refused to go into the parlour when ordered to bail up. After the blow the celestial went in as meek as a lamb. I was put with the others, of whom, at the time, there were about twenty. I was in the Hotel bailed up for the remainder of the time that the gang were in the township, with the exception of the short period during which Ned Kelly took me into the bank to hand over the money out of the treasury drawer. Hart stood at the door with my revolver and two of his own in his hands, while Dan Kelly paraded up and down on top of the bar, from which he could also command the room through the second door. Occasionally, if there was too much talking going on, Hart, who seemed to be most particularly anxious to shoot somebody, would interfere. He would say, 'There must be less noise'. Several times, when persons looked out of the windows, he went and pulled them back, saying that they would get themselves shot. He repeated the threat of shooting about twenty or thirty times altogether for different offences. I was sitting near Hart for a long time and I noticed that when his attention was attracted to another quarter it would be a perfectly easy matter to knock him down, but the trooper replied, 'If you look over your shoulder, you will see that Dan Kelly has us covered. If neither of us is shot, somebody on the other side of the room will be.' Dan Kelly was, as before stated, in the main bar, I can corroborate the J. G. Rankin incident, as related by Mr Living. Ned Kelly shouted very freely, and paid for every drink to Mr Cox, the landlord. They asked me to drink when I first came in, but I refused. Before going away Ned Kelly delivered an harangue in the bar, with the evident intention of exciting sympathy. He also said, 'I have come here, not so much to stick up the bank, but to shoot these two policemen. They are worse than any blacktrackers, especially that man Richards. They have followed me up closely; that man Richards particularly is one whom I have a down on. I am going to shoot him directly.' We all attempted to intercede for Richards' life, but Kelly repeated, 'No, he must die'. Richards seemed to take the matter very coolly, and notwithstanding all Ned Kelly's bloodthirsty threats, never once changed colour. Ned's speech was very much interrupted by a person who was inebriated. Ned then took Richards, Jefferson the postmaster, and his assistant, young Rankin, away in the direction of the police camp, telling us that we might go as soon as we liked. Dan Kelly and Hart mounted their horses and rode up the street, shouting and gesticulating. Dan Kelly flourished his revolver over his head in the most approved braggardoccio fashion.

Dan Kelly also carried a rifle slung over his shoulder. The two Kellys, it might be mentioned, were dressed in trooper's uniforms, while Hart and Byrne were habited in ordinary tweed. As soon as I had sent a messenger to Urana by a roundabout route to warn the bank manager there, I, having got a horse, started for Deniliquin. I was told the Kellys were engaged in making a bonfire at the police camp, and that they had set scouts in ambush to shoot anyone who attempted to leave the township before the restricted time . . . I told the people I thought I should be able to gallop away from any scouts . . . I left soon after Living and arrived at Deniliquin at a quarter to six a.m.

AFTER THE BANK HAD BEEN ROBBED

Ned Kelly, in company with Mr Lyving and Richards, went round to McDougall's Hotel. Kelly asked McDougall if he had a racing mare called Minnie. McDougall: 'Yes'. Kelly: 'I want her' ordering the groom to bring her out of the stable. Kelly:

The Jerilderie post and telegraph office was not put out of action until after the robbery, yet no warning was transmitted. Byrne captured the postmaster and assistant completely by surprise, cut and tangled all the office wiring, and Ned Kelly smashed the insulators on the nearest veranda post. Still not satisfied, they forced two men to chop down nearly half a mile of telegraph poles.

'What do you value the mare at?' McDougall: '£50'. Kelly: 'If I take the mare away with me I will give you that amount for her'. Kelly then took the mare away to the police barracks.

KELLY'S SPEECH AT THE ROYAL
After the robbery of the bank had been effected, and just before the prisoners were released from the Royal Mail, Edward Kelly delivered the following speech: 'Boys, I'll tell you how I'm an outlaw, and how I've been treated by the police in Victoria. When I was accused by Fitzpatrick of shooting him, I swear I was 400 miles away from home. When I heard of the way he treated my sister, I hurried home, and found that I was accused of shooting Fitzpatrick. I don't like to present a revolver at any man, as it naturally makes him tremble, unless I am compelled to do so, but what must have been the feelings of my sister – a mere child – when she had a revolver put to her head demanding her to submit her virtue, or be shot by the villain Fitzpatrick. I don't deny having stolen horses, and sold them, but of shooting Fitzpatrick I was entirely innocent. When outlawed I was only three weeks married. When we came upon the police they were fully armed. All I had was an old rifle, with a barrel shaking about. Enough of this, you will find it all in the paper I have left to be printed.

ADDITIONAL PARTICULARS
While Ned Kelly was in the town, the Rev. Gribble, who was passing along the street, accosted him, and informing him who he was, asked him, as a personal favour, to leave Miss McDougall's horse, which he was riding. He jumped off the horse, and in a most respectful manner said, 'It is not my fault, Sir, that the horse was not returned. If Mr McDougall or his daughter had asked me personally, they should have had it. But one of my chaps promised to send it back through the police, and I would not have that, so I determined not to give it up'. Mr Gribble then remarked, 'It is a pity to deprive the girl of her horse; perhaps before you leave you might call at McDougall's and speak to him about it'. Kelly said, 'I will', and springing into the saddle, rode off. When the mare was at the barracks Kelly sent word to Mary McDougall that if she came and asked for the mare herself, he would give her to her. Miss McDougall then went down to the barracks when Hart was going to give her the mare, but Kelly would not allow him to do so, saying 'You need not take her down, I will have her sent back which he did, with Mr Lyving's saddle, giving instructions that the saddle was to be restored to him.

THE PARSON STUCK UP
While the Rev. Gribble was engaged speaking to Mr McDougall about getting back his horse, Steve Hart came up, and without the least ceremony, bailed the Rev. gentleman up, and demanded his watch and guard. Mr Gribble wondered for a moment whether he could really be in earnest, and then said, 'Surely you cannot take a poor parson's watch?' Hart replied, 'A parson is no more to me than any other man, out with your watch', and Mr Gribble was, with great reluctance, compelled to deliver up the articles. He however, resolved to get them back; if possible, so he watched his opportunity for meeting Ned Kelly unobserved by Steve Hart, and said, 'One of your men has stuck me up, and took my watch and guard. I am a poor man and cannot afford to lose them; and moreover, the watch belongs to a friend'. In an excited manner Ned Kelly replied, 'One of my men stuck you up? Show me the man.' Mr Gribble then led him to McDougall's verandah, where Hart was busy saddling his horse, and said, 'There', pointing to Hart. Ned Kelly said, 'Did you take this man's watch?' Hart said, 'Yes I did'. 'What made you take it?' replied Kelly. 'Because I wanted it', replied Hart. Kelly then demanded the watch; and after examining it, said, 'Why, the watch you took from the other man (referring to the bank manager) is a better one than this. Why can't you be satisfied with the watch you've got, and if you stick a man up for a watch, stick him for a good one! Give the man his watch', handing it to Hart who gave it back to Mr Gribble, Ned Kelly making the remark, 'It's just his crossness, because I wouldn't let him have his own way today'.

ACCOMPLICES
There cannot be any doubt that the gang was assisted here on Monday, as we never remember seeing so many strangers about. At the hotel Kelly said he had a great many friends – and if anyone tried to shoot him the people would soon see who were on his side. In fact the town was full of them. Where they came from, and where they went, no one knows. It was supposed that the last of their confederates only left Jerilderie on Thursday afternoon, the 13th.

THE DEPARTURE
After all the old clothes of the Kelly gang had been burnt at the barracks, Ned Kelly and Hart came down to the town again for the last time, when Kelly went into McDougall's Hotel, shouted and paid for what drinks he called for. At this time the bar was crowded with strangers. Kelly also took two bottles of brandy, which he paid for, with him. Before he mounted his horse he said 'Anyone could shoot me; but if a shot was fired, the people of Jerilderie would swim in their own blood'. He also said he would not be taken alive, before he would allow the police to shoot him he would take his own life, at the same time pulling a small revolver from his breast, and showing those by him how he would do it. He added that he was not afraid to die at any time – all that he

had on his conscience was the shooting – in self-defence – of three unicorns. A short time after this Kelly got on his horse, and with Hart galloped off singing: 'Hurrah for the good old times of Morgan and Ben Hall!' the strangers giving a cheer. They went on the Deniliquin road a short distance, but suddenly wheeled round in the direction of Wunnamurra, joining Byrne and Dan Kelly about a mile from the town – the last two men having charge of the money taken from the bank – which was securely fixed on a spare horse.

AT WUNNAMURRA STATION

The gang went straight to Wunnamurra station and on the way held up Mr A. Mackie, brother of the bank assistant. Ned Kelly, in a defiant manner, demanded, 'Is your brother out on Wunnamurra station?' To which Mackie answered, 'I do not know'. Kelly said 'I am going to shoot him because he helped to catch the horses for Tarleton and Lyving, and I will go down and burn the homestead for giving them fresh horses to go on with'. The gang had evidently learned from some of their spies that Living and Tarleton had ridden off for Deniliquin, and they seemed to think Mr J. Mackie, on his release from the hotel, had gone to the station and provided fresh horses for them. At the Wunnamurra homestead Ned told Hart and Byrne to push on their way, which they did, taking the packhorse and the proceeds of the robbery. After some conversation Kelly asked one of the station people where Tarleton and Living were, to which the person answered 'I do not know'. Finding the bankers had not been there, Kelly at once became affable in his manner, and conversed freely. He said, handling his revolver, 'I will shoot that hound Living whenever I see him. I gave him everything he asked for that was his. He begged and prayed in the bank for me not to destroy his life policy, and when I was taking his saddle he almost cried and begged me to give it back, saying he was a poor man. I gave it back; and now as soon as he gets a chance, he rushes off to betray me to the traps.' He asked for a drink of water, and then he and Dan rode off in the direction of Berrigan station. That was the last seen of them on this side of the Murray.

DESCRIPTION OF THE OUTLAWS

While in Jerilderie Ned Kelly was asked who was his best and most reliable man in his gang, his brother being suggested as the most likely. Kelly, however, shook his head, and pointing to Byrne, remarked, 'No, that's the fellow. He's as cool and firm as steel.' Ned Kelly does not in any way resemble his likeness as shown in the Illustrated Journals. He stands nearly six feet high and wears a beard about two and a half inches long. He is well built and appears a very active and powerful man. He has a thorough command of the gang, and allows nothing to be done without his sanction. Without doubt he is the man who concocts all the plans and makes the others carry out his wishes. He appears to have the powers of a commander. His looks even infuse terror into his comrades. No one, from his appearance, would take him for a bushranger, and if dressed out in a black suit anyone would take him for a gentleman; at the same time when he is in a rage and disappointed, he looks a demon. He can also be very civil and courteous when he likes – this was proved on Monday when he was speaking to females. All the women he treated very courteously, and spoke to them kindly. Kelly treated the Rev. Mr Gribble with kindness, conversed with him in a reasonable manner, so much so that the Rev. gentleman was not at all afraid of him.

Joe Byrne stands nearly six feet high, long features, fair complexion, and an effeminate cast of countenance, and of a nervous disposition; his manner is quiet, and he appears to a casual observer an inoffensive man.

Dan Kelly could not be recognised from the likeness published; he is a moderate-sized man, about five feet seven inches high, sallow complexion, black hair, and a fine pair of dark eyes, and rather a pleasing look when smiling. About 20 years of age, Steve Hart is a small man, fair complexion, dark hair, small growth of whiskers, dark grey eyes, and appears as though he was 'on needles and pins', but not at all a frightened look or nervous.

12 THE GREAT DISAPPEARANCE, PART ONE

FEBRUARY–JUNE 1879

The first telegrams regarding the Jerilderie hold-up reached Sydney and Melbourne only hours after the gang left Wunnamurra station. These telegrams also brought fear and confusion. By the time the police reached the border they could not even find where the gang had crossed; newspapers were quick to level their customary abuse. That New South Wales had invited the raid by boasts of a superior police force was as clear as their humiliation. The Melbourne *Herald* reported: 'The Victorian police have been subjected to a great amount of "chaff" in connection with the doings of the Kellys, but they have now the satisfaction of knowing that the New South Wales police have been subjected to greater insult.'

Back in their home districts, the Kellys again went into hiding. The New South Wales–Victorian government reward for their capture inflated to £8,000, but was adequately countered by the outlaws distributing their bank proceeds among sympathisers from one locality to another. The gang continued to move about, never showed themselves openly and in turn, the hunt for them rambled on without any sign of drawing to a close. In the weeks following the Jerilderie raid, there were several incidents credited to the outlaws that were never explained. On 24 February, telegraph wires were cut in four places on each side of Howlong and police believed that it was 'done by Kelly confederates for the purpose of creating a sensation and concentrating police from other localities'. In March, police were given the startling news that the Kellys 'had procured some dynamite and intended blowing up

V. R.

£8000 REWARD

ROBBERY and MURDER.

WHEREAS EDWARD KELLY, DANIEL KELLY, STEPHEN HART, and JOSEPH BYRNE have been declared OUTLAWS in the Colony of Victoria, and whereas warrants have been issued charging the aforesaid men with the WILFUL MURDER of MICHAEL SCANLON, Police Constable of the Colony of VICTORIA, and whereas the above-named offenders are STILL at LARGE and have recently committed divers felonies in the Colony of NEW SOUTH WALES: Now, therefore I, SIR HERCULES GEORGE ROBERT ROBINSON, the GOVERNOR, do, by this, my proclamation issued with the advice of the Executive Council, hereby notify that a REWARD of £4,000 will be paid, three-fourths by the Government of NEW SOUTH WALES, and one-fourth by certain Banks trading in the Colony, for the apprehension of the above-named Four Offenders, or a reward of £1000 for the apprehension of any one of them, and that in ADDITION to the above reward, a similar REWARD of £4000 has been offered by the Government of VICTORIA, and I further notify that the said REWARD will be equitably apportioned between any persons giving information which shall lead to the apprehension of the offenders and any members of the police force or other persons who may actually effect such apprehension or assist thereat.

(Signed) HENRY PARKES,
Colonial Secretary, New South Wales.

(Signed) BRYAN O'LOGHLEN,
Attorney-General, Victoria.

Dated 15th February, 1879.

£8,000 REWARD!

Proclamation by His Excellency Sir Hercules George Robert Robinson, Knight Grand Cross of The Most Distinguished Order of St. Michael and St. George, Governor and Commander-in-Chief of the Colony of New South Wales and its dependencies, and Vice-Admiral of the same.

WHEREAS Edward Kelly, Daniel Kelly, Stephen Hart, and Joseph Byrnes have been proclaimed outlaws in the Colony of Victoria, and whereas warrants have been issued by James Bambrick, Esq., J.P., at Wodonga, Victoria, charging Edward Kelly, Daniel Kelly, and two men whose names were then unknown, with the wilful murder of Michael Scanlon, police constable, of the Colony of Victoria, and the said warrants have been duly endorsed by Captain Brownrigg, police magistrate at Albury, to have force in the Colony of New South Wales, and whereas Victorian warrants, duly backed for execution in New South Wales, were subsequently granted for the apprehension of Stephen Hart and Joseph Byrnes, charging them with the murder of the aforesaid Michael Scanlon, and whereas the abovenamed offenders are still at large, and have recently committed divers felonies in the Colony of New South Wales: now therefore, I, Sir Hercules George Robert Robinson, the Governor aforesaid, do by this my proclamation, issued with the advice of the Executive Council, hereby notify that a reward of four thousand pounds will be paid—three-fourths by the Government of New South Wales and one-fourth by certain banks trading in the colony—for the apprehension of the abovenamed four offenders, a reward of one thousand pounds for the apprehension of any one of them, and that, in addition to the above reward, a similar reward of four thousand pounds has been offered by the Government of Victoria. And I further notify that the said reward will be equitably apportioned between any person giving information which shall lead to the apprehension of the offenders and any member of the police force or other persons who may effectually effect such apprehension or assist thereat, and that if, in attempting to effect the capture of the said offenders, any member of the police force should be wounded, thereby incapacitating him from earning a livelihood, he will be pensioned, or in the event of any member of the police force losing his life in the execution of such duty, his widow or family depending upon him for support will be provided for by the Government.

Given under my hand and seal at Government House, Sydney, this eighteenth day of February, in the year of our Lord one thousand eight hundred and seventy-nine, and in the forty-second year of Her Majesty's reign.

By Command,

HENRY PARKES.

V. R.

MURDER OF POLICE.
£4000 REWARD.

WHEREAS, by a notice published in the *Government Gazette*, bearing date 13th December 1878, a Reward of TWO THOUSAND FIVE HUNDRED POUNDS was offered for the capture of four offenders charged with the murder of certain members of the Police Force, in the King River District: AND WHEREAS it is decided to increase the Reward to FOUR THOUSAND POUNDS (£4000): NOTICE IS HEREBY GIVEN that a Reward of ONE THOUSAND POUNDS (£1000) will be paid by the Government for the capture of or for such information as will lead to the capture of each of the said offenders as described in the *Government Gazette*, No. 113, 30th October 1878, and whose names are as under:—

EDWARD KELLY,   STEPHEN HART, and
DANIEL KELLY,   JOSEPH BYRNE.

BRYAN O'LOGHLEN, Acting Chief Secretary.

---

the railway line in revenge for the arrest of [sympathisers]'. Then, each night for a week, the Wangaratta–Beechworth telegraph line was mysteriously jammed – although never interfered with again. In the same month, the police were sure that the outlaws had moved on from their usual haunts.

During this period, the alleged Kelly sympathisers were still in Beechworth Gaol on successive remands – and still without evidence of guilt. But their court appearances were not without incident. On 11 February, relieving magistrate Alfred Wyatt took the bench and among remarks to other prisoners, said to Wild Isaiah Wright: 'Wright, you and I have met before.' Wright answered sarcastically but with meaning, 'There is no fear of the Kellys killing me if I was out. You will not get the Kellys until Parliament meets and Mrs Kelly is let go, and Fitzpatrick lagged in her place.' Judge Wyatt again remanded the sympathisers and caused a sensation when he added: 'I would give you fair play if I could'.

At the next remand, Wright said to Wyatt, 'Your Worship promised to give me fair play; it does not seem like it, I don't know how some of the men stand it!' Wright then turned to superintendent Hare and remarked, 'No wonder you blush to ask to keep us longer – are you not ashamed?' The other prisoners took his lead and impertinence became a regular part of the proceedings; the magistrates, knowing the law was under strain, overlooked the contempt.

The reward posters. Outraged banking houses and the New South Wales Government co-operated to double the £4,000 reward offered in Victoria after the Jerilderie robbery. The grand total of £2,000 per outlaw advertised on 15 February 1879 was the highest ever offered for bushrangers in the Australian colonies. The offer was even printed in Chinese because storekeepers and gold-buyers at the Woolshed and the upper King and Buckland rivers were known to be aiding them.

For Ned Kelly, their latest exploit was a mixture of success and failure. It appears that he was just as concerned with getting his statement published as with gaining extra funds. Ned Kelly's Jerilderie letter (see page 140) was suppressed like its predecessor. Edwin Living did not hand the document on to the local editor Samuel Gill as he had promised. When major newspapers in Melbourne and Sydney heard of the letter, they sent representatives to the town to purchase the article. The Melbourne *Argus* offered £10 and the *Age* offered ten guineas, but the New South Wales attorney general wired instructions to Jerilderie to prevent publication of the account. The only version of the letter to appear in the press was a brief synopsis by the schoolmaster William Elliott. His account was reproduced in the *Jerilderie Gazette* and the Melbourne *Herald*. The Kellys went back to Victoria unaware, for the meantime at least, that the second of their statements failed to receive serious attention.

The alleged sympathisers were not a happy or peaceful crowd. On one occasion, Wild Wright and John McElroy started fighting in the gaol exercise yard; McElroy was getting a sound thrashing until two others pinioned Wright while another knocked him unconscious. In another incident, Wright got into a savage brawl with two prisoners. All of them were lined up in the main yard waiting their turn at the washbasins. Wright had an annoying habit of ignoring the queue and would push anyone aside, saying, 'Men first, dogs come last!' Benjamin Gould and Francis Harty eventually lost patience and flew at him; Wright knocked both men out and fractured three of Gould's ribs. From then on he was kept in a separate division of the gaol. Joseph Ryan also broke his leg during this time, supposedly while 'sky-larking'.

On 18 February, application was made to the Melbourne Supreme Court for a 'writ of habeas corpus' on behalf of John McElroy, intended as a test case for his fellow sufferers — and Ned Kelly was supposed to have supplied the legal costs. Judge Redmond Barry rejected the application over a technicality — the prisoner's affidavit was not counter-signed by two witnesses. But the following week five more of the men were released without apology, John McElroy among them. Like the others (Thomas Lloyd senior, Michael Haney, Joseph Ryan and John McMonigal) McElroy probably went home more determined to support the outlaws. When the remaining men came up for remand, James Quinn yelled out, 'How many more eight days?' Wright gave reason to be remanded again by snarling at the magistrate, 'If I ever get out of this, I'll make my name a terror to you!' The remaining prisoners were finally released on 23 April 1879 after serving 107 days on no more than suspicion. A government report two years later referred to the arrests:

They were not salutary in their effects. They did violence to people's ideas of liberty . . . irritated and estranged many who might have been of service to the police, they failed to prevent the gang from obtaining supplies . . . and, what was of more significance, the failure of the prosecutions led the public to believe that the conduct of the affair had been mismanaged.

While newspapers condemned the waning police effort, and Kelly supporters aimed abuse at the law from the Beechworth dock, police leaders were bewildered to find that other relatives and connections had eagerly taken over supporting the gang. Superintendent Hare complained that: 'Hart had a sister and brother, and they were always on the move. Byrne had [two] brothers and [three] sisters;

the former were always riding about. Reports used to come in that Mrs Skillion used to be seen at all hours of the night riding about the bush, sometimes with large packs tied on her saddle.'

After the conviction of her husband and mother in October 1878, Margaret Skillion — the eldest surviving Kelly daughter — had taken over management of the Kelly and Skillion selections and provided for both families. Margaret and her two children lived in the Skillion hut with her siblings Kate and Grace Kelly and Ellen and John King. The Kelly homestead was only occupied intermittently by friends and relatives — James Quinn was staying there when he was arrested as a Kelly sympathiser and Francis Harty had been grazing stock on Mrs Kelly's land when he was taken on the same day in January. The men of the Kelly clan took it in turn to live at Mrs Skillion's or the Kelly hut, evidently to support and protect the women. Tom Lloyd was often there and Wild Wright stayed with the women after his release in April 1879.

The gang owed much of their survival to Mrs Skillion's support. There is no doubt that Margaret Skillion and Tom Lloyd were the main contacts for the gang; Margaret was one of only a few people to hold their complete trust. As early as November 1878, Margaret Skillion and Kate Kelly were seen

Main gates, Beechworth Gaol. In the month following the Jerilderie raid, local prison officials feared that the outlaws would rally support to attack the gaol and rescue their friends. As a precaution, an alleged £7,000 was spent replacing the wooden gates of the gaol with iron gates, thereby making it 'Kelly proof'. Ironically, the sympathisers had been released for months before renovations were completed.

Joseph Ryan was another of the infamous inner circle that dedicated nearly two years of his life to the Kelly cause. He was born at Beveridge on a small farm near the Kelly block; his mother, Anne, was Red Kelly's sister. He was only five years old when the Kellys moved north to Avenel; the Ryans followed some years later, settling near Lake Rowan in the north-east. The families maintained close connections, despite occasional friction between Anne Ryan and Ellen Kelly. Joe was nineteen years old when he was arrested as a sympathiser in January 1879. He was remanded in Beechworth Gaol, where he broke his leg, but upon release he was busy annoying and misleading police again.

buying extra quantities of provisions at Benalla stores; liquor and tobacco included in their shopping. 'Large bakings' were reported at the Skillion home and Margaret was known to be cooking far more meat than her large household could consume. Superintendent Sadleir confirmed that Mrs Skillion or Kate Kelly 'often went out early after dark and returned in the morning'.

The Kelly and Skillion selections were intermittently under surveillance, but police found it useless to keep constant watch or follow the women's nightly expeditions. Occasionally, the police did watch activities at the two huts from a ridge running along the north side of the Greta road. Legend has it that the gang or their scouts used to watch the troopers three kilometres away, from the peak of the Bald Hills.

The gang almost surely visited Mrs Skillion up until March 1879. During one observation, troopers saw horses tied up and heard the music of a concertina. They advanced and surrounded the small hut, but were kept at bay by a pack of barking dogs. Suddenly, the music stopped, the lights went out and men were seen moving about in the shadows. The constables panicked and retreated. On another occasion, a troop of twelve mounted police on patrol from Benalla passed the Skillion selection on their way to Greta. They left the road and went over to the north-west corner of the block near the hut, but turned at the last minute and cantered on. The Kellys were said to have been inside making hasty preparations for an expected battle.

Superintendent Hare, in charge of pursuing the outlaws until July 1879, detailed repeated attempts to follow up movements of Mrs Skillion and Kate Kelly:

Mrs Skillion and Katey Kelly were aware they were being watched, and nearly every night before they went to bed they would take their dogs and hunt round the bush within several hundred yards of the house. Very often the dogs discovered the police lying on the ground, and then commenced barking at them until the women came up. It appeared as if the dogs knew [we] were their natural enemies . . . the sympathisers' dogs and dogs belonging to relatives were a great nuisance to us.

One night, Hare tried to fix the problem:

I appointed a man with a few baits and a bag, Strychnine on pieces of meat, and told him to drop one here and there. But after that you could not poison the dogs about the place if you tried. They always had muzzles on day and night, and I have seen Mrs Skillion and Katey Kelly come into Benalla with the dogs muzzled . . . One morning before daybreak some policemen got within a short distance of Mrs Skillion's house and in some way she must have become aware of their presence. She went out into the paddock about three or four o'clock, caught her horse, and started off towards the mountains, the three policemen following. She made for a steep gap in the mountains, the men following on foot, thinking they had a good thing on hand. The sun was nearly up when they reached the top of the gap, and the first thing they saw was Mrs Skillion sitting on a log facing them, with her two hands extended from her nose, taking what is called a 'lunar' at them, with a grin of satisfaction on her face. They went up to examine a pack on her saddle and found it to be an old table-cloth wrapped up.

Poetic warning. Like Joe Byrne, Joe Ryan had a talent for balladry. The stanzas preserved on the battered copy-book page formed part of one composed by Ryan and sent as a warning to a local selector suspected of aiding police. Sympathisers favoured double-meaning ultimatums in the Fenian tradition of threatening letters: easily understood but unlikely to attract prosecution.

Initially, police regularly followed Mrs Skillion and would unwittingly show themselves, but eventually, police leaders claimed that it was useless following the women because they were so cautious, and they were left to come and go as they pleased.

In February 1879, other watch parties had been formed in the hope of ambushing the outlaws if they visited any of their families' selections. One was established south of Wangaratta near the Hart selection, and superintendent Hare joined seven troopers camped in caves on the Woolshed Valley near Mrs Byrne's place. The caves – on the range east of 'Byrne's Gully' – are supposed to have been used previously by the Kellys. They were pointed out to Hare by his valuable new helper, Aaron Sherritt, whose selection was about a two and a half kilometres further south. Their vigil lasted 25 nights and coincided with the most heated controversy regarding the remanded sympathisers at Beechworth. Each night, Hare and his men would sneak down the valley wall to take positions around Mrs Byrne's home. The risk they took was as great as the odds against their presence being kept secret.

On the reassurance that Joe Byrne would be spared, Sherritt began a more dangerous double game. He visited the Byrne family – and his sweetheart Catherine Byrne – as often as he hid outside with the police, all the while pledging loyalty to both sides. It seems hardly credible that Hare expected eight and sometimes nine men to stalk around the house for nearly four weeks without leaving obvious signs, or live within a mile of it without being seen. The caves were clearly visible from the valley and Sebastopol and the police had to walk down to Reedy Creek for their water supply.

Discovery was inevitable. Mrs Byrne need not have been a 'wry, suspicious woman' to discover the surveillance. Every day, Joe's brothers – Patrick and Dennis – and their mother would gather their cat-

No. 1—THE VICTORIAN POLICE.

THROUGHOUT Victoria's country towns
   Has gone an awful scare,
For rumour says the Kelly band,
   Are here and everywhere;
And country people's faces,
   Are blanched with very fear,
They tremble in their shoes to think,
   The Kellys may be near.

And all Victoria's Peelers,
   Have been upon their track,
They either can't catch up to them,
   Or else the pluck they lack;
And the Bobbies can't entice them
   Within their widespread net;
The Kellys snap their fingers, and
   Remain at large as yet.

And gallant Captain Standish marched
   Up-country with his men;
The Kellys wouldn't wait for him,
   So he marched back again.
In spite of martial Standish,
   And troopers trim and starch,
With all their counter marching,
   The Kellys steal a march.

And Kelly swears he'll go to town,
   And, spite of all demur,
Will seize on Captain Standish,
   And take him prisoner.
And Standish lets the whole police
   Be managed by his sub.;
To hunting robbers he prefers
   Whist playing at his club.

And managers in country banks,
   And every country town,
Look scowling at their customers,
   With too suspicious frown;
For the vision of the Kellys
   Before their eyes now stands,
And they always do their business with
   Revolvers in both hands.

No. 2—POLICE IN N. S. WALES.

HOW different is the story,
   And well may we exult
That our policemen brought about
   A different result;
No marching through the country,
   With half a hundred scouts,
And ending all the grand display
   By apprehending touts.

About the four bushrangers
   Our peelers heard the tale,
And three of them within the hour
   Were starting on the trail.
All day and night they travelled hard
   Without a wink of sleep,
And stedfast, for two hundred miles,
   Upon the track they keep.

At last the quarry to the lair,
   Was tracked over dale and hill,
By men who knew well how to act,
   And did not lack the will.
"Now yield" cried out the peelers,
   "Bail" cried the bandits four
But those bandits soon were handcuffed
   To trouble us no more.

They took their prisoners four with them
   Back to their starting place—
All honour to those plucky three,
   Who rode that winning race.
Four hundred miles they'd ridden
   In four and fifty hours;
Now, whose police have proved the best,
   Victoria's or ours?

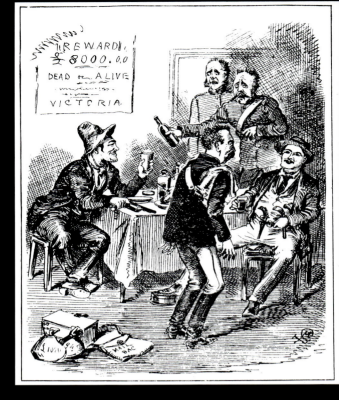

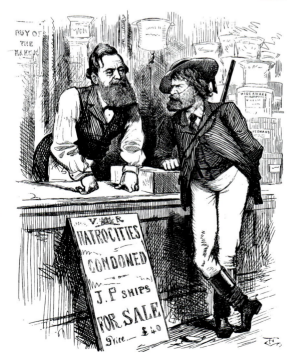

THE BERRY BROKER.

NED KELLY (to the Secretary of the National Reform League).—"£40 FOR A J.P.-SHIP, MR. YEOMANS: HOW MUCH FOR A FREE PARDON FOR ME AND MY MATES?"

Fringe benefits. While the Kellys cost the colonies more than £115,000 (not including bank funds, prison renovations and the reward) they brought brief prosperity to the north-eastern district and to the police who received double pay. Edmund Ryan's Camp Store in Benalla got the first contract to supply the Benalla police barracks; he employed thirteen hands and at his death, he left £38,000 – said to have been 'founded on the outbreak of the Kellys and quartering of 200 troopers close to his store'. Merchants between Benalla, Wangaratta and Beechworth all did good trade with troopers and sympathisers.

The police poems and illustrations appeared in Adelaide's *Frearson's Weekly*, contrasting the successful capture of a band of Kelly imitators in New South Wales.

The berry broker. The Kelly affair also sold newspapers and helped sharpen weary cartoonists' pens. Taken from the *Melbourne Punch* in March 1879, this illustration referred to allegations that J. P.'s were being reinstated (after the 'Black Wednesday' purge) at a price.

Mrs Skillion and Tom Lloyd junior comprised part of the inner circle of the outlaws' sympathisers. One honest police agent argued that though local gossip and rumours were always available 'there was an inner and more secret circle that he found difficult to reach'. Mrs Skillion, Tom Lloyd and Kate Kelly were three of the gang's closest contacts. Young Tom Lloyd was never imprisoned as a sympathiser, although police tried to bring other charges against him. In April 1879 a friendly test of strength ended disastrously when he accidentally killed his cousin Jack Lloyd outside O'Brien's hotel, Greta. Each had been testing their strength against chest blows — a charge of murder was subsequently thrown out of court. On the other hand, tolerance shown to the Kelly womenfolk was little short of amazing. After the Euroa robbery, Grace Kelly rode into Benalla to buy an expensive side-saddle and bridle which she paid for entirely in shilling pieces. Soon after, Mrs Skillion and Kate Kelly were seen in Wangaratta and Benalla buying clothing, hats, children's toys, household goods and other supplies.

After the robbery in Jerilderie, the north-eastern district was flooded with New South Wales bank notes. Police were shown notes that 'had an earthy smell . . . as if they had been planted'. Reports of the immediate family buying stores 'which undoubtedly reached the outlaws' came in regularly. Louis Stienwehr, a Benalla trader, said that 'Kate used to come to my store . . . and take a bundle of £10 notes from her blouse to pay me from it ... and £10 notes were scarce in those days.'

Kate Kelly was only sixteen in 1879 when a legend grew around her efforts to help the outlaws. Much of the credit she gained, however, was for the feats of her elder sister, Margaret Skillion. Maggie Skillion was only 22 years old but managed to support two families and play 'cat and mouse' with police. Her courage was illustrated by one incident in June 1879 when she travelled south with Tom Lloyd and Michael Nolan to buy ammunition. The trio caught a train at Benalla and visited several gun shops in Melbourne. At Rosier's in Bourke Street, they purchased a large supply and left a deposit for another brand they would pick up the following day. Rosier reported the purchase and the next morning, constables waited all day in the shop — only to find out that the trio had already left the city. Police apprehended Maggie and Tom as they got off the train at Benalla and searched the carriages, and even a stretch of line, but the goods had already reached their destination via Nolan. Possibly two or more such trips were made by the relatives. The photograph of Maggie Skillion was taken by D. Isley in the 1880s. The engraving of Maggie and Tom (who later became her de facto husband) was taken from a sketch made in the Beechworth court in 1880. The photograph of Kate Kelly was also taken during the 1880s.

THE GREAT DISAPPEARANCE, PART ONE

tle from the valley below the caves; they surely noticed the strange tracks. If they did not do so before, Mrs Byrne discovered the whole plot in the first week of March. One Saturday morning, she found a piece of soap and a whittled stick on the bank of Reedy Creek and then saw the reflected gleam of a sardine-tin carelessly dropped by a trooper. On the following morning, as the police lay about the cave, Mrs Byrne crept into the midst of them and bent over Aaron Sherritt as he slept under a police hat and overcoat. The sentry noticed her too late and allowed her to leave undisturbed. Sherritt was woken and told to clear off and establish an alibi. Not long after, Mrs Byrne was seen coming back up the boulder-strewn slope. Senior constable Mills was ordered to frighten her and he waited behind a rock and jumped out with a roar. Hare recalled that: 'the old woman lost her presence of mind and almost fainted, saying "What, What? I am only looking for cattle", and then she soon

Facing page: The parish of Beechworth. The Woolshed Valley runs west from the junction of Young's and Reedy creeks, from a point (top right) four kilometres north-west of Beechworth. The valley runs west toward Eldorado and beyond to Wangaratta. Contained in it were a series of localities, former bustling 'tent towns' during the gold rush. By the late 1870s, the centres of Woolshed (1), Devil's Elbow (2) and Sebastopol Flat (3) were virtually vacant and only worked by the last of a dwindling population of miners (mainly Chinese) and a number of Europeans who had stayed to farm the remaining arable land.

The Byrne home (4) was a slab and bark-roofed hut near a steep-sided gully cutting back into the south range below Sebastopol. There was no road to their home, but tracks ran along the south side of the creek to the Woolshed bridge and the stores. 'Byrne's gully', as it became known, contained about sixteen hectares (40 acres) behind their home. The family had no fenced land but grazed most of their dairy cattle on the 'common', north of the creek and main road. The Sherritt family's selection was nearly four kilometres away near the source of Sheepstation Creek (5). Aaron Sherritt's selection (6) was about three kilometres south of 'Byrne's Gully'. The caves used by the police during their watch were on the wall of the valley east of the Byrne hut (7) and near the rim of the south range on the east side of Devil's Elbow (8).

Top: The police caves. The upper caves commanded a view north across the Woolshed Valley to the main road, bridge and school. Aaron Sherritt sometimes slept with the police parties when they occupied this cave, but preferred curling up under a rock further down the hillside. Also shown are the lower caves, located only one kilometre east of the Byrne hut.

Above: Winter scene in north-eastern Victoria. In late February or March 1879 the Kellys disappeared from the settled districts and ranges surrounding the Oxley plains. Superintendent Sadleir recalled: 'There was a sudden drying up of the sources of information, when for a period no news whatever of the Kellys could be had. That they had actually fled the country seemed the most likely explanation. The [police agents] were sorely perplexed, and so also were [we].' The gang did not reappear until the end of June. During their four-month absence, they were rumoured to have gained passage on a ship to California, were thought to have gone to one of the other colonies, and were also reported in Melbourne. The gang actually retreated east into the snow-covered Alps for the winter. It seems almost certain that they were waiting for official response to their two written statements. They never revealed the exact locality of their hideout, but Ned Kelly said 'they had been amongst snow' and at times 'had to clear several feet of snow off a hut they lived in to prevent it falling in'. The hut was generally assumed to have been in the Buffalo Ranges, a belief strengthened when police interviewed a Chinese storekeeper on the Buckland River in 1880. He admitted the gang had: 'frequently bought plenty of previsions . . . had come down off the ranges two at a time and tied their horses outside . . . had plenty of money and always paid.' The storekeeper also said that he had been too frightened to tell police as the Kellys had threatened to 'shoot him and then burn him'. The storekeeper's admission was undoubted because of Byrne's reported drug addiction and subsequent dependence on the Chinese for supplies.

NED KELLY AND THE GANG

(Joe Byrne, a member of the notorious Kelly Gang, was reputed to have written the following, which we have taken from an old newspaper.)

The Kelly Gang will never hang,
  Nor yet be caught alive,
And against the police and troopers,
  They happily do thrive.

My name it is Ned Kelly, I'm known
  adversely well,
My ranks are free, my word is law,
  Wherever I do dwell.

My friends are all united, my mates
  Are lying near,
We sleep beneath these shady trees,
  No danger do we fear;

Out in the ranges of Strathbogie, we
  Fiercely do roam,
The caves we seek, our hiding place,
  Are a wild and barren home.

Two thousand pounds are on my head
  The bloodhounds on my track.
I'll make them pay and rue the day
  Their mothers gave them birth;

I'll shoot them down like prowling
  Dingo, Hawk, or carrion crow,
Or any other miscreant that seeks
  my overthrow.

I'll shoot them down like kangaroos
  That rove the mountain side,
I'll leave their carcase bleeding, all
  On the woodlong side.

* * *

They rode along together, undaunted
  Boys were they,
They crossed the united kingdom
  Long before the break of day;

They rode into Jerilderie town at 10
  O'clock at night,
They took those troopers from their
  Beds, they were in dreadful fright.

They took them in their nightshirts,
  Which I'm ashamed to tell.
Conveyed them with revolvers, and
  Locked them in their cell;

Next day, it being Sunday, of course
  They must be good.
They dressed themselves in troopers'
  Clothes, and Neddie chopped some
  wood.

Everyone suspected them as troopers
  On the pass,
And Dan, the most religious one,
  Took the sergeant's wife to mass;

Early on Monday morning, still
  Masters of the ground,
They took their horses to the forge
  And had them shod all round.

They backed their mounts and
  Mounted them, all plans thought
  out so well.
And with the assistance of the troops
  They stuck up Cox's hotel;

They bailed up all the servants, they
  locked them in a room,
Saying, do as I command, or death
  Will be your doom.

The Chinaman cook, no savee no,
  No knowing how to fear,
But Byrne fetched him to his senses
  With a punch beneath the ear;

This time across the Billabong creek
  On Morgan's ancient beat.
They robbed the bank of thousands
  And retired in safe retreat.

Throughout the whole affair, my
  Boys, they never fired a shot,
The work was done so splendidly, it
  Will never be forgot;

And now my song is ended, I've got
  No more to say,
We made a pile at Jerilderie, and
  Now we're going away.

June 26. 1879

Dear Aaron I write those few stolen lines to you to let you know that I am still living I am not the least afraid of being captured dear Aaron meet me you and Jack this side of Puzzel ranges Neddie and I has come to the conclusion to get you to join us I was advised to turn treater but I said that I would die at Ned's side first Dear Aaron it is best for you to join us Aaron a short tive and a jolly one the Lloyds and Quinns wants you shot but I say no you are on our side, If it is no thing only for the sake of your mother & sisters We sent that bloody Hart to your place twice did my mother tell you the message that I left for you I slept at home three days on the 24 of may did Patsy give you the booty I left for you I intend to pay old sandy doig and old Mullane Oh that bloody snob where is he I will make a target of him meet me on next thursday you and Jack and we will have another bank quite handy I told Hart to call last thursday evening I wold like to know If he obeyed us or not if not we will shoot him if you come on our tracks; close your puss you know; you were at Kates several times you had just gone one night as we came we followed you four miles but returned without success If you do not meet me where I ask you meet me under london you know I will riddle that bloody Mullane, If I catch him no more from the enforced outlaw till I see yourself

I remain yours truly
  you know ———

Top: Kelly songs, ballads, and even the Kelly letters, draw on the rich Irish prose tradition. Both Ned and Joe were avid readers and regular customers of Beechworth bookseller, James Ingram. Much of the gang's literary output appears to have come from Joe Byrne, who was the gang's scribe. Ballads were still the popular entertainment of the day and the Kellys provided ideal material for the Robin Hood image that grew around them. Byrne was said to have kept a detailed diary of all their experiences, but it has never been discovered. One of the police leaders of the time wrote, 'Joe Byrne was better educated than any of his companions and was very fond of writing, and was a bit of a poet. A great deal of his writings fell into our hands. They were chiefly directed against the police . . . He was, for a bushman, rather clever with his pen.'

Above and facing page: Letters to old friends. The pages dated 26 June 1879 were received through the mail by Aaron Sherritt and passed on to police through his mother. They were forwarded to superintendent Hare at Benalla with this covering memo: With reference to the attached letter: 'Mrs Sherritt handed it to me and said she knew the writing to be Joe Byrne's — enclosed is another letter Joseph Byrne wrote out of the Gaol at the time he was serving his sentence with Moses [police pseudonym for Aaron Sherritt], this was handed to me also by Mrs Sherritt. You will be able to judge for yourself if the handwriting is alike, Mullane says he could swear the writing in the enclosed is Joe's writing … these small scraps of paper written in pencil by Joe Byrne were shown to S. C. Mullane by the prisoner who conveyed the letter out of the gaol at the time.' The later note could be a Sherritt forgery, but there are distinct similarities between the writing of these two letters and large sections of the Jerilderie letter, strengthening the belief that Byrne was the gang's scribe.

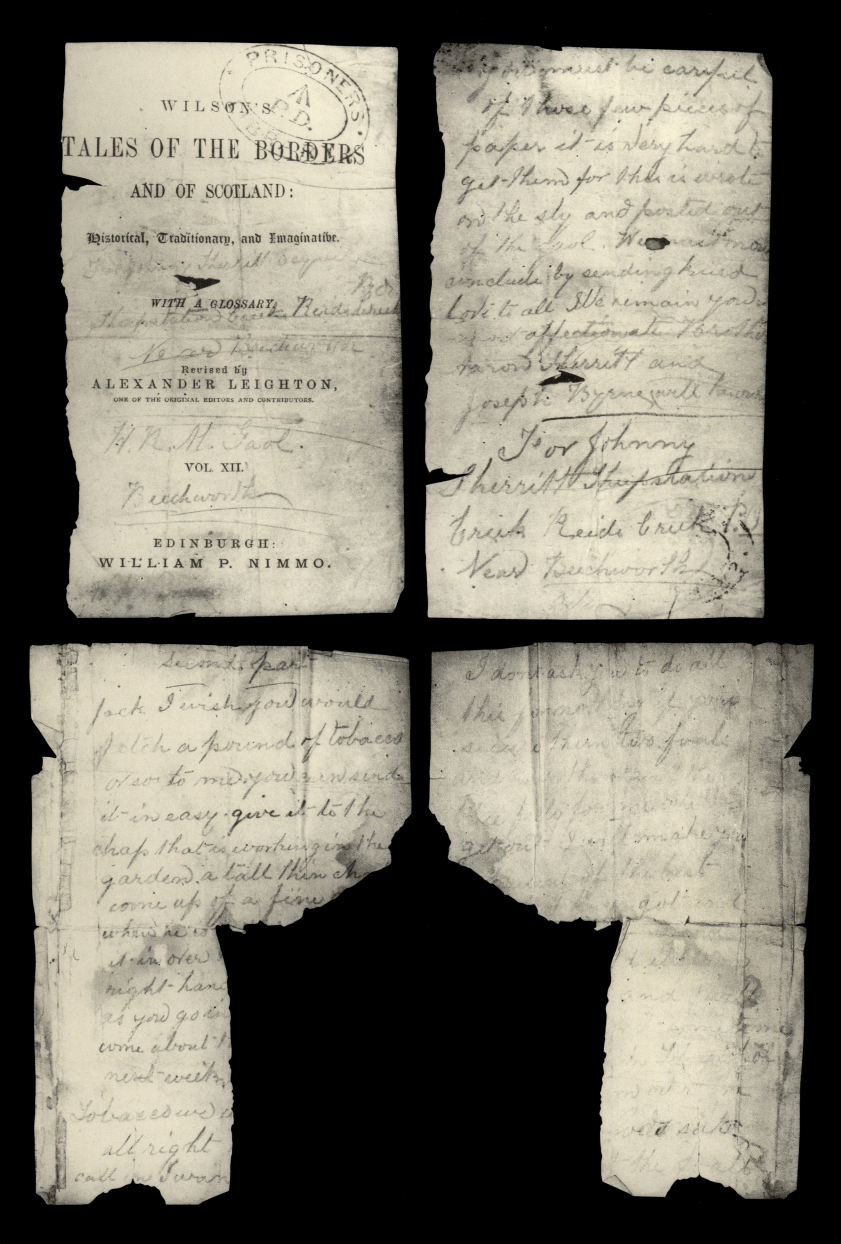

recovered her assurance and got impertinent and said, "I will get my son to shoot the whole lot of you!"'

Sherritt was either naive, as his mother thought, uncommonly brave, or just plain foolhardy. The same night that Mrs Byrne discovered the surveillance party, Sherritt went to the Byrne hut, 'taking a penny whistle, making music he hoped would bring out his girl . . . and enable him to learn what Mrs Byrne knew'. But Catherine did not show. With relief, he later told the constables that he had not been recognised. Mrs Byrne told him of her discovery and abused him for not finding the police sooner, but there is little doubt that Mrs Byrne knew of his treachery. Three days later, she went to his block while he was working and asked why police horses were grazing in his paddock. A heated and bitter argument followed, which put an end to his engagement to Catherine and his friendship with the family. The cave party withdrew a few days later. Then, still not worried, Aaron turned his efforts away from the Woolshed. He decided, possibly with some prompting, to try and win the heart of young Kate Kelly at Greta to gain entrance to the tight-knit Kelly clan. The manoeuvre must have been transparent as Sherritt had never met Kate Kelly, and was unknown to Margaret Skillion.

Margaret said Sherritt first came to her home and introduced himself in April 1879, offering to sell her a horse. Although she turned him down it was the start of repeat visits. Kate saw nothing suspicious in the particular attention Aaron paid to her, but Mrs Skillion and Wild Wright did. 'Mrs Skillion objected to his being about the place', Aaron's contact wrote. 'Kate and he got on very well, but she never mentioned her brother nor he to her. They became great friends'. It is doubtful whether Sherritt would have gained any information in the face of suspicion, but in late April his visits seemed promising. Kate was reported 'often visiting the Sherritts at Sheepstation creek', and on 2 May, Mrs Skillion agreed to buy the horse he had offered a few weeks earlier. But she insisted on going into Greta with Wright to have a receipt drawn out and witnessed.

While Aaron was courting Kate that autumn, he again showed indiscretion that was to have disastrous consequences. The police, perhaps through him, heard that the gang was expected to visit Tom Lloyd senior's home, nearly five kilometres south of Mrs Skillion's hut. 'Kate Kelly had been seen riding from her place to her uncle's with a large bundle in front of her saddle thought to be clean clothes and etc for her brothers.' With incredible nerve or stupidity, Sherritt went out with three police sent from Benalla to watch Lloyd's place. His selection was near the Greta–Lurg road, on a branch track running north around Bald Hill to the Skillions. The house was set at the base of a gap in Futter's Range, 'surrounded on three sides by steep mountains'. They took up position before daylight in a clump of trees looking down the slope.

They had a good view of Lloyd's hut and the surrounding country. Shortly after daybreak they saw two young boys come out and unfasten the dogs. They at first thought it was to fetch the cows for milking but in a very short time they discovered the boys had been sent out to see if anyone had been about the place during the night. To their horror they saw the dogs coming on their trail following their footsteps into the trees. One of the men jumped up so Aaron could not be seen. The dogs began to bark. The boys ran back to the hut, and shortly afterwards the inmates came out and looked in their direction . . . Lloyd himself came up and spoke to the men while Sherritt hid. He went back to his house, and immediately three shots were fired off, presumably as a signal. There was a hollow tree trunk lying on two logs, and an axe was taken and three distinct blows given upon this . . . you could hear the echo resounding from all sides of the hills. Kate Kelly was inside and when she came out it was evident that the whole thing was blown . . . the men had to stay in their position all day and left after dark so Aaron would not be seen.

Aaron Sherritt managed to keep visiting the Kelly sisters, but his mischief spoiled his efforts. The break-up was foreshadowed by another near miss.

One night, when Mrs Skillion went out to visit a friend, she left Kate and Aaron in the house together. Aaron induced Kate out for a walk with him and when Mrs Skillion returned she found them both away. She was most indignant and went to Oxley police station [Greta station had been closed since the Stringybark Creek shootings] and laid some charges against Aaron. The Constable went [to the house], and when Aaron saw him coming up to the door he bolted out the back. The Constable followed him and fired several shots, but could not overtake him . . . Aaron went to Beechworth and saw Detective Ward and said he feared he would be arrested . . . this occurrence never got into the papers and the policeman at Oxley was very much surprised at the leniency shown towards Aaron.

By mid-May, Sherritt found himself in even more trouble. Mrs Skillion later testified that Sherritt had been back, asked her to return the horse he had sold her, and was forced to admit it was stolen. The incredible fact was that he had stolen the animal from his ex-fiancée, Kate Byrne, and 'Mrs Byrne was [threatening] to get him five years [imprisonment]'. Mrs Skillion refused his plea, and took the horse and receipt to the police.

Efforts were made to avoid action over the theft. The horse was returned to Mrs Skillion with the excuse that no complaint had been submitted. When Mrs Byrne swore information for Aaron's arrest not long after, police were forced to issue a warrant in June 1879. While the police issued the warrant, Sherritt was offered for the second (and last) time to join the gang as a scout. Joseph Byrne allegedly wrote a letter to Sherritt asking him and his younger brother Jack to meet him the following week. They went but the outlaw made no appearance. If the letter was genuine, there is little doubt that the gang was testing his contact with police and fully expected Sherritt to lead a posse to the meeting. On 10 July, Ned Kelly appeared at Sheepstation Creek – the first time he had been seen in four months – and tried to contact Sherritt. Kelly would have first called at Aaron's own selection, then at Sherritt's parents' selection, but could not find him at either place.

Mrs Sherritt later gave an account of the visit, although she wasn't at home at the time.

There was only two children in, the eldest fifteen. He said to them he had a mob of cattle at the back of the hill, and that he wanted to get Aaron, as Aaron was a good bushman, to show him the way by the head of the King [River] . . . there was some dough in the dish, and he took some of the dough up, and he flattened it on the table and pulled out the fire with his foot and cooked two or three pieces. He was alone. And then he made some tea, and he said he was sending this tea up to his men that he had on the hill; and he had a flask of brandy in his pocket, and all the time he was inside he kept the baby in his arms, and he filled out a tumbler of brandy and put it on the cupboard and told the children to give that to Aaron, and say that a gentleman was there who wanted him to assist with some cattle, and he would be back in a fortnight or three weeks. He said he believed there was a warrant out for Aaron, and the best thing he could do was to come along with them; that he . . . would be of use to them.

At 4 p.m. the same afternoon 'the outlaw Byrne and his younger brother were seen together on horseback at Reed's Creek ranges' – five kilometres north-east of the Sherritt selections. Aaron made no attempt to contact the gang or to give any answer to Kelly's offer. He was arrested five days later and lodged in the cells in Beechworth. The Ovens and Murray Advertiser commented:

Aaron Sherritt, who is most unfavourably known in these parts as a purloiner of horses and cattle belonging to other persons . . . appears to have continued carrying on his little game; for a short time back Mrs Byrne of the Woolshed (near which place Sherritt also resides) took out a warrant saying he stole a horse belonging to her.

The following week, the *Ovens and Murray Advertiser* added again:

about two hundred persons attended the above [Beechworth] court to hear the case of horsestealing against Aaron Sherritt . . . Much interest is taken in the case, for Sherritt is well known in these parts, and Mrs Byrne, the prosecutrix . . . is the mother of Joseph Byrne, a member of the Kelly gang of outlaws. It was anticipated that some matters in connection with the latter would be elicited in evidence, and much importance was attached to the fact that Mrs Skillion, nee Margaret Kelly, was present in Court.

On 26 July, Sherritt had his day in court. Mrs Skillion and Kate Kelly attended the hearing and Mrs Skillion gave evidence in support of the charge. Mrs Byrne and her seventeen year-old son, Patrick, gave the main testimony for the prosecution. Sherritt's solicitor called five witnesses. There was no question of his guilt; he admitted giving a horse to Kate Byrne three years earlier. Kate told how she had swapped the horse for the one eventually stolen. The defence maintained that Sherritt's condition of giving her the horse was that if it was sold or disposed of, he could claim it. The defence also stated that during the argument between Sherritt and Mrs Byrne, she told him to take the horse back. Whether the case was rigged is a matter of opinion, but it is fairly certain that the evidence of Mrs Byrne and Mrs Skillion was discredited because of their connections. Sherritt was discharged and his breach with the Byrnes and Kelly sisters was public knowledge. Mrs Byrne was to confide in a friend that they thought the whole case 'was a dodge of that [detective] Ward . . . to bring Joe back again to have revenge on Sherritt, but it would not take . . . they, the outlaws, would wait their own time.'

13 THE GREAT DISAPPEARANCE, PART TWO

JUNE 1879–JUNE 1880

The game of waiting was refined to an art form on both sides of the Kelly pursuit. In July 1879, another change in police command brought the chase into a new phase. Superintendent Nicolson resumed charge from Standish and Hare, who had been conducting the Kelly pursuit since December 1878. Nicolson drew on his experience as a detective – opposing Hare's policy of search parties – and relied solely on a system of secret agents, spies and informers. Over the duration of the Kelly pursuit, police employed 26 men in the district. These included farmers, labourers, storekeepers and, among others, an ex-schoolmaster at Greta, a schoolteacher on the Woolshed, a Glenrowan railway porter and a Benalla stock auctioneer. All of them claimed to be in a position to hear of the outlaws' plans and movements. Many of them volunteered information out of a sincere regard for the law, but just as many were attracted by the easy income. The police paid for the information according to its importance, thereby encouraging spies to fabricate news when it was scarce. Subsequently, Nicolson's secret service reports became tangled with useless and misleading information.

Two of the most unreliable agents were James Wallace (a schoolmaster and former schoolmate of Aaron Sherritt and Joe Byrne) and 'Wild' Pat Quinn (the Kellys' uncle who had been selecting at South Hanson since 1873).

Wild Pat agreed to inform on his nephews and was employed by the police under the alias of 'Foote'. He gave information on a number of occasions, but most was unreliable. Nicolson was suspicious of him,

On 1 March 1879, six **Queensland trackers** joined the Victorian police under sub-inspector O'Connor. Their presence was one of the most effective measures in the pursuit. The trackers had a long record of success in Queensland and an almost uncanny skill in following old and faint tracks. Captain Standish, however, severely hampered their effective use. He alleged they were frail men, pointing out that on the first bush patrol, one of the men, corporal Sambo, had contracted pneumonia and died. Yet Ned Kelly said 'what told on them most was the perpetual dread of surprise . . . the black trackers robbed them even of sleep'. The photograph was taken in front of the Benalla police paddock prior to July 1879. From left are, constable King, sub-inspector O'Connor, Hero, Barney, Jacky, Jimmy, Johnny, superintendent

Another Kelly letter. To the despair of the outlaws, no further moves were made to institute a public inquiry into Mrs Kelly's sentence or their own plight when the Victorian parliament re-opened on 8 July 1879. They were surprised because premier Berry was considered to be a radical; feared by conservatives and property owners alike, and committed to protecting the small man and selector. He demonstrated his contempt for self-serving officials in 1878 by sacking over 200 magistrates. For this reason, the Kellys expected more than political posturing. In an attempt to create interest in their case, they sent another version of their manifesto to coincide with the opening of parliament in Melbourne, but this time it was addressed to the *Herald* newspaper and an abridged version was published and reprinted in the *Ovens and Murray Advertiser.* In the clipping shown, their demand for a full and open inquiry is considered 'apparently a justified one'. This would be the only occasion, other than brief reports of his speeches and remarks, when Kelly's version of events was given any public exposure.

The veil of writing as a sympathiser was obviously not important to the Kellys as the letter's phrasing was identical to the previous two letters. It also displayed a knowledge of their history unavailable to anyone but themselves.

While the gang waited near Mount Buffalo, Mrs Skillion also attempted to gain public attention. She wrote to the editor of the *Jerilderie Gazette* 'asking for the manuscript of the statement left . . . by Ned Kelly, as she [wanted] to see what he had to say of his life'. It was not difficult to see that she was writing on behalf of her brother and the request caused Gill and the bank teller Lyving considerable terror. If Gill replied, his excuses were not believed. In late July 1879, Wild Wright and another alleged sympathiser, Donnelly, made a visit to Jerilderie, evidently to obtain the Kellys' letter, but it had already been confiscated.

Ovens and Murray A

BEECHWORTH, SATURDAY, JULY 12, 1879.

THE KELLY GANG.

[HERALD.]

We have received from an anonymous correspondent who is evidently a sympathiser with, and a near associate of the Kellys and their companions, a long but rambling statement of the case as it is put by the outlaws. The document, which contains sixteen pages, came by post simply addressed to "The editor of the *Herald* newspaper, Melbourne." It is evidently written by an illiterate person, the orthography being defective, the caligraphy in some portions almost undecipherable, and the composition rambling and sometimes unintelligible. Sufficient can be gathered, however, to show that there is a very bitter feeling of animosity among the sympathisers of the outlaws against the police, and reasons are stated why this should exist. An inquiry is anxiously demanded, and as the statements made are of a serious character, and the demand for an inquiry apparently a justifiable one, we give some particulars from the effusion of our anonymous correspondent, who, for aught we know, may be one of the gang. He commences by drawing attention to the Monk inquiry, and, as might be expected, fully endorses the decision of Mr Panton, asserting positively that Monk's statements that he was shot at were false. In this matter the anonymous writer thinks the authorities acted with wisdom, as the statements were such as to demand inquiry. He then proceeds to argue that a similar inquiry into the whole circumstances that led up to the police murders is necessary, and that it would save the Government money if they appointed Mr Panton to make, not only that inquiry, but to also investigate the conduct of the police in the North-Eastern district, not only before, but since the outrage. In support of this, it is alleged, as has before been stated, that the whole cause of the tragedy and the subsequent events was the conviction of Mrs Kelly, Skillian and Williamson, on the unsupported testimony of Constable Fitzpatrick, which, it is affirmed, was false. Justice is claimed for these three persons, and it is boldly stated that had it been accorded in the first instance, there "would have been no necessity for persons like Monk to go in search of the bodies of police who were sent out to shoot men who, on false evidence, were banished to the wilds, and their mother, brother-in-law, and friends, on the word of one man alone, convicted of a serious crime." The writer goes on to say that on the jury that tried Mrs Kelly, Skillian and Williamson, was a discharged sergeant of police, "which is contrary to law." To quote again from our correspondent. "The Kellys were then outlawed, and a price of £200 offered for their apprehension, for firing three shots at Fitzpatrick, as he said, at a yard and a half distance; and yet he was hit only once, the bullet entering the middle of the back of his wrist, but not even injuring a sinew of touching the bone, but passing simply along the skin. Kelly's arm and a revolver would go a long way towards a yard and a half, and Fitzpatrick must have had good eyesight to see bullets and revolvers all round him. In fact his statement was simply ridiculous. From the 13th April, 1878, to the 23rd October in the same year, the Kellys were not seen or heard of. During that time they were not interfering with or harming anyone, but were digging on Bullock Flat, quietly trying to make a living, when the police came to shoot them down like dogs, as they stated they would do before they would ask them to stand. Three different parties of police, numbering in all some 12 or 15, supplied with the best firearms, were sent out to take the Kellys in dead or alive. Kennedy's party camped within a mile of the Kellys, and the latter had nothing for it but to coolly wait and be shot like dogs, or bail the police up and take their firearms from them. And when they called on the police to surrender, one obeyed, and was not injured, but the rest fought and were shot. If the Queen of England was in in the place of the Kellys, she could have done no less than they did. Let anyone consider the circumstances of the persecution of the Kellys. Their mother and friends convicted, and themselves banished and pursued by blacktrackers, police, and even English bloodhounds, on the evidence of Fitzpatrick; and for what cause? In the first place, if the Kellys intended to murder Fitzpatrick, they could easily have done so, as, according to his statement, there were enough of them to eat him without salt; and yet there was no mark on him but a small cut on the back of his wrist, which any man could see was never done by a bullet fired from a revolver. Fitzpatrick would not stand long before Mr Panton." Our anonymous correspondent then goes on to give his version of the characters of the Kellys. He says:—"The Kellys are termed thieves and cold-blooded murderers, but those that term them this would be guilty of far worse crimes than they are. No case of horsestealing was ever proved against any of the Kellys. Ned got six months for striking a man named McCormack, and three years for receiving a stolen horse. This was on the evidence of Constables ———and———. The swearing abilities of the first are well known, as he has been twice tried for perjury, and the latter has himself since been sentenced to three years for horsestealing. Dan Kelly was sentenced to three months for smashing a door with his fist. These are the only convictions on the roll against the Kellys. I guess there was not much cold-bloodness about the shooting of the police. It was the police who went out to murder for the reward. If other men were treated as the Kellys have been, they would not spare nothing in human shape, as both the public and the Government have done their best against them, and laws have been made to suit the police." Having thus lauded the outlaws, the writer comes to his great grievance—the conduct of the police in the North-Eastern District. He writes:—"The policeman business has been a good one during the last fourteen months that Kellys has been outlawed. Any scapgrace can get a pound a-day now. I know a great many of the special constables, not one of whom could earn their tucker before, but now can sport silk coats, and calls themselves mounted-constables. Two, in particular, I could mention. One is well-known in the Beechworth and Greta districts, and his character needs no comment. But he is a good man for Ned Kelly, as he can draw the police wherever he chooses, and clears the road for a man that knows how to work him better than all the police-detectives put together. When a drove of police are getting tired of watching about the Beechworth hills this man will steal a horse from some of the neighbors, ride him down to Greta or Sa[illegible]ly Creek, or some other place; there style himself Byrne, the bushranger; ride through a railway gate and threaten to shoot the gatekeeper, so that the police will make a rush in that direction after the Kellys. When they start on his tracks, he cuts the horse's throat and doubles back, while the police keep in hot persuit, especially when they find the dead horse, and hear the testimony of the people the supposed Byrne threatened to shoot. The special constable on his way back steals a couple of horses, takes them with him to near Byrne's house, and when the police return, tells them that Byrne has been visiting his home and has left strange horses. In fact, this man tries the mettle of the blacktrackers, and even the blood hounds, and gets great credit from the inspectors for his supposed cleverness in getting information of the Kellys. Some of the police [illegible] bad as this man himself, as they are aware that it was he who fired at several persons in the Beechworth district, and also that he rode a grey horse belonging to a Chinaman at the Woolshed. If an inquiry should be held there are plenty of members of the police force who could give important evidence, and could show the public the true character of the special constables and others supposed to be hunting for the Kellys. In fact, if things are not altered there will be plenty bushrangers besides the Kellys. As it is, the whole force ought to be outlawed instead of the Kellys. If the police are are allowed to threaten to shoot respectable men, women, and even children, break down fences, turn stolen horses into peoples' paddocks, and a lot of drunken police, dressed like bushrangers, to surround quiet homes, threatening to shoot the inmates and ransacking the house; yelling, roaring and galloping through the crops, shouting at the trees, who can tell if they are the police or the Kellys? It is the place of the public to insist that the police should wear their uniforms, or at least something to distinguish them from bushrangers or civilians. As it is, no man dare fire at anyone surrounding his house, for fear of shooting a policeman, as the police are in the habit of bailing people up and behaving in a most ruffianly manner. A certain inspector of police a fortnight before Fitzpatrick alleged he was shot at, told an editor that he knew the Kellys were armed, and that there would be shooting between the police and the Kellys before a fortnight. If he thought that it is very strange to me that he should send a drunken trooper to arrest them without a warrant. I believe I write the opinion of thousands, when I say an inquiry should be held, and all the particulars brought to light. Unless this is done the Kellys will certainly revenge the insult offered to themselves and their mother. At present they are painted as black as print can paint them, but they harmed no man, woman, or child. Their actions are more like those of four sisters of charity, than four outlaws. If they had robbed, and plundered, and ravished and murdered the public and every man and woman they met, it would have been a very different thing, but in the way they have acted, after being treated as they have been, they deserve to be called men instead of outlaws. Their robberies are confined to banks, the police, and the Government. If this sort of thing goes on, the Chief Secretary will soon have to go home for a new loan." Of course the above extracts are not given "verbatim et literatim," but they have only been altered sufficiently to render them intelligible. With the writer's opinions as to the angelic nature of they Kellys we have nothing to do, but the public is concerned to know whether his allegations against the police are true or false. Sooner or later a most searching inquiry will have to be made, and it is to be hoped that when the proper time comes, those who can give evidence will come boldly forward.

yet he continued to pay him as an informant. On the day the gang raided Euroa, Pat had gone into Benalla to persuade police that the Kellys were hidden on the upper King River. It was (and still is) generally accepted that Quinn was acting as a double agent – providing misleading information to the police as instructed by the outlaws.

Financial incentive certainly attracted James Wallace to Nicolson's service. Wallace lived with his family on the Woolshed and had grown up with the Byrnes and Sherritts. He convinced police he was in touch with the gang and could borrow Byrne's diary by saying he was writing a book on the outlaws. He sent in many lengthy and vague reports and earned £180 before the police realised his services were useless.

By August 1879 the Kellys had evaded capture for sixteen months. Under the weight of failure, the police's enthusiasm for the pursuit began to wane. After the Jerilderie robbery, police numbers in the north-east were reduced by 25 per cent and between May and July that year, the soldiers of the defence corps had been withdrawn from Beechworth, Chiltern, Wangaratta, Wodonga, Seymour and Avenel. The remaining police were concentrated at Benalla with the Queensland trackers. Random search parties were also discontinued as the government attempted to curb costs; Nicolson could only hope that the cutbacks would lull the outlaws into a false sense of security. While the change allowed them much easier movement around the country, it eventually wore down their morale and made them suspicious of supporters.

In September 1879, a Beechworth newspaper reporter observed:

One of the common beliefs is that the Kellys have made away with Hart and Byrne and have managed to leave the colony . . . During that time it is not pretended that the gang have ever been seen by the police, and now that the pursuit has slackened, it does not appear they will ever be. We no longer have the marching and counter marching of armed men, which at one time gave the town the appearance of a garrison settlement in war country . . . matters have now settled down to a very humdrum condition.

A month later, the reporter commented again:

A number of Benalla people . . . stated positively that the Kellys are not only in Victoria but they have been as comfortably housed all the winter . . . One partly acknowledged that if it were not for the Kellys, the North Eastern district would be in a bad way . . . He said he had netted £500 through them in his own business . . . we may reasonably imagine business folks are not over eager to have the Kellys caught.

A royal commissioner later reflected:

The alarm caused by the daring outrages of the gang had to some extent subsided, but a strong feeling of indignation prevailed at the spectacle of four young men, three of them only about twenty years of age, defying all the resources and powers of the Government, and remaining in almost undisturbed tranquillity in what one of them described as their mountain home.

The outlaws' existence was hardly tranquil – they survived by their skill and endurance. The Kellys

'Where are the Kellys?' The press regularly represented the uniquely Australian lack of sympathy for authority, in particular the police.

WHERE ARE THE KELLYS?
1. Captain Standish and the Victorian police on the *qui vive*. 2. After many weeks, they discover a clue to the whereabouts of the Kelly gang. 3. Who are discovered on the ranges by the light of the moon and the aid of a black tracker, who forthwith makes tracks, followed by the police, to the 4 Awful consternation of the bushrangers.—*Sydney Punch*.

Above: The marquis of Normanby, governor of Victoria 1879–84. The Kellys viewed the lack of parliamentary response to their statements as a major setback. Kelly might even have refrained from further robberies after Jerilderie if the inquiry he hoped would free his mother had eventuated. But nothing happened and by August, the gang were again testing banks in search of a suitable target. There were suggestions that Kelly also considered the capture of the governor at his holiday retreat on Mount Macedon. The alleged intention had been to hold him hostage and offer his freedom for Mrs Kelly, hopefully believing in the meantime that he could be 'converted into a sympathiser'.

Aaron Sherritt's contact in Beechworth was **detective Michael Ward**. He was well known to the Kellys, Byrnes and Sherritts after ten years as a policeman at Wangaratta and Beechworth, and it is often claimed that he was as notorious as many of the criminals he chased. Ward was also a remarkably brave man and Byrne went to great lengths to shatter the detective's nerve. He sent him a constant barrage of 'poison-pen' letters between 1878 and 1880. The most original were blank sheets with renderings of coffins and wreaths; other less subtle cartoons showed the outlaws despatching him and his comrades in a variety of ways. The most amusing was a pseudo-reward bill that Ward said was *a counter-blast to the Government reward offering £8,000 . . . for the apprehension and delivery in Strathbogie Ranges of Captain Standish, Senior Constable Mullane and [myself]*. As late as June 1880, Ward still rode alone with his greyhound and armed only with a small pocket Webley revolver.

'frequently rode from sixty to seventy miles in one night'. Byrne is said to have practised galloping straight down the sides of mountains through timber and rocks, knowing troopers would never risk their lives to follow. The outlaws 'never carried anything beyond an overcoat' and firearms; and the coats 'had to cover them night and day'. Even a police leader admitted 'it seemed wonderful that men could exist in this manner'. Another pointed out that they often travelled behind an advance guard:

They always used to travel at night until before daybreak . . . generally accompanied by sympathisers . . . One of them, I may mention their own sister Mrs Skillion, used to always go ahead, on the lookout, and the outlaws would follow at the usual distance, just within sight. The former would give signals if anyone appeared, and the gang would then avoid them.

The outlaws were just as cautious in camp. If they could safely enjoy a fire it was always small, and when they left they painstakingly disguised their presence – in case they needed to use the spot again. Nicolson described such a spot he found with the help of Aborigines:

A camp was discovered in the ranges between Chiltern and Beechworth, in a depression in low-lying ground alongside the creek, amongst some bushes. There were marks of their horses standing there, and the marks of bridles chafing bushes, and very small quantities of ashes spread over about a couple of yards, and no appearance of a fire. On removal of a heap of leaves and rubbish, there was a round fire – a black mark on the ground – which they had carefully concealed.

Superintendent Hare said he learned many of the outlaws' habits: 'from watching their former associate Aaron Sherritt. On one occasion when talking to [him] I inadvertently broke a twig and began breaking up the leaves. He immediately stopped me and said, "You would never do for a bushranger. If Ned Kelly saw any of his men break a twig off a tree when they were camped he would have an awful row with them."' Years later in England, Hare said: 'I hardly think that anyone out of Australia could possibly conceive the hardships that men of this stamp can endure . . . They have an extraordinary way of sleeping; they coil themselves up like dogs. I remember one night finding Aaron lying with his head between his knees, and [afterwards] he said, when camping out he always slept in that position.'

But if the hardships of the bush were no problem for the outlaws, the high cost of surviving was. By spring 1879 the Kellys were testing banks all over the district, hoping to find one with sufficient reserves that was not heavily guarded. They were still looking in April the following year, but without success. The gang supposedly considered raids on towns as far east as Walhalla in Gippsland and as far south-west as Trentham. As early as March 1879, a cousin of the Kellys spent a week looking over Trentham. The bank manager was quickly alerted and the branch was temporarily closed.

In late July, detective Ward sounded one of the many supposed hold-up alarms in Beechworth: 'I have received information that the Kellys are going to make a raid on one of the banks in the next few days, but they want to have some time amongst their friends. The Oriental Bank would be an easy place to effect entrance from the back . . . Have warned all the banks to be very careful for the next few days.' In October a report read, 'James or Jim Hall, a suspected confederate of the outlaws, asking about police strength in Yackandandah . . . known to be a resident of Millacoota [sic] near Mansfield where Wild Wright resides.' It was even believed that the outlaws went through with several attempts only to pull out at the last moment. Ward also said, 'We received information that they were going to take the Oxley Bank, but we afterwards heard that, on account of their seeing three policemen there in the morning when the bank opened, they thought it would not be worthwhile for the amount of money they would get there.' In April the following year, another report claimed: 'Alexandra was recently watched and examined on their behalf. The outlaws went, but returned, saying "They did not wish to throw their lives away", or words to that effect.'

After Ned Kelly's appearance at the Sherritt home in July 1879, the gang was reported moving about their old haunts. In late September, the four outlaws were seen south of Wangaratta. The two young men who saw them, Smith and Morgan, were so scared from their encounter with the gang that they would not tell police for a month. Smith's account was not published until nine months after the event.

As they were walking through the bush, near the three mile creek in the vicinity of a house tenanted by the parents of the outlaw Hart, they saw two men approaching them behind trees and they advanced on them. They then saw that one had a striking resemblance to Dick Hart. They first concluded that he was that individual, and sang out 'What is the use of larking in this way?' The two men then came out from behind the trees and bailed them up. Both carried firearms. One was then recognised as Steve Hart, the outlaw, and the other was a stranger, who was certainly not one of the outlaws. The stranger carried a rifle and two revolvers, and assisted Steve Hart to bail up Smith and Morgan. The four then went to Hart's house.

There Dan Kelly was found, washing his head and chest. Shortly afterwards Joseph Byrne turned up, and a general conversation ensued . . . supper was in the form of steak and onions. The strange man stayed outside most of the evening but he eventually entered the house, and reported that the 'Captain' was coming. Soon afterwards Ned Kelly entered, and the company passed a jovial evening. Ned stated that he had missed his way, and had almost walked into a lion's mouth, for he had stumbled on a railway crossing where a [certain] gatekeeper lived. Mrs Hart and her daughters were present, and it may be mentioned Morgan is a relative of the Harts . . . Smith was allowed to go at about 11 o'clock on account of his wife and family, but the sympathiser referred to first made him kneel down and swear that he would give no information to the police . . . until a month had elapsed, gave him two Sydney £5 notes, and firing a revolver over his head, said that if he split on them he would be shot like that. Ned Kelly was asked who the strange man was, and he replied that he was a man they had on trial as an associate, but one who he did not think would suit. The gang left at 2 o'clock in the morning and Morgan was kept under surveillance for several days.

Smith kept his promise to the day; the stranger turned out to be young Tom Lloyd, thought to have been away shearing. Charges would have been laid but Morgan could not be persuaded to testify. He left the colony soon after.

That September, the outlaws also visited Mrs Skillion and the Lloyds at Greta, the Ryans at Lake Rowan, and Mrs Byrne at Sebastopol. During this time, it was reported that 'Ned Kelly was suffering from sciatica'. Also in September, Joe Byrne indicated that he had overlooked Aaron Sherritt's treachery and the gang invited Jack Sherritt (Aaron's younger brother) to become one of their agents. Byrne sent several letters to Jack Sherritt in September, enclosing caricatures and threatening letters to police; one of them was the classic £8,000 reward for captain Standish, detective Ward and constable Mullane. Byrne had nothing to lose: Jack would either pin up the posters and mail the threatening letters or deliver them to the police – who would see the connection as an avenue to gain Byrne's trust. As it turned out, Jack was not connected with the police when he received the letters, but he took them to detective Ward nonetheless. Ward seized the opportunity, pinned up the caricatures on the veranda of the Beechworth police station, created a pseudo-reward notice and notified the Beechworth paper that he had received threatening letters. On 4 September, the Beechworth paper reported that Ward had been contacted by a 'member of the Kelly gang, telling him to prepare for his "latter end" as he would be murdered at the first opportunity'. The detective convinced Jack Sherritt that the gang would believe he had posted them. It seemed they did: on 19 September Byrne left £2 in silver at Mrs Byrne's 'for Jack, in payment for posting the letters'. Jack received several more letters from Byrne that month.

All the letters reached Jack Sherritt through the Byrne family, generally through his sister, Anne. The ties between the two families were closely interwoven; the children all went to school together and grew up on intimate terms. Joe Byrne was apparently engaged to Elizabeth Sherritt before his outlawry, and Aaron Sherritt was engaged to Catherine Byrne. In April 1879 a Woolshed resident wrote that 'Pat Byrne, the brother of the outlaw, is courting Anne Jane Sherritt and they are going to be married first of January next.' This courtship did not result in marriage, although Anne was still visiting the Byrne hut in May the following year. It was through these regular visits that Jack Sherritt received Joe Byrne's letters. In turn, he kept in contact with detective Ward and, like Aaron, was paid as a police agent under the alias of "Jones". A September police report mentioned 'Joe Byrne, outlaw, writes several letters to "Jones". Replies dictated . . . Requests in Byrne's letters acceded to as far as possible, with the view of "Jones" securing his confidence.'

A crucial test for Jack Sherritt came on 6 November when he was asked to meet the outlaws near Peechelba, 22 kilometres north of Wangaratta. The police were informed and told him to keep the appointment. Jack went but found no sign of them. He later said,

on the next morning coming back on a scrubby track through the ranges, Byrne the outlaw suddenly appeared and signed to me to follow into the bush. When out of sight of the track we had a long conversation. Byrne's mind seemed burdened over the murder of Sergeant Kennedy. He asked me to join them as a scout, and spoke about sticking up the Yackandandah bank . . . he said a lot about Mr Hare and Mr Nicolson. He asked me if I knew Mr Hare, and I said 'No' and he said, 'That is the old buck that caught Power'. I said, 'I do not know'. He said he believed he was a bloody smart old cove. And he asked me if I knew Mr Nicolson and I told him I knew no one. He asked me to go to Yackandandah and see how many police were stationed there, and to let him know . . . I was to see if I could detect any police in private clothes, and loaf round there and see where the police went in to have tea, and all particulars about their movements. Byrne said that Mr Hare and the search parties very nearly had them once, and that they were bloody well starved out. He told me he would give me money to spy for him – that is, to go to Yackandandah bank – but that he was short of cash at present but when he got a bank he would give me a hundred or two . . . He had no horse, but he had a pair of long boots, and his trousers were all over blood. He had long spurs . . . and he had the appearance of having ridden hard. I asked him where his mates were, and he said, 'Not very far off' I was to meet him at Evan's Gap a short time afterwards.

The meeting was a trap for Sherritt – the outlaws had already been informed of police strength and bank details at Yackandandah. Nicolson wrote that the gang's predicted appearance, like all of them, had been 'made with such precautions as to baffle any pursuit'. Had the police followed up the meeting they would have been seen coming and Sherritt would have been exposed as a spy. Nor did Jack have any doubts; Byrne's questions about police leaders made his danger seem certain. Jack did not have to keep the appointment at Evan's Gap and didn't: on 13 November he was working on his parents' selection when his sister came to tell him that Dan Kelly was at the house and wanted to see him. Sherritt panicked and rode straight into Beechworth to tell superintendent Nicolson. He was given 10 shillings and told to show himself on the Woolshed and establish an alibi. There was no doubt that Sherritt was telling the truth and Nicolson was censured for not having acted. Nicolson would have realised his oversight when other reports confirmed the gang were only five kilometres west of his office.

Close friends of Joe Byrne told him that they saw Sherritt going into Beechworth. By this time, the outlaws were as sure of his treachery as that of his brother's. Yet incredibly, Byrne made another visit to the Sherritt family and his former mates at Sheepstation Creek. The official police details are the only record; Aaron and Jack Sherritt are mentioned under their aliases.

On November 23rd Byrne visited Jones's hut about 8 p.m. Other members of the gang evidently outside. Dogs barked for two hours before he entered. He was well dressed. Shook hands with all, including Moses [Aaron]. Complimented Jones [Jack] upon the work he had done for them about posting letters and caricatures during past month. Said that Dan had been sent on the 13th to tell him not to meet him [Byrne] at Evan's Gap. That he and Ned had two separate plans for doing one of the Beechworth banks . . . Byrne said their horses were bad. His grey was still the best. A female present suggested if he would tell where the others were and give himself up he might get his pardon. He replied that the people would say he was worse than Sullivan and hunt him out of the colony. He remarked that the police were tired of watching his mother's place. Byrne looked as if fretting. Now looks under 10 stone weight. He left about 12 p.m. saying he would come again.

New South Wales police who captured Moonlite. The surviving nine troopers from the Moonlite affray were paraded in Sydney and given rewards totalling £525. According to one police officer at the time: 'when Scott . . . got together his youthful band of amateur bushrangers, he sent word to Ned Kelly that he wished to join forces with him. Kelly sent back word threatening that if Scott or his band approached him he would shoot them down.'

Byrne, however, made no further contact with the Sherritt brothers after that night. Jack returned to working his parent's selection, but lived in fear of reprisal. Aaron blissfully went on helping police, apparently unaware that he was provoking his own destruction.

For another six months, the Kelly campaign dragged on without visible incident. The Kellys and police kept up the game of hide and seek, which by this stage was fast losing any semblance of romantic adventure. Though a number of the gang's hideouts were reported and eventually found, the fugitives never returned to a camp known to police. In the summer and autumn of 1879–80 the gang were reported in every corner of 'Kelly Country'. In a single week, the outlaws managed to visit an orange grove near Glenrowan, Byrne's mother's home at Sebastopol, and be glimpsed fleeting across the Oxley plains and the Warby Range above the Hart selection. Their only predictable habit was a preference for hideouts near friends or relatives. They were known to camp on the ranges each side of the King River between Moyhu and Edi where their uncle, John 'Jack' Quinn, ran 300 head of horses. The gang also stayed further west near Lake Rowan – close to the Ryan family. A detective found that 'selectors on the direct route between Lake Rowan and Greta see and hear horsemen passing through at night and have found panels removed from their fences'. Such activity occurred in nearly every locality north of Benalla.

A remarkable revelation was that the outlaws spent most of their time from November 1879 to May 1880 in the vicinity of Greta and Oxley – within 35 kilometres of the Benalla police headquarters – without ever being sighted by a policeman. The Kellys regularly used a hut owned by one of the McAuliffes on the edge of the Greta swamp and often lived in a low bark hut in scrub near the

Captain Moonlite gained brief notoriety during the Kellys' career. On 15 November 1879, a wild-minded George Scott, alias 'Captain Moonlite', led five companions into the most dramatic and saddest attempt to follow Kelly's footsteps. Three days after crossing into New South Wales, they fought a fierce battle with ten troopers near Wantabadgery. Two of Moonlite's men – or boys – and one constable were fatally wounded and another of the gang was shot in the arm before they surrendered. Scott and another named Rogan were tried and hanged at Sydney's Darlinghurst Gaol in late January 1880; the two other survivors were given life imprisonment.

King River and Oxley, known as 'Skeehan's paddock'. In the same period, they also hid on land beside the Greta–Oxley road (rented by one of the McAuliffes). In March, five pairs of horse-hobbles were found on Kilfeera station near Tom Lloyd senior's selection; nearby was a camp concealed in a bank of ferns on the Fifteen Mile Creek. Wild Wright said the gang swam their horses out to shelter on an island in the Winton swamp (Lake Mokoan). James Quinn and another alleged sympathiser, John Hart, were working the Kelly selection in early 1880 when Tom Lloyd said the outlaws put a bark ceiling in their mother's hut and were literally living under their own roof for a time.

After the unsuccessful prosecution of sympathisers in 1879, the Kellys network of supporters enjoyed a strange amnesty – which often led to

Mounted police on duty at Greta. By 1880 the enormous, yet highly unsuccessful, Kelly pursuit had left the police demoralised and bored. The police were defeated by the unreliability of spies and the 'forces bred of kinship'. Fear of the gang also forced many selectors to shelter them. If a lonely farmer glimpsed the outlaws riding along a distant ridge, he dared give no sign. The likelihood of coming home to find sheds or haystacks on fire or waking to see fences down and cattle driven away was only too real. On the other hand, the police were up against a national tendency to idolise bushrangers and distrust or oppose authority. This characteristic caused more apathy than unwillingness to help police. For the working class, police represented authority, wealth and power. The 1870s and 1880s were times of extreme social imbalance and the Kellys actively encouraged people to see their stand as a fight against wealth and power. After the shock of the Stringybark shootings, they did nothing to jar the average bush consciousness. The robberies from banks expressed a common frustration and as poor selectors rarely, if ever, had money in banks, they possibly viewed them as fair game. This group is shown at the Greta police stables and includes at right senior constable Graham. They carry British Martini-Henry breech-loading single shot carbines and ammunition pouches hang at their sides.

amusing incidents. When a spy reported the Kellys were in a hut on the Ryan selection at Lake Rowan, police raided the property but only found young Tom Lloyd. Superintendent Nicolson said Lloyd 'chaffed the troopers as there was no ground whatever for arresting him – and they all came away good-humouredly'. Then Nicolson stopped Tom Lloyd senior on the Benalla road. The old man was carrying a bundle of new boots across his saddle, thought to be for his nephews; but again suspicion was not enough to support a charge. Detective Ward recalled another incident:

We started off for the Eleven Mile Creek and Mrs Skillion's residence one evening being of the opinion that Ned Kelly or his brother would come on that night to see their sister. The night was raining heavens hard and very dark, when about two miles from Winton on the Greta road we found a dray and two bags of flour and other articles, without a horse, in the middle of the road. We searched around and found Mrs Skillion and Kate Kelly sitting on a log. They were wet through, having very light clothes on. We went up and spoke to them. They said they were benighted, and could not find their way home – it was too dark. I had a flask with some whisky in it; I gave some to Kate Kelly and then left two men behind to show them the way to their own house.

Signs that people were supporting the gang often showed in indirect ways. Nearly all the Kellys' connections prospered in 1879. The McAuliffe brothers, lifelong friends and former Greta schoolmates of the Lloyds – and probably the Kellys – were among the many supposed to have done well out of the Kelly outbreak. Later that year, a Benalla police memorandum noted:

About twelve months ago the widow McAuliffe, Greta, was very ill, not being able to get the necessaries of life. Since then she has rented 300 acres of land, purchased £60 or £70 worth of cattle, has four men fencing, sent one of her sons to Tasmania and brought her daughter home who was in service there, and purchased a ladies saddle in Wangaratta for £10. Her sons are wearing top boots and have plenty of money and spend it freely about Glenrowan. Youngest Jack Lloyd lives at the McAuliffes and is constantly riding back and forwards to Mrs Skillion's . . . One of the Tanners [suspected sympathisers] is with the men fencing for McAuliffes.

Accounts of how the Kellys endured their two years as outlaws survive in two versions. Police spies optimistically reported in the first months of 1880 that the fugitives were extremely hard pressed. An informant for Nicolson told how Dan Kelly, upon visiting a friends' hut near Chiltern, 'was so emaciated that you could put your fists on his cheekbones'. In other reports of the time, Nicolson wrote:

During the past summer the outlaws have been in the habit of resting among ferns, long grass and in the open air during the day and visiting their few trusted friends unexpectedly at night . . . These friends are confined to their blood relations and a few chosen young men of the criminal class, who have known them since childhood; none of them, up to this date, can be induced to betray them, even for £8,000. They are accompanied by one or two scouts, who search the ground before them for ambuscades, and they use all their craft against leaving any trail for the trackers. When they do visit any hut or place, they watch it for several hours previously, and, after satisfying themselves that no strangers are within, one of them enters, and, if all is well, the others follow leaving one or two of their scouts outside. They have never shown themselves openly, as at Euroa and Jerilderie, since the arrival of the Queensland native trackers here. The presence of the latter, and the precautions taken against a successful raid, have baffled the outlaws. Their funds are almost exhausted, their prestige has faded considerably, and, consequently, the number of their admirers has decreased. They are depressed and very distrustful . . . I do not think there is much prospect of them making another raid if the present precautions and vigilance is maintained – neither do I think it likely that they will leave the colony as they seem to be thoroughly impressed with the idea that they are safest where they are, amongst their own people.

Joe Byrne, however, remarked that 'they had always lived well, but that the want of sleep, which they had often to endure, was very trying'. The Kelly relatives maintained that the outlaws were never harassed by police, but led a relaxed and comfortable existence behind a wall of friendship and loyalty. The outlaws, they said, moved about as they pleased. Besides being guests at parties among friends, the outlaws visited district race meetings, ploughing matches, drank at hotels and attended theatrical shows. Their greatest hardship was most likely boredom. The truth lies somewhere in between the two versions, as both Nicolson and the sympathisers were guilty of exaggeration.

It was March 1880 before the Kelly gang showed signs that some new move was being planned. On 22 March, a Glenrowan farmer named Sinclair reported mouldboards stolen from his ploughs. Within a week other selectors 'within a radius of eight miles' between Glenrowan, Greta and Oxley, complained of similar thefts. Benalla police, including the Queensland trackers, were sent to investigate what seemed a ridiculous crime. Traces of footsteps were found; 'one of them was described as that of a man with a very small boot; with what is called a "larrikin heel" upon it'. Ned Kelly was known to have very small feet, and the gang – like the Greta mob – favoured stylish footwear. The police had little doubt that the outlaws had been responsible.

During the week the mouldboards disappeared, and for nearly a month afterwards, Kelly sympathisers took over Glenrowan and Mrs Jones' small Glenrowan Inn as a meeting-place, for what was revealed afterwards as a diversion tactic. Police were puzzled because a rival publican, McDonnell, was a known friend of the Kellys. Months later, it was found that Joe Byrne had been regularly visiting McDonnell's during the same period under a nom de plume. On the day the first plough was found stripped, a Glenrowan railway porter acting as a spy informed police that 'Ettie Hart, sister of the outlaw, at Mrs Jones's Hotel, visited by sympathisers, but no sign of outlaws'. The Benalla paper reported 'riotous conduct' at Glenrowan in the weeks following. On 14 April another police despatch read:

Esther Hart still at Glenrowan. McAuliffes, Lloyd, and other sympathisers visit Mrs Jones's, and rowdy, especially to strangers. Suspicious movements of Dick Hart, elder brother of outlaw Steve Hart. He has returned to Mrs Jones's, Glenrowan. On the night of April 24th went up behind the hotel; absent two hours. Next night he came out in front of hotel, and cracked a stockwhip three times, like a signal.

While the sympathisers were making noise at Glenrowan, the outlaws were busily engaged five kilometres south near Greta on what was to be the fatal mistake of Ned Kelly's career. Whether his judgement and morale had been affected by two years of running, or whether he had been struck by a wild romantic brainwave, Kelly decided on the fantastic idea of making body armour for their protection in case of pitched battle. The armour was never intended for wearing on horseback, but was most likely designed for use if the gang were surrounded in one of their hideouts, or for fighting their way into a bank. However, it is more likely that Kelly had a specific project in mind.

When completed, the suits weighed between 25 and 30 kilograms – so heavy that even a strongly built man could only walk under the load. Kelly relatives and descendants have always taken great pride in the secret of exactly where the armour was made and who made it. Many people have claimed to be the tradesmen who shaped the suits; and a blacksmith at Greta was strongly suspected at the time. Tom Lloyd junior, however, maintained that he and Dan Kelly made the armour.

Recalling the armour as an old man, Lloyd said various materials were tested for suitability: among them indiarubber and sheet-iron, before the iron of plough mouldboards was chosen. Reports of the time said pitsaws were also stolen but were not used. Lloyd said the armour was made near Mrs Skillion's

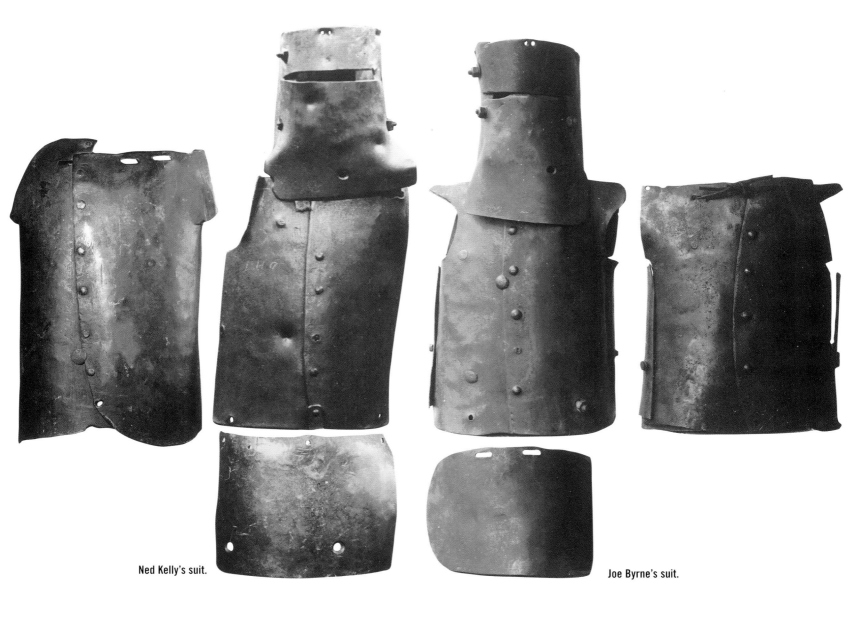

Ned Kelly's suit.

Joe Byrne's suit.

Dan Kelly and Steve Hart's suits.

The Kelly armour. Each of the four suits consisted of a helmet, back and front body-pieces and a lappet hanging from the front body-piece. Some of the suits may have had another lappet at the back and narrow side strips joining the breast and back-pieces — Ned Kelly's suit even had shoulder caps. The pieces shown are most of what survives of the original Kelly blacksmithing. A number of replicas have been made but they are easily discredited. The engraving and photograph (showing the armour worn by Hart and Dan Kelly) appeared immediately after Ned Kelly's capture.

The suit at top left was most likely Ned Kelly's; the lappet-piece that covered his groin has since been re-attached with an iron hinge. Byrne wore the suit beside it and the two below were those of Hart and Dan Kelly. A senior police officer recalled that the helmets were lined with padding or quilting to soften the impact of bullets — Ned wore the padded cap shown in the photograph with armour and his cut-down Colt carbine. The photograph also discounts the theory that only one helmet was ever made by the gang.

V. R.

MURDER OF POLICE.

NOTICE

OF

WITHDRAWAL

OF

REWARD.

WHEREAS by a Notice published in the *Victoria Government Gazette* bearing date the 18th February 1879, a Reward of One thousand pounds was offered by the Government for the capture of, or for such information as would lead to the capture of each of the following offenders, that is to say, Edward Kelly, Daniel Kelly, Stephen Hart, and Joseph Byrne: NOTICE IS HEREBY GIVEN that such offer of Reward will only remain in force for the period of three months from the date hereof, that is to say, that after the 20th day of July next the Government of Victoria will absolutely cancel and withdraw the offer of the Reward in question for the apprehension of the said offenders.

ROBERT RAMSAY,
Chief Secretary

Chief Secretary's Office,
20th April 1880.

N.B.—The Government of New South Wales has signified its intention of cancelling the offer of the Reward similarly issued by it on the same date.

Above: Another factor almost certainly unknown to the Kellys was the departure of sub-inspector O'Connor and his trackers — news that could have changed the Kellys plans that month. On Friday 25 June, the contingent left Benalla for Melbourne. The trackers [have] not only frightened the Kellys, it was claimed soon after, but [have] caused then much inconvenience and hard work . . . It is well known that bushmen of the Kelly type object to walking much, and always ride on horseback if they get the chance. The presence of the Queensland aborigines in the district often compelled the gang to walk in order to avoid giving the aborigines a chance of following horse's tracks, when they would otherwise have ridden . . . the blacks could follow [tracks] with unerring certainty; and their astuteness in that direction astounded and terrified Ned Kelly, other than whom there are few better white bushmen. The picture was either taken at Benalla or Essendon. From left are Barney, Johnny, Jimmy, sub-inspector O'Connor, Jack and Hero. The trackers are armed with English Snider .577 breech-loading single shot carbines.

Left: Daniel Kennedy, the 'diseased stock agent', was a teacher at Greta until 1874 when he began helping his sister-in-law (Bridget O'Brien) run her hotel. Many of the 'Greta mob' were customers and former pupils and this put him in a prime position to inform police. Kennedy had a bitter dispute with key sympathisers, the McAuliffes, and others, which may have prompted him to act as an informer. Nicolson considered Kennedy a most effective agent and without doubt — as it transpired — his most sensational piece of intelligence was that of the Kelly armour. One of Nicolson's colleagues wrote of him: 'He [Kennedy] had a professional standing in the district that brought him in contact with all classes of people; the talk and family gossip of the place came to him without seeking; he moved about without suspicion even amongst persons who favoured the Kellys . . . this agent's services were worth more than those of all others put together.' Nevertheless, when Hare was re-appointed, he dismissed Kennedy from service.

Facing page: Withdrawal of reward. If the gang had waited until after July for their next move, their career might have taken a different direction. If they were aware that the bounty was about to expire, the cause of their untimely actions remains a mystery. The proclamation was even highlighted in the press at the time: 'The Act [Felons Apprehension Act 1878] was only directed to be in force until the end of the last session of Parliament. As a matter of fact then the gang [after 2 February 1880] were not outlaws . . . the early prorogation of Parliament having really destroyed the validity of the Act.'

hut and in the Kellys' own forge by the Eleven Mile Creek. The twist was taken out of the mouldboards by heating them and then beating them out on a green log stripped of bark. The back, breastplates and helmet were riveted and shaped in a similar way while the cutting and joining was done on an anvil. Contrary to J. J. Kenneally's 1935 claim, four helmets were made by the gang – one for each suit. The finished result was as unique and impracticable as it was true to Kelly's spirit: a grand, misguided gesture.

Superintendent Nicolson learned of the Kellys' creative efforts from a spy named Daniel Kennedy, informing under the alias of 'Denny'. Nicolson received Kennedy's information in a letter dated 20 May 1880. He wrote this summation:

subsequently I heard that the mouldboards were being made into, and were intended for, armour. Agents communicated with me in a special way. Each had a special character given them. This one was supposed to be an Inspector of Stock; and the term 'diseased stock' was supposed to mean the outlaws, and under that veil he wrote to me as follows. 'Dear Sir – Nothing definite on the diseased stock of this locality. I have made careful inspection, but did find [sic] exact source of disease. I have seen and spoken to ——— and ——— on Tuesday, who were fencing near home. All others I have not been able to see. Missing portions of cultivators described as jackets are now being worked, and fit splendidly. Tested previous to using and proof at 10 yards. I shall be in Wangaratta on Monday, before when I may learn how to treat the disease. I am perfectly satisfied that it is where last indicated, but in what region I can't discover. A break-out may be anticipated, as feed is getting very scarce. Five are now bad . . . Other animals are, I fear, diseased.

If Nicolson believed the news – as he claimed – he did nothing about it. A week later, more important events distracted his attention. On the morning of 26 May, Aaron Sherritt's mother reported that one of the outlaws had threatened Aaron's life. The visit was apparently genuine, but seems pointless unless Byrne was trying to warn his former friend to leave the district.

My son John was doing a bit of ploughing at home. This evening he went into Beechworth. I got up very early in the morning and went out to his room to see if he had come home, and saw his bed had not been disturbed. Then I went out to see if I could hear the bells on the horses ploughing. I went along our own paddock fence . . . I then saw a man with a horse's bridle on his arm, and this was Joe Byrne. And as soon as he saw me he got up and came over. He spoke friendly enough to me; [but then] said he had come to take my son Aaron's life, and also Detective Ward's. He said, 'Oh, we could go anywhere were it not for your sanguinary son there . . . Those two had them starved to death . . . that Ward went about the hills like a blacktracker; and that if he had them two out of the way, and also Senior Constable Mullane . . . he could go where he liked'. I begged him not to take Aaron's life. I said, 'He has no harm; he would not hurt you'. And he said, 'You need not try to impress that on my mind, because I tell you now that there was Ward and him and Hare very nearly twice catching us, and that tells you whether they will hurt me or not.' Then I strove with him – I don't know what I said – not to take poor Aaron's life . . . So when he had done he went away.

Soon after, a police party with blacktrackers traced Byrne's horse from the Sherritt selection north to Mrs Byrne's and then up across the creek to the main road. During the same period, several shots were fired across the roof of Aaron Sherritt's new hut near the Devil's Elbow. Superintendent Nicolson organised yet another police party to be stationed permanently on the Woolshed – this time at Aaron's new home. Nicolson wrote at the time that he was sure the gang were now on the verge of another raid.

On 31 May 1880, however, Nicolson's role as commander of the Kelly pursuit ended due to lack of results. His rival, superintendent Francis Hare, was appointed – leaving Nicolson to return to Melbourne under a cloud of failure. Hare made no changes to Nicolson's system during his first four weeks at Benalla and the first three weeks of June 1880 passed uneventfully. The outlaws made no appearances in the district and were later found to have spent most of that month on the ranges somewhere above the Buckland River. The most significant incident during that time occurred on 25 June, when Nicolson's agent, 'Denny', brought in more detailed news of the Kelly armour. Superintendent Sadleir was present and wrote of the prophetic interview:

He [Kennedy] had a very important, not to say startling story to tell. The Kellys were now entirely out of funds and their friends . . . were putting pressure on them, and a fresh exploit was to be expected immediately. The Kellys had provided themselves with bullet-proof armour which they had tested with their own rifles, and part of their plan was to effect something that would cause the ears of the Australian world to tingle . . . I do not quite know what the man thought of the reception he met with. Hare treated him with scorn, dismissed him from all further service, and, turning to me, remarked; 'If this is the sort of person Nicolson and you have been depending upon, it is no wonder you have not caught the Kellys.

14 DEVIL'S ELBOW
THE DEATH OF AARON SHERRITT, 26 JUNE 1880

Within three days of dismissing Daniel Kennedy, Nicolson's key informant, superintendent Hare realised his mistake. After fourteen months of inactivity, the Kellys – driven by ever-decreasing funds and haunted by fear of betrayal – had decided to deliver the masterstroke of their career. It remains unknown whether their intention was to win back prestige and money, to try once more to force the release of their mother, to declare a republic in north-eastern Victoria or whether it was a combination of these motives. The armour was the visible sign of preparation for what Mrs Byrne boasted would be 'something that would astonish not only the colony, but the whole world'. The Kelly plan, as far as it was revealed, was simple, diabolical and ingenious. The exploit was to include three stages and satisfy a number of ends.

The first stage of the plan was the murder (or execution, as sympathisers called it) of their old friend and assumed traitor, Aaron Sherritt. Joe Byrne and Dan Kelly agreed to be his 'executioners' and their intention was to repay his deceit and discourage further traitorous behaviour. Sherritt's death also served another purpose. The gang calculated that if Sherritt was killed on a Saturday evening, news of the murder would reach police headquarters at Benalla and Melbourne by Sunday afternoon at the latest. Knowing that there was no Sunday passenger traffic, the Kellys estimated that the only train heading toward Beechworth would be a police special rushing to the scene of the crime. On this assumption, they decided on the second part of the plan: that Ned Kelly and Steve Hart

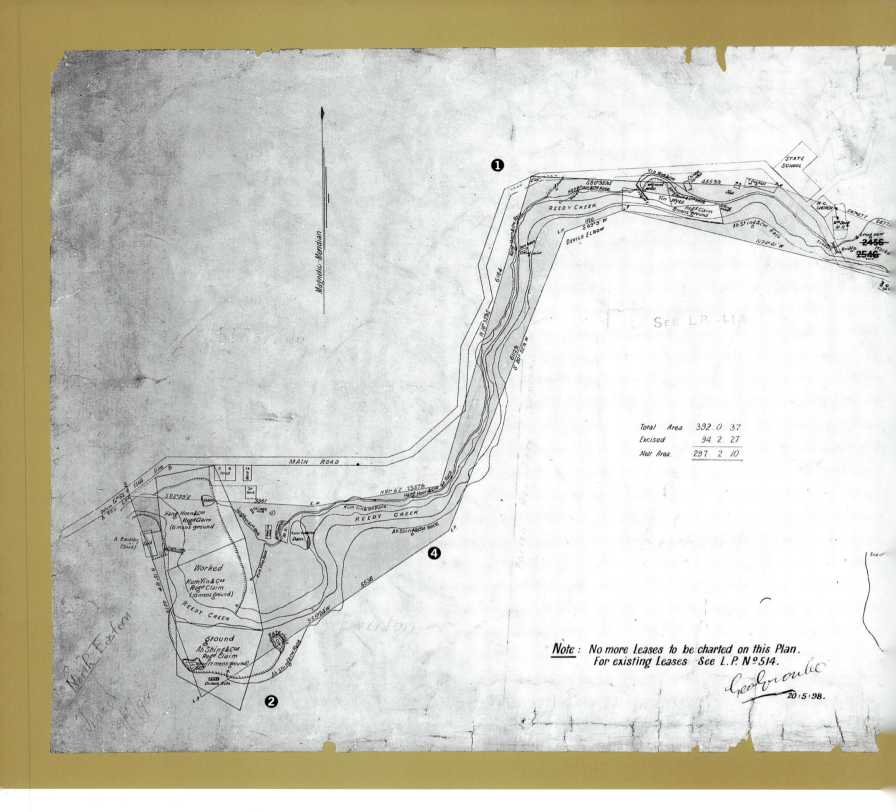

would prepare to stop the train at Glenrowan – midway between Benalla and Wangaratta and the start of the Beechworth branch of the line. They intended to tear up the track on the embankment and downhill grade just beyond Glenrowan railway station. Joe Byrne and Dan Kelly would join them there for the big surprise.

Two explanations have been given for what the Kellys had planned for the train's occupants. Some Kelly descendants support the argument that the gang's intention was to force the stationmaster to stop the train at Glenrowan station, capture the police leaders and hold them hostage to bargain the release of Mrs Kelly, Skillion and Williamson. Derailment was only to be a last resort. Police and journalists later believed a large-scale massacre was the sole intention, and that the gang intended letting carriages and human freight plunge over the embankment where they could 'rake the train with shot'. Three of the outlaws later made contradictory statements about their plans. At Glenrowan, Dan Kelly, Joe Byrne and Ned Kelly all said they would 'send the train and its occupants to hell'. Ned Kelly later changed his stand saying, 'I was determined to capture Superintendent Hare, O'Connor and the blacks for the purpose of an exchange of prisoners, and while I had them as hostages I would be safe, no police would follow me.'

Ned Kelly was deliberately evasive about the third stage of their plan – evidently protecting those who were to be involved. They intended to gather a small army of friends – one police officer suggested 30 men – who were to wait at Morgan's Lookout (overlooking Glenrowan Gap) until signalled by 'sky rockets' to join the gang. The rallying point was to be a hotel owned by a sympathiser, McDonnell, on the south side of the Glenrowan railway station. The gang almost certainly intended arming all their sympathisers with weapons taken from the police train. It is likely that Benalla and its unprotected banks were the ultimate targets after Glenrowan. Far more spectacular plans have been assumed, based on an alleged draft document for a republic attributed

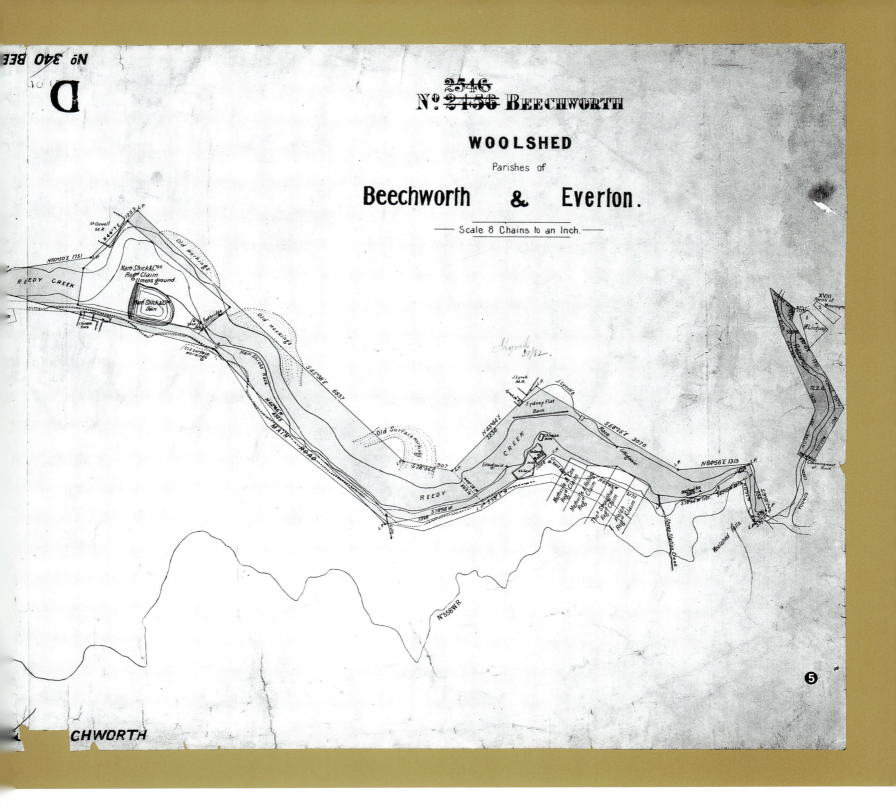

to the Kellys, but as yet it has not been relocated. Despite the uncertain final objective, the whole operation was planned like a military campaign.

In the last winter days of June 1880 events began to move toward a violent climax. By this time, Aaron Sherritt was 25 years old and had been married for six months. His wife, still in her teens, was Ellen Barry – daughter of a 'well known farmer on the Woolshed' whose family lived east of the Woolshed State School. The newlyweds initially lived with the Barrys as Aaron had sold his selection the previous year. After several months, the couple took over an abandoned miner's hut at the Devil's Elbow, between the Woolshed and Sebastopol. Sherritt had been employed 'at seven shillings a day' with the police since December 1879 and at the time he was stationed with a watch party overlooking the Byrne hut from the upper police caves. When these caves became too dirty, the police moved in with the newlyweds at the Devil's Elbow. Four troopers hid in the small Sherritt hut until 1

Beechworth and Everton. The hut occupied by the young Sherritts in March 1880 was 'at a spot directly in line with the Devil's Elbow' (1). It was less than three kilometres from the Byrne home (2) and clearly within sight from the range behind the hut. The Barry family, Aaron's 'in-laws', lived one kilometre west of them (3). Anton Wick also lived about one kilometre from the Byrnes (4). A visitor to the locality in August 1880 wrote: 'I had a run down to Sebastopol to see Aaron Sherritt's hut. It stands on the Eldorado road, about [seven] miles from Beechworth. [Three and a half] miles this side there is a bridge over Reid's creek [5]. At this bridge Sherritt used to meet Detective Ward, and give him information . . . The road, then having crossed a range, descends into a long valley, which extends westwards. In this valley is the place called the Woolshed, and further on Sebastopol. It has been pretty well torn up by diggers, and the bulk of the population now are chinamen. Sherritt's hut, which stands on an elevation a few yards from the main road is now tenantless, and presents a very deserted and dilapidated appearance. Just here the valley and the road takes a turn towards the south, and [under] two miles more brings the traveller to Mrs Byrne's house. Looking southward, Mrs Byrne's stands on the left hand side of the gully. On each side are steep rocky ranges, just behind the house there is a gap and a track, which were utilized by the Kelly gang.'

THE AGE, MONDAY, JUNE 28,

ANOTHER MURDER BY THE KELLY GANG.

A PRIVATE DETECTIVE SHOT.

FOUR CONSTABLES BESIEGED FOR TWELVE HOURS.

[BY ELECTRIC TELEGRAPH.]

[FROM OUR OWN CORRESPONDENT.]

BEECHWORTH, 27th June, 4 p.m.

Constable Armstrong, one of a police search party, rode into Beechworth at half-past one o'clock this (Sunday) afternoon, and informed the police that the Kelly gang had been at Sebastopol on the previous evening (Saturday), at six o'clock, and that Joe Byrne had shot Aaron Skerritt through the eye and killed him. The gang brought a German to Aaron Skerritt's hut handcuffed, there being a number of police in the hut at the time, and forced him to ask Skerritt the road to Sebastopol. As soon as Skerritt opened the door a ball was sent through his eye and another through his chest. The gang also fired seven balls into the sides of the hut, and kept the police prisoners for twelve hours.

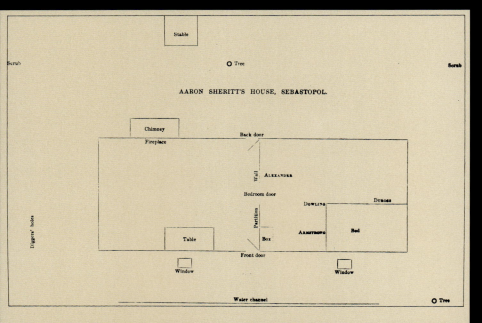

Top left: Age news item, 28 June 1880.

Above: Anton Wick (often misspelt 'Weekes') was a German miner, woodcutter and market gardener. He was 54 in 1880 and a long-term resident of the Woolshed Valley bringing up four children on his own. He was on good terms with Mrs Byrne, his nearest neighbour, and had known Aaron and Joe since childhood. The Barrys (Aaron's wife and mother-in-law) also knew Byrne and his family intimately. Seven years earlier, Wick had prosecuted Joe for illegally using his horse, but Byrne said he held no grudge. Wick considered Byrne 'was not a bad sort of chap' until that night when he expected he would be shot.

Left: Aaron Sherritt's home. The engraving appeared in newspapers at the time, but is inaccurate in that the doors were in the centre of the side walls. The view looks south, down the slope toward the main road. A journalist who visited the hut noted: The house is . . . a one storied weatherboard structure, with a shingle roof, and comprises two rooms. One of these rooms, which was used as a kitchen is 15 ft. by about 9 ft., and the other, the bedroom, about 11 ft. by 9 ft. There are two doors, one at the back; and the other at the front nearly opposite to each other. There is no passage formed through the house, both doors opening into the kitchen, which is partitioned off from the bedroom by a wooden screen having a doorway cut in the centre of it. The partition does not reach to the ceiling but there is a space of about [two] feet. There is no door in the partition, the opening being covered by a grey piece of calico . . . There are two windows both of which are in front of the house. The bed on which the three Constables were lying when the first shot was fired is a double iron one directly beneath one window. In front of the other window is the table on which the candle was burning . . . Directly opposite the table is the fire, which is an open one, for burning logs of large dimension. The chimney . . . is built of strong weatherboards, the upper portion of the flue constructed of pieces of kerosine tins.

Bottom left: Plan of Sherritt's home. This accurate detail was produced for the 1881 royal commission. The front door faced directly onto the main road 'about five yards from the hut'.

April 1880 before the watch was abandoned. By June 1880, four troopers once again moved in with the young couple after Joe Byrne's visit to Aaron's mother at Sheepstation Creek.

By Saturday 26 June, the men living hidden in the Sherritt household were senior constable Armstrong and constables Duross, Dowling and Alexander. Also visiting that night was Aaron's mother-in-law, Ellen Barry. The first news report of what followed that night, hastily wired from Beechworth on Sunday afternoon – as expected – appeared in the Melbourne *Age* on Monday 28 June 1880. Mistakes in the article are corrected by the following accounts of those present that night.

8.00 P.M.

A party of five police left here at three o'clock in charge of Senior Constable Mullane, but no further particulars are to hand yet. Mr Foster, the police magistrate, proceeded to the scene of the affray to hold an inquest, but he has decided to postpone it until tomorrow. The police are very reticent. It is thought that Sherritt was shot in order to check the disaffection amongst the outlaws' friends. He was an old resident of the Beechworth district. For some months past he has been known by the Kellys to be a private detective in the service of the police.

8.46 P.M.

The house at which the affray took place is situated about seven miles from Beechworth, on the Eldorado road, and is within half a mile from the residence of Byrne's mother. It is a two-roomed slab house, and at the rear there is a stable; in front there are several large trees between the house and the main Eldorado road. At the time of the outbreak, about half past eight o'clock, there were six [sic] people in the house, namely Constables Armstrong Alexander, Duross and Dowling and Aaron Sherritt and his wife. The German, Anton Weekes [sic], who was brought to the house by the gang is a resident of the place [sic]; and Sherritt, it is supposed, recognised his voice and immediately opened the door and was shot down by Byrne, who said, 'You'll not blow what you will do to us any more'. Sherritt died instantaneously, without a struggle. About eight shots were fired by the outlaws. The marks of five balls are visible on the outside wall of the house, three of which passed through. After Byrne shot Sherritt, the gang retired behind trees and called upon the police to 'Come out of that you dogs and surrender'. The police said they would sooner die than surrender, and one of the gang then threatened to burn down the house and roast them inside. It is reported that the police concealed themselves under the bed, but the rumour is discredited. Numbers of persons have visited the scene of the murder this afternoon, and the greatest excitement prevails amongst those present. At Sherritt's house this afternoon was one of the sympathisers who was in Beechworth Gaol some time ago; when he saw that he was recognised he slunk away.

THE MURDER OF AARON SHERRITT

Anton Weekes said: I am a market gardener. I remember last Saturday . . . On that evening I went out to go to John Weiner's. I went as far as the house, and as I saw no light there I went back again. Weiner's house is close to Sherritt's place, about ten or fifteen yards away. I returned to my own place about ten minutes past six o'clock and about a hundred yards away I met two bushrangers, Byrne and Dan Kelly. They were on horseback Byrne was riding one horse and leading another. I think I said 'Good evening' as they passed me. They did not answer, but Byrne rode about five yards past me, then turned round and came back again. He asked me, 'What is your name?' I said, 'Weekes, from the Woolshed'. He drew up close, looked into my face, and asked if I knew him. I said 'No'. He said 'I am Joe Byrne'. I replied, 'I do not believe you'. He put his hand back and showed me a revolver, at the same time saying 'Will you believe it now?' He pointed to his mate and said, 'That is Mr Kelly'. He next told Kelly to put the handcuffs on me. Kelly came off his horse and put the handcuffs on me. Byrne told me not to be frightened, for although I had summoned him once for using a horse he forgave me. I had in fact summoned him for such an offence in this [Beechworth] Court. He said, 'You must go with me to Sherritt's, and if you do what we tell you we will do you no harm'. They walked me between them to Sherritt's, and when we got about twenty yards from the place we turned off into the bush on the right. We went about half-a-dozen yards into the scrub and the bushrangers got off their horses. One of them tied his animal to a bush. Byrne said to me, 'Now you have nothing to do except what we tell you'. Kelly went out from the bush on the main road. Byrne stopped with me and said, 'You go with me and knock at the door'.

We went to Sherritt's house, and he placed me in front of the back door, about a yard away. He said, 'Knock'. He was standing just behind me. When they left the bush both of them took a rifle from off the packhorse. When Byrne told me to knock I did so. He then said 'Call Aaron'. I called Aaron. He said 'Call louder'. I did so, and I received an answer from inside, 'Who is there?' Byrne told me to say 'Weekes' and I obeyed. He told me when I was asked what I wanted to say, 'I have lost myself'. Aaron opened the door and came out. Byrne, when he heard the door opening, moved a yard or two away, and stood behind the chimney. When the door was fully opened he stepped from behind the chimney and got under cover of me again. Aaron sang out 'Who is there?' Byrne then shot him at once. He fired from the right side of me. I am not sure whether he fired a second shot. I think he did, but I was so frightened I could not say. Aaron fell inside the house upon the floor. Byrne looked into the place and said 'That's all, that is the man I want'. He next saw Mrs Barry and Mrs Sherritt, and asked

Left: The murder of Aaron Sherritt. The legend in the Kelly family is that Sherritt's death was not the result of his treachery, but retaliation for a remark made to Mrs Byrne. Aaron had met Mrs Byrne on the main road between their homes and the old woman remarked angrily as they passed, 'What would Joe think of you now?' Sherritt is supposed to have answered, 'I'll shoot Joe Byrne, and I'll ——— his body before it gets cold'. Yet there is no doubt that allowing the police to live in his hut was sufficient to seal his doom. It is still contentious whether the constables showed cowardice or good sense by not firing a shot during the siege. Aaron's wife and Mrs Barry later admitted that two of the troopers hid under the bed and forced them under with them. The outlaws left the scene no later than 9 p.m. that night, yet the constables stayed inside until daybreak. The 1881 royal commission noted: 'Never was there a more conspicuous instance of arrant cowardice than was exhibited by these men on [that] night'. However, all witnesses stressed that it would have been suicide to rush for the doors. Ned Kelly told one of the troopers later, 'To have gone out in that light would have been foolhardy. You would all have been shot but one. It was not our game to shoot you all. We wanted one man to go and draw the police away from the barracks.' The engraving is fairly accurate except for some minor points: the door swung from the left and Dan Kelly and Anton Wick were both clean-shaven.

Below: Superintendent Hare commanded the third Woolshed watch party in June 1880, but it was organised by superintendent Nicolson. Hare's faith in the value of the Woolshed group was principally based on the reports of detective Ward and Aaron Sherritt — despite both misleading him. It is hard to believe that a senior officer like Hare was gullible, but clearly he was easily flattered. He wrote of that period: 'After I found out all I could concerning the movements of the outlaws at Benalla I started off to Beechworth and saw Aaron Sherritt . . . I had a long interview with him, finding out all that had taken place during my absence, and the different interviews he had had with the outlaws whilst I was away from the district. He expressed himself pleased at my return, and told me he did not get on with the Inspecting Superintendent as he did with me, and he would set to work with fresh zeal and endeavour to find out where the outlaws were to be found.' One of the troopers in the hut party pointed out that Sherritt lied to Hare, telling him that the outlaws 'often came about after his [Hare's] departure'. When confronted, Sherritt said, 'Well, I must use a little policy'. When Hare made a surprise twilight visit to check that Sherritt and the police were on duty, detective Ward made them rush off to their places. Several constables revealed that Ward 'manipulated [their] reports' and persuaded them not to report that their presence was known to the outlaws, adding that the detective was 'intimate with a storekeeper in Beechworth who was getting £30 a month for provisions, spirits and porter' supplied to the various watch parties.

Facing page: No agent on either side of the Kelly outbreak took more risk or paid more dearly for his work than **Aaron Sherritt**. Inevitably likeable, Sherritt's behaviour was a mass of contradictions. In one moment he could show unfeigned loyalty and in the next an utter lack of principle. Aaron betrayed the outlaws for the money it was worth, but always refused to carry weapons against them or for his own protection. He also admitted exploiting his police employers and yet, according to the police who lived with him, he showed consistent loyalty to his obligations. During 1880, he received a number of written and verbal threats but kept all of them from his young wife and showed no inclination to abandon his job. Nearly all the police distrusted him, but liked him nonetheless. Even C. H. Nicolson, who Sherritt described as 'a cranky Scotchman', parted 'good friends' with Sherritt when he left. Superintendent Hare made no secret of his infatuation and left this admiring description that is an insight into both of them. 'He [Sherritt] was a remarkable looking man, if he walked down Collins street, everybody would have stared at him — his walk, his appearance, and everything else was remarkable . . . he was a man of the most wonderful endurance . . . He would be under a tree without a particle of blanket of any sort in his shirt sleeves, whilst my men were all lying wrapped up in furs . . . I saw him one night when the water was frozen in the creeks and I was frozen to death nearly. I came down and said, "Where is Aaron Sherritt?" and saw a white thing lying on the ground uncovered — I said, "Are you mad Aaron, lying there?" and he said, "I do not care about coats." I said to him . . . "Can the outlaws endure as you are doing?" He said, "Ned Kelly would beat me into fits; I am a better man than Dan Kelly or Steve Hart, I have always beaten Joe [Byrne], but I look upon Ned Kelly as an extraordinary man; there is no man in the world like him, he is superhuman . . . I look on him as invulnerable, you can do nothing with him."' The undated portrait was taken in James Bray's Camp Street studio in Beechworth. Aaron is shown wearing a waist sash and chin strap under the nose 'in the Greta fashion'.

Superintendent Hare claimed this was a portrait of **Joseph Byrne**. However, it has also been suggested that it is actually Patrick Byrne – Joe's nineteen year-old brother. Sub-inspector O'Connor recalled, 'On the 31st of May [1880] an agent sent in word that he had seen Joe Byrne up a gully about a mile from his [Byrne's] mother's house. We got on the man's track, and, after following it for some distance, found it was only a man collecting cows . . . Aaron Sherritt, who was acting as our guide saw at once that it was Joe Byrne's brother Patsey, who was very like the outlaw.' Patsey, or 'Paddy' as he was called, left little doubt that the family knew the police were in the Sherritt hut. Large supplies of food and necessaries for the hidden men were often delivered to the hut in broad daylight and the men were often seen to 'answer calls of nature'. Ellen Sherritt's young brother often visited the hut and 'hailed Denny Byrne and his sister' from the front door as they went home from school. On one occasion he invited Denny inside while the four police hid breathless behind the partition. On the Sunday before the murder, 'Paddy Byrne stood on his grey mare in front of the hut, looking in; [the troopers] were all watching him through the joints of the door'. Even as late as the morning of 26 May, Aaron told the constable in charge: 'Armstrong you are discovered. Denny Byrne passed in the rear of the hut and looked in twice. They can set fire to this hut, and shoot you one by one as you run out.'

them to send the men out. The women were close to where Aaron fell, near the chimney. Mrs Barry came out, Byrne kept her out for half or three quarters of an hour. After he shot Aaron he put a shot through the bedroom. Fifteen minutes afterwards he put another shot through the bedroom, and said 'I want those men out, or I'll burn the place down'. I heard two shots fired from the front. Byrne then took the handcuffs off me, and made me go away from the house. He did not let me go out of his sight. Some little time afterwards he sent Mrs Barry into the house.

I heard some person speaking near a bush a short distance from me. This was after some shots were fired from the front. Byrne called out to Kelly, 'Shall I send Weekes in too?' Kelly said, 'No, don't send him in'. They both waited about for some time. They next went a little way into the bush. I remained there about three quarters of an hour and then left. I did not hear the bushrangers leave. I think they left before me, but I cannot say, as I heard nothing. I reached home about half past nine the same night. I had been absent about three hours. I had no chance to send information. When Byrne took the handcuffs off he asked me if my horse was at home. I said, 'No'. He then said, 'Give no information about this'.

Ellen Sherritt stated: I am the wife of the deceased Aaron Sherritt, and resided with him at Sebastopol. On Saturday evening last my husband and myself were present at our home. The other persons in the house were four constables and my mother. A knock came to the back door and a voice called out, 'Aaron'. I knew it was Mr Weekes' voice, and I told my husband so. My husband went to the door and asked what he wanted. Weekes said, 'I am lost, come out and show me the road'. He opened the door and went outside. As he did so he heard a man move behind the chimney, and he sang out, 'Who is there?' Just then Joe Byrne said something and fired off his rifle. My husband endeavoured to make his way back into the room. Byrne followed him to the door and fired a second shot at him. He [Sherritt] staggered and fell down near the table. He moaned once, but that was all. No word or other exclamation escaped him. After the second shot I ran into the bedroom out of the way. Byrne appeared at the [back] door again and I asked why he had shot Aaron. He said, 'If I had not shot him, he would have shot me if he could get the chance'. He heard one of the Constables going into the [bed] room, and he asked who the man was. I said he was a person staying with us for the night; that he was looking for work. He told me to bring him out. Before this he directed my mother to go and open the front door. She did so, and just then Dan Kelly made his appearance there. He had a revolver with him, which he kept pointed at me.

Byrne then called my mother out to the back door and he stood talking to her with Weekes between them. He asked me why I had not brought the man out I told him the man would not come. He then sang out to Dan Kelly, 'Look out, there are windows at the front'. Dan replied, 'It's all right' and stepped to the corner of the [front] door, pointing his rifle into the room all the time. He fired two shots into the bedroom where the men were. Byrne sent me in two or three times to get the men out, but kept himself covered by the forms of Weekes and my mother. About the same time he went up towards the bush at the back whistling and calling to someone, and asking them to come on, as there were men in the place. When he came back he must have heard the policemen doing something with their rifles, for he said to my mother, 'There's more than one man there and if you don't tell me the truth I will shoot both you and your daughter'. He also said he would burn the place down, and Dan Kelly went about gathering bushes. They did not set fire to the bushes. We then went in and remained inside the house all the night. About two hours after my husband was shot, one of the policemen came out of the bedroom, closed the doors, and shifted the box against which the head of my husband's dead body was resting. The first message sent to Beechworth was at eight o'clock. It was given to Mr O'Donohoe. Before that they tried to send a Chinaman, but could not do so, as they could not make him understand what was wanted. They then sent the Chinaman to Mr O'Donohoe's with a letter. Mr O'Donohoe came to the place and said he would go straight to Beechworth. He, however, soon came back and said he could not go. I heard afterwards that a man galloping up and down the bush had prevented him from going. The policemen said they were afraid to leave the place earlier because there were few enough of them if the place was attacked again. When O'Donohoe came back they sent a message by another man; but Constable Armstrong said he would not trust this person and so left the place himself to go to Beechworth. There were no shots fired at the police. I was in the bedroom with the police. Two of them were standing with their rifles ready. In order to fire on the outlaws they would have had to come out through the calico door, which if they had attempted to disturb, they would have at once been shot down by Dan Kelly. On the other hand, if they had rushed out to shoot Byrne at the back door, they would have either shot the German Weekes, or my mother.

There were about five or six shots fired in addition to the two which killed my husband. These were fired from the front of the house. About half an hour elapsed between the time when my husband was shot and when my mother returned after speaking to the outlaws. We thought the other two confederates of the outlaws were there because Dan Kelly and Byrne made themselves so bounceable. We had no other reason for thinking so. The police did not come out of the bedroom until two hours after my husband was shot. When it was daylight they went out and looked round the house to see if the gang were about. This was the first time they went out of the house. The outlaws would have been able to see the police, but the police could not see them.

W. H. Foster, Beechworth police magistrate and coroner, also gave an outline of his visit to the scene that Sunday afternoon. A little before one o'clock Mr Cheshire, who was then in charge of the telegraph station, came to me. He was very much excited, and said, 'The Kelly gang have shot one of the watch party down at Sebastopol!' I said, 'One of the police?' And he said, 'No, a man who is helping!' I said, 'Aaron Sherritt?' and he said, 'Yes, Aaron; that is the name'. I knew he was operating with the police, and it occurred to my mind that he would be the man. I enquired where it was, and immediately ordered a vehicle, and took down the clerk with me and my papers, and got to the spot as quickly as possible. When I got there, I found a crowd of about 100 or 120 men, women and children about and the hut closed. I demanded admission. I announced that I came there as Coroner, and was admitted by the police, and went into the hut, and found it in darkness, or almost dark. I asked for a light – no, first the question I asked was, 'Who is in charge?' and one of the Constables said, 'I am'. At that time I could not make out one man from another. I said, 'I want a light'. He said, 'Well, we do not much care about a light here, sir'. I said, 'Well, you must get it'. A light was then procured. While the light was being got I said, 'Where is the body?', and one of them said, 'You are almost standing on it'.

I turned round, and by this time my eyes had become accustomed to the darkness, and I saw the corpse close to me. I distinguished the man's teeth, and one of his eyes, all the rest was blood. I then interrogated the men there, two or three of them, and I also spoke to Mrs Barry, made such enquiry as I could. I cannot remember exactly what questions I put, but they were with the object of ascertaining how the thing occurred, and how it came that the police had not made any attack upon the Kellys . . . I should like to explain that – I drew this sketch of the building just now. I would like to explain the position of the parties. My opinion is, had the men made a rush and gone out they would have met a certain death, because those men had only to step a yard or two back and they would be invisible on account of the darkness of the night. The police would naturally suppose there were four outlaws there. This room, according to the enquiry I made immediately after, had a bright fire in it and a lighted candle. One of the Constables stooped down and pointed to the left eye of the corpse and said, 'That is where he got his death wound'. As a matter of fact I learned (afterwards) that he received two shots; one entered just above the collar bone and passed backwards through his body, the other went in just above the navel and broke two ribs and went through the kidney. I took that to be the second shot, and he fell back then. As a matter of fact he had no wound in the head at all, but it looked just as if that was where he had been shot, as it was covered with blood. Before I left the hut I made what enquiry I could, and asked the men if they wanted anything, that I was going back to Beechworth and would convey any message, and they said no; and I said also to one of the men, 'I feel sorry for you men, you seem to have been caught in a trap without any show', and the Constable I spoke to said, 'Thank you'. I was struck with the position myself, they were placed at great disadvantage.

Before I left, the crowd, somewhat over one hundred, were so clamorous to get in and I asked the police what they were going to do about them, and they said it would be better to keep them out; and I said, 'Yes'. I said, 'Keep them out, I am in charge of the body as coroner'; and I announced to the crowd, 'There are four armed police inside; they have my orders not to let anyone enter, so you had better go home, and fully half of them started before I left. I then started for Beechworth and about a mile from the hut I met the police [coming] from Beechworth – Senior Constable Mullane and Constable McColl, and others I forget.

15 THE LAST STAND
GLENROWAN, 26 JUNE 1880

By the time magistrate Foster departed the scene of Aaron Sherritt's murder, the Kellys had already prepared for the next stage of their campaign – 45 kilometres away below the grey timbered slopes of Morgan's Lookout. Dan Kelly and Joe Byrne left the Woolshed on Saturday night and rode hard to join their mates at Glenrowan by early on Sunday morning. Ned Kelly and Steve Hart had arrived outside Glenrowan on Saturday evening – in time to watch the last passenger train pass through. Then they walked into Glenrowan and bailed up some navvies camped in tents near Glenrowan railway station before calling at Mrs Jones' hotel.

Mrs Jones commented after the event:

I well remember Kelly coming to my place that dreadful night. It was raining and very wet. He took me and my dear little girl [Jane] away, and locked my two little boys up in a room by themselves. He made me turn the key – said he would shoot me if I refused to do everything that he told me. I begged him to lock myself and my daughter in my own room, but he wouldn't. He took me and my little girl – she was 15 then – together with seven men, over to the [railway] station. These were the men who were to take up the line and wreck the train that was coming up with the police from Melbourne. Kelly said to me, 'I'll show you a sight now! I'll kill all your ———- traps!' Then they went away up the line towards Wangaratta. My daughter saw them pulling up the railway line, but I did not.

After the line was destroyed, the Kellys took the other men to the gatehouse. They had no down on any of them – only on me and Reardon [the line-repairer]. They used to think Reardon was spying on them – with me. My daughter

Facing page: Weapons in the Kelly saga. Joe Byrne and Ned Kelly carried police-issue Webleys (one taken from sergeant Kennedy) similar to that second from top left. Top right is shown an 1856 model Tranter .45 calibre – popular among the Kelly gang and their pursuers. Ned carried three revolvers at Glenrowan: a Webley and two Colts: pocket and navy models. The Colt at top left (pocket model) was claimed to be Ned Kelly's and it is held, along with a Webley, by the Victorian police historical unit. The Colts at bottom, a shorter 1849 .31 calibre pocket model and the large 1849 .36 navy model were also allegedly taken from Ned Kelly at Glenrowan and are preserved by the State Library of Victoria. Railway guard Jesse Dowsett also carried a pocket Colt when he confronted Ned Kelly.

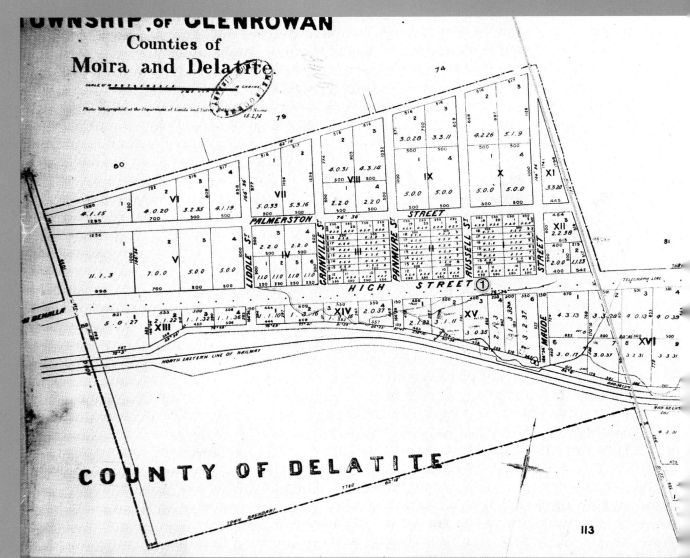

Glenrowan is in the heart of Kelly country – only seven kilometres from the Eleven Mile Creek selection and within close range of their final objective at Benalla. The shoot-out did not take place in the township – in 1880, the railway station was one kilometre from the town centre. At that time, the town was comprised of a post office, police station, State school and several stores located on the old Sydney road (1). There were only four buildings, including Mrs Jones' hotel, in the vicinity of the railway station (2). The meridian line (3) indicates the direction of Morgan's Lookout and (4) is the point where the rails were dismantled.

Thomas Carrington's **'Bird's-eye view'** shows the railway station and surroundings. (1) Mrs Jones' hotel, (2) outhouse, (3) railway station, (4) stationmaster's house, (5) McDonnell's hotel, (6) platelayers' [sic] tents, (7) positions taken by police, (8) post taken by sub-inspector O'Connor and the blacktrackers, (9) spot where superintendent Hare was shot, (10) paddock where horses were shot, (11) tree where Ned Kelly was captured, (12) road to Glenrowan police barracks, (13) Carrington believed the rails were torn up less than one kilometre from this point.

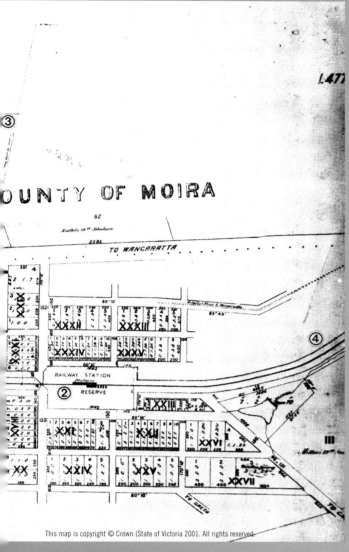

Ann Jones earned the disfavour of police and the Kellys during the outbreak. There is little doubt that she played to both sides and each in turn realised the game. When the outlaws chose her hotel as their headquarters it was not out of friendship. Mrs Jones was apparently delighted and encouraged her children to show similar hospitality. Tragically, her imprudence made the disaster that followed far worse. One bitter captive recalled, 'just before the train came up, Dan Kelly asked Mrs Reardon if she would like to go home. She said she would. We all got up to go out by the back door, when Mrs Jones rushed to the door, put up her hands, and said, "No. You must not go. Ned will be here shortly to give you all a lecture." A great many of us could have left the hotel when Dan Kelly gave us leave — only Mrs Jones prevented us.' Mrs Jones paid for her shortcomings: she lost her son, home, business and was charged, although not convicted, of 'receiving, harbouring, and maintaining' the gang at Glenrowan.

The place where the rails were pulled up 'is exactly half a mile beyond the station . . . The line takes a sudden turn down an incline and is then carried over a gully on an embankment. There is a little creek in this gully, and to carry it under the line a substantial culvert had been built . . . just at the end of the sharpest part of the curve and at the foot of the incline . . . the rails were torn up.' These men stood where Ned Kelly forced two line-repairers (Reardon and Sullivan) and a group of navvies to remove the rails at about 3 a.m. on Sunday. The line was repaired by 9 a.m. on Monday and the photograph was possibly taken the same day. The view looks north-east toward Beechworth and the man at right is pointing to where the dismantled rails were hidden.

Thomas Curnow's first post as a schoolteacher was to Glenrowan in 1876. At the time of Kelly's capture, Curnow, a Cornish immigrant, was 25, married, had an infant daughter and the young family lived in rooms attached to the school. Tom was small man with a lame leg, but was a shrewd and brave citizen. He duped the Kellys into trusting him so that he could escape and meet the police train before it could be captured. He received £1000 for his effort but in fear of retaliation, he fled the district and changed his name.

The outlaws stabled their horses at Mrs Jones' hotel and also at McDonnell's Railway Tavern, located on the southern side of the railway. They collected the occupants of the few buildings within sight of the station, forcing everyone to the gatehouse and Mrs Jones' hotel. The outlaws were cautious that word did not get out about their intentions, and they calmly bailed up anyone passing in the vicinity of the station. Eventually, 62 people were captured as they waited for the police train to roar through the town on that fateful Sunday. Among them was the Glenrowan schoolmaster, Thomas Curnow.

On Sunday morning, 27th of June 1880, I determined to take my wife, sister, and child out for a drive along the road from Glenrowan to Greta. We left the school in a buggy at about eleven o'clock in the morning accompanied by David Mortimer, my brother-in-law, who rode on horseback. When we got in sight of Jones's hotel, and opposite the railway crossing through which we intended to pass, we noticed a number of people about Jones's Hotel, and at the crossing. I said, 'Mrs Jones must be dead; she has been very ill'. I drove past the hotel to the crossing and, seeing Mr Stanistreet [the stationmaster] asked him, 'What's the matter?' He replied, 'The Kellys are here; you can't go through.' I thought he was joking and made a motion to drive through the gates, when a man on horseback, who blocked up the crossing and was talking to a young man whom I knew to be named Delaney, wheeled his horse around and said to me, 'Who are you?' I saw then that he had revolvers in his belt . . . I replied that I was the teacher at Glenrowan. He said, 'Oh, you are the schoolmaster here, are you, and who are those?' pointing to my wife, sister, and brother-in-law.

came to me at the gatehouse. I might say that Steve Hart was sick, and didn't want to go out that night, but they made him. They were all strangers to me at first. I knew nothing at all about them.

I told him . . . He then said, 'I am sorry but I must detain you', and directed us to get out of the buggy, which we did . . . I directed Mrs and Miss Curnow to go to Mr Stanistreet's, which they did.

There were, including those who had just been taken over, about fifty persons in and around the hotel, all of whom appeared to be prisoners of the gang. We were allowed to go about in the hotel, excepting one room, which the outlaws used, and of which they kept the key, and we were allowed outside, but were forbidden to leave the premises. Dan Kelly, a short time after I entered the hotel, asked me to have a drink, and I drank with him at the bar. I said to him that I had been told that they had been at Beechworth during the previous night, and had shot several police. I asked him whether it was true. He replied that they had been near Beechworth last night, and had done 'some shooting' and that they had burned the 'b———— out' alluding to the police. Byrne came in the bar, and, looking at Dan Kelly's glass, said, 'Be careful old man.' Dan Kelly replied, 'All right' and poured water into his brandy.

While talking with Byrne and Dan Kelly, I expressed surprise at Glenrowan being stuck up by them, and they said they had come to Glenrowan in order to wreck a special train of inspectors, police, and black trackers, which would pass through Glenrowan for Beechworth, to take up their trail from there. They said they had ridden hard across country, often being up to their saddle-girths in water, to get to Glenrowan, and that they had the line torn up at a dangerous part, and were going to send the train and its occupants to hell. About one o'clock I was standing in the yard, Dan Kelly came out of the hotel and asked me to go inside and have a dance. I said that I could not dance in the boots that I had on. Ned Kelly then came out of the hotel, and hearing me object, said, 'Come on; never mind your boots.' I said to him that it was awkward for me to dance in those boots as I was lame, but that I would dance with pleasure if he would go to school with me to get a pair of dancing boots. It flashed across my mind that, in passing the Glenrowan police barracks to reach my house, Bracken, the trooper stationed there, might see us and be able to give an alarm. I knew that Bracken had been stationed at Greta, and felt sure that he would recognise Ned Kelly . . . Someone else . . . said my house was near the police barracks. Ned Kelly . . . then said that we should not go, and I went into the hotel, and danced with Dan Kelly. After we had finished dancing Ned Kelly said that he would go down to the police barracks and bring Bracken and Reynolds, the postmaster, up to Jones's. I laughed and said to him that I would rather than a hundred pounds that he would, and asked to be allowed to accompany him when he went, and to take home my wife, sister and child. He made no reply . . . The intention to do something to baffle the murderous designs of the gang grew on me, and I resolved to do my utmost to gain the confidence of the outlaws, and to make them believe me to be a sympathiser with them.

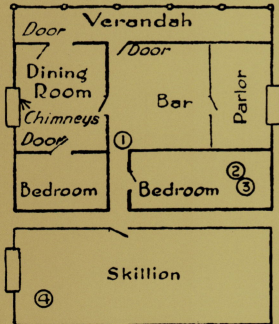

PLAN OF INTERIOR OF GLENROWAN HOTEL, drawn from descriptions by people imprisoned there by the Kellys. The numbers represent (1) where Joe Byrne's body was found, (2) and (3) where the bodies supposed to be those of Dan Kelly and Steve Hart were lying, and (4) where Martin Cherry was found.

Above: Mrs Jones' licensed house, otherwise known as the Glenrowan Inn, was a small, unimposing five-roomed weatherboard building with a detached slab and bark kitchen at the rear. The interior was lined with hessian and sparsely furnished.

On Sunday morning, Steve Hart guarded the first captives at the stationmaster's gatehouse until Joe Byrne and Dan Kelly arrived — visibly jubilant about their success on the Woolshed. After a breakfast of 'porridge and pig's cheek', the outlaws transferred most of their male prisoners to Mrs Jones' hotel. During the following few hours, 62 residents and passers-by were rounded up in the vicinity of the railway crossing. From all accounts, the Sunday was pleasant enough, despite the gang's stated intentions. Mrs McDonnell said, 'the outlaws were very civil and joked and laughed with us constantly . . . and none of us were afraid'. David Mortimer explained, 'we knew we could do nothing and therefore we did not take any steps to warn those in the train of the danger'. Mrs Jones claimed that the 40 male prisoners could have easily overpowered the outlaws, but the fact that at least five of the gang's known sympathisers were among the crowd probably explains why they did not.

Left: Plan of Mrs Jones' hotel.

Curnow stops the pilot engine. The rejoicing press called the meek schoolteacher the hero of Glenrowan for his bravery in saving the occupants of the train and contributing as much as anyone to the capture of the outlaws. The engraving was featured on the cover of the *Australasian Sketcher*. It is reasonably accurate, however, the pilot engine that joined the expedition at Benalla was actually pulling a guard's van.

Locomotives at the Benalla sheds. Among them is the one that preceded the special train.

The outlaws kept a very sharp watch on their prisoners without seeming to do so. About three o'clock in the afternoon Ned and Dan caused several of their prisoners to engage in jumping and in the hop, step, and jump. Ned Kelly joined with them, and used a revolver in each hand as weights. After jumping was concluded I went to Mr Stanistreet's house to see my wife and sister . . . I saw Hart lying down on a sofa. He had three loaded guns by his side, he complained to me of having swollen and painful feet, caused, he said by not having had his boots off for several days and nights. I advised him to bathe them in hot water, and requested it for him. It was brought and he did so . . . Shortly after, Mr Stanistreet and I were walking about at the back of the house, and Mr Stanistreet expressed a wish that an alarm could be given . . . I asked if it would be wrong to break a promise given to the outlaws. [He] said it would not. I then asked Mr Stanistreet if the outlaws had taken his revolver from him. He said they had not. I saw what use this fact could be made of by me . . . [later] I was near the door of Jones's kitchen and requested Dan Kelly to tell Ned Kelly that I wanted to speak with him. He went into the hotel and brought Ned Kelly out, and I told him that Mr Stanistreet possessed a loaded revolver . . . They thanked me, and I perceived that I had in a great measure obtained their confidence . . . In speaking of and to one another the outlaws had assumed names.

About dusk I heard Ned Kelly saying to Mrs Jones that he was going down to the police barracks to capture Bracken . . . I advanced to them, and said to Ned Kelly that I thought it would be better for him to take Dave Mortimer, my brother-in-law, to call Bracken out, because Bracken knew his voice well, and by hearing it, would suspect nothing . . . Ned Kelly, after a pause, said that he would do so. He then went to Mrs Jones's stable, and I followed him, and asked would he allow me to take my party home when he went down for Bracken . . . Ned Kelly said that we must wait till he was ready to go. I found, on going back to Jones's, that a log fire had been made on the Wangaratta side of the hotel yard, and that many of the prisoners of the gang were standing around it. It was soon dark. Other prisoners were in the hotel, and the outlaws encouraged them to amuse themselves by playing cards. I waited . . . I believe, two or three hours before Ned Kelly directed me to put my horse into the buggy. He and Byrne then went into the room which they had reserved for their own use. I drove to the front of Jones's hotel, and put my wife and sister and Alec Reynolds, who was seven years of age and the son of the postmaster into the buggy . . . We waited for about an hour. Ned Kelly then came to us on horseback, and told me to drive on. It was then, I believe, about ten o'clock.

As we got into the road, I found that we were accompanied by Ned Kelly, Byrne, and my brother-in-law, each on horseback, and by a Mr E. Reynolds and R. Gibbins on foot, both of whom resided with Mr Reynolds the postmaster. On the road down Ned Kelly said that they were going to fill the ruts around with the fat carcasses of the police. The outlaws each had a light-coloured overcoat on, and I was amazed at the bulky appearance which they presented. I had then no knowledge that the outlaws possessed iron armour [underneath]. Each one carried a bundle in front of him, and in each one had a gun or rifle. We reached the barracks, and were directed by Ned Kelly to halt about twenty yards distant from the front door of the barracks. Ned Kelly got off his horse and fastened him to a fence, ordering my brother-in-law [Mortimer] to do the same, and he did so. Kelly then ordered him to advance to the barracks door and knock, which he did. Ned Kelly got behind an angle of the walls, and levelled his rifle and revolver at Dave Mortimer or at the door. No reply came from the knocking or calling, though they were often loudly repeated at Ned Kelly's whispered command . . . We neither saw nor heard anything for, I think, more than an hour, when Ned Kelly appeared, having Bracken, E. Reynolds, and Bracken's horse with him. Kelly stopped when he reached us and ordered Bracken to mount the horse brought round, and Bracken did so. Ned Kelly put a halter on the horse, which he kept hold of, saying – 'I can't trust you with the bridle, Bracken.'

Ned Kelly then said that I could go home and take my party with me. He directed us to 'go quietly to bed, and not to dream too loud' and intimated that if I acted unwise we would get shot, as one of them would be down to our place during the night to see that we were all right. I then left them and rode home, distant from the barracks one hundred or two hundred yards . . . As soon as we were out of hearing of the outlaws I announced to my wife and sister my intention to go to Benalla and give information as to the intentions and whereabouts of the outlaws. They both earnestly opposed my purpose, saying it was not at all likely that we would be allowed to come home unless some of the friends of the gang were watching. While the discussion was going on I quietly prepared everything including the red lama scarf, candle and matches, to go to Benalla, intending to keep as close to the railway line as I could, in case of the special coming before I could reach there . . . At length Mrs Curnow consented to go to her mothers to obtain advice . . . My sister engaged her attention while I went out to harness my horse to go . . . I heard the train coming in the distance while I was harnessing the horse, and I immediately caught up the candle, scarf and matches, and ran down the line to meet the train. I ran on until I got to where I could see straight before me along the line, and where those in the train would be able to see a signal for some distance . . . Every second I stood there I expected a bullet . . . I then lit the candle and held it behind the red scarf. As the guard's van got opposite me I caught sight of the guard, who shouted, 'What's the matter?' I yelled, 'The Kellys' and the Pilot engine then stopped a little past me and the guard jumped down. I told the guard of the line being torn up and of the Kellys' lying in wait at the station.

Constable Bracken, who tried to stop the gang's plan of his own volition, was escorted back to Mrs Jones' hotel. He gave this account of the gang's final hours waiting for the special train.

When we were held prisoners in the hotel Ned Kelly began talking about politics. 'There was one b——r in Parliament', he said, 'whom he would like to kill, Mr Graves.' I asked him why he had such a desire, and he replied, 'Because he suggested in Parliament that the water in the Kelly country should be poisoned, and that the grass should be burnt. I will have him before long.' He knew nothing about Mr Service, but he held that Mr Berry was no b—-dy good, as he gave the police a lot of money to secure the capture of the gang; too much by far.

He then asked me, 'What was the policeman's oath?' I replied that 'Policemen were sworn to do their duty without malice or favour, and to deal even-handed justice all round.' He rejoined, 'Constable ——— of Greta, once told me that the oath was that policemen had to lag any person, no matter whether it was father, mother, brother, or daughter, if they were but arrested.' He also asked if there were not 19 or 20 men in the force who were as great a rogues as himself. I of course concurred with him. He then said, 'We are just after shooting one ——— traitor', alluding to Aaron Sherritt, 'and we now want that ——- Detective Ward, but he is not game to show up. The next I want are those six little demons', alluding to the black trackers, 'then O'Connor and Hare, if I had them killed, I would feel easy and contented.' He questioned the ability of the blacks to track in the Victorian bush, and said he himself could track an emu in Queensland.

The prisoners were then all called together, and Ned said, 'If any of you ever hear or see any of us crossing the railway, or at any other place, and if the police should come and ask if you have seen any such party, you must say, "No, we saw nobody", and if I ever hear of any of you giving the police any information about us I will shoot you down like dogs.'

Between 12 and 1 o'clock on Monday morning one of Mrs Jones's sons sang the Kelly song for the amusement of the gang and his mother occasionally asked him to sing up louder. Most of the prisoners were then cleared from the front parlour and the gang had a dance. They danced a set of quadrilles, and Mr David Mortimer, brother-in-law of the schoolmaster, furnished the music with a concertina. Ned Kelly had the girl Jones for a partner, Dan had Mrs Jones, and Byrne and Hart danced with male prisoners. Thinking they heard a noise outside, the gang broke away from the dance abruptly, and Dan went outside. It was at this time that I secured the key of the door. Doubling up my trousers at the feet, I placed the key in the fold, and when I heard the special arrive I raised my leg picked out the key stealthily, unlocked the door and bounded away. When the train was heard stopping Kelly said, 'You will see some play now boys. We will shoot them all.'

The events that followed were the antithesis of the outlaws' plan: Curnow's warning had ruined the gang's surprise attack. In addition, appalling inefficiency had delayed the police special train for more than 24 hours, though this fact is not admitted to in the following report. By the time the train arrived, the gang were intoxicated and exhausted from lack of sleep. Subsequently, they were unable to make decisive moves in order to regain the upper hand. Despite their elaborate preparations, the gang were caught in their own trap.

Joseph Melvin, reporter for the *Argus*, gave the following sensational report.

DESTRUCTION OF THE KELLY GANG
THE FIGHT AT GLENROWAN AND ANNIHILATION OF THE GANG

GLENROWAN, Monday night, June 28th 1880

At last the Kelly gang and the police have come within shooting distance, and the adventure has been the most tragic of any in the bushranging annals of the colony. Most people will say that it was high time, too, for the murders of the police near Mansfield occurred as long ago as the 26th of October, 1878, the Euroa outrage on the 10th of December in the same year, and the Jerilderie affair on the 9th and 10th of February, 1879. The lapse of time has induced many to believe that the gang was no longer in the colony, but these sceptics must now be silent. The outlaws demonstrated their presence in a brutally effective manner by the murder of the unfortunate Aaron Sherritt at Sebastopol. Immediately [sic] on the news being spread the police were in activity. A special train was despatched from Melbourne at 10.15 on Sunday night. At Essendon Sub Inspector O'Connor and his five black trackers were picked up. They had come recently from Benalla, and were en route for Queensland again. Mr O'Connor, however, was fortunately staying with Mrs O'Connor's friends at Essendon for a few days before his departure. Mrs O'Connor and her sister came along, thinking they would be able to pay a visit to Beechworth. After leaving Essendon the train travelled at a great speed, and, before the passengers were aware of any accident having occurred, we had smashed through a gate about a mile beyond Craigieburn. All we noticed was a crack like a bullet striking the carriage. The brake of the engine had, however, been torn away, the footbridge of the carriage destroyed, and the lamp on the guard's van destroyed.

The train had to be pulled up, but after a few minutes we started again, relying on the brake of the guard's van. Benalla was reached at half past 1 o'clock, and there Superintendent Hare with eight troopers and their horses were taken on board. We were now about to enter the Kelly country, and caution was necessary. As the moon was shining brightly, a man was tied on upon the front of the engine

Above: A dance at the Glenrowan Inn 'was organised [but] Ned could not go through the waltzes. He was laughing and amused all around him. He said he would have to knock off as he was no dancer. David Mortimer played the concertina and said he would be master of ceremonies.' The gang, apparently convinced that the train was not coming, joined in the dancing. Ned Kelly is shown as the tall figure in the foreground, supposedly with armour under his coat, and wearing the quilted cap he later wore under his helmet. The girl beside him is Mrs Jones' daughter, Jane. Also among the captives at Mrs Jones' hotel were some of the gang's sympathisers. Ned later suggested that the presence of Patrick and Dennis McAuliffe and the Delaney brothers was merely coincidental. James Kershaw, another Greta friend, was among those helping the gang during the day. Kershaw was not prosecuted for his involvement, and while the McAuliffe brother's were arrested on Monday morning, they were released that afternoon.

Left: Constable Hugh Bracken had been in bed suffering from a bilious attack when he was captured by the gang. He was unarmed when he escaped from the hotel to alert superintendent Hare and travelled sixteen kilometres to Wangaratta for reinforcements. He returned with Steele and party in time to take part in the capture of Ned Kelly.

Right: The night attack. The police rushed to the Glenrowan gatehouse where Mrs Stanistreet told them the gang had escaped in the direction of the Warby Ranges. They returned to the railway platform and were mustering men and horses when constable Bracken escaped and gave them more accurate directions. During this time, Ned Kelly had left Mrs Jones' hotel and rode toward the station where he was seen by police but not recognised. After returning to the hotel, the gang waited calmly on the front veranda for the police to close in on them, apparently confident in the protection of their armour. Superintendent Hare recalled, 'Had they been without their armour when we first attacked, and could have taken proper aim at us, not one of us could have escaped being shot, [But] they were obliged to hold their rifles at arm's length [because of the armour] to get anything of a sight.'

Joe Byrne was shot in the leg in the initial firing, Ned Kelly in the foot and Hare in the wrist. Despite the screams of civilians who were in the line of fire, both sides continued shooting. During this initial volley of shots, two fireworks were seen exploding in the sky above McDonnell's hotel — thought to have been a signal to sympathisers waiting at Morgan's Lookout. As the second rocket lit up the ground outside the hotel, Ned Kelly was seen walking into the bush beyond the hotel. He said later that 'when he returned to the hotel and signalled his mates to join him by rapping on his armour, Byrne crawled on his hands and knees as far as the kitchen at the back of the hotel with the object of joining him, but . . . must have fainted from loss of blood or the weight of his armour.' Kelly's statement was confirmed by constable Phillips, who overheard the following: 'Is that you Joe? — Yes. Is that you Ned? Come here. — Come here be damned; what are you doing there? — Come with me and load my rifle; I'm cooked. — So am I, I think my leg is broken. — Leg be damned; you've got the use of your arms. Come on, load for me; I'll pink the buggers. — Don't get so excited, the boys will hear and get disheartened; it's a case with us this time Ned. — Don't you believe it. — Well, it's your fault, I always said this bloody armour would bring us to grief. — Old Hare is cooked, and we'll soon finish the rest.'

As it turned out, both sides were without leaders only minutes after the fighting started. Superintendent Hare left by train about fifteen minutes after the first volley of fire seeking medical attention — he did not even hand over command. Ned Kelly also vanished — either to escape the police cordon or to turn back sympathisers summoned by the rockets.

to keep a lookout for any obstruction of the line. Just before starting however, it occurred to the authorities that it would be advisable to send a pilot engine in advance, and the man on the front of our engine was relieved. A start was made from Benalla at 2 o'clock, and at 25 minutes to 3, when we were travelling at a rapid pace, we were stopped by the pilot engine. This stoppage occurred at Playford and Desoyre's paddocks, about a mile and a quarter from Glenrowan. A man had met the pilot and informed the driver that the rails were torn up about a mile and a half [sic] beyond Glenrowan, and that the Kellys were waiting for us near at hand. Superintendent Hare at once ordered the carriage doors on each side to be unlocked, and his men to be in readiness. His orders were punctually obeyed, and the lights were extinguished. Mr Hare then mounted the pilot engine, along with a constable, and advanced. After some time he returned, and directions were given for the train to push on. Accordingly, we followed the pilot up to Glenrowan station, and disembarked.

THE FIRST ENCOUNTER

No sooner were we out of the train [sic], than Constable Bracken, the local policeman, rushed into our midst, and stated, with an amount of excitement which was excusable under the circumstances, that he had just escaped from the Kellys, and that they were at that moment in possession of Jones's public-house, about a hundred yards from the station. He called on the police to surround the house, and his advice was followed without delay. Superintendent Hare with his men, and Sub Inspector O'Connor with his black trackers, at once advanced on the building. They were accompanied by Mr Rawlins, a volunteer from Benalla, who did good service. Mr Hare took the lead, and charged right up to the hotel. At the station were the reporters of the Melbourne press, Mr Carrington of 'The Sketcher', and the two ladies who had accompanied us. The latter behaved with admirable courage, never betraying a symptom of fear, although bullets were whizzing about the station and striking the building and train. The first brush was exceedingly hot. The police and gang blazed away at each other in the darkness furiously. It lasted for about a quarter of an hour, and during that time there was nothing but a succession of flashes and reports, the pinging of bullets in the air, and the shrieks of the women who had been made prisoners in the hotel. Then there was a lull, but nothing could be seen for a minute or two in consequence of the smoke. In a few minutes Superintendent Hare returned to the railway station with a shattered wrist. The first shot fired by the gang had passed through his left wrist. He bled profusely from the wound, but Mr Carrington, artist of 'The Sketcher', tied up the wound with his handkerchief, and checked the haemorrhage. Mr Hare then set out again for the fray, and cheered his men on as well as he could, but he gradually became so weak from loss of blood that he had reluctantly to retire, and was soon afterwards conveyed to Benalla by a special engine. The bullet passed right through his wrist, and it is doubtful if he will ever recover the use of his left hand. In his departure Sub Inspector O'Connor and Senior Constable Kelly took charge, and kept pelting away at the outlaws all the morning. Mr O'Connor took up a position in a small creek in front of the hotel, and disposed his blackfellows one on each side, and stuck to his post gallantly throughout the whole encounter. The trackers also stood the baptism of fire with fortitude, never flinching for one instant.

Facing page: Press carriage in the special train. Remarkably, the gang's plan failed as a result of their over-estimation of police efficiency. After Aaron Sherritt's murder, shortly before 7 p.m. on Saturday 27 June, there was a gap of 32 hours before the special train rattled into Glenrowan at 3 a.m. on the Monday morning. This delay in the Kelly pursuit, plus elements of chance and the courage of schoolteacher Thomas Curnow, actually resulted in the capture of the Kellys.

Four news reporters were provided with their own compartment on the journey to cover the murder of Aaron Sherritt. Thomas Carrington, the only artist of the group, made the sketch illustrated, and probably drew himself into it as the silhouetted figure. The fifth person shown on the far right was most likely Charles Rawlins – the police agent who joined the train at Benalla with superintendent Hare's party.

Ned Kelly's 1856 model .56 calibre Colt percussion carbine, which he used to fire on police in the opening exchange. The foresight was removed (or barrel shortened) and the stock was tied with waxed string.

Mrs Stanhope O'Connor and her sister, Mrs Proute Webb, were the only female passengers on the police special. When asked to rejoin the pursuit, sub-inspector O'Connor asked for a first-class carriage so that his wife and sister-in-law could go with him — both ladies were looking forward to holidaying in Beechworth.

Mrs Proute Webb recorded in her diary: 'Mr Hare had already left and a few moments later bursts of gunfire began to hit the train, and then the noise of the police fire hitting the walls of the hotel . . . We didn't look out and we pulled out our dressing-cases and piled them against the windows. Presently the train porter came along and said he had to put out our carriage-lamps as the lighted train was a target.' The ladies were supposed to leave with the wounded superintendent Hare, but in the confusion of the shooting, one locomotive steamed off with only a driver and the second with only Mr Hare perched on the coal tender. The ladies were left to wait out the long night in their railway carriage.

At about 5 o'clock in the morning a heart-rending wail of grief ascended from the hotel. The voice was easily distinguished as that of Mrs Jones, the landlady. Mrs Jones was lamenting the fate of her son, who had been shot in the back, as she supposed, fatally. She came out from the hotel crying bitterly and wandered into the bush on several occasions, and nature seemed to echo her grief. She always returned, however, to the hotel, until she succeeded, with the assistance of one of the prisoners, in removing her wounded boy from the building and in sending him on to Wangaratta for medical treatment [sic]. The firing continued intermittently, as occasion served, and bullets were continually heard coursing through the air. Several lodged in the station buildings, and a few struck the train. By this time the hotel was completely surrounded by the police and the black trackers, and a vigilant watch of the hotel was kept up during the dark hours.

At daybreak police reinforcements arrived from Benalla, Beechworth, and Wangaratta. Superintendent Sadleir came from Benalla with nine more men, and Sergeant Steele, of Wangaratta, with six, thus augmenting the besieging force to about 30 men. Before daylight Senior Constable Kelly found a revolving rifle and a cap lying in the bush, about a hundred yards from the hotel. The rifle was covered with blood, and a pool of blood lay near it. This was evidently the property of one of the bushrangers, and a suspicion therefore arose that they had escaped. That these articles not only belonged to one of the outlaws, but to Ned Kelly himself, was soon proved. When day was dawning the women and children who had been made prisoners in the hotel were allowed to depart. They were, however, challenged individually as they approached the police line, for it was thought that the outlaws might attempt to escape under some disguise.

The wounded Black Tracker

CAPTURE OF NED KELLY

At daylight the gang were expected to make a sally out, so as to escape, if possible, to their native ranges, and the police were consequently on the alert. Close attention was paid to the hotel, as it was taken for granted that the whole gang were there. To the surprise of the police, however, they soon found themselves attacked in the rear by a man dressed in a long grey overcoat and wearing an iron mask. The appearance of the man presented an anomaly, but a little scrutiny of his appearance and behaviour soon showed that it was the veritable leader of the gang Ned Kelly himself. On further observation it was seen that he was only armed with a revolver. He, however, walked cool-

A Queensland tracker was the only other member of the police force wounded at Glenrowan — a scalp wound received while peering from a drain in front of the hotel. In contrast to the amount of attention given to superintendent Hare, not even the name of the Aboriginal officer was recorded. More than £600 was paid to treat superintendent Hare's wrist, yet when a Benalla doctor requested four guineas for stitches and treatment to the tracker's scalp, the Victorian government claimed the bill was excessive.

The Wangaratta contingent of police present at the capture, photographed by W. E. Barnes. Only three of the party have been identified: sergeant Steele is kneeling in the centre with shotgun in hand and wearing the saddlebag he claimed to have taken from Ned Kelly. Constable Cawsey is at extreme left and constable O'Dwyer is seated at extreme right. The others are constables Moore, Montford, Walsh, Healey and Dixon. In addition to revolvers, five of the group carry double-barrelled shotguns, two have Martini-Henry rifles and one, standing second from right, holds an obsolete muzzle-loading carbine.

ly from tree to tree, and received the fire from the police with the utmost indifference, returning a shot from his revolver when a good opportunity presented itself. Three men went for him – viz., Sergeant Steele, of Wangaratta, Senior Constable Kelly, and a railway guard named Dowsett. The latter, however, was only armed with a revolver. They fired at him persistently, but, to their surprise, with no effect. He seemed bullet-proof. It then occurred to Sergeant Steele that the fellow was encased in mail, and he then aimed at the outlaw's legs. His first shot of that kind made Ned stagger, and the second brought him to the ground with the cry, 'I am done – I am done'. Steele rushed up along with Senior Constable Kelly and others. The outlaw howled like a wild beast brought to bay, and swore at the police. He was first seized by Steele, and as that officer grappled with him he fired off another charge from his revolver. The shot was evidently intended for Steele, but from the smart way he secured the murderer the Sergeant escaped. Kelly became gradually quiet, and it was soon found that he had been utterly disabled. He had been shot in the left foot, left leg, right hand, left arm, and twice in the region of the groin. But no bullet had penetrated his armour. Having been divested of his armour he was carried down to the railway station, and placed in a guard's van. Subsequently he was removed to the Stationmaster's office, and his wounds were dressed there by Dr Nicholson of Benalla. What statements he made are given below.

THE SIEGE CONTINUED

In the meantime the siege was continued without intermission. That the three other outlaws were still in the house was confirmed by remarks made by Ned, who said they would fight to the last, and would never give in. The interest and excitement were consequently heightened. The Kelly gang were at last in the grasp of the police, and their leader actually captured. The female prisoners who escaped during the morning gave corroboration of the fact that Dan Kelly, Byrne and Hart were still in the house. A rumour got abroad that Byrne was shot when drinking a glass of whisky at the bar of the hotel about half-past 5 o'clock in the morning and the report afterwards turned out to be true. The remaining two kept up a steady defence from the rear of the building during the forenoon, and exposed themselves recklessly to the bullets of the police. They, however, were also clad in mail, and the shot took no effect.

At 10 o'clock a white flag or handkerchief was held out at the front door, and immediately afterwards about 30 men, all prisoners, sallied forth holding up their hands. They escaped whilst Dan Kelly and Hart were defending the back door [sic]. The police rallied up towards them with their arms ready, and called upon them to stand. The crowd did so, and in obedience to a subsequent order fell prone on the ground. They were passed, one by one, and two of them – brothers named McAuliffe – were arrested as Kelly sympathisers. The precaution thus taken was highly necessary, as the remaining outlaws might have been amongst them. The scene presented when they were all lying on the

Left: John Jones. Lack of leadership and consideration for civilians was only too evident on both sides. Three innocent people were hit by police fire within the first few minutes of shooting. The first two were Mrs Jones' own children – eleven-year-old John Jones was shot in the first volley. David Mortimer recalled, 'I put my fingers in my ears, so as not to hear his screams of agony, and the lamentations of his mother and Mrs Reardon, who had a baby in her arms. We could do nothing, and the bullets continued to whistle through the building.' Neil McHugh carried the wounded boy out of the hotel, through the line of fire and delivered him safely to McDonnell's hotel. He was taken to Wangaratta hospital the next day, but died the following night.

Far left: Jane Jones, fifteen-year-old sister of John Jones, was struck on the forehead by a spent bullet not long after her brother was hit. Mrs Jones recalled, 'My brave little girl was shot too, shot with a big rifle bullet that had gone through half the house first, or it would have killed her.' Later in the gunfire, another boy, Michael Reardon, was severely wounded; both he and Jane Jones recovered.

Bottom left: Glenrowan line-repairer **James Reardon, his wife Mary** and their eight children were among the people trapped in Mrs Jones' hotel when the police arrived. Reardon testified afterwards, 'The Kellys said they would allow us to go if the police would. There was a tall chap – I forget his name – he put a white handkerchief out of the window, and there were three bullets sent in at once . . . Ryan and his wife and three or four children and three of mine, and a strange woman from Benalla then rushed out [about 3.30 a.m.] and the firing was on them as hard as it could be blazed. My wife and I got out and we had to go back into the house because of the firing . . . from all directions. The most part of it from the drain . . . We went back again and said to Dan Kelly; "I wish to heaven we were out of this." Byrne said. "Mrs Reardon, put out the children and make them scream and scream yourself;" and she was coming past the rifles in the passage, and one of the rifles tangled in her dress, and Dan Kelly said to Byrne, "Take your rifle or the woman will be shot;" and I came out and she screamed, and the children, they came out. The [gun] fire was blazing and a policeman called out – I thought it was Sergeant Steele – "Come this way;" and he still kept firing at her – at my wife with the baby in her arms . . . She has a shawl with a bullet hole through the corner of it she can show . . . Constable Arthur was standing close to Sergeant Steele and he said, "If you fire on that woman again, I am ——— if I don't shoot you. Cannot you see she is an innocent woman?" These were Arthur's own words. I crept on the ground and went back [once more] to the [hotel] with the children, and as my son Michael returned he got wounded in the shoulder, and fell on the jamb of the door . . . I lay down among the lot inside, and put the children between my knees, when a bullet scraped the breast of my coat and went across two other men, and through the sofa at the other end. We remained there expecting every minute to be shot until about half past nine in the morning.'

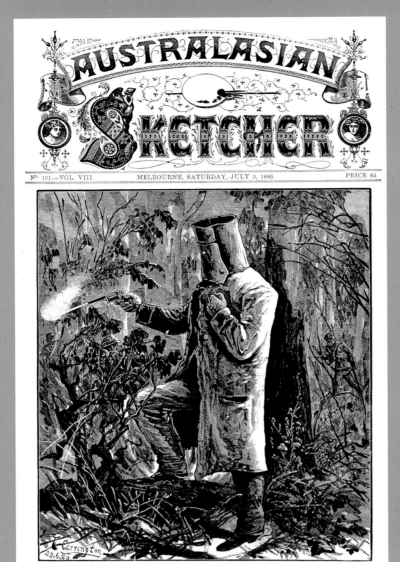

NED KELLY AT BAY.
FROM A SKETCH DRAWN ON THE SPOT BY MR. T. CARRINGTON.

Ned Kelly's grey mare. 'Shortly after [Kelly's appearance] a horse with saddle and bridle came towards the place where the man (whom we had by this time ascertained to be Ned Kelly) was lying, and we fully expected to see him make a rush and mount it, but he allowed it to pass, and went [on] towards the hotel . . . His mare was found on the railway line, a few miles from Glenrowan, saddled and bridled. The saddle resembled that of Byrne, and bore the name of the same Wangaratta manufacturer, Mr Bullivant.'

The last stand; Ned Kelly at bay (Australasian Sketcher). There is some doubt about the exact time Ned Kelly left Mrs Jones' hotel — more uncertain are his reasons for doing so. He most likely headed through the timber towards Morgan's Lookout not long after the first exchange of shots and he was absent from the fight for at least three hours. It was assumed he either slept or lay unconscious near police lines on the Wangaratta side of the hotel, where his cap and rifle were found. Legend among Kelly sympathisers claims that Ned made his way to the shoulder of Morgan's Lookout to turn back armed sympathisers — an explanation strengthened by the fact that he disappeared immediately after fireworks were seen above McDonnell's hotel. Whatever Kelly's reason for leaving the battle there was never any doubt that he 'made up his mind to break through the cordon of police [to] rejoin and die with his companions in the hotel.'

A reporter watching from the railway platform gave this colourful description of Ned Kelly's amazing final act in freedom. It was then shortly after 6.30 a.m. on Monday. 'Suddenly we noticed one or two of the men, with their backs turned to the hotel, firing at something in the bush. Presently we noticed a very tall figure in white stalking slowly along in the direction of the hotel. There was no head visible and in the dim light with the steam rising from the ground it looked for all the world like the ghost of Hamlet's father with no head, only a very long thick neck. Those who were standing with me did not see it for a time, and I was too intent on watching its movements to point it out to others. The figure continued gradually to advance, stopping every now and then, and moving what looked like its headless neck slowly and mechanically round, and then raising one foot onto a log and aiming and firing a revolver. Shot after shot was fired at it, but without effect, the figure generally replying by tapping the butt end of its revolver against its neck, the blows ringing out with the clearness and distinctiveness of a bell in the morning air. It was the most extraordinary sight I ever saw or read of in my life, and I felt fairly spellbound with wonder, and I could not stir or speak. Presently the figure moved towards a dip in the ground near to some white dead timber and, more men coming up, the firing got warmer. Still the figure kept erect, tapping its neck and using its weapon on its assailants. At this moment, I noticed a man in a small round tweed hat stealing up on the left of the figure, and, when within 30 paces of it, firing low two quick shots in succession. The figure reeled and staggered like a drunken man and in a few moments fell near the dead timber. The iron mask was torn off and there in the light of day were the features of the veritable bloodthirsty Ned Kelly himself.'

Sergeant Arthur Steele was the first to reach Kelly when he fell; but Ned's last stand was a completely one-sided affair. Constable Arthur said Ned was 'more dead than alive' as he staggered down the slope toward them. He was so impaired by his wounds that he could not even lift his revolver to take aim. Arthur also maintained that Ned Kelly had tripped and was already falling when Steele fired twice into his legs.

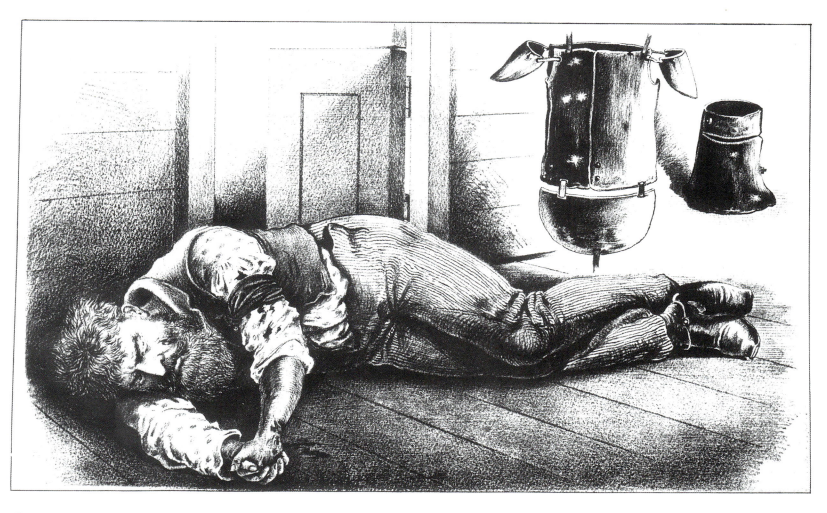

Above: Ned Kelly in the station building. Superintendent Sadleir wrote: 'There was some very vicious shooting from the hotel on the place where Kelly was being attended to . . . Some shots struck the van into which he was first taken, and he was then removed into one of the station buildings not so open to the view of the remaining bushrangers in the hotel.'

There is a legend that a rough draft of a declaration for the 'Republic of Victoria' was found in Ned Kelly's coat pocket, which was supposedly confiscated or souvenired. Sadleir added, 'All who saw Ned Kelly while he lay helpless were struck with the gentle expression on his face . . . but the old spirit . . . was there notwithstanding.' Julian Ashton recalled the same occasion: 'As the outlaw lay wounded, his face bruised by the bullets that had thudded on his helmet, he smiled and said, "It was as good as Waterloo, wasn't it? As good as Waterloo."'

Right: Railway guard Jesse Dowsett reached Ned Kelly just in time to prevent Steele shooting him. He testified: 'I ran up, and jumped over the log and saw Steele and he on the ground. I grasped the revolver from [Ned Kelly] as he fired, and Senior Constable Kelly, coming up almost at the same moment, pulled his headgear off. Steele at once recognised him, and would have shot him, but [we] said, "No, take him alive." Another added, When I reached the place, he was in a sitting posture on the ground, his helmet lying near him, and a most extraordinary and pitiable object he looked. A wild beast brought to bay, and evidently expecting to be roughly used. His face and hands were smeared with blood. He was shivering with cold, ghastly white, and smelt strongly of brandy. He complained of pain whenever he was jolted in the effort to remove his armour . . . operations materially hastened at this time by being fired on from the house [Mrs Jones' hotel], one bullet striking close to us. He was then carried over the railway fence to the station.'

Left top: The 30 men who escaped from Mrs Jones' hotel. Though all of the women and most of the children escaped within the first hours of firing, nearly all the male prisoners were kept in captivity until late on Monday morning. Nearly seven hours after the fight started, superintendent Sadleir called out to the remaining townspeople. The two surviving outlaws promised not to fire until the people were safely away and even shook hands with everyone as they left.

Left middle: Police in position to fire. At least three other photographers – making a total of five – competed with Madeley and Bray for the scoop of their lives, but only Madeley and Bray appear to have witnessed the siege. W. E. Barnes of Wangaratta photographed police engaged in the affair, and well-known Melbourne operators, John. W. Lindt and Arthur Burman took pictures at Benalla. Only Burman and Lindt signed their 'Kellyana' prints, so in many cases the actual operator is unknown, such as this print that has since been attributed to Oswald Madeley. The group here includes three of the Queensland trackers and the view look south toward the railway crossing. The line-repairers' tents can be seen in the background.

Left bottom: Madeley's second plate looks north-west and shows **police standing at the tree where Ned Kelly was captured.** 'By midday hundreds of people had collected, including not a few of the outlaws' friends. Wild Wright and his brother Tom, Steve Hart's brother [Dick], Kate Kelly, [Grace Kelly and Margaret Skillion] and several of the Lloyds were watching events from a ridge on the Greta side of the station.' One artist wrote, the day was 'cold and dreary, and was an appropriate setting to the last episode in the great man-hunt'.

Facing page top: Mrs Jones' hotel at daylight. As news of the shoot-out reached Benalla, Wangaratta and Beechworth, people flocked to Glenrowan. Among the spectators was an almost forgotten Benalla photographer, Oswald Thomas Madeley, who set up his camera near the station buildings – dangerously close to the line of fire. The proofs of the exposures he took that day, together with those of James Bray who arrived soon after, form a remarkable record. As Jack Cato noted, it is 'perhaps the first full news coverage by the camera of a national tragedy [in Australia]'. A friend of superintendent Sadleir mentioned Madeley and his series years later: 'I had several conversations with the little man who took them and he described himself as skipping about . . . under fire and very likely in your and everybody's way.' This plate was his first and looks north-west shortly after sunrise. Ned Kelly had been captured not long before in the timber outside the right of the picture. Dan Kelly and Hart had appeared in the passageway between the front building and detached slab kitchen, firing heavily at police as they carried Ned away, but were driven back by return fire.

Facing page bottom: The death of Byrne. Superintendent Sadleir wrote: 'We were told that Byrne was firing briskly, and was in great spirits, boasting of what the gang were going to do. The work was hot, so he went to the counter for a drink. Finding the weight of his armour prevented him throwing back his head to swallow the liquor, he lifted the apron-shaped plate with one hand while with the other he lifted the glass to his mouth. In this attitude a chance bullet struck him in the groin, and spinning round once, he fell dead.'

James Mortimer stated, 'Dan Kelly told us we had better remain in the house because the police would shoot us if we attempted to leave. Someone said to him, "you had better go out and surrender," and he replied, "We will never surrender, but most likely we will leave directly". I think that they intended to do so, but shortly after five o'clock in the morning Byrne was shot . . . this seemed to dishearten Dan Kelly and Hart. They had been calling for Ned all night, and now renewed their calls for him.' Julian Ashton made this drawing of Byrne's corpse by candlelight as the body lay in a cell at Benalla. He said 'it was the most miserable assignment I ever had'.

Above: This third plate by Madeley looks south to the **station buildings** and was taken east of Mrs Jones' hotel. McDonnell's hotel is above the group at centre. In the background is Futter's Range — stretching south toward Greta and the Kelly selection.

The Glenrowan battle was mismanaged by both police and the outlaws. The police fired indiscriminately into the hotel after the arrival of Sadleir's contingent from Benalla at 3 a.m. and Steele from Wangaratta shortly after. While it resulted in the death of Joe Byrne, civilians Michael Reardon and Martin Cherry were also shot. When the Beechworth contingent arrived at about 9 a.m., discipline got even more out of hand. Of the eleven men from Beechworth, four had been present at the murder of Aaron Sherritt and were anxious to clear the stigma of cowardice from their names. Jack Sherritt, Aaron's brother, also came to avenge his brother's death. Superintendent Sadleir finally passed an order to 'fire high' — attempting to spare the innocent people lying trapped inside. Many misinterpreted the order, thinking that it meant the outlaws were hiding under the rafters and commenced riddling the iron roof. Others thought it was an order to fire harder. This and the enthusiasm of the Beechworth men started a tremendous burst from all around the cordon. One Beechworth constable testified that he fired 100 rounds at the hotel within an hour. Inside, elderly civilian Martin Cherry slowly bled to death.

Facing page top: Railway station and Mrs Jones' hotel looking north. James Bray captured the recklessness of spectators as they nonchalantly stood within clear view of the bushrangers. One wrote, 'We were on the platform, watching the proceedings, sometimes exposed to the fire from the house in our eagerness to get a clear view of everything, and then, suddenly remembering that we were in easy range, quickly seeking shelter.' Under the station's veranda, men can be seen with their backs to the camera — evidently peering into the stationmaster's office where Ned Kelly was being treated. Dr Nicholson, who attended him said, 'I dressed the wounds as well as circumstances would permit. He complained of the coldness of his feet, and said they would never get warm again. He was being questioned all this time, sometimes by the police, sometimes by the reporters, and sometimes by the general public, who were inconveniently crowding the room. He was besieged with questions, and very seldom had less than three to reply to at the same time. He was very weak, and replied in a listless way to most of the enquiries . . . He must have lost much blood during the night, as he said that the [serious] wound in his foot and the one in his arm were received at the first volley.'

Facing page bottom: Glenrowan station and Jones's hotel, by James Bray. The man standing fifth from left is thought to be Father Mathew Gibney — the priest who heard Ned Kelly's confession and administered the last unction of the dying. It was initially assumed that Ned would not survive his wounds. Later in the afternoon, when he had recovered slightly, Ned's three sisters, the Wright brothers, Tom Lloyd and several other friends were allowed to see him and bid their last goodbyes. Father Gibney said, 'After I had attended him, I asked him did he think it would be safe for me to go up to the house and get this man, his brother, I think, to surrender. He looked very steadfastly at me, seemingly reading me, and he said, "I would not advise you to go, they will certainly shoot you".'

ground, and demonstrating the respectability of their characters, was unique, and, in some degree, amusing.

THE END — THE HOTEL BURNT

The siege was kept up all the afternoon, and till nearly 3 o'clock in the afternoon. Some time before this the shooting from the hotel ceased, and opinions were divided as to whether Dan Kelly and Hart were reserving their ammunition or were dead. The best part of the day having elapsed, the police, who were now acting under the direction of Superintendent Sadleir, determined that a decisive step should be taken. At 10 minutes to 3 another and last volley was fired into the hotel, and under cover of the fire, Senior Constable Charles Johnson, of Violet Town, ran up to the house with a bundle of straw, which [having set alight] he placed on the ground at the west side of the building. This was a moment of intense excitement, and all hearts were relieved when Johnson was seen to regain uninjured the shelter he had left. All eyes were now fixed on the silent building and the circle of besiegers began to close in rapidly on it, some dodging from tree to tree, and many, fully persuaded that everyone in the hotel must be 'hors de combat' coming out boldly into the open. Just at this juncture Mrs Skillion, sister of the Kellys, attempted to approach the house from the front. She had on a black riding-habit, with a red underskirt, and white Gainsborough hat, and was a prominent object on the scene. Her arrival was almost simultaneous with the attempt to fire the building. Her object in trying to reach the house was apparently to induce the survivors, if any, to come out and surrender. The police, however, ordered her to stop. She obeyed the order, but very reluctantly, and, standing still, called out that some of

Mrs Jones' hotel beginning to burn. While no shots were fired from the building after 1 p.m. on Monday, there was considerable risk of being struck by police fire coming from the opposite side of the cordon. Thomas Carrington was making drawings at the same time this plate was taken and complained afterwards, 'I went down during the day to the Beechworth end and knelt behind a log with one of the police, and while we were sitting there – I was making a drawing – a rifle ball came over our heads. I will swear it was not fired from the hotel, because I was looking at the hotel at the time.' The hotel was set on fire just before 3 p.m. – five hours after the last townspeople had been allowed to leave the building. By that time, the whole spectacle resembled some kind of macabre sporting match – people watched from vantage points around the police cordon and waited for a gruesome climax to the event.

Mrs Jones' hotel at the time Father Gibney entered. 'I stepped forward and asked [Mrs Skillion] would she go to her brother [Dan] and tell him there was a Catholic priest here who was anxious to come and see him, and to ask him would he let me in, She said, "Of course I will go up and see my brother," she was very excited. She then started for the house but was stopped by some police authority . . . The house was being set fire to. My feelings revolted very much at the appearance it had . . . when the fire seemed to have taken well, just as it seemed to break through the house here and there, there was a volley fired into the house, and I then said to myself, "These men have not five minutes to live". I was then close down to the gate at the railway crossing and I started from there direct for the front of the house. I think I might have been about half the distance when I was called to, Mr Sadleir called to me not to go there . . . I said something to the effect, "I am not in the police service, I am going to do my duty, and there is no time to lose". So he did not interfere with me further, and I walked on.'

the police were ordering her; to go on and others to stop. She, however, went to where a knot of besiegers were standing on the west side of the house. In the meantime, the straw, which burned fiercely, had all been consumed, and at first doubts were entertained as to whether Senior Constable Johnson's exploit had been successful.

Not very many minutes elapsed, however, before smoke was seen coming out of the roof and flames were discerned through the front window on the western side. A light westerly wind was blowing at the time, and this carried the flames from the straw underneath the wall and into the house, and as the building was lined with calico, the fire spread rapidly. Still no sign of life appeared in the building. When the house was seen to be fairly on fire, Father Gibney, who had previously started for it but had been stopped by the police, walked up to the front door and entered it. By this time the patience of the besiegers was exhausted, and they all, regardless of shelter, rushed to the building Father Gibney, at much personal risk from the flames, hurried into a room to the left and there saw two bodies lying side by side on their backs. He touched them, and found life was extinct in each. These were the bodies of Dan Kelly and Hart, and the Rev. gentleman expressed the opinion, based on their position, that they must have killed one another. Whether they killed one another, or whether both or one committed suicide, or whether, both being mortally wounded by the besiegers, they determined to die side by side, will never be known. The priest had barely time to feel their bodies before the fire forced him to make a speedy exit from the room, and the flames had then made such a rapid progress on the western side of the house that the few people who followed close on the Rev. gentleman's heels dared not attempt to rescue the two bodies.

It may be here stated that after the house had been burned down the two bodies were removed from the embers. They presented a horrible spectacle, nothing but the trunk

Mrs Jones' hotel burning, by Oswald Madeley. Father Gibney continued, 'I went in then on what I think was the room on the right-hand side, and it was quite vacant . . . It was the other end of the house the fire was set to, and then when I came inside I called out to the men that I was a Catholic priest, and came to offer them their life. I got no answer . . . Then I found first the body of Byrne . . . lying there in a straggled kind of way, quite stiff. When I found this man's body, the house was blazing just before me . . . Then when I came in that passage down from the bar towards the back of the house there was a little room to the left hand, and I spoke again to the men inside. I got no answer of course, and I looked in upon the floor and found two corpses lying together. Both dead, and a dog was lying dead alongside of them. My impression is that they were certainly not killed by the fire . . . they were composed looking both lying at full stretch, side by side, and bags rolled up under their heads, the armour on one side of them off. I concluded they lay in that position to let the police see when they found them that it was not by the police they died . . . I took hold of the hand of the one that was near me to see whether or not they had recently killed themselves – whether there was life in them, and I found it was quite lifeless. Then I looked at his eyes, and I found they showed unmistakable signs that he was dead for some time; and then I went to the other to touch him. I satisfied myself that life was completely extinct in both of them before I left, and at the time this little room they were in the fire was just running through it . . . I did not see any weapons, and I cannot say that I saw any sign of blood. I did not see any wounds about the bodies. They lay so calm together, as if layed out by design.'

Left: Father Mathew Gibney, who was one of the few heroes that day, arrived with other spectators on the midday train and observed the 'evident want of Generalship . . . firing at the house was the only thing that anyone could say there was uniformity about'.

Pages 204–205: Ned Kelly's bloodstained green silk sash. Dr Nicholson removed the sash without anyone else knowing and kept it as a memento. The sash was one of Ned's treasured possessions, given to him when he was a boy – a gift from Esau Shelton of Avenel for rescuing his son from drowning.

Mrs Jones' hotel burning. When Father Gibney reappeared, the crowd cheered again and surged forward to surround the blazing hotel. Police dragged Byrne's body clear but could not reach Hart or Dan Kelly. Other police found Martin Cherry, the fourth wounded civilian, lying in the detached kitchen and he died soon after. A rumour spread that Ned Kelly shot Cherry for not holding aside a window blind, but Father Gibney reported that one of Cherry's friends told him that he was shot by police. The Melbourne *Herald* commented, 'In all conscience Ned Kelly's crimes are more than sufficient for one wretch to bear without being charged with another infamous and cold blooded act, which he did not commit.' A wave of horror passed through the crowd when they realised that two bodies were still inside. 'Whilst the fire was doing its work Mrs Skillion said, "Thank God they are burned. I would rather see them burned than shot by the police." ' The photograph was taken by Oswald Madeley.

and skull being left, and these almost burnt to a cinder. Their armour was found near them. About the remains there was apparently nothing to lead to positive identification, but the discovery of the armour near them and other circumstances render it impossible to be doubted that they were those of Dan Kelly and Steve Hart. The latter was a much smaller man than the younger Kelly, and this difference in size was noticeable in their remains. Constable Dwyer, by the by, who followed Father Gibney into the hotel, states that he was near enough to the bodies to recognise Dan Kelly.

As to Byrne's body, it was found in the entrance to the bar-room, which was on the west side of the house, and there was time to remove it from the building but not before the right side was slightly scorched. This body likewise presented a dreadful appearance. It looked as if it had been ill-nourished. The thin face was black with smoke, and the arms were bent at right angles at the elbows, the stiffened joints below the elbows standing erect. The body was quite stiff and its appearance and the position in which it was found corroborated the statement that Byrne died early yesterday morning. He is said to have received the fatal wound, which was in the groin, while drinking a glass of whisky at the bar. He had a ring on his right hand which had belonged to Constable Scanlon [sic], who was murdered by the gang on the Wombat ranges. The body was dressed in a blue sac-coat, tweed strapped trousers, crimean shirt, and very ill-fitting boots. Like Ned Kelly, Byrne wore a bushy beard.

In the outhouse or kitchen immediately behind the main building the old man Martin Cherry, who was one of the prisoners of the gang and who was so severely wounded that he

Mrs Jones' hotel prior to collapse, by James Bray. Onlookers ignored their safety to get a close look or be in the photograph. Their curiosity led to sudden and desperate retreats as unused ammunition began to explode from the heat. The roof later collapsed with a tremendous crash, throwing out clouds of smoke and sparks. The detached lamp-post and signboard were not burned; beneath the sign are two empty barrels of alcohol from Sunday's celebrations. By Monday afternoon Mrs Jones was at the bedside of her dying son in Wangaratta Hospital and did not see her premises razed.

could not leave the house when the other prisoners left, was found still living but 'in articulo mortis' from a wound in the groin. He was promptly removed a short distance from the burning Hotel and laid on the ground, when Father Gibney administered to him the last sacrament. Cherry was insensible, and barely alive. He had evidently suffered much during the day, and death released him from his sufferings within half an hour from the time when he was removed from the hotel. It was fortunate that he was not burned alive. Cherry, who was unmarried, was an old resident of the district, and was employed as a platelayer, and resided about a mile from Glenrowan. He was born at Limerick, Ireland, and was 60 years old. He is said by all who knew him to have been a quiet, harmless old man, and much regret was expressed at his death. He seems to have been shot by the attacking force, of course unintentionally.

While the house was burning some explosions were heard inside. These were alarming at first, but it was soon ascertained that they were cartridges burning. Several gun barrels were found in the 'debris', and also the burnt carcass of a dog which had been shot during the 'melee'. All that was left standing of the hotel was the lamp-post and the signboard bearing the following device, which, in view of the carnage that had just been perpetrated within the walls of the hostelry, read strangely – THE GLENROWAN INN. ANN JONES. BEST ACCOMMODATION.

In a small yard at the rear of the buildings four of the outlaws horses, which had been purposely fired at earlier in the day, were found and were killed at once, to put them out of their agony. They were poor scrubbers. Two of them were shod. The police captured Byrne's horse, a fine animal. About the same time that Mrs Skillion appeared on the scene, Kate Kelly and another of her sisters were also noticed, as were likewise, Wild Wright and his brother Tom,

Mrs Jones' hotel burned down. 'The black ashes were covered in part by the sheets of corrugated iron that had formed the roof. The iron was pierced with innumerable bullet and slug holes, and the chimneys also bespattered with bullet marks, showing how fierce and constant the firing of the attacking party had been. The wrecks of two iron bedsteads, a sewing machine and a few tin cans, some of which bore shot marks, were the only recognisable objects in the debris.'

and Dick Hart, brother of one of the dead outlaws. Mrs Skillion seemed to appreciate the position most keenly, her younger sisters appearing at times rather unconcerned. Dick Hart, who was Steve Hart's senior, walked about very coolly.

INTERVIEW WITH NED KELLY

After the house had been burned Ned Kelly's three sisters and Tom Wright were allowed an interview with him. Tom Wright as well as the sisters kissed the wounded man, and a brief conversation ensued, Ned Kelly having to a certain extent recovered from the exhaustion consequent on his wounds. At times his eyes were quite bright, and, although he was of course excessively weak, his remarkably powerful 'physique' enabled him to talk rather freely. During the interview he stated: 'I was at last surrounded by the police, and only had a revolver, with which I fired four shots. But it was no good. I had half a mind to shoot myself. I loaded my rifle, but could not hold it after I was wounded. I had plenty of ammunition, but it was no good to me. I got shot in the arm, and told Dan and Byrne so. I could have got off, but when I saw them all pounding away, I told Dan I would see it over, and wait until morning.'

'What on earth induced you to go to the hotel?' inquired a spectator. 'We could not do it anywhere else,' replied Kelly, eyeing the spectators who were strangers to him suspiciously. 'I would,' he continued, 'have fought them in the train, or else upset it if I had the chance. I didn't care a —— who was in it; but I knew on Sunday morning there would be no usual passengers. We first tackled the line, and could not pull it up, and then came to Glenrowan station.'

'Since the Jerilderie affair', remarked a spectator, 'we thought you had gone to Queensland.'

'It would not do for everyone to think the same way,' was Kelly's reply. 'If I were once right again,' he continued, 'I would go to the barracks, and shoot every one of the —— —- traps, and not give one a chance.' Mrs Skillion (to her brother), 'It's a wonder you did not keep behind a tree.'

Ned Kelly: 'I had a chance at several policemen during the night, but declined to fire. My arm was broke the first fire. I got away into the bush, and found my mare, and could have rushed away, but wanted to see the thing out, and remained in the bush.'

A sad scene ensued when Wild Wright led Mrs Skillion to the horrible object which was all that remained of her brother Dan. She bent over it, raised a dirge-like cry, and wept bitterly. Dick Hart applied for the body of his brother, but was told he could not have it until after the 'post-mortem' examination. The inquest on the bodies will be held at Benalla.

Michael Reardon, aged 18 years, was shot through the shoulder; but it is apparently only a flesh wound. The boy Jones was dangerously shot in the thigh. Both have been sent to the Wangaratta Hospital. A cannon was brought up as far as Seymour, but as the burning of Jones's Hotel had proved successful, it was countermanded.

THE ATTEMPT ON THE TRAIN

According to Ned Kelly, the gang after shooting Sherritt at Sebastopol, rode openly through the streets of Beechworth, and then came on to Glenrowan for the purpose of wrecking any special police train which might be sent after them, in the hope of destroying the black trackers. They descended on Glenrowan at about 3 o'clock [sic] on Sunday morning and rousing up all the residents of the township, bailed them all up. Feeling unable to lift the rails themselves, they

Above: Police with Joe Byrne's horse, by James Bray. After the battle, four horses belonging to the gang were found in the stables of McDonnell's hotel and several more were found in the vicinity of the station. 'A very fine upstanding chestnut horse was identified as the property of Mr Ryan . . . It was the horse ridden by Joe Byrne on the night Sherritt was murdered. A brown mare was identified as the property of Mr Fitzsimmons, stolen from his farm at the Ten Mile creek.' Among other things, the gang's packhorses carried a complete set of tools for shoeing horses and over ten metres of blasting fuse. An oil can containing 20 kilograms of blasting powder was found behind a log in the vicinity of McDonnell's hotel. Ned Kelly explained later that the explosives were intended for the special train or their planned visit to Benalla. While in the stationmaster's office, Kelly admitted 'his intention was to send the police on to Beechworth, wreck the train at the place where the rails were dismantled, and on Monday morning, whilst the troopers were away, take possession of Benalla barracks.' At the feet of the trooper at right is Ned Kelly's quilted cap.

Left: Dr John Nicholson treated Kelly in the stationmaster's office. According to three doctors who eventually examined the outlaw, he had nineteen separate bullet and slug wounds and his face and body were covered with bruises from his armour. Superintendent Sadleir noted, 'He would have died but for the care of Dr John Nicholson of Benalla, who steadily supplied him with stimulants. It is quite true . . . that Ned must have swallowed two or three bottles of whiskey while he lay between life and death.' Nicholson found him wearing a remarkable 'green silk sash with a heavy bullion fringe'. Apart from three revolvers, the only other effects found on the outlaw were a silver Geneva ladies' watch and chains, some ammunition and one threepence.

Overleaf: Kelly taking the attacking force in the rear. Colour lithograph, *Illustrated Sydney News*, August 1880.

compelled the line-repairers of the district and others to do so. The spot selected was on the first turning after reaching Glenrowan, at a culvert and on an incline. The diabolical object in view was the destruction of the special train.

Having performed this fiendish piece of work Kelly returned to the township, and, bailing all the people up, kept them prisoners in the Station-master's house and Jones's hotel. By 3 o'clock on Monday morning they gathered all their captives into the hotel, and the number of those unfortunate people amounted by that time to 47, as already stated. The police then arrived, and the prisoners escaped at intervals during the night [sic].

The first attack by the police was a brilliant affair. They approached the house quickly, but stealthily. Their arrival, however, was expected, and they were met with a volley from the verandah of the hotel. Special trains were run during the morning between Glenrowan and Benalla, and Mrs O'Connor and her sister – who may justly be called the heroines of the day, for they behaved bravely – were taken on by one of them to Benalla. Ned Kelly, after being secured, quietened down, and became absolutely tame. He is very reserved as to anything connected with his comrades, but answered questions freely when his individual case was alone concerned. He appeared to be suffering from a severe shock and exhaustion, and trembled in every limb. Now and again he fainted, but restoratives brought him round and in his stronger moments he made the following statements:

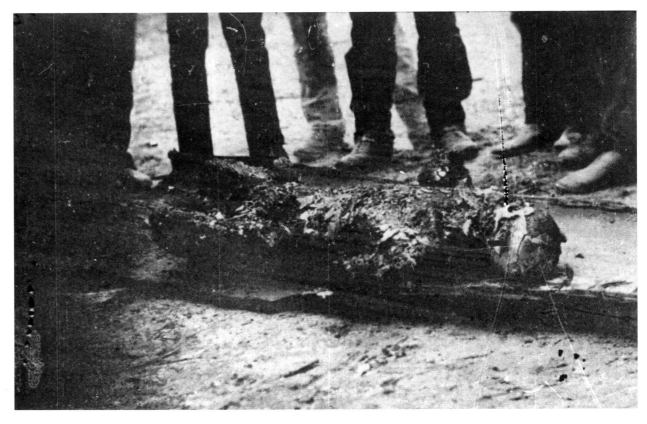

Burned body, by Oswald Madeley and James Bray. Senior constable Johnston, who had set fire to the building, raked out the corpses and armour with an iron pole and forked stick. He also found the carcass of a dog belonging to one of the outlaws. The stoic among the crowd pressed round to gaze at the gruesome sight and superintendent Sadleir noted 'not even his sisters could have recognised their brother'.

Opportunists and impostors would later exploit the bodies' questionable identities, but there is no doubt who they are. Sadleir added, 'I was greatly gratified at getting this trouble over that we had on our hands for two or three years and I was inclined to act liberally . . . the bodies were brought down to the platform. I offered to Isaiah Wright, if the friends wished it, to give them over the bodies of Steve Hart and Dan Kelly. This seemed to please them much, as an unexpected favour. They all began to come up at this moment; Mrs Skillion, Kate Kelly, Dick Hart, and several of their friends.' The women ran forward, dropped to their knees and cried and wept bitterly. Kate Kelly repeated in heartbroken sobs 'My poor, poor brother' while Tom Lloyd, Dick Hart and Wild Wright wrapped the corpses in blankets and carried them away.

NED KELLY'S STATEMENTS

'I was going down to meet the special train with some of my mates, and intended to rake it with shot; but it arrived before I expected, and I then returned to the hotel. I expected the train would go on, and I had the rails pulled up so that these ———— black trackers might be settled. I do not say what brought me to Glenrowan, but it seems much. Anyhow I could have got away last night, for I got into the bush with my grey mare, and lay there all night. But I wanted to see the thing end. In the first volley the police fired I was wounded on the left foot; soon afterwards I was shot through the left arm. I got these wounds in front of the house. I do not care what people say about Kennedy's death. I have made my statement of the affair, and if the public don't believe me, I can't help it; but I am satisfied it is not true that Scanlon was shot kneeling. He never got off his horse. I fired three or four shots from the front of Jones's hotel, but who I was firing at I do not know. I simply fired where I saw police. I escaped to the bush, and remained there overnight. I could have shot several constables if I liked. Two passed close to me. I could have shot them before they could shoot. I was a good distance away at one time, but came back. Why don't the police use bullets instead of duck-shot? I have got one charge of duck-shot in my leg. One policeman who was firing at me was a splendid shot, but I do not know his name. I daresay I would have done well to ride away on my grey mare. The bullets that struck my armour felt like blows from a man's fist. I wanted to fire into the carriages, but the police started on us too quickly. I expected the police to come.' Inspector [sic] Sadleir: 'You wanted then, to kill the people in the train?' Kelly: 'Yes, of course I did; God help them, but they would have got shot all the same. Would they not have tried to kill me?'

McDonnell's Railway Tavern.

McDonnell's hotel, coffins and reporters, by Oswald Madeley. The charred bodies were taken to McDonnell's hotel by relatives and then to Mrs Skillion's selection near the Eleven Mile Creek on the Monday night. Tension between police and the grief-stricken relatives increased when news spread that the police intended retrieving the bodies for an inquiry. Dick Hart told police at the hotel: 'If you want the bodies back, you will have to fight for them'. The police, with unusual tolerance, made no immediate move to force the issue. 'John Grant, undertaker of Wangaratta, was employed by their friends to provide coffins of a first-class description, the cost being a matter of no consequence. He arrived with them in a buggy at Glenrowan and they were seen to be high-priced articles. The lid of one lettered "Daniel Kelly, died 28th of June 1880, aged 19 years", and the other "Stephen Hart, died 28th of June 1880, aged 21 years". How the remains are to be distinguished from each other is a problem that will not easily be solved.'

Overleaf: 'Ned Kelly at bay'
by H. Hunt, *Illustrated Sydney News*.

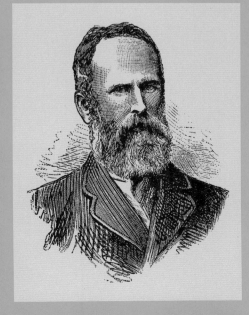

Above: Group at the Kelly tree. The group, a mixture of participants and spectators including some of the Wangaratta police and Queensland trackers, pose for a photograph after defeating the gang.

Far left: Sergeant Arthur Steele.

Left: Sub-inspector Stanhope O'Connor.

Bottom left: Constable Hugh Bracken. Wangaratta photographer W. E. Barnes missed out on the action but took a number of portraits of notables after the affray. While praise for police in capturing the gang was short-lived, all police shared the reward for the gang's destruction — even though it had technically been withdrawn. Hare received £800, Steele £290, Sadleir £240, and O'Connor £237. Within twelve months, however, a royal commission had left few associated with the Kelly pursuit with any semblance of a career. Steele, sporting a walrus moustache by 1880, became well known if little respected for his part. The commission recommended he be 'reduced to the ranks'. Sub-inspector O'Connor was even less fortunate. His Queensland police commissioner wrote to him after the battle: 'so far as I can judge from the very meagre information contained in your report, and the more fully detailed accounts given by newspaper correspondents, I am unable to find any cause for congratulation.' O'Connor resigned and sought admission into the Victorian force, but was rejected. Historian C. H. Chomley wrote, 'Altogether, Bracken's is the only name in the Victorian police force, which derived any added lustre from the events'. He was, however, one of several police who were promoted following the police purge. He received £275 for his part in the destruction of the Kelly gang.

Bottom right: Superintendent John Sadleir was severely criticised for his 'conduct of operations against the outlaws at Glenrowan'. Defending his actions 30 years later, he overlooked the seven hours taken to find an alternative to the field gun being sent up at his request from Melbourne. 'In the light of later knowledge, it is possible that a sudden rush in upon the two men might have been effected without serious loss, but at the time the view I took was different . . . I resolved instead to burn the building over them.' In other respects, Sadleir acted with tact and compassion towards the captured outlaw, his sisters and relations on that fateful day.

16 AFTERMATH OF A TRAGEDY
JUNE–JULY 1880

An estimated 1,000 spectators watched the final act in the Glenrowan shoot-out on that dismal winter afternoon on 28 June 1880. The following day, the Melbourne *Herald* announced almost hysterically: 'The excitement in the city yesterday over the Kelly affair was so intense . . . our circulation was nearly double that of any occasion'. Artist Julian Ashton commented wryly: 'When I returned to Melbourne Mr Syme told me it was the first week the *Illustrated Daily News* had shown a profit'.

News reached the other capital cities by electric telegraph within hours – with great excitement. In Sydney, the streets were crowded with people anxious for the latest items of news in connection with the tragedy . . . Altogether, 90,000 words were sent across the wires for Sydney alone, of which the *Evening News* received 8,500. That journal published five editions. In the following days, the Kelly affair gained publicity throughout Australia and abroad unequalled by anything in the country's history. Messages of congratulation from one official to another flashed over the wires in an unending stream. The Victorian police basked in the brief glory of success while the Kelly sympathisers distantly voiced threats of revenge.

At Glenrowan on the Monday night after the fight, occasional showers drifted through the gap in Futter's Range – extinguishing the smouldering remains of Mrs Jones' hotel. Chief commissioner Standish arrived on the 5.30 p.m. train from Melbourne to take command – well after the whole affair was over. He immediately arranged for a special train to carry the weary police and a heavily guarded

The Kelly log, where Ned Kelly was captured. The guard's van, visible in the background (top right) shows just how close Kelly got to the railway — about 50 metres from the hotel. 'The trees behind which Kelly stood when fighting in the morning are all pierced with bullets and slugs, and the place where he fell is saturated with blood. He had evidently passed the night under a fallen tree.'

Above: Wood-block engraving of the ruins of Mrs Jones' hotel. 'The debris of Jones's hotel was still smouldering and a crowd of people [were] fossicking among the ruins for mementos of the gang. Two brick chimneys were all that remained standing.' The view looks south-east towards the level crossing and stationmaster Stanistreet's home, where women and children were held by the gang.

Right: The log where Ned Kelly fell, photographed by James Bray on the Tuesday or Wednesday after the shoot-out.

Ned Kelly back to the Benalla barracks. The bodies of Joe Byrne and Martin Cherry went too; Byrne was laid in the cell next to his captured leader and Cherry was taken to the Victoria Hotel to await an inquiry. On Tuesday morning, Ned Kelly was transferred to Melbourne Gaol – out of the reach of would-be rescuers. Feelings still ran at fever pitch in the district after his departure, as the Melbourne *Herald* reported on Wednesday 29 June:

ANNIHILATION OF THE KELLY GANG
LATEST DETAILS
FIFTY SYMPATHISERS ARMED
ANOTHER OUTBREAK THREATENED

The interest in the details of the events which led to the destruction of the Kelly Gang still continues and any additional items are eagerly looked for and discussed. Our reporters who are on the spot have been able to send us some late particulars, which are given below. We are also able to supply information as to the condition of Ned Kelly.

SUPERINTENDENT HARE

This gentleman, it will be heard with pleasure, is much better this morning. The fever has abated and he will probably be moved to Mr W. J. Clarke's house this afternoon, and remain as that gentleman's guest till restored.

The Melbourne *Age* reported: 'the scene of the encounter was, this morning [Tuesday], visited by a number of persons from Benalla. Photographic operators from Melbourne were also present, and took same excellent views of the locality.' These three photographs by Oswald Madeley were all taken from the south side of the railway line. The first, from the slope directly opposite the ruins, shows more than 20 people standing between the chimneys of the burnt-out hotel, overlooked by Morgan's Lookout. The second was taken earlier while the fire was still smouldering from the slope opposite the station buildings. The third view, by James Bray, looks from a point further east, past the station. The cross on the print is supposed to indicate where Kelly was taken, but is incorrect. Interestingly, Mrs Jones' signboard has been removed.

AFTERMATH OF A TRAGEDY 221

Right: Byrne's body on display at Benalla, Tuesday 29 June 1880. This widely published photograph by John W. Lindt shows fellow operator Arthur Burman making his series of close-ups. Also captured in Lindt's picture is artist Julian Ashton, at left with sketchbook under arm.

Bottom: Joe Byrne's corpse photographed by Arthur Burman. 'During the forenoon the body of Byrne was brought out of the lock-up where it lay, and was slung up in an erect position on the outside of the door, the object being to have it photographed by Mr Burman, of Melbourne. The features were composed in a natural way, and were easily recognised. The face was small, with retreating forehead, blue eyes, the upper lip covered with a downy moustache, and a bushy beard covering the chin, whilst his hair had recently been cut. The figure was that of a tall, lithe young fellow.' The spectacle, however, was very repulsive. The hands were clenched and covered with blood, whilst blood also covered his clothes. All the members of the gang were comfortably clad and wore boots which were evidently made to order. Ned Kelly had riding boots which showed well how he prided himself on having neat feet. When the doctor was dressing his wounds the boots had to be cut off. It was found that he wore no stockings. The gang all have the appearance of being well-fed, and Byrne stated to one of their prisoners that 'they had always lived well, but that the want of sleep which they had often to endure was very trying . . . It was quite evident that he [Byrne] was fully determined never to be taken alive, as on his remains was found a parcel labelled "poisons".' On one of his right hand fingers was found a topaz ring worn by trooper Lonigan at the time he was shot by the gang. On a left hand finger was a gold ring with a large white seal in it.

Facing page left: Arthur Burman ignored the repulsiveness of the scene and went to considerable trouble to get his **macabre close-ups** — he even washed the smoke-blackened features of the corpse for better detail. He sold the photographs as part of a carte-de-visite (100 x 60 mm) 'Kellyana' series — forerunner of the postcard.

Facing page right: Senior constable John Kelly questioned Ned Kelly at the Benalla lockup on the night after his capture. By this time, the outlaw lay exhausted, critically wounded and unable to sleep — in the cell next to Joe Byrne's body. John Kelly claimed that the outlaw made a startling admission during their conversation, which was later corroborated by sergeant Steele and constable McIntyre. According to the policeman, he said, 'Look here Ned, now that it is all over, I want to ask you one question before you go, and that is, did you shoot Constable Fitzpatrick at Greta when he went to arrest your brother?' Ned allegedly replied: 'Yes, I did. I shot him in the wrist, and the statements which have been made that Fitzpatrick inflicted the wound himself are quite false.' Despite defence council protests this statement was reported in the news and later admitted as evidence against the outlaw. Kelly sympathisers and historians dispute this neat self-condemning confession because the only witnesses were policemen. The importance of the remarks, if true, is that they undermine Ned Kelly's justification in taking to the bush two years earlier.

AFTERMATH OF A TRAGEDY 223

John Lindt photographed the police, trackers and gentlemen present at the encounter soon after Byrne's body had been removed from public gaze. (Detail on facing page.) Superintendent Sadleir is pictured centre in the tall hat and long, light-coloured jacket. Kneeling second left of him is the bearded constable Bracken of Glenrowan. At the rear beside the tree at left, with bowler hat, heavy beard and dark tie, is the only survivor of the encounter at Stringbark Creek – constable Thomas McIntyre. Excluding the constable on duty beside the cell door (partly visible behind Sadleir) none of the police are in uniform – an unsuccessful disguise tactic used in the Kelly pursuit.

LATEST POLICE TELEGRAMS

The following telegram has been received by the Chief Commissioner this morning.

BENALLA 12.30

No truth in the rumour about Steele [being shot]. I have heard from him half an hour since. There is a deal of ill-blood stirring and I cannot at present reduce the strength of the force stationed here.

JOHN SADLEIR. Superintendent of Police

It may be mentioned that there was no intention on the part of the authorities to at present remove any of the police from the neighbourhood, even prior to the receipt of Mr Sadleir's telegram.

THE SCENE AT GRETA – THREATS OF REVENGE

BENALLA, This day.

The scene at Greta when the charred remains of Hart and Dan Kelly were carried in by their friends was perfectly indescribable. The people seemed to flock from the gum trees. There were some of the worst looking people there I ever saw in my life. The two bodies were carried into Mrs Skillion's hut amidst the wailing and groaning of over 200 people. They were laid down on the table side by side – a dreadful sight. Their friends rushed the hut to catch a glimpse of them, but Mrs Skillion took down a gun and threatened to blow out the brains of the first person that entered the house without her permission. She then allowed only three at a time to enter, and after they had remained only sufficient time to walk around the table and look at the bodies they were turned out again. The first who went in were two girls and an old man, a relative of Hart's: he cried like a child. Then Tom Lloyd and Quinn went in. They looked at the bodies for a moment, and then Tom Lloyd took hold of Kate Kelly's hand and, lifting his right arm to heaven, swore a most dreadful oath that he would never leave their deaths unavenged. All day long scenes like these continued. Drink was brought over from Mrs O'Brien's Hotel (Greta), and they were all more or less in a state of intoxication and dangerously inclined. Lloyd seemed to be the most sober of the lot, though he was drunk enough. He went out into the clearing at the back of the hut with Mrs Skillion, and the two kept in conversation for a long time. A number of papers were passed between them both. Then Lloyd got on his horse, and rode off to Benalla. He came to beg the body of Byrne. Of course this was denied him until after the magisterial inquiry has been held, and he hung about the police station attempting to enter into conversation with every Constable he could. He kept appealing to their good nature, and asking them not to be too hard. He was in a state of greatest anxiety to know what the police were going to do next, and seemed to be afraid that he and some others would be arrested as sympathisers – 'What are you going to do with us now, Mr Kelly?' he asked of the Constable there, 'Oh I don't know, Tom; you had better keep out of the way and behave yourself'. 'Oh! For God's sake don't interfere with us; we have done you no harm. Be satisfied with the work you have already done and leave us and the poor girls in peace; our load is hard to bear.'

Tears actually started out of his eyes when he spoke. To look at the man then and to see him at Mrs Skillion's hut when he swore to be avenged, an ordinary observer would be puzzled to judge his character. To a close observer, however, it is apparent that he is a mere boaster. Another per-

Seven men from the Benalla contingent display their weapons for Oswald Madeley on Monday 28 June. Ian Jones identifies those engaged in the first attack under superintendent Hare as, from left, constables Barry, Bracken (from Glenrowan), Phillips, Arthur (a skilled marksman and the first officer encountered by Ned Kelly during the shoot-out), senior constable Kelly (involved in Ned's capture), constables Gascoigne (who seriously wounded Ned in the first exchange of fire) and Canny. They carry an assortment of shotguns, Martini-Henry breech-loading rifles and carbines.

son who appeared to act under instructions from Mrs Skillion was Wild Wright. He stayed at Mrs McDonnell's hotel, at Glenrowan, all Monday night and all day yesterday. He sat up with her in the bar and conversed in earnest whispers with her all Tuesday night. They had a number of papers spread out on the counter, which they were constantly arranging and re-arranging. Wright kept writing memoranda on the back of telegraph forms; he covered over twelve slips of paper. Yesterday afternoon he counterfeited drunkenness, would insist on singing rough songs, and made himself a nuisance to everybody. When expostulated with he retorted in such apparent good humour that it was impossible to get out of temper with him. When the Kellys came to Glenrowan they put horses in the stable at McDonnell's hotel, and left them there. They remained there until a late hour on Tuesday without having any food or drink. Mrs McDonnell says she was afraid to tell the police they were there for fear of being molested. Mrs McDonnell left after the outlaws were captured, and did not turn up again until yesterday, some hours before Ned Kelly was taken to Melbourne.

The police, now the affair is all over, conduct matters more secretly than they did when necessity required it of them. After the Magisterial inquiry had been held on Byrne's body yesterday, the friends of the deceased were extremely anxious to get possession of it. They came to the station and the courthouse, and begged hard to be allowed to bury it at Greta. They were put off from time to time, and after dark the body was sneaked out by the back way from the police camp, and, with only an undertaker's man and a well-armed Constable, was taken to the Benalla cemetery, and privately buried in a snug corner there. The Constable and the undertaker marched back again, saluted each other and went home. It was a great disappointment to the friends. They appeared to be in doubt as to whether they would be allowed to keep the other bodies or not. There are a number of them here making anxious inquiries. A number of miscellaneous articles belonging to the outlaws were brought in to Benalla last night, amongst which were a keg of powder and some fuse. The wildest rumours are current here. It is believed that another gang of bushrangers will soon be out headed by Dick Hart.

MORE VIOLENCE THREATENED — ANOTHER GANG SPOKEN OF
BENALLA, This day. (Wednesday, June 30th).
The police are making preparations to escort Mr Bickerton, the police Magistrate at Wangaratta, from that place to Greta, to hold an inquiry on the remains of Dan Kelly and Steve Hart. A large body of armed troopers has been despatched to Mrs Skillion's hut, and it is reported that there are at least fifty sympathisers there all armed and determined to resist the holding of the inquiry. Dick Hart is very conspicuous by his conduct, and swears that he will head another and stronger gang than that of Ned Kelly and take to the bush.

A trooper poses in a suit of armour taken from the fire and holds Kelly's Colt carbine. Superintendent Hare wrote of the gang's weapons: 'It is a strange coincidence that none of the rifles stolen by the outlaws at Jerilderie or the Wombat Ranges were used by them at Glenrowan, but they had most inferior and obsolete repeating rifles which had been cut short, and no proper aim could be taken with them, as they were not sighted.' According to Tom Lloyd junior, the better weapons were distributed to sympathisers for their planned revolt.

THE DESTRUCTION OF THE KELLY GANG: SCENE AT THE WAKE AT GRETA.

The wake at Mrs Skillion's hut was illustrated on the cover of the Australasian Sketcher and is a crude attempt to demonise the family. The ill-proportioned man at left is supposed to be – but looks nothing like – Tom Lloyd. There was much talk of retaliation among the relatives. The threats enlivened newspapers and worried police, who were anxious to keep the peace. Superintendent Sadleir was in a dilemma for having handed the bodies to relatives without the necessary magisterial inquiries. On Tuesday 29 June, Sadleir sent a request to Mrs Skillion to return the bodies, but the family refused. Sixteen troopers were then sent to retrieve them, but were recalled after only going a few kilometres. Police sent another message to the relatives indicating that an inquiry would be held at Glenrowan, but a magistrate could not be persuaded to attend so it was not held. Finally, a magistrate authorised a burial. Sadleir explained afterwards, 'I had the thanks of those people afterwards for following a fair and moderate course towards them; they have conveyed their message direct that if I had pursued the course anticipated . . . there were eight or nine men ready to break out and we should have had the same trouble in an aggravated form again.'

The funerals for Steve Hart and Dan Kelly were held at Greta cemetery on 30 June without police presence. About 100 friends and relatives of both families attended – including Jim Kelly, who had disappeared after release from prison in late 1879. Daniel O'Keefe, a Glenrowan farmer, read the service and Tom Lloyd junior acted as undertaker. After the graves were filled, the O'Brien brothers ploughed the area to conceal their location.

NED KELLY IN GAOL

Ned Kelly, the vanquished leader of the now historical Kelly Gang of bushrangers, has been in Melbourne Gaol since yesterday, and is a patient in the hospital of the establishment, under treatment for the wounds he received in his encounter with the constituted authorities. He lies in a ward where there are two other prisoners, and a fourth prisoner, who is not a patient, is told to watch him unceasingly. The door of the ward is kept constantly locked, and thus proper precautions are taken against his making an attempt on his own life or effecting his escape. Indeed, under existing circumstances, either would be a matter of impossibility. Last night Ned slept well. During yesterday he partook of no food, not from mere sullenness, but no doubt from natural inability, consequent of the state of his health from the wounds which he received from the firearms of the police. He is dull in manner and spirit, but quiet in disposition and evidently in his right mind. It has erroneously [sic] been stated that seven or eight bullets were removed from Kelly's body. The fact is that only one piece of lead – a slug – has been removed and that from his right hand. If he received any more lead in that desperate encounter it must have passed from his body . . . or must still be secreted beyond the surgeon's ken or the reach of his probe. The most severe wound from which Kelly suffers is one in the left arm. Perhaps it might be more correctly described as two wounds resulting from the same shot. There is one gunshot wound under the left arm, and the bullet seems to have travelled along the arm and gone out half way between the elbow and the shoulder. It is very probable that this wound was received while the arm was bent in some use. Ned has been ordered by the surgeons in attendance only farinaceous food, and even this he is not likely to partake of in other than small quantities for some little time to come. Yesterday he seemed to lack a little stimulant more than food, and of course the directions of the surgeon are rigidly adhered to. There can be no doubt that Kelly, now that his companions-in-arms have been annihilated, that he has been removed from exciting surroundings, and has had time for reflection, as well as being subjected to religious influences, to which he is not wholly insusceptible, feels deeply his position, and perhaps regrets the past. He still expresses regret that he did not fall with his companions and shared their grave. Kelly was visited yesterday by the Rev. P. J. Aylward of St Patrick's Cathedral, whose visit and ministrations he is understood to have received well.

MRS KELLY INFORMED OF HER SONS' FATE

Subsequently Father Aylward had an interview with Mrs Kelly, Ned's mother, who is also a prisoner in the same gaol with her son. It may be here explained that Ellen Kelly, on the 9th of October 1878, was sentenced, at the Beechworth Circuit Court, by Mr Justice Barry, to three years hard labour [sic] for having wounded Constable Fitzpatrick, at Greta, while he was arresting her son Dan, on a charge of

Left: Kelly's arrival in Melbourne. 'By the ordinary train this morning Ned Kelly was forwarded from Benalla to Melbourne, in the custody of a number of police . . . Mrs Skillion and Kate Kelly were on the platform prior to the departure of the train. The scene was very affecting between the two women and their brother, Ned Kelly. The outlaw, too, was evidently moved as they said good-bye, though he struggled to avoid exhibiting any weakness . . . Miss [Kate] Lloyd and Miss McElroy also saw Kelly prior to his departure. Miss Lloyd bade him an affectionate farewell, and at the station she appeared dreadfully agitated.' Doctor Charles Ryan travelled with Kelly to Melbourne. '[Kelly] spoke very little, and seemed like a man in a trance, and glared at any strangers he saw. He had had no sleep all the previous night. Most men wounded as he was would have been far more prostrated than he was, but he has a splendid constitution. Moreover his body looked as if it had been well nourished. When I asked him if he had been pretty well fed, he said he had, but he did not add where he had got the food. I expected to find him, after the life he had been leading, very dirty; but his skin was as clean as if he had just come out of a Turkish bath. I attended to his wounds, and now and then gave him some brandy and water. He seemed grateful, but gave me the idea he wished to die.'

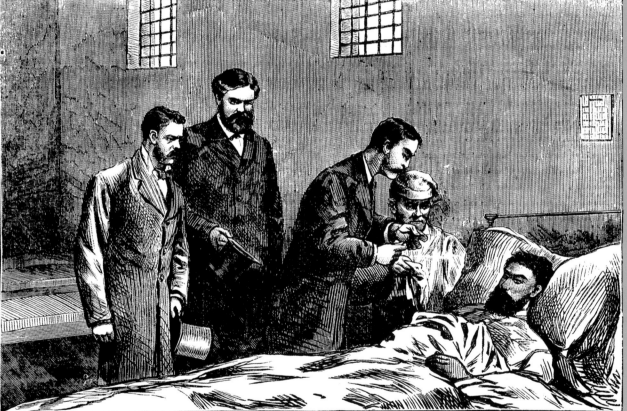

Under intensive care, Kelly slowly recovered strength in the Melbourne Gaol hospital. His day-to-day condition was reported widely to satisfy an interest more befitting a hero than a captured criminal. One paper reported two days after his arrival in Melbourne: 'Ned Kelly, who is still a patient in the hospital of the Melbourne Gaol, slept well last night, and today is stronger. His recovery to perfect health will of course be slow, but it is now perfectly certain that he is out of danger. He is still allowed none but farinaceous food; but of this he partakes in moderately large quantities. He is not communicative except when spoken to, and then he converses freely. Except immediately after his reception at the gaol he has not expressed the wish that he had shared the fate of his companions. Kelly continues to be continually watched by another prisoner, and the door of the ward in which he lies is still kept locked. He is attended by Doctor Shields, the medical officer of the Gaol. The interview between Kelly and his mother, which took place yesterday, was of a very affecting character to those who witnessed it. Ned, though not demonstrative towards his mother, or exhibiting very much emotion, nevertheless showed that he was sensible of the painfulness of the meeting. He exhibited a proper filial affection according to his own rude nature; and she, on her part, though of that class known as bushwomen, hardened by a rough and almost savage life, exhibited that maternal instinct and solicitude which is hardly ever absent . . . Mrs Kelly has now returned to her former occupation in the workroom of the Gaol. She is not to see her son today, but it is probable she will be allowed to have another interview with him for a short time tomorrow.' The engraving, from the Illustrated Sydney News, shows Dr Shields and a prisoner attending Kelly.

> H.M. Gaol, Melbourne
> July 19th 1880
>
> The Hon.
> The Chief Secretary
> Sir
>
> I beg most respectfully to request your permission to send for my sister Mrs Skillion to visit me at the Hospital of the above Gaol, to enable me to confer with her respecting the provision of a Solicitor to prepare my Defence at my forthcoming Trial and likewise for her to procure me the necessary Clothing to appear thereat.
>
> I would also ask you to allow me to see my Mother. I have only seen her once
>
> Your obedient Servant
> Edward x Kelly
>   his mark
>
> Witness
> Geo. Voston
> Hos. Att'd

An unsigned request. During Kelly's first five weeks in gaol, he was remanded several times and continually denied his right to legal advice. Despite verbal and written requests, Kelly was not allowed to see relatives to arrange for his defence; finally they had to engage a solicitor without his knowledge or approval. Tom Lloyd and Margaret Skillion arrived in Melbourne on Friday 29 July, believing the trial would be held in Melbourne, and briefed David Gaunson MLA to defend Kelly. While they were in Melbourne, Ned Kelly was transferred to Beechworth to stand trial. As a curious precaution, Ned did not sign the letter illustrated, or any he dictated after his capture.

horsestealing. That occurrence was the commencement of all the Kelly troubles, which have since stained the criminal annals of the colony, and brought death, misery and sorrow into a number of families. Mrs Kelly has now been an inmate of the female division of the Melbourne Gaol for nearly two years. She is a well conducted woman in the establishment, and will probably have nine months remitted from her sentence. She would therefore be discharged in January next – little more than six months hence. Father Aylward was the first person to communicate to Mrs Kelly some intelligence of the dreadful occurrences of the last few days. He told her in gentle words that her son Dan was dead, and that Ned was lying wounded, and a prisoner, only a few yards from where she then was. Mrs Kelly is an unimpassioned woman, but it was evident she was terribly grieved at the tragical news. Father Aylward told her of the desperate encounter with the police on Monday last, and she immediately told him that on the same night she dreamt that such an encounter had taken place. Mrs Kelly had come from the work-room where she had been employed, to see the clergyman, but after her interview with him she requested not to be taken back, and to be left alone in her grief. This request was of course complied with, and up to the time of our going to press today she was still alone, and had not resumed her normal occupation. Mr Castieau, the Governor of the Gaol, visited the woman, and told her that as soon as her son Ned had so far recovered as to bear an interview, she would be taken to see him. That meeting of mother and son will doubtless . . . excite even strong men to emotion.

NED KELLY'S TRIAL

A widespread impression prevails that Kelly, being an outlaw, can and will probably be summarily executed without trial, or at most after a Magisterial investigation as to his identity. This impression is incorrect. It is stated on the best authority that being now in legal custody, he is under protection of the law, which must be precisely carried out. His present position is that he now lies under a warrant of remand until the 5th prox., issued by Mr Wyatt, the local Police Magistrate. He will then have to be brought before a magisterial bench and committed for his trial before a jury, which trial must take place at Beechworth, unless some Judge or Judges of the Supreme Court change the venue to the Central Criminal Court, Melbourne, which course will probably be adopted.

Left: On Saturday 31 July, **an impromptu court was held in the kitchen of the gaol hospital** in order to remand Kelly to Beechworth. 'Kelly was brought forward, and Mr C.A. Smyth, the Crown prosecutor, with whom was Mr Gurnor, Crown solicitor, formally applied for his remand to Beechworth. Kelly, who appeared to regard the whole matter with indifference, asked if the proceedings constituted a trial. He was informed that such was not the case, but that the intention was simply to remand him. He then said that when he was tried he should require ex-Constable Fitzpatrick and several others to be present, and concluded by remarking that he had no desire to live . . . Constable McIntyre, who escaped when his comrades were murdered at Mansfield, was then called, and being sworn, identified Kelly as one of the men who had taken part in the murders, Mr Call then remanded Kelly to appear at Beechworth on the 6th inst., to answer the charge of wilful murder preferred against him.'

Bottom left: Sergeant Steele guarding Kelly as the train passes through the Strathbogie Ranges. On the morning of Sunday 1 August, Kelly was escorted from Melbourne Gaol to Newmarket station, then by special train to Beechworth. A reporter who accompanied the escort wrote: 'the prisoner was taken into the guard's van, where seats had been provided in the form of platform chairs. His right leg being still unable to bear him, he sat most of the time; occasionally, however, he desired to look out at the window, and was allowed to do so. When passing Donnybrook he pointed out the spot where he first drew breath; and when he came in sight of the Strathbogie ranges, he exclaimed, "There they are; shall I ever be there again?" He gazed intently at Glenrowan, said that a good man [Byrne] had fallen there, and pointed out the tree where he himself fell. There were no spectators at any of the intermediate stations except Wangaratta, and there only a very few were found on the platform. During the journey Kelly argued that he was illegally in custody, as he had never seen any warrant, and that he could never be hanged. Pointing to Constable Bracken, he said, "There is a man I did not have heart to shoot"; and the time passed in conversation of that kind. The train arrived at Beechworth at half-past 3 o'clock. Superintendent Sadleir now took charge, and saw Kelly safely lodged in Gaol. Somehow it leaked out that Kelly was coming, and about 100 awaited his arrival at the railway station. This crowd pressed forward on the guard's van, but troopers were there who kept them back. Kelly had to be lifted out of the van, and carried to a cab which was in attendance. Just as he was near the cab, a trooper came within his reach, and he gave the horse a kick on its leg. Having been deposited in the cab, he was driven at once to the local Gaol.'

17 THE PRELIMINARY HEARING
BEECHWORTH, 6 AUGUST 1880

As a cavalcade escorting Kelly's cab rattled down Ford Street Beechworth, the scene would have been reminiscent of Harry Power's arrival in chains ten years earlier. Power's misdeeds, however, had faded from memory in light of the exploits of the boy he described as a coward.

Ned Kelly's reputation was now at its peak. Since being outlawed, he had aroused public interest to a degree of excitement not previously experienced in the Australian colonies. The extraordinary fight at Glenrowan, his capture in strange armour and the death of his mates fanned excitement to fever pitch. As a result, a large proportion of the public were more interested in the Kelly who had been shot down trying to rescue his comrades than in the man responsible for the deaths of three policemen two years earlier. His return to Beechworth more closely resembled the visit of a celebrity than that of a murderer.

Kelly's case was not presented until five days after his arrival. During that week, he was denied all personal contact with relatives but was interviewed by local barrister, Mr Zinke, who had so unsuccessfully defended his family on earlier occasions. On the night of Thursday 5 August, only hours before the hearing, Kelly decided to put his trust in more prominent hands. Mr David Gaunson MLA arrived from Melbourne that evening at the request of Tom Lloyd and Margaret Skillion. He was allowed an interview immediately and, with Ned's consent, Gaunson took over the defence – offending Zinke who retired from the case altogether.

Early the following morning, as he walked down

Ned Kelly the bushranger.
'A number of people who saw him in court recognised Kelly as a man they had seen during the career of the Kelly Gang. At the Oxley coursing matches last easter he was seen sitting on a fence, and about four months ago he was drinking in the bar of Dreyer's Hotel, Beechworth, but no one who saw knew him then except sympathisers.' When this engraving appeared in the July 1880 issue of the *Australasian Sketcher*, a woman wrote to the editor saying she had seen him in Melbourne. A reporter asked Kelly in Beechworth Gaol if he had been there; Ned denied it but asked to see the drawing. A journalist wrote, 'He was evidently much gratified by the sight of a newspaper . . . intently studied the picture which had appeared in the Sketcher, and said, "it is a mere fancy sketch of a bushman, and in no way like me".'

Kelly's lodgings in Beechworth Gaol. Ned justifiably complained: 'I have been kept here like a wild beast. If they were afraid to let anyone come near me they might have kept at a distance and watched, but it seems to me to be unjust when I am on trial for my life, to refuse to allow those I put confidence in to come within cooey of me; why they won't so much as let me have a change of clothes brought in. When I came into the Gaol here they made me strip off all my clothes except my pants, and I would not do that.'

The Melbourne *Argus* commented, 'The probability that some relative or sympathiser of the gang will attempt to hand Kelly some means of evading the gallows is so great that the strictest precaution has to be exercised. The Melbourne *Age* also mentioned that Kelly was anxious to have a change of clothing, but so far anything he has asked in that direction has been denied him. The authorities told Mrs Skillion that Ned wanted a shirt. She accordingly purchased one, and took it to the gaol, when she was informed that it could not be handed to the prisoner. Mrs Skillion then offered to buy what was necessary in the presence of a warder, and let the warder take the clothes away so that she would not have a chance of touching them, but this request was also denied.'

the stairway in the gaol, Ned Kelly saw the gallows and remarked, 'what a pity that a fine fellow like Ned Kelly should be strung up there'. He then cheerfully added to his escort, 'well gentlemen, you were not so ready to meet me [two] months ago'.

At 10 a.m. on Friday morning, the Beechworth court opened the first stage of the Kelly trial. The preliminary examination was designed to give the prisoner notice of his case and enable the magistrate to decide if the Crown's evidence justified a full trial. In Kelly's case, it was simply a formality. There was no doubt that he had charges to answer, of which he was sure to be found guilty. Ned was charged with only two of the many misdeeds that police alleged he had committed. First, that on 'the 26th day of October in the year One thousand eight hundred and seventy eight at Stringybark creek in the Northern Bailiwick [Ned Kelly] feloniously, wilfully and with malice aforethought did kill and murder one Thomas Lonigan.' The second charge was that he had dealt similarly with constable Michael Scanlon.

Heading the judiciary was police magistrate Foster – the man who presided over the remand of Kelly sympathisers in 1879. Beside him was chief commissioner of police, captain Frederick Charles Standish. The Crown case was presented by Mr C. A. Smyth, assisted by Chomley and Gurner. The large stone-walled courtroom was crowded to 'suffocation point' on that August morning. A large number of people also gathered in the street, trying

Ford Street and Beechworth Gaol. The view looks north-east from the Church of England tower and shows the town centre as Kelly knew it. Although taken some time before the trial, the town was unchanged when Kelly's guarded cab grated between the courthouse and gaol at the end of the main street. The main gate of the gaol can be seen above and to the left of the post office tower, and the courthouse is among the group of government buildings between the post office and gaol on the right hand side of Ford Street.

Left: The Beechworth courthouse 'did not open till 10 o'clock but by 9 many persons managed to secure admission to the building, and by 10 o'clock every part was crowded. Respectable persons and ladies were admitted by the side and back doors, and the front entrance was kept closed. There was quite a rush of ladies, and whilst over a hundred of them were crowded into the gallery, about thirty more were accommodated near the Bench . . . The great bulk of the crowd were excluded, but they remained all the time in front of the courthouse, and making a good deal of good-humoured noise.'

Bottom left: Interior, Beechworth courthouse. The picture is taken from the front entrance below the gallery and looks toward the bench. On the left wall is the dock, and on the right is the jury box.

THE PRELIMINARY HEARING 235

Beechworth court during the Kelly hearing. The engraving shows only half of the courtroom looking from the jury box, where the press where accommodated. Ned Kelly is shown in the dock (extreme left); the door behind him leads to the court cells. Police magistrate Foster is shown at extreme right and captain Standish is seated beside him. The man addressing the court is thought to be the Crown prosecutor, Smyth. 'Intense interest is depicted in the faces of the people who throng the chamber . . . the general public [make] the most of the limited space around and behind the dock. That there are many sympathisers present there can be little doubt, especially amongst the ladies, many of whom made no secret of the matter. Indeed, one young girl of good looks and respectable attire showed questionable taste in going to the extent of kissing hands to the outlaw, who returned the compliment with interest.'

Above: Ned Kelly in the dock, guarded by sergeant Steele. 'I was sent to sketch him during his trial . . . It was a cold day, and he was wearing an overcoat. He took it off, and put it over his head. His action caused a stir in court, and counsel for the defence spoke to him. Turning to the judge, counsel complained that somebody in the court was sketching the prisoner, and he objected to it. The judge addressed the reporters and asked that the person who was sketching Kelly should desist. I had a good outline of him, and I left the court.' The engraving was based on a watercolour by Julian Ashton.

Facing page below: Mrs Skillion and Tom Lloyd. 'Mrs Skillion is the eldest sister of Ned Kelly. Her husband is at present undergoing a sentence of imprisonment for horsestealing and for many years was known at Greta as a struggling cockatoo, or small farmer. Mrs Skillion is a woman of considerable astuteness, force of character and determination. She is an excellent horsewoman, and although there is nothing to prove that to her attention the Kelly Gang were indebted for the supply of necessary provisions during their concealment, there exists a shrewd suspicion that she knew something about the matter. She is the mother of a large family, and about 33 years of age, trials and hardships making her look older, as her face presents a wizened, sharp, careworn aspect . . . Tom Lloyd . . . interested himself in arranging for his defence, and accompanied by Mrs Skillion, visited Melbourne and consulted several lawyers, the selection finally falling upon Mr David Gaunson.'

Facing page below: Some of the friends. 'Kate Kelly is a younger sister of the bushranger, and is about 17 years old. She is supposed to have assisted Mrs Skillion in her labours on behalf of her outlawed brothers . . . She appears to be of a lively temperament, and to have often indulged in humorous chaff at the expense of the police, who were told to keep her under surveillance . . . Dick Hart is an [elder] brother of the outlaw who was shot at Glenrowan. There is nothing against his character . . . The brother of Joseph Byrne has also been classed as a sympathiser, but there seems nothing to identify him with the criminal acts.'

Facing page below: Thomas McIntyre giving evidence. Kelly said, 'I do not call McIntyre a coward for I reckon he is as game a man as wears the jacket as he had the presence of mind to know his position'. But the 34-year-old Irish trooper had lost three comrades and his reputation, so he did not return the favour. McIntyre perjured himself on vital details of Lonigan's death to misrepresent it as cold-blooded murder. In his first statement to superintendent Sadleir, he explained (as Kelly consistently maintained) that Lonigan drew his revolver, dropped behind a log and was taking aim when shot. In later statements, he omitted Lonigan's attempt to fire on the Kellys. McIntyre was fully aware of his deceit and intimidated witness George Stephens (groom at Faithfull's Creek station and later a detective) during the hearing to alter his evidence on these details.

VICT

PETTY SESSIONS at Beechworth

Before: William Henry Foster Esq., Chairman, and a Magistrate

No.	Complainant.	Defendant.	Mileage.	Fees.
333	The Queen on the information of Thomas McIntyre Constable of Police	Edward Kelly	On remand from 6th inst	
334	The Queen on the information of Thomas McIntyre Constable of Police	Edward Kelly	On remand from 6th inst	

...ORIA.

the 7th day of August 1870.

_____ Esqre.

Cause.	Decision.	Date of Issue.	Remarks.

[wil]ful murder of Thomas
Lonigan at Stringy
Bark Creek in the
Northern Bailiwick of
the Colony of Victoria
on the 26th day of
October 1878.

Remanded till the 9th inst

[wil]ful murder of
Michael Scanlan
at Stringy Bark Creek
in the Northern Bailiwick
of the Colony of Victoria
on the 26th day of
October 1878.

Remanded till the 9th inst

W. Foster P.M.

to follow the proceedings. Police guards were present to maintain order and to ensure that no one passed Kelly any means of cheating the law. Superintendent Sadleir and inspector Baber were among other senior police officials in the crowd.

Mr Foster, PM having taken his seat on the bench, the court was declared open, and Kelly was carried into the dock. The prisoner limped into the end of the dock and looked furtively round the court until his eyes fell on Mrs Skillion and Tom Lloyd, and then mutual signs of recognition passed between them. Mrs Skillion and Lloyd first took seats at the attorney's table, but before the proceedings commenced they shifted to the front seat in the body of the court, within a few feet of the prisoner.

David Gaunson opened proceedings by applying for a further remand: 'I may say that until Wednesday I had no idea of being called upon to defend the accused, and I have not read up the case. If I ever read the evidence it has faded from my memory, and therefore I am not instructed with sufficient accuracy to go on with the case.' He also complained that refusing visitations to Kelly was 'not only a departure from rule but an injustice. It is monstrous the he should be denied such a privilege.' Mr Smyth opposed the application, reminding the court that Mr Zinke had already been engaged for the defence some time earlier. He also denied that the ordinary legal course had not been followed and claimed the responsibility for Kelly's isolation rested with the government. He added: 'This is a preliminary investigation to make out a "prima facie" case ... and the prisoner's defence will be made in another court, for the preparation of which there will be ample time.' Gaunson answered: 'if you Sir [Mr Foster] are not satisfied that there is a 'prima facie' case your clear duty would be to discharge the prisoner. How can I cross-examine the witnesses unless I am seized of all the facts?' The remand was refused.

Mr Smyth opened the case for the Crown by indicating the line of evidence he intended bringing forward for the prosecution. He called Thomas McIntyre as his first witness, who gave a long and detailed account of the expedition to the Wombat Ranges under sergeant Kennedy and his conversations with Kelly. McIntyre remained calm throughout his testimony, giving a clear and unwavering account. Kelly listened with what seemed disinterest except to turn and glare at him on occasions or 'smile and look significantly to his friends whenever a point was made' in cross-examination. The entire first day was given to McIntyre's description of events.

As the court was adjourned for the day, 'Mrs Skillion and Tom Lloyd stepped forward and shook hands with [Ned]'. He remarked to Margaret Skillion, 'It looks as if they won't let me see you – goodbye'. Mrs Skillion replied, 'Never mind, Ned, they are a lot of curs', to which the prisoner rejoined, 'There's one native that's no cur, and he will show them that yet'.

The court was resumed on Saturday morning with David Gaunson complaining of newspaper references to the case. 'The *Argus* had a paragraph in reference to the case, the whole of which was absolutely untrue ... stating that he [Gaunson] had been employed for a political purpose ... The *Ovens and Murray Advertiser* alluded to the prisoner as a "thing" and he asked that they be cautioned for contempt.'

Thomas McIntyre continued his narrative to another packed courtroom and was cross-examined at length by David Gaunson. The inconsistency in McIntyre's account of Lonigan's death was pressed but the trooper held to the more incriminating version, except to inadvertently quote Dan Kelly's remark that Lonigan 'caught for his revolver'. Gaunson drew admissions that Kennedy opened fire when called on, that they expected 'resistance' and carried an unusually large amount of weapons and ammunition. His last question to the constable was on police attitude towards the prisoner, to which McIntyre replied, 'some of the men have said he should be hanged. I cannot say what the feeling of others is.' Mr Foster then addressed the witness: 'I think it only right that I should inform you that it is my opinion that you have given your evidence in an intelligent and honest manner'. Gaunson replied indignantly, 'I need not say that it is very unusual to make such a statement before a prisoner has been dealt with'. Doctor Samuel Reynolds then gave evidence relating to the post-mortem of constable Lonigan and the nature of his wounds before the court was adjourned until Monday.

On Sunday 8 August, David Gaunson followed up on a sympathetic report by the Melbourne *Age* and released another interview with the demonised Kelly. The transcript indicates Gaunson's polish but the structure and content is clearly that of the prisoner. Ned was able to reveal how he had been kept isolated and unable to brief relatives or legal advisers. He once more outlined his grievances and the history of his case going back to the Fitzpatrick incident, including the belief that Kennedy's party 'only wanted the slightest pretext to shoot both my brother and myself'. As Ian Jones pointed out, this piece represents some of the most powerful expressions of his case. It was a considerable coup on Gaunson's part as it broke through the wall of silence unfairly erected around the prisoner when

Previous pages: Beechworth court records of August 1880 Kelly hearings.

he should have been allowed contact with family to prepare a defence.

At his first meeting with Gaunson, Kelly had said quite reasonably:

All I want is a full and fair trial, and a chance to make my side heard. Until now, the police have had all the say, and have had it all their own way. If I get a full and fair trial I don't care how it goes; but I know this – the public will see that I was hunted and hounded on from step to step; they will see that I am not the monster I have been made out. What I have done has been under strong provocation.

In a later interview Kelly added:

I do not pretend that I have led a blameless life, or that one fault justifies another, but the public in judging a case like mine should remember that the darkest life may have a bright side, and that after the worst has been said against a man, he may, if he is heard, tell a story in his own rough way that will perhaps lead them to intimate the harshness of their thoughts against him, and find as many excuses for him as he would plead for himself.

For my own part I do not care one straw about my life now or for the result of the trial. I know very well from the stories I have been told of how I am spoken of, that the public at large execrate my name; the newspapers cannot speak of me with that patient toleration generally extended to men awaiting trial, and who are assumed according to the boast of British justice, to be innocent until they are proved to be guilty; but I do not mind, for I have outlived that care that curries public favour or dreads the public frown.

Let the hand of the law strike me down if it will, but I ask that my story be heard and considered; not that I wish to avert any decree the law may deem necessary to vindicate justice, or win a word of pity from anyone. If my life teaches the public that men are made mad by bad treatment, and if the police are taught that they may not exasperate to madness men they persecute and illtreat, my life will not be entirely thrown away. People who live in large towns have no idea of the tyrannical conduct of the police in country places far removed from court; they have no idea of the harsh and overbearing manner in which they execute their duty, or how they neglect their duty and abuse their powers.

The proceedings lasted another three days, with eight more witnesses called for the Crown. These witnesses generally supported McIntyre's testimony, but they also reiterated Ned's version of events. Curiously, unless reserving argument for the later trial, Gaunson did not pursue their inconsistencies. On Monday, George Stephens, a groom at Faithfull's Creek who had since been employed as a detective, recalled Kelly's remarks about the shootings. Stephens repeated the Kelly's version of the shooting of Lonigan, Scanlon and Kennedy. He offered that he did not think Ned would 'be acquitted. I think he will be hanged.' On hearing this, Ned Kelly laughed loudly. More supporting evidence was given by James Gloster, the hawker bailed up at Euroa on the same day, his assistant Beecroft, the Euroa bank manager Scott, and also Robert McDougall and Henry Dudley who had been among the captured party. Edward Living and senior constable Kelly also testified for the Crown.

When all the evidence relating to Lonigan's death had been heard, the same witnesses were called again to testify for the charge of murdering constable Scanlon; this process lasted until Wednesday 11 August. With the formalities of judiciary satisfied, Mr Foster reached the expected decision and committed Kelly to stand trial at the next Beechworth general sessions on 14 October. 'When Mr Foster asked the prisoner the formal question, if he had anything to say, it was evident from the expression on his face he intended to speak. Mr Gaunson at once urged that he should say nothing, and the prisoner restrained himself, simply saying to his adviser, "If he wants me to say anything I'll very soon speak".' When Mr Foster had adjourned the court, the police bodyguard was surprised to see that 'Kate Kelly rose from her seat and walked to the side of the dock over which her brother leaned and kissed her affectionately. They clasped hands and for a moment gazed at each other. They were then separated.' Ned was escorted from the court and into a police cab. As it drew away from spectators outside the courthouse, Ned learned out the window and pretended to shoot a crowd of children running along behind.

Good behaviour leg-irons of the type worn by Kelly in prison.

Overleaf: Eleven Mile Creek and Glenrowan Gap from Kelly's Lookout.

18 THE TRIAL, MELBOURNE
18 OCTOBER 1880

While Ned Kelly had been a thorn in the side of justice for a long time, the judiciary was not in a hurry to deal with him. Nevertheless, they were determined to convict him and he was eventually brought to trial in late October – nearly four months after his capture. He was not tried in 'Kelly Country' because the prosecution claimed that this would be to the prisoner's advantage. Immediately after committal, application was approved to conduct the trial in Melbourne. The reasons were given in view of suspicious movements of known sympathisers between Greta and Beechworth and the general tenor of spectators at the hearing. In Melbourne, 'with feeling . . . running very high against the accused, the chances of an acquittal were very remote'.

Despite the presence of Kelly's closest friends and sympathisers in Beechworth, he was removed quietly and without notice. Instead of using a special train, the outlaw was escorted from Beechworth by road in a cab loaded with police and guarded by a mounted escort. At Wangaratta, they boarded a train where 'a large crowd on the platform [were] eager to see the bushranger', but his arrival in Melbourne was unexpected and went unnoticed. He was quiet and said little on the journey but remarked to Constable Bracken, 'if it was his fate to be hanged he would be . . . He did not expect to get off'.

Kelly spent the following six weeks in the recesses of Melbourne Gaol, recovering from the wounds he sustained at Glenrowan. The chief secretary's order refusing visitations continued to upset efforts to organise his defence.

West Melbourne from parliament house. The view looks from Spring Street, past the old Princess Theatre to the old Central Criminal Court and Melbourne Gaol on the centre skyline. Ned Kelly's trial preceded the spring racing season, one with more than normal festive spirit because of the city's first International Exhibition — then in full swing. According to the *Illustrated Australian News*: '[his] case excited little interest, as there was little fresh to be extracted from the witnesses, and the result, it might be said, was a foregone conclusion . . . A large number of sympathisers from the Greta district attended the court, but nothing like a demonstration of feeling was attempted. The prisoner demeaned himself quietly, and with a sort of cynical indifference. At times he exhibited even levity . . . Throughout both days the court was densely crowded . . . A large crowd of people were also assembled in front of the courthouse . . . Kate Kelly and Mrs Skillion were present, and an unusually large contingent of constables were stationed in the court to guard all the means of exit.'

While the gang had gained about £5,000 from the Euroa and Jerilderie raids, Kelly had only threepence when captured. His boast that he 'had left his mother well provided' was an empty one. Apparently, he did not have enough to pay for his defence. David Gaunson MLA, acting for Margaret Skillion, made desperate efforts to raise money on the Kelly selection at Greta, on which all rents had been paid under the seven-year lease. But her application for title was refused by the Lands Department at the request of the police.

If the odds were mounting against Kelly, one final factor ensured his conviction. The judge presiding at the Central Criminal Court was Sir Redmond Barry – the same man who had sentenced Mrs Kelly to three years imprisonment just prior to the Stringybark Creek shootings. According to family legend, Barry had denounced Kelly at his mother's trial 'in the most scathing and virulent terms'. Ned was surely bitter when he learned who would preside his case.

On 15 October, Mr Hickman Molesworth, an experienced Melbourne barrister acting on the defence counsel, made an application to Barry for an adjournment until November. The defence were hoping for a trial before a judge 'less obviously hostile' and was also based on the grounds that Kelly had no financial means to proceed with his defence.

Top: The old Central Criminal Court at the corner of Russell and Latrobe streets. Kelly was led into court through a gate in the wall of the Melbourne Gaol (extreme right).

Above: Interior of the court. The judge's high-backed chair is shown centre. The dock, were Kelly sat throughout the trial, is on the right.

Molesworth read an affidavit by the prisoner's attorney outlining discrimination by the chief secretary in not allowing Kelly contact with relatives, and by the Lands Department in not releasing title to his sister's land to finance the defence. The Crown opposed the application on the grounds that Gaunson had known of the trial's proposed date since 25 August and that it was not too late to apply to the Crown for financial assistance. The application was then refused.

The trial commenced on 18 October in the Central Criminal Court on the corner of Russell and Latrobe streets. A huge crowd gathered to witness the event and a large number of police were stationed to maintain order. Jurors, witnesses and all connected with the case were admitted through back entrances and Margaret Skillion was allowed to take a seat in the gallery before the building was opened to the public. At 10 a.m. the court was declared open and Ned Kelly was brought in and placed in the dock before Sir Redmond Barry. The prosecution was conducted by Mr C. A. Smyth and assisted by A. Chomley. The defence was handled by Mr Gaunson and Henry Massy Bindon – a young barrister who had had only ten months experience at the bar. Bindon was retained for seven guineas at the Crown's expense – Mr Molesworth had refused to act for less than 50 guineas.

Kelly's counsel immediately applied for a further postponement to enable further preparation and for Gaunson to seek funds from the Crown to retain Molesworth for the defence. The Crown prosecutor opposed the application, pointing out that the customary fee had been provided, but concluded by saying he was 'loath to do anything which would convey the impression that the prisoner had been improperly treated; and if his honour thought counsel for the defence had made a case ... he would not oppose the application.' Judge Barry said he would not be available until 28 October, and so adjourned proceedings until then.

Kelly's trial finally got under way on Thursday morning 28 October, just prior to the Melbourne racing week. Coincidentally, it was nearly two years to the day since the death of Lonigan, Scanlon and Kennedy. The courtroom was filled to capacity; the lighting was dim, the ventilation was poor and an air of tension and suppressed excitement hung in the atmosphere. Tom Lloyd junior and a heavily veiled Kate Kelly and Margaret Skillion were among the spectators. The sombre scene was dominated by the contrasting figures of Redmond Barry and the accused: the judge in his imposing red robes and Kelly, reserved and solemn in the face of hostile surroundings. The event encouraged sensational

Above: The Kelly trial. Sir Redmond Barry is shown at left; Ned Kelly stands in the dock against the far wall; his attorney, David Gaunson, is below him. Henry Bindon is seated at Gaunson's left, wearing traditional black robe and horsehair wig. On the extreme right is the Crown prosecutor, Mr Smyth. Over the two-day trial, sixteen witnesses gave evidence for the Crown, but not one was called on the prisoner's behalf. Kelly, according to the law at that time, was unable to give sworn evidence on his own behalf, yet curiously his earlier remarks amounting to admission to the charge could be used as hearsay evidence against him. Kelly could have made an unsworn statement but did not — at the insistence of his attorney. The defence rested entirely on cross-examination of Crown witnesses and Bindon's final address to the jury. Their case, inadequately argued for Kelly, was that Lonigan's killing was in self-defence; that Kelly believed the police were acting on false evidence given by Fitzpatrick and intended — from the remarks made by Brooke Smith and other police — not to arrest him but to shoot him on sight. When he saw the police heavily armed and disguised in plain clothes, it confirmed his belief and so he took defensive action. Bindon pointed out and questioned McIntyre's remarkable memory for detail, but overlooked the significant inconsistency of his earlier statements, particularly in relation to Lonigan's death.

Left: Mr David Gaunson MLA acted as Kelly's attorney and later organised support for a petition of reprieve — an act that almost cost him his seat in parliament. Gaunson would have been well aware of the political danger of his actions, but was convinced that the accused deserved fair treatment. He went to great lengths on Kelly's behalf — both before and after the trial. Probably the greatest setback in his efforts was the inexperienced Henry Bindon — a result of the failure to raise funds for Mr Molesworth's expertise. Bindon gained little credit for his part in the trial, although under the circumstances his task was virtually hopeless. J. A. Gurner, who assisted in the Kelly prosecution, wrote unkindly of Bindon, '[he] was furnished with an exceptional belief in his own capacity and a superlative contempt for all other members of the legal profession . . . It was thought, however, that his defence did nothing to assist his client, and that, I was informed, was the opinion of Ned Kelly, expressed by him in very forcible terms.'

reporting: McIntyre's graphic description made an impact only possible from the mouth of a sole survivor of such a tragedy. Kelly's pluck, in the face of an unsympathetic jury, and his remarkable dialogue with Barry after the verdict had been delivered, made sure of his legend's survival. The following is the *Argus*'s report of the two-day trial.

TRIAL OF EDWARD KELLY

At a special sitting of the Central Criminal Court yesterday, before his Honour, Mr Justice Barry, Edward Kelly was brought up for trial on a charge of having at Stringybark Creek, in the Wombat Ranges, on the 28th October, 1878, wilfully and maliciously murdered Thomas Lonigan, a police constable.

Mr C. A. Smyth and Mr Chomley appeared for the prosecution, and Mr Bindon for the prisoner.

Mr Bindon applied for a further postponement of the trial until next sessions, on the ground that the defence of the prisoner had only been placed in his hands on Monday night, and that he had consequently been unable to make himself thoroughly acquainted with the voluminous depositions taken in the case.

His Honour said he would not be justified in postponing the case any further. The prisoner received notice of his trial two months ago, and how the procrastination had occurred he (His Honour) could not tell. The case would now proceed.

A jury having been sworn in, Mr C. A. Smyth opened the case by narrating the circumstances of the police murders and explaining the nature of the evidence he would submit. He called the following witnesses: Michael Edward Ward said he was a detective stationed in Melbourne. A document produced was a warrant for the apprehension of Edward Kelly, of Beechworth, for horse stealing. It was dated 15th March, 1878. The person accused therein was the prisoner in the dock. He also proved the warrant which was issued for the arrest of Daniel Kelly on a similar charge. He had been in pursuit of the Kelly gang since the 9th September, 1878 until they were captured on the 29th of June.

Patrick Day, police constable, stationed at Benalla, proved the issue of warrants for the arrest of the prisoner and his brother Daniel Kelly for attempting to murder Constable Fitzpatrick.

Thomas McIntyre deposed – I am a police constable, at present stationed in Melbourne. In October, 1878, I was stationed at Mansfield, and on Friday the 25th of the month, left with Sergeant Kennedy and Constables Lonigan and Scanlon to search for the prisoner and his brother Dan, on a charge of attempting to murder Constable Fitzpatrick. Knew that there were warrants issued. They were notified in the Police Gazettes. The party were in plain clothes, and Sergeant Kennedy was in charge. We started at about 5 o'clock in the morning, and camped in the Wombat Ranges, 20 miles from Mansfield, pitching our camp in a small cleared space. There were the remains of a hut there, and some dead logs lying on the ground. On the following morning the 26th, Sergeant Kennedy and Scanlon left the camp to patrol on horseback, leaving me and Lonigan in charge of the camp. Sergeant Kennedy had a Spencer rifle and revolver, Scanlon a revolver. Lonigan had a revolver and I a revolver and fowling piece. During the day, in consequence of a noise having been heard down the creek, I searched the place but found no one, and on returning to the camp fired two shots at parrots. I and Lonigan, at about 5 o'clock, lit a fire in the angle formed by two large logs which crossed each other, and proceeded to prepare our tea. We were standing at the fire with one of the logs between us. Lonigan alone was armed, and he only had a revolver in his belt. My revolver and fowling piece were in the tent. There was a quantity of speargrass 5ft high about 35 yards from the fire, and on the south side of the clearing. I was standing with my face to the fire and my back to the speargrass, when suddenly a number of voices from the speargrass sang out, 'Bail up, hold up your hands'. Turning quickly round, I saw four men, each armed with a gun, and pointing these weapons at Lonigan and me. The prisoner, who was one of the men had the right-hand position, and he had his gun pointed at my chest. I, being unarmed at once threw my arms out horizontally. Lonigan was in my rear and to my left. Saw the Prisoner move his rifle, bringing it in a line with Lonigan, and fire. By glancing round I saw that the shot had taken effect on Lonigan, for he fell. A few seconds afterwards he exclaimed, 'Oh Christ, I'm shot'. The four men then advanced on me, running three of them with their guns lowered, the prisoner drawing a revolver, and all calling out, 'Keep up your hands'. At a distance of three yards they all covered me with their weapons. On ascertaining that my firearms were at the tent, the prisoner took the revolver from Lonigan, who had in the meantime expired, and also secured the firearms in the tent. The four men then went into the tent, leaving me outside. Dan Kelly returned to me with a pair of handcuffs found in the tent, and said he was going to handcuff me. Prisoner, who followed him, said that was unnecessary, as his rifle was better than handcuffs, threatening at the time to track me, even to the police station if I tried to escape. In the conversations that followed prisoner called my attention to the gun with which he had shot Lonigan, He said, 'That's a curious old gun to carry about the country'. It was an old gun with stock and barrel spliced together with waxed string. The prisoner then took up my fowling piece, drew the charges, abstracted the shot and substituted them with bullets, reloading the gun the same. He gave the fowling piece to Byrne, whose body I identified at Glenrowan. I recognised the prisoner and his brother from their likeness to their mother and sisters. Did not know Hart, the other member of the gang. Prisoner, jerking his head towards Lonigan's body, asked 'Who is that?' Witness replied, 'Lonigan'. Prisoner at first said, 'No, I know Lonigan well'; but afterwards, 'Oh, yes it is. I am glad of that for the ——— once gave me a hiding in Benalla.' Prisoner had now two guns, the one he received from Byrne in exchange for the fowling piece and his own weapon. He remarked that one was for me if I attempted to escape. The prisoner then arranged his men, placing two in the speargrass [Dan and Byrne] and one [Hart] in the tent. The prisoner himself lay down behind a log at the fire, and called me to the log. We had some conversation in which the prisoner expressed a belief that the police had come out to shoot him. The prisoner and his mates were now waiting for the return of Kennedy and Scanlon, and with regard to their absence and probable time of return he closely questioned me. He asked me to request them to surrender, and promised not to shoot them if they did. He stated, however, that there were four men in the police force he intended to roast viz., Flood, Fitzpatrick, Steele and Strong. He said, 'What gun is it? A breechloader?' I said, 'Yes, it is'. He said, 'That looks very like as if you came out to shoot me'. I said, 'You can't blame the men, they have got their duty to do, and they must come out as they are ordered'. He said, 'They are not ordered to go about the country shooting people'. He then said, 'What became of the Sydney man?' – he referred to a man who murdered Sergeant Walling in New South Wales. I said, 'He was shot by the police'. He said, 'If the police shot him, they shot the wrong man. I suppose if you could you would shoot me some day, but before you do it I will make some of you suffer for it. That fellow Fitzpatrick is the cause of all this. Those people lagged at Beechworth the other day no more had revolvers than you have at present – in fact, it was not them who were there at all.' I said, 'You can't blame us for what Fitzpatrick did to you'. He said, 'I have almost sworn to do for Fitzpatrick, and if I let you go now you will have to leave the police force'. I said, 'I would, that my health was rather bad, and I intended to go home'. I asked him what he would do to the men if I got them to surrender. He said, 'You had better get them to surrender, because if they get away we will shoot them and if they don't surrender we will shoot you. We don't want their lives, only their firearms. We will handcuff them all night, and let them go in the morning.' I thought I could possibly get a gun by a sudden spring, and I made a short step towards them. Hart cried out from the tent, 'Ned, look out, or that fellow will be on top of you'. Prisoner said, 'Don't do that mate; if you do you will soon find your match, for you know there are not three men in the police force who are a match for me. About this time (half-past 5 or 6 o'clock) Kennedy and Scanlon came up. Prisoner cried out, 'Listen lads, here they come'. (This evidence was objected to as relating to another offence, but the objection was overruled on the ground that the evidence was admissible to show the intent with which the first shot was fired.) Kennedy and Scanlon came up horseback. They were 150 yards from us. The prisoner was still kneeling behind the log. He stooped to pick up a gun. Kennedy was on horseback. Prisoner said, 'You go and sit down on that log' (pointing to one), and added 'Mind you don't give any alarm, or I'll put a hole through you.' The log was about 10 yards distant from the prisoner, in the direction of Kennedy. When they were 40 yards from the camp I went to them and said, 'Sergeant, we are surrounded; I think you had better surrender.' Prisoner at the same time rose and said 'bail up'. Kennedy smiled, and apparently thought it was a joke. He put his hand on his revolver. As he did so prisoner fired at him. The shot did not take effect. The three others came from their hiding place with their guns, and cried out, 'bail up!' Prisoner picked up the other gun. Scanlon, when Kennedy was fired at, was in the act of dismounting. He became somewhat flurried and fell on his knees. The whole party fired at him. Scanlon received a shot under the right arm. He fell on his side. Kennedy threw himself on the horse's neck, and rolled off on the offside, putting the horse between him and the prisoner. I caught Kennedy's horse, and looked round and saw the others running past. I attempted to mount the horse to get away. The last I saw was Kennedy and Scanlon on the ground. I got away. I heard shots fired. I can't say if they were fired at me. I got thrown off the horse in the timber when I had ridden two miles. I remained in the bush all night, and got to Mansfield next afternoon (Sunday), about 3 p.m. I reported the matter to Inspector Pewtress, and a search party was organised. We started from Mansfield about 6 o'clock. Never saw the prisoner again till after his arrest at Glenrowan. I arrived at Glenrowan on the Monday afternoon. Saw the prisoner at the railway station, and recognised him.

Cross-examined by Mr Bindon – We went out with Kennedy to arrest the prisoner and his brother. I did not see the warrants for their apprehension. I can't swear that any of our party had a warrant. I knew of the warrants by the Police Gazette. Kennedy did not roll off his horse through being wounded by the prisoner. From the time the sergeant came in sight till Scanlon was shot was about a minute. Kennedy's horse was restive after I caught him. I thought nothing of the horse till I saw Scanlon was shot, and then I did not think I could get away. Scanlon was shot immediately after Kennedy was fired at. When they were firing all round I thought no mercy would be shown to any of us. If I had known Kennedy would have fought I would not have left. I did not consider there was any opportunity for a fight.

George Stephens, groom, said he was at Faithfull's Creek station when it was stuck up by the prisoner, and Hart, Byrne, and Dan Kelly. He said prisoner gave him the following account in answer to a question about shooting the police. Prisoner said, 'We were behind a log. I told Dan to cover Lonigan and I would cover McIntyre. I then called on them to throw up their hands, and McIntyre immediately did so. Lonigan made for the log and tried to draw the revolver as he went along. He laid down behind the log, and rested his revolver on the top of the log and covered Dan. I then took my rifle off McIntyre and fired at Lonigan, grazing his temple. Lonigan then disappeared below the log but gradually rose again, and as he did so I fired again and shot him through the head. I then sent two men back to our own hut, fearing a surprise there. I sent Dan over to the rise to watch for the police coming. While I was talking to McIntyre the men appeared in the open, and I had just time to fall down by the fire. The fire was very nigh scorching my knees. McIntyre went over and spoke to Kennedy, and Kennedy smiled. I immediately sang out for them to throw up their hands. Scanlon swung his rifle round and fired at me. I then fired, and Scanlon fell forward on the horse's neck. I still kept him covered, thinking he was shamming. When the horse moved, he rolled off.

Cross-examined – I have been in the police. I left in 1868. I was discharged for being absent for two or three days without leave. I am going to try to get employed by the police.

Re-examined – I repeated my evidence to Detective Ward shortly after the prisoner went away.

Wm. Fitzgerald, labourer, at Molongolong, who was present at the conversation between Stephens and prisoner, gave evidence similar to that of the last witness.

Henry Dudley, employed in the Government Printing-office, gave evidence as to having been stuck up by the prisoner at the Faithfull's Creek station, in December, 1878. Referring to a conversation he had with prisoner, he said that the prisoner pulled out a gold watch in a double case. He said, 'That's a good watch, is it not? It belonged to poor Kennedy. What would be best for me – to shoot the police, or for the police to shoot me and carry my mangled body into Mansfield?'

Robert McDougall, bookbinder at the Government Printing-office, who was with Dudley, gave similar evidence.

James Gloster, draper at Seymour – I was hawking goods in December last in the neighbourhood of Mr Younghusband's station, when I was locked up by the prisoner at the station with 14 other persons. The prisoner in one conversation described the shooting of the police at the Wombat. One of the prisoners, out of curiosity, asked him about it. Prisoner said that he had shot Lonigan, and had also shot Sergeant Kennedy. He said, 'Lonigan ran to the log and was trying to screen himself behind it when I fired at him. He fell. I was sorry afterwards that he didn't surrender.' He said that Lonigan was struck in the head, and killed. He said, people called it murder, but he had never murdered anyone in his life. I said, 'How about Sergeant Kennedy?' He said, 'I killed him in fair fight; as Kennedy came up I told him to throw up his arms, but instead of surrendering he showed fight, and during the fight he retreated from tree to tree. Kennedy must have been a good shot as well as a brave man, for one of the shots went through my whiskers.' He added that Kennedy turned round, and he (Kelly) thought he was going to shoot him, and he fired, and shot him. He was sorry he had fired that last shot, as he had thought since that Kennedy was going to surrender, and not fire. He said that he had afterwards had a long conversation with Kennedy, and seeing from his wounds that he could not live, he shot him. He said that the party were going to leave the ground, and as he did not wish Kennedy to be torn by wild beasts while he was dying he shot him. He added that it was no murder to shoot one's enemies, and the police were his natural enemies. He said he had stolen about 280 horses, and that if the police had taken him for any of these cases he would not object, but that the police had persecuted him.

Cross-examined by Mr Bindon – Prisoner said he was 200 miles away at the time of the alleged shooting at Greta; that his mother had struggled up with a large family, that he was very much incensed at the police, that his mother had been unjustly imprisoned, and that Fitzpatrick's testimony was prejudiced. He referred to his mother having an infant at the breast when she was taken to gaol. Prisoner said he was sorry Lonigan had not surrendered. I said at the Police Court that my impression was that he took the whole of the shooting on himself to screen the others.

At this stage the further hearing of the trial was adjourned till next day, at 9 o'clock.

The jury were taken to the Supreme Court Hotel, where quarters for the night were prepared for them.

TRIAL AND CONVICTION OF EDWARD KELLY
SENTENCE OF DEATH

The trial of Edward Kelly on the charge of murdering Constable Lonigan was resumed in the Central Criminal Court yesterday, before His Honour Mr Justice Barry. The Court reassembled at 9 o'clock.

Mr C. A. Smyth and Mr Chomley prosecuted, and Mr Bindon appeared for the defence.

Frank Beacroft [sic], draper's assistant living at Longwood, said that he was with Mr Gloster at the time the Faithfull's Creek station was stuck up. He gave evidence similar to that of Gloster in reference to the statements made by the prisoner as to the manner in which Lonigan had been shot.

Robert Scott, manager of the National Bank at Euroa, gave evidence as to the prisoner sticking up the bank on the 10th December, 1878. He asked Kelly who shot Lonigan. Kelly said, 'Oh, I shot Lonigan'.

Cross-examined by Mr Bindon – The prisoner treated me and Mrs Scott well.

Henry Richards, police constable stationed at Jerilderie, New South Wales, said that in February 1879, the police station there was stuck up by the prisoner and three other men. Prisoner said he had come to shoot him because he had tried to shoot him (Kelly) on the punt at Tocumwal two months before. He said he also intended to shoot Constable Devine, as he was worse than a black tracker, and was always following him about. Constable Devine asked the prisoner about the shooting of the police in Victoria. The prisoner said that a reward of £100 had been offered for him for shooting Constable Fitzpatrick. He was not guilty of that, as he was 200 miles away at the time that Fitzpatrick was shot in this way. He had gone to arrest Dan Kelly; that his mother asked him if he had a warrant, and he said he had not, and his mother then said that Fitzpatrick could not arrest Dan if Ned was there; that Dan tried to take the pistol from Fitzpatrick, and in the scuffle the pistol went off. Prisoner also said that he had not gone out to shoot Kennedy, Scanlon, and Lonigan, but was determined to get their arms. The reason he shot them was that they were persecuting him. He said he had Sergeant Kennedy's watch, and he intended to return it in course of time.

Cross-examined – Kelly told Mrs Devine that he would not shoot her husband. The remark about the shooting at Tocumwal referred to this. About two months before, while he and another constable were on patrol duty on the New South Wales side of the Murray, they saw four men in a punt, and he called out that he would shoot them if they did not answer. The men proved to be Victorian Police.

Edward M. Lyving [sic], clerk in the Bank of New South Wales, Jerilderie, said that after the bank was robbed, in the course of a conversation with him, prisoner said that he had shot the police with a gun he had. 'It was an old one, but a good one, and would shoot round a corner'. Prisoner went to the newspaper office to give a written statement for publication. The proprietor was not in, and his wife refused to take it. Prisoner gave him the statement, and he afterwards handed it to the police.

The statement was tendered in evidence, but was not received.

John Wm. Tarlton [sic], clerk in New Zealand, was clerk at the Bank of New South Wales, Jerilderie, in February, 1879. Prisoner stated that people talked about their shooting the police, but they had done it in self-defence. They had been persecuting him ever since he was 14, and he had been driven to become an outlaw. He had a revolver which he said was taken from Lonigan after he was shot. He said he shot Kennedy and Lonigan, and that Hart and Byrne were miles away at the time. The prisoner left the impression that he had done all the shooting himself.

John Kelly, senior constable of police, gave evidence as to the Glenrowan affair, and produced the armour the prisoner had on when he was wounded. Prisoner said to Constable Bracken, 'Save me; I saved you.' He (witness) replied, 'You showed little mercy to Sergeant Kennedy and Scanlon'. Prisoner said, 'I had to shoot them or they would have shot me'. Asked him where Kennedy's watch was, and he said he didn't care to tell. The witness corroborated Constable McIntyre's version of the conversation between him and the prisoner at the lockup. Between 3 and 6 o'clock the same morning had another conversation with prisoner in the presence of Constable Ryan. Give him some milk-and-water. Asked him if Fitzpatrick's statement was correct. Prisoner said, 'Yes, I shot him'.

Arthur Steele, sergeant in charge of the Wangaratta police station, gave evidence as to the arrest of the prisoner at Glenrowan. When he was captured he said, 'Don't kill me; I never hurt any of you'. Constable Kelly said, 'You did not show Scanlon and Kennedy much mercy'. Prisoner said, 'If I had not shot them they would have shot me'. In reply to other questions, the prisoner said he had intended to shoot everyone that escaped from the wreck of the train. Prisoner was asked if it was true about his shooting Fitzpatrick. He said 'Yes, it is true; I shot him'.

Cross-examined by Mr Bindon – I arrived at Glenrowan about 5 o'clock in the morning. First saw the prisoner about a quarter-past 7 o'clock. There was some firing. There were about a dozen constables there in the morning besides the black trackers. There were 53 in the evening. I fired at a young fellow named Reardon. I fired at him because I thought it was one of the outlaws. The police fired into the hotel. I believe there were a number of people in the hotel, but I did not know of it at the time. After the boy was shot and I understood that there were people in the house, I called on them to come out. We fired in answer to firing from the house. Martin Cherry and a boy named Jones were shot. I was accused of shooting the boy. There was nothing but slugs in my gun. That boy was shot before I arrived. Never said to Mrs Jones that if she would say that Ned Kelly shot her son I would forward her application for a portion of the reward to the Government. Never heard of such a thing before today.

Re-examined – The boy Reardon recovered. Can't say who shot Cherry.

Samuel Reynolds, medical practitioner at Mansfield, made a 'post-mortem examination on the body of Thomas Lonigan. There were two wounds – the one in the eye, the other on the temple, which was merely a graze. He had also a wound on the left arm, and one on the left thigh. They were all gunshot wounds. The wound through the eye was the cause of death.

Cross-examined by Mr Bindon – The ball that struck the eye must have come slightly slanting. Did not think the other wounds were inflicted after death. I should say that Kennedy was standing up when he was shot, as he had the wound right in the centre of the chest. I did not make a regular 'post-mortem' examination of Kennedy's body. I extracted a bullet from Lonigan's thigh. It was an ordinary revolver bullet.

Re-examined – If wounds were inflicted before the circulation had actually ceased, it would be impossible to state accurately whether they were before or after death.

This closed the evidence for the prosecution, and the Court adjourned for an hour to allow Mr Bindon an opportunity of considering whether he would call any witnesses. On the Court resuming.

Mr Bindon stated that in the course of the case he had objected to certain evidence that had been tendered, and he wished to know whether his Honour would reserve a special case on the points for the consideration of the full Court. He referred more particularly to the evidence given after Lonigan had been killed. He contended as the prisoner was not being tried for the murder of Kennedy or Scanlon, that therefore no evidence should have been given in regard to them.

His Honour said that if an act were doubtful or ambiguous, or capable of two meanings, the conduct of the person

Judge Sir Redmond Barry was highly respected in his day, but more for his activities in public life than his work on the bench. His treatment of the Kelly family definitely discredited his achievements in other spheres. According to one biographer, 'he considered the presence of many former convicts in the colony and the occurrence of many crimes of violence called for rigorous repression to the point of harshness. He was in the habit of accompanying his sentences with florid and, at times, sanctimonious speeches . . . but he was in general fair and judicial in court and invariably courteous . . . He was not, however, a great lawyer or a great Judge . . . He [also] seems to have been quite without humour.' Barry has often been under fire for his apparently vindictive dealings with Ned Kelly. The fact that he was intimately acquainted with his history and had publicly expressed strong opinions of him, yet did not hand Kelly's case to a more impartial colleague invited such criticism.

Legal opinion, like that of professor Louis Waller (1968) and justice John Phillips (1987) supports the view that Barry did not handle the case impartially. Nor did he put the case squarely before the jury when summing up. It was quite clear that Barry saw no case for self-defence by Kelly. He allowed evidence objected to by Bindon relating to the shooting after Lonigan's death on the grounds that it was admissible to establish intent and rule out accident – which is now seen as unfair to the accused. The engraving accompanied an article announcing the death of Barry on 23 November 1880, four weeks after the trial – supposedly significant in the light of Kelly's promise to see him in a higher court.

before, at the time or after the time of doing the act was admissible to show the motive and reason for his conduct. This evidence was admissible to show whether the shooting of Constable Lonigan were accidental or justifiable.

Mr Smyth then addressed the jury, reviewing the evidence on behalf of the Crown.

Mr Bindon then addressed the jury on behalf of the prisoner. The evidence, he said, was in one sense most elaborate, but the great bulk of it was quite extraneous matter. It would be the duty of the jury to exclude every thing from their minds but what related to the death of Constable Lonigan. What occurred at Euroa, Jerilderie, and Glenrowan was altogether irrelevant, and with regard to what occurred at Stringybark Creek, they had only the evidence of one witness. That one witness (Constable McIntyre), had given a very consecutive and well prepared narrative after the event, but he was in such a state of trepidation at the time of the affray, that he could not have made the minute observations he professed to have done, and could not possibly have picked out the prisoner from amongst the gang as the particular person who shot Lonigan. His statement was therefore to be received with discredit. The prisoner and his three mates were following a lawful pursuit in the bush, when a party of men in disguise, fully-armed policemen in plain clothes, as they afterwards turned out to be – came upon them, and an unfortunate fracas occurred, in which Constable Lonigan lost his life. Who shot that man no one could tell. McIntyre said that he saw the prisoner fire at him, but there were shots fired by others at the same time and to tell which was the fatal bullet was a matter of impossibility. Only two men were alive who were in the fray, and it was simply a question of believing the statement of the one or that of the other. Unfortunately for the prisoner, his mouth was closed, and they had only the statement of McIntyre before them. That statement, moreover, was not only that of a prejudiced witness, but the corroborative evidence given was of most peculiar and unreliable character, being simply a variety of remarks made by the prisoner himself – remarks made either 'ad captandurn', for the purpose of screening others, or for keeping the persons he had in durance in subjection. Evidence of this character was of a most illusory nature, and ought to have no weight with the jury. The prisoner was not the bloodthirsty assassin the Crown prosecutor had endeavoured to make out. Both before and after the shooting of the police he showed that he had the greatest possible respect for human life, for he had many previous opportunities of assassinating policemen, if that was his desire, and at Euroa and Jerilderie he never harmed one of the persons who fell into his power. The jury had an important and serious duty to discharge, and he had to urge them not to take away the life of a man on the prejudiced evidence of a single man.

His Honour, in summing up, said that the prisoner Edward Kelly was presented against for that he, on the 26th October, 1878, at Stringybark Creek, in the northern bailiwick, feloniously, wilfully, and with malice aforethought, did kill and murder Thomas Lonigan. Murder was the highest kind of homicide. It was the voluntary killing of any person in the Queen's peace by another person of sound mind, with malice prepense and aforethought, either expressed or implied. Malice was twofold. It might be proved by expressions made use of by the prisoner, which showed a malevolent disposition, and that he had an intention to take away the life of another man without lawful cause. It might also be proved by the prisoner procuring materials to cause the death of another, such as purchasing a sword, or a knife or poison, and if those weapons or the poison were used, it was evidence from which malice might be inferred, unless there was some justification for their use. As, for instance, if a man bought a pistol intending to shoot A and went out intending to shoot him, and if on the way he was assailed and overpowered by another with whom he had no intention of

quarrelling and should kill him, he would be justified in using the pistol in self defence. If however, having bought the pistol, he proceeded to carry out his original intention, and did so, it would be murder. And if two or three or more persons went out together with an intention of an unlawful character, they were all principals in the first degree, and each was liable to account for the acts of the others. So if four men went out armed intending to resist those in lawful pursuit of an object, and one of these four men interfered with those on their lawful business, and killed them, the four would be equally guilty of murder, and might be executed. Here four constables went out to perform a duty. It was said they were in plain clothes. But with that they had nothing to do. Regard them

The accused. 'Throughout the examination of the witnesses who were condemning him he stood silent, a stocky powerful figure, with piercing eyes, which looked out with quiet intelligent interest from beneath a heavy shock of hair that grew well down on his forehead. The lower part of his face too, was hairy, and a longish beard, turning from dark brown to ginger, gave him an appearance of wildness in keeping with his violent history. In the witness box he exhibited one curious mannerism. Every now and then he would raise his right arm almost level with his shoulder and spit over it on to the floor of the court — a trick that was fairly common in those days among bushmen and coach drivers.'

as civilians – he used the word because it had been made use of in the course of the trial, although he thought it inappropriate – what right had four other men armed to stop them? They had the evidence of the surviving constable as to what had occurred – that two were left by their companions at the camp – what right had the prisoner and three other men to desire them to hold up their hands and surrender? But there was another state of things which was not to be disregarded. These men were persons charged with a responsible and, as it turned out, a dangerous duty, and they were aware of that before they started. They went in pursuit of two persons who had been gazetted as persons against whom warrants were issued, and they were in pursuit of these two persons; therefore they had a double protection – that of the ordinary citizen, and that of being ministers of the law, executive officers of the administration of the peace of the country, Whether they were in uniform or not, there was no privilege on the part of any person to molest them, and still less was there power or authority to molest them as constables. The jury had been invited to be extremely careful before relying upon the evidence of Constable McIntyre. He went further, and told them to be careful in considering the evidence of all the witnesses. According to the law of this country, the principles of evidence were the same on all sides of the Court, at the common law, at the equity, and at the criminal side, with some few exceptions. As, for instance, in treason there must be two witnesses, although not necessarily to the same overt act. In perjury there must be generally two witnesses, or one witness sworn and certain circumstances deposed to on oath to corroborate him. There must be two witnesses to a will. Some documents must be signed by an attorney, some documents must be attested by a notary public; but with these and some other unimportant exceptions one witness was sufficient to prove a case on either side of the Supreme Court. McIntyre was the only survivor of this lamentable catastrophe. The jury would have to consider the manner in which he had given his evidence, and say whether they thought from his demeanour or mode of giving his evidence that he was stating what was not true. It was not his province to land or to censure him, but if he had not escaped there would have been no survivor to give evidence today. The jury were properly told that the prisoner was not on his trial for the murder of either Scanlon or Kennedy, but he had admitted the evidence of what had occurred prior to the shooting of Lonigan, because the jury might infer from it what was the motive for shooting Lonigan, or whether the shooting was accidental or in self-defence. Besides the testimony of McIntyre there were also the admissions made by the prisoner himself at different times, and at different places, to different persons. Two classes of those admissions were made at Euroa and Jerilderie, and the other at the time of his capture. On the first two occasions, the prisoner was not under any duress, and it was for the jury to say what motive he had in making the admissions. There was no compulsion upon him; he answered questions which were put to him when he might have held his tongue. These admissions were spoken to by five different persons at one place, by three at the other, and by three at the third, and it was for the jury to say whether these witnesses had concocted the story or not.

The jury then retired, and after deliberating about half-an-hour returned into Court with a verdict of guilty.

The prisoner, having been asked in the usual way if he had any statement to make, said: 'Well, it is rather too late for me to speak now. I thought of speaking this morning and all day, but there was little use, and there is little use blaming any one now. Nobody knew about my case except myself and I wish I had insisted on being allowed to examine the witnesses myself. If I had examined them, I am confident I would have thrown a different light on the case. It is not that I fear death; I fear it as little as to drink a cup of tea. On the evidence that has been given, no juryman could have given any other verdict. That is my opinion. But as I say, if I had examined the witnesses I would have shown matters in a different light, because no man understands the case as I do myself. I do not blame anybody – neither Mr Bindon nor Mr Gaunson; but Mr Bindon knew nothing about my case. I lay blame on myself that I did not get up yesterday and examine the witnesses, but I thought that if I did so it would look like bravado and flashness.'

The court crier having called upon all to observe a strict silence whilst the judge pronounced the awful sentence of death,

His Honour said – Edward Kelly, the verdict pronounced by the jury is one which you must have fully expected.

The Prisoner – Yes, under the circumstances.

His Honour – No circumstances that I can conceive could have altered the result of your trial.

The Prisoner – Perhaps not from what you can now conceive, but if you had heard me examine the witnesses it would have been different.

His Honour – I will give you credit for all the skill you appear to desire to assume.

The Prisoner – No, I don't wish to assume anything. There is no flashness or bravado about me. It is not that I want to save my life, because I know I would have been capable of clearing myself of the charge, and I could have saved my life in spite of all against me.

His Honour – The facts are so numerous, and so convincing not only as regards the original offence with which you are charged, but with respect to a long series of transactions covering a period of 18 months, that no rational person would hesitate to arrive at any other conclusion but that the verdict of the jury is irresistible, and that it is right. I have no desire whatever to inflict upon you any personal remarks. It is not becoming that I should endeavour to aggravate the sufferings with which your mind must be sincerely agitated.

The Prisoner – No, I don't think that. My mind is as easy as the mind of any man in this world as I am prepared to show before God and man.

His Honour – It is blasphemous for you to say that. You appear to revel in the idea of having put men to death.

The Prisoner – More men than me have put men to death, but I am the last man in the world that would take a man's life. Two years ago, even if my own life was at stake, and I am confident if I thought a man would shoot me, I would give him a chance of keeping his life, and would part rather with my own. But if I knew that through him innocent persons lives were at stake I certainly would have to shoot him if he forced me to·do so, but I would want to know that he was really going to take innocent life.

His Honour – Your statement involves a cruelly wicked charge of perjury against a phalanx of witnesses.

The Prisoner – I dare say, but a day will come at a bigger court than this when we shall see which is right and which is wrong. No matter how long a man lives, he is bound to come to judgement somewhere, and as well here as anywhere. It will be different the next time they have a Kelly trial, for they are not all killed. It would have been for the good of the Crown had I examined the witnesses, and I would have stopped a lot of the reward, I can assure you; and I do not know but I will do it yet, if allowed.

His Honour – An offence of this kind is of no ordinary character. Murders had been discovered which had been committed under circumstances of great atrocity. They proceeded from motive other than that which actuated you. They have had their origin in many sources. Some have been committed from a sordid desire to take from others the property they had acquired, some from jealousy, some from a desire for revenge, but yours is a more aggravated crime, and one of larger proportions, for with a party of men you took up arms against society, organised as it is for mutual protection, and for respect of law.

The Prisoner – That is the way the evidence came out here. It appeared that I deliberately took up arms of my own accord, and induced the other three men to join me for the purpose of doing nothing but shooting down the police.

His Honour – In new communities, where the bonds of society so well linked together as in older countries, there is unfortunately a class which disregards the evil consequences of crime. Foolish, inconsiderate, conducted, unprincipled youths unfortunately abound, and unless they are made to consider the consequences of crime they are led to imitate notorious felons, whom they regard as self-made heroes. It is right therefore that they should be asked to consider and reflect upon what the life of a felon is. A felon who has cut himself off from all decencies, all the affections, charities, and all the obligations of society is at helpless and degraded as a wild beast of the field. He has nowhere to lay his head, he has no one to prepare for him the comforts of life, he suspects his friends, he dreads his enemies, he is in constant alarm lest his pursuers should reach him, and his only hope is that he might use his life in what he considers a glorious struggle for existence. That is the life of the outlaw or felon, and it would be well for those young men whom so foolish as to consider that it is brave of a man to sacrifice the lives of his fellow-man in carrying out his own wild ideas, to see that it is a life to be avoided by every possible means, and to reflect that the unfortunate termination of your life is a miserable death. New South Wales joined with Victoria in providing ample inducement to persons to assist in having you and your companions apprehended, but by some spell which I cannot understand – a spell which exists in all lawless communities more or less – which may be attributed either to a sympathy for the outlaws, or a dread of the consequences which would result from the performance of their duty – no persons were found who would be tempted by the reward. The love of country, the love of order, the love of obedience to law, have been set aside for reasons difficult to explain, and there is something extremely wrong in a country where a lawless band of men are able to live for 18 months disturbing society. During your short life you have stolen, according to your own statements, over 200 horses.

The Prisoner – Who proves that?

His Honour – More than one witness has testified that you made the statement on several occasions.

The Prisoner – That charge has never been proved against me, and it is held in English law that a man is innocent until he is found guilty.

His Honour – You are self-accused. The statement was made voluntarily by yourself. Then you and your companions committed attacks on two banks, and appropriated therefrom large sums of money, amounting to several thousands of pounds. Further, I cannot conceal from myself the fact that an expenditure of £50,000 has been rendered necessary in consequence of the acts with which you and your party have been connected. We have had samples of felons and their careers, such as those of Brady and O'Connor, Clark, Gardiner, Melville, Morgan, Scott, and Smith, all of whom have come to ignominious deaths; still the effect expected from their punishment has not been produced. This is much to be deplored. When such examples as these are so often repeated society must be reorganised, or it must soon be seriously affected. Your unfortunate and miserable companions have died a death which probably you might rather envy, but you are not afforded the opportunity.

The Prisoner – I don't think there is much proof that they did die that death.

His Honour – In your case the law will be carried out by its officers. The gentlemen of the jury have done their duty. My duty will be to forward to the proper quarter the notes of your trial and to lay, as I am required to do, before the Executive any circumstances connected with your trial that may be required. I can hold out to you no hope. I do not see that I can entertain the slightest reason for saying you can expect anything. I desire to spare you any more pain, and I absolve myself from anything said willingly in any of my utterances that may have unnecessarily increased the agitation of your mind. I have now to pronounce your sentence.

His Honour then sentenced the prisoner to death in the usual form, ending with the usual words, 'May the Lord have mercy on your soul'.

The Prisoner – I will go a little further than that, and say I will see you there where I go.

The court was cleared, and the prisoner was removed to the Melbourne Gaol.

19 TO A HIGHER COURT
TWO WEEKS TO 11 NOVEMBER 1880

Melbourne's attention turned to the Melbourne Cup carnival, the influx of foreign visitors to the International Exhibition and the accompanying festivities. In Russell Street, the dust swirled up past the gloomy gaol walls, and warders kept guard from lonely vantage points. Inside the cells near Latrobe Street, Ned Kelly pondered the awful nature of his sentence — one that had been given to 74 convicts before him in the same prison. The solid iron door of his cell was left ajar and a lamp kept burning above it as a warder kept constant watch. He was allowed to exercise daily in an adjoining yard — always accompanied by two warders. During the last two weeks of his life, relatives said their goodbyes and priests came to give spiritual comfort. Adding to Ned's discomfort was the knowledge that his mother was a fellow prisoner. His nerves were also buffeted by the well-meaning (however futile) efforts of friends seeking a reprieve. The strain he was under was visible in his last three letters to the governor of Victoria, the marquis of Normanby.

On a daily basis, the Melbourne newspapers traced Ned Kelly's progress through what would have felt like the shortest two weeks in his short life. On Saturday 30 October, the day after his trial:

He is dressed in prison clothes and ironed. He is supplied with the usual prison fare. His hair has not been cut, nor his ample beard been taken off . . . last evening the prisoner engaged in the pastime of singing secular songs, as he has done on other occasions since his reception into the establishment, and one of the warders reminded him that his con-

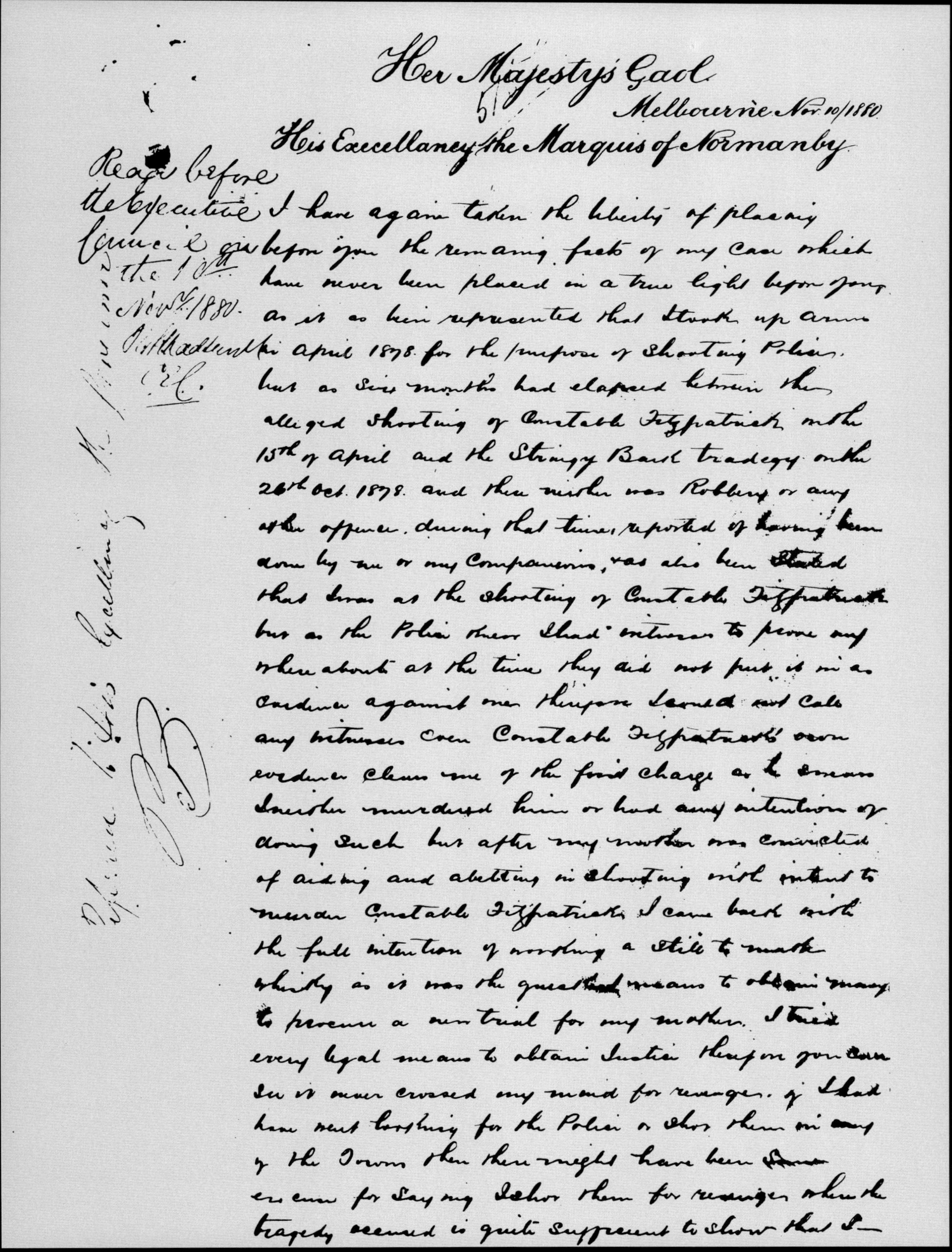

Her Majesty's Gaol
Melbourne Nov 10/1880

His Excellency the Marquis of Normanby

Read before
the Executive
Council
the 10th
Novr 1880.
[illegible]
RC

I have again taken the liberty of placing before you the remaining facts of my case which have never been placed in a true light before you, as it as been represented that I stuck up [illegible] in April 1878 for the purpose of shooting Police. but as six months had elapsed between the alleged shooting of Constable Fitzpatrick on the 15th of April and the Stringy Bark tradegy on the 26th Oct 1878. and there neither was Robbery or any other offence, during that time, reported of having been done by me or my Companions, as also been stated that I was as the shooting of Constable Fitzpatrick but as the Police knew I had intentions to prove my whereabout at the time they did not put it in as evidence against me therefore I could not call any witnesses even Constable Fitzpatrick's own evidence clears me of the first charge as he swears I neither murdered him or had any intention of doing such but after my mother was convicted of aiding and abetting in shooting with intent to murder Constable Fitzpatrick I came back with the full intention of working a Still to make whiskey as it was the quickest means to obtain money to procure a new trial for my mother. I tried every legal means to obtain Justice therefore you can see it never crossed my mind for revenge. if I had been went looking for the Police or shot them in any of the Towns then there might have been an excuse for saying I shot them for revenge when the tragedy occured is quite sufficent to show that I—

Please hand to His Excellency the [illegible]

Letters to the governor. During the last two weeks of his life, Kelly dictated several letters to the governor and Executive Council outlining what amounted to the defence he did not give at his trial. The mood of these letters was quite different from the Cameron and Jerilderie letters: the rage, bitterness and wild bluster had gone, but even from beneath the shadow of the gallows, he made no effort to repent or express regret. He maintained his story of injustices and provocation as justification for his actions, pausing only to point out discrepancies in police evidence. The Melbourne *Age* commented: 'At the end of the last document prisoner requests that his mother may be released from gaol, and his body handed over to his friends for burial in consecrated ground. (Neither request will be granted).'

duct was hardly becoming of a man in his position. The prisoner, however, soon discontinued his vocal amusement. On the whole Kelly conducts himself quietly and in a decorous manner . . . This morning Mr William Gaunson had an interview with Mr Graham Berry, Chief Secretary, with the object of procuring an order to allow the convict to see his sister and relatives. Mr [Sir Graham] Berry, after fully considering the matter, granted the necessary order. The [visiting] party consisted of three young men named [Dennis, Patrick and Thomas] McAuliffe, [Joseph] Ryan and [Thomas] Lloyd, together with Miss [Bridget] McAuliffe, Miss Kate Lloyd, and Mrs [Margaret] Skillion, the prisoner's sister. The interview between the condemned man and his relatives was of a very touching nature. He was quite calm in his demeanour, and expressed a hope that he would meet his doom in a proper manner; and also that his execution might lead to an investigation into the whole conduct and management of the police . . . The prisoner expressed a desire to see Kate Kelly, and also his little sister Grace Kelly.

Monday 1 November: Yesterday afternoon he was visited by his mother, who was allowed to converse with him through the iron grating. During the day he was visited by the visiting Catholic priest with whom he had a short conversation . . .

Thursday 4 November: He and his mother were visited today by Kate Kelly and James Kelly, his sister and brother. A man known as 'Wild Wright', was also refused admission to the gaol . . . The very rev. Dean Donoghy [gaol chaplain] also visited the convict today, and remained with him a very long time. By some means it became known outside that Kate Kelly was in the gaol, and about 100 idle persons of either sex assembled outside for the purpose of seeing her. He [Kelly] is calm and collected in manner . . . The parting between sister and brother was of a painful nature.

Wednesday 10 November: Mrs Skillion and [Patrick] Quinn, an uncle, visited the prisoner yesterday afternoon. Today Kate Kelly and her sister Grace, a girl of fourteen, who has been wired for from Greta, will pay their last visit to their brother. Mrs Skillion returns home by the midday train . . . it is the intention of the family to apply for the clothes of the condemned man as souvenirs, not wishing them to fall into other hands. They will also apply for the body, which they wish to inter at Greta cemetery by the side of his brother Dan . . . the condemned prisoner is in a state of nervous unrest . . . largely brought about by the false hopes engendered in his mind by persons agitating on his behalf outside. He has already written two statements, which have been taken down by a prisoner told off to perform this duty. Yesterday he made a request that he might dictate another statement; this was granted at once, and he proceeded to make a further statement, which was duly taken down. The process appears to give the prisoner considerable relief. When left alone he suffers much mental and nervous depression.

The considerable efforts made to gain a reprieve, dismissed as 'agitation' by unsympathetic journalists, was

The Melbourne Gaol looking east across Victoria Street to the main entrance. The prison is seen from the north and obscures the old Central Criminal Court on the opposite corner. Until the morning of his execution, Kelly was housed in the far block; its roof can be seen behind the main wings. The drop and condemned cells were located under the skylight where the three wings converged, behind the main entrance and chapel block. At capacity, the gaol could hold 600 prisoners. The photograph was taken by Charles Nettleton.

largely due to the efforts of Kelly's former attorney, David Gaunson, and his brother William, who had also become interested in the case. Not satisfied with the outcome of the trial, the brothers gained the support of politician J. P. T. Caulfield and A. S. Hamilton, chairman of the Society for the Abolition of Capital Punishment. With Kelly's sisters, they formed what the newspapers described as the 'Reprieve Committee'. They did not have much time to effect change as the Executive Council announced that Kelly would be executed on Thursday 11 November – two weeks after the trial – which as Kelly said was 'very short notice'. The Melbourne press unanimously opposed the efforts to save Ned Kelly from the gallows, but despite their scathing commentary a remarkable response was gained from the public. It is hard to say what section of the community responded to the campaign, in view of editorial bias, but even this unsympathetic article shows how busy Kelly friends were on the outside and to what extent the plea for mercy was supported.

KELLY, THE BUSHRANGER

A meeting of persons desirous of obtaining a reprieve for the condemned man Edward Kelly was held on the night of November 5th in the Hippodrome, Stephen-street. It was convened by the brothers Gaunson, and was attended by at least 6,000 persons. Only 4,000 were able to secure admittance, and the remainder had to remain outside in the street. The crowd was of a miscellaneous description, comprising 200 or 300 women from Little Bourke street and the vicinity, large numbers of the larrikin class, and hundreds of working-men and others who were attracted by mere curiosity. Mr Hamilton, Phrenologist, acted as chairman, and the speakers were Messrs. David Gaunson, William Gaunson, and J.P.T. Caulfield. Mr David Gaunson reviewed the convict's case at great length, and argued that Kelly conscientiously believed that the police came after him and his brother for the purpose of shooting them down like dogs; that he did not intend shooting any of them, but simply wanted to make prisoners of them, and appropriate their horses and arms; that he fired on none of them until they refused to surrender; and that his whole career showed that he was not the bloodthirsty character he was generally represented to be. For these reasons he contended that he should not suffer capital punishment, and he therefore moved – 'That this meeting having considered the circumstances of Edward Kelly's case, believes it is one fit for the exercise of the Royal prerogative of mercy, and therefore earnestly prays His Excellency the Governor in Council to favourably regard the prayer of this meeting, viz., that the life of the prisoner may be spared. The resolution was seconded by Mr Caulfield, and was carried unanimously. It was also resolved that the resolution should be presented to His Excellency next morning at half-past 10 o'clock. The original intention was to form the meeting into a procession, and

Kate Kelly, like all Kelly relatives and friends, was before the public gaze wherever she appeared. Detective Ward described her as 'aged about eighteen, five feet four inches high, slender build, dark complexion and hair – thin features, dark piercing eyes, very small chin and a reserved manner, when in Victoria generally dressed in dark clothes.' On 10 November, before Kate and her younger sister, Grace, were to pay their final visit to Ned, a reporter described her presence: 'Miss Kelly appears well in health, though pale. She was tending a child, which she, however, consigned to its mother [Margaret 'Maggie' Skillion], and conversed pretty freely. A habit of cautious reticence seemed, however, to have become her nature, and while her eyes gleam with intelligence, they had a certain shy sense of pleasure she felt in baffling inquiry . . . with regard to either herself or any other member of her family. She denied that there was ever any offence to be laid to her charge, unless it was that of sympathising with her brother, and said that the way the whole family had been harassed for years made her wish "she had never been born".' The photograph, one of a series, was most likely taken in 1880.

march direct to Government House, but as the regulations of the City Council had not been complied with, this would have been illegal.

Some 200 persons of both sexes gathered on the following morning at the Town-Hall for the purpose of accompanying the brothers Gaunson to Government House on behalf of the murderer Edward Kelly. The crowd was, however, of a nondescript character, and, being apparently ashamed to travel in such company, the Gaunsons – along with Mr Hamilton, young Caulfield, and Kate Kelly – secretly left in a cab, and proceeded by themselves to Government House. His Excellency said that the resolution they had presented would be laid before the Executive at a meeting to be held on Monday, but told them it would be deception on his part to hold out the faintest hope of a reprieve. In reply to W. Gaunson, he also pointed out that it was no case for petitions. The Executive had come to their decision after due deliberation and care, and the law had to be carried out, otherwise the responsible authorities would have to answer to the country. In spite of this very plain speaking the Gaunsons still continued agitating. At the instance of W. Gaunson petitions were hawked about the town and suburbs on Sunday, and their emissaries even intruded into church grounds canvassing for signatures. At St Patrick's Cathedral some of them were found obtaining signatures from a number of boys, and were ordered off. Fully 1,000 idle persons collected in front of the Treasury buildings on November 8th, in the expectation of seeing some members of the Kelly family, and hearing the result of the petitions to the Governor for the reprieve of the condemned man. Shortly after 2 o'clock a cab, containing Mr W. Gaunson, Mr J.P.T. Caulfield, Kate Kelly, and Mrs Skillion, drove up to the Treasury steps, and Mr Gaunson conducted the convict's two relations into a retiring room. Mr Gaunson then saw the Governor's Aide-de-camp, and left with him for the presentation to His Excellency of the petitions for Kelly's reprieve which have been in course of signature during the last two or three days. Mr Gaunson afterwards waited on the Chief Secretary, and informed him that the petitions contained 32,424 signatures, and that he believed had the time been a little longer 50,000 signatures could have been obtained . . . The decision of the Executive that the Law would take its course was received by the crowd outside without any expression of feeling whatever.

A meeting of persons desirous of obtaining the reprieve of the prisoner Edward Kelly, or a reconsideration of his case, was held on [Tuesday] November 9th in Carlton, and a resolution was passed asking the Chief Secretary to have the case reconsidered by the Executive Council. A deputation, headed by Mr William Gaunson, waited on Mr Berry at the Treasury at 10 o'clock, and Mr Berry promised to lay the case before the Executive Council again next day, but at the same time held out no hope whatever of any alteration of the decision already arrived at.

By the time of this last meeting — just two days before the execution — tempers frayed on both sides. The *Age* reported:

A large crowd of people assembled on the Supreme Court reserve last night for the purpose of hearing speeches on behalf of Kelly, the condemned bushranger. A strong posse of police was marched on to the ground, and they compelled the crowd to move back onto the road. This step was taken by virtue of a provision setting forth that no assemblage of persons shall meet together within the precincts of the Gaol. On the arrival of Mr William Gaunson, the crowd expectantly looked on, evidently anticipating that he would lead the way through the police barrier, but the members of the force refused to admit Mr Gaunson to enter the reserve. He asked the reason why, but the police were reticent, and, obtaining no satisfaction, he led the crowd to a vacant piece of land in Madelaine street, where he and Mr Caulfield addressed them. The crowd was composed principally of the lowest characters, and a few persons of apparent respectability being attracted by curiosity. A resolution was proposed to the effect that the Executive Council should be requested to further consider the case of Edward Kelly, and that if a reprieve could not be granted his execution should be stayed until public opinion could fully express itself. The crowd then proceeded to the Treasury, where at ten o'clock Mr Berry received the deputation.

The Executive Council still stood firm on its decision — Kelly was to hang. In what was to be his last letter to the governor, Ned Kelly again attempted to move officialdom. The letter was read before the Executive Council but the sentence remained.

One of the official guests who filed through the cold corridors of the gaol to watch the final scene in the young criminal's career was J. Middleton. These are his impressions as quoted from his newspaper, the Melbourne *Herald*, on 11 November 1880.

THE EXECUTION ETC

Of all the unpleasant duties to fall to the lot of the journalist none more unpleasant can be conceived than that of witnessing and recording the execution of a fellow being. It has to be undertaken, however, by some members of the press; for while that was a highly desirable reform which made all executions semi-private, it is far from being desirable that the public should be excluded from all knowledge of what goes on on such awful occasions, even if it be simply as a guarantee that the poor doomed creatures are not cruelly treated.

Apart from this, there is also the consideration that the dreadful last sentence of the law should in some manner be brought home to the criminal classes of the community without the disgusting and degrading surroundings of public executions. A graphic report of an execution written in all decorous spirit enables those who are tempted to appreciate the awful consequences they expose themselves to

Above: Kate Lloyd. The identity of Ned's sweetheart was a well-kept secret and so far, no evidence has surfaced to confirm his claim that he was married. Steve Hart's sister, Ettie, and Kelly's cousin, Mary Miller, were noted admirers, but family legend suggests his sweetheart was seventeen year-old Kate Lloyd. She tearfully farewelled him at Benalla station after his capture, attended his court appearances (where they blew kisses to each other), and later visited him in prison. Kate's mother (Ned's aunt Jane, née Quinn) also came to Melbourne to help on the reprieve committee. Ned and Kate said their last goodbyes on the day before his execution.

Left: John McElroy was a poor selector from Swanpool. He was married to Ned's cousin, Mary Lloyd, and was a close friend of the outlaws (he was also imprisoned as a sympathiser in 1879). McElroy bought a day-return ticket to Melbourne, which was out of his means, in order pay Ned a final visit. However, along with 'Wild' Isaiah Wright, he was refused entry without explanation. Eventually, premier Berry overruled the decree restricting visitations to Kelly in his final days. McElroy, however, didn't get to say goodbye.

One of Kelly's last walks would have been along the eastern wing of the new cellblock. This view, looking towards Russell Street, was taken from the catwalk of the first floor tier – near the condemned cells and drop. A second tier is above and another is on the ground floor. An atmosphere of hardship and grimness has survived in the old prison. The only lighting available was natural daylight through the long skylight and tall windows at the end of the block. The floor was made of large paving stones polished smooth and worn down in tracks where thousands of chained feet have shuffled along the dim corridors. The last of Ned's family to visit him on the Wednesday was his mother – given a final interview that evening. Her legendary parting words to him were, 'Mind you die like a Kelly, Ned'. The next morning he walked into this corridor for the last time. 'He was conducted from his cell in the old wing to the condemned cell alongside the gallows in the new or main building. In being thus removed, he had to walk through the garden which surrounds the hospital ward, and to pass the hand-cart in which his body was in another hour to be carried back to the dead-house. Making only a single remark about the pretty flowers in the garden, he passed in a jaunty manner from the brilliant sunshine into the sombre walls of the prison.'

Previous pages, left: The last portraits. 'At his own request his photograph was taken by a departmental operator, and copies will be given to his friends'. On that same Wednesday, his mother, sisters, brother and cousin saw him for the last time. Here, in the cool light of the prison exercise-yard he did not give any hint of emotion. For this close-up, a cloth backdrop hid the stone wall of the gaol. He is wearing the white scarf he asked to wear at his trial. The portrait conveys a certain dignity unusual in prison pictures; with this version hand-tinted colouring was added later.

Previous pages, right: Ned Kelly in irons. The subject stand necessary to keep him steady during the lengthy exposure is noticeable behind his legs, and the camera seems to have caught Kelly winking. Kelly's right hand, crippled from gunshot wounds, rests on the sling holding up his leg-irons. Each day 'persons in the yard of the Supreme Court about noon could hear the clanking of the convict's chains, as he took his hour's exercise in the yard adjoining the old wing of the gaol.' The departmental operator who took both portraits was the pioneer photographer, Charles Nettleton. He photographed Ned's old tutor, Harry Power, in irons against a wall in Pentridge prison ten years earlier. Nettleton held the government contract for penal department photography for nearly 25 years and had cells specially fitted out as darkrooms for his work.

when outraging the laws of this country, and in this aspect may be thus expected to act as a deterrent. In this spirit, we trust, the following account of the final scene in the life of the notorious Edward Kelly, the bushranger and, for a long time, outlaw, who expiated his crimes this morning within the walls of the Melbourne gaol will be read. First, for a full realisation of the awful scene it may be necessary to give some faint idea of the gallows, the approaches to it, and its surroundings. Those furnished with tickets admitting them to the execution present themselves at the main entrance to the gaol facing Victoria street, and knock at the little wicker door under the archway over the iron-studded main door. Through a wicker a warder replies, and a due inspection of the card results in admission to the first yard, which is set apart for persons who are detained simply for contempt of court. In this yard, and under the cool shade of the vast frowning arch inside the great gates the visitors stand and talk in subdued tones, until the dread hour appointed arrives, and then headed by the sheriff under sheriff and governor of the gaol, they walk generally with due solemnity up the yard towards the main inner buildings. All pass through an iron-grated gate and into a corridor running parallel with Russell street, and then through another iron-grated gate and in a few steps they confront the grim gallows. This is situated at a point where long corridors branch off to the left and right in the most northerly block of buildings in the shape of a cross. Coconut-matting is laid down on the stone floor of the corridors, and all is silent and grim as the visitors stand awaiting the appearance of the sheriff in the iron balcony round the upper tier of cells. As the spectators stand on the floor below they have to gaze upwards, and there in the southern corridor, which is but short, they see a huge beam stretching across from one side to the other, round which coil a number of turns of rope somewhat about the thickness of a stout man's thumb. This rope reaches with something to spare to a handle below, closely resembling the lever handles used to move railway switches. The end of the rope is furnished with a running noose. This is all that is seen from where the spectators stand below, save a 28 lb weight attached to a rope which runs through a pulley at the far back of the underneath side of the platform. It may be convenient here to explain that the rope is that used in the execution. The lever handle withdraws a bolt that supports a drop in the center of the platform, and the rope to which the weight is attached is also fixed to the drop; in such a manner that when the bolt is drawn and the drop falls, the latter cannot swing back, as it otherwise would, and strike the hanging man. This is all the paraphernalia nowadays, and very simple it looks, but yet what awful effects can be produced. On either side of the platform above is an ordinary cell door. These are the two condemned cells, into one or the other of which the convicts are placed after sentence of death is passed upon them. Edward Kelly occupied the one to the left from the spectators point of view. Glancing round as the last of the visitors entered, the reporter, who has been present on such similarly mournful occasions could not help being struck with the small number of persons compared with what is ordinarily the case. Including perhaps a dozen warders and other gaol officials and the sheriff and under sheriff there were not fifty witnesses of the last moments of the bushranger who for so long kept half the colony in terror. Besides the officials mentioned there were two police officers, two detectives and four policemen. The remainder consisted of a few representatives of the police, a number of justices of the peace, and several medical men. There was hardly a citizen present outside of these. Before proceeding to describe what took place at the execution itself it may be convenient to give some few particulars as to the conduct and bearing of the condemned man during the

LAST FEW DAYS

of his life. After his committal he was undoubtedly much depressed, but he recovered his mental equilibrium somewhat, and even went into excesses on the other side by indulging in profane songs and ribald jests. After this he became calmer, and appeared as though resigned to his fate, and desirous of meeting his doom in a proper form of mind until he became aware of the very ill-advised efforts being made to secure a reprieve even after it must have been apparent that such an event was, humanly speaking, outside the bounds of possibility. The condemned man, however, was of a sanguine temperament, and besides this a man condemned to die will naturally clutch at any hope, however slight, as will the drowning man at a straw. Edward Kelly, therefore, had the last few days of his life upset, and directed from what should have been his thoughts in such a time by a nervous anxiety engendered by the unwise efforts being made on his behalf. Yesterday, however, he seemed to become aware that all hope was out of the question, and calmed down somewhat. He dictated another long statement, and then seemed calmer still as he approached his

LAST HOURS.

He retired to rest at last about half past 1 o'clock this morning, but was very uneasy and restless till about half past 2 o'clock, when he fell asleep, and slept quietly till about 5 o'clock this morning. He then rose, and occupied about twenty minutes in his devotions. After this the convict appeared tolerably contented and calm, for he went so far as to indulge in a little vocalisation. Although the songs he sang were not sacred, they were of the better class of secular compositions, and contained nothing in themselves offensive. During the time intervening between half past 5 o'clock and 9 o'clock Kelly occasionally lay down and rested for a while, but at 9 o'clock the Very Rev. Dean Donoghy, the chaplain to the gaol, who had been in constant attendance on the condemned man arrived to administer the last rites of the church, and to be present with him in

HIS LAST MOMENTS.

The Very Rev. Dean was, of course, left alone with the condemned man, and equally of course what passed between them will never be revealed. At about half past 9 o'clock the Very Rev. Dean O'Hea, of Coburg who knew Kelly in his boyhood, and therefore anxious to comfort him as far as possible in his last moments arrived, and was at once conducted to the condemned cell where he remained with Dean Donoghy and the culprit until the tap at the door announced the

ARRIVAL OF THE SHERIFF.

Colonel Rede, the sheriff for the Central Bailiwick, was attended by Mr Ellis, the under sheriff, and presented himself at the door of the condemned cell punctually at 10 o'clock to demand the body of Edward Kelly in order to carry out the awful sentence of death. Mr Castieau, the Governor of the gaol had some little time previously visited the prisoner, and seen his irons knocked off, and the necessary warrant being presented by the sheriff he tapped at the door and the prisoner was made acquainted with the fearful fact that his last hour had arrived. All this time

UPJOHN THE HANGMAN,

who for the first time officiated in this horrible capacity, so far as is known, in this colony, had been unseen; but upon the door of Kelly's cell being opened, the signal was given, and Gately's successor emerged from the condemned cell opposite that occupied by his first victim. He stepped across the scaffold quietly, and as he did so, quietly turned his head, and looked down upon the spectators, revealing

A FEARFULLY REPULSIVE COUNTENANCE.

Those who have seen Gately know how dreadfully forbidding were that miscreant's features. If it be possible his successor is even more repulsive in appearance. He is an old man about 70 years of age, but broad shouldered and burly. As he was serving a sentence when he volunteered for his present dreadful office, and as that sentence is still unexpired, he is closely shaved and cropped and wears the prison dress. Were it not for the prison cropping he would probably have a heavy crop of hair, for thick bristles, of a pure white, stick up all over his crown and give him a ghastly appearance. He has heavy lips and heavy features altogether, the nose being about the most striking and ugly. It is large in proportion, and appears to have a huge carbuncle on the end. Altogether the man's appearance fully sustains the accepted idea of what a hangman should look like. As this was his first attempt at hanging, Dr Barker was present alongside the drop, to see that the knot was placed in the right position. Upjohn disappeared into the condemned cell, and proceeded to pinion Kelly with a broad and strong leather belt. The prisoner, however remarked,

'YOU NEED NOT PINION ME',

but was, of course, told that it was indispensable, and the hangman rapidly performed this portion of his task.

Overleaf: Condemned cell and wing of the old Melbourne gaol.

Preceded by the crucifix, which was held up before him by the officiating priests, Kelly was then led on to the platform. He had not been shaved or cropped, but was in prison clothes. He seemed

CALM AND COLLECTED,

but paler than usual, but this effect might have been produced by the white nightcap placed over his head, but not drawn down over his face. As he stepped on the drop, he remarked, in a low tone,

'SUCH IS LIFE.'

The hangman then proceeded to adjust the rope, the Dean in the meantime reading the prayer proper to the Catholic church on such occasions. The prisoner winced slightly at the first touch of the rope, but quickly recovered himself, and moved his head to facilitate the work of Upjohn in fixing the knot properly. No sooner was the rope fixed than without the prisoner being afforded a chance of saying anything more, the signal was given, and the hangman, pulling down the cap, stepped back and

WITHDRAWING THE BOLT

had done his work. At the same instant the mortal remains of Edward Kelly were swinging some eight feet below where he had been previously standing. At first it appeared as if death had been instantaneous, for there was for a second or two only the usual shudder that passes through the frame of hanged men but then the

LEGS WERE DRAWN UP

for some distance, and fell suddenly again. This movement was repeated several times, but finally all motion ceased, and at the end of

FOUR MINUTES ALL WAS OVER

and Edward Kelly had gone to a higher tribunal to answer for his faults and crimes. The body was allowed to remain hanging the usual time, and then the formal inquest was afterwards held, when the remains were buried within the precincts of the gaol . . . An application by the relatives for the body was refused. This is the last melancholy act in the history of the Kelly gang led by Edward Kelly, during the career of which many lives have been sacrificed.

THE OUTSIDE SCENE

There has been seldom seen so peculiar an assemblage (nearly 3,000) as that which mixed itself before the gaol door this morning. Not that larger crowds have not gathered and more impressive demonstrations been noticeable, but the general aspect of those assembled was the reverse of what might have been expected. Each one there in point of fact seemed to have been attracted by the idea that a disorderly mob would be present, and came to see the sight, instead of which the intending sightseers, with few exceptions, formed the crowd. The assemblage was singularly orderly, for a large crowd of any nation, as assembled for any purpose, is never free from the larrikin elements which make themselves visible by horseplay, oaths, and loud, coarse laughter. All this so painfully conspicuous at other times was singularly absent, and the crowd appeared to be pervaded by a general spirit of inquiry and curiosity. There were not ostensibly a large number of police on the ground, but detectives were numerous, and every precaution seemed to have been taken should there be any attempt to riot or unseemly conduct. As the time rolled on and the fatal hour of ten grew near the mob thickened, and while before scattered along the sidewalks on either side of the road, they now drew round the gaol gates in a close mass. Suddenly a neighbouring clock struck, and by a simultaneous feeling all present hushed and counted the strokes as they slowly fell upon the ear. One silent moment and the buzzing resumed, but the topic was different. The idlest, most ignorant, the most dissipated realised at that moment the solemn fact that a fellow-creature had been passed from this world to the unknown in obedience to the just dictates of the outraged laws of his country.

Above: Dean Charles O'Hea took a special interest in the soul he had baptized at Beveridge. Crediting with re-directing teenage Kelly towards an honest life after release in 1874, he returned to minister to him in his last dark hours, blessing his entry and exit from a short, spectacular life.

Facing page: 'The last scene of the Kelly drama; the criminal proceeding to the scaffold'. One *Argus* reporter wrote, 'He walked steadily on the drop; but his face was livid, his jaunty air gone, and there was a frightened look in his eyes as he glanced down on the spectators. It was his intention to make a speech, but his courage evidently failed him and he merely said, "Ah well, I suppose it has come to this", as the rope was being placed around his neck. A writer for the *Illustrated Australian News* said, Kelly was visibly impressed by the awful nature of his position, but he stood firmly on the drop. The day being bright, the warm summer sun had penetrated through the gaol windows and made itself felt . . . It was such a day as would make a young man in the prime of manhood and in the full bloom of health keenly realise the dearness of life. Kelly evidently felt it, but displayed no levity or bravado. He had intended to make a speech, but he uttered no audible sound. While the prayers were yet being said, the condemned man glanced at the sky, the cap was drawn over his face, the signal given and he went to his account.'

Ned's family did not wait outside with the assembled crowd — and his mother had no choice about being under the same roof. 'At the Robert Burns Hotel, the headquarters of the Kelly family and those who sympathise with the executed criminal, things were singularly quiet this morning. Outside were the usual crowd, inside the hotel all was quiet and the friends and relatives of Ned Kelly hardly spoke above a whisper, and were evidently considerably affected Between 10 and 11 o'clock, Jim Kelly glanced at the clock and remarked, "Ah, well, the poor devil is out of his misery anyhow by this time". Wild Wright muttered something about the police, but it was impossible to catch what. It was probably not of a laudatory nature.'

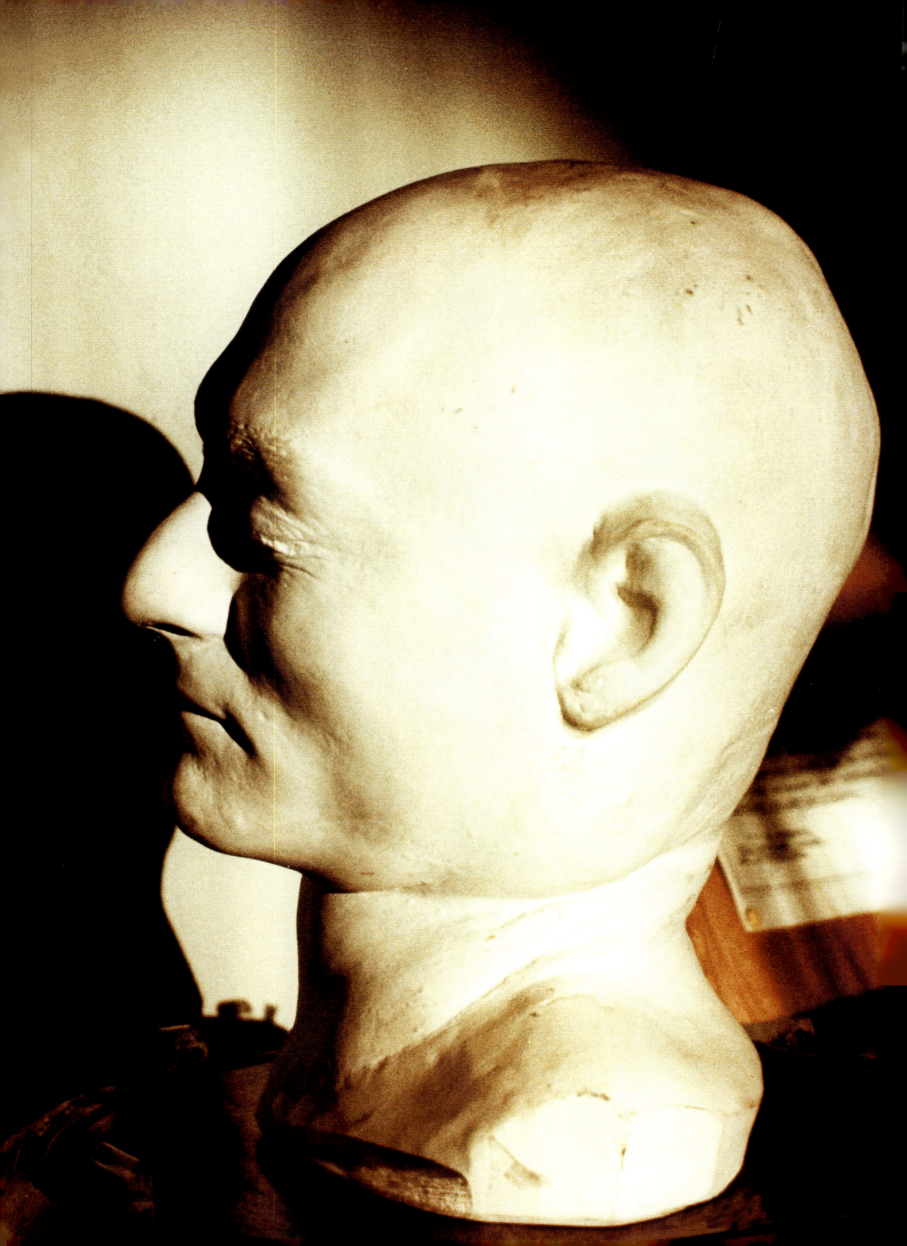

The Kelly story did not end with Ned's death or the clan's retreat into the anonymity of private life. Ned's plea for an inquiry into police conduct was partly realised with the 1881 royal commission into the Kelly outbreak – less than twelve months after his execution. The inquiry, however, was far from impartial. Only one of the 66 witnesses involved – Pat Quinn – was from the Kelly clan, and only one of the commissioners – Benalla newspaper editor George Wilson Hall – was at all sympathetic to the family's version of events. The inquiry focused on police administration and revived old grievances among relatives – creating fear of more trouble in 'Kelly Country'. Nevertheless, some satisfaction was achieved when the inquiry substantiated Ned Kelly's repeated claims of police persecution, corruption and incompetence.

The royal commission strongly censured police chief commissioner Standish and inspector O'Connor (who had already left the force). It also called for the retirement of superintendents Hare and Nicolson, and inspector Brooke Smith. It recommended demotion of superintendent Sadleir, sergeant Steele and detective Ward, and the constables who had formed the watch party at Sherritt's hut were sacked. Constable Fitzpatrick had already been acknowledged as a 'liar and a larrikin' and dismissed by this time. Judge Barry died soon after Kelly and the disgraced Standish and Brooke Smith both died in 1882. To the satisfaction of Kelly sympathisers and the general public, the Victorian police force was reformed as a result of the royal commission.

'Even-handed' policing did not spare some of the clan. James Kelly was released from Darlinghurst Gaol at the end of 1879 and police generally suspected that he joined his brothers' gang during 1880 – although there was never any proof of this assumption. But before settling down in the 1880s, Jim Kelly, Wild Wright and James Quinn all saw the inside of gaols again for stock theft.

No simple conclusion can be drawn about Ned Kelly's story – it remains open to interpretation. The events were not a chain of cause and effect: accidents, mistakes and chance also contributed to Kelly's actions and eventual demise. He was a complex character – and certainly not without contradictions. His writing and statements have to be treated cautiously, as he always protected friends and sympathisers and sometimes intentionally misled others. Equally, some police were less than honest in their reports, shielded colleagues and exaggerated the severity of cases for political gain.

The gaps in our knowledge, the contradictory interpretations of people and events offered by police and sympathisers preclude an unequivocal understanding of the motives behind Ned Kelly's actions. For example, the list of arrests and convictions of the Quinns, Kellys and Lloyds can be interpreted in many different ways. On first glance, the Quinns, Kellys and Lloyds look like habitual criminals. The offences, however, are mostly minor or trivial. More than two thirds of them were to do with disorderly conduct – only one case related to grievous harm. Most importantly, two thirds of the cases were dismissed as unproven. While the list proves how often the Quinns, Kellys and Lloyds were charged, it can also highlight how minor their offences were and the extent of police harassment and inefficiency.

It is clear that some of the Quinns, Kellys and Lloyds were occasional public nuisances, but they were certainly not the brutal hillbillies depicted by police. Ned deserved appropriate punishment for his early misdeeds (almost always for brawling, assault or stock-theft) but he and his family did not deserve the planned policy of harassment admitted by Nicolson and specifically prohibited in police regulations.

Above: Adding insult to injury. As though the family had not suffered quite enough, Kate and James Kelly and Ettie Hart were duped into appearing on stage in Melbourne on the night after the execution. An ingenious showman persuaded the Kellys that it would be a fitting way to express appreciation and to thank in person the many who supported their appeals to the government for a reprieve. Instead, the affair was like a human circus, and a huge crowd attended to see the prize exhibits.

Facing page: Kelly's death mask. An inquest was held before burial, the head was removed for examination, and a mould for a death mask was taken. The Melbourne *Herald* reported: 'Mr Kreitmeyer has just placed in the waxworks a wax cast from the mould taken from the face and head of Edward Kelly after death. The face is quite calm and composed, and is reproduced with great fidelity.' Ex-constable Thomas McIntyre wrote bitterly in his recollections: 'To say that Ned Kelly had no courage would be a reflection upon the citizens whom he bailed up in fifties and hundreds, and the police whom he defied so long. I cannot understand any man effecting the big robberies which he did without having some courage or some other quality very much like it yet the manner in which he shot Lonigan and Scanlon betrayed apprehension and was cowardly . . . A close acquaintance with him gives you a feeling of contempt for his inordinate vanity, and renders it difficult to find in him a hero of romance.' Years later, another of Kelly's enemies, ex-constable Alexander Fitzpatrick, told a journalist: 'Considering his environment he [Kelly] was a superior man. He possessed great natural ability, and under favourable circumstances would probably have become a leader of men in good society.'

Mrs Kelly arrives home at the Eleven Mile Creek, 1881. Ellen Kelly was finally released from prison in February 1881 with only eight months remission, despite good behaviour. Kate travelled down to Melbourne by train to escort her home. The family dressed in their best clothes and ignored the summer heat to commemorate the occasion with this photograph. From left are Alice King, Kate Kelly (wearing the black hat and dress worn in the previous portrait) and Grace Kelly patting her dog, Faith. Ellen is sitting between the children: to her right is young John 'Jack' King. Granddaughter, Anna Gunn junior, is feeding her pet lamb. Standing at right in best top hat is the Methodist Reverend William Gould, who had married Ellen to George King in 1874.

There is substance in Kelly's assertion that he was 'exasperated to madness by bad treatment'. As he maintained, the Fitzpatrick incident caused the Kellys to graduate from horse-stealing to homicide, and the single reason he gave was the unjust treatment of his mother and neighbours. At least one magistrate and the chief commissioner of police at the time publicly declared that they considered judge Barry's sentence harsh and inappropriate. While Fitzpatrick was later exposed as a liar, it was on his evidence that the two heavily armed (and disguised) police parties set out to capture the Kelly brothers – dead or alive. At this stage, it was horse-thieves – not bloodthirsty degenerates – who were chased and threatened with summary execution. Kelly might well have retreated but he retaliated 'madly', trying to disarm his attackers –resulting in the fatal shooting of three police officers.

When he was declared an outlaw, Kelly lost the basic rights of citizenry – he could be shot on sight by anyone. Immediately, he would have considered himself at war with the police. He had nothing to lose, but behaved decently and honourably to the public and police he captured. While Aaron Sherritt's murder was a deplorable waste of life, it was not carried out by Ned Kelly. The senseless and tragic deaths of Martin Cherry and John Jones at Glenrowan resulted from unnecessary police fire – not the outlaws, who held their fire while the civilians escaped. Better management and discipline on the police cordon would have spared their lives.

When Ned Kelly was finally brought to trial, it was far from fair or impartial. In addition, his sentence seems inordinately harsh for what was a spontaneous and unpremeditated act. But regarding police deaths, manslaughter was not an option as the law applied in 1880. When the Gaunsons presented their extensive petition for a reprieve, the governor failed to act fairly – sealing Kelly's fate as a forgone conclusion.

While the law and popular opinion do not always agree, the colonial administration – police, judiciary and government – held its verdict and condemned Kelly to the maximum penalty. After all, he had taken the lives of police officers, held up whole towns and embarrassed officialdom for nearly two years. As it turned out, execution made him a martyr and his positive qualities elevated him to legend. Ironically, the social hierarchy that applied in his life has subsequently been inverted in various recollections of the Kelly outbreak – the rough, poorly educated bush larrikin from the 'criminal-class' (the poor) became a popular symbol of tragic heroism. Meanwhile, the governor, judges, officers and gentleman involved in Kelly's life are only remembered for their contribution to his development. What Ned Kelly failed to get in his lifetime – justice and a fair go – has, to some extent, been reversed with historical analysis and interpretation.

Despite the dramatic elements in his story, Kelly's significance is not about the triumph of an underdog or of a poor, downtrodden hero outwitting the establishment – the Kelly saga had no winners. It involved the very real and terrifying deaths of four civilians, three police and four outlaws. In addition, a tracker died of pneumonia, three more civilians were wounded and many more lives were ruined as a direct result. While the Kelly saga is a popular bushranging folk story and a significant example of class warfare, it is also an enduring lesson that administrative power can be abused and that a society should be judged by how it treats its most unfortunate members – even its outlaws.

Mrs Kelly in later life. This photograph is believed to have been taken more than two decades after the 'Kelly Outbreak'. While Ned Kelly became a national folk-hero, survivors in the immediate family continued to experience tragedy and hardship. Maggie Skillion, unsung heroine and mainstay for her brothers during their outlawry, became Tom Lloyd's de facto and raised ten more children. She died in 1896. Kate Kelly married William Foster in 1888 but tragically drowned at Forbes, New South Wales in 1898. Kate's son Fred, brought up by Mrs Kelly and Jim, volunteered and died in World War I. Grace Kelly became Mrs Edward Griffiths and raised eight children beside the Eleven Mile Creek. Ned's mother and his only surviving brother, Jim, continued to live in poverty in the remote district where they had seen so much excitement and misery. Ellen, feisty and remarkable mother of twelve, died in 1923 aged 91; Jim lived as a recluse until his death in 1946 aged 87.

Below: The grave in the gaol yard. The request by the Kellys for Ned's body to be returned to them was denied and he was buried in the yard of the Melbourne Gaol on Friday 12 November. The broad arrow and initials chiselled later in the prison wall may or may not have been above the grave but they were far from being his only epitaph.

ABBREVIATIONS

AC	Author's collection
ADB	*Australian Dictionary of Biography*
AOT	Archives of Tasmania
AS	*Australasian Sketcher*
BC	Birth certificate
BE	*Benalla Ensign*
CC	copyright collection
CAE	Council of Adult Education
const.	constable
CLD	Crown Law Department
det.	detective
det. insp.	detective inspector
DC	Death certificate
GSOM	Government Statist Office, Melbourne
IAN	*Illustrated Australian News*
INF	Illustrated Newspaper File
insp.	inspector
ISN	*Illustrated Sydney News*
JP	Justice of the Peace
jr	junior
KP	Kelly Papers
LCSLV	Latrobe Collection, State Library of Victoria
LPC	Latrobe Picture Collection
LV	Land Victoria
MDHC, CAM	Melbourne Diocesan Historical Commission, Catholic Archdiocese of Melbourne
MLA	Member of the Legislative Assembly
MLC	Mitchell Library collection
MM	Memorial Records
MUP	Melbourne University Press
NTV	National Trust of Victoria
O&M	*Ovens and Murray Advertiser*
PC	Police correspondence
PD	Private Donor
q.	quote
Q.	Question in Royal Commission 1881
RC	Roman Catholic
RCVP	Royal Commission on the Police Force of Victoria, 1881
RHSV	Royal Historical Society of Victoria
sgt	sergeant
SLV	State Library of Victoria
SMH	*Sydney Morning Herald*
sr	senior
sr const.	senior constable
sub-insp.	Sub-inspector
Sun	*Sun*, Sydney
supt	superintendent
TOM	Titles Office, Melbourne
VCLD	Victorian Crown Lands and Survey Department
VGG	*Victorian Government Gazette*
VHM	*Victorian Historical Magazine*
VPC	Victorian Police Correspondence
VPHU	Victoria Police Historical Unit
VPG	*Victorian Police Gazette*
VPR	Victorian Police Records
VPRO	Victorian Public Records Office
VRA	Victorian Railway Archives
WD	*Wangaratta Dispatch*
WT	*Weekly Times*

NOTES

The following notes are revised from the first edition and include corrections and additions.

1 Formative Years, Beveridge 1850–64

Ned Kelly's birthday was apparently not registered and his baptism record has been mislaid. Family members, including Ned, gave different estimates. John Kelly on birth certificate (hereafter BC) of Catherine, 12 July 1863, gave Ned's age as eight years, indicating December 1854. On BC for three other children he consistently indicated June 1855. Ned provided his age on death certificate (hereafter DC) of his father, John Kelly, 29 December 1866 (illustration 2.15) as eleven and a half; indicating June 1854. Ellen Kelly, on BC for Daniel, 1 June 1861, gave Ned's age as six years; indicating December 1854. On BC for Ellen (Frost) 25 March 1870, she gave Ned's age as fifteen and a half, indicating June 1854. At Avenel school, on 30 March 1865, school inspector Wilson Brown recorded Ned's age as ten years three months; indicating end of 1854. The 1854 estimate is consistent with Kelly–Griffith family descendants who suggest he was born at the time of the Eureka stockade, see also Ian Jones, *Ned Kelly: A short life*, 1995, p. 346, (hereafter Jones 1995). **Midwife, Mrs D. Gorman**, *Euroa Gazette* 28 January 1953. **Baptized by Father O'Hea**, see *Herald* 11 November 1880. Biographical details, *Australasian* 27 July 1891. *Cyclopedia of Victoria*, Melbourne 1891, Vol. I, p. 268. **Location of birth.** Kelly pointed out 'the little hill' but probably meant Mt Fraser or what locals call Big Hill from the train 'at Beveridge', see *Age* 29 June [1880] and *Australasian Sketcher* 14 August [1880].
John Kelly's Beveridge land purchases. Forty-one acres, part of portion 22, 11 February 1854, Titles Office, Melbourne (hereafter TOM), memorial book 7, folio 963. Township allotment 6, section 7, fronting Lithgow St 27 October 1854. Transfer of part of portion 22 as 'mortgage in fee' 10 May 1855, book 26, folio 832; sale of same to A. Fraser 8 May 1857, book 60, folio 491. Sale of part township allotment 6 to A. Fraser, 8 May 1857, book 48, folio 815. Purchase of township allotment 12, section 6, fronting Arrowsmith St 4 May 1858. Purchase from Charles McDougall of two half-acre township allotments (9 and 10), section 9, with two nine-acre allotments (38 and 39) and one three-and-a-half acre allotment (41), (approximately 21 acres in total) 10 February 1859, memorial book 82, folio 806. Sale of township allotment 12, 21 March 1861, book 104, folio 482. Sale part allotment 6, 3 October 1861. Sale allotments 9 and 10, 4 February 1862. Sale allotments 38, 39 and 41 to James Stewart 16 January 1864, book 135, folio 645 TOM. John 'Red' Kelly's signature, matching those on marriage and children's birth certificates, distinguished him from other John Kelly in the area.
Ellen Kelly's marriage and history. Marriage at St. Francis's Church 18 November 1850, certificate no. 985, Government Statist Office, Melbourne (hereafter GSOM). Assisted Migrant shipping lists 1841, Victorian Public Records Office (VPRO) give names and ages of Quinns and children. Births of Kelly children from certificates, GSOM. See also G. Wilson Hall, *The Kelly Gang: The outlaws of the Wombat Ranges*, Hall, Mansfield 1879. See also letter of Mrs W. Cook (née Ratcliffe) in *Weekly Times* 25 November 1964, B. W. Cookson, 'The Kelly Gang From Within' in *Sydney Sun*, 27 August–24 Sept. 1911 (hereafter Cookson 1911). **John 'Red' Kelly's history,** for recent and detailed research see Bob Reece, 'Ned Kelly's father' in *Exiles From Erin: Convict lives in Ireland and Australia*, Macmillan Academic UK 1991. See also Tasmanian Archives Convict Records 1842–48 and Jones 1995, Pp. 346–47. **Kelly house at Beveridge**, still exists on Allotment 41 at time of publication. Author surveyed and photographed house and construction details in early 1960s. Interviews with Miss Patience Stewart, youngest daughter of James Stewart, who purchased from John Kelly, added to detail. **Red's prosperity,** 'made some money on the goldfields', Ellen Kelly q. by Cookson 1911. 'Dealt in horses', Hall, *op. cit.*
Births of Kelly children, other than Ned, see registry certificates, GSOM, also baptismal records for Mary Jane, 28 February 1851 and siblings. **Beveridge historical details** see Payne, J. W., *The History of Beveridge*, Lowden 1974 and Tudehope, C. M., 'Kalkallo; A link with the past' in *Victorian Historical Magazine* 32 (hereafter VHM), 1961, pp. 99–115. Also based on interviews with Mr M. Quinlan, Mrs Patience Stewart, former Beveridge residents, Mr Rupe Hatfield and Lewis brothers of Beveridge. See also Sands & McDougall's Melbourne Directories, Sands, Melbourne 1860–70. Maps, Victorian Crown Lands and Survey Department (hereafter VCLD) and *Bailliere's Victorian Gazetteer and Road Guide*, Whitworth, R. P., Bailliere, Melbourne 1865. Letters, *Walkabout* 1965. **Difficulties of immigrant settlers on small holdings**, see Broome, R. *The Victorians – Arriving*, Fairfax, Syme & Weldon 1984. Dingle, T., *The Victorians – Settling*, Fairfax, Syme & Weldon 1984.
Quinn family prosperity at Wallan East. Records of crown grants TOM. See also Hall 1879, Royal Commission in the Victorian Police 1881 (hereafter RCVP). For description of Quinn homestead – q. 'it is evident, even today' *Tractor Talk*, journal of Chamberlain industries, July 1963. Quinn forge door was given to author by owner of property, Mrs F. Cleve, in early 1960s and was passed on to Ian Jones. The homestead still exists at time of publication. Author surveyed and photographed it in early 1960s when in possession of Cleve family. Colour photograph taken for author by Peter Gough in early 1980s when Brown family owned property. **Kilmore as market town for Irish district**. Historical details, see Maher, J. A., *The Tale of a Century: Kilmore, 1837–1937*, Spectator, Melbourne 1938. Author interviews with long-term residents of Kilmore and district, Hoban, Johnston and Laffan families.
Catholic Church School Beveridge was intact but in poor condition when surveyed and photographed by author in 1960s; it has since been renovated as a private residence. For historical details see National and Catholic Board of Education files 1858–64 VPRO. See also Payne 1974, and Finn, W. M., *Glimpses of North Eastern Victoria and Albury, New South Wales*. Catholic bookselling & printing Depot, Melbourne 1870. **Kelly school mates,** Ned as 'tall and active youngster' from letter by Mr Frederick Hopkins in possession of Ian Jones. School rolls have not survived but according to Stewart, *op. cit.*, Mr R. Hatfield, Wallan, and Mr Quinlan, the Kellys and their cousins, the Ryans, attended.
Ryans at Beveridge. These sources claimed neighbour to Kellys, Timothy Ryan, shown on allotment 4, two blocks west of them, was a relative, married to Ellen's sister Helen. I have not been able to confirm this connection. Research by descendant of Anne Kelly, Mrs Marie Donnelly of ACT, has confirmed that Ned's cousin Joe Ryan was the son of John Ryan and 'Red' Kelly's sister, Anne. They farmed at Beveridge until 1875. Anne lived temporarily in Avenel after her brother's death, see chapter two. This Ryan family moved to Lake Rowan where they were selectors during later Kelly troubles.
'Red' Kelly's siblings. According to shipping records, Edmond, Thomas, Mary, Anne, James and Daniel Kelly arrived from Tipperary on the ship 'Maldon' on 8 July 1857. Several settled at Beveridge and Merriang. According to Jones 1995 some of Red's uncles also emigrated. Ellen Kelly acted as mid-wife to Anne's third child John, born 24 October 1860.
Kelly reputation at Beveridge. 'Rough characters' according to Kyle, W. *'Reminiscences from 1841 of William Kyle, a pioneer'*, VHM 10, 4, 1925. See also RCVP 1881. Red owning an illicit poteen still, Hall 1879, *op. cit.* Contrary view of Kelly family as poor but respectable, by schoolmates Fred Hopkins, see Jones 1995 *op. cit.*, and John Quinlan, author interview with his son, Mat Quinlan. Interview with Mr R. Hatfield, Wallan East, see also Tudehope, *op. cit.* Quote 'just an ordinary family', letter from Mrs W. Cook, (née Ratcliffe) 1964 to author. See also McQuilton, J., *The Kelly Outbreak 1878–1880*, MUP 1979, pp. 74–76 (hereafter McQuilton 1979), Moloney, J., *Ned Kelly*, Penguin 1980 (hereafter Moloney 1980), pp. 12–21 and Jones 1995, pp. 7–16.
Quinn troubles with the law, see RCVP for official line. For an accurate and thorough review see McQuilton 1979. James Quinn case with Lands Board, executive minutes, 1860–61 VPRO and Payne, J. W., 'The Merriang Road: It's discovery and development (1824–60s)', VHM 38, 2, 1967, pp. 60–63. Development of the railway, *Kilmore Examiner* November 1864. The line first surveyed through Quinn's land in 1863–64, see also Victorian Railways Board records and strip maps, Lands Department maps and Payne 1967, *op. cit.* Quotes 'in this country everyone', diary of Frederick Standish, LCSLV. 'We found the company of our Irish partners hard to take'. Wilhelm Gayer, q. in Broome 1984, p. 80. For character and social status of Irish–Australians see O'Farrell P., *The Irish in Australia*, University of New South Wales Press 1986, Jupp, J., (ed.) *The Australian People: An encyclopaedia of the nation, its people and their origins*, Angus & Robertson 1988, also Broome 1984, and Dingle 1984. Quinns mustering un-branded horses, Ward, RCVP, Q3140. Police correspondence Benalla district 1872, letters of Montfort, McBean, Nicolson, Barclay, VPRS 937, unit 414, VPRO. For Irish as police see Haldane, R., *The People's Force: A history of the Victoria Police*, MUP 1986, pp. 78–101 (hereafter Haldane 1986). Eldest son, Patrick Quinn, drowned in the Murray River at Echuca in 1850, see Hall 1879. Youngest son, William Quinn, was mentioned in VPC 1872, re: fire at the Glenmore police stables but was never in trouble with the law. Married Mary Comerford, had three children and died at the Kelly's, Lurg in 1914.
Ned's first appearance as witness in Kilmore court, trial of uncle

James, *Kilmore Examiner* 23 April 1863. **Sale of Kelly farm at Beveridge** to James Stewart family, TOM, *op. cit.* Details, condition of the house, oral tradition, author interview with Miss Patience Stewart.

2 Luck of the Irish, Avenel 1864–67

Historical details of Avenel. Property valuation book (1863–70), possibly the first in the area, was in possession of Mr P. Kelly in 1967. Entries described improvements and buildings, nature of construction etc. including 40 acres of grassland, Longwood, electoral division of Murray, rented by John Kelly from John (but actually his widow) Mutton for £14, recorded 18 March 1864. By 1865 record described 'unfenced grassland and hut, Avenel'. By 1866 rent reduced to £10, land then 'fenced'. Historical detail provided in interviews, Mr C. F. Lefoe, retired teacher, and Mr A. Wilson, then Avenel schoolmaster in 1960s. Information and photographs relating to Shelton family were kindly supplied by Ethel Middleton through Mrs E. Archer. Also see Burgoyne, A. J., *Memories of Avenel*, Halstead press, Sydney 1954, and Martindale, H. G., *New Crossing Place: Seymour and it's shire*, Cheshire, Melbourne 1958. Arrival of the police coach was of great interest, and quote 'especially to children' as retold by Burgoyne, *op. cit.* Maps of Avenel, VCLD.
Kellys' first rented house near Campion's store, Lefoe *op. cit.* Location of rented 40 acres from Land Surveys and Valuation Book, *op. cit.*
School, details, drawings and description, Avenel state school, building file, correspondence 1859–68, application to Board of Education for aid 17 Sept. 1864, 64/9145, building files VPRO, also Blake, L.J., 'Young Ned' in *Educational Magazine* 27, 8, 1970, pp. 350–55. School inspector Brown, G. W., reports and description of school from his diary 1864–66, Education Department of Victoria archives. Interviews with descendants of fellow pupils, Mr P. Kelly, Ethel Middleton, Mrs A. Burgoyne, *op. cit.* Schoolmaster James J. Irving, quote 'all the Kellys behaved well', Mr Peter Smith. **Quinn purchase of Glenmore lease** 1865, see Billis, R. V., & Kenyon, A. S., *Pastoral Pioneers of Port Phillip*, Stockland Press 1974. **Quinns as fine horsemen and competitive foot-runners**, regularly won prizes such as saddles and bridles at picnic races in Wallan and Greta districts, Mr J. Spencer, descendant of Pat Quinn and Tom Lloyd. See also WD and O&M 1865-70.
Ned Kelly saves Richard Shelton, detail from Ethel Middleton (née Shelton), *op. cit.* 'At the risk of his own life', Burgoyne, *op. cit.* Location given by Mr W. Ewing and Mr C. Lefoe, Avenel, *op. cit.* Kenneally, J. J., (schoolmaster who grew up at Lurg, near Kellys where his father was a selector) in his *Inner History of the Kelly Gang and their Pursuers*, 7th edition, Robertson & Mullins, Melbourne 1935, gives detail. The green silk sash is now preserved by the Benalla Historical society, see illustration 15.45.
Bushrangers careers, for more critical assessments see Sadleir, J., *Recollections of a Victorian Police Officer*, George Robertson, Melbourne 1913, Haydon, A. L., *Trooper Police of Australia*, Melrose, London 1911 and Haldane, R., *The People's Force: A history of the Victoria Police*, MUP 1986.
Morgan connection to Quinns, see police correspondence 1865 VPRO and Benalla district files August–Sept. 1869. Belief still popular, see 'Historical Account of the Kellys' *Age* 29 June 1880. Kelly family 'knew what it was to go hungry', Burgoyne, *op. cit.* Drought recorded in contemporary newspapers.
Red Kelly's scrape with the Morgans and the law, details of Morgan family, valuation book 1864–66, *op. cit.* Avenel and Burgoyne, *op. cit.* Charge book and court records 1865, now missing, provided detail cited in Clune, F., *The Kelly Hunters*, Angus and Robertson, 1954, pp. 52–54. See also list of arrests and convictions of Kellys, Quinns and Lloyds RCVP, Appendix 10, p. 699. Files of Kilmore police district 1864–66, police department correspondence VPRO. Quote, 'they were light-fingered people', P. Kelly, descendant of John 'Black' Kelly of Avenel. See also, Avenel case list book VPRS 287, Unit 2, VPRO.
Ned's first mention in police matters, see *Victorian Police Gazette* October 1866. **Red's declining health**, Kenneally, *op. cit.*, repeats Kelly family claim that mistreatment by authorities accelerated his decline, but there is no firm evidence. There is more indication that alcoholism was the problem. See DC illustrated 2.14–15. Details of Dr Heeley, Seymour, see Martindale, *op. cit.* There are apparently no surviving cemetery records, location deduced from Lefoe and Middleton, *op. cit.* The Country Roads Board was prevented from taking the south-west corner of cemetery for road widening as locals claimed Kelly's grave was directly inside fence. Grave has since been marked with a head stone.

Ellen and Anne Kelly court appearances. Case list book Avenel petty sessions 20 June 1865 to 28 July 1870, VPRS 287, Unit 2, VPRO *op. cit.* Anne Kelly case 19 February 1867, Thomas Ford case 28 May 1867. **Ned supposedly 'charged with horse stealing'** see *Victorian Police Gazette* description 6 June 1867,p. 224 and 'charged', index. **Kellys leave Avenel.** Indicated to have been after May and before September 1867 when their rented land was recorded in Avenel valuation book as vacant, P. Kelly, *op. cit.* The Kellys move in with Lloyd aunts at Greta. Depositions by all three in Crown brief for trial of James Kelly, 9 April 1868, confirm details, Crown Law Correspondence files VPRO.

3 Return to the Clan, Greta 1867–70

Ellen and family living with Lloyd sisters. See depositions and brief for prosecution of James Kelly sr on charge of arson, 9 April 1868 at Wangaratta, Crown Law correspondence files, VPRO. Depositions by all three women show the widow was living in the Lloyd home in late 1867. **Greta details**, see directories, *op. cit.* and *Bailliere's Victorian Gazetteer*, *op. cit.* 1860–70s entries; also schoolmaster's report 22 September 1866 regarding application for aid for a non-vested common school at Greta, education correspondence files, VPRO. Description and location of Lloyd home given in trial of James Kelly. **Details of the trial of Tom Lloyd sr and Jack Lloyd sr** given in coverage of their case in O&M, Beechworth, October 1865. Directories, *op. cit.* listed Quinn brothers as squatters residing at Greta 1867–68. See also report of school-inspector Wilson Brown, VPRO, *op. Cit.* **James Kelly sr trial details**. Hearing at Wangaratta 9 April 1868 and trial at Beechworth 18 April 1868, reported in O&M and BE. For Ashmead's reference to Ellen living in Wangaratta, see Jones 1995, p. 351.
Character and background of Sir Redmond Barry. Quotes, 'to be taxed and kept down' and 'little faith in rehabilitation … hanging Judge' see Galbally, A., *Redmond Barry, An Anglo-Irish Australian*, MUP 1995, pp. 76, 107, 109. 'Intoxicated with the awful power of his position' see Barry, J. V., *Life and Death of John Price*, MUP 1964; Clark, M., *A History of Australia*, MUP 1980, vol. III, pp. 272–73; Nairn, N., Serle, A., Ward, R., *ADB*, MUP 1969, vol. III, pp. 108–11.
Kellys settling at the Eleven Mile Creek. Ned testified in June 1869 that he had been living there for 'about twelve months', see O&M 19 June 1869. It seems they moved there between April and October 1868. VCLD file on Ellen Kelly's land, section 57A, has disappeared. According to Jones 1995, p. 351, rent rolls show that from June 1869 she paid rent every six months. These were not maintained while her sons were fugitives and she was in prison. See David Gaunson's claims for Kellys, *Herald* 19 October 1880. VCLD maps, *op. cit.*, for the Parish of Lurg, shows section 57A under both Ellen Kelly and Ellen King and that she completed payment in 1891. Descriptions of hut, q. 'about twelve feet across and built of slabs', const. Whelan, evidence at Ah Fook case, Benalla, in BE 29–30 October 1869. For weekend festivities, interviews with Mr T. Lloyd, son of Tom Lloyd jr, Broadmeadows 1964; also Mr John Spencer, descendant of Pat Quinn. See also Kenneally1929, 1955. For Ellen Kelly's character, see Lake, M., and Kelly, F. (eds) 'The Trials of Ellen Kelly' in *Double Time: Women in Victoria – 150 Years*, Penguin 1985, pp. 86–96. McBean acknowledges that he was trying to buy Ellen Kelly out, see VPRS, letter of McBean to Standish 8 May 1872, KP, box 414, VPRO.
Land selection conditions. There were a number of Land Selection Acts from 1860, but it was not until the *Longmore Act 1878* that the system was adequately liberalised. Licence and lease periods were doubled, rent was halved and selectors were allowed to be absent from their property for three months each year. This allowed the surviving Kellys longer to complete purchase. See McQuilton 1979, pp. 17–47, 191–3. For selection and rural life, see Dingle 1984, pp. 58–76 and Priestley 1984, pp. 80–89. For insights on the experiences of itinerant rural workers, see Evans, J., *Diary of a Swagman, 1868–1894,* abridged and notated by William Evans, Sun Books 1977.
Ellen running her home as a 'shanty' or 'sly grog-shop'. See O&M 4 May 1870. Claimed in constable Hall's evidence concerning capture of Wright in O&M 10 and13 May 1870, see also O&M 2–5 August 1871 for evidence of inspector Montfort and William Williamson, at trial of Edward Kelly. **James Quinn's time as a fugitive**. BE 17–19 September 1868. Ned had left school by 1869, see his evidence at trial of Gunn and Stewart, where he described his occupation as 'a splitter', BE 17–18 June 1869. James Kelly working for hawker Ben Gould by 1870, see letter of Robert Scott to manager, National Bank, December 1878, regarding Ben Gould, KP, VPRO.

Local 'children … growing up wild for want of education'. See application for establishment of a school north of the Kelly block in 1879, q. letter of Dennis O'Halloran. Kelly children listed among those who were without a school in the area. School correspondence files, VPRO. **Harry Power as a Kelly visitor.** See Morris, G., *Devil's River Country: Selections from the History of the Mansfield District*, Advertiser, Shepparton 1952. See letter insp. Nicolas to commissioner Standish 10 September 1869, VPC 1854–90, Benalla files 1869, VPRO. **Anne Kelly's wedding to Alex Gunn,** RC church Wangaratta, 9 April 1869, marriage certificate, GSOM. Alex Gunn loses selection, VGG 1869, vol. I, p. 288. In 1871 he was said to have lived 'at various places in Greta' during the previous year. For description, see VPG 25 August 1873. Anne was apparently living at home seven months after their marriage (as reported in Ah Fook case) **Anne Gunn and cons. Flood**, see VPRS937, unit 414, 21 February 1872, complaint of James Short against Flood, memo Standish to Supt Barclay, Beechworth, police inquiry 29 February includes statements of witnesses. Birth of Anna Gunn jr 9 November 1872, Anne died at Eleven Mile Creek, 11 November 1872; described in DC as 'housekeeper'. Certificates, GSOP. **Ellen and William Frost**, boundary rider at Laceby. See O&M 21 September and 21 October 1871, BE 21 October 1871. Frost shot, see VPG 22 February 1870, pp. 43–44; 1 March 1870, p. 51. Birth of Ellen Kelly (Frost) 25 March 1870 but recorded 6 July, district of Benalla no. 867, GSOM. Boundaries of stations neighbouring Kelly selection, see Billis & Kenyon, 1974. Tom Lloyd sr case 10 May 1869, Wangaratta, see WD. Gunn and Stewart case, 17 June 1869, Benalla, see BE.
Ellen Kelly's social rebellion. Physical characteristics, scars on forehead, left cheek and right hand, on prison record sheet 3520, p. 197, VPRO. Ellen was described as 'notorious' by Nicolson (RCVP, *op. cit.*), other police and the press'; notoriously bad woman', see O&M 31 October 1878. She assaulted her sister-in-law, Anne, 19 February 1867 (Avenel Case List Book, *op. cit.*) convicted of using 'abusive and threatening language' towards Thomas Ford 28 May 1867, *op. cit.* Chased her brother-in-law, James Kelly, through Greta hotel with a stick, see O&M 21 April 1868, *op. cit.* She could defend herself when fights broke out, such as at Malyron's restaurant in Benalla 6 July 1870, see BE 15 July 1870. Accused of 'furious riding' in Benalla 24 October 1871, see BE, also Benalla Court of Petty Sessions, Case List Book, in LCSLV. Convicted of 'wounding with intent' 9 October 1878. I have paraphrased a balanced and sensitive review by Lake, M., 'The Trials of Ellen Kelly' in Lake, M. & Kelly, F. (eds) *Double Time: Women in Victoria – 150 years*, Penguin 1985.
Kelly sisters. In January 1879, BE editor G. Wilson Hall offered a rare and reasonable assessment: *'Kate Kelly and her married sister Mrs Skillion are both harmless, well-behaved young women and conduct themselves with propriety, and the frequent attempts to bring them into notoriety by questionable allusions to their conduct are both unmanly and cowardly'.*
Death of James Quinn sr, registered 25 August 1869, district of Oxley, no. 58, GSOM. The family's earlier prosperity had evidently been reversed in the north-east. Quinn sr died intestate with property valued at £655 but debts and expenses of £658, register of wills and administration papers, 11/332, VPRO. Quinns, Lloyds and Power. See PC Standish to Nicolas 10 July 1869, VPRO. Quote James Quinn sr and family, 'the deceased is the father', report of det. Harrington VPC Benalla district September 1869, VPRO. For view that Quinns did not deserve reputation, see report of supt Barclay to Standish 19 April 1872, 'no crime exists' at Glenmore station. See particularly, report of det. Berrill, Detectives Office Melbourne 24 April 1872: *'I can not look on them (Quinns) as being the notorious men that they have got the name of, if they had committed half the horse and cattle stealing … they could not have been so long without being convicted'*. Glenmore station was sold to a neighbour, Lewis, in August 1875. 4 months later the police station was disbanded. **Descriptions of John and James Quinn**, VPRS, reports of Harrington, August–September 1869; Montfort, Barclay and Berril April 1872. Descriptions given at arrest of sympathisers 1879, KP VPRO. James' list of charges and convictions listed in RCVP, 10, p. 699. Quote, John 'it is notorious' and 'they are known horse and cattle stealers', letter Evans Brown to supt Furnell and Jameison; see also letter of James Curr, Degamero station 1869, VPRS Benalla files 1869, VPRO. **William Quinn**, born 1843, youngest brother of Ellen Kelly, was living at Glenmore at time police stables were burnt down in February 1872, but not implicated. He was visiting Kellys in November 1872 at time of Anne Gunn's death, and acted as undertaker. He married Mary Comerford, had three children, but at the time of his death at 'Mr James Kelly's of Lurg, Greta' 12 December 1914, he was described as single and a labourer. DC GSOM.
Henry Johnstone alias Harry Power's career, escape reported VPG

18 February 1869. Ellen Kelly not impressed with 'brown paper bushranger', Morris 1952, p. 38. See Power interview with Stanley J., 'The Vagabond', in *Argus*, 10 March 1877. For incident at Dr Rowe's Mt Battery station see Hare, F. A., *The Last of the Bushrangers*, Hurst & Blackett, London 1892, p. 94 (hereafter Hare 1892). See Sadleir, J. *Recollections of a Victorian Police Officer*, George Robertson & Co. Sydney 1913, pp 155-165 (hereafter Sadleir 1913). Also Passey, K., & Dean, G., *Harry Power, Tutor of Ned Kelly*, Victorian Bushranger Enterprises 1991. See male prison register vol. 13, p. 159, no. 2643, series 515, VPRO. Boxall, G. E., *History of Australian Bushrangers*, Home Entertainment Library, Sydney 1935, gives description of Power's lookout tree at Glenmore. **McBean holdup**, VPG 22 March 1870, pp. 57 & 70, BE 18 March and O&M 19 March 1870. See also Robert McBean's affidavit tendered by Nicolson in RCVP Q. 16861, p. 624. McBean's wife helps Lloyds, *Ovens Spectator* 8 June 1870. **McBean attempts to buy Ellen Kelly's selection**, see letter to Standish 8 April 1872, VPRS, *op. cit.*, VPRO. Nicolson's description of capture, and q. 'throwing myself into the gunyah', *Age* and *Argus* February 1892; see also Fitchett, W. H., 'The Story of the Kellys', *Life* 1 September 1909 – 1 February 1910, p. 270. **Description of Kelly by senior police**, see Hare 1892, p. 93, Nicolson's impression given in Sadleir 1913, p. 207, Standish's disdain in his diary, MS 9502, entry for 5 May 1870, LCSLV. Kelly's 'peculiarity of never washing', Standish to Winch 7 May 1870, PC VPRO. Nicolson's offer to get employment for Kelly cited in Lofting, H., *Bail Up!: Ned Kelly, bushranger*, Sydney 1939, p. 171 (hereafter Lofting 1939). See Robert McBean's affidavit re: Power capture, submitted by supt Nicolson to RCVP, p. 624, Q. 16681. Hare, F., reports in Melbourne newspapers 8–20 June 1870 give descriptions of Power's gunyah. For Nicolson's version of the capture, see Fitchett 1909–10, p. 270. This seems the most reliable account. Hare's man, later insp. William Montfort, described aspects of capture in RCVP, Q. 3370, p. 171-2. **James' Quinn involvement** in reward, Standish to chief secretary 19 August and 27 September 1870, chief secretary correspondence, series 1189, box 573, VPRO.

Jack Lloyd sr. Sadleir 1913, p. 155, detailed and named as a betrayer. Hare and Nicolson referred to him simply as L——. Power quote 'first and last they had heaps of money from me'. Stanley, J., *The Vagabond Papers*, Melbourne 1879, vol. III, p. 143. Jack was given four years imprisonment 3 Feb 1873, for maliciously killing a Greta farmer's horse. He died in October 1877 while on his way home from Benalla, accompanied by son Tom Lloyd jr. He was intoxicated, fell headfirst from his horse and was taken to Lindsay's public house, Winton. Died from concussion, 13 October 1877. Inquest 16 October VPRS 24, box 362 VPRO.

Ah Fook case reported in BE 22 & 29 October 1869, see also O&M. Quote, 'left the dock inwardly rejoicing', BE *op. cit.* **Ned's arrest and remands for aiding Power**, see BE 18 6 March & 13 May 1870. Kelly's condition, see PC Standish May1870, VPRO *op. cit.* See Kyneton Guardian 14, 15 & 18 May 1870 , also Kyneton Observer 4 & 28 June 1870. See also PC Nicolson to Standish 24 October 1870, VPRS 937, unit 272, VPRO. Quote 'he smiled complacently and assumed a jaunty air'. O&M 6 May 1870. See also affidavit of McBean at RCVP, Q. 16861, p. 624. Ned's letter to Babington, the only document in his handwriting, VPRS 937, unit 272, VPRO. Kelly portraits ordered from Melbourne, PC, Kyneton office 1870, VPRO. Rumours that Kelly was the betrayer, Power's view in Stanley 1879, Vol. III, see also *Argus* 10 March 1877. **Ellen charged with serving illegal spirits**, reported O&M 12 May 1870 *op. cit.*

Kelly's brawl with uncles James and Pat Quinn, reported BE 2 September 1870, quote 'young Kelly was being pursued..' BE ibid. See also O&M 1–3 & 9 September 1870. See trials of two Quinns and Kenny. Police version, criminal offence reports 26 August 1870, Hall to supt Nicholas 28 August, sub-insp. Montfort to Nicholas 27 August, Standish to Nicholas 29 August 1870 in VPRS 937, unit 49, VPRO.

Sr const. Hall's character, PC memo sub-insp. Dobson to supt Wilson 15 January 1870, re: Hall 'too hot tempered'. See also Standish to Wilson 31 January 1870, in VPRS 937, unit 412, VPRO. Hall charged with perjury and assault at Eldorado, see O&M, 5, 6 & 18 January 1870. Hall again accused of perjury, Tighe case at Broadford O&M 9 June 1870. See also letters in VPRS, 937, unit 411, VPRO.

Greta. The original township buildings have all disappeared. Location of streets and properties of old settlement on banks of Fifteen Mile Creek found in maps, VCLD. And police correspondence 1870–81. See also Ellis, S. E., *A History of Greta*, Lowden, Kilmore 1972. **Glenmore police station**, maps and description in VPRS, VPRO *op. cit.* Stables burnt down 2 February 1872, Quinns were suspected but were attending Beechworth court at the time, McBean opposed closure May 1872, Nicolson and Montfort supported continuance. Isolation of site, no crime or useful work for troopers, see memo supt Barclay to Standish 19 April 1872, see VPRS 937, unit 414, 1870–74. For const. McEnery going insane, see RCVP evidence of Montfort p. 167.

Pat Quinn. To the confusion of historians and others, Patrick married Ellen's sister Margaret at Mansfield in 1866 and first settled with the extended family at Glenmore. They later selected land at South Hansen, seven miles beyond Greta. To confuse matters further, he had a volatile and not always friendly relationship with Ned Kelly. During the Kellys outlawry he offered to provide information to Supts. Hare, Sadleir and Nicolson but often let them down, and his information was not productive. Some of the clan believed that he was a police spy, see Kenneally 1929, p. 26. Within Pat's own family, interview with Mr J. Spencer, descendant, 1963, he was considered a sympathiser. In November 1880 he travelled to Melbourne, visited Ned and assisted the Reprieve Committee by personally appealing to premier Berry. He was the only member of the clan to testify at RCVP, pp. 669–73, but was not considered a reliable witness.

4 A Secondary Education for the Kelly Children, 1870–74

The McCormick incident. For record floods see BE during winter; Greta was completely surrounded with water at one stage. See O&M, WD and BE, 11 November 1870. James was Gould's assistant, interview with Cookson 1911, also letter of Scott to National Bank management, December 1878, KP, VPRO. Ned's version and quote 'Mrs McCormick struck my horse' in Jerilderie letter, SLV. Tom Lloyd's jr's evidence O&M 12 November 1878. He was thirteen years old. The accusation that Kelly had caught McCormick's horse to help Gould was admitted in Gould's account given to Kenneally 1929, p. 13. Quote of Nicholas, 'Young Kelly was a terror', VPRS June–December 1870, VPRO. Convict record of both Mr and Mrs McCormick given by Jones 1995, p. 354, see CON 40/4 (Catherine) and CON33/38 (Jeremiah), AOT. Catherine was married previously to a convict constable, Joyce. **Ben Gould history**. Details provided in interview with his only surviving son Mr W. Gould, Wangaratta 1968. Description, including tattoos etc. provided in PC January1879, among descriptions of Kelly sympathisers, VPRO. The fact that Ben was also an ex-convict transported to Tasmania was revealed by Jones 1995, pp. 61 & 354. Recorded CON33/102 (convict record), and CON 14/42 (indent), AOT. **Wangaratta courthouse.** In the previous edition, I inadvertently included the building with 1892 renovations. It is replaced here by the view taken in 1866.

The postmaster's chestnut mare and pistol-whipping by Hall. Kelly's version, and quote 'chestnut mare, white face, docked tail' and 'when Wild Wright and my mother came', Jerilderie letter, LCSLV. For news coverage see O&M 2 & 13 May, 4 & 5 August 1871. See Hall correspondence, report to supt Barclay, Standish to Barclay, etc April 1871, VPRS 937, unit 413, VPRO. **Kelly's movements in prison**. Brown, M., *Australian Son*, Georgian House 1948, 1956, p. 41 outlines transfers during sentence (which he mentioned in 'The Hide of Ned Kelly', *People* 5 July 1950, came from a ledger then in the Treasury Building, Spring St Melbourne). He evidently misread term 'Battery' to indicate another hulk instead of the shore battery gun emplacements. Mention of battery, hulks, and prisoner's quarters, in *Royal Commission into Penal Discipline 1870–72*. Description of hulks given in Barry 1964. Flood quote 'They seemed to have', RCVP evidence given by him. Ellen Kelly quote 'the land was very poor', Cookson interview 1911.

Const. Ernest Flood was also 'hand-picked' for Greta station. He was a mischievous official and scoundrel who relied on fear and intimidation. See McQuilton 1979, pp. 63, 65. Moloney 1980, pp. 70–75, described him as 'a liar, thief, and drunk'. In 1872 the married trooper had an ill-concealed affair with Ned's eldest sister Annie, taking advantage of husband Alex's and brother Ned's absence in prison. See complaint of James Short, Benalla, re: Flood's behaviour 29 January 1872, Standish to Barclay 21 February 1872, PC series 937, box 414, VPRO. Flood was merely cautioned. To curry favour with superiors he brought a number of unsuccessful charges, and succeeded on several others against the Kelly family in Ned's absence. Flood was a horse thief, as Kelly had claimed (Jerilderie letter, *op. cit.*). He escaped conviction but was transferred out of the district after being caught with a squatter's horses in 1874, see VPRS, complaint of shire president John Brown to Standish VPRO, also entry on Flood's record sheet, 'assisting' removal of horses, VPHU. See Flood's evidence to RCVP and Hall, G. W. 1879, p. 28. Also PC to supt Wilson of Beechworth and to Standish 27 May 1869, Flood to Wilson 5 June 1869, series 937, box 412, Barclay to Standish 16 June & 26 July 1871, February 1872 and August 1874, series 937 *op. cit.*,VPRO. See also police muster rolls, series 55, vol. 1–9, VPRO.

Jim and Dan Kelly case brought by Flood, see Wangaratta Sessions, O&M 15 September 1871. Quote, 'on account of their youth', Flood evidence RCVP *op. cit.* **'Furious riding',** Ellen suing William Frost 19 September – 13 October 1871, BE. Ellen, Anne Gunn, James and Anne Murdoch charged with furious riding 24 October, BE.

Williamson and Quinn convictions, BE and O&M 16 & 23 January, 2 February 1872. Flood charging Ellen Kelly and Jane Graham, BE 12–13, 19 November 1872. Directive re: Kelly clan, quote 'without oppressing the people', Nicolson in evidence, RCVP, p. 47. James Kelly and Tom Williams case 17 April, reported O&M 18 April 1873.

Kelly household and relations in prison in 1873. Ned Kelly 'for receiving', 1871–74; James Kelly for 'cattle stealing', 1873–78; Alex Gunn for 'horse stealing', 1871–74; Williamson 'for assault', 1872–73; Williams for 'cattle stealing', 1873–78; Pat Quinn for 'assault', 1870–73, James Quinn, two cases of 'assault', 1870–77.

5 The Coming of Age, 1874–78

Maggie marries William Skillion (Skilling or Skillen, see BE 21 October 1871), Jones 1995. Margaret was sixteen years old when married 17 September 1873. First child, Ellen, born six weeks later, certificates, GSOM. Skillion was a hard worker and decent citizen, labourer and bullock-driver. Jury duty (inquest of Jack Lloyd 1877), formerly lived at Beveridge, where he had known the Kellys. He boarded at Kellys from 1871, took up block 56 at Lurg, held by him until 1878 when Maggie and Kate were the only adults left on the Kelly and Skillion selections. The Skillion hut was in the north-west corner, indicated on Bricky Williamson's map, illustration 8.4. After Bill's imprisonment Maggie became *de facto* partner of Tom Lloyd jr in 1880, raising another family. See William Wye, 'The Kellys', *Albury Border Mail* 29 November 1944.

Ellen's marriage to George King. Certificate GSOM. See also letter to Moir from Rev. Gould's brother, in J. K. Moir papers, LCSLV. All PC and news reports refer to 'Mrs Kelly' after 1874. VCLD records show her selection at different times under Kelly and King. Her name and those of King children recorded by Maggie Skillion as 'Kelly', Glenrowan West State School file 1879, *op. cit.* Ellen was buried as Ellen King 27 March 1923. She was evidently always called 'Mrs Kelly' by family but at times recorded her name as King in official documents. Ned swears never to go to gaol again, recounted by Brown1950, *op. cit.*

Ned works in sawmills, see Kelly, Jerilderie letter *op. cit.* See also 'The Years Ned Kelly went straight', *Walkabout* June 1962 and Jones 1995, p. 76. For wages of rural workers see Evans, J., *Diary of a Welsh Swagman 1869–94*, abridged and annotated by William Evans, Sun books 1977. **Kelly fight with Wild Wright,** August 1874. See Jones 1962 *op. cit.* and Jones 1995, p. 77. **Building ventures**, see Jones *op. cit.* and Balcarek, D. & Dean, G., *Ned Kelly and Others*, Glen Rowen Cobb. & Co. 1995, pp. 89–91. **Ned Kelly described favourably by Beechworth bookseller and JP, James Ingram**: 'I was well acquainted with Ned Kelly long before he took to the bush. He was, in his usual manner, of a quiet unassuming disposition – a polite and gentlemanly man. I would not have been at all afraid to have met [him] in the bush anywhere.' Kenneally 1955, p. 17.

Michael Woodyard case, warrant auctioned by Leonard Joel, Melbourne 1969, see *Age* 24 October 1969. Trial of Woodyard at Beechworth 28February 1877. Further detail, and quote 'dragged into the trouble' in letter from Woodyard to supt F. Winch 1 November 1878 from Pentridge, with information re: Kellys, KP VPRO. Kelly descriptions, Hare quote, 1892 *op. cit.* 'Wild and reckless life', RCVP. For more objective assessments see McQuilton 1979 and Jones 1995.

Kelly's physical prowess, 'ejected from church, but a grand rider', reminiscences of ex-detective Ward to Cookson 1911. See evidence of Pat Quinn, RCVP, *op. cit.*, also press reports of Kelly trial 1880. Interviews with Mr T. Lloyd and Mr J. Spencer. See Jones 1962 and 1995, Ashmead manuscript. **Ned and the wild bull**, see Kelly's version in Jerilderie letter, *op. cit.* Quote 'he told me distinctly', ex-constable Fitzpatrick evidence RCVP. Quote 'I visited the notorious Mrs Kelly's', supt Nicolson evidence RCVP, which also includes his admission of harassment. Quote 'wholesale and retail', Jerilderie letter, LCSLV. Quote, Benalla barman, 'Ned Kelly was of a cordial disposition', *Herald* 20 February 1922. **Ned passing cheques in Benalla** under alias of 'Thompson', see O&M 10 October 1878. Kellys 'under arms', Woodyard letter 1878, VPRS, VPRO *op. cit.* Skillion buying 'ammunition … revolvers' and 'had it in mind for a long time', Williamson letters RCVP. Quote, 'more horses were stolen from Greta', evidence of sgt Steele, RCVP. Quote 'James Whitty', Alex Fitzpatrick to Cookson 1911.

Ned claimed to have stolen 280 head, evidence of Gloster at Kelly trial 9 August 1880. Judge Barry made reference to it in summing up, see *Argus* 30 October 1880. System used by the gang, outlined by supt Nicolson, Montfort and sgt Steele before RCVP. See also Elliott, W., 'Kelly Raid on Jerilderie' in Lundy, H. C., *History of Jerilderie*, Jerilderie Shire 1958, recalled that some of the Kelly horses were sold in Jerilderie by Steve Hart. Aaron Sherritt described the operation, q. 'used to steal horses wholesale' to Hare, Hare 1892, *op. cit.*, p. 170. Ex-detective Michael Ward described their techniques to Cookson 1911 *op. cit.*, and maintained there was also a NSW gang involved. For other members of horse stealing gang, O&M 12 October 1878, Hare 1982 *op. cit.* and Woodyard letter 1878, KP, VPRO. Quote 'they had ample paddock space', Ward to Cookson 1911. Quote 'good-looking, well-dressed men', Hare 1892, p. 170. **Jim Kelly's arrest at Kiandra**, see *Wagga Wagga Advertiser* 30 June 1877; supt Nicolson entry in crime report book, RCVP, Q. 16222, p. 590, letter Singleton, Q. 1041, p. 47. **O'Brien and Hart charged**, see O&M 24 & 31 July 1877, 14 August 1877. Stolen horses traced, see evidence of Whitty and Baumgarten trial Beechworth, O&M 12 October 1878. Ward to Cookson 1911 *op. cit.*, Kelly identified, see evidence of Ward at Kelly trial 29 August 1880. Quote 'when the horses were found', Kelly's Jerilderie letter, *op. cit.* **Steve Hart** descriptions see PC, VPRO. Quote, 'Steve Hart used to wear', Edwards, W. H., q. Brown, M., 'Portrait of Max Brown' AM June 1949, p. 6. **Joe Byrne, descriptions**, PC *op. cit.* Reminiscences of Kyle, W., *op. cit.* See also AS 17 July 1880; Lundy, *op. cit.*, p. 111; Woodyard letter 1878, KP, VPRO. Quote 'eldest son of a respected dairy farmer', Kyle *op. cit.*, 'a person who would rather follow', Lundy, *op. cit.*
George King's disappearance. An unlikely legend repeated by Kenneally 1955, p. 26, held that Ned Kelly murdered King for ill-treating his mother. Kelly, however, spoke of King with affection in his letters, *op. cit.* It seems quite clear that King left the district to avoid conviction for horse-stealing and did not return because of later developments. He may have been present at the Fitzpatrick incident.
Dan's farm on Bullock creek, Woodyard *op. cit.*, stated 'I know the place where the police were murdered ... the Kellys were in hiding there once before when they wanted to keep out of the way of police'. Jones, 1962 & 1995 writes that Kelly took some of the Greta mill workers there to help clear the farm and repair the hut in 1876, evidenced by name carved in tree, J. Martin, an employee. Ned Kelly and the incident in the Benalla boot shop. Evidence of ex-constable Fitzpatrick, RCVP *op. cit.* Details are given by Kelly in O&M and *Age* 9 August 1880. RCVP listed offence, fine details are given in report of sgt Whelan, CLD files, KP, VPRO.
Case re: Dan and Lloyd cousins, q. 'I told him', evidence of Fitzpatrick RCVP *op. cit.* See also O&M 20 October 1877 and 29 February 1878, trial held at Benalla. Kelly mentions Goodman in Cameron letter and claims his brother was unlawfully imprisoned in Jerilderie letter *op. cit.* Description of Dan, q. 'looked quite a youth', Lundy, H. C. 1958 *op. cit.* p. 111.
Fitzpatrick incident. See evidence of Whelan, Fitzpatrick and Steele at RCVP *op. cit.* Nicolson went to great lengths to avoid mentioning his presence in the locality at the time of the Fitzpatrick visit. See also PC Benalla 1878, KP VPRO; Davies, J. M. S., 'The Kellys are Out' in *Herald* November 1930, mention of 'Strahan over the Murray trying to get up a case against Kelly'. For Fitzpatrick's version of events and times, see trial of Kelly, Williamson and Skillion, O&M 9 October 1878.

6 An Ill-fated Visit to the Kelly Hut: The Fitzpatrick Incident, 15 April 1878

New Kelly hut. Author surveyed and photographed the remains of Kelly homestead, still intact but collapsing, from beginning of 1960s. Colour photograph illustrated, taken at that time, kindly provided by Graeme Moore. Internal partitions were of horizontal timber slabs, as exterior walls. Kitchen area, where Fitzpatrick incident took place, was the last section surviving. According to oral tradition, Griffith and Lloyd descendants, it was built by Ned Kelly and friends between 1877 and early 1878. Building was photographed from various angles during 1900s but another gable and brick chimneys were added by Griffith descendants. See photographs of the building, *Sun* 11 February 1923, and from the rear, see Kenneally serialised in *Stead's Review* 1 February – April 1928. By the time of Fitzpatrick visit, the old hut, close to the road, was being used as men's quarters. Mrs Kelly q. 'before that day', Cookson interview 1911 *op. cit.* Ned Kelly q. 'my mother has seen better days', 'An interview with Ned Kelly' 1880 *op. cit.* See also, Gloster evidence at Kelly preliminary hearing, *Age* 9 August 1880.

Cause of Fitzpatrick's visit, and supt Nicolson's presence in district. Clune, F., *The Kelly Hunters*, Sydney 1954, pp. 138–39, hints that sr const. Strahan of Greta may have been included in a deliberate conspiracy which took Fitzpatrick to the Kelly hut, prompted by police insecurity over **'Black Wednesday'** threats of Sir Graham Berry. Details and implications of 'Black Wednesday' are given in Turner, H. G., *A History of the Colony of Victoria*, London 1904, vol. II, p. 198. **Supt Nicolson was in the district and appears to have orchestrated the affair.** See Sgt Steele's evidence, p. 319, RCVP. Quote 'police were never to go near the [Kelly] house alone', Nicolson evidence, p. 47, RCVP. See also Sadleir 1913, p179–81 for 'the shadow of Black Wednesday'. Kelly quote 'Berry would have sacked a great many of them', Jerilderie letter, LCSLV.
Const Fitzpatrick's record given in his evidence to RCVP. Details in Meredith, VPRS 937, unit 144, 145, VPRO. His record, length of service, postings and history also given, from police records in Davies, J. M. S., 'The Kellys are Out' *Herald* 1 November – 16 December 1930. **Fitzpatrick's version of events**, q. from *Chiltern Federal Standard* 25 May 1878. Further information on police activity, see sgt Whelan's evidence RCVP, and Crown prosecution brief, Queen v. Ellen Kelly et al., KP, VPRO. **Photographs of 'Mounted Constable Alex. Fitzpatrick'** Bray portrait included in first edition came from police files in early 1960s but turned out to be incorrect. Bray print included here was from papers of ex-constable McIntyre, identified by him on back of mount-card. He knew and worked with Fitzpatrick. Kindly provided by Martin Powell, VPHU 1985. Later photograph of ex-constable Fitzpatrick appeared in *Herald* in response to Davies series 1930, *op. cit.*
Dr. Nicholson's evidence reported O&M 10 October 1878. Tom Lloyd's version of incident in Kenneally 1929, pp. 34–35. Mrs Kelly's admission that Ned was present in Cookson 1911 *op. cit.* Steele q., 'we watched Mrs Kelly's', evidence to RCVP, p. 319. Arrest of John Lloyd on Tuesday 16 April, see BE 19 April 1878. Beechworth news q. 'on Monday evening last' and 'the poor fellow arrived', O&M 18 April 1878. Doctor Nicholson's opinion, O&M 18 April 1878. Under cross-examination at the trial, he 'could not swear it was a bullet wound'. Kellys mentioned in *Herald, Argus*, AS April–May 1878.
Hearings, first of 17 May, see BE and O&M. Zinke's request, q. 'asked that Mrs Kelly', *Chiltern Federal Standard* 18 May 1878. Quote 'MRS KELLY. A day or two since', O&M 6 June 1878. **No act of charity**, two Greta farmers, William Dinning and Robert Graham, stood bail of £50 each – a very considerable sum – and Ellen had to provide a personal surety of the same amount to enable her to return home before trial in the coldest winter for many years, see O&M 16 June 1878. Dan and Ned seen at Bald Hill, Lurg, in July, see Sadleir evidence RCVP, p. 609.
Trial reports in news coverage, O&M and BE 6–12 October 1878. Dr Nicholson q., 'I did not probe the wound', ibid. **David Lindsay of Winton** was identified by Ned in Jerilderie letter, *op. cit.*, as a shanty keeper and police informant. However, he and his 'public-house' were mentioned at inquest into death of Jack Lloyd in October 1877 *op. cit.*
Harty and Ryan indicate Ned was present at Fitzpatrick incident, see O&M and BE; evidence, Ellen Kelly to Cookson 1911 *op. cit.* Tom Lloyd version given in Kenneally *op. cit.* Harty q. given second-hand by Whelan in VPRS 1878, prior to Ellen's trial: 'Ned Kelly is the best bloody man that has been', report of const. Fitzpatrick to officer-in-charge, Beechworth 22 May 1878, prosecution brief, Queen v. Ellen Kelly et al., KP, VPRO *op. cit.*
View of Redmond Barry's sentence being excessive, O&M 15 October 1878, Quote 'hoped this would lead' and 'the only pity is', O&M 10 October 1878. **Barry's alleged remark** at Fitzpatrick trial, q. 'If your son Ned was here', cited in Kenneally 1929, p. 45. Jones 1995, p. 362, cites another source in Hall 1879, p. 15. Quote of Benalla magistrate Alfred Wyatt, 'thought that sentence upon the old woman', Wyatt, A., evidence to RCVP, p. 131. See also Wyatt, RCVP Q. 2275. Quote 'if policy had been used or consideration', evidence of E. Downes to RCVP, p. 487. Standish q. 'I believe the outrages would never have occurred', evidence to RCVP, p. 10.
William 'Bricky' Williamson boarded at the Kelly hut from approximately 1872. His selection was block 57, illustrated 8.4. According to his prison record sheet, no. 9441, VPRO, he was an Anglican native of Newcastle on Tyne and arrived as a free immigrant in 1862. Some of Williamson's statements from Pentridge are included as appendices to RCVP. See also KP and prison record sheet, vol. 14, p. 228, no. 9441, series 515, VPRO. Williamson said he 'had heard that the police had since discovered that Byrne was present at the fight at the Eleven Mile'. In statement, 29 October 1878, he describes Byrne but conceals his identity, calling him 'King', VPRO. In his letter to Kenneally 1929, pp. 36-38 he describes the incident and Joe Byrne as 'Burns' and confirms Skillion's innocence as he was not present.
Sergeant Whelan, Benalla. See evidence of Whelan, Steele and Fitzpatrick, RCVP. **Gaol and Ford Street, Beechworth.** Fitzpatrick q. 'it was known that Ned', evidence of Fitzpatrick, p. 467, RCVP. Kelly seen at Woolshed, evidence of Ward, RCVP, pp. 162–63. Fitzpatrick transferred to Melbourne for his safety, see his record given by Davies 1930. Williamson q. 'After we were sentenced', Kenneally 1929, p. 37.
Ned Kelly's attempts at peaceful settlement, see evidence of Benalla magistrate Alfred Wyatt to RCVP, p. 272. Williamson q. 'Ned sent word to us', Kenneally 1929. Interior of Beechworth court. Mrs Kelly as 'a notoriously bad woman', O&M 31 October 1878. Quote 'The Kelly family are notorious in this district', BE 31 October 1878. Quote 'The Judge never read the evidence', Williamson letter in Kenneally 1929. The warrant Fitzpatrick was not carrying. For John Lloyd jr's case at Beechworth 25 April, see *Chiltern Federal Standard* 27 April 1878.
Record of the Quinns, Kellys and Lloyds. This listing was given as appendix 10, RCVP, p. 698. Author has deleted cases after 1880 as irrelevant to present study. For a more comprehensive, if still incomplete listing of cases, see Jones, G. & Bassett, J., 1980, pp. 116–20; Jones, G. 1990, pp. 130–55.

7 From Horse-stealing to Homicide: Stringybark Creek, 28 October 1878

Byrne's presence at Fitzpatrick incident. Established by Williamson letters, *op. cit.* also confirmed later by Kelly in Cameron and Jerilderie letters, part written by Byrne. Joe had to avoid Beechworth after April as Fitzpatrick was transferred there and would have recognised him. Tom and John Lloyd jr's and Dan Kelly were sentenced to three months gaol 20 October 1877 at Benalla (Tom had another three months added 28 February 1878, for assault). They were in Beechworth Gaol together with Steve Hart (who received four months, Wangaratta court 24 July 1877, and additional 8 months on 30 July 1877).
Tom Lloyd and Hart joined the visitors to Bullock Creek after April 1878. Quote, 'I heard how the police used to be blowing', Cameron letter, *op. cit.*
Stephen Hart biographical details, see prison record sheet, VPRO, also letter Clow, R. J., to Kenneally 1955, p. 16. See reminiscences of Mrs Beecroft (née Gardiner); Davies, 'The Kellys are Out' in *Herald* 22 November 1930. See also, RCVP. Quote, 'he was slightly built and looked wiry', Elliott's narrative in Lundy, Rev. H. C. *History of Jerilderie 1858–1958*, Jerilderie Shire 1958. See police descriptions, KP, VPRO.
Joseph Byrne, biographical details. James Ingram JP, in letter of Clow, R., to Kenneally 1955, p. 17 recalled 'Joe Byrne, when he was a lad, frequently came into my shop. He was a very nice little fellow; he was well behaved, and there was never anything in his deportment that anyone could take exception to.' Byrne was born in 1857 and was a Roman Catholic. In 1876 he was 5 ft 9 in., fair complexion, light brown hair and blue eyes. See evidence of sr const. Mullane, RCVP; physical characteristics on prison record sheet, register vol. 24, p. 99, no. 13890 (does not include a photograph). See also, Harvey, R., *Background to Beechworth, 1852–1952*, Beechworth centenary publicity committee and Ovens and Murray Advertiser, Beechworth 1952; reminiscences of descendant of Ellen Barry in 'Portrait of Max Brown' in *A.M.* June 1949, p. 6. **Byrne's misdemeanors**, O&M 25 June 1876 and January 1877, see det. Ward evidence in RCVP, also 'Incident of assaulting the chinaman. Joe Byrne and Aaron Sherritt as boys' in *Argus* August 1880, and Ward's reminiscences given to Cookson 1911 *op. cit.* Byrne's engagement to Elizabeth Sherritt, mentioned in 'Charge of Sebastopol', *Age* 7 November 1878, but see Jones, I. *The Friendship That Destroyed Ned Kelly*, Lothian 1992, a remarkable study of Byrne and Sherritt. Could speak Mandarin, PC 1878–80, KP, VPRO, also Clune 1954, p. 115, and Brown 1949, p. 61. Addicted to opium, Sadleir telegram, Benalla 27 December 1878, KP, VPRO. Sgt Steele in Fitchett, W. H., 'The Story of the Kellys', *Life*, 1 February 1910, p. 146 refers to Byrne as a 'half chinaman'. See letter from det. Berril, Wangaratta 10 January 1879, PC KP, VPRO. Quote 'There is a man named Billy King – but that is not his proper name', W. Williamson letter, in RCVP, p. 702.
Tom Lloyd jr, see PC October 1878 for descriptions of Tom and John Lloyd (jr's) 'thought to be with the Kellys at the Wombat'. See prison record sheet, VPRO. After Byrne, Tom was Ned Kelly's most trusted ally and friend. Tom shared a tragic history with other members of the clan, *op. cit.* On 12 October 1877 he was escorting his father

home from Benalla when his father fatally fell from his horse, *op. cit.* On 28 April 1879 some of the Greta mob were testing their strength on the verandah of O'Brien's hotel, Greta when John jr invited cousin Tom to punch him on the chest – he collapsed and died a few minutes later. Police charged him with manslaughter, he was tried at Beechworth 6 May 1879 and acquitted; see O&M. From 1880 Tom raised a family of ten children with Maggie Skillion, who died in 1896 aged 39. He was the 'inner-circle' source for Kenneally's writing, the first published work defending the Kelly's against several decades of denigration by retired and sacked police. See evidence of Thomas Bolan and supt Nicolson before RCVP. Jones 1992 and 1995 gives a thorough outline of Tom's contribution to Kelly affairs. Jones and McMenomy spoke to Tom's son (also Tom) 1964–69.

Wombat Ranges, q. 'unimaginably impractical nature', Hall 1879, *op. cit.* **Descriptions of Dan's farm** in the Wombat ranges. See Kelly Jerilderie letter, *op. cit.* Quotes, 'Immediately surrounding the hut' and 'Situated on a small rise', *Argus* 18 November 1880. **Fortified hut of the gang**. Quote, 'I came back with the full intention', Jerilderie letter, *op. cit.* **Kelly's admission**, q. 'our horses were poor and our firearms were bad', const. McIntyre swore that Kelly made this remark to him at Glenrowan, see *Age* 9 August 1880.

Kellys warned of approaching police parties. Kelly indicated in his letters that he was patrolling the area when finding tracks. Kelly wrote 'we thought the country was woven with police', Cameron letter, and in Jerilderie letter he mentions the Greta police party: 'We knew our doom was sealed if we could not beat those [Mansfield police] before the others would come as I knew the other party of police would soon join them'. Henry Perkins, the only selector in area [later arrested as a sympathiser], was the suspected informant. Quotes, 'I was not there long' and 'On the morning of the 25th', Cameron letter *op. cit.*

Sr const. Strahan's threat provoked Kelly's actions. Strahan reportedly threatened Kelly that he 'would not ask me to stand but would shoot me like a dog', Jerilderie letter, LCSLV. See also, *Argus* 10 November 1880, affidavit of Patrick Quinn; supt James' letter to Sadleir 24 June 1898, confirmed Kelly's story and observed that Strahan's threat 'would in a measure, account for the murder of the police ... Strahan's ill-judged speech caused the mischief', Sadleir Papers, KP, H209 LCSLV.

McIntyre's deposition given at Mansfield 20 October 1878 at magistrate's inquiry into deaths of Lonigan and Scanlon, PC, KP, VPRO. **Kelly's account of Scanlon and Kennedy's deaths**, q. 'While I was talking to McIntyre', combines what he told George Stephens and James Gloster at Euroa, December 1878, recounted in their evidence at Kelly's preliminary hearing at Beechworth 9 August 1880, reported 9 August 1880 O&M. **Thomas Lonigan**. Details of history and q. 'both constables Scanlon and Lonigan', given in Hall 1879, *op. cit.* Biographical details in news reports October 1878. Sadleir to Kennedy 21 October 1878, both Lonigan and Scanlon can recognise Kelly, KP VPRO.

Police party very heavily armed and carried 'body straps'. Kelly mentions 'long firearms' more than usual ammunition, weapons and impression that they intended to shoot them in his letters, *op. cit.* See McIntyre evidence 12 August 1880, reported *Age*, on unusual armament and ammunition, Kennedy borrowed shotgun from vicar, Spencer carbine from sr const. Kelly, Kelly evidence to RCVP, Q. 7978, p. 299. See Kelly Jerilderie letter, *op. cit.* Confirmed in list of property stolen from police party at Stringybark Creek, file 06650, VPHU. Jones 1992, p. 210 reveals that 'body straps' were especially manufactured by Boles, Mansfield saddler, supplied to Kennedy's party to carry back corpses of Kelly brothers, cites Kinnear Papers as source.

Thomas Newman McIntyre. Biography and q., 'created a cloud' and 'Ned Kelly and the two strangers' from McIntyre's unpublished memoirs, typescript 'A True narrative of the Kelly Gang' copies in VPHU and LCSLV. McIntyre was haunted by the experience and guilty for leaving his comrades, but evidently perjured himself over details of Lonigan and Scanlon's shootings to further incriminate Kelly. See McIntyre's first account, given in Sadleir 1913 *op. cit.* See also McQuilton 1979, pp. 219–21, McIntyre's claim that gang had four guns but heard only revolver shots as he left. See Jones 1995 for a thorough and balanced analysis. McIntyre's sketch in PC accompanying McIntyre's sworn statement, KP, VPRO. **The clearing on Stringybark Creek**. Influence of summary execution of 'Midnight' mentioned by Kelly to McIntyre, reports O&M 18 October 1878 were clearly seen by Ned. Troopers disguised as diggers, *Age*, *Herald* and *Argus* November 1878. Quote by artist accompanying photographer, 'The two troopers stood at the fire' and 'From trooper McIntyre I get the following descriptions', AS November 1878. Burman's photograph of Stringybark Creek was produced at Kelly trial 1880 and its accuracy confirmed by McIntyre, who evidently positioned the men shown.

Constable Michael Scanlon and Sergeant Michael Kennedy. For background details see Morris 1952, *op. cit.* See also Hall 1879, *op. cit.* Stringybark not on their intended route, see evidence of McIntyre, RCVP, *op. cit.* See Sadleir 1913, *op. cit.* For news spreading before McIntyre's return see Sadleir evidence at RCVP, p. 111, and 1913,p. 184 and Hare 1892, *op. cit.* **Old gun used by Ned Kelly** at Stringybark Creek was on display at the Melbourne Aquarium, has since disappeared and may have been burnt in the fire which gutted the building. In Brown 1948, p. 64, it is shown with Kelly armour. McIntyre mentions it in evidence at Kelly hearing August 1880, *Age* 6 August 1880. Quotes, 'A bloody old crooked musket', Jerilderie letter, *op. cit.* 'I asked McIntyre why they carried', Jerilderie letter, *op. cit.* 'Aaron told me it was quite by accident', Hare 1892, *op. cit.* 'Cut up at the turn of things', McIntyre cited in Hare, *op. cit.* **Discovering Sergeant Kennedy.** Quote 'a young man, Sparrow, sang out', deposition Henry G. Sparrow, overseer of Mt Battery station 1 November 1878, KP, VPRO. Quote of Bishop Moorhouse, cited in Morris 1952, p. 42. Burman's photographs show the same men in all plates, Sgt Kennedy had a cloak, not a blanket left covering him. Also unlikely he would have worn hob-nailed boots. See Fitchett, *op. cit.* 1 February 1910, p. 146. Wild Isaiah Wright and Mansfield police, q. 'Dogs! Curs! cowards!', reported in *Mansfield Guardian*, reprinted in Morris 1952, *op. cit*, p. 39. Lonigan photograph pre-dates the Stringybark shootings; British style helmets were introduced in 1877–78. **Second police party**, see evidence of Ward, RCVP, *op. cit.* **Search parties**, press reports, AS gave details of packhorses and the night ride. **Reynolds' medical reports** on the bodies are in CLD correspondence files with depositions taken at Mansfield magisterial inquiry 29 October, VPRO *op. cit.* The fact that Kelly reloaded his gun with 'swan-drops' promoted the idea that wounds were caused by a number of separate shots. Details on Reynolds, see Gillison, J., *Colonial Doctor and his Town,* Cypress Books, Melbourne 1974.

8 From Obscurity to Outlawry, October–December 1878

Police numbers in north-east. Evidence of Nicolson, RCVP. News reports in *Age, Argus* and *Herald* November–December 1878. ***Felons Apprehension Act*** October 1878, Proclamations published in press 31 October 1878 and 2, 9 November 1878. Quote, 'At the time we could get little or no assistance', Nicolson RCVP, p. 16. McMonigle message from Ashmead, Jones 1962. Quote 'they have a tent' and 'The Kellys are certain to get' Williamson, appendix 13, RCVP. 'Typical Kelly country', RCVP, p. ix.

Kelly Gang postcard. Doubts on authenticity are due to image being a dry-plate, allowing rapid exposure, indicated by sharp image of horses. In addition, postcards were not popular until the 1890s. Dry-plates were developed in 1878, used in Tasmania in 1879, but apparently not widely available in Australia until 1880. Madeley used them at Glenrowan, June 1880. Group is not 'composed' (grey horse should have been positioned against dark hillside) and operator has left tripod and plate-box in frame at left, indicating haste. See McIntyre's report, VPRO, of leather leggings stolen at Stringybark, Hare 1892, p. 324, and Curnow evidence at RCVP for outlaws' method of carrying firearms. Carlyon, L., *The Last Outlaw*, Wilke 1980, p. 39. Thanks also to David Corke 1991, for his informative letter.

Field of Operations. Quote, 'Kelly Country ... as that tract lying between points'RCVP, *op. cit.* Quote 'The Kellys had not one but three vast ranges', Hare 1892, pp. 96–97. **Search party on the Kelly track.** Quote from Brooke Smith's censure, 'Two days were allowed', evidence of Steele, RCVP, p. 321. **Victorian police engaged in pursuit.** Murray police skirmish, see Lundy *op. cit.*, p. 65. Quote, 'The Kellys have endeavoured to pass themselves off', *Age* 25 November 1878. My thanks to Nannette Green for identifying 'troopers' as the Strickland brothers, illustration 10.20–21.

Attempted surprise. Quote, 'The rumbling noise' evidence of Nicolson RCVP, p. 16. Details in evidence of Nicolson, Standish and Hare, ibid. **Reward poster** from Jameison, printed after outlawry of 15 November 1878. **Uncle Thomas Lloyd sr,** photograph by James Bray at Beechworth 1879. Tom farmed his selection on the south side of Bald Hill or Kelly's Lookout, blocks 30 and 31. Quote, Sadleir, *op. cit.* p. 191.

Movements, sightings, listed as appendix IV, RCVP. Lloyd meeting the Kellys after Stringybark, Kenneally 1929, p. 71.Visiting Tanner, report of Flood, 23 September 1879, VPRS, KP, VPRO. Oxley, Pioneer Bridge Hotel and Everton appearances, Ward, RCVP, p. 164. At the Murray River, q. from 'labourer' in telegram det. Kennedy of Wodonga, KP, VPRO. Kellys caught in flooded river, Tom Lloyd to Kenneally 1955 *op. cit.* At Baumgartens, Nicolson evidence RCVP, p. 15. Quote 'The woman of the house blamed Ned Kelly', Sadleir *op. cit.* p. 194. Gang at Sherritt's, 'horses pretty well worn out', ibid., p. 195, Sadleir's appearance date wrong. At Wangaratta, quote 'I got up to the window ... heard the noise of galloping', Chomley 1900 *op. cit.*, pp. 42–44. Police talk to widow Byrne 7 November, q. her son had 'his head in a halter' and 'he has made his bed', Nicolson evidence RCVP, Chomley 1900, p. 49. Movements to 11 November 1878, evidence of Nicolson RCVP, p. 18 and appendix IV, ibid.

Outlawed on 15 November, q. 'if found at large armed', cited in Chomley 1900 *op. cit.* where he gives details, pp. 42–44, revoked their citizenship, see *Age, Herald* and *Argus* November 1878. **Gang hiding** on Frank Harty's farm near Winton and on Emu station, as told by Tom Lloyd to Kenneally 1955,pp. 92–94. Supplied by Maggie Skillion and other sisters, see Williamson letters, RCVP, *op. cit.* School correspondence file, Glenrowan West, VPRO *op. cit.* April 1879 notes that 'Kellys and Skillion children live together on block 56 (Skillion's selection) during the temporary incarceration of parents'. Gang sighted south of Benalla, Lloyd in Kenneally, *op. cit.*, getting supplies from Ben Gould, see Scott correspondence, KP, VPRO.

9 The Euroa Hold-up, 9 December 1878

***Argus* coverage 12 December 1878.** I have made some deletions for the sake of continuity; descriptions of bank and township used under illustrations. Seven Creeks Hotel and store. Pat Quinn information in RCVP, *op. cit.* Kellys' knowledge of bank hours and procedure, see Blainey, G., *Gold and Paper: The history of the National Bank of Australia limited*, Georgian House 1958. Magistrate Wyatt's warning, see evidence of Wyatt, Nicolson and Sadleir, RCVP.

Benjamin Gould. Scott q. 'I am still more of the opinion', KP, VPRO. Arrests and remands reported in BE and O&M. December 1878–March 1879. Biographical details, from author interview with Mr W. Gould, Wangaratta.

Chance presence of Gloster contrived by gang, see report of const Gill 13 October 1879, KP. As pointed out by Jones 1995, p. 369, Gill's report rejected by Standish, which allowed Gloster and his assistant to be called as witnesses at later Kelly trial, VPRO *op. cit.* **Gould letter to Mr Raines**, KP, VPRO, *op. cit.* **Younghusband's station**. Details in Billis & Kenyon 1974, *op. cit.* Quote 'Ned Kelly said', narrative of Robert Scott, *Argus* 12 December 1878. **Demanding refreshments.** Details *Age* 12–16 December 1878, also Davies in *Herald* 22 November 1930, re: Gill's report of Gloster's complicity.

The new rig-outs. Ned and Dan Kelly descriptions, reports of det. Ward and Robert Scott re: hold-up, KP, VPRO, *op. cit.* **'The prison' and 'cutting of the telegraph wires'.** Details in Scott narrative, *op. cit.* Quote 'none of the women were molested', Scott, ibid., and 'although domineering in giving their orders' and 'Before leaving they amused themselves', McDougall narrative, *Argus* report *op. cit.*

Railway street, Euroa. Quote, J. H. Graves, 'Byrne was in the town', evidence RCVP, *op. cit.* Hart, the trooper and Wyatt, evidence of Wyatt, RCVP. The National Bank, *Age* 12 December1878, q. 'He then forced his way', Scott narrative, *op. cit.* Haul represented a fortnight's profit, see Blainey 1958, *op. cit.* Quote of Mrs Scott from Hare 1892, *op. cit.*; see also Mrs Scott's narrative, Mitchell Library.

Railway station, quote 'One of the men engaged at the new railway buildings', *Herald* 12 December 1878.

10 Evading the Police Force: December 1878–February 1879

Nicolson and Sadleir at border, see RCVP. Quote 'At daybreak they attempted', Hare 1892, p. 136. Police officers and dates of arrival, see evidence RCVP. Military presence, see news reports *op. cit.* and RCVP list of principal dates in Kelly pursuit. Quote 'as long as police strange to the districts', sec. source in evidence Of Hare and Standish, RCVP.

Kellys in hiding; *Australasian Sketcher*. Quote 'Our artist has given', AS December 1878. Supt Hare and the Kelly pursuit. Quote 'there were peculiar difficulties', Hare 1892, p. 3, 'The Kelly family are the most prolific', from Hare's evidence, RCVP p. 76. Seventy-seven direct relatives in area, evidence of Wyatt JP, RCVP p. 134. The Kelly hunters, q. 'I had a splendid lot of fellows', Hare 1892, p. 228 and evidence at RCVP p. 682. Quote, 'Ned Kelly knew all our camps', RCVP, p. 68.

Captain Standish. Details of his history, social affectations, political connections, favouritism and failings given in de Serville, P., *Pounds and Pedigrees. The Upper Class in Victoria 1850–80*, Oxford University Press 1991, pp. 42–76. Royal commissioners were particularly unimpressed, Sadleir 1913,pp. 266-268. Sadleir was particularly critical, q. 'dismissed from consideration officers of a more serious disposition', ibid., Clune 1954, *op. cit.* details the view that Standish and his favourite officer, Hare, conspired to profit from the Kelly pursuit, and in fact drew large amounts from expenses during their period in charge. This allegation is supported by difference between Nicolson's expenditure and theirs, given during RCVP, p. 31. **Moses**. Hare quote ' wonderful powers these blacks have', Hare 1892, p. 228.

Mr D. Cameron MLA. See Victoria, parliamentary debates 1878, vol. 29, p. 1793. Kelly would have read the debates in news reports, such as *Age* 14 November 1878. *Age, Herald* and *Argus* 14 November referred to letter being received by Cameron on 18 December 1878. **Cost of pursuit.** Hare 1892, p. 325 refers to cost being nearer to £115,000 including salaries and wages. Quinn and Wright transmitted first opportunity of negotiation to Wyatt JP at time of Fitzpatrick trials.

Mention of Cameron letter, *Argus* 12 December 1878. The pencil note on the Crown Law copy, correspondence files, KP, VPRO, is the only reference to the postage mark of 14 December at Glenrowan. *Argus* 12 December reported that Mrs Fitzgerald at Euroa was induced to get the stamps for its postage. Hall 1879, *op. cit.* said the outlaws gave the letter to Mrs Fitzgerald to post. Letter q. from CLD copy. **Bank in the bushranging district**. Quote 'One effect of the Kelly scare', *Argus* 7 January 1879.

Significance of Kelly's writing. The (Cameron, Jerilderie, and *Herald*) letters reveal Kelly – with the help of Byrne who was the scribe, poet and 'literary' member of the gang – to be considerably more justified in his actions than the stereotype, cunning criminal externalising blame. There are omissions of detail, wild threats, and invectiveness. He displays the racial prejudice that he accuses his enemies of practicing. Nevertheless, the list of grievances can be substantiated to the degree of comprising a forceful defence and critical indictment of the police and authorities: Brooke Smith, Hall, Flood, and Fitzpatrick were villains. The writing amounts to a defence never considered formally in his lifetime. On another level it was a significant example of vernacular poetic prose, threaded with wry humour. Joe Crowley, in his insightful honours thesis, 'If words be louder, I will oppose your Laws – An analysis of the Jerilderie Letter', (University of Queensland 1999), identified the literary subtleties of the Jerilderie letter. Lyrical sensibility and passionate Irish nationalism contributed to the rhetorical power of the documents. Murray Smith 1981, p. 54, saw the Jerilderie version as a remarkable piece of demotic writing.

Arrest of alleged Sympathisers. Press reports Melbourne and north-east, *op. cit.* 4–8 January gave details. Quote 'Both here and at Benalla' *Argus* 6 January 1879. The names and details of those arrested are from press reports, confirmed by list of particulars – ages, birthplaces, records (if any), and personal descriptions – from Victoria Police Archives 1960s, courtesy Sgt P. Wilson. Some press reports made mistakes; William Strickland was reported as 'William Woods', an alias given at time of arrest. Harty was described as 'Francis Hart'. Hare revealed in evidence, RCVP, *op. cit.* that police were assembled at Benalla in presence of Standish, Hare and Sadleir and asked to give names of those suspected in each district. Some volunteered names of unpopular people who were not sympathisers to show their own efficiency.

Sympathisers photographed. James Bray contracted to record the 'likenesses' of the unlucky group. Quote re: Robert Miller, 'this man is a hard-working respectable farmer', *Herald* and *Argus* 27 January 1879. Walter Stewart mentioned in O&M 14 January Daniel and James Clancey, q. 'One of the Clanceys', O&M 11 January 1879. Richard and William Strickland, see PC, KP, VPRO, *op. cit*; Woodyard, *op. cit.* Michael Haney, see *Argus* 6 January 1879. Daniel Delaney, brothers John and Patrick were held in the Glenrowan hotel in June 1880. See evidence of Curnow, RCVP, *op. cit.* Morrissey, D. 'Ned Kelly's Sympathisers', *Historical Studies,* Melbourne, vol. 17–18, October1977–April 1979,pp. 288–96 provided a detailed study of social implications of the gang's active supporters. It included small errors; for example, the accidental death of John Lloyd jr did not result from a fight but a misguided test of strength. Morrissey compiled a list of 124 Kelly sympathisers. This provided a valuable base for ethnic and sectarian study but it was problematic. The 'short-list' was originally based on local police volunteering uncontested suspects and it resulted in public ridicule when examined in court. Morrissey included several in his extensive list, like James Kellys jr and sr, who were in prison preceding and during the 'outbreak'. Several, like Ellen and Grace Kelly were young children. Even the outlaws were included.

Old Tom Lloyd's telegram re: the four bulls. See Hare evidence RCVP, *op. cit.* p. 90. Quote 'It was found these sympathisers', ibid, pp. 63, 72. Mansfield telegram re: sympathisers, *Argus* 7 January1879. Press reports, see O&M 14, 18 January; Hare 1892, p. 63. Quote, 'The whole affair was making a laughing stock', O&M 18 January 1879. **Sympathiser proceedings were illegal**, according to evidence of Wyatt, JP at RCVP *op. cit.* and Sadleir, evidence ibid., p. 120. The Standish initiative came in for scathing criticism by the royal commissioners in 1881.

Kelly letter to Bryan O'Loghlen. Letter q. in Brown 1949, pp. 112, 113, but not acknowledged. A facsimile is preserved in the Burke Museum, Beechworth. Phrasing bears close resemblance to other Kelly letters but better grammar and punctuation indicate that it may have been dictated (like other efforts) to a literate sympathiser. **Byrne offered a free pardon**, see evidence of Standish, Nicolson and Sadleir, RCVP, *op. cit.* Sherritt recruited as a spy, q. 'He told me Joe Byrne jumped off his horse', Hare, RCVP, pp. 63, 682. **Sherritt information misleading**: date and location of crossing-place given by Tom Lloyd jr to Kenneally 1955, pp. 133, 134. It is not known if Sherritt deliberately misled police or was given incorrect information.

11 The Jerilderie Hold-up, 8 February 1879

Crossing the Murray, Tom Lloyd in Kenneally 1929, p. 113. **At Woolpack Inn**, Elliott in Lundy, *op. cit.*, p. 67. **Quoted news coverage of town capture, composite** drawn from *Jerilderie Gazette* and *Herald* 18 February 1879. Order of paragraphs adjusted for improved sequence. Lyving's statement has been abbreviated. Direct quotation of Lyving in *Age* and *Herald*, ibid. and White, C. & G. S., *History of Australian Bushranging*, Bathurst 1893. Tarleton's narrative: added detail from *Age* 12 February 1879. 'The Surprise': added detail following 'Shortly after 11 a.m. Ned and Dan', from versions in other Melbourne papers, Elliott also q. in Lundy 1958, *op. cit.* and WT 24 and 31 January 1931. 'At Wunnamurra Station': added detail from *Herald* 18 January 1879, information supplied by Mr A. Mackie, the man held up. 'Description of the Outlaws': added detail from *Jerilderie Gazette, op. cit.*, see *Herald* 19 February 1879 for reprint. **The town of Jerilderie, plan.** Quote 'settlers around Jerilderie', *The Australian Handbook and Almanac and Shippers' and Importers' Directory* 1879, Gordon & Gotch London 1878. 'It is situated on the Billabong', Elliott in Lundy 1958, *op. cit.* **Bailing up the police**. Quote 'Week ending 15th', occurrence book preserved in the Mitchell Library. See also Archives of New South Wales. **The Jerilderie courthouse**, see Dunne, P.A., in Cookson 1911, *op. cit.* **Jerilderie Street.** Gill q. 'the three of us walked into the bank', from Gill's narrative, 'The Kelly Gang at Jerilderie', *Life* 1 March 1910. **The Royal Mail Hotel,** Elliott q. 'There is no doubt that the outlaws had spies', Elliott in Lundy 1958, *op. cit.* **The Bank of New South Wales,** see Holder, R., *The Bank of New South Wales: A history,* two volumes, Angus & Robertson 1970. See also Elliott in Lundy 1958, *op. cit.* Quote 'When it was rented by the bank', Elliott in Lundy, ibid. Sherritt q. 'when the Kellys contemplated a robbery', Hare 1892, p. 320. Quote 'while walking with Ned Kelly', Lyving's narrative in *Age* 12 February 1879. Ned Kelly and Hart were not strangers to Jerilderie, Elliott in Lundy 1958, p. 65. Ned stayed at the Royal Mail previously, *Herald* 15 January 1879, asked at Davidson's Hotel if Collier and Maslin still lived there, and was told it was four years since they were did. Ned also asked after 'Larrikan Mary', one of the Davidson's. Steve Hart on previous visits, *Argus* 13 February 1879, and Gill 1910, *op. cit.* **John Monash** claimed to have met Ned Kelly, see 'Sir John Monash talks to Ned Kelly' – Cabbages and Kings column, *Table Talk* 18 April 1929, p. 10. Father ran a store in the town (1874–80) and Elliott, *op. cit.* p. 99, confirmed that Louis was present during raid. Monday 10 February was the last day of holidays for John's school, Scotch College in Melbourne. However, biographers have since cast doubt on Sir John's claim, hence photograph has been deleted. **Schoolteacher William Elliott**, q. 'when told that his latest capture', 'only his example kept the four' and 'He said that he and his family had been persecuted', Elliott in Lundy 1958, pp. 88, 89, 105, 111. **Jerilderie letter.** Original has recently been acquired by SLV. Most of the document appears to be in Byrne's handwriting. For an illuminating study, see Crowley 1999, original pages first published by Jones 1992, see also Jones 1995. See Stephen Murray-Smith, introduction to 'Ned Kelly and the Jerilderie Letter', *Overland* 84, July 1981, p. 54; Morrissey, D. 'Ned Kelly's World' in *Royal Historical Society of Victoria Journal* (RHSVJ) vol. 55, no. 2, June 1984, pp. 29–34. Previous comments on Cameron letter apply, but the Jerilderie letter contains more details, with added florid and wild rhetoric. For suppression of letter see Elliott in Lundy, *op. cit.*

12 The Great Disappearance, Part One, February – June 1879

Quote, 'The Victorian police have been subjected to', *Herald* 13 February 1879. Quote 'done by Kelly confederates to create a diversion', *Herald* 25 February 1879. Quote 'had procured some dynamite', Hare 1892, p. 194. **Kellys vanished from their usual haunts**, see list of reported appearances, RCVP, appendix 5. No appearances of outlaws between March and July. See also Sadleir 1913, p. 218, mentions they camped at the head of the Buckland River.

Reward posters, Boxall G. E., *History of Australian Bushrangers*, Home Entertainment Library 1935, p. 353, PC, KP, VPRO. Mention of posters in Chinese, PC, ibid. 19 June 1879. **Kelly sympathisers**. Quotes 'Wright, you and I have met before', 'There is no fear of the Kellys killing me' and 'I would give you fair play if I could', reported in O&M 12 February 1879. Quotes 'Your worship promised to give me fair play' and 'No wonder you blush', *Herald* and O&M 15, 18 February. See also evidence of Wyatt, RCVP, *op. cit.* p. 136. Wright brawling with others, q. 'Men first, dogs last', Ben Gould recollections to Kenneally, 1955, p. 127. Joe Ryan broke a leg in prison, O&M 22 April 1879. McElroy case, press reports, O&M 15 February; others 18–22 February 1879, see also CLD correspondence, VPRO. Quote 'How many more eight days?' James Quinn, 'If I ever get out of this' Wild Wright, ibid. Quote 'They were not salutary in their effects', RCVP, p. xv. Quote 'Hart had a sister and brother', Hare 1892, p. 203. **Main gates, Beechworth gaol**. For details see O&M 28 June 1879. **The fringe-benefits**. Prosperity in north-east, see evidence of Patrick Allen at RCVP, *op. cit.* also interviews with Cookson 1911 *op. cit.* See also evidence of Armstrong, RCVP. Benalla prosperity, see 'History of Benalla' in *Leader* 23 August 1930. **Joe Ryan details**, see report on movements of Joe Ryan in PC, KP 24 August 1879 including 'Ryans lived at Donneybrook neighbourhood until about eighteen months or two years ago' before selecting three miles out of Lake Rowan, VPRO. See news reports at sympathiser appearances, such as O&M 22 April 1879. More detail provided in research of descendant, Mrs Marie Donnelly. For Ryan's Camp store see 'History of Benalla' in *Leader* 23 August 1930. For Beechworth storekeeper Patrick Allen, see Cookson 1911, *op. cit.* and evidence of Allen and Armstrong, RCVP, *op. cit.* **Mrs Skillion and Tom Lloyd**. Quote 'there was an inner and more secret circle', Daniel Kennedy cited in Sadleir 1913, p. 217. Grace buying saddle and bridle with bag of shilling pieces, Clune 1956, *op. cit*, p. 205, notes 'which had an earthy smell', report of Whelan, Benalla 19 October 1879, PC, KP, VPRO. See also evidence of Hare, Nicolson and Sadleir, RCVP, *op. cit.* Louis Steinwehr q. 'Kate used to come to my store' recounted in *Sun* 21 February 1923. **Maggie Skillion, Tom Lloyd and Michael Nolan buy ammunition**, see telegram of Sadleir, Benalla 18 June 1879, PC, VPRO; Tom Lloyd's version in Kenneally 1955, *op. cit.* Grovenor gave details to Cookson, *op. cit.* 13 September 1911.Two more trips known of, see Hare evidence, RCVP, p. 91. **Kate Kelly portraits**. Appearance of the head and shoulders portrait of Kate reproduced here, courtesy Edgar Penzig, made it clear that the engraving in first edition might have aimed to portray Ned's sister but the 'Kate Kelly' (head and shoulders) photograph in first edition was not her.

Parish of Beechworth and Woolshed Valley. Some idea of the Woolshed diggings is gained from the *Ovens Directory* 1857, reprinted in Harvey, R., *Background to Beechworth 1852–1952, op. cit.* See also *Argus* 2 August 1880, article covering a visit to Aaron Sherritt's hut. The location of Mrs Byrne's home was still pointed out by old identities of the area like Mr Bill Knowles, grandson of Anton Wick, in 1968. Its location is confirmed by news reports like *Argus* 2 August 1880. Brown, *op. cit.* incorrectly locates the Byrne home on the eastern side of the 'Devil's elbow'. Evidence of Sherritts and Ward, RCVP, *op. cit.* mention Batchelor's Hotel and a Chinese store at Sebastopol Flat, north of the Byrne's, in 1879. 'Byrne's Gully' is marked on plan E/87/4, VCLD, and mentioned frequently in RCVP evidence. The caves are well known and were located for me by Mr Knowles. They are mentioned frequently in evidence of Mrs Sherritt sr, Hare, Mullane, Ward, and members of the hut party, Armstrong, Duross, and Dowling at RCVP, *op. cit.* Location of Sherritt selections on Lands Department surveys, north-west section, Parish of Beechworth, including Aaron's selection with name replaced by Crawford.

Winter scene in North Eastern Victoria. Quote, 'There was a sudden drying up of information', Sadleir 1913, p. 218. Quote 'they had been amongst snow', see article *Argus* 6 August1880. Quote, 'frequently bought plenty of provisions', report of Const. Falkiner, RCVP, appendix 15. **Byrne's addiction to opium**, see telegram from Sadleir 27 December 1878, PC, KP, VPRO. For Byrne's connections with Chinese community on Woolshed see evidence of J. Sherritt, RCVP.

The Kelly songs and ballads. Kelly and Byrne, frequent customers of bookseller James Ingram, see letter of Clow in Kenneally 1955, pp. 16–17. See Crowley J. 1999, *op. cit*; Jones 1992, *op. cit.* Quote 'Joe Byrne was better educated', Hare 1892, *op. cit.* p. 320. Scribe of the

gang, AS 17 July 1880, and evidence of James Wallace at RCVP, p. 537. Two poems attributed to Byrne, second poem includes a detail that could authenticate it. Byrne referred to Ned as 'Neddie'. **Letters to old friends.** Sherritt often communicated with Ward, Hare et al, through his mother or Beechworth storekeeper Patrick Allen. See Cookson 1911, *op. cit.* 4 September 1911. Quote, 'With reference to the attached letter', memo from det. Ward to supt Hare, KP, VPRO. Jones 1992, illustrations following pp. 60, 126, doubts the authenticity of the 26 June 1879 letter. This does not have the flourishes or returns on last character of words noticeable in 'Tales of the Borders' note but does resemble style in pages of Jerilderie letter. The earlier note from Beechworth Gaol might have been written by Byrne or Sherritt, which makes conclusive analysis difficult. **Maggie Skillion looking after the remaining family at her selection, block 56,** see evidence and writings of Hare, Sadleir, Nicolson, and Building Files, Glenrowan West State School, *op. cit.* VPRO and Lands Department maps. Visitors to Kelly and Skillion selection. See press reports on arrests and remands of sympathisers, PC, KP, VPRO, evidence of sr const. Strahan O&M 18 January re: Harty and Quinn at the Eleven Mile Creek. See evidence of Hare, RCVP, p. 92, also depositions of Sherritt horse-stealing case, CLD correspondence files, *op. cit.* and O&M 29 July 1879. **Activities of the Kelly women**. 'Large bakings', Kate 'often went out after dark', evidence of Sadleir, RCVP, p. 113. See also evidence of Hare and Nicolson, ibid. Outlaws and sympathisers watched police watch-parties from Bald Hill, Kenneally 1955,pp. 173–74 , and Hare, evidence RCVP, p. 74. Quote 'Mrs Skillion and Katey Kelly', Hare evidence RCVP,p. 98. Quotes, 'I appointed a man with a few baits' and 'One morning before daybreak', Hare, ibid. p. 74, 98. Mrs Skillion too clever for police, see evidence of Sadleir, RCVP,pp. 113–14. Also evidence of Hare and Nicolson. **Caves used by watch parties at the Woolshed.** See evidence of Hare, Ward and Mullane, RCVP, *op. cit.*
Aaron Sherritt's double game. The deal between police and Sherritt was that Byrne's life would be spared if Aaron helped. Details, evidence of Sadleir and Hare, RCVP. Hare gives further detail in his book, 1892, p. 20, relations with Byrne family and engagement to Catherine Byrne. At Sherritt's trial Mrs Byrne denied the engagement, saying 'He was not in a fair way to becoming my son-in-law'. O&M 29 July 1879. Discovery by Mrs Byrne, see Fitchett 1909, *op. cit.* 1 November 1909, p. 499. Quote 'The old woman lost her presence of mind', Hare evidence RCVP, *op. cit.* Sherritt was naïve, according to his mother, evidence of Mrs Sherritt sr. RCVP, pp. 476–79. Sherritt at Byrne's hut 'taking a penny whistle', Hare evidence RCVP, *op. cit.* Mrs Byrne asking Sherritt about police horses, see evidence of Mrs Byrne at Sherritt trial for horse-stealing 29 July 1879. Aaron courting Kate Kelly. Sadleir evidence RCVP, p. 217, Hare evidence ibid. p. 201, claimed it was Sherritt's idea. See evidence of Maggie Skillion at Sherritt hearing, Beechworth O&M 29 July 1879. 'Mrs Skillion objected to him being about the place ... Kate and he got on very well', Hare 1892, p. 201–03. Quote 'Kate often visiting the Sherritts', in anonymous letter to Hare 16 April 1879, KP, VPRO. Quote 'Kate Kelly had been seen riding from her place to her uncles', Hare 1892, p. 199.
Tom Lloyd sr's selection and Sherritt, q. 'They had a good view of Lloyd's hut' and 'One night Mrs Skillion went out to visit a friend', Hare 1892, *op. cit.* pp. 200–01 and evidence RCVP. Sherritt and Kate Byrne's horse. Quote, 'Mrs Byrne was [threatening] to get him five years', evidence at hearing O&M 29 July 1879. Ned Kelly appears at the Woolshed on 10 July, q. 'I was not in the house', evidence of Mrs Sherritt sr, RCVP, *op. cit.* Joe and Paddy Byrne seen at Reed's Creek ranges the same day, ibid. also appendix 5, RCVP. Sherritt arrested 15 July 1879, evidence of Mullane at Sherritt hearing, O&M 29 July 1879. Quotes 'Aaron Sherritt, who is most unfavourably known' and 'About two hundred persons attended', O&M 15 July, and 24 July 1879. Quote 'A dodge of that [detective] Ward', O&M 29 July 1879.

13 The Great Disappearance, Part Two, June 1879–June 1880

Systems of police pursuit detailed in evidence to RCVP. Most witnesses favoured Nicolson's methods. The two systems outlined in royal commissioners' report 1881, *op. cit.* **Police spies.** Names and aliases were listed in a confidential memo compiled for the reference of the royal commissioners, preserved VPHU file 06650. See evidence of Chomley, p. 355; Nicolson, p. 20, 32 and Quinn, p. 669, RCVP. Overall costs of agents, see Nicolson evidence, RCVP p. 31. Chomley mentions threats on the life of Pat Quinn because of cooperation with police revealed at RCVP. See evidence of Wallace, p. 526. **Nicolson cuts back on search parties,** see evidence, RCVP *op. cit*, pp. 30–34, 40. Quote 'One of the common beliefs', O&M 16 September 1879, 'A number of the Benalla police', O&M 18 October 1879, 'The alarm caused by the daring outrages', report under 'Mr. Nicolson resumes search', RCVP *op. cit.* Kellys frequently rode 60 to 70 miles in one night, ibid. under heading 'Queensland Trackers'. Byrne riding down precipitous slopes, ibid. See also evidence of Armstrong, RCVP, p. 438. **Queensland trackers** under sub-insp. O'Connor. See evidence of O'Connor, RCVP, *op. cit.* For remarkable ability, see Sadleir 1913, p. 211. Standish severely hampered their usefulness, reports of commissioners and evidence of Standish RCVP, *op. cit.* Kelly's dread, reported in press covering Euroa hold-up, December 1878. Trackers planning to leave 29 June for Queensland, Sadleir 1913, p. 221. Quote 'The trackers have not only frightened the Kellys' AS 17 July 1880. Group photograph taken at Benalla or Essendon, after the death of one trooper in winter.
Another Kelly letter. Mrs Skillion writing to the Jerilderie editor, O&M 10 July 1879. Telegram quoted 'Isaiah [Wild] Wright has been in town since Monday', O&M 5 July 1879. This statement, first appeared in the *Herald*, and has most of the contents of other Kelly letters but was either dictated to a more literate sympathiser than Byrne, or, more likely the Melbourne editor improved grammar and punctuation for its publication. See first passage for description of original sixteen pages, unfortunately not preserved. **Plan to capture the governor**, marquis of Normanby. See Kenneally 1929, p. 170.
Detective Michael Ward, history, see Ward recollections in Cookson 5 September 1911, and evidence to RCVP, *op. cit.* The most serious allegations against Ward were made by schoolmaster James Wallace, const. Mullane and others in the hut party at Sherritt's: Armstrong, Duross, Dowling and Alexander, RCVP. Quote re: pseudo reward bill 'was a counter-blast to the government', evidence of Ward, RCVP, p. 501. **Kelly imitators**. The Lancefield bank was robbed in August 1879, two men were caught and imprisoned. The Moe bank was the scene of another attempt on 8 November 1879 where the assailants were also captured. In New South Wales on the Murrimbidgee in February 1879, four men were captured after a short career posing as the Kellys. **George Scott, alias 'Captain Moonlite'.** IAN and ISN, November issues 1879. Also in Melbourne dailies 16 November 1879. **New South Wales police who captured 'Moonlite'**. See Boxall, *op. cit.*, pp. 323–34. Quote 'When Scott ... got together', Sadleir 1913, p. 191.
Outlaws habits and endurance, see Hare evidence RCVP and 1892, p. 320, 321. Quote 'They always travelled at night', Nicolson evidence RCVP, p. 33. Quote, 'A camp was discovered', Nicolson evidence, *op. cit.*, pp. 32, 33. Quote 'On one occasion when talking to him', Hare 1892, p. 321. **Outlaws 'gallop down ranges'** and Byrne 'used to practice riding down steep ranges' in evidence of Armstrong, RCVP, *op. cit.*, p. 438. **Kellys checking banks** by Spring 1879, see Blainey 1957, *op. cit.* Quote, 'I have received information', telegram from det. Ward 10 July 1879, VPC, KP, VPRO. Quote 'James or Jim Hall', VPC October 1879, KP, VPRO. Quote 'We received information they were', Ward evidence RCVP, p. 501. Quote 'Alexandra was recently watched', Nicolson 4 April 1880, VPC,KP,VPRO. Gang's movements, q. 'As they were walking through the bush', 'A Kelly Incident', *Argus* 6 July and August 1880. Ned suffering from sciatica, VPC, KP, VPRO. **Byrne contacts Jack Sherritt.** Evidence of John Sherritt and Michael Ward, RCVP, *op. cit.* See also O&M 4 September 1879, and list of reported appearances of the Kellys, RCVP, appendix 5, p. 692. **Byrnes and Sherritts**. Joe engaged to Elizabeth Sherritt, Aaron engaged to Catherine Byrne, see evidence of John Sherritt, RCVP, *op. cit.* p. 540, see 'Charge of Sebastopol' *Herald* 10 November 1878; Jones 1992, *op. cit.* Quote 'Pat Byrne, the brother of the outlaw' anonymous letter, April 1879, to supt Hare, VPC, KP, VPRO. See evidence of const. Mullane, RCVP, p. 49 re: Falkiner that 'the Sherritt [girls] have been continually backwards and forwards together at Byrne's' during 1880. See evidence of Mrs. Sherritt sr, John Sherritt ,ibid. Jack Sherritt as agent 'Jones'. **Mounted police on duty at Greta**. Police attributed lack of co-operation from the public to fear. See evidence of Nicolson, RCVP, p. 41, also ex-detective Ward to Cookson 1911. Jacob Wilson, evidence, RCVP, and Daniel Kennedy, see Pryor, L., 'The Diseased Stock Agent' in *Victorian Historical Journal*, December 1990,pp. 243–69, were among those driven out of the district when their police connections were revealed. The gang certainly used fear and intimidation to survive but there was also widespread support among the poorer selectors, who the police termed the 'criminal' class. See Ward 1958 for national tendency to idolise bushrangers and oppose authority. See Kenneally 1929, McQuilton 1979, Jones 1992, 1995. **List of agents and aliases**, file 06650, VPHU, *op. cit.* List of reported appearances of the Kelly outlaws, RCVP, *op. cit.* and evidence of John Sherritt gives details of work. Quote 'Joe Byrne, outlaw, writes several letters to "Jones"' 30, 31, October 1879, RCVP, p. 693. Quote, 'On the next morning', evidence of John Sherritt, RCVP, pp. 540–41. See also list of reported appearances, RCVP, and evidence of Ward and Nicolson. Yackandandah bank already checked, report of James Hall of Nillacootie [sic], neighbour of Wild Wright, KP, VPRO, *op. cit.* Nicolson on the gang's appearance 'made with such precautions', evidence RCVP, p. 693, item 5. Byrne's questions about police leaders, see evidence of John Sherritt, *op. cit.* and list of reported appearances, RCVP, p. 693. John Sherritt panicked by appearance of Dan Kelly at his parents' house, see RCVP, p. 693, 13 November1879. **Byrne visits the Sherritt home again**, quote 'On November 23rd Byrne visited Jones's hut', ibid. Quote, 'Jack Quinn, uncle of the Kellys' detective reports dated 22, 24 August 1879, VPC, KP, VPRO. Quote, 'Selectors on the direct route', ibid. Kelly hideouts within 32 km (20 miles) of Benalla headquarters. See Grovenor to Cookson, *op. cit.* 9 September 1911; report of Whelan, Benalla, October 1879, containing information from Mrs McCormick, wife of the hawker at Greta. Information not acted upon but confirmed by later police intelligence, PC,KP, VPRO. See list of reported appearances, RCVP, p693, first item, p694, last item. See evidence of Nicolson and Sadleir and Jacob Wilson, ibid. See Tom Lloyd reminiscences, Kenneally, 1955 *op. cit.* p173.
Incidents with sympathisers. Quote, Lloyd 'chaffed the troopers' evidence of Nicolson RCVP, p. 34. Tom Lloyd sr and new boots, evidence of Nicolson and Wilson, neighbour of Tom sr, RCVP, *op. cit.*, p. 203. Quote 'We started off for the eleven mile creek', evidence of Ward, RCVP, p. 160. Benalla police memo quoted 'About twelve months ago the widow McAuliffe', report of Whelan, Benalla 19 October 1879, VPC, KP, VPRO. **Fugitives extremely hard pressed.** Evidence of Nicolson, and list of reported appearances, appendix 5, RCVP, *op. cit.* Quotes 'My informant told me' and 'During the past summer', Nicolson evidence and report 'as to the Whereabouts of the Gang' in RCVP, p. 34. Byrne's remark, q. **'They had always lived well'** *Argus* 30 June 1880, p. 6. Detail given to Kenneally, *op. cit.* by Gould and Lloyd. Sign of outlaws next move. List of reported appearances, RCVP, *op. cit.* Farmers complaining of losing plough mouldboards. ibid., 22 March 1880. Traces of footsteps, q. 'one of them was described', list of appearances, ibid. **Sympathisers at Mrs Jones's**, ibid. and statement of Mrs McDonnell, *Herald* 29 June 1880. See also report of police agent 'Smith' 22 March 1880 in list, appendix 5, and evidence of Nicolson RCVP, p. 34. Quote 'Esther Hart still at Glenrowan'. List of reported appearances, by agent 'Renwick' 17 April 1880. **Threats to Sherritt**. Quote, 'My son John was doing a bit of ploughing', evidence of Mrs Sherritt, RCVP, p. 476. Byrne's tracks followed, evidence of Nicolson, RCVP, p. 35. Shots fired across the roof of Aaron's hut, evidence of Armstrong, RCVP, *op. cit.* Another hut party established to guard Aaron Sherritt, Nicolson sure the gang were on verge of another raid, evidence of Nicolson, RCVP, *op. cit.*
The Kelly armour. See Tom Lloyd's recollections, Kenneally 1929, *op. cit.*, pp 155–60. See also evidence of Sadleir, RCVP,p. 617. See Grovenor in Cookson 1911 *op. cit.* Contrary to Kenneally, four helmets were made, see photographs at Glenrowan and evidence of Mrs Jones and supt Sadleir, RCVP, p. 152. **Daniel Kennedy, 'Denny' or 'Diseased Stock Agent'**, q. 'subsequently I heard that the mouldboards', evidence of Nicolson, RCVP, p. 33. Nicolson claimed he believed 'Denny's' information but did nothing about it, ibid. For detail on Kennedy see Pryor 1990, pp. 243–69. Quote, 'He [Kennedy] had a professional standing in the district', Sadleir 1913, p. 217.
Armour elements. Ian Jones has invested considerable time researching Kelly armour, and generously shared his advice to correct oversights in my previous edition. See Jones in Carlyon 1980, pp. 68, 69, also Jones 1992, 1995, *op. cit.* The SLV and Ken Oldis have published a summary of their research on www.slv.vic.gov.au
Ned's suit is identified from Thomas Carrington's drawing, made on Monday 29 June. Sadleir 1913, p. 233, mentions a bullet mark on the helmet above the eye-slit. Only one helmet has such a mark above the slit and a deep bullet dint below. Constable Arthur, in his account to the press on 2 July and 3 July 1880 and evidence, RCVP, *op. cit.*, mentions hitting Kelly's helmet twice with a Martini Henry rifle, which matches the helmet in the Latrobe Collection, SLV. On all suits the front plates have armholes cut into top corners, with right side deeper to allow rifle butt to be rested on shoulders. Kelly's front body plate and helmet have distinct bullet dints. Carrington's sketch shows what he called a back lappet, but is more likely the original front lappet. Sadleir 1913, p. 233, claimed there was only one back plate to Ned's iron suit. The front apron attached with an iron hinge was added at some point, and belongs to Dan Kelly or Steve Hart's suit. Shoulder plates have been mislaid, like one displayed at Museum of Applied Science. In 1967, another was in possession of Mrs K. Davenport, daughter of const. Gasgoine of Hare's

party, see *Sun* 1 November 1967. Ned's helmet and front body piece is included in the set preserved in the Latrobe Collection, SLV. **Joe Byrne's suit** was the only other set not burnt. It is the most refined piece of blacksmithing craftsmanship, including side plates that connected front elements to back plates. This was kept, almost intact, 'souvenired' by supt Hare, donated to his friends, the Clarke family, and since preserved by descendants, the Hammonds. The front lappet preserved by Hammonds may not belong to the suit; it is shown background left in the Bray photograph. According to Sadleir, 1913, p. 233, the helmets were lined with padding or quilting to soften the impact of bullets. **Dan and Steve Hart's suits** are identified from the photograph by James Bray taken after suits were raked from the ashes. Dan and Steve's individual sets can only be re-assembled on size of elements, Hart being the smallest of the pair, and matching of attachment holes. Most of these elements are preserved by the VPHU. **Brand marks.** The Kelly suits comprised at least seven or eight pieces, or 28 mould boards taken off single furrow ploughs. The mould board is a large twisted iron plate (approximately 10mm or one quarter-inch thick) which turns the sod ripped up by the plough's point; the cast-iron share. Replica suits were made in 1880 and since for Kelly films but these are easily differentiated. A correspondent, Sydney *Sun* 12 September 1911, claimed the Kelly armour came from Hornsby ploughs, Sadleir, 1911, p. 234, said Kelly's suit showed the brand of Melbourne manufacturer Lennon. The part considered to be Ned's front body piece bears the brand M&A at centre on the lower edge. Byrne's front body piece is branded 'LH2' in the same place. See Jones in Carlyon, *The Last Outlaw* 1980,pp. 68–69. **James Bray's photograph of armour** and Kelly's rifle may have been taken at Glenrowan or at the Benalla police barracks. It is valuable primary reference, along with Carrington's drawing. This plate includes one of Ned's shoulder pieces, centre, his padded cap and Colt carbine. It also shows the front lappet, rear left, until recently, with Byrne's suit.
Aaron Sherritt's hut, taken over during absence of owner. Sherritt sold his selection in April 1880, four months after marriage to Ellen Barry, see AS 3 July 1880. Hut is described in *Argus* 2 August 1880, location described in evidence of Nicolson, Ward, Armstrong and Mullane, RCVP *op. cit.* Hare resumes command, RCVP, *op. cit.* Kellys near Buckland river, report of Falkiner re: information about Kelly gang, Appendix 15, RCVP. 'Denny' or Kennedy dismissed by Hare, q. 'He [Kennedy] had a very important, not to say startling story', Sadleir 1913, p. 222. **Withdrawal of reward**. Quote, 'The Act [*Felons Apprehension Act*] was only directed', *Herald* 30 June 1880.

14 Devil's Elbow: The Death of Aaron Sherritt, 26 June 1880

Kelly's motive for Glenrowan. Reminiscences of Tom Lloyd jr in Kenneally, *op. cit.* and by son, Tom Lloyd of Broadmeadows, 1964, was that it was intended as a master stroke to bargain the release of Ellen Kelly. The Benalla banks appear to have been part of their wider plans, which included the sympathisers. **Kelly plan to stop train at station**, see Kenneally 1955, pp. 192–213. As Jones points out, 1995, p. 225, the location of lifted rails on the high embankment, and the gang's actual prohibiting of any warning to stop the train beforehand, indicates they intended a first decisive strike. It indicates they intended to overturn and not simply derail or stop the train. Ned's various and contradictory comments made when he was gravely ill, q. in news reports like *Age* 29 June: 'I intended ... to go down with my mates and meet the special train and rake it with shot. The train arrived, however, before I expected it [sic], and I had to return to the hotel. I thought that the train would go on, and on that account I had the rails pulled up so that these ———- black trackers might be settled. It does not much matter what brought me to Glenrowan. I do not know, or I do not say. It does not seem much anyway.' **Kellys considered they were at war with the authorities**, see letter of cousin James Ryan in Kenneally 1955, p. 314, 'The Outlawry Act gave my relatives the same right to use the privileges and forms of war as used by the Government'. Quote, 'I was determined to capture Superintendent Hare', Kelly's letter to governor of Victoria 10 November 1880, attorney general's department records, VPRO. The lost draft for a republic, mentioned by Jones, ibid., would clarify their wider motives. **Mrs Byrne's comment**, Hare 1892, *op. cit.*p. 235, Brown 1949, p. 173. **Aaron Sherritt's 'execution'** part of the wider plan, see Lloyd as told to Kenneally, 1955, *op. cit*, p. 192. **Kelly knew there would be no ordinary trains**, see AS 3 July 1880, reports that Kelly said, 'I knew there would be no usual passengers on Sunday'. **Small army of friends in waiting**. Kelly distinguished from his 'mates', those who were to help him at Glenrowan, and his 'associates', the other gang members. In Melbourne Gaol, he said 'I had plenty of mates in the neighbourhood ready to join us'. Sadleir 1913, p. 237 mentions the sympathisers and sr const. Johnson's reports and evidence of Glenrowan adds detail (see chapter 15). When Dick Hart cracked a stock-whip outside Jones's Hotel in April (chapter 13) he was testing whether it could be heard from the shoulder of Morgan's Lookout. Brown 1949, *op. cit.* p. 176, Kelly briefed 'upwards of a dozen men' to assist in the strategy, Sadleir 1913, p. 228 estimated some 30 armed supporters were in the vicinity. Hare in evidence, RCVP and 1892, *op. cit.* mentions how poorly armed the gang were at Glenrowan, suggesting better weapons were given to supporters. See evidence of const. Arthur, RCVP,p. 339. Kelly intended to rob Benalla banks, for Kelly's admissions see *Age* 29 June and *Herald* 30 June 1880. AS 17 July 1880 claimed Kelly 'after destroying the blacktrackers and police, [intended] to proceed to Benalla and blow up the police camp and a bank', Curnow's evidence, RCVP, *op. cit.*
Aaron Sherritt. DC, GSOM. See evidence of const. Barry, RCVP, *op. cit.* mentions marriage on Boxing Day, confirmed on DC. See evidence of Ellen Sherritt, RCVP, *op. cit.* Maps confirm selection taken over by H. Crawford. Details of hut, AS 3 July 1880, also memoirs of P. Allen in Cookson 4 September 1911. Ellen, fifteen year-old daughter of 'a well known farmer', see AS, 3 July, *op. cit.* and evidence of const. Armstrong, RCVP,p. 438. See also evidence of Ellen Barry, RCVP, *op. cit.*pp. 432–585. **News report of murder**, *Age* 28 June 1880. Personal accounts were not given with the first *Age* report, but in 1 July 1880 issue. Evidence of Durross before RCVP, *op. cit.* appears the most accurate. Mistakes, name of **Anton Wick** was often misspelled 'Wicks' or 'Weekes'. School records, Woolshed Common School, show Byrne and Wick children attending, VPRO. *op. cit.* See evidence of Anton Weekes [sic] at RCVP, *op. cit.* Details added by descendant Mr. Ron Wick 1989. **Magistrate W.H. Foster's account** from evidence at RCVP, *op. cit.*
Aaron as a double agent. Physically impressive, see AS 3 July 1880, evidence of Armstrong and Falkiner, RCVP, *op. cit.*, p. 219, 438. Would not carry weapon, see evidence of const. Duross RCVP, p. 179. Admitted exploiting police, Armstrong evidence RCVP, p. 438. Showed consistent loyalty to obligations, evidence of Alexander, Armstrong, Dowling, Duross and Hare, RCVP, *op. cit.* Received threats, ibid. See also, evidence of Mrs Sherritt sr and Ellen Barry, RCVP, *op. cit.* Liked but distrusted, Nicolson a 'cranky scotchman ... who would know your thinking', but parted friends, evidence of Armstrong, ibid., p. 437. Supt Hare was infatuated with Aaron, just as Standish was infatuated with Hare, see Sadleir 1913, p. 220. Quote 'He was a remarkable looking man', Hare, evidence RCVP, *op. cit.*, p. 65. Aaron wears a waist sash and chinstrap under the nose 'in the Greta fashion', anonymous letter to supt Hare, from resident of Woolshed 30 April 1879, VPC, KP, VPRO, *op. cit.* **The murder of Aaron Sherritt.** Legend of Aaron threatening to kill and defile Byrne's body. James Kelly to Cookson 5 September 1911, repeated by Kenneally, *op. cit.*, 1955, p. 191. Jones, in an exemplary study of Kelly, Sherritt and Byrne 1992, p. 161, doubts the veracity of the threat. Troopers forced women under the bed, evidence of Armstrong, RCVP, *op. cit.*, p. 434. Quote, 'Never was there a more conspicuous', RCVP. Ned Kelly disagreed, q. 'To have gone out in that light', Kelly's remark cited in evidence of Armstrong, RCVP, *op. cit.*, p. 437.
Joseph or Paddy Byrne. Hare 1892, *op. cit.*, facing p. 192. See Jones, 1992, 1995, *op. cit.* Quote, 'On the 31st of May [1880]', evidence of sub-insp. O'Connor, RCVP, *op. cit.*, p. 52. Police presence at Sherritt hut known to Paddy, supplies delivered to hut, police answering calls of nature, see evidence of hut party constables, and storekeeper Patrick Allen, RCVP, *op. cit.* See also Allen in Cookson 4 September 1911. Denny Byrne came to Sherritt hut while police hid, see evidence of hut party constables, Armstrong RCVP, *op. cit.*, p. 433. Quotes, 'Paddy Byrne stood on his grey mare' and 'Armstrong, you are discovered', evidence of Armstrong, ibid. **Superintendent Frank Hare**. See Sadleir 1913, *op. cit.*, p. 206, 220, 221. Quote, 'After I found out all I could', Hare 1892, *op. cit.*, p. 233. Sherritt and Ward deliberately lied to Hare, Sherritt using 'policy', evidence of Armstrong, RCVP, *op. cit.*, p. 431, 432, 436.

15 The Last Stand, Glenrowan, 26 June 1880

Byrne reached Glenrowan early on Sunday morning, statement of Mrs McDonnell, *Herald* 29 June 1880. Ann Jones told Cookson 3 September 1911 that Dan was present when the line was being dismantled at about 3 a.m. Ned Kelly and Steve Hart arrived early Saturday evening, Kelly letter to governor 5 November 1880, attorney general's department files, KP, VPRO *op. cit.* Quote, 'I well remember Kelly coming to my place', Ann Jones to Cookson 3 September 1911. Bailing up the townspeople, evidence of James Reardon, RCVP, *op. cit.*, pp. 276–81, 383; see also *Age* 30 June 1880. Quote, 'On Sunday morning', Curnow, evidence, RCVP, *op. cit.*, pp. 662–67, answer to Q. 17635. Quote, 'When we were held prisoners', const. Hugh Bracken's account in *Argus* 30 June 1880.
Outcome the complete opposite of the outlaws' plans. See J. Reardon evidence, RCVP, *op. cit.*, and Robert Gibbons account in *Age* 29 June, 'prior to that [arrival of the train] the gang drank quite freely', confirmed by Ann Jones to Cookson 1911, *op. cit.* James Mortimer, in *Age* 30 June, mentioned 'at half past two on Monday morning Ned Kelly said something to the effect that he did not think the train was coming'. **'Destruction of the Kelly Gang' report by Joseph Melvin, *Argus* 29 June 1880,** reprinted in AS 3 July 1880. There are **inaccuracies** in the account. Distance between station and rails torn up, see map. Police went to Stanistreet's and returned to platform and were unloading horses when Bracken met them. Although supt Hare left the scene with conspicuous haste in the first few minutes of battle, John Jones was taken to McDonnell's and lay for nine hours before some means was found to convey him to hospital. **Escape of the male civilian prisoners.** According to evidence of townspeople, Steve and Dan were standing in the passageway as they left, and agreed to hold their fire, see evidence of Reardon, RCVP, *op. cit.* Byrne's body found in bar. Melvin's report originally, incorrectly put it on the east side, see plan of hotel. See Mrs Reardon's and Father Gibney's evidence RCVP, *op. cit.*, p. 379, 442. Rings on Byrne's hands. One was identified as belonging to const. Lonigan and was returned to his widow, VPC, Montfort, Benalla 31 May 1881, KP, VPRO. In interview with Ned Kelly Tom Wright is mentioned, but although Wild Wright was present it seems likely reporter meant Tom Lloyd jr. Arrival of gang incorrectly given as 3 a.m. on Sunday morning. Mrs Jones told Cookson 1911, *op. cit.*, that the line workers, the first held up by Ned and Steve, 'had been out since 1 o'clock'. Ned, in letter to governor 5 November 1880, said they arrived in time to wait for the 9 p.m. [Saturday evening] passenger train to pass. Civilians released earlier by the gang. Curnow and party were not the only ones released by Kelly. Nearly 20 were let go by the gang before the police arrived, see evidence of Mr & Mrs Reardon, RCVP, *op. cit.*, p. 227. The women and most of the children, except Mrs Reardon and her children, escaped within the first hour of the battle, see Mrs Reardon's evidence, ibid., p. 379–83. 'The first attack by the police was a brilliant affair', incorrect. It was in fact very nearly a disaster. See evidence presented, ibid., and RCVP, *op. cit.*, p. xxv. Hare did not wait for his men to assemble and attack in a body, he fired into the hotel, knowing that it was full with civilians. Then, with a minor wrist wound, he left the scene without giving any orders.
Weapons in the saga. The Colt with label, the .45 Tranter and police issue Webley were photographed at VPHU, the two Colts being held were photographed at the SLV by author in 1964–65. For expertise on Kelly weapons see Jones 1995, *op. cit.* **Glenrowan.** See *Argus* 30 June 1880. **Carrington's 'Bird's eye view'**. From ISN 5 August 1880. Several literals have been corrected. **The place where the rails were torn up.** Quote 'is exactly half a mile beyond the station', *Argus* 30 June 1880. Times and details, *Argus* 1 July 1880. **Thomas Curnow**. See evidence at RCVP, *op. cit.*, pp. 663–67. See biography by Pryor, L. J., *Thomas Curnow,* Pryor, Burwood 1986. As Pryor, ibid., pp. 32–33, and Jones 1995, p. facing 212, point out, Curnow successfully lobbied to have his reward increased from £550 to £1000. **Mrs Jones' licensed house or Glenrowan Inn.** Details, *Argus* 30 June 1880, further detail news reports and evidence at RCVP, *op. cit.*, from civilian captives. **The building layout** is confirmed by evidence of Rev. Gibney and Mrs. Reardon, p. 379, 442. Relative scale shown on plan is approximate. Plan modified from J. Davies 'The Kellys are Out', *Herald*, November 1930.
Gang jubilant at success of Byrne and Dan Kelly, account of Mrs McDonnell, *Herald* 29 June, also Mortimer's statement *Age* 30 June 1880. Quote, 'The outlaws were very civil', Mrs McDonnell, *op. cit.* Quote, 'We knew we could do nothing', Mortimer, *op. cit.* **Ann Jones as a young woman**. See interview in Cookson 1911, *op. cit.*, evidence Anne Jones at RCVP, *op. cit.* Quote, 'Just before the train came up', evidence of John Delaney, trial of Ann Jones, Beechworth Assizes 10 November 1880, KP, VPRO. Mrs Jones' claim that civilians could easily have overpowered the gang, in application for compensation 5 December 1880. Mentions she had two sons and two daughters at the time of Kelly visit. One daughter and two boys present at time of battle.
Curnow stops the pilot engine, AS 31 July 1880. See evidence of Curnow, RCVP *op. cit.* **Constable Hugh Bracken**. His account given in *Argus* 29 June 1880, and in evidence RCVP, *op. cit.* Also see Kelly Reward Board Papers, *op. cit.* Amounts given in Kenneally 1955, *op. cit.*, but not final sum for Curnow. **Dance at the Glenrowan Inn.**

Quote, 'was organised but Ned Kelly could not go through the waltzes', application of Mrs Jones for compensation, Kelly Reward Board Papers, *op. cit.* Sympathisers present, see evidence of Curnow, RCVP, *op. cit.*, p. 663. For details about McAuliffes and Delaney brothers see VPC, VPRO, *op. cit.* **The night attack.** Quote, 'Had they been without their armour', Hare evidence RCVP, *op. cit.* For movements of police in first minutes see also evidence of Arthur, re: sky rockets, McWhirter, Carrington and Melvin, ibid. Sympathisers moving about McDonnell's, see evidence of Curnow, ibid., p. 667, Q. 17626. Outlaw leader seen leaving rear of hotel, evidence of Arthur, *op. cit.*, p. 399. Quote, Ned said 'when he returned to the hotel', ibid.; see also evidence of Hare p. 595. Quote, 'Is that you Ned?', sworn declaration of const. W. Phillips, tendered in evidence by supt Hare, RCVP, *op. cit.*, p. 674.
Combatants left leaderless in first few minutes. See evidence of Hare, Sadleir and Whelan, RCVP, pp. 88, 148, 238, also evidence of O'Connor, McWhirter, Carrington and Melvin RCVP, *op. cit.* Mrs Stanhope O'Connor and Mrs Proute Webb. Quote, 'Mr. Hare had already left', diary of Mrs Proute Webb, in possession of descendants, South Yarra 1967. Left in train during battle, see evidence of Hare and O'Connor, RCVP, *op. cit.* **A Queensland Tracker**. See Chomley 1900, p. 154, also evidence O'Connor et al, RCVP, *op. cit.*
Wangaratta contingent of police present at capture. Saddlebag, claimed to have been taken from Kelly, said to be in collection of VPHU.
John Jones. Quote, 'I put my fingers in my ears', David Mortimer in *Age* 30 June 1880. **Jane Jones.** Quote, 'My brave little girl was shot too', Ann Jones to Cookson 1911, *op. cit.* Evidence of Mr and Mrs James Reardon, const. Arthur, Phillips, Rawlings, Dwyer and Dowsett, RCVP, *op. cit.* Jane Jones died in 1882 but not as direct result of wounding. Jones 1995, p. 386 points out that **George Metcalf was wounded in the eye at Glenrowan and died** in Melbourne 15 October 1880. Despite claims that it was not caused by police fire his board and lodging and medical expenses were paid by police dept, see Nicolson to chief secretary 9 December 1880, KP, VPRO. **James and Mary Reardon.** Details in press and RCVP evidence, *op. cit.* Also interview with daughter, Mrs Bridget Griffiths, Benalla 1963, the baby carried by Mary Reardon at Glenrowan. Quote 'The Kellys said they would allow us to go', James Reardon's evidence, RCVP, p. 278. The last stand. **Oral tradition, that Kelly left Jones' hotel to turn back sympathisers**, see Jones in *Ned Kelly, Man and Myth*, Cassell 1968, p. 173 gives the version handed down in Lloyd family; interview Tom Lloyd 1964; see also Wye 1944, *op. cit.* Wye was a former north-east resident and friend of Tom Lloyd jr, the McAuliffes and Jack McMonigle. Quote, 'He ... made up his mind', RCVP, *op. cit.*, p. xxvii.
Ned Kelly at bay. Quote, 'Suddenly we noticed one or two of the men', Joseph Melvin in AS 3 July 1880. **Ned Kelly's mare.** Quote, 'Shortly after [Kelly's appearance] a horse with saddle and bridle came', Dr J. Nicholson in *Argus* 2 July 1880 and 'His mare was found on the railway line', ISN July–August 1880. Ian Jones 1992, *op. cit.*, p. 225, and1995, *op. cit.*, p. 260 has pointed out that **the grey mare belonged to Joe, but also answered to Ned**. It was kept at the Byrne's home stable and exercised by Paddy Byrne until 21 June. See evidence of Hare, referring to reports of Armstrong and Ward, RCVP, *op. cit.*, Q. 1515, p. 89. **Sergeant Arthur Steele**. See evidence of const. Arthur, RCVP, *op. cit.*, pp. 398–99. **Railway guard Jesse Dowsett.** Quote, 'I ran up, and jumped over the log', Dowsett, evidence RCVP, *op. cit.*, p. 335, 389. See also his narrative in *Argus* 1 July 1880. Quote, 'When I reached the place', John Nicholson, *Argus* 2 July 1880. **Ned Kelly in the station building**. Quote, 'There was some very vicious shooting', Sadleir 1913, *op. cit.*, p. 234.
Draft for a republic of Victoria said to have been found in Kelly's pocket. First mentioned in *Cavalcade*, March 1947, pp. 113–14; cutting preserved in Moir collection, LCSLV. See also 'Declaration of a Republic found in Ned's pocket at Glenrowan', *Herald* 2 December 1952, quoting an unsubstantiated article in *Belfast Sunday Independent*, Ireland. Oral tradition that such a document existed and some details confirmed by Tom Lloyd, 1964, to author, Ian and Daren Jones. Jones 1995, p. 377 cites Leonard Radic viewing 'Ned's Declaration of the Republic of North Eastern Victoria' at London's Public Records Office in 1962. So far, it has not been relocated. Quote 'All who saw Ned Kelly', Sadleir 1913, *op. cit.*, p. 238. Quote, 'As the outlaw lay wounded', article referring to Julian Ashton, Moir collection, LCSLV. **Jones's hotel at daylight**. Quote, 'I had several conversations', letter in papers of John Sadleir, LCSLV. Details on O. Madeley, J. Kerr (ed.), *The Dictionary of Australian Artists, Painters, Sketchers, Photographers and Engravers to 1870*, Oxford 1992, p. 508.
The death of Byrne. Quote, 'We were told', Sadleir 1913, *op. cit.*, p. 235. Quote, 'Dan Kelly told us we had better', James Mortimer account in *Age* 30 June 1880. Quote, 'by candlelight as the body lay in a cell at Benalla', Julian Ashton 'The Kelly Gang' in SMH 25 January 1934. **The thirty men who escaped.** See evidence of James Reardon, RCVP, *op. cit.*
Photographers at Glenrowan and Benalla. Bray arrived on Monday and took one view, two plates, of the railway station before the fire. He took views of the station and hotel and other plates in the police paddock at Benalla. These and later images were registered for copyright in Melbourne by **John Bray**, presumably James's son, see CC, envelope 5, LPCSLV. Photographer **James E. Bray** (1832–91) ran the photographic business in Camp Street, Beechworth from approximately 1871 until his death in 1891 and photographed many portraits of Kellys, relations, friends and police. Either James or John could have taken the photographs at Glenrowan. **Oswald Thomas Madeley**, (1832–1913) was based at Benalla but moved to Melbourne by the time he registered his Glenrowan images for copyright. According to J. Cato in *Story of the Camera in Australia*, Georgian House, 1955, p. 97, 'Wadeley' [sic] was among the first in the country to use dry-plate process for this coverage. Cato claims that Barnes and Lindt were also present. **Lindt's teenage assistant, Carl Krutli**, in McLardy, M. 'Our Oldest Living Photographer', *A.P.R. for September 1947*,pp. 484–87, said he and Lindt set up their wet plate tent on Glenrowan railway station 'after the arrest' and their photographs were used as reference for a newspaper woodcut artist. However, **John William Lindt** (1845–1926) and Arthur Burman probably travelled from Melbourne on the train with chief commissioner Standish on Monday afternoon. Wangaratta photographer **William Edward Barnes** (1841–1916) may not have attended the battle. He is not credited on any views but took portraits of police afterwards. Ashton, *op. cit.*, mentions that by Tuesday morning 'numerous photographers had reached the scene ... My friend Lindt was there'. *Argus* 30 June 1880, p. 6 also mentions Burman taking photographs of Byrne at Benalla For **Arthur William Burman** detail (1851–1915) see Kerr 1992, *op. cit.*, p. 115. Arthur Burman's father **William Insull Burman** (1814–90), patriarch of the photographic family, was probably the entrepreneur who obtained material from Bray and Madeley for his series 'Kelly Tragedies: A complete series of photographic views, in connection with the Kelly Outrages'. This included eighteen images, from Wombat Ranges to McDonnell's Hotel and the coffins. He also sold photographs of Dan Kelly, copied from Bray images. It was William who registered the reworked police identity portrait of Ned in 1880, to which a suit and beard had been added.
Watching and waiting, Madeley image. Quote, 'By midday hundreds of people had collected', Hare 1892, *op. cit.*, p. 220. This must have been based on police intelligence, as he was not present by this time. Quote, day was 'cold and dreary', Ashton, *op. cit.* **Watching and waiting, second plate,** Madeley. **Glenrowan battle disgracefully mismanaged.** See evidence of police lower ranks, and Father Gibney, RCVP, *op. cit.* Beechworth const. fired 100 rounds into the hotel in one hour, evidence of Duross, RCVP, *op. cit.*, p. 187. **Railway station and Jones' Hotel Glenrowan, looking north, James Bray plate.** Quotes, 'We were on the platform' and 'I dressed the wounds as well as circumstances would permit', Dr Nicholson, *op. cit.* **Station and hotel, second Bray plate**. Quote, 'After I had attended him', Gibney evidence RCVP, *op. cit.*, p. 441.
Jones' Hotel just beginning to burn, by James Bray. Quote, 'I went down during the day', T. Carrington in evidence to RCVP, *op. cit.*, p. 365. **Jones' Hotel at the time Father Gibney entered, Madeley.** Quote, 'It would be some considerable time', evidence of Gibney, RCVP, *op. cit.*, p. 442. **Father Mathew Gibney**. Quote, observed 'evident want of generalship', Gibney evidence, ibid. **Jones' Hotel burning. Image by Madeley**. Gibney q. continued, 'I went in then on what I think was the room on the right-hand side', ibid. **Jones' Hotel burning, Madeley image.** Quotes, 'In all conscience Ned Kelly's crimes are more than sufficient' and 'Whilst the fire was doing its work', John McWhirter, *Age* 30 June 1880. **Jones' Hotel before it collapsed, Madeley image. Jones' Hotel burned down. Bray image.** Quote, 'The black ashes', evidence of const. Johnson, RCVP, *op. cit.*, and evidence of Sadlier, ibid. **Police with Joe Byrne's horse;** may not have belonged to Byrne, see Jones 1995, *op. cit.* Quote, 'A very fine upstanding chestnut', *Age* 30 June 1880. See also *Herald* and *Argus* ibid., and Kenneally 1955, *op. cit.*, p. 270. **Nineteen bullet and slug wounds**, see Dr Nicholson *Argus* 2 July, Dr Ryan and Dr Shields in *Argus* 30 July. Quote, 'He would have died but for the care of Dr Nicholson', Sadleir 1913, *op. cit.*, p. 238. Contents of Kelly's pockets, IAN, July 1880, p. 107; *Argus* 30 June, p. 6.
The burned body, Madeley and Bray. See evidence of Johnson, raking out bodies and dog RCVP, *op. cit.* Quotes, 'Not even his sisters' and 'I was greatly gratified at getting this trouble over' evidence of Sadleir, RCVP, *op. cit.*, p. 153. Sisters and friends taking bodies, see AS 3 July, IAN, July 1880, and evidence of Sadleir, RCVP, ibid.
Implausible impostors. There is no basis to believe Dan or Steve escaped from Glenrowan. Impostors have never approached surviving members of the family. See evidence of Gibney, RCVP, *op. cit.*, also letter from James Kelly in Kenneally 1955, pp. 314–15. Ned Kelly confirmed Father Gibney's belief that Dan and Steve had committed suicide. Kelly said in Melbourne Gaol: 'I am sure they finished one another ... we had all sworn to', see evidence of Hare, RCVP, *op. cit.*, p. 595; also statement of H. G. Weston, ibid. The belief that they took poison strengthened by the fact that Byrne was found to be carrying a small parcel of it when his clothing was searched (see chapter 16). **McDonnell's hotel and coffins.** Dick Hart's challenge to police, reported in *Argus* 1 July 1880. Quote, 'John Grant, undertaker of Wangaratta, was employed', *Argus* 30 June 1880. The damaged carte-de-visite print is from the Kelly series marketed by William and Arthur Burman. **Kelly taking the attacking force in the rear.** Colour lithograph from supplement to ISN 5 August 1880. Unfortunately, this impression is not accurate in detail, although it captures the bush atmosphere and early morning light. Kelly approached from the east and rear, heading towards the side of Jones' Hotel. None of the illustrations indicate that Kelly was exhausted, close to collapse, staggered through the last exchange and was unable to take effective aim because of previous gunshot wounds. **Ned Kelly at bay.** Tinted lithograph by H. Hunt from supplement in *Sydney Illustrated News*, July 1880. Again, this is a masterly drawing but obscures Kelly's debilitated state as he tried to rejoin his mates in the hotel.
Superintendent John Sadleir. Criticisms, see evidence of Gibney, and report of RCVP. Defended his actions and quote, 'looking at the matter in the light of later knowledge', Sadleir 1913, *op. cit.*, p. 236. **Group at the Kelly tree**. Image by Oswald Madeley. Group of police with Byrne's horse. Barnes' publicity photographs: **Sergeant Arthur Steele**. See Reward Board Papers, VPRO. Kenneally 1955, *op. cit.*, pp. 298, 299, gives list of amounts distributed, but does not include extra paid to Curnow. For censure of Steele see RCVP report, *op. cit.* **Sub-inspector Stanhope O'Connor**, brother-in-law of supt Nicolson, was discredited in letter from Queensland commissioner, included in evidence, and report of commissioners, RCVP, *op. cit.*
Constable Hugh Bracken, q. 'Bracken's is the only name', Chomley 1900, *op. cit.*, p. 143.

16 Aftermath of a Tragedy, June–July 1880

One thousand people watched the spectacle, and q. 'The excitement in the city', see *Herald* 29 June 1880. Quote, 'When I returned to the city', Ashton 1934, *op. cit.* Quote, in Sydney 'the streets were crowded', *Herald* 29 June 1880.
Standish arrived after the affair was over. Evidence of Standish, Sadleir and O'Connor, RCVP, *op. cit.*, pp. 56, 425. Annihilation of the Kelly gang. Latest details from *Herald* 29 June. **The 'eye-witness' account** of the wake and 'the scene at Greta' can only be taken at face value. It is neither substantiated nor contradicted by any other account. **The Kelly Log.** Quote, 'The trees behind which Kelly stood', *Herald*, ibid. Ruins of Jones' Hotel, day after the fire. Quote, 'The debris of Jones's hotel was still smouldering', *Argus* 30 June 1880.
Aftermath and **smoke rising from the ruins**, taken by Oswald Madeley. **Railway station after the battle,** taken by James Bray. Quote, 'the scene of the battle was', *Age* 30 June 1880. **Senior Constable John Kelly**. Quote, 'Look here Ned, now that it is all over', *Argus* 30 June 1880, see depositions, prosecution brief, KP, VPRO, *op. cit.*; also Kelly's evidence at RCVP, *op. cit.* **Byrne's body on display at Benalla**. Quote, 'During the forenoon the body of Byrne was brought out of the lockup', *Argus* 30 June 1880. Quote, 'It was quite evident that he [Byrne] was fully determined', *Herald* 29 June 1880. For Ashton, see SMH 26 January 1934, *op. cit.* Policeman poses in Kelly armour. Quote, 'It is a strange coincidence', Hare 1892, *op. cit.*
Police, trackers and gentlemen present at the encounter, *Argus* 30 June 1880. This cabinet size, half-plate John Lindt image was preserved by descendants of *Argus* reporter Joseph Melvin, seen holding a revolver, second from extreme right. **Seven men from Benalla contingent**. Identified, Jones 1995, *op. cit.* facing page 213. **The wake at Mrs. Skillion's hut.** Quote, 'I had the thanks of those people', Sadleir evidence RCVP, *op. cit.*, p. 154. See *Argus* and *Herald* 1 July 1880. Sadleir mentioned James Kelly's release date in evidence, RCVP, *op. cit.*, p. 158. **Kelly's arrival in Melbourne.** Quote, 'By the ordinary train this morning', *Age* 30 June 1880. Quote '[Kelly] spoke very little', Ryan account in *Argus* 30 June 1880.

Under intensive care. Quote, 'Ned Kelly, who is still a patient', *Herald* 1 July 1880. **An impromptu court in Melbourne Gaol.** Quote, 'Kelly was brought forward', AS August 1880. Sergeant Steele guarding Kelly as the train passes through the Strathbogie Ranges. Quote, 'The prisoner was taken into the guard's van', ibid.

17 The Preliminary Hearing, Beechworth, 6 August 1880

Mr Zinke retired in a huff, *Age* 6–7 August 1880. Quotes, **'What a pity that a fine fellow'**, *Argus* 9 August 1880, and **'Well gentlemen'**, *Age* 7 August. Charge 'that he on the 26th day of October in the year', ibid. Quote, 'Mr. Foster PM, having taken his seat', *Argus* 7 August 1880. Mr. Gaunson MLA. Quotes, from 'I may say that until Wednesday' to include 'if you Sir [Mr Foster] are not satisfied', *Argus*, ibid. **Remarks between Ned and Maggie**, *Argus* 7–8 August 1880. **David Gaunson complaining of newspaper references** to the case. Quotes, 'The *Argus* had a reference ... absolutely untrue', McIntyre's reply to question q. 'Some of the men'; **Foster quote** 'I think it only right that I should inform you' and **Gaunson's reply**, 'I need not say that it is very unusual', *Argus* 7 August 1880. Quote, 'When Mr Foster asked the prisoner', *Age* 11 August 1880. Quote, 'Kate Kelly rose from her seat and walked over to the side of the dock', *Age* 12 August 1880. Kelly taken away in coach, Harvey 1952, *op. cit.*, p. 49. Ned Kelly's plea for a fair hearing, q. 'All I want is a full and fair trial', *Age* 9 August 1880.
Ford Street Beechworth and Gaol. Photograph taken in 1869. Details from Harvey 1952, *op. cit.* Kelly's lodgings in Beechworth. Quotes, 'I have been kept here like a wild beast' and 'Kelly was anxious', *Age* 7 August 1880. **Ned Kelly the bushranger.** Quote, 'A number of people who saw him in court', *Age* and *Argus*, ibid. Quote, 'He was evidently much gratified', *Age* 9 August 1880.
Beechworth courthouse. Quote, 'did not open till 10 o'clock', *Argus* 7 August 1880. **Beechworth court during the Kelly hearing.** Quote, 'intense interest is depicted in the faces', IAN 28 August 1880. The young lady referred to was Ned's sweetheart, Kate Lloyd. **Mrs Skillion and Tom Lloyd.** Quote, 'Amongst the sympathisers in court', *Age* 11 August 1880. **Some of the friends,** q. ibid. Trooper **Thomas McIntyre**, q. ibid. Ned Kelly in the dock, q. 'I was sent to sketch him during his trial [sic]', Ashton 1934, *op. cit.*

18 The Trial, Melbourne, 18 October 1880

Trial shifted to Melbourne, q. 'with feeling ... running very high against the accused', P.A. Jacobs, *Famous Australian Trials and Memories of the Law*, Robertson & Mullens, Melbourne 1944, p. 77. For movements of sympathisers and relatives between Greta and Beechworth, seen as potential danger, see VPC June to August 1880, KP, VPRO, *op. cit.* Kelly's remark to Bracken q. 'if it was to be his fate to be hanged', *Age* 13 August 1880. **Mrs Skillion's application for title to the Kelly selection refused by Lands Department on advice of police**, *Age* 16 October 1880. Barry, as trial judge, denounced Kelly 'in the most scathing and virulent terms', and hope for someone 'less obviously hostile', see Jacobs 1944, *op. cit.*, p. 76. Hickman Molesworth application for adjournment refused by Barry, *Age*, ibid. Bindon hired for seven guineas, Molesworth refused to act for less than 50 guineas. Trial started 18 October, q. crown prosecutor 'loath to do anything', IAN 6 November 1880; trial adjourned nonetheless to 28 October, *Age* 19 October. Coverage of trial q., possibly by Joseph Melvin, *Argus* 29, 30 October 1880.
West Melbourne from Parliament House. Quote, '[his] case excited little interest', IAN 6 November 1880. The old Central Criminal Court. Mr. David Gaunson MLA. Quote, Bindon 'was furnished with an exceptional belief in his own capacity', J. A. Gurner, *Life's Panorama: Being recollections and reminiscences of things seen, things heard, thing read,* Lothian, Melbourne 1930. **The Kelly trial.** For expert analysis see professor Louis Waller, 'Regina v. Edward Kelly' in Cave C. (ed.), *Ned Kelly. Man and Myth,* Cassell 1968, *op. cit.* and justice John H. Phillips, *The Trial of Ned Kelly,* Law Book Co., North Ryde 1987. Their complex argument can only be touched briefly here. Waller concluded not surprisingly, p. 126, that Bindon never put clearly or coherently that defence which had seemed apparent to the Crown prosecutor. Kelly was acting in self-defence. Police were in plain clothes and heavily armed. The Kellys were not hiding but following their ordinary occupation when they fell in with this armed party [the police]. Barry did not consider this defence adequate and admitted evidence relating to shootings other than Lonigan's. Barry, according to Waller, p. 131, was incorrect in directing the jury that a verdict of manslaughter was not an option. Phillips differed on some issues. He criticised Bindon's failure to consider Kelly's plea of self-defence, p. 78, to question McIntyre's description of the critical event – Lonigan's death. He could have pointed out that Kelly did not ambush, but challenged the police in the open and only fired after being fired on. Kelly's aim was to disarm and not to kill. Also, p. 81, a 'proper analysis of the doctor's [Reynolds] evidence would have proved of great value in Kelly's defence'. Bindon addressed none of these issues. John Phillips found it puzzling that Bindon did not call on the experienced Gaunson for advice. In contrast to Waller, Phillips suggested manslaughter was not an available option, p. 92: 'In 1880 any person who, even without intending death to result, caused the death of a constable of police while resisting or escaping a lawful arrest was guilty of murder ... Thus, the real issue for the jury in Kelly's trial was, in factual terms, the nature of the police expedition. What were the police really about? ... if Kelly could show that their real purpose was to shoot him down and that in those circumstances he inflicted no greater injury on Lonigan than he in good faith and on reasonable grounds believed to be necessary in order to defend himself, then the defence of self-defence had been made out and he was entitled to be acquitted'. Phillips concluded, 'Sir Redmond should have told the jury that it was for them to decide ... Instead, the matter was put to the jury in terms that were conclusive in favour of the prosecution. Accordingly, the conclusion is inescapable that Edward Kelly was not afforded a trial according to law'.
Judge Sir Redmond Barry has attracted increasing critical scrutiny. Manning Clark, in *A History of Australia*, vol. IV, MUP 1978, p. 337 recognised his cultural contribution but referred to him as one of those 'who clothed their sadism towards the common people in the panoply of the law'. John McQuilton 1979, *op. cit.*, p. 172, 229, acknowledged his community service and leadership, but observed that Barry was 'bewildered by the Outbreak' and 'incapable of understanding rural problems, he was reduced to attacking their most extreme lawless manifestation ... He was an Orangeman, a member of the transplanted English aristocracy who feared and detested the bog-Irish ... [and who were] firm believers in a system of law and order which guaranteed them their social pre-eminence ... Ned Kelly represented the epitome of the Anglo-Irish nightmare'. Ann Galbally 1995, *op. cit.*, p. 189, added, 'By June 1880 the Kelly Gang had a legendary status in rural areas. Which was why, after capture, the system was manipulated to ensure that the trial was transferred to Melbourne. The trial was indeed a questionable one ... Kelly's telling reply, "More men than I have put men to death", was directed at Barry, notorious since the 1850s for invoking the death penalty ... He [Barry] was unable to recognise and accommodate the deep cravings for social democracy that characterised the new country.' Quote, in caption 18.6, 'he considered the presence of many former convicts', Dean, A., *Multitude of Counsellors: A history of the bar of Victoria*, Cheshire for the Bar Council, Melbourne 1968.
The Accused. Quote, 'Throughout the examination', Atkinson, R., 'Ned Kelly at the bar of justice' in *Australasian Post*, February 1947.

19 To a Higher Court: Two Weeks to 11 November 1880

Number of prisoners hanged in Melbourne Gaol, listed with crimes and dates, held in VPHU, *op. cit.* **Kelly watched constantly** through an iron barred door, *Argus* 12 November 1880. Quote, 'He is dressed in prison clothes', *Herald* 30 October 1880. Kelly's daily routine, q. 'Yesterday afternoon he was visited, ... The parting between sister and brother was of a painful nature', *Herald* 1–5 November 1880. Wednesday 10 November q. 'Mrs Skillion and [Pat]Quinn, an uncle, visited the prisoner yesterday afternoon', *Age* and *Herald* 11 November. **Reprieve Committee,** included eminent citizens mentioned, who were impressed with Kelly's case. A female friend of Standish published 'Kelly's Defence', a pamphlet outlining the case for self-defence, printed W. H. Williams, Melbourne, see LCSLV. Another, Lucy Dashwood, wrote to Queen Victoria in September pleading his case, see secretary of state to the governor, series 1087, no. 54. Friends, relations and opposing factions of the clan rallied, including James, Kate, Maggie and Grace Kelly; Tom Lloyd, Kate and aunt Jane Lloyd; Dennis and sister Bridget McAuliffe and Isaiah Wright and Pat Quinn. Eight thousand people gathered at the hippodrome on 5 November calling for a reprieve. It was claimed that the petition, initially with 32,000, finally contained 50,000 signatures. 1500 people rallied at the treasury building to appeal to premier Berry. Another deputation begged the governor, lord Normanby, for re-consideration. For detail, see press reports. However, some press, particularly the *Argus* and *Age* 10 November, denigrated Gaunson and those involved in reprieve efforts. See Dean 1968, *op. cit.*, Gurner 1930, *op. cit.*, Waller 1968, *op. cit.* Quote, 'Kelly the Bushranger', AS and ISN, November 1880. Quote, 'A large crowd of people assembled', *Age* 10 November 1880. **The execution**, *Herald* 11 November 1880.
Kelly's letters to the governor, 3, 5 and 10 November 1880, Kelly Capital Case File, VPRO. Quote, 'At the end of the last document', *Age* 12 November 1880. The **Melbourne Gaol.** Details *Police Life*, July 1965. Kate Kelly. Quote, 'Victorian, aged about eighteen years', report of det. Ward 12 December 1880, VPC, KP, VPRO. **Kate Lloyd** later married William Cleve. Her descendants owned the former Quinn property at Wallan East for many years. Mrs F. Cleve and son John were very generous to researchers in the 1960s. Once again, I am indebted to Ian Jones for details on Kate, see Jones 1995, *op. cit.*, p. 229, 230, p. facing 309. Many thanks to M. Brolan, for the portrait. **John McElroy**, selector and 'native' of Victoria, was 32 years old in 1880, married Kate's eldest sister Mary Lloyd. He had been arrested as a sympathiser and was the target of police harassment. Gaunson's request for permission on McElroy's behalf, with notation added that request be denied, KP, VPRO, *op. cit*; see also *Herald* 4 November 1880.
The last portraits, head and shoulders plate. Quote, 'At his own request', *Argus* 11 November 1880. **Ned Kelly in irons**. Quote, 'persons in the yard of the Supreme Court', *Herald* 1 November 1880. **Charles Nettleton**, see Cato 1955, *op. cit.*, and Kerr 1992, *op. cit.*, p. 567. He was a major recorder of Melbourne, its early citizens, heroes and villains. According to Peter Cudmore and Joan Kerr, 1992, ibid., 'usually taking his identification photographs outdoors, near a cell ... which he had fitted out as a darkroom ... his most famous photograph is probably a close-up portrait of Ned Kelly taken the day before the bushranger was hanged'. **One of Kelly's last walks; eastern wing of Melbourne Gaol.** Quote, 'Mind you die like a Kelly', *Herald* 10 November 1880; 'He was conducted from his cell in the old wing', *Argus* 12 November 1880.
The last scene of the Kelly drama. Quote, 'He walked steadily on the drop', *Argus*, ibid. Quote, 'Kelly was visibly impressed', IAN, November 1880. Quote, 'At the Robert Burn's Hotel', *Herald* 11 November 1880. Kelly's death mask. Quote, 'Mr Kreitmeyer has just placed in the waxworks', *Herald* 12 November. **The grave in the gaol yard,** arrow and initials 'EK' carved in third bottom coarse of south wall, accuracy debatable. Section included area that served as graveyard for 'more than 100 murderers'. Photographed and reproduced in Melbourne *Truth* 9 March, *Herald* or *Argus* 13 April 1929, during demolition of south west of old gaol to provide site for Royal Melbourne Technical College. Quote, 'To say that Ned Kelly had no courage would be a reflection', T. McIntyre, manuscript, n.d., *op. cit.*, VPHU & LCSLV. Quote, 'Considering his environment he [Kelly] was a superior man', A. Fitzpatrick, interview Cookson, *op. cit.*, 16 September 1911. **Mrs Kelly arrives home in 1881.** See Jones in Carlyon 1980, *op. cit.* p. 24 for identity of those included.
Troubled times continued, Jim Kelly received five years in 1881, see prison registers, vol.17, no. 10861, p. 221, series 515, VPRO ; Wild' Wright got six years in 1883, see also *Geelong Advertiser* 4 June 1929; uncle Jimmy Quinn was back in prison in 1886, see prison registers, vol. 15, no. 9757, p. 521, series 515; Kate married William Foster at Forbes, NSW 25 November 1888, died 1898, inquest 18 October, see letter from her nephew Edward Foster, *Forbes Advocate* 21 October 1955. Kate's son Fred Foster, raised by Ellen and Jim, enlisted and was killed in action 17 March 1916. Ellen and James moved to section 69, on the north side of the Greta road and on top of the 'Gap' in the 1890s. They sold their original selection to Grace Kelly and her husband, Edward 'Ned' Griffiths. Maggie Skillion died 22 January 1896 (DC registered by Tom Lloyd as Skillan). Ellen Kelly died 27 March 1923, DC 'Ellen King', *op. cit.* James Kelly died in 1946, see *Sun*, 19 December 1946. For interesting detail on Ellen and family, see Balcarek, D., *Ellen Kelly*, Farlell, Glenrowan 1984. **Portrait of Ellen in later years**, courtesy of descendants Leigh Olver and Elsie Pettifer, cropped from one including son-in-law, Ned Griffiths. Identity of Ellen in photograph of 'Mrs Kelly and James at Greta' in previous edition has been discredited and so deleted.

PICTURE SOURCES

Note: A Full list of abbreviations is given before endnotes. The author's own photographs of landscapes, buildings and artefacts are abbreviated as 'AP'. Author's collection of early material is given as 'AC'. Donors who asked to remain anonymous are shown as 'PD'. The figures in **bold** in the first column refer to the page numbers.

1 Formative Years, Beveridge 1850–64

1	**Township of Beveridge**, B309, with permission of the Surveyor General, Land Victoria hereafter, LV.
1	**John 'Red' Kelly's signature,** TOM.
2–3	**Quinn homestead at Wallan East.** Colour photo 1983, Peter Gough, courtesy of the Brown family.
4	**Interior of Quinn kitchen**, 1963 AP, courtesy Cleve family.
4	**Quinn forge door,** 1963 AP, Cleve family.
5	**Quinn family tree to 1880,** AC.
5	**Farmhouse of a dairyman**, 1964 AP.
5	**Elevation of original house**, author's drawing from field survey.
6	**Father Charles O'Hea,** from *Cyclopedia of Victoria*, 1891.
6	**St. Francis's Church Melbourne,** courtesy Bernard Laffan.
7	**Beveridge Catholic School exterior,** 1964 AP.
8	**Bevereridge Catholic School interior,** 1964 AP.
9	**Kilmore, as it was in the 1860s,** H. Vanheens 1861, Latrobe Picture Collection, hereafter LPC, H1834, State Library of Victoria, hereafter SLV.
9	**Kilmore courthouse,** courtesy Vern Jewell (née Johnson).
10	**Settlers travelling up-country,** *Australasian Sketcher* 20 February 1875.

2 Luck of the Irish, Avenel 1864–67

13	**Avenel bridge and toll-gate on Hughes Creek,** T. Washbourne photo, courtesy of Ethel Middleton (née Shelton).
13	**Avenel Common School,** reproduced by permission of the Keeper of Public Records, hereafter VPRO.
14–15	**Hughes Creek (colour),** by Peter Gough.
16	**Avenel township and surrounds,** A74, LV.
17	**Schoolmaster James J. Irving,** courtesy Peter Smith.
17	**Elizabeth Shelton,** courtesy Ethel Middleton.
17	**Esau Shelton,** Ethel Middleton.
17	**Richard Shelton,** courtesy Ethel Middleton.
18	**A matter of example; the death of Morgan,** *Illustrated Australian News* 25 April 1865.
19	**The Avenel lock-up,** T. Washbourne photo, LPC, H27573, SLV.
19	**Campion's store,** courtesy Ethel Middleton.
20	**Ned and his father's entries in the births and deaths register,** GSOM.
21	**On the Tallarook Ranges,** from Morris, E. (ed.) *Cassell's Pictureque Australasia,* London 1888.
22	**A Family Hut,** by L. H. Dacey, early undated postcard, AC.
23	**'Bush burial'** by Frederick McCubbin, 1890, courtesy of the Geelong Gallery.

3 Return to the Clan, Greta 1867–70

25	**Greta and district,** AC.
25	**Proeschel's desk and traveller's map,** AC.
26	**Redmond Barry,** *Cyclopedia of Victoria*, 1891.
27	**Bush farm, Victoria 1876** (colour), H. L. Houten, photo by Jenni Carter, courtesy of Art Gallery of New South Wales.
28	**Unidentified neighbour at Lurg,** courtesy of Benalla Historical Society.
29	**James 'Jimmy' Quinn; three portraits,** Bray plate 1879, PD, others in prison register (hereafter PR), Series 515, Vol. 15, p. 52, VPRO.
30–1	**Colony of Victoria in 1870** (colour), William Collins, Sons & Co. London 1870, AC.
32	**Henry Johnstone alias 'Harry Power'; two portraits,** CC, 24, number 34 & 35, LPCSLV.
32	**Robert McBean,** from J. Sadleir 1913, *op. cit.,* facing p.156
33	**John Quinn,** 1879, by J. E. Bray, VPHU.
35	**Power's lookout,** postcard, AC.
36	**Wangaratta police barracks and courthouse,** City of Wangaratta.
37	**Capture of Power, the bushranger,** *Australasian Sketcher*, June–October 1870.
38	**Kelly's note to sergeant Babington,** Babington file, VPC, KP, VPRO.
39	**Wild Pat Quinn, the Dubliner,** tintype, undated, PD.

4 A Secondary Education for the Kelly Children, 1870–74

42	**Murphy Street, Wangaratta** 1866, City of Wangaratta.
42	**Benjamin Gould,** James Bray 1879, PD.
43	**Police barracks, Greta,** from S. E. Ellis, *A History of Greta,* Lowden 1972, courtesy North-Eastern Historical Society.
43	**Township of Greta,** Samuel Calvert, wood engraving from *Illustrated Australian News* July 1880, Illustrated newspaper Files, Latrobe collection, State Library of Victoria, hereafter IAN, INF, LCSLV.
43	**Curlewis Street, Greta,** courtesy Ian Jones.
44	**Senior constable Hall,** with permission of the Victorian Police Historical Unit, hereafter VPHU.
45	**Ned Kelly's record sheet, prison register,** VPRO.
46–7	**Prison life at Pentridge Gaol,** AS, October–November 1873.
47	**One of the prison hulks,** detail, 19th Cent. view of Hobson's Bay, AC.
48–9	**The many false faces of Ned Kelly,** 4.14 William J. Burman 1880, CC, 5, no. 1481, LPCSLV; 4.15-16, PR, VPRO; 4.17 from Chomley 1900, *op. cit.* p. 1; 4.18, *Illustrated Sydney News* July 1880.
50	**James Kelly,** PR series 515, vol. 17, no. 10861; also, series 522, vol. 1, p. 38, 45, VPRO.
51	**Victorian selector's homestead,** AC.

5 The Coming of Age, 1874–78

53	**Ned Kelly's prison portrait (colour)** PR, VPRO.
54	**Another of Ned Kelly's prison sheets** (colour) PR, VPRO.
55	**James Kelly's prison portrait (colour)** PR, VPRO.
56	**Edward Kelly in boxing trunks** by John J. Chidley, courtesy of Ian Jones.
57	**Wild Wright,** PR series 515, vol. 20, no. 12313, VPRO.
57	**Kelly at Beechworth** by James Bray, courtesy of the Lloyd family.
58	**John McMonigle,** by James Bray 1879, VPHU.
58–9	**View from Bald Hill** AP.
60	**James Whitty,** from composite by Henry Hansen, 1899, Burke Museum, Beechworth.
60	**Aaron Sherritt** by James Bray, Hare 1892, *op. cit.,* facing p.140
60	**Joseph Byrne** by Arthur Burman 1880, courtesy E. W. Swan.
61	**Jim Kelly;** two later prison portraits, Museum of Applied Science, Melbourne, hereafter MAS.
61	**Steve Hart** by James Bray, *Herald* November 1930.
62–3	**Bird's-eye-view of Benalla (colour),** by Francis Niven 1882, courtesy of Colin Boyd.
64	**Constable Lonigan,** from Sadleir 1913, *op. cit.,* facing p. 183.
65	**Dan Kelly; full-length portrait** by James Bray, copied by Burman studios, *Argus file*, AC.
66	**William Baumgarten,** PR series 515, vol. 28, p. 277, VPRO.

6 An Ill-fated Visit to the Kelly Hut: The Fitzpatrick Incident, 15 April 1878

69	**Constable Alexander Fitzpatrick,** J. E. Bray, Beechworth 1878, VPHU.
70–1	**Ruins of Kelly homestead** in the 1960s, courtesy of Graham Moore.
72	**Selections on the Greta road,** area of Winton, first survey 1866, courtesy LV.
72	**Constable Fitzpatrick, later in life,** *Herald* November 1930.
73	**Dan Kelly,** 6.5 photograph by J. E. Bray, Beechworth, copied by Burman studios, AC; 6.6 wood engraving ISN July 1880, INF, LPCSLV.
74	**Kate Kelly,** *Argus* file, AC.
75	**The new Kelly homestead,** courtesy Ian Jones.
75	**Kelly house, from the rear,** author drawing based on later photographs, collection of Leigh Olver.
76	**Ellen Kelly in 1911,** courtesy of Elsie Pettifer and Leigh Olver.
77	**William Skillion,** PR series 515, vol. 28, p. 272, VPRO.
77	**William 'Bricky' Williamson,** PR series 515, vol. 14, no. 9441, VPRO.
77	**Superintendent C. H. Nicolson,** VPHU.
77	**Sergeant James Whelan,** Benalla, from Sadleir 1913, *op. cit.,* facing p. 209.
77	**Sergeant Steele,** VPHU.
78	**The gaol and courthouse,** Ford Street, Beechworth, Burke Museum, Beechworth.
78	**The warrant,** VPRO.
78	**Two-storey Beechworth courthouse,** AP.
78	**Interior of the Beechworth court,** AP.
80	**The cause of an outbreak,** VPRO.
81	**Francis Harty** 1879, by J.E. Bray, VPHU.
81	**Sir Redmond Barry,** by T. Chuck, from *The Explorers & Early Colonists of Victoria,* 1872, AC.
81	**The record of the Quinns, Kellys and Lloyds,** RCVP, appendix 10, p. 699.

7 From Horse-stealing to Homicide: Stringybark Creek, 28 October 1878

83	**Wombat Ranges,** AS November 1878.
83	**The Kelly farm,** T258, LV.
84	**Dan Kelly's house, Bullock Creek,** Captain Cook Museum.
85	**Stephen Hart,** W. E. Barnes 1877, LPC, CC, 5, no. 38, SLV.
86–7	**Police graves in Mansfield cemetery,** AP.
88	**Joseph Byrne,** wood engraving, ISN July 1880, INF, LPC-SLV.
88	**Tom Lloyd junior,** James Bray 1879, MAS.
89	**Thomas Lonigan,** MAS.
89	**Thomas Newman McIntyre,** from Sadleir 1913, *op. cit.,* facing p. 185.
89	**Sketch,** thought to have been made by McIntyre, KP, VPRO.
90	**The clearing on Stringybark Creek** 1878, VPHU.
90	**Stringybark Creek clearing, second plate,** courtesy Harold Baigent, CAE.
91	**Mounted-constable Michael Scanlon,** courtesy VPHU.
91	**Sergeant Michael Kennedy,** MAS.
92	**The first map surveyed of the area,** T258, LV.
93	**Mansfield from the Longwood road,** AS November 1878.
93	**The old gun used by the gang,** *Argus* file, AC.
94	**Discovering Sergeant Kennedy's body,** VPHU.
94	**Discovering Kennedy's body, second plate,** CAE.
95	**Sub-inspector Pewtress,** Royal Victorian Historical Society, hereafter RVHS.
96	**The first news to reach Melbourne,** KP, VPRO.
96	**The brief details of 'the murder of two constables',** *Age* 28 October 1878.
97	**The Mansfield police station,** *Weekly Times* 17 May 1930.
97	**Doctor Samuel Reynolds,** from Sadleir 1913, *op. cit.,* facing p. 183.

8 From Obscurity to Outlawry, October–December 1878

99	**The notorious bushrangers,** *Frearson's Weekly*, November 1878.
99	**Supreme Court proclamations,** O&M November 1878.
99	**1873 identification plate of Edward Kelly,** MAS.
100	**Sketch of the Kelly selection,** KP, VPRO.
100	**Typical Kelly country,** undated postcard, AC.
101	**Portrait of the Kellys,** n.d., Regal Post Card Co. courtesy Ian Jones.
101	**Kellys inset, detail,** Ian Jones.
102	**A field of operations,** *County Maps of Victoria* 1884.
103	**Victorian mounted trooper in uniform** (colour), AC.
103	**Victorian police engaged in the Kelly pursuit [in plain clothes],** VPHU.
104	**Search party on the track,** *Frearson's Weekly* 10 May 1879.

284

104	**Attempted surprise**, AS 21 December 1878.	
105	**The cost of living**, AC.	
106	**Uncle Thomas Lloyd**, J. E. Bray 1879, PD.	
107	**A Bush Home** by L. H. Davey, early postcard, AC.	

9 The Euroa Hold-up, 9 December 1878

109	**Seven Creeks Hotel and store**, courtesy of Mrs Lomer, Euroa.
110	**Benjamin Gould**, Howship, Benalla, approx. 1903, courtesy of William Gould.
110	**Aiding the outlaws**, KP, VPRO.
111	**Younghusband's station**, IAN January 1879, INF, LCSLV.
111	**Demanding refreshments**, IAN January 1879, INF, LCSLV.
112	**The new rig-outs**, IAN January 1879, INF, LCSLV.
112	**Gloster's wagon in Euroa**. Detail from larger photograph, Victorian Railway Archives (VicRail), hereafter VRA.
113	**Railway Street, Euroa in the 1870s**, Euroa Camera Club.
114	**'The prison' and 'cutting the telegraph wire'**, IAN January 1879, INF, LCSLV.
115	**Sticking up the bank**, IAN January 1879, INF, LCSLV.
115	**Euroa National Bank**, IAN January 1879, INF, LCSLV.
116	**Euroa railway station**, Euroa Camera Club.

10 Evading the Police Force, December 1878–February 1879

119	*Australasian Sketcher*, 'outlaws in camp', AS 21 December 1878
120	**Superintendent Hare**, from Sadleir 1913, *op. cit.*, facing p. 217.
121	**The Kelly hunters**, Harold Baigent, CAE.
121	**Chief commissioner captain Frederick Charles Standish**, VPHU.
122	**Standish in camp**, RHVS.
123	**Moses**, PD.
124	**Mr Donald Cameron**, supplement to *The Leader*, May 1880.
125	**The Cameron letter** [attach Standish telegram], KP, VPC, VPRO.
125	**Standish telegram** to Chief Secretary, VPRO
126	**Melbourne Punch cartoon**, 16 January 1879.
127	**Bank in the bushranging district**, AS 15 March 1879.
128	**Police caves on the Woolshed**, colour, AP.
129	**Wild Isaiah Wright's prison record**, VPRO.
130–31	**Some of the alleged sympathisers**, by J.E. Bray 1879, VPHU.
131	**'Wild' Wright**, PR series 515, vol. 20, p. 341, no.12313, VPRO.
132–33	**Scene near the Buffalo Mountains**, no. 22, *Views of Victoria* by Nicholas Caire (later hand-tinted), AC.

11 The Jerilderie Hold-up, 8 February 1879

135	**Jerilderie, New South Wales**, town plan, Shire of Jerilderie.
136	**Bailing up the police**, IAN 21 February 1879, INF, LCSLV..
137	**Jerilderie courthouse**, AP.
137	**Jerilderie Street**, *Sun* 7 September 1911.
137	**The Royal Mail Hotel**, Shire of Jerilderie.
138	**Bank of New South Wales, Jerilderie** 1875, Bank of NSW Archives.
139	**Schoolteacher William Elliott**, Shire of Jerilderie.
140	**Kelly's Jerilderie letter**, Ian Jones, original now in LCSLV.
141	**Jerilderie post and telegraph office**, AP.

12 The Great Disappearance, Part One, February–June 1879

145–46	**The reward posters**, £8000 combined Victorian and NSW governments, Shire of Jerilderie; £8000 proclamation VPHU; £4000 reprinted in *Sun*, 27 August 1911.
147	**Main gates, Beechworth Gaol**, AC.
148	**Joseph Ryan**, by J. E. Bray 1879, VPHU.
149	**Poetic warning**, KP, VPRO.
150	**The fringe benefits**, *Fearson's Weekly*, 29 March 1879.
150	**The berry broker**, from *Melbourne Punch*, March 1879.
151	**Mrs Maggie Skillion**, by D. Isley, photograph approximately 1881, courtesy of Elsie Pettifer and Leigh Olver.
151	**Maggie and Tom Lloyd**, wood engraving from IAN August 1880, INF, LCSLV..
151	**Kate Kelly**, n.d., courtesy Edgar Penzig.
152	**Beechworth, map** 1868, L.3883 but now B621, LV.

153	**Upper police caves**, AP.
153	**Lower police caves**, AP.
153	**Winter scene in north-eastern Victoria**, Benalla Historical Society.
154	**Kelly songs**, MLC, SLNSW.
154–55	**Letters to old friends**, VPRO.

13 The Great Disappearance, Part Two, June 1879–June 1880

159	**Queensland trackers at Benalla**, courtesy Colin Boyd.
160	**Another Kelly letter**, O&M 12 July 1879.
161	**Where are the Kellys?** *Fearson's Weekly*, 9 August 1879.
162	**The marquis of Normanby**, by Thomas Chuck, Ref. No.H11, LPCSLV.
162	**Detective Michael Ward**, *Sun* 5 September 1911.
165	**New South Wales police who captured Moonlite**, *Trooper Police of Australia*, A. L. Haydon 1911.
165	**George Scott** alias 'Captain Moonlite', AC.
166	**Mounted police on duty at Greta**, courtesy Ian Jones.
168	**Ned and Joe's armour pieces**, AP, Ned's suit, LCSLV, Joe's suit courtesy Mr R. Hammond.
168	**Steve and Dan's armour pieces**, AP, courtesy VPHU.
169	**Armour taken from ashes, rifle and padded cap**, by O. Madeley, CC, 5, no. 20, SLV.
169	**Carrington drawing of Ned's armour**, by T. Carrington, wood engraving, AS, 3 July 1880.
170	**Withdrawal of reward**, AC.
171	**Queensland contingent, O'Connor and trackers**, RHSV.
171	**Daniel Kennedy alias 'diseased stock agent'**, courtesy Leonard Pryor.

14 Devil's Elbow: The Death of Aaron Sherritt, 26 June 1880

174–75	**Beechworth and Everton, Woolshed map**, Victorian Mines Department Archives.
176	**Age news item** 28 June 1880.
176	**Anton Wick**, courtesy of Ron Wick.
176	**Aaron Sherritt's home**, wood engraving from AS 17 July 1880.
176	**Plan of Sherritt's home**, RCVP.
178	**Aaron Sherritt**, by J. E. Bray, n.d. Beechworth, *Argus* file, AC.
179	**The murder of Aaron Sherritt**, wood engraving from ISN 10 July 1880, INF, LPCSLV.
179	**Superintendant Hare**,VPHU.
180	**Joseph Byrne, or brother Paddy**, by J. E. Bray, but here from Hare 1892, *op. cit.*, facing p. 192.

15 The Last Stand, Glenrowan, 26 June 1880

183	**Weapons in the Kelly saga**, VPHU and LCSLV.
184	**Glenrowan map**, G921, LV.
184	**Carrington's bird's-eye-view of railway station and surrounds**, IAN 17 July 1880, INF, LCSLV.
185	**Ann Jones as a young woman**, *Sun* 1 September 1911.
185	**Place where the rails were pulled up**, courtesy of Harold Baigent, CAE.
186	**Thomas Curnow**, MC P1/C, SLNSW.
187	**Mrs Jones' Hotel**, detail from plate by J. E. Bray, June 1880, courtesy Mr B. Hiscock.
187	**Plan of hotel**, modified from J. M. S. Davies, 'The Kellys are Out', *Herald* , 1 November – 16 December 1930.
188	**Curnow stops the pilot Engine**, AS 17 July 1880.
188	**Engines at Benalla**, VRA.
191	**Dance at the Glenrowan Inn**, wood engraving from AS 17 July 1880.
191	**Constable Bracken** by W. E. Barnes 1880, LPC, CC, 5, no. 32, SLV.
192–93	**The night attack**, wood engraving from AS 3 July 1880.
192	**Press carriage in the special**, AS 17 July 1880.
194	**Kelly's 1856 model .56 calibre Colt percussion carbine**, AP, courtesy R. Hammond.
194	**Mrs O'Connor**, Mrs Proute Webb.
194	**Mrs Proute Webb**, Mrs Proute Webb.
195	**Wounded tracker**, engraving from IAN 3 July1880, INF, LCSLV.
196	**Wangaratta contingent**, by W. E. Barnes, Wangaratta, LPC, CC, 5, no. 1, SLV.
197	**Jane Jones**, by W.E. Barnes, AC.
197	**John Owen Jones**, by W. E. Barnes, *Sun* 1 September 1911.

197	**James and Mary Reardon**, n.d., courtesy of Bridget Griffiths.
198	**Ned Kelly at bay**, wood engraving, AS 3 July 1880.
198	**Kelly's grey mare**, AS 17 July 1880.
198	**Sergeant Arthur Steele**, by W. E. Barnes, LPC, CC, 5, no. 3, SLV.
199	**Ned Kelly in the station building**, ISN 10 July 1880, INF, LPCSLV.
199	**Jesse Dowsett**, ISN August 1880, INF, LPCSLV.
200	**Jones' hotel at daylight**, by O. Madeley, LPC, CC, 5, no. 8, SLV.
200	**Death of Byrne**, by Julian Ashton, ISN 5 August 1880.
201	**Thirty men who escaped**, wood engraving, AS 3 July 1880.
201	**Police in position to fire**, by O. Madeley, LPC, CC, 5, no. 19, SLV.
201	**Watching and waiting**, by O. Madeley, LPC, CC, 5, no. 15, SLV.
202	**Watching and waiting, view south to station**, O. Madeley, LPC, CC, 5, no. 18, SLV.
203	**Railway station and Jones' hotel**, by J. Bray, LPC, CC, 5, no. 24, SLV.
203	**Second plate, Jones' hotel**, by J. Bray, LPC, CC, 5, no. 25, SLV.
204–5	**Ned's blood-stained green silk sash**, AP, Benalla Historical Society.
206	**Hotel just beginning to burn**, by J. Bray, LPC, CC, 5, no. 26, SLV.
206	**Jones' hotel at the time the priest was entering**, by O. Madeley, LPC, CC, 5, no. 9, SLV.
207	**Jones' hotel burning**, by O. Madeley, MAS; also LPC, CC, 5, no. 10. SLV.
207	**Father Mathew Gibney**, MDHC Catholic Archdiocese of Melbourne.
208	**Hotel burning, crowd at front**, by O. Madeley, LPC, CC, 5, no. 12, SLV.
209	**Hotel prior to collapse**, by J. Bray, LPC, CC, 5, no. 13, SLV.
210	**Jones' hotel burned down**, by J. Bray, LPC, CC, 5, no. 30, SLV.
211	**Police with Byrne's horse** [sic] by J. Bray, LPC, CC, 5, no. 31, SLV
211	**Dr Nicholson**, *Cyclopedia of Victoria* 1891.
212–13	**Kelly taking the attacking force in the rear** (un-attributed colour lithograph) ISN 5 August 1880, copy P3/K, Mitchell Library, Sydney.
214	**A burned body**, by O. Madeley, LPC, CC, 5, no. 14, SLV.
214	**Burned body, second plate**, by J. Bray, LPC, CC, 5, no. 28, SLV.
215	**McDonnell's tavern and coffins**, by O. Madeley, courtesy Elsie Pettifer and Leigh Olver.
215	**McDonnell's hotel, coffins and reporters**, by O. Madeley, LPC, CC, 5, no. 16, SLV.
216	**Ned Kelly at bay**, colour tinted lithograph by H. Hunt, ISN July 1880, INF, LPCSLV.
217	**Group at the Kelly tree**, by O. Madeley, LPC, CC, 5, no. 17, SLV.
217	**Superintendent Sadleir**, wood engraving, IAN 17 July 1880, INF, LCSLV..
217	**Steele** (full length portrait) by W. E. Barnes, LPC, CC, 5, no. 5, SLV.
217	**Sub Inspector O'Connor**, by W. E. Barnes, LPC, CC, 5, no. 37, SLV.
217	**Constable Bracken**, by W. E. Barnes, LPC, CC, 5, no. 36, SLV.

16 Aftermath of a Tragedy, June–July 1880

219	**The Kelly log**, anonymous, courtesy Mr. J. T. Parkinson.
220	**Ruins on the day after the fire**, wood engraving, ISN 3 August 1880.
220	**The log where Kelly fell** (second plate) by J. Bray, LPC, CC, 5, no. 29, SLV.
221	**Aftermath**, by O. Madeley, LPC, CC, 5, no. 23, SLV.
221	**Smoke rising from the ruins** by O. Madeley, LPC, CC, 5, no. 13, SLV.
221	**Railway station after the battle**, by J. Bray, LPC, CC, 5, no. 27, SLV.
222–23	**Byrne's body on display at Benalla**, (wide view) by J. W. Lindt, courtesy Ian Jones and Cyril Pearl.
222	**Joe Byrne's corpse**, (side view) by A. Burman, courtesy E. W. Swan.

223	**Byrne,** (close-up), A. Burman's second plate, VPHU.
223	**Senior Constable John Kelly**, wood engraving, ISN 3 August 1880.
224	**Police, trackers, gentlemen present at encounter**, by J. W. Lindt, courtesy E. W. Swan.
225	**Men at the barracks after the encounter** (detail by J. W. Lindt).
226	**Seven men from the Benalla contingent**, by O. Madeley, LPC, CC, 5, no. 22, SLV.
227	**Policeman in Kelly armour,** by O. Madeley, LPC, CC, 5, no. 21, SLV.
228	**The wake at Mrs Skillion's hut**, wood engraving, AS 17 July 1880.
229	**Kelly's arrival in Melbourne**, wood engraving, IAN 17 July 1880, INF, LCSLV..
230	**Under intensive care,** wood engraving, ISN August 1880.
230	**An unsigned request,** CLD files, KP, VPRO.
231	**Impromptu court in the gaol kitchen**, wood engraving, AS 14 August 1880.
231	**Sergeant Steele guarding Kelly** as the train passes through the Strathbogie Ranges, wood engraving, AS 14 August 1880.

17 The Preliminary Hearing, Beechworth, 6 August 1880

233	**Ned Kelly the bushranger**, wood engraving, AS 31 July 1880.
234	**Kelly's lodgings in Beechworth Gaol**, AC.
235	**Ford Street and Beechworth Gaol**, courtesy Bill Knowles.
235	**Beechworth courthouse,** 1962 AP.
235	**Interior of Beechworth court**, 1962 AP.
236	**Beechworth court during the Kelly hearing**, wood engraving, ISN August 1880.
236	**Mrs Skillion and Tom Lloyd,** ISN August 1880.
236	**Some of the friends**, ISN August 1880.
236	**Trooper Thomas McIntyre**, ISN August 1880.
237	**Ned Kelly in the dock,** wood engraving from drawing by J. Ashton, IAN 28 August 1880, INF, LCSLV.
238–39	**Beechworth court records**, 1962 AP.
241	**Good behaviour leg irons**, AP.
242–43	**Eleven Mile Creek and Glenrowan Gap from Kelly's lookout** (colour), 1989 AP.

18 The Trial, Melbourne, 18 October 1880

245	**West Melbourne from parliament house**, by C. Nettleton, AC.
246	**The old central criminal court**, Harold Baigent, CAE.
246	**Interior of the court**, ibid.
247	**The Kelly trial**, wood engraving, ISN November 1880.
247	**Mr David Gaunson MLA**, by J. W. Lindt, ML, P1/G, SLNSW.
252	**Judge Sir Redmond Barry**, AS, 4 December 1880.
253	**The accused**, wood engraving, AS, 6 November 1880.

19 To a Higher Court: Two Weeks to 11 November 1880

257	**Letters to the governor,** Capital Case file, KP, VPRO.
258–59	**The Melbourne Gaol**, by C. Nettleton, composite of two plates, *Argus* file, AC.
260	**Kate Kelly**, *Argus* file, AC.
261	**Kate Lloyd**, courtesy Ian Jones and Myra Brolan.
261	**John McElroy**, by J. E. Bray 1879, PD.
262	**The last portrait** (head and shoulders, hand-tinted colour) by C. Nettleton, courtesy John Payne and Annette Hall.
263	**Kelly in leg-irons**, by C. Nettleton, courtesy Ian Jones.
264	**One of Kelly's last walks**, AP, NTV.
266–67	**Condemned cell and wing of Melbourne gGaol** (colour) photographed by Peter Gough.
268	**The last scene of the Kelly drama**, wood engraving, AS 20 November 1880.
269	**Dean O'Hea,** MDHC, CAM.
270	**Kelly's death mask** AP, courtesy Burke Museum, Beechworth.
271	**Adding insult to injury,** J. K. Moir collection LPC, SLV.
272	**Mrs Kelly arrives home at the Eleven Mile Creek** 1881, Ian Jones.
272	**Detail of Kelly family,** Ian Jones.
273	**Mrs Kelly in later life**, courtesy Elsie Pettifer and Leigh Olver.
273	**The grave in the gaol yard**, *Herald* 13 April 1929.

BIBLIOGRAPHY

1 Manuscripts

Burke Museum Beechworth
Beechworth Court of Petty Sessions, case list book.
Kelly, Edward. Letter to the chief secretary, January 1879.
Education Department of Victoria Library
Brown, Gilbert. Notebooks 1864–66.
State Library of Victoria, La Trobe Collection
Barry, Redmond. Papers. M58380.
Benalla Court of Petty Sessions, case list book 1868–78.
Copyright collection of photographs, Kelly papers and miscellaneous photographs.
Croll, R. H. *Before I Forget*. Croll papers, ch. 3. M58910.
Kelly, E. The Jerilderie Letter. Original manuscript. MS SAFE 1.
McIntyre, T. E. *A Narrative of My Experience with the Kelly Gang and a Short Account of Other Bushrangers.* N.D. M56343.
Moir, J. K. Papers.
Sadleir, John. Collection of correspondence and diaries.
Smith, C. P. [investigator]. *Game as Ned Kelly!: An epic in crime.*
Standish, Frederick. Manuscript copy of diary. M59502.
Mitchell Library Manuscript collection
Browne, Thomas Alexander. Diary.
Cameron, T. H. Letter to his brother 8 July 1880.
Jerilderie police station, occurrence book.
Scott, Mrs. *The Kelly Gang at Euroa.*
St Paul's Roman Catholic Church, Coburg
Baptismal Records 1850–70.
University of Melbourne Archives
Hare, Francis. Personal papers.
Victorian Attorney General's Department
Kelly, Edward. Letters dictated from Melbourne Gaol 1880.
Victorian Crown Lands and Survey Department
Map collection 1850–90.
Victorian Railways Department
Historical collection.
Wangaratta courthouse
Records 1860–80.
Wangaratta Shire Offices
Historical collection and records.

2 Official records

New South Wales Archives
Colonial secretary of New South Wales' correspondence with the chief secretary of Victoria 1878–81.
Police files and correspondence 1878–81.
Tasmanian Archives
Convict records 1841–48.
Victorian court records 1850–80.
During research, most records were still preserved by the courthouse concerned with the relevant case.
Victorian Government Statist
Birth, death and marriage certificates 1843–78.
Victorian Government Titles Office
Title and memorial records under old law and Crown grant systems 1850–80.
Victorian Police Historical Unit Archives
Euroa police station, criminal offence reports.
Glenrowan police station, occurrence book.
Greta police station, occurrence book.
Mansfield police station, occurrence book.
McIntyre, T. E. *A Narrative of My Experience with the Kelly Gang and a Short Account of Other Bushrangers.*
Victorian police, inspecting superintendents' reports. Victorian police officers' and constables' record sheets.
Victorian Public Records Office
Assisted migrant shipping lists 1840–55.
Chief secretary's correspondence. Series 1189.
Crown law files and correspondence. Series 266.
Department of Education, records and correspondence 1860-80.
Executive Council minutes. Series 1080. Governor's despatches to the secretary of State. Series 1084.
Jerilderie Letter (copy).
Kelly, Edward. Capital case file. Without series.
Kelly papers. Without series. Includes: Cameron Letter (copy).
  Chief secretary's correspondence 1878–82 and 1906–30.
  The controversy surrounding the unearthing of Ned Kelly's body and the search for the skull.
  Correspondence between the Victorian and Queensland authorities on the black trackers 1878–80.
  Curnow's account of Glenrowan.
  Kelly's defence by a lady.
  Constable McIntyre's reward claim 1881.
  Superintendent Nicolson's defence of his conduct of the Kelly pursuit 1880.
  Nicolson, O'Connor and Standish call for an inquiry.
  Petition to ban the film *The Story of the Kelly Gang.*
  Prosecution of Anne Jones 1880–85.
  Setting up the police commission 1881.
  Superintendent Sadleir's report on Glenrowan.
  Captain Standish's defence of his conduct of the Kelly pursuit and arrest of sympathisers 1879.
  Detective Ward's reward claim 1881.
  William Williamson's information about the Fitzpatrick incident and the whereabouts and likely haunts of the Kelly gang.
The Kelly Reward Board, papers.
  Decisions made by the board.
  Individual claims submitted.
  Minutes of evidence 8–21 March 1881.
Police correspondence 1878–81.
  Detective reports by Ward, Egan and Fook Sing 1878–80.
  Individual police reports by the cave party 1880.
  Individual police reports on Glenrowan.
  McIntyre's reports October–November 1878.
  Montfort and Graham on Kelly Country 1880–85.
  Ned Kelly's prison record and photographs with general reports on the probable composition of the gang.
  Petitions for the reprieve of Ned Kelly.
  Police reports on Euroa.
  Police strength 1878–80 (also in the commission papers).
  Reports by Nicolson to Standish July 1879–June 1880.
  Reports submitted by Euroa prisoners.
  Sub-inspector Pewtress' reports 1878.
  Sympathiser surveillance reports 1879.
  Victorian and New South Wales police reports on Jerilderie.
Prosecution briefs.
  Queen v. Ellen Kelly, William Skillion and William Williamson charged with aiding and abetting the attempted murder of constable Alexander Fitzpatrick, Beechworth Court of Assizes October 1878.
  Queen v. Edward Kelly charged with the murder of Thomas Lonigan, Beechworth Court of Petty Sessions and City Court August and October 1880.
Police department correspondence 1854–90.
  Benalla police district report and correspondence 1869–80.
  The establishment of the Greta and Glenmore police stations 1867–75.
  The McBean–Standish letters 1870–75.
  Senior Constable Hall's report on the arrest of Ned Kelly April 1871.
  Answers to stock theft allegations by regional superintendents 1871–78.
  Confidential reports on the Quinn clan 1876–78.
Police muster rolls. Series 55.
Prison registers. Series 515.
Royal commission on the Victorian police force. Papers.
  Minutes of evidence and proceedings 1881–83.
  First progress report 5 July 1881.
  Second progress report and preliminary recommendations 1881.
  Ad interim report 11 October 1882.
  Detective branch report 11 January 1883.
  General report 6 April 1883.
Secretary of State's despatches to the governor. Series 1087.
Victorian Shire Valuation Records
During research, records were preserved at various shire offices and in several instances, by local historians.

3 Official government publications

New South Wales
  Government Gazette 1878–80.
  Parliamentary Debates 1878–80.
  Police Gazette 1865–80.
Victoria
  Government Gazette 1877–80.
  Papers Presented to Both Houses of Parliament. Sessions 1870–72. Royal commission into penal discipline 1870.
  Papers Presented to Both Houses of Parliament. Sessions 1881. Vol. III, Folio VII. Royal commission of into the circumstances of the Kelly outbreak and organisation of the police force 1881–83. (Also held at Victorian Public Records Office, see Royal commission on the police force of Victoria papers.) *Parliamentary Debates*, Acts of parliament votes and proceedings 1878–83.
  Police Force Gazettes 1860–90.
  Statistical Register 1873 and 1878–80.

4 Contemporary newspapers and periodicals

Metropolitan
Advocate 1878–80.
Age 1878–80.
Argus 1877–81.
Australasian Sketcher 1880 and 1891 (*Australasia* after 1891).
Australian Pictorial Weekly 1880. (Facsimile edition. Queensbury Hill Press, Melbourne, 1982.)
Federal Standard 1875–80.
Herald 1878–80.
Hobart Town Courier 1842.
Illustrated Australian News 1865 and 1878–80.
Illustrated Sydney News 1879–80.
Melbourne Punch 1878–80.
Port Phillip Patriot and Melbourne Advertiser 1841.
Sydney Mail 1878–80.
West Australian Catholic Record 1880.
Regional
Benalla Ensign and Farmers' and Squatters' Journal 1869–71.
Examiner and Kilmore and McIvor Journal 1860–63.
Jerilderie Gazette February 1879.
Kyneton Guardian 1870.
Kyneton Observer 1870.
Mansfield Guardian 1872–79.
Mansfield Independent 1869–71.
North Eastern Advertiser 1874.
North Eastern Ensign 1872–75.
Ovens and Murray Advertiser 1864–81.
Wagga Wagga Advertiser 1877.
Wangaratta Dispatch 1873–77.
Wangaratta Star 1874.

Secondary sources

1 ARTICLES

Ashton, Julian. 'The Kelly gang'. *Sydney Morning Herald* 26 January 1934.
Atkinson, R. 'Ned Kelly at the bar of justice'. *Australasian Post* February 1947.
Bartlett, G. 'Sir Graham Berry (1822–1904)'. In *Australian Dictionary of Biography*, Melbourne University Press, Melbourne 1969. Vol. III. Pp. 151–56.
Bate, W. 'Ned Kelly rides again'. *Overland* 84, July 1991. Pp. 48–50.
Beard, W. 'Exploits notorious: A narrative in verse of the adventures of the notorious Kelly gang'. *Parramatta Cumberland Newspaper* 1953.
Blake, L. J. 'Young Ned'. *Educational Magazine* 27, 8, 1970. Pp. 350–55.
'The Case for Constable McIntyre'. *Australian Post* 9 February 1961.
Buckley, V. 'Ned Kelly'. *Overland* 84, July 1981. Pp. 51–52.
Cobley, J. 'William Bland (1789–1868)'. In *Australian Dictionary of Biography*, Melbourne University Press, Melbourne 1966. Vol. I. Pp. 112–15.
Cook, W. (née Ratcliffe). Letter to *Weekly Times* 25 November 1964.
Cookson. B. W. 'The Kelly gang from within'. Sydney *Sun* 27 August–24 September 1911.
Coughlan, N. 'The coming of the Irish to Victoria'. *Historical Studies: Australia and New Zealand*. 12, 45, 1965. Pp. 68–86.
Davies. J. M. S. 'The Kellys are out'. Melbourne *Herald* 1 November–16 December 1930.
'Declaration of republic found in Ned's pocket at Glenrowan'. *Herald* 2 December 1952.
Dunn. E. J. 'The Woolshed Valley, Beechworth'. *Bulletin of the Geological Survey of Victoria*, 25, 1913. Pp. 3–16.

Forde, J. M. 'Casual chronicles: In the early days'. Melbourne *Truth* 1915.
Fitchett, W. H. 'The story of the Kellys'. *Life Magazine* September 1909 – February 1910.
Gill, S. 'The Kelly gang at Jerilderie'. Melbourne *Life* 1 March 1910. P. 264.
'Hide of Ned Kelly'. *People* 5 July 1950.
'History of Benalla'. *Leader* 23 August 1930.
Jones, I. 'The years Ned Kelly went straight'. *Walkabout* June 1962.
Legge, J. S. 'Frederick Standish (1824–83)'. In *Australian Dictionary of Biography*, Melbourne University Press, Melbourne 1976. Vol. VI. Pp. 172–73.
Linane, T. J. 'With revolver and breviary'. *Footprints* 3, 7, 1979. Pp. 3–6.
McLaren, I. F. 'Henry Power (1820–91)'. In *Australian Dictionary of Biography*, Melbourne University Press, Melbourne 1974. Vol. V. P. 455.
McLardy, M. 'Our Oldest Living Photographer' (Lindt's assistant, H. C. Krutli) *A.P.R.* for September 1947. Pp. 484–89.
McQuilton, J. 'The legend of Ned Kelly'. *Overland* 84, July 1981. Pp 38–41.
Morrissey, D. 'Ned Kelly's sympathisers'. *Historical Studies: Melbourne*. Vol. 17–18, October 1977–April 1979. Pp. 288–96.
Morrisey, D. 'Ned Kelly's world'. *R. H. S. V. Journal*. Vol. 55, 2, June 1984. Pp. 29–34.
Nicholson. J. 'Capture of Power'. *Life Magazine* September 1909.
O'Malley, P. Social bandits: modern capitalism and the traditional peasantry. A critique of Hobsbawm'. *Journal of Peasant Studies*. Vol. 6, 1978. Pp. 489–501.
O'Malley, P. 'Class conflict, land and social banditry: bushranging in nineteenth century Australia'. *Social Problems*. Vol. 26, 3, February 1979. Pp. 271–83.
Payne, J. W. 'The Merriang road: its discovery and development (1824–60)'. *Victorian Historical Society Magazine*, 38, 2, 1967. Pp. 243–69.
Phillips, J. 'A case for Ned Kelly' in *Herald Sun*, Melbourne 3 Jan. 1994, p15.
Pryor, L. J. 'Daniel Kennedy: diseased stock agent'. *Victorian Historical Journal*, December 1991. Pp. 243–69.
Queale, A. 'Harrisville's link with the Kelly gang'. *Royal Historical Society of Queensland Journal*, 10, 1975–76. Pp. 24-29.
'Reminiscences from 1841 of William Kyle, a pioneer: as communicated to and transcribed by Charles Daley'. *Victorian Historical Society Magazine*, 10, 4, 1925.
Ryan, J. 'Ned Kelly: the flight of the legend'. *Australian Literary Studies*, 3, 1967. Pp. 98–115.
Ryan, P. 'Sir Redmond Barry (1813–80)'. In *Australian Dictionary of Biography*, Melbourne University Press, Melbourne 1969. Vol. III. Pp. 108–11.
Serle, G. 'The Victorian Legislative Council: 1856–1950'. *Historical Studies: Australia and New Zealand*, 6, 22, May 1954. Pp. 186–203.
Shaw, A. G. L. 'Violent protest in Australian history'. *Historical Studies: Australia and New Zealand*. Vol. XV, 60, 1973. Pp. 545–61.
'Sir John Monash talks to Ned Kelly'. *Table Talk* 18 April 1929.
Strahan, F. The iron mask of Australia'. *Overland* 84, July 1981. Pp. 42–47.
Sutherland, Alexander. 'Sir Redmond Barry'. *Melbourne Review*, 7, 1882.
'The best bushranger we've seen!'. *Truth* 9 March 1929.
'The shooting of Sherritt'. *Australasian Post* 21 April 1983.
Tudehope, C. M. '"Kalkallo": A link with the past'. *Victorian Historical Magazine*, 32, 126, 1961. Pp. 99–115.
Walker, R. B. 'Bushranging in fact and legend'. *Historical Studies: Australia and New Zealand*, 11,42, 1964. Pp. 206–22.
Woranna, 'Bushranging days – the Kelly gang'. *Australian History Pamphlets*, 5, 1944.
Wye, William. 'The Kellys'. *Albury Border Morning Mail* 28–29 November 1944.
Wynn, B. 'Woolshed revisited'. *Holy Name Monthly* 1 June 1962. Pp. 3–4.
'Young Victoria'. *The Journal of Scotch College*, 10, 1879.

2 BOOKS

Adam Smith, P. *Romance of Australian Railways*. Rigby, Adelaide 1973.
The Amazing History of the Kelly Gang, Melbourne. n.d.
Andrews, A. *The First Settlement of the Upper Murray*. D. S. Ford, Sydney 1920.
Ashton. J. *Now Came Still Evening On*. Angus and Robertson, Sydney 1941.
Bailliere's Victorian Gazetteer and Road Guide. Compiled by K. P. Whitworth. Bailliere, Melbourne 1865.
Background to Beechworth, 1852–1952. Compiled by Roy Harvey for Beechworth Centenary Publicity Committee, *Ovens and Murray Advertiser* 1952.
Baker, S. J. *The Australian Language*. Melbourne 1966.
Balcarek, D. *Ellen Kelly: A biography in novel form*. Farlell, Glenrowan 1984.
Balcarek, D. & Dean, G. *Ned and the Others*. Cobb & Co. Pty Ltd, Glenrowan 1995.
Barry, J. V. *The Life and Death of John Price*. Melbourne University Press, Melbourne 1964.
Billis, R. V. & Kenyon, A. S. *Pastoral Pioneers of Port Phillip*. Stockland Press, Melbourne 1974.
Blainey, Geoffrey. *Gold and Paper: The History of the National Bank of Australasia Limited*. Georgian House, Melbourne 1958.
Blair, D. *Cyclopedia of Australia*. Fergusson & Moore, Melbourne 1881.
Blake, L. J. (ed.) *Vision and Realisation: A centenary history of State education in Victoria*. Education Department of Victoria, Melbourne 1973.
Blake, L. *Young Ned*, Neptune Press, Belmont 1980.
Bond, G. *Ned Kelly, the Armoured Outlaw*. Arco, London 1961.
Boxall, G. E. *History of Australian Bushrangers*. Home Entertainment Library, Sydney 1935. (Facsimile edition edited by Michael Cannon, Penguin, Melbourne 1974.)
Bridges, R. *By Mountain Tracks*. Bookstall, Sydney 1924.
Broome, R. *The Victorians: Arriving*. Fairfax, Syme & Weldon, McMahons Point 1984.
Brown, M. *Australian Son: The Story of Ned Kelly*. Georgian House, Melbourne 1948.
Burgoyne, A. *Memories of Avenel*. Hallstead Press, Sydney 1954.
Carghill. E. A. *Stories of Glenrowan West, Greta and the Eleven Mile*. Privately printed 1972.
Carnegie, M. *Morgan: the bold bushranger*. Hawthorn Press, Melbourne 1975.
Carroll, B. *Ned Kelly, Bushranger*. Lansdowne Press, Sydney 1976.
Carlyon, L. *The Last Outlaw*, Pegasus Productions for the Seven Network, Melbourne 1980.
Castieau, J. B. *The Reminiscences of Detective Inspector Christie*. George Robertson, Melbourne 1925.
Cato, J. *Story of the Camera in Australia*. Georgian House, Melbourne 1955.
Cave, C. F. (ed.) *Ned Kelly Man and Myth: The Wangaratta seminar*. Cassell, Melbourne 1968.
Chomley. C. H. *The True Story of the Kelly Gang of Bushrangers*. Pater, Melbourne 1900.
Clarke, M. *A History of Australia*, Vol. IV. Melbourne University Press, Melbourne 1978.
Clow, R. J. *The Cause of Kelly: A complete history of the primitive colonial war between the Kelly family and the police, in blank verse*. Baxter and Stubbs, Ballarat 1919.
Clune, F. *The Kelly Hunters*. Angus and Robertson, Sydney 1954.
Clune, F. *Ned Kelly's Last Stand: The life and times of Australia's ironclad outlaw*. Angus and Robertson, Sydney 1962.
Clune, F. *A Noose for Ned: Reprint of a very rare pamphlet*. Hawthorn Press, Melbourne 1948.
Cowen, Z. *Isaac Isaacs*. Oxford University Press, Melbourne 1967.
Cronin, B. & Russell. A. *Bushranging Silhouettes*. Angus and Robertson, Sydney 1932.
Crowe, C. *One Big Crime – Startling Stories of Australian Crime and Corruption: Reminiscences and reflections*. Ross' Book Service, Melbourne 1920.
Davies, A. & Stanbury, P. *The Mechanical Eye in Australia: Photography 1841–1900*. Oxford University Press, Melbourne 1985.
Dean, A. *Multitude of Counsellors: A history of the bar of Victoria*. Cheshire for the Bar Council of Victoria, Melbourne 1968.
de Serville, P. *Pounds and Pedigrees. The Upper Class in Victoria 1850–80*. Oxford University Press, Melbourne 1991.
Dingle, T. *The Victorians: Settling*. Fairfax, Syme & Weldon, McMahons Point 1984.
Ebsworth, Rev. W. *Pioneer Catholic Victoria*. Polding Press, Melbourne 1973.
Ellis, S. F. *A History of Greta*. Lowden, Kilmore 1972.
Evans, J. *Diary of a Swagman*. Abridged and notated by William Evans, Sun Books, Melbourne 1977.
Evans, W. P. *Port of Many Prows*. Hawthorn Press, Melbourne 1969.
Farwell, G. *Ned Kelly: The life and adventures of Australia's notorious bushranger*. Cheshire, Melbourne 1970.
Finger, C. J. *Bushrangers*. George and Harrop Co., Sydney 1924.
Finn, William M. *Glimpses of North Eastern Victoria, and Albury, New South Wales*. Catholic Bookselling and Printing Depot, Melbourne 1870.
Fitchett, W. H. *Ned Kelly and His Gang*. Fitchett Brothers, Melbourne 1938. Serialised in *Life* September 1909–February 1910.
Frost, L. *Dating Family Photos 1850–1920*, Valient Press, Essendon 1991.
Galbally, A. *Redmond Barry, an Anglo-Irish Australian*. Melbourne University Press, Melbourne 1995.
Garryowen [Finn, E.] *The Chronicles of Early Melbourne 1835–52*. Two volumes. Fergusson and Mitchell, Melbourne 1888.
Gillison, J. *A Colonial Doctor and his town*, Cypress books Melbourne 1974
Gould, N. *Stuck Up!* G. Routledge, London 1894.
Gurner, J. A. *Life's Panorama: Being recollections and reminiscences of things seen, things heard, things read*. Lothian, Melbourne 1930.
Haldane, R. *The People's Force: A history of the Victoria Police*. Globe Press, Melbourne 1986.
Hall, G. Wilson. *The Kelly Gang: The outlaws of the Wombat Ranges*. G. Wilson Hall, Mansfield 1879.
Hare, F. A. *The Last of the Bushrangers: An account of the capture of the Kelly gang*. Hurst & Blackett, London 1894.
Hatherley, F. *Ned Kelly*. Jackdaw Publications, London 1970.
Haydon, A. L. *The Trooper Police of Australia*. Andrew Melrose, London 1911.
A History of Benalla: Highlights of progress and notable events from the exploration of north west Victoria by Hume and Hovell 1824 to 1968. Two volumes. Benalla City Council, Benalla 1969.
Holder, Reginald. *The Bank of New South Wales: A history*. Two volumes. Angus and Robertson. Sydney 1970.
Howitt, W. *Land, Labour and Gold*. Longman, Brown, Green & Longmans, London 1855.
Hunter, F. *The Origin, Career and Destruction of the Kelly Gang: Also the adventures of Captain Moonlight*. A. T. Hodgson, Adelaide 1895.
Geoffrey C. Ingleton. *True Patriots All*. Angus and Robertson, Sydney 1952.
Isaacs, A. *Ned Kelly: The ironclad Australian bushranger, by one of his captors*. Alfred J. Isaacs & Sons. London 1881.
Jacobs, P. A. *Famous Australian Trials and Memories of the Law*. Robertson & Mullens, Melbourne 1944.
Jennings, M. J. *Ned Kelly, the Legend and the Man*. Hill of Content, Melbourne 1968.
Jones, G. & Bassett, J. *The Kelly Years*. Charquin Hill Publishing, Wangaratta 1980.
Jones, G. *Ned Kelly – The Larrikin Years*. Charquin Hill Publishing, Wangaratta 1990.
Jones, G. B*ushrangers of the North East*. Charquin Hill Publishing, Wangaratta 1991.
Jones, I. 'The Kellys and Beechworth' and 'A new view of Ned Kelly'. In Cave, C. (ed.) *Ned Kelly – Man and Myth*, Cassell, Melbourne 1968.
Jones, I. *The Friendship That Destroyed Ned Kelly – Joe Byrne and Aaron Sherritt*. Lothian, Melbourne 1992.
Jones, I. *Ned Kelly: A short life*. Lothian, Melbourne 1995.
Jupp, J. (ed.) *The Australian People: An encyclopaedia of the nation, it's people and their origins*. Angus & Robertson, Melbourne 1988.
Keesing, N. (ed.) *The Kelly Gang*. Ure Smith, Sydney 1975.
Kenneally, J. J. *The Complete Inner History of the Kelly Gang and Their Pursuers*. Robertson & Mullens, Melbourne 1929. Seventh edition (revised) 1955.
Kerr, J. (ed.) *The Dictionary of Australian Artists – Painters, Sketchers, Photographers, and Engravers to 1870*. Oxford University Press, Melbourne 1992
Lake, M. 'The trials of Ellen Kelly'. In Lake, M. & Kelly F. *Double Time: Women in Victoria – 150 Years*. Penguin, Melbourne 1985.
La Nauze, J. A. & Crawford, R. M. (eds) *The Crisis in Victorian Politics, 1879-81: A personal retrospect*. Melbourne University Press, Melbourne 1957.
Lane, Rev. L. *A History of the Parish of Beechworth, l854–1978*. Parish of Beechworth, Beechworth 1978.
The Life and Adventures of the Kelly Outlaws: The daring Australian bushrangers. Frearson & Brother, Adelaide c. 1881.
Leitch, B. *The Fatal Dice: Lifting the lid on the cause of persecution of Ned Kelly*. B. Leitch, Wangaratta 1993.
Lofting, H. *Bail Up!: Ned Kelly, bushranger*. New Century Press, Sydney 1939.
Lundy, Rev. H. C. *History of Jerilderie, 1858-1958*. Jerilderie Shire Council, Jerilderie 1958.

McDermott, A. (ed.) *The Jerilderie Letter, Ned Kelly,* Text Publishing, Melbourne 2001.
McGuffin. W. *Australian Tales of the Border.* Lothian, Melbourne 1920.
McQuilton, J. *The Kelly Outbreak 1878–1880: The geographical dimension of social banditry.* Melbourne University Press, Melbourne 1979.
Madgwick, R. B. *Immigration into Eastern Australia, 1788–1852.* Sydney University Press, Sydney 1969.
Maher, James A. *The Tale of a Century: Kilmore, 1837–1937.* Lowden, Kilmore 1972.
Martin, A. P. *True Stories from Australasian History.* Griffith, Farran & Co., London 1893.
Martindale, Harold G. *New Crossing Place: The story of Seymour and its shire.* Cheshire, Melbourne 1958.
Maxwell, C. F. *The Law List of Australasia: Comprising the judges and officers of the different courts of justice, counsel, attorneys, notaries, etc., and rules of the supreme courts in Victoria, New South Wales, South Australia, Queensland, New Zealand, Tasmania and Western Australia.* Charles F. Maxwell, Melbourne 1880.
Meredith, John. (ed.) *Songs from the Kelly Country.* Bush Music Club, Sydney 1955.
Molony, John. *I Am Ned Kelly.* Allen Lane, Melbourne 1980.
Morgan, W. *Ned Kelly Reconstructed.* Cambridge University Press, Melbourne 1994.
Morris, E. E. (ed.) *Cassell's Picturesque Australasia.* Volume IV. Cassell, London 1890.
Morris, G. *Devil's River Country: Selections from the history of the Mansfield district.* Advertiser, Shepparton 1952.
Nairn, N., Serle, A.G., Ward, R.B. (Eds.) Australian Dictionary of Biography. Melbourne University Press 1969
O'Callaghan, T. *List of Chief Constables, District Constables, Police Cadets and Police Officers in Victoria 1836–1907.* Government Printer, Melbourne 1907.
O'Farrell, P. *The Irish in Australia.* New South Wales University Press, Sydney 1986.
Osborne, C. *Ned Kelly.* Blond, London 1970.
O'Sullivan, M. *Cameos of Crime.* Jackson & O'Sullivan, Sydney 1935.
Passey, K. & Dean, G. *Harry Power – Tutor of Ned Kelly.* Victorian Bushranger Enterprises, Wodonga 1991.
Payne, J. W. *The History of Beveridge.* Lowden, Kilmore 1974.
Phillips, C. *The Cry of the Dingo.* Arthur Barker, London 1956.
Phillips, J. H. *The Trial of Ned Kelly.* Law Book Co., North Ryde 1987.
Pratt, A. *Dan Kelly, Outlaw: Being the memoirs of Daniel Kelly (brother of Edward Kelly), supposed to have been slain in the famous fight at Glenrowan.* Bookstall, Sydney 1911.
Proeschel, F. *Desk and Traveller's Map of Victoria.* Brown and Slight, Emerald Hill 1863.
Pryor, L. J. *Thomas Curnow.* L. J. Pryor, Burwood 1986.
Radcliffe, E. T. (ed.) *Iron Ned Kelly and his Gang. A personal history of Australia's most notorious bushrangers and a record of their most eventful career of highway robbery, horse stealing romance and murder.* Modern Publishing Company, Sydney 1902.
Reece, B. 'Ned Kelly's father'. In Reece, B. *Exiles from Erin – Convict Lives in Ireland and Australia.* MacMillan Academic, London 1991.
Royal Commission on the Police Force of Victoria,. *Police Commission: Minutes of evidence, together with appendices and tables.* Government Printer Melbourne 1881, re-printed Heinemann, Melbourne 1968.
Ryan, P. *Redmond Barry: A Colonial Life 1813–1880.* Melbourne University Press, Melbourne 1980.
Sadleir. J. *Recollections of a Victorian Police Officer.* Penguin, Melbourne 1973.
Sands and McDougall's Melbourne Directories. Sands and McDougall, Melbourne 1860–70.
Seal, G. N*ed Kelly in Popular Tradition.* Hyland House, Melbourne 1980
Seccombe, T. (ed.): *Lives of Twelve Bad Men: Original studies of eminent scoundrels by various hands,* London 1894.
Serle, G. *The Rush to be Rich: A history of the colony of Victoria, 1883–89.* Melbourne University Press, Melbourne 1971.
Smith, P. *Tracking Down the Bushrangers.* Kangaroo Press, Kenthurst 1982.
Sowden. Henry R. (ed.) *Australian Woolsheds.* Photographs by Henry R. Sowden. Cassell, Melbourne 1972.
Stanley, J. S. *The Vagabond Papers.* Volume III. Melbourne University Press, Melbourne 1969. Hyland House, Melbourne 1973.
Turnbull, C. *Kellyana.* Hawthorn Press, Melbourne 1943.
Turnbull, C. *Ned Kelly: Being his own story of his life and crimes.* Hawthorn Press, Melbourne 1942.
Turner, H. G. *A History of the Colony of Victoria from its discovery to its absorption into the Commonwealth of Australia.* Volume II. Melbourne Heritage Publications, Melbourne 1973.
Turton. K. W. *The North East Railway: A lineside guide, Melbourne to Wodonga.* Australian Railway Historical Society, Victorian division, Melbourne 1973.
Voyageur. *Kamboola and Other Tales.* Sydney 1891.
Wannan, B. *Australian Bushrangers.* Universal Books, Sydney 1970.
Wannan, B. *The Wearing of the Green: The lore, literature, legend and balladry of the Irish in Australia.* Landsdowne Press, Melbourne 1965.
White, C. *Australian Bushranging: The Kelly gang.* Bookstall 1921. Rigby, Sydney 1978.
Ward, R. *The Australian Legend.* Oxford University Press, Melbourne 1958.
Watson. F. (ed.) *Historical Records of Australia.* Series 1. Vol. XIX. Library Committee of the Commonwealth Parliament, Sydney 1923.
Was Ned Kelly a Hero, Robin Hood, Outlaw, Cold Blooded Killer or Just A Rebel Forced to Turn Outlaw? Australian Publishing Company, Brisbane n.d.
Westgarth, W. *Personal Recollections of Early Melbourne and Victoria.* George Robertson, Melbourne 1888.
White, C. *History of Australian Bushranging.* No. 7. C. & G. S. White, Bathurst 1893.
White, H. A. *Tales of Crime and Criminals in Australia: Based principally upon reminiscences of over thirty years official experience in the penal department of Victoria.* Ward & Downey, London 1894.
Whittaker, D. M. *Wangaratta: Being the history of the township that sprang up at the Ovens crossing and grew into a modern city 1824–1838–1963.* Wangaratta City Council, Wangaratta 1963.
Woodhall, E. T. *The Kelly Gang.* Mellifont Press, London 1938.
Woodham–Smith, C. *The Great Hunger: Ireland 1845–49.* Hamish Hamilton, London 1962.

3 UNPUBLISHED WORKS
Ashmead, J. The True Kelly Story (as told to him by J. McMonigle). Collection of Ian Jones. Melbourne.
Bartlett, G. Political Organisation and Society in Victoria 1864–83. Ph.D. thesis. Australian National University 1964.
Crowley, J. If Words Be Louder, I Will Oppose Your Laws. An analysis of Ned Kelly's Jerilderie Letter. BA Honours thesis, University of Queensland 1998.
DeBoos, G. L. Recollections of Euroa and the Kellys. Collection of Mrs. N. Lomer, Euroa.
Hopkins, F. Letter. Possession of Ian Jones. Melbourne.
Lefoe, C. H. & Kintag, B. Rough Draft for a History of Avenel. Possession of C. H. Lefoe, Avenel 1933.
Proute Webb, Mrs. Diary (including recollections of the siege at Glenrowan). Preserved by family descendants, South Yarra 1967.
Shelton. Esau, Album of family photographs. Possession of Ethel Middleton, Melbourne.
Stewart, F. Items of Euroa History. Collection at Mrs. N. Lomer, Euroa.

4 NEWSPAPERS AND PERIODICALS
Advocate 1946.
Australasian Post 9 February 1961.
Benalla Standard 30 July 1964.
Evening Sun 27 December 1924.
Everybody's 10 November 1965, p. 4.
Forbes Advocate 21 October1955.
Geelong Advertiser 4 June1929.
Herald 20 February 1922, 6 January 1958.
Orange Stock and Station Journal 28 October 1955.
Police Life July 1965.
Sun Herald 10 July 1960.
Sun [Melbourne] 19 December 1946, 1 November1967.
Sun [Sydney] 8 November1923.
Tractor Talk, journal of Chamberlain Industries July 1963.
Truth, 9 March 1929
Victorian Railways Magazine, 3, 3, March 1926.
Walkabout 1965.
Weekly Times 1931.

INDEX

Age newspaper (Melb) 96, 146, 176, 177-81, 221, 257, 261
Ah Fook 34, 65
Albion Hotel, Jerilderie (NSW) 139–41
Albury (NSW) 118
Alexander, Senior Constable 177
Archdeacon, Constable 40
Argus newspaper (Melb) 108–17, 126, 146, 190–217, 234, 240, 248–55, 269
Armstrong, Senior Constable 177, 181
Ashmead, Joseph (farmer) 26, 60
Ashton, Julian (artist) 218, 237
Australasian Sketcher 118, 187, 198, 228, 232
Avenel 12–23, 120
Aylward, Reverend 228, 230

Bald Hill (Kelly's Lookout) 57, 72, 74, 147, 242–43
Bank of New South Wales, Jerilderie 138
Barker, Dr 265
Barkly, Superintendent 44
Barnawatha 64, 67
Barnes, W.E. (photographer) *vi*, 85, 196, 201, 217
Barnett, Mr 44
Barney (black tracker) 159
Barry, Ellen see Sherritt, Ellen
Barry, Mrs 177–80
Barry, Sir Redmond 26, 50, 76, 79, 81, 147, 228, 245, 246–48, 252–55
Baumgarten, Gustav 67
Baumgarten, Mrs 106
Baumgarten, William 66, 67, 79
Beechworth 88, 120, 152–53
Beechworth court *ix*, 26, 40, 44, 74, 76, 78–9, 147, 228, 234–36
Beechworth Gaol 40, 42, 44, 49, 66, 78–9, 126, 127, 146, 147, 234–36
Beecroft, Frank 241, 250
Benalla 37, 52, 62, 73, 161
Benalla court 29, 33, 38, 66, 73, 74
Benalla Ensign 34, 40
Berry, Sir Graham 74, 120, 126
Beveridge 1–11
Beveridge Catholic School 7–8
Bickerton, Mr (police magistrate) 226
Billabong Creek (NSW) 134
Bindon, Henry Massy 246, 248–52
Black Wednesday 74, 76, 77
Booth, Mr (Euroa bank clerk) 116–17
Bowen, Sir George Ferguson 107
Bowman, Mr (solicitor) 76, 79
Bracken, Constable Hugh 186, 189–91, 193, 217, 225
Bradley, Mr (Euroa bank clerk) 116–17
Bray, James (photographer) *vi*, 57, 61, 69, 130–31, 178–79, 201, 202–3, 209, 211, 214
Brown, Detective 73, 122
Brown, Mr (barrister) 44
Brown, Schools Inspector 17, 26
Bullock Creek 84
Bungawunnah 106
Burke, Mr (publican) 134
Burman, Arthur (photographer) *vi*, 65, 73, 90, 94, 222–23
Burns, Mr 121
Burramine 134
Butler, Mr (police magistrate) 125
Byrne, Catherine 156–57
Byrne, Joe 67, 82
    alias Billy King 88
    armour 167
    balladry 154–55
    body displayed 222
    death 200, 208, 220, 224
    description and character *ix*, 61, 65, 88, 143
    Faithfull's Creek 1 14, 131
    in hiding 151–57, 158–72
    Jerilderie hold-up 135, 138–40, 143
    Sherritt 1 31, 157, 163, 173–81
    Glenrowan siege 174, 182–90, 196, 210
    stealing horses 64
    Stringybark Creek 82, 127

Byrne, Mrs 147, 153, 157, 172, 173
Byrne, Patrick 157, 180

Cameron letter 120–26
Cameron, Donald (MLA) 120, 124
Campion's store 12, 19, 22–23
Carr, Mr (publican) 62, 121
Carrington, Thomas (artist) 184, 193
Casement, Mr 113
Castieau, Mr (governer of Melbourne Gaol) 230, 265
Cato, Jack (photographer and historian) 49
Caulfield, J.P.T. 259
Ceallaigh, Sean (Red) see Kelly, John
Cherry, Martin 208–9, 220, 273
Cheshire, Mr 181
Chevalier, Nicholas (artist) 18
Chiltern 120
Chomley, A. 76, 79, 107, 234, 246, 248, 250
Clancey, Daniel 126
Clancey, James 126
Clarke, W.J.T. 220
Cohen, Mr 44
Cooke, William 67, 122
Cookson, B.W. (journalist) *vii*
Cox, Mr (Jerilderie publican) 138
Curnow, Miss 186
Curnow, Mrs 186, 189
Curnow, Thomas (Glenrowan schoolteacher) 186–89, 190

Davey, L.H. 22, 51
Davidson, Mrs 134
Day, Constable Patrick 248
De Boos' Hotel 113
De Boos, Mr 113
Degamero station 21
Delaney, Daniel 26, 186
Delatite River see Devil's River
Denny see Kennedy
Devil's Elbow 175
Devil's River 106
Devine, Mrs 135–36
Devine, Senior Constable 135–36
Donald (black tracker) 40
Donoghy, Dean 265
Dowling, Senior Constable 177
Dowsett, Jesse (railway guard) 199
Doxy, Constable 22
Dudley, Henry 113, 241, 250
Duffy Selection Act 12
Duross, Senior Constable 177
Dwyer, Constable 208

Eleven Mile Creek *viii*, 27, 28, 40, 44, 50, 52, 55, 67, 242–43
Elliott, William 138, 139
Ellis, Mr 265
Emu station 107
Euroa 108–9, 113, 115, 116
Euroa bank robbery 108–17; see also Faithfull's Creek station
Evan's Gap 164
Evening News' (Sydney) 218
Everton 106

Faithfull's Creek station 109, 111, 117; see also Euroa bank robbery
Farrell, Constable 62, 121
Felons Apprehension Act 98, 126
Fifteen Mile Creek 26, 33, 165
Fitzgerald, Mrs 109–11, 120
Fitzgerald, William 109–11, 250
Fitzpatrick, Constable Alexander *viii*, 65, 67, 120, 228, 271, 273
    attitude to Kelly gang 64
    Cameron letter 120–26
    description and character *viii, ix*, 69, 72
    incident in Benalla 65–6
    incident at Kelly hut 68–79
    Ned Kelly's trial for murder 240, 248–51

Flood, Constable 50–1
Foote see Quinn, Patrick
Ford, Thomas 23
Foster, W.H. 74, 177, 181, 234, 240
Frearson's Weekly (Adelaide) 99, 150
Frost, William 33, 37, 38, 50
Futter's Range 23, 25, 107

Gardiner, Frank (bushranger) 21
Gaunson, David 232, 240, 247, 254, 259–61
Gaunson, William 259–61
Gibbons, R. 189
Gibney, Father Matthew 207–9
Gilbert, John (bushranger) 21
Gill, Mrs 136, 139
Gill, Samuel 139
Glenmore station 24, 33, 34, 36, 40
Glenrowan 60, 120, 184–85
Glenrowan Inn 167, 186–210, 214
Glenrowan Range see Futter's Range
Glenrowan siege 182–217
Gloster, James 109, 111–12, 241, 250
Goodman, David 66, 125
Goodman, Mrs 67
Goulburn River 109
Gould, Benjamin 41, 42, 107, 110, 124, 126, 147
Gould, Reverend 52
Graham, Jane 50–1, 63
Green, Inspector 105
Greta *vii*, 23, 24, 25, 41, 43, 50
Greta mob 43, 65, 171
Greta wake 228
Grey, William 34
Gribble, Reverend 142
Gunn, Alexander 33, 44, 51, 124
Gunn, Anne see Kelly, Anne
Gurner, J.H. 234

Hall, Ben (bushranger) 21
Hall, Senior Constable 40, 44, 124–25
Hamilton Spectator 127
Hamilton, A.S. 259
Haney, Michael 147
Hare, Superintendent Frank A. 118, 147, 179
    capture of Harry Power 33
    description of Ned Kelly 39
    Euroa arrests 126
    Glenrowan siege 190–93
    pursuit of Kelly gang 120, 121, 147, 153, 158, 162, 164, 172
    Royal Commission recommendation 271
    use of police informers 149, 172–73, 179
Harkin, Mr (policeman) 106
Hart, Dick 167
Hart, Esther 167
Hart, John 126, 165
Hart, Mrs 141
Hart, Richard 65, 163, 210, 226
Hart, Stephen 82
    armour 167
    death 207–8, 210, 214, 224
    description and character *ix*, 61, 85, 143
    Faithfull's Creek 117
    Glenrowan siege 174, 186, 182, 189, 190, 196, 202
    in hiding 151–57, 158–72
    Jerilderie hold-up 135, 139, 140, 142–43
    stealing horses 65
    Stringybark Creek 82, 127
Harty, Francis 73, 79, 81, 107, 126, 147
Hastings, Dr see Hester, Dr
Heeley, Dr 23
Herald (Melb.) 144, 146, 160, 218, 220–30, 261, 271
Herne's Swamp 6
Hester, Dr (described by E. Kelly incorr. as Hastings) 44
Houten, H.L. 27
Howlong 144
Hughes Creek 13, 14–15

Illustrated Australian News 136, 245, 269
Illustrated Daily News (Melb.) 218
Illustrated Sydney News 73, 212–13, 216, 229
Irving, James (schoolteacher) 17
Isley, D. (photographer) 151

Jacky (black tracker) 159
Jefferson, Mr (Jerilderie postmaster) 139, 141
Jerilderie Gazette 134, 146, 160
Jerilderie courthouse 137
Jerilderie letter 140
Jerilderie robbery 134–43
Jewitt, Mr 44
Jimmy (black tracker) 159
Johnny (black tracker) 159
Johnson, Henry *see* Power, Harry
Johnson, Senior Constable Charles 202, 207
Jones' hotel *see* Glenrowan Inn
Jones *see* Sherritt, Jack
Jones, Mrs 167, 182, 185, 189, 190, 195
Jones, Jane 182, 190, 197
Jones, John 197, 273

Kelly, Anne *viii*, *xii*, 7, 17, 33, 34, 51
Kelly, Catherine (Kate)
    assistance to Kelly gang 147–48, 151
    birth 7
    death 273
    description and character *viii*, 74, 237, 260
    Fitzpatrick incident 74
    Glenrowan siege 209–10, 224
    Greta wake 228
    Ned Kelly's trial and death 229, 241, 258, 160
    Sherritt 1 56
Kelly, Daniel *viii*, 63, 110–12
    armour 167
    arrests 50, 66–7
    Beechworth Gaol 66
    birth *ix*, 7
    Cameron letter 122, 125
    death 207–8, 224
    description and character *ix*, 65, 73, 112, 143
    employment 55
    Faithfull's Creek 117
    Fitzpatrick Incident 68, 73–4
    Glenrowan siege 174, 182–90, 196, 202, 210
    in hiding 151–57, 158–72
    Jerilderie hold-up 135–41
    outlawed 107
    Sherritt's death 173–81
    Stringybark Creek ambush 82–95
Kelly, Ellen (née Quinn):
    Cameron letter 122
    children's births *xii*–7, 22, 37
    court appearances 23, 36, 38, 50
    death 273
    description and character *vii*, *ix*, 50, 76, 272–73
    Eleven Mile Creek 27–8, 50, 63
    Fitzpatrick incident *viii*, 68–9, 73–9
    imprisonment 74, 79, 228, 230
    marriages *xii*, 52
    Ned Kelly's trial and death 228–31, 258, 264
Kelly, Grace *vii*, 22, 147
Kelly, James (junior) *viii*, 41, 50, 51, 55, 65, 271, 273
Kelly, James (senior) 6, 9, 26
Kelly, John (Red) *viii*, *xii*, 1–7, 22–3
Kelly, Margaret *see* Skillion, Margaret
Kelly, Mary Jane *xii*
Kelly, Michael (Black) 23
Kelly, Senior Constable John 195, 196, 223, 251
Kelly, Edward (Ned)
    armour 167
    ballads 154–55
    Baumgarten affair 67
    birth *ix*, *xii*
    boxing ability 55, 56
    capture 195–96
    death 214, 261–69
    description and character *ix*, 36, 40, 57, 60, 65, 112, 253, 262–63
    education 7, 17
    employment 55–60
    fight with Fitzpatrick at Benalla 66
    first Kelly gang 63
    Fitzpatrick incident 68–79
    Glenrowan siege 174, 182–217, 210–14
    Harry Power 29–40
    imprisonment 42, 44, 49, 228, 229
    in hiding 151–57, 158–72
    James 'Jimmy' Quinn 11
    Jerilderie hold-up 134–43
    letters 38, 88, 120–26, 127, 140, 154, 160, 230, 257
    outlawed 107
    Redmond Barry's opinion 252–55
    Richard Shelton's life saved 21
    Sherritt's death 173–81
    stealing horses 42–4, 55, 63–4
    Stringybark Creek ambush 82–95
    trial 240–51
Kelly armour 167–72
Kelly guns 182–83
Kelly's Lookout *see* Bald Hill
Kenneally, J.J. (Kelly historian) 168
Kennedy (Denny) 168, 171, 172
Kennedy, Samuel 67, 79
Kennedy, Sergeant Michael 89–95, 124, 240
Kiandra (NSW) 65
Kilfeera station 27, 36, 165
Kilmore 9
Kilmore courthouse 9
King River 62, 161
King, Billy *see* Byrne, Joe
King, Ellen (junior) 147
King, George 52, 63, 67, 121
King, Mr (Benalla bootmaker) 65
King, Mrs Ellen *see* Kelly, Ellen
Krafft, Mark 50
Kyneton 39

Lake Mokoan *see also* Winton swamp 165
Lake Rowan 107
Lake Winton *see* Winton swamp
Land Selection Acts 24, 27, 28
Lauriston 36, 40
Lewis, Mr 4
Lindsay, David 68, 76, 126
Lindsay's shanty, Winton 67, 73, 76
Lindt, John (photographer) *vi*, 201, 222, 224, 225
Lloyd, Catherine (junior) 26, 261
Lloyd, Jane 8, 23, 24
Lloyd, John (junior) 64, 66, 73, 79, 126, 166
Lloyd, John (senior) 9, 10, 26, 33, 37, 39–42, 51
Lloyd, Mrs Catherine 18, 23, 24, 37
Lloyd, Tom (junior) 42, 51, 82
    armour 167
    arrest for assault 66–7
    assistance to Kelly gang 147, 163–66
    description and character 88, 151
    Fitzpatrick incident 73
    Glenrowan siege 209–10, 224
    Greta wake 228
    in hiding 106
    Jerilderie robbery 134
    Ned Kelly's trial and death 232, 240, 246, 258
    stealing horses 64
    Stringybark Creek 82
Lloyd, Tom (senior) 9, 10, 26, 33, 106, 107, 126, 147, 156, 166
Lonigan, Constable Thomas 64, 89
    Benalla fight 66
    Cameron letter 124
    death 89–95
    Ned Kelly's trial for murder 240, 246–52, 254
    Stringybark Creek ambush 82–95
Lowry, Frederick 22
Lydicher, Mr 62, 121
Lyons, John 26
Lyving, Edwin 138, 140, 143, 241, 251

Mackie, A. 143
Mackie, J. 138, 143
Madeley, Oswald (photographer) *vi*, 201, 202, 207–8, 214–15, 221
Mansfield 97, 107
Martin, Peter 44
May Day Hills 49
McAuliffe, Dennis 166, 196
McAuliffe, Patrick 166, 196
McAulifffe, Mrs 166
McBean, Robert *ix*, 27, 28, 32, 33, 36–8
McCaulay, Mr 111, 114, 117
McColl, Constable 181
McCormick, Jerimiah 41–2, 124–25
McCormick, Mrs 41–2, 124–25
McCubbin, Frederick (artist) 23
McDonnell, Mrs 226
McDonnell, Mr 174
McDonnell's Hotel *see* Railway Tavern
McDougall, Mary 142
McDougall, Mr 113
McDougall, Robert 141, 142, 241, 250
McDougall's Hotel *see* Albion Hotel
McElroy, John 126, 146, 261
McInnes, William 66, 124
McIntyre, Constable Thomas Newman 89, 225, 237
    Cameron letter 123
    evidence at Ned Kelly's trial 240, 248–50
    Stringybark Creek ambush 82–95, 127
McMonigle, John 57, 60, 105, 126, 147
Melbourne Gaol *vii*, 220, 228, 230, 244, 259, 264, 266–67, 273
Melbourne Punch 126, 150, 259
Melvin, Joseph 190
Merrijig 106
Middleton, J. 261
Miller, Robert 126
Mills, Senior Constable 153
Molesworth, Hickman 245
Montfort, Constable 40
Moonlite, Captain *see* Scott, George
Morgan, Dan (bushranger) 18, 21
Morgan, Mr 141
Morgan, Phillip 22
Morgan's Lookout 174, 182
Mortimer, David 186, 189, 190
Moses (black tracker) 123
Moses *see* Sherritt, Aaron
Mount Battery 34
Mount Feathertop 24
Moyhu 60, 64
Mullane, Senior Constable 163, 172, 177, 181
Murdoch, James 44, 50
Murray, J. *ix*
Mutton, Eliza 22

National Bank at Euroa 108, 113–16
Nettleton, Charles (photographer) *vi*, 259, 264
Newman, Mr 122
Nicholas, Superintendent 37, 42
Nicholson, Dr John 76
Nicholson, Superintendent C.H. 38–40, 51, 62, 67, 77, 118, 158, 162–66, 172, 211, 271
Nolan, Michael 151
Normanby letters 256–57
Normanby, Marquis of 162, 256

O'Brien, John 65
O'Brien's Hotel, Greta 26, 171, 224
O'Connor, Mr (bushranger) 171
O'Connor, Mrs 191, 194, 211
O'Connor, Sub-Inspector Stanhope 190, 193, 271
O'Donohue, Mr 181
O'Hea, Father 6, 18, 49, 265, 268
Old Melbourne Gaol *see* Melbourne Gaol
O'Loghlen letter 127
O'Loghlen, Bryan 127
Oriental Bank, Beechworth 163
Ovens and Murray Advertiser 74, 157, 160, 240
Oxley 55

Pentridge Gaol 21, 26, 33, 46–7, 49, 105
Perkins, Henry 126
Pewtress, Sub-Inspector 95, 97

Pioneer Bridge hotel, Ovens River 106
Point Gelibrand 47, 55
Power, Harry (bushranger) *vi, viii*, 29, 32, 33–40
Power's lookout 25, 34–6

Quinn, Catherine, *see* Lloyd, Catherine
Quinn, Ellen *see* Kelly, Ellen
Quinn clan family tree 5
Quinn, James 'Jimmy' 9, 10–11, 23, 28–9, 33, 40, 50, 60, 73, 126, 147, 165, 224, 271
Quinn, James (senior) 7, 11, 33
Quinn, Jane *see* Lloyd, Jane
Quinn, John 'Jack' 9, 23, 29, 33, 60, 62, 79, 106, 126
Quinn, Margaret 39, 50
Quinn, 'Wild Pat' (alias Foote) 39, 40, 42, 109, 158
Quinn, William 33, 62

Railway Tavern, Glenrowan 186, 215, 226
Rankin, James G. 139,140
Rawlins, Charles 193
Reardon, James (line-repairer) 182, 197
Reardon, Michael 197, 210
Reardon, Mrs Mary 197
Red Camp station 55
Rede, Colonel 264
Reedy Creek 153
Reynolds (postmaster) 186
Reynolds, Alec 189
Reynolds, Dr Samuel 97, 240, 251
Reynolds, E. 189
Richards, Constable Henry 135, 136, 141, 250
Robert Burns Hotel 269
Rowe, Dr 34
Royal Commission, 1881 *viii*, 270
Royal Mail Hotel, Avenel 13,21
Royal Mail Hotel, Jerilderie 137, 138, 140, 142
Ryan, Anne (née Kelly) 6, 23
Ryan, Joseph 73, 79, 107, 126, 147, 148

Sacramento 47, 49
Sadleir, Superintendent John 118, 225
    Glenrowan siege 202
    Ned Kelly's Beechworth hearing 240
    police informers 172
    Royal Commission recommendation 217, 271
Saunders, Mr (sawmiller) 55
Saunders and Rule sawmills 55, 60
Scanlon, Constable Michael 91
    Cameron letter 123–24
    death 89–95
    evidence given at Kelly trial 248–51
    Kelly's version of death 95
    Stringybark Creek 89
Scott, George (Captain Moonlite) 165
Scott, Mrs 116
Scott, Robert 116–17, 241, 250
Sebastopol 64, 107
Seven Creeks Hotel, Euroa 109
Seymour 120
Sheepstation Creek 156, 157, 164, 177
Shelton, Elizabeth 17
Shelton, Esau 17, 21
Shelton, Richard 17, 21
Shelton, Sarah 21
Shepparton 120
Sherritt, Aaron 64, 67, 138, 157
    death 173–81
    description and character 60, 179
    Joe Byrne 131
    Kate Kelly 156
    marriage 175
    police informer 131, 149, 153, 154, 157, 162, 172
    stealing horses 64, 157
Sherritt, Anne 164
Sherritt, Ellen (née Barry) 175, 180
Sherritt, Jack (alias Jones) 157, 163, 164
Sinclair, Mr 167
Skeehan's paddock 165

Skillion Margaret (née Kelly) *viii*, 88, 120, 151
    Aaron Sherritt 156–57
    assistance to Kelly gang 105, 107, 147–48, 162–63
    birth 6
    description and character 237
    education 17
    Fitzpatrick affair 79
    Glenrowan siege 202, 224–26
    Greta wake 228
    marriage 52
    Ned Kelly's trial and death 232, 240, 245–46, 258–60
Skillion, William 34, 50, 52, 63, 68, 74, 77, 79, 122
Smith, Inspector Brooke 67, 123, 271
Smith, Mr (resident of Wangaratta district) 141
Smyth, C.A. 234, 240, 246, 248, 252
South Hanson 158
Standish, Captain 118, 122
    causes of Kelly outbreak *ix*
    first meeting with Kelly 38
    Kelly's Beechworth hearing 234
    pursuit of Kelly gang 121, 158, 163
    pursuit of Harry Power 37
    Royal Commission recommendation 271
    Fitzpatrick incident 69, 73, 79
Stanistreet, Mr (Glenrowan station master) 186, 189
Steele, Senior Constable Arthur 77, 198, 217
    Cameron letter 122
    Glenrowan siege 196
    Kelly trial and captivity 231, 251
    Royal Commission recommendation 271
Stephens, George (groom, Younghusbands' station) 241, 249
Stewart, James (of Beveridge) 11
Stewart, John 126
Stewart, Mrs James 11
Stewart, Walter 126
Stienwehr, Louis 151
Still, Thomas (printer) 105
Story of the Camera in Australia 49
Strahan, Senior Constable 67, 6 8, 73, 122
Strathbogie Ranges 109
Strickland, Richard 103, 126
Strickland, William 103, 126
Stringybark Creek 90
Studders, Mr (charged during Baumgarten trials) 67
Sullivan, Mr (line repairer) 185,
Swanhill, Mr *see* Swannell, Mr
Swannell, Mr (Lake Rowan townsman) 122
Sydney Sun *vii*
Syme, Mr 218

Tanner, William 106
Tarleton, John (bank employee) 138–40, 143, 251
Tennant, Mr 113
Thompson, Mr 44
Thompson, Mr (alias used by E. Kelly) 67
Trentham 163

Upjohn, Mr (hangman) 265, 269
Urana (NSW) 141

Victoria Hotel, Benalla 220
Violet Town 23, 107, 120

Walhalla 163
Wall, Sarah (schoolteacher) 7
Wall, Thomas (schoolteacher) 7
Wallace, James (of the Woolshed) 158, 161
Wallan *ix, xii*
Walling, Sergeant 93
Wangaratta 26, 27, 33, 42, 44, 120
Wangaratta court 36, 37, 38, 41, 50, 51
Warby Ranges *see* Futter's Range
Ward, Detective Michael 162, 163, 166
    harassment of Kelly family 123
    police informers 172
    Royal Commission recommendation 271
Webb, Mrs Proute 194
Weekes, Anton 177–81
Weiner, John 177
Welshe, J. 122

Whelan, Sergeant James 34, 65, 66, 67, 77, 124
Whitty, James (squatter) 60, 62, 64, 67, 106, 121
Williams, Tom 50, 51
Williamson, William (Bricky) 77
    association with Kellys 44, 50, 55, 63
    Cameron letter 120, 122
    Fitzpatrick incident 68–74
    police informer 105–6
Williamstown 50
Winton 27, 66, 72
Winton swamp 55, 165
Wodonga 120
Wombat Ranges 64, 67, 82, 83, 107
Woodyard, Michael 55
Woolpack Inn, near Jerilderie 134
Woolshed Diggings 64, 107, 131, 161, 164
Wright, Isaiah (Wild) 42, 79
    arrests 124, 126, 146–47, 271
    boxer 55
    description and character 42, 57, 130
    Glenrowan siege and aftermath 209–10, 226
    stealing horses 44
Wunnamurra station 143, 144
Wyatt, Alfred 146, 230

Younghusband's station *see* Faithfull's Creek
Zinke, Mr (Beechworth barrister) 74, 232, 240